W9-ABC-985

CHICAGO PUBLIC LIBRARY

Forest Fires

SD
421
.F84
1991

Fuller, Margaret.

Forest fires.

$12.95

DATE			

BUSINESS/SCIENCE/TECHNOLOGY
DIVISION

© THE BAKER & TAYLOR CO.

The Wiley Nature Editions

At the Water's Edge: Nature Study in Lakes, Streams and Ponds, by Alan M. Cvancara

Mountains: A Natural History and Hiking Guide, by Margaret Fuller

The Oceans: A Book of Questions and Answers, by Donald Groves

Birding Around the World: A Guide to Observing Birds Everywhere You Travel, by Aileen Lotz

Birding Around the Year: When to Find Birds in North America, by Aileen Lotz

Walking the Wetlands: A Hiker's Guide to Common Plants and Animals of Marshes, Bogs and Swamps, by Janet Lyons and Sandra Jordan

Nature Nearby: An Outdoor Guide to America's 25 Most Visited Cities, by Bill McMillon

Wild Plants of America: A Select Guide for the Naturalist and Traveler, by Richard M. Smith

Forests: A Naturalist's Guide to Trees and Forest Ecology, by Laurence C. Walker

Forest Fires

• • •

An Introduction
to Wildland Fire Behavior,
Management, Firefighting,
and Prevention

Margaret Fuller

Wiley Nature Editions

John Wiley & Sons, Inc.
New York • Chichester • Brisbane • Toronto • Singapore

SD
421
.F84
1991

In recognition of the importance of preserving what has been
written, it is a policy of John Wiley & Sons, Inc. to have books of
enduring value published in the United States printed on acid-free
paper, and we exert our best efforts to that end.

Copyright © 1991 by John Wiley & Sons, Inc.

All rights reserved. Published simultaneously in Canada.

Reproduction or translation of any part of this work beyond that
permitted by section 107 or 108 of the 1976 United States
Copyright Act without the permission of the copyright owner is
unlawful. Requests for permission or further information should be
addressed to the Permissions Department, John Wiley & Sons, Inc.

Library of Congress Cataloging-in-Publication Data
Fuller, Margaret.
    Forest fires : An introduction to wildland fire behavior,
management, firefighting, and prevention / Margaret Fuller.
        p.   cm.—(Wiley nature editions)
    Includes bibliographical references and index.
    ISBN 0-471-52189-2 (paper)
    1. Forest fires.   2. Fire ecology.   I. Title.   II. Series.
    SD421.F84   1991
    634.9'618—dc20   90-46331
                                                             CIP

Printed in the United States of America

91 92 10 9 8 7 6 5 4 3 2 1

Acknowledgments

This book would not have been possible without the help of the many people who granted interviews and provided information and assistance. I would especially like to thank my editor at John Wiley & Sons, David Sobel, and his assistant, Nancy Woodruff. In addition, Linda Hieb of the Caldwell, Idaho, library, the staff of the Boise State University Library periodical room, and Rozella Hopkins of the Boise Interagency Fire Center Library provided most of the library materials I needed to complete the book. I would like to thank the people at the Boise Interagency Fire Center who helped by granting interviews and providing information. Researchers at the Intermountain Fire Sciences Laboratory in Missoula, Montana, played a special role in editing the manuscript and making sure that it was technically accurate. In addition, I would like to thank Jack Wilson, director of the Bureau of Land Management (the host agency) at the Boise Interagency Fire Center, for writing the foreword, and I would like to thank the many people whom I interviewed for the book, who edited the manuscript, or who otherwise helped me: Bill Adams, Ed Allen, Mary Allinger, Jay Anderson, Steve Arno, Bob Barbee, Wintauna Belt, Gene Benedict, Doug Brown, Jim Brown, Lonnie Brown, Merlin Brown, Frank Carroll, Bob Cathcart, Eleanor Cathcart, Wallace Cathcart, Jerry Chonka, Elsie Cunningham, Wayne Dawson, Don Despain, Sue Douglas, Mary Dudley, Bill Fischer, Lynn Flock, Doug Fuller, Hilary Fuller, Wayne Fuller, Michael Galvin, Steve Gauger, Rolf Goerke, Jamie Haines, Bobbie Hartford, Arnold Hartigan, Marilyn Hemker, Dave Hettinger, Dick Hodge, Karen Holcomb, Rozella Hopkins, Roy Inskeep, Anne Marie Jehle, Marsha Karle, Beth Lund, Bill Meadows, Paul Moroz, Dennis Oaks, Dave Olson, Paul Smith Color Lab, Ron Pierce, Richard Pine, Evelyn Pogue, Joel Pomeroy, Stanley Potts, John Pritchard, Lynn Reinig, F. Dale Robertson, Ron Rochna, John Russell, Kevin Ryan, Merrill Saleen, Stark's Photography, Janice Strachan, Richard Rothermel, Conrad Smith, Bert Strom, Dick Terry, John Varley, Joe Wagenfehr, Bob Webber, Paul Werth, Cyd Wieland, Bill Williams, Steve Williams, Wayne Williams, George Wuerthner, Ron Yacomella, and Greg Zschaechner.

Contents

Foreword

Fire is one of the great forces of nature, both everyone's great friend and deadly enemy. That is, we may enjoy a hamburger from the grill, but the same fire that cooked it could also burn our house. We know surprisingly little about fire. For example, even after all our years of dealing with it, we have not yet arrived at an acceptable understanding or definition of smoke. Furthermore, we learned in Yellowstone—and will probably learn more in the fires that will burn the trees snapped off by Hurricane Hugo—that in certain situations, most of what we think we know about fire can also go up in flames. And despite all our resources and technology, we cannot control all fires.

Likewise, we know a great deal about lightning, but we do not know how to predict whether a particular stroke will cause a fire. And even though we have learned much about fire effects, we still know little about such effects on a large scale. For example, introducing 2 trillion Btus from a fire into our closed-world ecosystem must have some effect. Also, in the 1980s about 1 percent of the earth's surface burned every year, and even this may be a conservative estimate. The sheer loss of productive timber resources alone is cause for great concern.

Margaret Fuller has done research and talked with people in the "fire world." She has threaded her way through the sensitive and complex issues regarding forest fires and has brought to light the fundamental problems that need to be addressed. This book describes today's experiences with fire as well as the people who have been shaping tomorrow's experiences with fire. The details, though generally not technical, enable the reader of this book to understand the basic issues. Firefighters, fire managers, and, indeed, anyone interested in wildland fire will enjoy reading *Forest Fires*.

Jack Wilson, Director, Bureau of Land Management, Boise Interagency Fire Center

Preface

In the United States in 1985, wildfires destroyed 1400 homes and killed 44 people. Each year since then, fires have burned more than 300 homes, and in June 1990, wildfires destroyed more than 600 homes. In northern China in 1987, the Great Black Dragon Fire burned 3 million acres, devastating several towns and killing more than 200 people. This fire also consumed 15 million acres in Siberia, making it the world's largest forest fire in recorded history.

At Old Faithful in Yellowstone National Park, the gloom in midafternoon of September 7, 1988, resembled twilight. To the west a wall of orange flame touched towering clouds that rolled and tumbled, mixing with the flames. Embers from the flaming wall sailed over the open area toward an immense log inn. As the embers landed on the roof and flared up, firefighters with hoses successfully doused the blaze. That summer, forest fires covered nearly half of Yellowstone National Park.

In 1989, a forest fire burned 49 homes outside Boulder, Colorado, and a few weeks later a firestorm whipped through Lowman, Idaho, destroying 25 homes and a lodge. How did all these fires start? Some believe that drought caused it. Others cite the fuel buildup from fire suppression as the reason. This book explores these and other causes of the recent fires.

Forest Fires tells the story of the 1980s' drought fires and discusses what might happen if the drought continues. This book also covers the science of wildland fires, including physics, chemistry, behavior, weather, and ecology—fire's effect on plants and animals—as well as the technology used to fight fires. It describes the effects of weather on both forest fires and forest fuels and how they, in turn, influence a fire's behavior. The

Twenty years or more after a fire on Mosquito Ridge in the Frank Church–River of No Return Wilderness, young trees cover the ground between the old snags.

Here in Olympic National Park is an old snag in a forest that grew up after a fire long ago.

book also explores firefighting methods and equipment, including the new minimum-impact techniques and compressed-air foam, as well as prescribed burning, both natural fire and planned ignitions. The author advocates respect for fire, not only for its power, but also for its relationship with ecosystems, and she outlines steps that homeowners and those who enjoy outdoor recreation can take to protect themselves and their homes from wildland fire.

Finally, *Forest Fires* offers a brief history of forest fire policies in the United States, discusses the current policies, and presents some ideas for solving wildland fire problems around the world.

We hope that this book will tell you enough about the science and technology of wildland fires, the effects of fires on forests, and the difficulties of controlling wildfires that you can evaluate the United States' current wildland fire policies and even try to change those policies when necessary.

Introduction

During the Lowman Fire in Idaho in 1989, a firestorm trapped a fire engine crew on the hillside behind the Haven Lodge, a hot springs resort, located across state Highway 21 from the South Fork of the Payette River. The resort included a two-story log lodge, a cinder-block and tin gas station, and a cement swimming pool enclosed by a board fence.

Ron Rochna, the driver of the fire engine, explained that when he arrived at the Haven Lodge, just before the firestorm, "the fire on top of the ridge just above us was spinning, and the clouds were already red-orange." He and his partner, Clarence Grady, had driven up to the ridge to save a man who had earlier refused to leave his home. But Rochna and Grady could not persuade the man to leave. He told them: "I'd rather die than leave. Everything I own is here. [If it all burned down] I would have nothing to live for." In addition to saving lives, Rochna had been ordered to try to save all buildings in the area, so he started spraying fire-retardant foam on the man's house. Even when some of the foam splashed this would-be martyr, he still would not leave. But finally, when foam had covered the house and yard, the man climbed in his pickup truck and left.

To make sure everyone had left, Rochna and Grady stayed in the area but moved about 100 yards down the canyon to where the fire was nearing two houses next to a couple of propane tanks. Luckily, no one was in the houses. When Carl Dorsey, the driver of a second fire engine, called him on his radio, Rochna suggested that Dorsey drive up to meet him. When Dorsey arrived, Rochna asked him to work on a spot fire

On a day when the air was unstable, fire spotted into the heavy
fuels of an old blowdown and triggered the Lowman firestorm.
Courtesy of the Boise Interagency Fire Center.

that threatened several homes as well as both of the men's own
escape. Rochna then began to foam the first house and its yard.
As he did this he threw the firewood stacked against the house
out into the yard and sprayed it with foam. Over the radio he
heard, "Get out of there, she's blowing up."

About that time the wind knocked Rochna to the ground,
and at first it blew too hard for him to get up. So he lay on the
ground; Grady was still in the truck between the house and the
fire. The flames were traveling horizontally, gobbling up trees
and power poles in their path. One of the nearby sheds was
blown apart by the fire. Power lines fell on the truck, which was
about 10 feet from the house. Then the house caught fire. As
Rochna described it, "Everything turned pure red. It was like
something you see on television and where you say, Geez! 'That
could never really happen!'" Flames enveloped the truck but
did not burn it; they just melted the rubber around the windshield. Then with a roar, flames from the propane tank next
to the house shot up 50 feet in the air. With so many other
propane tanks so close by, Rochna thought his fire shelter—a

pup tent made of aluminized cloth—would be useless. During his training he had learned that the shock wave from an exploding propane tank would kill a person as far away as 1000 feet. Not surprisingly, Rochna felt "this hollow feeling in my stomach, this knot."

But his luck held, and after the flames had moved beyond the truck, Rochna climbed back into it. Grady was still there. They both put on their respirators as a precaution, and Grady drove the truck down into a vegetable garden away from the buildings.

In the garden they got out of the truck and at first sat on its downwind side, closed in by dense smoke and burning buildings. Now and then they sprayed the truck with foam to keep it cool. But because there were at least ten propane tanks within 1400 feet of them, one only 50 feet away, after a few minutes they decided to leave the truck.

Still wearing their respirators, they tried to reach the river canyon but found their way obstructed by burning vehicles and trailers and the flames of the Haven Lodge. Small explosions, probably from fuel containers, kept showering them with shrapnel. Nonetheless, they kept moving for about an hour, taking shelter where they could, until the fire quieted down. When they finally emerged from the fire zone, they found their vision hazy; their eyes burned and felt as though they were full of rocks. Even after a medic washed the bits of charcoal out of their eyes, it took five days before their vision cleared.

Dorsey had driven his engine out when the warning came, trying to foam the lodge on the way until everything turned red. He and his assistant, Allen Olson, had driven through the flames with Olson lying on top of the truck and spraying foam ahead to clear (and cool down) a passage.

Rochna, the leader of the foam project at the Boise Interagency Fire Center, explained that working on a fire like this one is difficult psychologically for the firefighters because they must save people, in addition to the forest. He and Grady had spent the morning of that day inventorying the buildings in the canyon and planning how to protect them. They had knocked on doors to warn as many people as possible of the danger, telling them to shut and board up the windows and move flammable materials away from their homes. Rochna recalled that

Spraying firefighting foam on houses in Lowman saved several of them from the 1989 fire. Courtesy of the USDA Forest Service.

some of them looked at him with disbelief, as though he were telling them that Martians were coming. He also feared that "a stupid house would take precedence over my priorities and plans for myself and my family."

Rochna's story is just one view of the Lowman Fire. How did the people whose homes burned feel? Karen Holcomb, her husband Dale, and her in-laws Feild and Evelyn Pogue owned the Haven Lodge. Holcomb remembered that on Saturday, July 29, 1989, she and two helpers were cooking steaks for the fire-fighters when the receptionist at the ranger station called and told her to leave. All of the lodge guests had already left because of the fire. Her husband then drove up the road to look for their water truck, which they had lent to a logging company. Karen telephoned her 19-year-old son, Randy, at their house above the lodge and asked him to rescue their photo albums. He brought them down to the lodge, but when he got there, Forest Service personnel ordered everyone out of the lodge and would not let him go back to rescue his stereo. Holcomb took time only to gather up her younger son, Denny, 13, their dog, her purse, her EMT radio, and two bank bags. Holcomb said that when they came out of the lodge, it felt like a blast furnace and that stuff was flying everywhere as if it were in a tornado.

They drove up to the turnout opposite Kirkham Hot Springs and waited. When Dale Holcomb came back with the water truck, some of their neighbors jumped in and went with him back to the lodge. They came right back, though, as they could do nothing more to save it. Although Feild Pogue had put sprinklers on the roof, they were not working because there was no power. In a few minutes the Forest Service officers advised the group to go farther up the highway. That night, Saturday, they stayed at a house up the river owned by a small telephone company. By Sunday the smoke was so bad they went on to Stanley, 50 miles away, and there they rejoined many of their neighbors, like Mary Allinger.

Mary Allinger lived in a mobile home up on the hill behind the Haven Lodge. She and her husband, Jerry, had built a roof over the mobile home and a two-story addition on one end of it, roofed with metal. They also had put in a lawn, an orchard, and a huge garden. Sprinklers were running somewhere on their land all the time. On that same Saturday morning the Allingers could see that the flames across the river had moved toward them. Their neighbors came over and watched the fire with them from their porch. Mary Allinger had heard that if the fire reached the dead trees—blown down in a 1987 windstorm—it would just take off, and so she was worried.

In the afternoon Jerry left to work on a water system for a family down the river. About 2:30 P.M. Mary and a friend noticed fire on the hill behind the house. Soon after, the Forest Service people knocked on her door and told her to evacuate. Allinger changed into long pants, collected her diamond ring and other jewelry, and began to look for her cat and dog.

Outside, someone told her, "Get in your car, and get out of here now." Allinger recalled that the heat felt like an inferno, the wind blew so hard it nearly knocked her over, and the roar of the fire deafened her. Everything looked red, red, red, and she had never felt so scared in her life. She joined the other evacuees at the Kirkham turnout and then proceeded upriver beyond the fire and eventually to Stanley.

When she called her husband and told him their house was gone, he did not believe it at first. He was trapped at Lowman and could not join her, as all the roads were closed. Mary wondered afterward why the Forest Service had not warned them earlier so that they at least could have rescued the pictures from their walls. But her husband had kept telling her not to be foolish; he was sure the fire could not cross the river.

Likewise, the Holcombs also had always believed the river and the highway would protect them from any fire across the river. Indeed, they had worried more about a kitchen fire. The previous owners of the Holcombs' Haven Lodge still held all the insurance on the buildings, and so the Holcombs had insurance only for their personal property, all of which they lost. Nothing was left, not even coins and rings, except for a lot of beer buried under the ashes. The fire even had melted the steel grill in the restaurant. And nothing was left of the lodge itself but ashes, pieces of rusty metal, the cement chimney, and the metal outdoor stairs to the upper rooms.

Photographs of the Allingers' home after the fire show a pile of crumpled corrugated tin roofing with a cinder-block chimney in the middle. Although Mary's old-fashioned black-iron piggy bank survived the fire, the pennies inside it had melted. The fire also took her husband's fishing equipment and collection of 18 guns. Everything else was gone, including their dog and all of their cats except one mother cat and one kitten. Although the Allingers had insurance, it did not cover the full value of their home or property. According to Mary, "So many of the things you have when you are my age you know you'll never have again." Indeed, when she went back to see the damage, it made her sick and she has not returned.

Although Mary Allinger admits that by Saturday morning the Forest Service could not have done any more than it did do, she said she still felt bitter toward the officials, except for Fire Management Officer Beth Lund, who, Mary remembered, came up and said she was sorry and gave her a hug.

Most of the people in Lowman either do not plan to rebuild or cannot afford to do so. The community tried to raise enough money to rebuild the Haven Lodge (a financial asset of the town), but the money they collected amounted to only a fraction of what would be needed. Although the Allingers officially moved to Boise, Jerry still lives during the week in a camper on their lot at Lowman because he is employed on a road construction project near there. Mary misses the people

In 1989 a firestorm destroyed 25 buildings in Lowman, including the Haven Lodge.

The Lowman firestorm caused such a severe burn on these slopes that erosion and flooding were feared. To prevent it, the Boise National Forest undertook the most extensive postfire rehabilitation to date in a U.S. national forest.

in Lowman, especially those in the community church, which still stands.

When a house burns in a fire like this, it turns into lumps of melted, twisted metal, shards of glass, and masses of blackened rubble. Unlike a house, however, a forest is not ruined by fire, because it can grow back on its own. A forest is continuously changing, in the same way that the seasons do or rock forms and erodes over time. To see the effect of fires on forests, you must visit Yellowstone or the site of one of the other recent fires. Then you will need to go back every few years for 100 or more years. But because you are unlikely to live that long, it would be more practical to look at forests that burned 100 years ago.

What does a forest look like right after a fire and 1, 2, 5, 10, 50, and 100 years later? If you fly over a forest in a small plane, you can see the patterns that fires make.

From a plane on a September day in 1989, Dave Olson, a public information officer for Idaho's Payette National Forest, made a video on wilderness fire, using the Frank Church–River of No Return Wilderness as an example of the patterns left by fire. At each burn Olson talked to the pilot, Lynn Clark, on the radio, telling her where to turn and what he wanted to photograph. Ed Allen, the assistant fire management officer for the district, commented on the fires as they flew along.

From the air, burns of different ages formed a tapestry of gray, black with rust-colored edges, and shades of green. Allen first pointed out the 25-year-old Flossie Lake burn. Here an immense carpet of young, short trees met a taller forest on a ridge, showing that one recent fire had stopped at the edge of the older burned area, because young lodgepole pines usually will not carry fire.

Allen next called attention to the 1986 Hand Meadows Fire. Here a few pale green patches of grass, brush, and seedlings showed beneath feathery gray snags. Nearby, the Hand Creek Fire sent up a small white plume of smoke from one edge of a blackened area. Allen and the Payette Forest officials were still monitoring this fire, but it had burned little in the last few weeks. Allen pointed out another blackened area as that summer's Game Creek Fire, which had burned out earlier. The Forest Service managed this fire by confining it to about 3000 acres. To do this it sent in a crew who used minimum-impact

A forest is a tapestry of burns of different ages. Here the 30-year-old Flossie Lake burn meets an even older burn.

methods, which leave little or no trace on the land. The crew built no fire line but just used water to keep the fire contained.

After a stop at the Chamberlain Ranger Station, the plane flew on to Cold Meadows. As it approached, Allen pointed out the large blackened area of the Sliver Creek Fire of 1988. Near Cold Meadows, the gray slopes held only a few blackened spars and branches and the pale stripe of a trail. Here the fire had burned intensely in the run it made on the same day that the North Fork Fire overran Old Faithful.

After stopping at Cold Meadows to film the burn from the ground, the plane flew over the Steep Cabin Fire of 1988. Allen explained that most of these other fires had destroyed so many trees that they were referred to as *stand-replacing fires*, fires that kill all the trees in an area. Although these fires had burned some older lodgepole pine and Douglas fir, the predominant species were subalpine fir and Engelmann spruce. On the other hand, the Steep Cabin Fire had only nibbled at the trees, mostly because it occurred in open forests of Douglas fir and ponderosa pine. This fire, on the south canyon wall of the Salmon River, showed only a few black spots where some trees—whose pitchy bases had made them vulnerable—had burned. The prevailing picture, however, was of straw-colored grass under living, albeit charred, trees.

On the way back from filming the video, Allen pointed out patches of older burns. Shorter and paler green trees covered the 40- or 50-year-old burns. "See where the trees are a slightly different shade of green?" Allen asked. "That's an even older burn—I have no idea how long ago [it happened.]" The plane flew on over the patches of black, gray, pale green, bright green, and dark green. Bright gold aspens highlighted this tapestry crafted by fire.

A fire mosaic like this shows a healthy forest, a fact that many people today fail to understand. Instead, they worry about the unusual number of large fires that have occurred in the 1980s in North America and elsewhere. The fires accompanying the recent drought in many areas of the United States have indeed burned homes and killed and injured firefighters, homeowners, and others. But even though burned homes are static—that is, they are damaged and will not recover—burned forests are dynamic—that is, they usually are not damaged and will progress through a series of stages back to what they were before the fire.

Chapter One

■ ■ ■

Drought Fires of the 1980s

The Butte Fire in Idaho's Salmon National Forest in 1985 threatened the lives of two fire crews. But Ron Yacomella, of the Challis National Forest, and the two crews in his charge survived by using aluminized pup tents called *fire shelters*, which have flaps by which the occupant holds the shelter down as he or she lies under it. Fire shelters protect firefighters from surface burns, and more important, the shelters protect the firefighters' lungs from being seared by breathing the intensely hot air. The Butte Fire was the first fire in which a large number of shelters had been used.

Yacomella had been working on top of a ridge with two crews preparing to do a burnout to a *cat line*, a fire line made by a bulldozer. They planned to set fire to some of the fuels that lay between the line and the fire, until they heard on the radio that the fire was "blowing up," that is, suddenly increasing in size and intensity. Thus they had 5 to 10 minutes before the fire from the heavy timber would reach them, and so they set a smaller fire to enlarge their safety zone, a 200-foot square of bare ground.

When they saw 400-foot flames, they popped into their shelters, but as Yacomella tried to secure himself in his, the wind blew him over before he could lie down properly in a prone position. The wind sounded like a jet plane taking off. In the shelter he felt the fire's heat but was not burned. At first Yacomella saw the fire glowing fluorescent orange through the walls of the shelter; then everything turned black with smoke. After the fire "spotted," that is, threw embers that started new fires, across the cleared area, it burned back uphill and overran the crews a second time. When Yacomella and his crew realized that the fire was returning, most of them crawled—in their shelters—across to the opposite side of the safety zone. Five firefighters who had abandoned their shelters after the first wall of flames suffered smoke inhalation and had to be hospitalized.

Afterward, while Yacomella was checking to see whether everyone was all right, some of his crew noticed that the handles had burned off their shovels and *Pulaskis* (special fire tools resembling a combination of hoe and axe). Yacomella was convinced that he and his crew survived because they were on a ridge top where the flames rose into open sky instead of into the trees, as the flames on the slopes below did.

The shelters saved 73 lives in the Butte Fire, and consequently the Forest Service produced a video about the episode. Bill Adams of the Wind Cave National Monument, who helped film the video, explained the Forest Service made the video to demonstrate that firefighters should use these shelters only as a last resort but that they also could depend on them to save their lives. In fact, since 1974, the Forest Service has required firefighters to carry shelters, but until this episode many of them did not realize just how important they were. Indeed, before this experience, Yacomella had always regarded his shelter as unnecessary weight.

Drought Fires in North America

By the end of the summer of 1988, fire had overrun 1,585,600 acres of the 12-million-acre Greater Yellowstone Area (see Figure 1.1). Even though not all of the area within the fire perimeter burned, that perimeter covered nearly half of Yellowstone Park. The final Park Service report, compiled from satellite images and aerial photography, revealed that the fires had scorched 793,880 acres of the 2.2 million-acre park. Because the fires threw embers as far as 1½ miles away, firefighters could not stop them.

During that same summer in the United States, more than 70,000 drought fires consumed over 5 million acres, 2 million acres of which was in Alaska. The last time so much land had burned was during a drought in 1910 when fires in northern Idaho and western Montana seared 3 million acres and killed

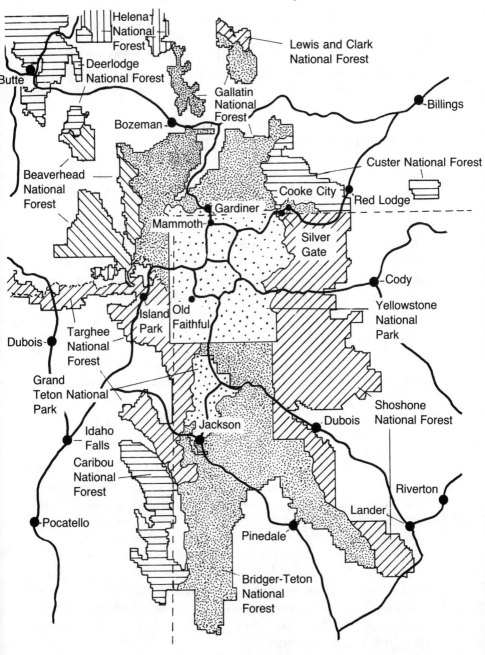

Figure 1.1

This map of the Greater Yellowstone Area shows the places mentioned in the accounts of the Yellowstone fires.

85 people. In a later drought in 1977, 2 million acres were burned.

The most recent drought fires in North America began in 1980 when 12 million acres burned in Canada. Then in 1981 an additional 13 million Canadian acres caught fire. In 1984 the Rosie Creek Fire threatened the suburbs of Fairbanks, Alaska, and on the fifth day, the fire jumped the Alaska Parks Highway and turned into a firestorm that snapped off trees in an experimental forest. (A *firestorm* is a fire that is so large and intense that it creates violent winds within its perimeter. In Chapter 2 we shall describe firestorms more fully.) Finally, in 1989, a record 16 million acres burned in Canada, and officials had to evacuate 24,500 people in Manitoba alone. Farther south, in Mexico, 1.2 million acres burned in 1988 and another 1.2 million acres in 1989. Of the trees that burned in 1989, 300,000 acres of them had been blown down by Hurricane Gilbert on the Yucatan Peninsula in September 1988.

Drought Fires in Australia

In the 1980s, Australia suffered devastating fires caused by the drought, the Ash Wednesday fires of February 16, 1983. Many of these so-called drought fires—which followed 10 months of no rain—started when high winds blew trees onto power lines. The subsequent fires destroyed 2500 homes and killed 75 people in Victoria, South Australia, and Tasmania.

On one memorable day in 1983, 23 fires consumed 846,100 acres, destroying seven towns and seaside resorts in their path. Strong winds blowing from a high-pressure area over the continent toward a cold front out at sea drove the fires: A video taken of the fire from an airplane at night showed that it resembled the unzipping of a black curtain over an inferno.

Australia frequently has fires because its most common trees are eucalyptus, which burn more easily than do most trees, because of the oils they contain. Tasmania, which has similar vegetation, also has many bushfires, and in times of drought, such fires can cover huge areas.

The Great Black Dragon Fire in China

The Great Black Dragon Fire incinerated 3.2 million acres in China and another 15 million acres in Siberia. There had been almost no rain during the summer of 1986 and no winter snow during the winter of 1986–1987, which meant that the drought was severe by the spring of 1987, when the fire started.

The Chinese called it the Black Dragon Fire because the Chinese name of the Amur River, which forms the Chinese–Soviet border, means Black Dragon. Actually several fires burned on both sides of the river. The first Soviet fire started 15 days before the first fire caught on the Chinese side of the river.[1]

The Soviet Union has never acknowledged the fire, but satellite photos revealed its presence. Apparently the Soviets were not concerned, as few people live in the area and they do not yet need its timber, according to a Soviet forester, Aleksandr Sergeyevich Isayev, who visited the Boise Interagency Fire Center in July 1989. He noted, too, that usually Soviet firefighters try to put out only those fires that threaten life and property.

The Chinese blamed an itinerant brush cutter, Wang Yu-feng, for starting the Black Dragon Fire on May 6 when gasoline he spilled from his brush-cutting machine caught fire. In reality, however, several other fires started at about the same time, from various sources. But by the evening of the day that Wang's fire started, 1000 firefighters were already attacking it.

By the next morning the firefighters had contained the fire, but then that afternoon a high wind of 50 or 60 miles an hour moved the fire into the treetops. As the town of Kilinji burned, its mayor, political director, and an army battalion leader were able to save all but 57 of the 22,000 people. Later the Chinese also seeded the clouds with dry ice, creating two rainstorms and enabling the government to credit the seeding with putting out the fire.

---

[1]Because of its frequent drought, northern China has the most forest fires of any area in that country. During the April/May fire season winds over 25 miles an hour usually blow for more than 10 days. Seven fires of over 163,000 acres each had burned in the preceding 10 years. Because more forest burns here each year than managers can replant, and in 25 years, 21 million acres have burned, the Chinese felt it was a disaster to lose so much timber in the Great Black Dragon Fire. To help with the disaster the World Bank approved a loan to China for fire rehabilitation.

At the time of the fire, the Chinese detected fires with patrols and lookout towers and maintained crews of professional firefighters. Some of the firefighters and fire managers had taken training provided by Canada in a joint program started in 1983.

Only because the fire straddled the Soviet border did the Chinese allow their reporters to view it; they did not let in any outsiders to report on the fire until Harrison Salisbury, formerly of the *New York Times*, was allowed into the area a year later to write a book about the fire. At that time the brush cutter, Wang, was still in jail. The TV hero of the fire, Wu Changfu, commanded the 36,000 troops fighting the fire. From the time he arrived until the fire was finally put out 26 days later, Wu did not shave; hence his name, Changfu, or "Black Beard."

Drought Fires in the United States in 1987

In 1987, drought also led to fires in the United States. The Klamath and Stanislaus national forests in northern California had two of the biggest fires that year. The Klamath fires came after three years of drought and a winter of no snowpack. They started on August 30 when 2400 lightning strikes accompanying dry thunderstorms hit California in 8 hours, igniting over 900 fires. Soon after, despite the efforts of 22,000 firefighters, fires were raging over 1000 square miles.

During the Stanislaus fires, near the town of Sonora, the Forest Service evacuated five small towns and closed the forest. The 86 Klamath National Forest fires burned 254,000 acres, but the firefighters took advantage of unusual resources to put out the fires, such as traveling to the fire lines by jet boat (a boat with a jet engine, all of whose working parts are contained inside the hull and so cannot be damaged by rocks). Doug Brown, a crew leader on the Elk Complex Fire, used jet boats to reach places along the river where the crew could ignite fires that would burn toward the main fire, thus forming a fuel break. Crews farther down the river had to travel by rubber raft, however, as the rapids prevented their using the jet boats.

Because of the steep riverbanks—slopes averaging 27 degrees—firefighters found it difficult and dangerous to work. They had trouble keeping burning logs from rolling downhill past the fire lines, even when they had dug trenches, and so they ignited back burns instead of constructing fire lines.

A *temperature inversion*—in which the warm air above traps the cold air below—trapped the smoke, thereby making the Klamath fires even more difficult to fight. The morning after he and his crew arrived at the fire camp for the Elk Complex,

Temperature inversions trap smoke in the valleys and create poor visibility for the firefighters. Courtesy of the USDA Forest Service.

Brown observed, "It was so smoky, it looked like the workshop of Hades." Away from the lighted area, the thick smoke forced the firefighters to use headlamps, even in the daytime. The temperature inversion also meant that the fires burned on the ridges all night long but the canyons remained cold. The firefighters could see so little that they could tell when the fire "crowned" only by the ashes falling on their heads.

Also because of the smoke, air tankers could seldom be used. Roy Inskeep, a fire management officer for the Middle Fork District of the Challis National Forest who ran the air support for the fire, remembered that in the 21 days he spent there, only one helicopter, which flew for 5 hours, ever got into the air. In addition, the zero visibility made it difficult to drive. On September 9, the level of particulates at Happy Camp, the nearest town, reached 4600 micrograms per cubic meter, 30 times the level the Environmental Protection Agency (EPA) considers unhealthful.

Firefighters suffered from both carbon monoxide and smoke inhalation. Exposure to carbon monoxide leads to greater-than-normal fatigue. For example, when one young man walked into the planning unit of the Happy Complex fire camp and complained of being worn out after 21 days of work without respite, the plans chief handed him a form to fill out so that he could be sent home. A minute later the chief noticed him asleep, with his head on the form.

In Idaho in 1987, when the Deadwood Fire in the Boise National Forest started, the Forest Service declared it a pre-scribed natural fire, that is, a fire caused by lightning and al-lowed to burn itself out if it does not spread outside certain areas or threaten life or property. Since the policies permitting prescribed natural fires were implemented in 1976, several of these fires have caused controversy, among which was the Dead-wood Fire. When first detected on August 4, the fire was burn-ing less than 2 miles from the border of the Frank Church Wilderness. Soon after, an air tanker plane dropped a load of chemical fire retardant on it, but "smokejumpers" could not jump because of the high winds.

Because the firefighters already were fighting two other large fires and this fire was heading for the wilderness, the fire managers decided to try to confine it. After it reached the wil-derness on August 6, Boise Forest officials sent crews to guard the private Sulphur Creek Ranch and others nearby. Then when 1 inch of rain fell on August 13, they removed the crews. The rain, however, put out the fire only in the light fuels, not in the logs, stumps, and large trees, where it continued to burn.

On August 20 when the fire began to burn fiercely again, the owner of the Sulphur Creek Ranch hired his own fire-fighters. But because the fire was a wilderness fire, the Forest Service requested that he remove them, which he did but grum-bled to reporters about the request. At about the same time, some people in Boise also began to complain, especially about the excessive smoke. Toward the end of August the fire made runs for several days but died down again in September. Then on October 4 the fire roared along for 5 miles to the Boundary Creek Campground at Dagger Falls, the launching point for the Middle-Fork-of-the-Salmon raft trips. Here the fire trapped a party of hunters who had taken refuge at the boat ramp after riding through a tunnel of fire to reach it.

The news media gave much publicity to this episode, so much that when the officials of the Intermountain Region reviewed the fire, their solution to controversy caused by wilderness fires was to ask for the intercession of a public information officer. These officials believed that any time the fire suppression strategy was less than total extinction, the officer could avoid a public uproar by building support for the strategy.

The Yellowstone Fires in 1988 _____

In 1988, drought parched Yellowstone, as it did most of the rest of the West. Earlier, in December 1987, the Palmer Drought Index had showed Yellowstone to be in a mild drought. Then the winter brought a record-low snowpack of only 16 percent of normal. (The Palmer index for an area is based on the actual precipitation compared with the average. It calculates this comparison by assuming that a normally wetter area needs more moisture to sustain itself than a normally drier area does. A normal index reading thus is zero, with negative readings indicating drought and positive readings pointing to a wet year.)

By May 1 the index showed that the drought was severe to extreme. Even though park officials had seen the drought data, they ignored them because they expected the 200-percent-of-normal July rains that had fallen during each of the last six Julys to fall in 1988 as well. In fact, as late as July 11 the National Weather Service predicted normal July rainfall for the area. Unfortunately, however, the driest summer in park history followed, after seven winters of below-normal snowpack and a wet spring. April and May recorded 150 percent and 180 percent of the normal rainfall, and so it was a surprise when only 20 percent fell in June, 79 percent in July, and 10 percent in August. By midsummer the moisture of the dead fine fuels (dry grass and twigs) sank to 2 to 3 percent and that of the larger fuels to 7 percent.

The Yellowstone fires began on May 24 with the Rose Fire in the Lamar Valley. (That fire was started by lightning and put out by rain in the same day.) On June 14, lightning started the Storm Creek Fire in the Absaroka–Beartooth Wilderness northeast of the park. On June 23 lightning ignited the Shoshone Fire near Yellowstone Lake. In its first 30 days this fire burned only 160 acres but by June 23 had consumed 4500 acres. Then on June 25 when the Fan Fire started in the Gallatin Range in Montana, in the park's northwest corner, local residents asked the Park Service to put it and the other fires out, and when the service did not comply, their resentment grew.

Over the July 4 holiday, lightning started three more fires and from July 9 to 12, seven more fires broke out. One of these, the Clover Fire, burned 2000 acres in the first three days. On July 12, even though the Shoshone Fire leapt the river 6 miles from Grant Village, Yellowstone's fire managers decided to let it remain a prescribed natural fire. They considered this decision appropriate because Yellowstone's fire management plan stated that only if a fire threatened human lives, buildings, or special features, should it be fought.

On July 15, however, when nine fires were burning inside the park, the park officials followed a procedure in their natural fire policy to allow no new natural fires to burn except those next to existing fires. On July 20 when the Shoshone Fire had extended 2 more miles toward Grant Village, the park declared it and two other nearby fires to be wildfires (which would be fought). On July 21 the Clover and Mist fires joined and ran toward the Shoshone National Forest. Because the forest management wanted nothing to do with the Clover–Mist Fire, the park declared it a wildfire. Finally, by July 21, when the fires, now covering 17,000 acres, alarmed U.S. Interior Secretary Donald Hodel sufficiently that on July 21 he ordered all the fires to be actively fought, they were already being fought.

The next day a recreation worker reported seeing a woodcutter throw a lighted cigarette into dry grass 300 yards outside Yellowstone Park, just after the North Fork Fire had started nearby; this fire eventually grew into the largest of the Yellowstone fires.

Within an hour four pumpers were working on the fire, and smokejumpers had arrived but could not jump because of 20- to 35-mile-an-hour winds. Bulldozers and a hand crew constructed a fire line around the rear of the fire, and tankers dropped five loads of retardant on it, but the winds were too strong to risk putting planes or firefighters ahead of the fire. By the end of the day it was spotting one-half mile ahead as it ran into the park toward Old Faithful, and ten 20-man crews, two bulldozers, nine fire engines, and a helicopter were fighting the fire.

That evening the fire died down when the winds calmed. At this time the person in charge of the fire, called the *initial-*

The 1988 Yellowstone fires burned at a frequency and intensity that was natural for lodgepole pine forests. Courtesy of the Boise Interagency Fire Center.

attack incident commander, asked for permission to bulldoze a fire line within the park. He felt that the firefighters had a 50–50 chance of putting a line around the fire that night. His request was denied.

By the next morning the fire had grown to 460 acres and, by the following day, to 1300 acres. When the area commander for the Yellowstone fires, Troy Kurth, and the chief park ranger, Dan Sholly, looked at the fire on July 24, they concluded that even if a fire line could have been built on the night of July 22, the fire would still have crossed it the next day. Kurth and Sholly therefore decided not to try to put it out but only to monitor it, because of the danger of putting firefighters in front of it, the probability of not being able to stop it anyway, the high costs of trying to, and the impact of suppression on the land. Crews continued working along the park's boundary to keep the fire from burning back into the Targhee National Forest, but fire managers concentrated most of their effort on trying to keep the fire from reaching Old Faithful.

People complained because they thought that the bulldozers could have prevented the fires from becoming so large. But no fire line is effective when fires spot—or when they throw embers, as they were doing—a half mile or more ahead of the fire. The last week in July, all the fires were spotting far ahead. In addition, the humidity was not rising at night, as it usually does, and so the fires remained active all night instead of slowing down.

On July 23 the Shoshone Fire forced the evacuation of Grant Village, and on July 24 the North Fork Fire advanced 5 miles toward Old Faithful. Then on July 25 the fire jumped the road near Grant Village, and so the fire camp, West Thumb, and the Lewis Lake campground had to be evacuated. By that time, 1500 firefighters were fighting the fires, a number that later in the summer rose to 9700.

On July 27 when Interior Secretary Hodel actually visited the park, he announced that the Department of the Interior would reexamine its natural fire policy. This natural fire policy allows lightning fires in wildernesses and national parks to burn as long as they stay within certain areas and do not threaten lives or property. By the time of Hodel's visit, however, 34 fires in the greater Yellowstone Area had burned 88,000 acres, and on July 31 the North Fork Fire jumped the Madison River.

On August 2, Richard Rothermel, the best-known fire behavior researcher in the United States, and other experts calculated that the fires would grow by 25 to 50 percent in the next 30 days. But in the next five days alone the fires grew more than 50 percent. Information given out by more than 55 public information officers could not prevent a public outcry over the fast-spreading fires. Even though other fires were burning without notice, the Yellowstone fires were the ones receiving all the public attention.

A Lack of Firefighting Resources   That summer, an additional 2.2 million acres were burning in Alaska. The United States was already using one-third of its firefighting resources on these fires. Dick Hodge, who served as plans chief for the first area command team at Yellowstone, explained that the area command sent the most resources to those fires with the top priority. Because the extreme fire behavior made the fires too dangerous to fight conventionally, the area command concentrated instead on saving developments.

When Hodge first arrived on July 23, the command gave first priority to the Shoshone Fire because it threatened Grant Village. The second week it transferred top priority to the Fan Fire in the northwest corner of Yellowstone Park because it was threatening to leave the park and invade the land owned by the Church Universal and Triumphant. When firefighters stopped this fire 200 yards outside the park, church members said they were sure it had stopped because they had just completed 24 hours of high-speed chanting.

For two weeks the firefighting also kept the North Fork Fire from reaching Old Faithful, thus meeting the goal of the area command at that time. Firefighters saved buildings by reducing fuel, backfiring, spraying firefighting foam on them, and using irrigation sprinklers. They also saved a million-dollar power line by covering the bottom 15 feet of the power poles with fire shelters and setting up irrigation sprinklers along the line.

In August, dry cold fronts brought high winds that fanned the fires. After the first front brought 40-mile-an-hour

Firefighters saved some buildings and power poles in Yellowstone by plastering them with old aluminized fire shelters. Courtesy of the Boise Interagency Fire Center.

winds, 45 fires were burning, and so many other fires were burning elsewhere that on August 13 the Forest Service decided to fight all fires nationwide, including the prescribed natural fires in large wilderness areas. The fire managers, however, had only enough resources to monitor the wilderness fires to see that they did not escape from their predetermined confines. On August 15 another dry cold front with 25-mile-per-hour winds caused the North Fork Fire to jump the Firehole, Gibbon, and Madison rivers. And on that day the Hellroaring Fire started next to an outfitter camp in the Absaroka–Beartooth Wilderness.

Black Saturday   On August 20, later nicknamed Black Saturday, 30- to 40-mile-per-hour winds with 70-mile-per-hour gusts lifted 100- to 300-foot flames. These winds blew a tree across a power line south of the park, thus starting the Huck Fire, which spread over 4000 acres in only 2 hours. Indeed, on that one day the Yellowstone fires covered 165,000 acres, five times as much as had burned in the park in the preceding 16 years and more than had burned since the park was created in 1872.

On Black Saturday the Clover–Mist Fire ran 11 miles, covering 55,000 acres and coming within 4 miles of the resort communities of Cooke City and Silver Gate, just northeast of the park. That day the Storm Creek Fire ran 10 miles in 4 hours to within 3 miles of Cooke City, and the Hellroaring Fire ran 8 miles in 8 hours.

On Black Saturday Tom Shorten and his dog took refuge in a shallow creek in the Absaroka–Beartooth Wilderness as the fire raged over them. Also on that day Pat Hedges and his two children and dog spent several hours in Horseshoe Creek in the same wilderness. The next day, except for the road in from West Yellowstone, Montana, park officials closed the park. And for the next week the winds continued, pushing the fires over an additional 30,000 to 90,000 acres a day.

On August 30 the area command decided that it needed to divide the North Fork Fire in order to manage it better. Not surprisingly, on that day its northeastern section, the Wolf Lake Fire, ran 2 miles along the edge of Hayden Village and leapt the Yellowstone River.

At the beginning of September, the fire again threatened the nearby towns. On September 1 the North Fork Fire came within 1¼ miles of West Yellowstone, but firefighters were able to save the town with the aid of bulldozers, backfiring, and fire lines dug with explosives. Irrigation sprinklers set up by Idaho farmers also helped. That day the extreme fire hazard throughout the state led Montana's governor, Ted Schwinden, to close the entire state to outdoor recreation. On Sunday, September 4, the day that Silver Gate and Cooke City had to be evacuated, a backfire—which had been set in order to try to save the towns—destroyed a few cabins near Cooke Pass.

Fire at Old Faithful   The best-known episode of the Yellowstone fires was the North Fork Fire's run on September 7 that threatened Old Faithful. News reports, even accounts in scientific magazines, called it a firestorm, although it did not fit the classic pattern. Firefighters, the sprinkling system, and the enormous parking lot saved the inn when the fire jumped the entire area, burning a storage shed and 16 shake-roofed cabins. If the wind had shifted only slightly, the fire would have burned even more.

Even though the Park Service evacuated the inn, it let reporters and tourists remain in the area. That day the Yellowstone fires burned 100,000 acres and threatened eight communities, such as Crandall Creek, east of the park, where the Clover–Mist Fire burned a store and 13 mobile homes.

On September 11, the threat to Old Faithful led President Ronald Reagan to send Interior Secretary Donald Hodel and Agriculture Secretary Richard Lyng to Yellowstone. The two promised more troops for firefighting and a review of all fire policies. By then the North Fork Fire was burning within 1 mile of Mammoth, Tower Junction, and Roosevelt Lodge. After the Park Service evacuated the park's headquarters and other buildings at Mammoth, all the next week it rained, and snow fell at the higher elevations. Even so, by mid-September, nine of the fires were still burning out of control. By September 26 when parts of Yellowstone were reopened, newspaper and TV stories were emphasizing the ecological rebirth of the park. Not until October 17 did the firefighting stop, and it took until November 10 before snow had finally smothered the fires.

Other Fires in 1988 _____

Many fires besides those in Yellowstone scorched the West in 1988. One was the Forty-niner Fire near Grass Valley, California, which burned 360 homes on September 12. Not a week earlier, the Canyon Creek Fire burned 267 square miles in Montana's Scapegoat Wilderness on September 6—more than had burned in Yellowstone on Black Saturday. And the Red Bench Fire in Glacier National Park was the most severe fire in that park in more than 50 years. Indeed, there were so many fires in 1988 that in late August when the Boise Interagency Fire Center tried to send some Yellowstone firefighters to other fires, they first had to train troops to replace them. (The Boise Interagency Fire Center, BIFC, pronounced "biff-see," is the national center for fire management. When a federal land-managing agency or state forestry department needs more resources to put out a fire, it orders them through BIFC.) All of the fires in the United States that year lacked adequate resources. Wintauna Belt, an employee of the Boise National Forest who worked on the Fayette Fire in the Bridger–Teton Wilderness in Wyoming that summer, commented that many times when they ordered a helicopter it would end up in Yellowstone instead. The reason was that the Yellowstone fires were given higher priority, even though the Fayette Fire doubled in size one day from 7000 to 15,000 acres, burning a "spike camp" (subordinate fire camp) in the process.

By summer's end fires also had burned 10 percent of Idaho's 2.3-million-acre Frank Church–River of No Return Wilderness. Like Yellowstone, this wilderness also contains developed areas such as ranches, lodges, ranger stations, and airstrips. Also like Yellowstone, lodgepole pine covers much of the area, so the same kinds of large intense fires can burn here. Rafters and kayakers who float the Salmon River and its Middle Fork are the main recreation users. On August 11, because of the Battleaxe Fire, the Indian Creek airstrip, a major launch point for rafting trips, had to be closed. And on September 6 the Sliver Creek Fire ran 7 miles from the Root Ranch to Cold Meadows through lodgepole pines.

Fires in 1989

Following the Yellowstone fires, the Forest Service and the Interior Department ordered that the policy of letting natural fires burn themselves out be discontinued until all their units had submitted new fire plans. Fire managers were to suppress all fires until the new plans were approved. But when lightning started hundreds of fires in the West in 1989, fire managers found that they simply could not fight all of them at once. The firefighters and equipment would not have been able to reach all the fires right away even if there had been enough to go around.

Even though an average amount of snow fell in parts of the West in the winter of 1988–1989, its water content was not high enough to make up the water deficit. Unusually warm weather in the spring of 1989 melted the snow early. So once again drought dried out the forests and led to fires in the western United States.

One of the first of these fires began on July 9, when a cigarette started a fire in the Sugarloaf area above Boulder, Colorado. Strong winds helped the fire cause $10 million of damage, destroy 39 homes, and damage 28 others, even though firefighters arrived within 45 minutes. Although the fire did not kill anyone, it burned a resident trying to save a neighbor's home. After Colorado Governor Roy Romer toured the area, he suggested that residents of areas like this replace their wood-shake roofs with nonflammable ones; clear away dry grass, shrubs, and trees around their homes; and move propane tanks.

On July 25 and 26, 1989, thunderstorms ignited hundreds of fires in the West, with the automatic lightning detectors at the Boise Interagency Fire Center registering as many as 2000 lightning strikes per hour. Normally only 1 percent of lightning strikes start fires, but because of the drought this percentage rose. On those two days in the Payette Forest in Idaho, 234 fires started, but at first the Forest Service had resources enough to fight only 70 of them. The Boise Forest reported 120 fires, and the Nez Perce Forest, 100. On July 28, when more than 500 lightning fires were burning in Idaho, Governor Cecil Andrus declared a state of emergency.

The Lowman Firestorm   On Saturday, July 29, light winds, unstable air, low humidity, and high temperatures caused many of the Idaho fires to threaten towns, cabins, and highways. As mentioned, that day a firestorm burned 25 buildings at Lowman, including several homes and the Haven Lodge. The firestorm also incinerated the narrow canyon of the South Fork of the Payette River above Lowman.

Paul Werth, a fire weather meteorologist in the Boise

office of the National Weather Service, observed that heavy fuels rather than high winds caused the firestorm. It happened when two of the four fires in the complex joined and then spotted into a big area of dead timber killed by an April 1987 windstorm. Although salvage logging had removed some of the dead trees, the hot, dry weather of the past two summers and the lack of personnel caused by the Klamath and Yellowstone fires had delayed the prescribed (planned) burning of the rest of them. Before the fire, this area resembled a strip of trees from canyon crest to river that had been mowed down by a giant lawn mower, each tree snapped off 20 feet above the ground.

Beth Lund, who commanded the initial attack on the fire, stated that on July 29 she had ordered structure protection crews but that only the Odin foam trucks arrived. That morning she asked Ron Rochna to start at the South Fork Lodge and go up the river warning people and planning how to protect the buildings. Because she and the district ranger, Morris Huffman, knew the local pattern of the winds, they were worried. They knew how steep the drainages of Huckleberry and Steep creeks were and that they entered the river at a curve. Fire behavior analyst Greg Zschaechner, who had arrived with the overhead team the night before, also predicted extreme fire behavior—which was to begin about noon—due to extreme fuel dryness, fuel loads as high as those of logging slash, steep slopes, and a humidity forecast of 13 percent. Lund, Huffmann, and the incident commander, Bill Williams, started evacuating people beginning one-quarter mile west of the Haven Lodge as soon as they saw the fire spot into the "blowdown" on Steep Creek sometime between 3 and 4 P.M. First they alerted Beth's two children and husband, and then they drove up the river. When they reached the Haven Lodge, the fire was showering embers, and the winds were tossing around 4-by-8-foot pieces of plywood.

Evelyn Pogue, coowner of the Haven Lodge, attributed the firestorm to the Forest Service's leaving the wind-killed trees lying on the hillside ready to burn. She said the fire leapt across from the other side of the canyon to the trees behind the lodge and then raced down the hill with the wind just before the deputy sheriff, Chuck Richards, evacuated those at the lodge. She said that the only thing not destroyed in the lodge was some beer that she had not yet put in the cooler and that it tasted pretty good, "a little fire-brewed Milwaukee."

Bill Williams, the first incident commander (person in charge of the team of managers of a large fire) for the Lowman Fire, told his story about checking the houses upstream from the Haven Lodge and across the river from it near Kirkham Hot Springs: As he was checking them, the fire caught up with him, so he crossed back to the highway side of the river. When he reached that side, a couple from Boise, Randy and Sandy Geer, pointed across the river at the end of the access road for those houses, where they could see an elderly man trapped by the fire.

Williams and Geer waded back across the river, which at that point runs in a steep canyon at least 50 feet below the roads, to help the trapped man wade across the river. To do this they locked elbows with him and used sticks to brace themselves with their free arms against the armpit-deep current. As they brought the 82-year-old man across the river 100 yards ahead of the fire, Williams said that at times he felt his feet floating off the river bottom. Meanwhile Sandy Geer drove first the Geers' car, and then Williams' Forest Service truck farther along, to keep them just ahead of the fire. Williams recalled that by the time they rescued the man, the firestorm was over. Of the group of houses Williams had checked, only one still stands, the one with a metal roof and green lawn. Williams stated that in 30 years on the job, he had never worked on a more difficult or dangerous fire.

On Tuesday, August 1, Lowman was evacuated again, and another home burned. In addition, the Fleming Creek Fire jumped the south fork of the Payette River west of Lowman and threatened the town of Garden Valley and the resort of Banks. Other blazes threatened the Warm Lake resort area east of Cascade and the mountain village of Warren, which had to be evacuated.

On Thursday, August 3, the Red Cross declared Idaho a disaster area, so that victims of the fires could receive national aid. By Friday, August 4, 38 major fires were burning in Idaho, but the Steamboat Fire had spared Warren. By Sunday, August 6, the list of threatened communities had grown to include Yellow Pine and Stibnite, north of Warm Lake. On August 10, a half-inch of rain followed by moister air helped calm the fires,

In 1988 firefighting efforts in Yellowstone were directed at saving developments, such as these cabins that are being foamed by a compressed-air foam system. Courtesy of Ron Rochna, the Boise Interagency Fire Center.

and a week of moderate-to-heavy rain beginning on August 20 allowed firefighters to contain the last major fire, the Dollar Fire near Warm Lake.

The major U.S. fires of 1989 were in Idaho. Also, many more acres burned in 1988 than in 1989 in Idaho, but most of the 1989 fires threatened communities. If the weather had remained hot, dry, and windy as it did in 1988, the Idaho fires would have consumed many more acres and many more homes.

Causes of the 1980s' Drought

Because 1988 was the hottest summer on record worldwide and the driest in the United States since 1894, the *greenhouse effect* was suggested as a cause of the drought. (The greenhouse effect is a predicted warming of the earth's atmosphere, from a rise in carbon dioxide and other gases that trap in the heat leaving the earth.) But the greenhouse effect did not lead to the lack of moisture in 1988. Rather, it will bring a more gradual change, according to Stephen H. Schneider of the National Center for Atmospheric Research in Boulder.

Schneider and other meteorologists believe instead that the interaction between ocean temperatures and currents and the atmosphere may have caused the drought. They blame La Niña, the opposite of El Niño, the abnormal warming of ocean temperatures along the equator. The cool water of La Niña drives tropical thunderstorms to the north. In 1988 the heat caused by these warm storms pushed to the north the jet stream that usually brings storms to the United States. As a result, a strong high-pressure area formed over the central and mountainous parts of the nation, and the Southwest also received some of the tropical thunderstorms.

Gene Benedict, a fire management officer for the Payette National Forest in Idaho, said that by June 1989 the Payette Forest was down by 24 inches in total precipitation, including water from winter snow and summer rain. Even though the winter of 1988–1989 produced a normal amount of snow, it was not enough to allow the region to catch up. In addition, in the winter of 1989–1990, only 35 to 70 percent of the normal amount of snow fell in much of the West. So the drought is continuing.

Some meteorologists think that drought years often succeed one another because once a drought begins, it prolongs itself. That is, the loss of soil moisture means that plants grow more slowly and therefore release less moisture back into the air. Also, because evaporating water absorbs heat and cools the air, the reduced amount of moisture causes the air to become warmer, which in turn dries out the soil more than usual. As water evaporates, it absorbs heat and so cools the air. Therefore when less evaporates, there is less to cool the air, and the resulting warmer air dries out the soil even more.

Prospect of Fires in the Future _____

In the early 1990s, soils in the West were still dry from the lack of water, and therefore the prospects for more large, intense fires in the 1990s resembled those of the last few seasons. Accordingly, the 1990 fire season started ominously on May 9 with the burning of 65 homes near Grayling, Michigan. On June 26 a wildfire near Payson, Arizona, killed six firefighters and destroyed 50 houses. On that day it was 112 degrees in Los Angeles, the warmest day ever recorded there. The next day, fires in Southern California destroyed 637 buildings and killed two people, one a homeowner who was trying to escape on foot. The two most destructive fires, in Goleta near Santa Barbara and in Glendale near Los Angeles, were thought to have been started by arsonists. And in August, three large fires and hundreds of smaller ones forced the U.S. Park Service to close Yosemite National Park for the first time in history.

Even with heavy rain and snowfall, it will take a few years for the forests and rangeland to recover from the drought. But as the earth begins to feel the greenhouse effect, drought will be more likely to parch the land in the 1990s and beyond, and so even more fires are likely.

As the population increases in the United States, the number of fires will increase as well. Because more people are enjoying outdoor recreation and are building houses at the edges of towns in forests and rangeland, more people are at risk than ever before. It is important, therefore, to know how wildland fires behave, how they are fought, and what firefighters can accomplish during the coming fire seasons.

Chapter Two

■ ■ ■

How Forest Fires Ignite and Burn

W hen my son Stuart and I hiked down to the green oval of First Lieutenant Lake in Idaho's Salmon River Mountains, we smelled smoke, but when we reached the shore no one was there. At the first campsite, a small fire was burning in decayed wood and pine needles several feet from a fire ring. We yelled, "Hey, anyone here?" but no one answered, nor was anyone fishing on the gray ledges across the lake.

So we filled our canteens and pots in the lake and carried them back 50 yards to dump them on the foot-high flames. Two hours later the fire had cooled enough to leave. That evening we poured more water on nearby areas to douse any possible underground fire and camped on the other side of the lake next to the ledges. Luckily the flames were not any higher, or we could not have put the fire out without help.

If you have seen a similar fire, you may wonder how fire can move invisibly from a fire ring and come up somewhere else. How can the decayed wood catch fire so easily, when on rainy days you find it so difficult to start a camp fire?

Ignition

Knowing how something can catch fire may answer some of these questions. When burning, cellulose (found in plants) and other carbohydrates react chemically with oxygen. This reaction, called *combustion*, produces carbon dioxide, water vapor, and heat. That is, in combustion, oxygen and fuel combine in the presence of heat. Combustion may or may not continue after the heat source is removed, and it can also occur without any external source of heat if the material can produce its own heat. Paint-soaked rags igniting in a closet are an example of this type of ignition, called *spontaneous combustion*.

How do such fuels catch fire in the first place? To begin with, they must heat to a certain temperature (called the *ignition point*) in the presence of oxygen. Three things—fuel, heat, and oxygen—make up the *fire triangle*; if you remove one, the fire cannot burn. For example, if something cooking on a stove catches fire, pouring salt on it will put it out because it removes the air.

While the fuel heats to the ignition point, two things happen: First, the fuel dries out, because the heat boils away the water and drives off the volatile substances, like the resin in the pitch of pine trees. Second, the heat breaks down the chemical structure of the fuel, producing flammable gases, droplets of liquids called *tars*, charcoal, water, and ash. The amounts vary according to the temperature, with higher temperatures required to produce flammable gases. To ignite, or burst into flame, the wood must become hot enough to produce combustible gases on its surface and must produce enough of these gases to keep a flame burning. Wood will only glow or smolder if heated to 400° to 700° F, but at about 800° F it will burst into flame. Note that even though the flame of a match burns at 2300° F, it is so small that it can heat up only a small amount of dry fuel.

One of three methods heats fuels to ignition temperature. The first, *conduction*, moves heat from one molecule to another, as happens when a person touches the hot handle of a frying pan. This method has little importance in wildland fires, however, because wood is a poor conductor. In the second method, *convection*, the motion of air or fluid heats the fuel, as when hot air rises above a wood stove. Most of a fire's heat is produced by this method. Finally, the third method, *radiation*, transmits heat by means of rays from a heat source. For example, outdoors on a sunny day, a person can feel warmth from the sun even when the air is cold. But radiation decreases rapidly the farther it is from a heat source coming from one point only. Because a fire usually is many points forming a row of flames, it radiates heat well.

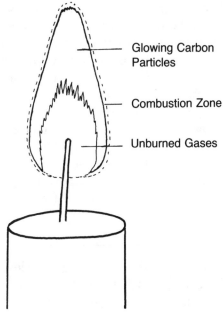

Glowing Carbon
Particles

Combustion Zone

Unburned Gases

Figure 2.1 _____
Combustion occurs in the bluish area surrounding the flame.

Combustion _____

What produces a fire's flames? The yellow part of the flame is formed by carbon particles that have not yet burned. The heat from the combustion makes them glow, or give off light. The invisible part of the flame in the center contains a cloud of gases that have vaporized but not yet burned. And the actual combustion takes place in a narrow bluish band that encircles the outside of the flame (see Figure 2.1).

Flaming combustion eventually turns the surface of the wood into charcoal. As the flames die down, the outer surface of the wood disappears, leaving a pattern of cracks. Some of the wood glows red with glowing combustion, but some of it has become too cold to combust. *Glowing combustion* occurs only in the cooler sections of the fire. It is the same chemical reaction as flaming combustion but burns solids rather than gases. Sometimes glowing combustion proceeds until only ash, water, and carbon dioxide remain, and at other times the wood cools off enough to stop burning before all the charcoal is consumed.

Types of Fire   When lightning or some other source ignites a forest or other wildland vegetation, three types of fire can result: surface, ground, and crown, often in combination. *Surface* fires move over the ground burning the litter on the surface, such as grasses, other plants, called forbs, and shrubs. They also burn dead branches and logs and small trees. The flames in a surface fire burn in a band called a *flaming front*, which is followed by glowing combustion. A surface fire also may "torch," or burn, all of a few isolated trees. *Ground* fires burn the duff and organic material in the soil beneath the surface litter of needles or leaves, usually by glowing combustion only. *Crown* fires burn the crowns or tops of trees or shrubs.

Fire Spread

A fire spreads horizontally by igniting a series of particles of fuel at or near its edge. At first the flames burn at one point, the source of ignition, and then move outward, accumulating enough heat to keep burning on their own. As the flames move out from the point of ignition, either wind or slope elongates the perimeter of the flames into an ellipse with a burned-out center (see Figure 2.2). (Note that this ellipse is a prototype; not all fires burn in this way.) The *head* of the fire is the end of the ellipse that the wind blows ahead into new fuels. The head of the fire advances faster than do its sides or flanks because the leading flames are first to reach the unburned fuel preheating the fuel and drying it. Conversely, the rear of the fire is slanted toward the already-burned center, and so the flames move outward more slowly. As the speed of the wind increases, the ellipse becomes more elongated.

Slope affects a fire in a way similar to that of wind but, instead, stretches it uphill. Fire can also spread downhill or against the wind, but such a fire will be the flanks or rear of the ellipse formed by the main fire. Hence a *flanking* fire advances crosswind or across a slope, and a *backing* fire advances against the wind or downslope. In any case, the shape of a fire seldom remains elliptical, because barriers, slope, changes in fuel, and spotting cause it to develop fingers and even multiple heads. A fire with an expanding perimeter is a *line* fire.

In timber, crown fires can spread 5 or more miles per hour, but in grass, fires spread at a rate of only 2 to 4 miles an

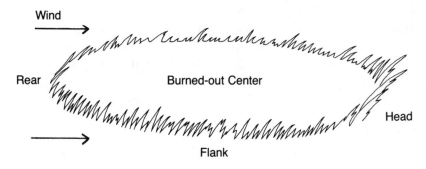

Figure 2.2 _____
Wind and slope elongate a wildland fire into an ellipse with a head, flanks, and a rear.

hour. In forests in the West, fires usually advance less than one-quarter mile an hour. Perhaps surprisingly, high winds, like those in Yellowstone in 1988, may push along a fire too fast to permit it to do as much damage as it would if it moved more slowly. But the fuels—plants, shrubs, and trees—left behind may still burn after the flaming front has passed.

Fire Behavior _____

As seen in Yellowstone, prolonged drought lowers the moisture content of the fuel to the point that fire may spread quickly and burn with enormous flames. Park officials described the "behavior" of the Yellowstone fires as extreme. By *fire behavior* they meant the ways that the fuels ignited, the flames developed, and the fire spread. Greg Zschaechner observed that typical fire behavior is controlled by the environment but that extreme fire behavior controls the environment.

Scientists studying the behavior of the Yellowstone fires in the fire behavior unit at the Intermountain Research Station's Fire Sciences Laboratory in Missoula, Montana, are constructing maps which show how far the fires spread each day. When drawing these maps they use images photographed from the planes that flew when the fires were burning, using special infrared cameras. When the planes were not able to fly into some areas because the fires were so large, the researchers gathered information from weather and fire records and fire managers.

First the lab associates digitized (put onto the computer) the tentative maps and then overlaid them with computerized terrain and fuels maps to verify the information. In a few places where they still could not determine the daily perimeters, they overlaid other fire-severity maps of Yellowstone made from satellite images. When they finish their maps, they will be able to analyze the fires' behavior by comparing their daily advances with other data.

The scientists in Missoula also are working on relating fire behavior to its effects. To do this, they measure flames with markers of known height that were installed before the fire. With a stopwatch, they also calculate how fast the fire spreads between markers. In addition, they estimate flame length, duration, and other characteristics of the fire, from their effects on the forest. (Such fire effects are discussed in Chapter 5.)

What influences the behavior of fires like those at Yellowstone? The three main influences are the particular fuels being burned, the weather, and the topography. Among these, fuel moisture, wind speed and direction, and slope steepness seem to have the greatest effect. Fuels with low moisture levels cause fires in fine dead fuels like grass to spread rapidly. Fuels with a high content of flammable oil, resin, or wax burn faster and at a lower moisture content. Wind speed is also important because strong winds can carry embers farther ahead of the flaming front, causing spot fires that accelerate the rate of spread. Spotting produced the fastest spread rates in the Yellowstone fires.

Topography

Topography is the physical shape and features of a region, and it affects fires by varying the weather within just a small area. (Weather and fuels, two other components of the fire environment, are discussed in Chapters 3 and 4.) Because warm air rises, preheating uphill fuels, fires advance uphill faster than they travel downhill. A slope raises the fuels in front of the fire, thus bringing them closer to the flames (see Figure 2.3), and also acts like a chimney carrying heat and flames uphill. Thus, depending on slope angle and wind speed, slope can be more important than wind in determining the rate of a fire's spread.

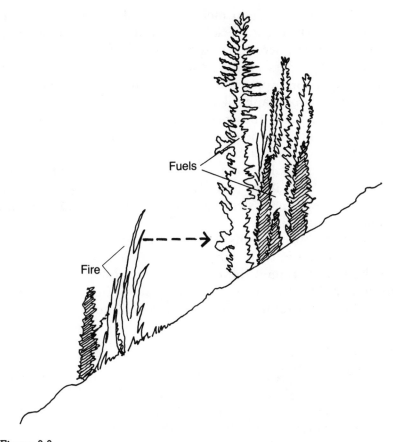

Figure 2.3 _____
A slope raises fuels and thereby puts them closer to the fire below.

Topography also affects fires by means of elevation, the shape of the land, and the direction in which slopes face. High elevations have a colder and wetter climate, and so there the fire season is shorter. The direction of a slope determines how much sunlight it receives. South and west slopes receive the most sunlight, and so they are much warmer and drier than north slopes are, which get the least amount of sunlight. South and west slopes therefore have a longer fire season, a longer daily burning period, and a greater number of fires than north slopes do, and more of the fires that start there become large.

This variation in sunlight means that all slopes have different *microclimates*. Different species and amounts of vegetation grow in the different microclimates. Because north slopes and deep canyons receive less sun, they hold more moisture and so stay green longer and support more vegetation than south slopes do.

Other topographical features, such as canyons, ridges, and bare areas, also influence fires. For example, a fire starting at the bottom of a slope is more likely to become large because more fuels are situated above it, and—remember—fire burns more easily uphill. Fires in narrow canyons preheat fuels across the canyon from them and also send embers across, as happened at Lowman. A steep, narrow canyon pulls up heat and flames as in a chimney.

Where two canyons join, fire spreads unpredictably because the winds in both canyons form eddies where they meet. At the tops of ridges, the fire may meet upslope winds from the other side, which slow it down. Accordingly, firefighters often build control lines along or near ridge tops.

Fire Intensity

Another characteristic of a fire is its *intensity*, or the rate at which a fire releases heat. Intensity also is determined by the amount of heat energy produced. Heat intensity is measured in *Btus*, or British thermal units. One Btu is the amount of heat required to raise 1 pound of water 1 degree Fahrenheit. Fire intensity is expressed in different ways, according to how the figures will be used. One way, called *fire-line intensity*, is the number of Btus per foot per second, or per unit length. A high rate of spread in light fuels like grass produces a high-intensity fire. In heavy fuels, however, even a low spread rate can produce a high-intensity fire.

The intensity of a fire is also related to the length of its flames, which limits the possible methods of suppressing it. When the flames are no more than 4 feet in length firefighters can usually attack the fire with hand tools. But when the flames are over 8 feet long, no control of any kind is likely to be effective. And when the flames are longer than 11 feet, fires often crown, spot, and make runs. (A *run* is rapid spread through surface or crown fuels.)

Wind

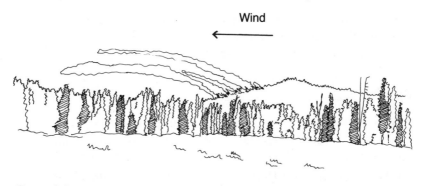

Figure 2.4 _____
Crown fires usually are found only in the presence of strong winds.

Crown Fires and Conflagrations _____

A *crown* fire is one that attacks the crown, or head of foliage, of a tree or shrub (see Figure 2.4). The three kinds of crown fire are passive, active, and independent. A *passive* crown fire burns primarily surface fuels but occasionally consumes an entire tree. An *active* crown fire consumes both the surface fuels and the tree crowns, and fires at both levels feed each other. An *independent* crown fire moves through treetops independently of any surface fire and may even race yards ahead of it.

To climb into the crowns of the trees, a fire first needs a *ladder*, in the form of a small tree or shrub or the dead lower branches of a larger tree. A crown fire also needs thick fuels and tree crowns in close proximity. Low moisture in fine fuels and low moisture and flammable chemicals in foliage also make crowning more likely. For a crown fire to stay in the tree crowns and keep moving, strong winds, steep slope, or high fire intensity must be present.

Because crown fires usually travel rapidly, they do not stay in one place long and so may be less destructive than the length of their flames would indicate. But when crown fires become very large and intense and spread quickly, fire managers rename them *conflagrations*, which are large destructive fires with moving fronts and rapid rates of spread. This type of fire occurred in Yellowstone in 1988. The extreme fire behavior of a conflagration differs from a firestorm because it moves faster. In addition, crown fires, conflagrations, and fire-storms often throw embers a long distance ahead of themselves. This phenomenon is called *spotting*.

Spotting

Spotting occurs when the hot air rising from the fire carries embers or firebrands (pieces of burning wood) upward and over to stands of trees ahead of the fire, where they start new fires. Long-range spotting requires firebrands large enough to travel long distances and to stay burning until they hit the ground. When the temperature is high and the humidity and fuel moisture are low, almost all the firebrands can start fires. In Yellowstone, spotting embers flew as much as 1½ miles ahead of the fires, but even 5 miles is not uncommon. In Tasmania in 1983, one ember spotted 47 miles from the source, according to Tony Mount, a fire research specialist. In this fire, curled strips of eucalyptus bark that were burning inside were transformed into flaming javelins by 100-mile-an-hour winds.

Convection Columns

Smoke is the combination of gases, water vapor, soot, and other hydrocarbons distilled by the heat of the fire. Smoke rises because heated air rises. A small fire can burn with a pale, almost transparent smoke plume that shows no real motion, or it can burn intensely, giving off a dense plume of smoke with definite edges that expand as it rises. Fire managers call this dense plume a *convection column* because it is formed by convection, or the motion of hot air. Although moderate winds may tilt the column, stronger winds prevent a column from forming at all.

When a convection column becomes large, so much warm air rises that it pulls the cool air around the fire into it, creating a noticeable indraft into the fire and giving birth to a veritable whirlwind of fire (see Figure 2.5).

Jack Wilson, the director of the Bureau of Land Management at BIFC, counted one evening in Yellowstone in 1988 five convection columns at or above the 35,000-foot altitude of the plane he was in. Around sunset one evening when flying over a ridge at the head of Slough Creek, Doug Brown, a helitack crewman for the Sawtooth National Forest, saw the eve-

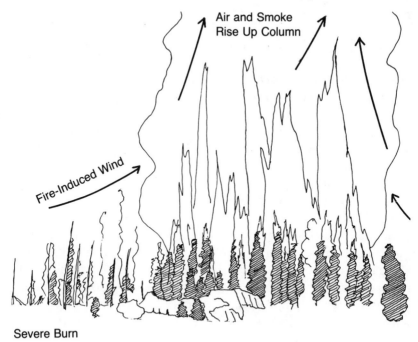

Air and Smoke
Rise Up Column

Fire-Induced Wind

Severe Burn

Figure 2.5 _____
When the smoke rising from a fire is strong enough to pull into it
the air around the fire, it has formed a convection column.

ning winds pushing fire with 300-foot flames and huge
convection columns down the canyons. Indeed, the heat and
winds caused by these columns' sucking in air forced him and
his pilot to leave the area, but when they tried to leave, the 60-
mile-an-hour winds at first held the helicopter at a standstill.
Later, when the fire forced them to evacuate the helibase for
the main Storm Creek Fire camp, winds from the fire tossed
around medium-sized helicopters like chunks of bark. As the
wind blew the tail of the helicopter in which Brown was riding
at a 30 degree angle, the helicopter kept dropping, 50 to 100
feet at a time.

When conditions in the fire environment are severe,
sometimes nothing can control the wildfires that result, even if
firefighters reach them right after they start. As Frank Carroll
of the Boise National Forest observed, "We don't manage large
wildfires; they do whatever the hell they please."

Firestorms

We heard a lot about firestorms in the news reports from Yellowstone in 1988, even though those fires were really conflagrations. What is the difference? Fire managers define a *firestorm* or a mass fire as a large area of intense heat that causes violent convection. This definition also applies to heavy aerial bombing, such as the firestorm created in Hamburg, Germany, during World War II. According to fire behavior expert Richard Rothermel, a firestorm is a very high intensity event with a large convection column that throws off embers in a shower of short-range spotting all around itself.

Such a fire acts as though a whole area of trees, rather than just one tree, were torching, or it may appear that the flame front has suddenly grown much wider. Whether or not a fire is a firestorm, however, depends on its actions rather than its size. Firestorms often include destructive, violent surface indrafts and sometimes contain tornadolike whirls. In fact, they may act as though several large whirlwinds or convection columns have combined.

Several convection columns merged in the Lowman firestorm.
Courtesy of the USDA Forest Service.

What causes firestorms? In a study[1] of blow-up fires in the South, George Byram concluded that the principal cause is a buildup of heat in one area, but fire scientists still know little else about firestorms. They believe that a wind speed decreasing with height above the fire, unstable air, and the advance of the fire into heavy fuels may add to the buildup of heat. This in turn strengthens the winds whirling up the convection column, enabling them to overcome any horizontal winds. Therefore, a firestorm can occur without the prerequisite of a large fire. As seen at the Lowman Fire, in the right weather, a fire of moderate size spotting into an area of heavy fuels can cause a firestorm.

Firestorms are unpredictable because they can develop suddenly when large wind-driven fires slow down. Jack Lyon, a research biologist at the Intermountain Research Station Forestry and Sciences Laboratory in Missoula, Montana, studied a firestorm that arose along the Pack River in the 1967 Sundance Fire in the Selkirk Mountains of northern Idaho. Lyon's study combined observation of the fire effects, official records, and eyewitness accounts. The firestorm was created when the fire ran 16 miles in 9 hours as it burned 50,000 acres. A prolonged dry spell, high temperatures, a 4-mile-long fire front, unstable air, and a dry cold front combined to cause the run, which was considered a conflagration. It then became a firestorm when it stalled in the Pack River Valley. During the storm, 80-mile-an-hour winds snapped off trees 60 to 75 feet above the ground. Lyon calculated the peak fire intensity as equal to a 2000-kiloton nuclear bomb.

Sliver Creek Fire   On the same day in 1988 that Old Faithful in Yellowstone was threatened, the rapid advance of the Sliver Creek Fire was termed a firestorm by those who saw it, as it drew near the Cold Meadows Guard Station in the Frank Church–River of No Return Wilderness. Before the fire, lodgepole pine covered the hills surrounding Cold Meadows. Rolf Goerke, manager of the guard station, recalled that he and his

_____

[1]Hundreds of studies have been conducted on the various aspects of wildland fire; only a few can be cited in this book as examples. Different studies produce varying results, so it follows that many studies must be completed before once-observed phenomena can be considered "usual cases."

wife thought the fire was still at the Root Ranch, 7 miles away, until they saw it coming over the hill on the other side of the meadows.

Fifteen minutes after they radioed that the fire was roaring toward them, a helicopter picked them up. Goerke then persuaded the pilot to land farther up the meadow to pick up two guides at an outfitter camp. But when he asked the pilot to pick up a horse party in a nearby branch of the meadows, the pilot refused, pointing out, "No, we've got only 2 minutes to get out of here." Rolf feared when they took off that they had left two people to burn to death and so feels that in the future when fire conditions are ripe for a fire run or a firestorm, a forest should consider closing its borders to the public. (A few hours later, however, District Ranger Earl Kimball, in a surveillance plane piloted by Lynn Clark, found the missing horse party safe in an open area near Papoose Lake, 10 miles from Cold Meadows. Later they found out when the horseback party saw the fire coming, they had turned their pack string loose, abandoned their gear, jumped bareback on their horses, and galloped across the meadows and up the trail to safety.)

Fire Whirls

A spinning, moving column of air, called a *fire whirl*, carries flames, smoke, and debris aloft and forms a *vortex* (spinning air that forms a vacuum in the center). The vacuum draws in flames and debris. Such fire whirls can range in size from dust devils to tornadoes. Small fire whirls do not have much effect on fire, but larger whirls cause spotting and increase the fire's intensity, because when a fire whirl forms, the combustion rate inside it increases dramatically.

A fire whirl needs two things to form: a heated surface that causes a vertical flow of air and an eddy in the airflow. Eddies can result where outside winds meet a convection column, where indrafts meet winds going up the column, or where the topography provides suitable conditions, such as the lee sides of ridges.

Predicting Fire Behavior

Fire behavior analysts still watch the weather and the characteristics of the fire itself, but today they also use mathematical and

The formation of a convection column signals the absence of strong surface winds and an increase in the intensity of a fire. Courtesy of the Boise Interagency Fire Center.

computer systems. In 1972, from studies of many experimental fires, Richard Rothermel of the Intermountain Research Station's Fire Sciences Laboratory in Missoula constructed a mathematical model called the Rothermel model, which combines data regarding the fuels, weather, and site of the fire to predict the spread of surface fires. The model can be used with a computer in a Fire Behavior Prediction Systems program called BEHAVE, with graphs called *nomograms*, or with tables and a hand-held calculator.

Fire managers using the Rothermel model or the BEHAVE program feed in data on the wind speed, slope, and properties of the fuels. They compare the vegetation of the fire site with descriptions of different fuel models, estimate the moisture of live fuels from how much of the grasses have cured or dried out, and gauge the moisture of dead fuels from the time of day, relative humidity, temperature, degree and aspect of slope, and amount of shade. With a hand-held meter, they measure the wind speed and calculate the temperature and relative humidity with an instrument called a *sling psychrometer*. To estimate the percentage of slope in the field, they may use instruments or figure the increase in elevation over a certain distance. Finally, fire managers select the fuel type from 13 standard fire behavior fuel models, or they feed in information on the fuels so that BEHAVE can design its own model. From the fuel type, time since ignition, topography, fuel moisture, and weather measurements, BEHAVE can describe many aspects of fire behavior, including its rate of spread, future perimeter, area, length-to-width ratio, and flame lengths. It is helpful for fire managers to have a trained fire behavior analyst interpret the results. BEHAVE can accurately predict surface fires in continuous fuels but cannot predict fire behavior when fires begin spotting or crowning.

Chapter Three

...

The Weather and Forest Fires

When Paul Werth, a fire weather meteorologist for the National Weather Service at the Boise Interagency Fire Center (BIFC), served as a fire weather specialist for the 1989 Lowman Fire, he took with him when he went to the fire early in the morning an automatic weather station, a satellite dish, weather balloons, helium, and a *theodolite* (a surveying instrument with a telescope for tracking the balloons). He also took a portable computer with two monitors and a printer. When Werth returned to the fire camp from Lowman about 11:30 A.M. the next day, smoke was still clogging the air, and the humidity was 60 percent. About 15 minutes later after the temperature inversion broke, another reading of the humidity showed that it had dropped to 18 percent. By noon when the overhead team held a briefing, the temperature had risen to 80° F. That morning Werth had warned the team that if the humidity dropped below 20 percent, the fire would start acting up. Not surprisingly, then, at 2 P.M. after he saw the smoke column building up, a report came that the Smoky and Sawmill fires had joined and spotted into the "blowdown" timber along Huckleberry Creek.

At this point, he and Greg Zschaechner, a fire behavior analyst, became worried, and so using a hand-held calculator, Zschaechner started drawing projections on a map to predict where and when the fire would go. Werth gave him current information on the humidity and the wind speed and direction for his calculations. From this, Zschaechner figured the fire would get down to the river by 4 P.M. Werth tried to radio the fire boss at Lowman to start evacuating people, but the radio system was not set up yet. By the time Werth was able to reach him, people were already being evacuated. As he later recalled, "As soon as the fire spotted into that downed timber, the smoke column literally exploded like an atomic bomb. It rose to 25,000 feet in 15 minutes." Zschaechner had predicted the high fire activity but not its severity. "Once it gets to that point, the fire prediction models go haywire," Werth commented.

Werth believes that the accumulation of heavy fuels caused this firestorm when the fire spotted into them. The fire burned at a high temperature, creating a huge column of hot air and smoke similar to the air rising in the bubbles of water boiling on a stove. In turn, the fire sucking the air around it into the rising column caused the strong winds reported in the canyon. With such low humidity, Werth explained, the column showers out every piece of burning material caught up in it, thereby igniting other fires. Thus, "you end up not having one fire to work with but literally hundreds." The conditions he saw showed that the fire had become a firestorm. Even with all available crews, all they could do was move people out of the way. In Werth's opinion, the spotting into the blowdown, together with the instability of the air, caused the firestorm.

The Weather and Fire Behavior

Fire weather meteorologists like Paul Werth can supply information that helps fire managers predict a fire's behavior. Certain weather factors, such as temperature, humidity, air stability, and wind speed and direction, directly affect the way that fires burn. Other factors, such as the weather's long-term climatic influence on the fuels and their dryness, indirectly affect fires. Both short-term and long-term effects are part of the *fire environment*.

Because the weather largely determines how fires behave and when and where they occur, fire managers have named *fire weather* the weather characteristics that influence fires. For example, hot dry weather with gusty winds and intense lightning storms means fire. During the fire season, to help them, the National Weather Service provides daily fire weather forecasts, and it also makes special forecasts during times of high fire danger or when fire managers request them.

The climate of each geographical region determines the

fuel (vegetation) types and the length of the fire season or the time of year when most fires occur.

The differences in the sun's heating of the earth's surface lead to the major weather and climate variations that contribute to fire danger. As the sun warms the earth's surface, it also heats the air above it. The heated air then creates air pressure differences that cause the basic wind patterns, that is, air flowing from higher-pressure to lower-pressure zones.

Moisture and pollutants in the air, the angle and duration of the sunlight, and the properties of the earth's surface combine to determine how much the air heats. One such property affecting the heating is the color of the earth's surface. Colors like black absorb heat better than others do. Texture also affects the surface heating; for example, a rough surface absorbs heat better than a smooth one does. And a transparent material, like water, distributes heat more evenly rather than keeping it on the surface. Furthermore, some substances, like rock, conduct heat better than others do. Materials also vary in the heat they can absorb, that is, their *specific heat*, the ratio of the heat absorbed or given off by a material to its rise or fall in temperature. Water has a high specific heat, and so wet surfaces heat more slowly than dry ones do. Accordingly, differences in air moisture can greatly affect fire weather.

Air Moisture

At low humidity, fuels (vegetation) dry out, therefore catching fire more easily and burning faster. (Fire managers define fuels as the herbaceous plants, shrubs, and trees, and the dead material within or below them, that will support a fire.)

The moisture in the air comes from evaporation from the ground, bodies of water, and the transpiration of plants. When the air holds as much water vapor as it can at its prevailing temperature, it is *saturated*. Usually air holds less than it can and so is *unsaturated*. Meteorologists describe air moisture with the term *relative humidity*, or the ratio of the amount of water vapor in a given volume of air to what it could hold if it were saturated at the same temperature. This ratio is expressed as a percentage, and saturated air has 100 percent relative humidity.

Because more water vapor is needed to saturate warm air than cool air, when the air temperature rises, the relative humidity drops. Conversely, when the temperature drops, the relative humidity rises. Because air cools as it rises, at higher elevations air with the same amount of water vapor as air lower down has a higher relative humidity and is closer to saturation.[1]

Clouds   When more water vapor is added to saturated air— which cannot hold any more—some of it condenses, forming clouds. Clouds can indicate that the wind speed or direction, or the stability of the air, has changed, and they also show the likely changes in precipitation and temperature.

Meteorologists classify clouds into families according to their elevation above the ground. *Cirrus* clouds form above 20,000 feet; *alto* clouds form between 6500 and 20,000 feet, and *stratus* clouds begin with fog on the ground and rise as high as 6500 feet. Cumulus or thunderstorm clouds usually start low and then build to towers as high as 30,000 feet.

Within these families three cloud types predict weather changes important to firefighters. The first is *castellatus*, a type of cumulus cloud. When these clouds form in the morning, they predict a thunderstorm during the afternoon. These high-level clouds—12,000 to 18,000 feet—resemble castles with turrets. The second type is the lens-shaped *lenticular* clouds that result from wave motion in strong winds that may drop to the surface by evening. The third type of cloud is the high rippling *cirrostratus* clouds, which indicate that rain is possible within 48 hours.

Air Stability

Fire managers keep track of the air's stability, its ability to resist vertical motion. This ability, which influences the development

---

[1]Fire managers find that knowing the humidity is useful in planning fire suppression, so they measure it in the field. Often they use a *psychrometer*, an instrument with two thermometers: one with a plain bulb, and the other with a cotton wick on it. The operator first dampens the wick with water, then whirls the psychrometer to cool the wick to its lowest temperature. After reading the temperatures of both thermometers the humidity can be read from a table.

of winds, depends on how fast the air cools with elevation. Scientists measure air stability by examining how much an invisible balloon of air cools as it rises, as compared with the air around it, if they do not mix, even though in the real world they do mix. This cooling with altitude without any mixing is called the *adiabatic lapse rate*.

The adiabatic lapse rate for unsaturated air is 5.5° F per 1000 feet. Unsaturated air seldom cools at this rate, however, because of mixing and other factors. Saturated air cools at an even lower rate, 3° F per 1000 feet, called the *moist adiabatic rate*. The reason that it is lower than the dry rate is that as air cools, some of its water vapor condenses, and the condensation warms the air, thereby slowing the cooling rate.

If the air cools at less than the dry adiabatic rate, it is considered stable; that is, if something pushes this air up or down, it will return to its original level. Stable air seldom moves vertically. Stable air will hold in smoke but reduce fire activity. As the earth's surface cools the air next to it at night, it makes the air more stable, enabling fires to "lie down" at night, especially in valleys. You can identify stable air by noticing haze, layered clouds, steady winds, or fog; any smoke columns tend to drift apart after only a short rise.

If the air stays at the same location when lifted or forced downward, it is *neutral*. Neutral air usually remains stationary because its temperature lapse rate equals the dry adiabatic rate.

But once set in motion, either up or down, if the air continues to move in the same direction, it is *unstable*. The temperature lapse rate of unstable air exceeds the dry adiabatic rate. Unstable air usually rises and, if lifted, keeps going up until it reaches air its own temperature. On a hot day the air is so hot near the ground that it cools much faster than does air cooling at the dry adiabatic rate, so heating is one cause of unstable air. Gusty winds, cumulus clouds, tall smoke columns, turbulence, and good visibility all are signs of unstable air. When air becomes unstable, fire activity increases, and the tall smoke columns carry firebrands aloft. Finally, the sun's warmth causes air to be more unstable during the day than it is at night.

Air stability simply means that the air tends to move up or down until it reaches air its own temperature. Above the earth's surface, the various layers of air may have different degrees of stability or instability. When an air layer is lifted, the lifting stretches the top of the layer farther from the bottom. This stretching then increases the difference in temperature throughout the layer, which makes the air less stable. Surface heating, cold fronts, and mountains all can lift air layers.

Air traveling over mountains becomes more unstable as it cools with height. It also develops updrafts and downdrafts that affect fires, and the moisture in it condenses. This condensation produces local thunderstorms and increases the precipitation of general storms.

Because air stability is so important to fires, Paul Werth at the National Weather Service in Boise is studying it. Using weather data and satellite photographs he examines the relationship of the stability of the air well above the earth's surface to extreme fire behavior. He and Richard Ochoa are basing their work on a study by Donald Haines of the North Central Experiment Station. On days of high fire spread in the western states, Haines found temperatures much colder than normal at 18,000 feet. Such temperatures mean that the air is unstable well above the earth's surface. In addition, Haines noticed that the equivalent elevation in the eastern states is 5000 feet, because the terrain there is so much lower.

Werth is trying to find a way to determine when a fire will go beyond the standard fire prediction models. He wants to be able to say, "Well, today it looks like we could have extreme fire behavior."

Although unstable air causes fire problems, stable air can lead to dangerous fire behavior as well, when a high-pressure system enters an area. In a high-pressure system, the air sinks to the earth's surface, diminishing fire activity, because it reduces vertical motion. As the air sinks, however, it warms, and the relative humidity drops, which increases fire activity. This sinking can also cause strong, turbulent winds as it interacts with the topography. Furthermore, if the sinking air is forced over a mountain range, it will tear down the other side of the range as a foehn or chinook wind.

In a high-pressure area, the air high above the ground can be warmer than that on the surface; that is, it is a *temperature inversion*. Inversions often occur at night when the ground cools off and cools the air just above it. This cool air runs downhill and collects in the valleys. Because night inversions usually do not extend to the ridge tops, they can slow a fire in a valley that still is burning actively on the ridge tops.

Because of this tendency for inversions to form, the areas halfway up the slopes are the warmest and driest. Called *thermal belts*, they are warm because they are above the nighttime inversions but below the ridge tops' cool winds and temperatures. Fires, therefore, are more active in these belts than in the areas above and below them.

Inversions also trap smoke in the valleys, and so planes spraying fire retardants or helicopters with water buckets must wait for the inversion to end before they can fly. But when an inversion does end, the air often becomes unstable, which can cause a sudden increase in fire activity.

Winds

Air stability and temperature inversions help determine local winds, as do large-scale general winds caused by patterns of air circulation well above the earth's surface. The combination of these general and local winds in an area is its *surface* winds; its usual surface winds are its *prevailing* winds.

The general winds are caused by the circulation of heat between the equator and the poles, modified by the heat differences between the oceans and the continents and by the roughness of the terrain. These heat differences result in wide variations in air pressure, which cause a complicated system of air circulation.

The local winds are generated by the terrain and local differences in heating and cooling. The friction and heating of the earth's surface make these winds turbulent. Turbulent air moves up and down as well as horizontally, blowing in gusts and in circles, called *eddies*.

General winds sometimes dominate local winds. An example is a band of strong winds dipping down from high in the atmosphere to just above the earth's surface. Fire managers call the resulting strong winds *low-level jets*. In the circulation system of general winds, the air heated at the equator rises and flows north and south at high altitudes. But the Coriolis force, caused by the earth's rotation, deflects any moving object on the earth's surface, including air. The Coriolis force thus deflects air moving toward the poles toward the east and deflects air moving away from the poles toward the west.[2]

By the time the heated air from the equator reaches a latitude of 30 degrees, it has cooled enough to sink to the surface. Then, because it has lost most of its moisture, the sinking dry air at these latitudes creates deserts, and it also causes cells of high pressure, or *high-pressure air masses*. Some of this warm air continues aloft to sink later at the poles, and from the poles it flows along the surface toward the equator to meet warm air flowing toward the poles from the deserts. Where these two opposing air currents meet, at a 50-degree latitude, they rise in stormy areas known as the *polar fronts*.

Because the Coriolis force deflects all these winds, the winds flowing north along the surface from the deserts blow toward the northeast or east. Winds are named by the direction from which they blow, and so these are *westerlies*. The winds near the equator and the poles blow in the opposite direction, from the east to the west. These *easterly* winds are called *trade winds* near the equator and *polar easterlies* near the poles (see Figure 3.1).

At high altitudes the belt of westerlies forms a pattern of waves called the *circumpolar vortex*. Its position meanders toward and away from the poles with the seasonal migration of the polar front. Sometimes strong winds called the *jet stream* form a core within the vortex, and storm systems migrate along the jet stream, close to the surface. At high altitudes the storms smooth out into troughs of low pressure, with ridges of high pressure on either side.

High-Pressure Air Masses and the Yellowstone Fires   Paul Werth observed that in 1988 a high-pressure air mass over the central

---

[2]You can test this by spinning the lid of a kettle on a table from left to right. Keep spinning the lid and draw a line with a marker from the center outward and another from the rim inward. Notice the curves. The directions in which the winds are deflected are different in the Southern and Northern Hemispheres because a person standing in the Southern Hemisphere is "upside down" relative to the one in the Northern Hemisphere. Therefore, to someone in the Southern Hemisphere, the directions will appear opposite.

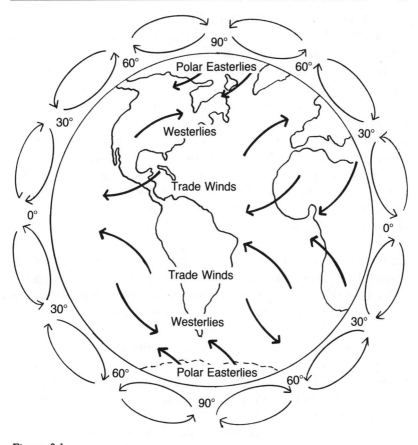

Figure 3.1 _____
Temperature differences in the sun's heating of the earth cause a
complex system of air circulating around the world.

Rockies, plus the prevailing winds, blocked the usual summer
moisture from Yellowstone. Ordinarily the monsoons that
drench Arizona and New Mexico bring storms to Yellowstone,
but in the summer of 1988 the winds of this air mass kept the
monsoons from moving that far north. In 1989 also, an upper-
level high-pressure ridge over the Rockies kept away the normal
rainstorms, thereby drying out the forests. Then when one
storm managed to break through at the end of July, its lightning
easily ignited several fires.
    The effects of high-pressure air masses and ridges on the
weather are typical. When a large body of air remains over one

area of land or ocean for several days, it adopts the same temperature and humidity as that area and becomes known as an *air mass*, named for its region of source. When air masses move away from their sources, they displace other air masses, which can cause bad fire weather.

A continental polar air mass moving over the northeastern and north central regions of the United States during the fire season causes bad fire weather because this type of air mass often becomes unstable as the summer sun heats the earth's surface and in turn heats the lower layers of air. Continental tropical air masses that form over the Southwest and Mexico and move elsewhere in the western states also raise the risk of fire because this hot, dry air is unstable and dries out fuels.[3]

Convective or Local Winds Fire managers call the local winds caused by heating differences *convective winds*, because the heating causes the air to move. These winds blow harder in the mountains and near the ocean. In the mountains they blow upslope during the day and downslope at night: As the sun warms the slopes in the mornings, the air above them warms and rises, and the cool air from the base of the slopes moves uphill to replace it. At night the air over the slopes cools faster than does that in the valleys, becomes heavier than the air below it, and slowly moves back down the slopes as a downslope wind. When it flows into the valley, it pushes the air down the valley (see Figure 3.2). Upslope winds may reach 15 miles an hour and contain turbulence, but downslope winds blow smoothly at only 2 or 3 miles an hour.

The times when upslope change to downslope winds, and the strength of those winds, depend on the number of hours

---

[3]These discussions attempt to simplify the descriptions of worldwide winds and air masses. At any one time the atmosphere contains a complex of winds traveling in different directions, horizontally and vertically, and at varying speeds at different altitudes. To find the wind speed at or near a fire for fire behavior calculations, meteorologists make use of *anemometers*, small cuplike devices that whirl on a rod. As these "cups" whirl, they measure the speed of the wind by counting revolutions per minute.

Because surface winds are affected by winds aloft, meteorologists also send up balloons with *radiosondes*, electronic units that measure and transmit temperature, moisture, pressure, elevation, and angles and distances from landmarks, to measure them.

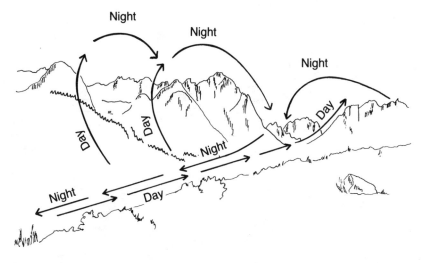

Figure 3.2
The heating of mountain slopes and ridges causes the air to rise above them and to pull the air up from the valleys below. At night, the cooling air sinks and flows down the slopes and then down into the valleys.

of sunlight that the slope receives. Because south and west slopes receive sunlight for more hours of the day, the air above them is hotter and so produces stronger slope winds. Upslope winds here also begin earlier in the day and change to downslope winds later than do winds on north slopes, which get less sun.

Similar convective winds near the seacoast affect fires on coastal ranges. Here, during the day the sun heats the air over the warm land more than it heats the air over the cool ocean. This warm air rises, and the air over the ocean moves inland to replace it, causing a convective wind called a *sea breeze*. At sunset the land and the air above it cool more rapidly than do the ocean and the air above it, and so the air over the land blows back downhill and then out over the ocean in a wind called a *land breeze* (see Figure 3.3). The upslope and downslope winds and the land and sea breezes interact with the general winds to produce the surface winds.

On hot days, when the air heats above the slopes and spirals up in columns, it draws in the surrounding surface air. These whirlwinds, or *dust devils*, are caused by very unstable air

Figure 3.3
Because the land heats faster than the ocean does, as the morning sun heats the land, the air rises above it, and cool air from over the ocean flows inland to replace it, thereby creating a sea breeze. At night the process reverses, and the cooling air flows from the land out over the ocean in a land breeze.

and obstacles like big rocks or isolated trees that start the air spinning. They can span 100 feet, rise to 4000 feet, and spin at 50 miles an hour. Within a fire, they are called *fire whirls*, which we discussed earlier. Another convective local wind occurs in thunderstorms, when rain or hail cools the air and causes severe downdrafts, or *downbursts* or *microbursts*. Slope winds, downdrafts, and foehn winds are the three winds most responsible for fire problems.

Foehn Winds   A *foehn wind* is produced when air descends a mountain range, warming as it falls and speeding up in response to gravity. The Santa Ana winds in Southern California and the chinook winds in the Rockies are examples of foehn winds (see Figure 3.4) Foehn winds are usually much warmer than normal for the season. They may develop in several ways. In the first, prevailing winds force a layer of moist air from a low-pressure area over a range into a high-pressure area. The air loses its moisture through precipitation as it climbs and cools at the moist adiabatic rate because it is saturated. As the air

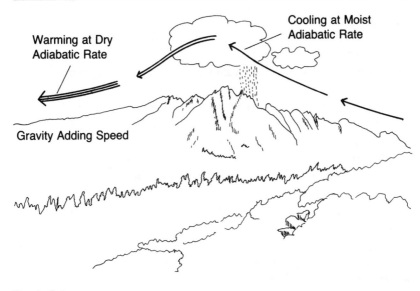

Warming at Dry
Adiabatic Rate

Cooling at Moist
Adiabatic Rate

Gravity Adding Speed

Figure 3.4
When the air is lifted over a mountain range, it loses moisture and
so will be much warmer when it descends on the other side by
means of gravity, in a wind called a foehn, chinook, Santa Ana, or
other local name.

goes down the lee side of the range, it is no longer saturated,
and so the increasing air pressure warms it at the much faster
dry adiabatic rate. Therefore, the air becomes much warmer
and drier than it was on the windward side.

The second type of foehn wind is caused by a low-pressure area on one side of a mountain range and a cold high-
pressure area on the other, but with only gentle prevailing
winds. In this case the wind blows naturally from the high
pressure toward the low pressure. The air warms in the same
way as it descends and, under the force of gravity, pushes out
the surface air as fast as 90 miles per hour. This kind of foehn
wind often occurs in the West when a cold high covers the Great
Basin and a low sits offshore along the Pacific coast.

In the third kind of foehn wind, a high-pressure area
extends across an entire mountain range. As the air of the high-
pressure area rises and cools, it loses moisture, then warms, and
speeds up as it descends. All foehn winds cause fires to spread
rapidly, just as winds associated with warm and cold fronts do.

Fronts

Fronts occur at the edges of air masses where air of one temperature and moisture is replacing that of another temperature and moisture. Because the air pressure at the edges is lower than that at the centers, the air at the edges of two adjoining air masses forms a line of low pressure called a *trough*. The air on either side of a trough shows higher pressure, and different wind directions, temperatures, and humidities.

As the wind blows in opposite directions on opposite sides of a trough, it usually evolves into a storm system, with a center called a *low* (see Figure 3.5). The storm system develops from a vertical wave effect, in which one air mass acts as if it were a lake tipped on its side and the winds of the other air mass were making a big wave in it. Meteorologists call one side of the wave—where warm air follows cold air—a *warm front* and the other side—where cold air follows warm air and pushes it upward—a *cold front*. In the Northern Hemisphere the air following these fronts circles around the low in a counterclockwise direction. As it does so, it moves inward along the surface and rises. In contrast, the air within an air mass, which has high pressure, revolves clockwise, sinks, and spreads out along the surface.

The flow of wind from high-pressure to low-pressure areas balances the diversion of wind by means of the Coriolis force, and so winds tend to blow along lines of equal pressure. Because these lines usually curve, centrifugal force causes the winds to move in spirals around the highs and lows.

When a front approaches, the wind speeds up and its direction shifts. Frontal winds blow harder near cold fronts than near warm fronts, and the wind shifts are more abrupt. The thunderstorms and strong winds that accompany cold fronts cause problems with fires. If there is too little moisture for precipitation, the winds may be the only effect of a front, and thus it is called a *dry cold front*.

Because dry cold fronts cause strong gusty winds for anywhere from 12 to 24 hours, they may drive fires in runs. The wind shift accompanying the front also may cause the fire to start moving at right angles to the direction in which it moved before, thereby transforming one flank of a fire into an enormous head. A series of at least six dry cold fronts brought the

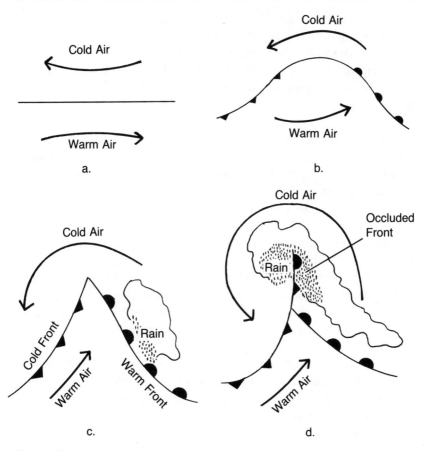

Figure 3.5

When an air mass meets another of differing temperature, the winds blowing in opposite directions cause a wave, similar to the way in which winds blowing over the water make waves. This wave then becomes a storm system with warm and cold fronts.

winds that spread the Yellowstone fires, with some of these winds blowing up to 60 miles an hour.

Thunderstorms

Cold fronts often bring thunderstorms that can ignite fires and increase the spread of fire. For a thunderstorm to form, a column of moist air is lifted by, perhaps, heating or a mountain range, and the lifted air forms cumulus clouds, which resemble masses of cotton balls. When these cumulus clouds grow large, they develop the flat top and pointed ends of the anvil-shaped thunderstorm clouds called *cumulonimbus clouds*. When one of these clouds forms, the air may be sucked into it as fast as 50 miles an hour. Thunderstorms also need unstable air, that is, air cooling more than 5.5° F per 1000 feet.

A thunderstorm passing over a fire can add to the updraft of the fire column or cause a downdraft. Both of these effects increase the wind at a fire and thus its rate of spread. A downdraft occurs when the rain or hail of a thunderstorm pulls down the air as fast as 70 miles an hour. The air in a downdraft hitting the ground spreads out in all directions, causing strong horizontal winds. A pilot flying beneath a downdraft will find the wind suddenly reversing direction. This reversal of the wind also can make the head of a fire suddenly change direction and trap firefighters. And in rugged terrain, downbursts can descend drainages with great speed, as one did at Lowman in 1987. As the downdrafts continue, the updrafts weaken and the thunderstorm cell disintegrates. As it disintegrates, a new cell may form to the side of the first.

When a cumulonimbus cloud grows into a thunderstorm, different sections of the cloud accumulate positive and negative electrical charges. When the charges have built up, the negative charges (electrons) flow toward the positive charges in a lightning flash that travels within the cloud or between the cloud and the ground.

Most lightning goes from cloud to cloud, but 20 percent of it travels from cloud to ground. Each lightning flash has two parts, a leader and one or more return strokes. The leader is an electrically charged or ionized path made by the electrons when they begin to flow. Once formed, this path allows bursts of electrons, or return strokes, to run along it. A lightning flash between a cloud and the ground can be either negative or positive. Negative lightning occurs when the discharge of energy runs from a negatively charged area in the cloud to a positively charged area on the ground. In positive lightning the discharge runs from negatively charged ground to a positively charged region of the cloud. Positive lightning is more powerful and thus is more likely to start fires than negative lightning is.

When lightning strikes a tree, it gouges a path, often a

When lightning strikes a tree, it often burns a spiral path down the trunk. Courtesy of the Boise Interagency Fire Center.

spiral one, down the grain of the wood. The force of the strike can break the tree into enormous splinters, flinging them as far as 100 yards away, but a strike will not start a fire unless it meets easily ignited fuel, like pine needles, grass, or pitch. If the lightning ignites decaying wood or duff, the fire can burn unnoticed as a "sleeper" for a long time before it grows large enough to be detected. According to Roy Inskeep, a fire management officer for the Challis National Forest, the 1973 Allison Creek Fire in that forest burned for ten days before they found it: the fire took that long to travel from one end of a rotten log to the other where dry grass allowed it to flare up.

Lightning ignites fires more often when it occurs during a dry thunderstorm. A dry thunderstorm is the result when the base of the thunderstorm clouds is at least 15,000 feet above the ground. It is dry because the rain it contains evaporates before it reaches the ground.

Fire Weather Terminology and Research

Many weather terms are familiar because they often appear in the daily weather reports; others are used only to describe weather as it affects forest fires. Fire managers have named the time when fires are most active, usually from 10 A.M. to 5 P.M., the *burning period*. The months each year when wildland fires are common are called the *fire season*. The typical fire season in an area is its *fire climate*. The fire climate plus the fuel and ignition patterns make up the *fire regime*.

These terms have resulted from research on fire weather. Researchers at the Forest Fire Laboratory of the Pacific Southwest Forest and Range Experiment Station in Riverside, California, have found that the short-range variations in weather make it difficult to forecast it for longer periods. Because small variations do not show up in the large-scale processes that influence the variations, errors can multiply rapidly. Because the measurements sometimes contain errors and data are lacking for some parts of the country, the longer the computer models run, the greater such errors become. Therefore, weather forecasts usually are accurate for only one to three days. At the Riverside lab, researchers also are trying to find out how weather creates large areas of high fire danger, by correlating past weather records with fire records and by gathering statistics on the relationship of conditions in the upper atmosphere to those of the surface weather.

Other Fire Weather Tools Two tools have been developed to help make fire weather forecasts. The first one is RAWS, remote automatic weather stations that contain solar-powered microprocessors. These stations transmit, by satellite, measurements from weather data sensors to various earth stations.

RAWS measure precipitation, usually by means of a rain gauge called a *tipping bucket*. The stations also calculate wind speed, direction, wind gusts, air temperature, relative humidity, fuel temperature, fuel moisture, and the voltage on their own batteries. These stations must be located away from objects that could produce weather readings unrepresentative of the area, such as asphalt parking lots, lakes, or granite cliffs. Because such sites also must be typical of the area, have only low veg-

Portable remote automatic weather systems (RAWS) are available to fire managers to take to fires. Courtesy of the Boise Interagency Fire Center.

etation, and receive full sun many hours a day, any slopes on which stations are located must face south or west.

The RAWS stations belonging to the BLM (Bureau of Land Management) feed data via satellite into computer-controlled receiving stations. One class of RAWS stations sits permanently on a 75-mile grid that will eventually cover the 11 western states. Fire managers move the other stations every few months to gather data for planning prescribed burns. For use at fires, BIFC keeps a few portable RAWS or micro-RAWS stations that transmit weather data to fire managers by means of computerized voice.

The other tool to help forecast fire weather is the automatic lightning detection system called ALDS. The Bureau of Land Management operates 33 of the 36 ALDS sensors in the western United States. Each sensor unit looks like a giant morel mushroom. It contains two 60-inch-long magnetic antennae formed into loops and encased in a removable fiberglass dome on a steel pole. The units detect whether the electromagnetic impulse released by the return stroke of lightning is negative or positive and from what direction it is coming. The detectors measure only cloud-to-ground strikes and can measure them from up to 225 miles away. At the Boise Interagency Fire Center, position analyzers, tied to the sensors by satellite, analyze and store the data from two sensors to calculate the location of each strike.

Every day in the western United States, the ALDS system detects 20,000 lightning strikes, 99 percent of all that occur. From the data they have gathered with this system, meteorologists have calculated that lightning causes 65 percent of the wildfires in the West. Lonnie Brown, manager of the ALDS system at BIFC, revealed that one summer day in 1988 the sensor detected 60,000 strikes and that during only one hour of this day it detected 11,000 strikes. At BIFC on a computer screen, visitors can see maps of recent lightning strikes that the ALDS system has recorded.

In 1983 the ALDS system was integrated by the BLM into a larger system called the Initial Attack Management System (IAMS), which contains data from the RAWS stations, maps of the area, data regarding the terrain, satellite maps of fuels, smoke dispersion models, ignition probability calculations, and dispatching plans. Fire managers receive all these data through the state and district BLM offices or from a regional forest service office in Fort Collins, Colorado. Computers map the lightning strikes and print out the maps if needed. Dispatchers with access to the Initial Attack Management System can call up data from ALDS, RAWS, and other information on the computer screen to use in planning the resources to send out.

In addition, researchers based at the State University of New York at Albany have set up a nationwide system of 115 lightning detectors that transmit data to computers by satellite. The electrical utility industry funds this project, and the FAA (Federal Aviation Administration) and the National Weather Service also have access to the data.

Chapter 4

■ ■ ■

Wildland Fire Fuels

C ost-conscious homeowners who plan ahead make written inventories of their household possessions to give to their insurance company in case of fire or theft. Those who don't, like myself, may find themselves for days after a fire puzzling over a large blackened lump, which turns out to be a coffeemaker. I had put off making such an inventory because there seemed to be just too many items to list.

Now a square foot of forest contains far more objects than a square foot of most houses. Because the managers of forests and rangelands also are concerned with the economic effects of fire, they take inventories of the *fuel* that is there, trying to estimate its volume. Wildland fuels are any organic materials living or dead, in or on the ground or in the air, that can ignite and burn. The inventories enable managers to determine the number of board feet burned in a fire, and, more importantly, fuel inventories can help them predict fire behavior.

Look closely at a small patch of forest. Notice all the trees, shrubs, plants, logs, branches, and cones on the forest floor. Now think what it would be like to measure and count them— that's just one aspect of wildland fire management. But fuels specialists have developed methods of inventorying in the forest without counting every twig. Because forests are so complex, it is still tedious, but luckily, fire managers can sometimes compare the fuels in their forests with photographs instead of conducting inventories.

Types of Fuel

Fire managers divide fuels into, ground, surface, and aerial. *Ground* fuels include the decayed organic matter, called *duff* or *humus*, on the forest floor below the surface litter, as well as buried pieces of wood and tree roots, because fire can travel along them and start a surface fire yards away. Fires in ground fuels are hard to extinguish because when these fuels dry out, they tend to repel water.

Surface fuels comprise dead needles, leaves, twigs, bark, cones, and small branches, all of which are called *litter*. Fire managers also consider dead logs, stumps, large branches, herbaceous plants, shrubs, and trees shorter than 4 or 6 feet above the forest floor as surface fuels.

Fuels in the tree or shrub canopy higher than 4 to 6 feet above the ground are *aerial* fuels. Again, a fire in this layer is a crown fire. Fine fuels in this layer, such as conifer needles, lichens, and mosses, carry the fire. In fact, these fuels burn so well that campers often use them for tinder. Note, however, that deciduous tree crowns burn only when many of the leaves have died and conditions are extremely dry.

Fuel Inventories

Fire managers use fuel inventories and stylized fuel models to simplify the complexity of forest fuels. They are complex because even stands of the same kind of trees differ from one another in appearance, which means that they contain differing amounts of fuels that react differently to fire. Fuel inventories also are used to detect areas of hazardous fuels, to plan prescribed burning, and to predict fire behavior.

To inventory fuels, scientists or fire managers choose an area with relatively uniform vegetation of the type they want to sample and with natural boundaries, like changes in the vegetation, around it. Such areas may range from less than an acre to a few hundred acres. One common method of inventorying is to establish a series of permanently marked points within the area of interest. By marking the points, fuels can be measured at the same place before and after a fire to calculate the amount of fuel consumed. Using a heavy cloth measuring tape, the fire managers run a line called a *transect* in a random direction from each point. Various methods of sampling along the transects are used, some of which were devised by Jim Brown of the Intermountain Fire Sciences Laboratory in Missoula, Montana.

Usually those taking inventory count and measure all the downed and dead fuels along the transect line and measure the depth of the duff. They may establish imaginary vertical planes at random distances and directions along the transects and count and measure the downed woody fuels intersecting those planes. Fire managers sometimes inventory standing fuels as well as the downed woody ones. Using one method that Brown developed, they locate 15 to 20 points in a grid pattern. They then sample different fuels at a specified distance and direction from these points. They count all the small trees inside a circle of ⅟₃₀₀ of an acre around the sample point, and also smaller fuels inside smaller circles. In addition, they estimate the weight of the litter and herbaceous plants inside small squares called *quadrats*.

Instead of conducting on-the-ground inventories to appraise downed woody fuels, fire managers may use photographs representing various common fuel complexes. Bill Fischer of the Intermountain Fire Sciences Laboratory wrote several booklets illustrating common fuel conditions in the northern Rocky Mountains. Each booklet contains photos of many different examples of downed woody fuels in each forest type, together with information about each example and estimates of potential fire behavior. (Fischer doesn't expect the booklets to have the precision of an inventory taken on the ground; however, they will have more precision than trying to estimate which stylized fuel model a particular forested area belongs to.)

To make these estimates, inventory crews, using three transects from each photo point, first gather fuel data at the sites. They measure both the sizes of the downed woody fuels along the transects and the depth of the duff. By boring holes in some of the dominant standing trees, they can determine their ages, from the rings in their trunks.

Fire scientists study fuels in the laboratory as well as in the field. To determine the fire chemistry of fuels, researchers take tiny samples of fuels such as wood or pine needles, grind them up, and analyze them. They put a sample onto a tiny balance in a heat chamber and heat it up to more than 1000° F, watching how it loses weight. One of the researchers, Ron Susott, has linked certain chemicals in the plant tissues with those times that they lose weight quickly. Other tests determine how much oxygen a fuel sample requires to burn completely and the amount of heat it generates.

One of the researchers has remarked, "We do everything on such a small scale, a lot of people don't see how it relates to fire. Even the fireplace in your living room is big compared to what we're doing."

All these data will help make a new fuel model system, a system that classifies wildlands by the type, size, depth, and amount of their vegetation, rather than by the species they contain. Fire managers use fuel models in mathematical and computer systems that help them predict fire danger and fire behavior. The hope is to construct a system that will enable scientists to assess fire danger from fire behavior. The system could then provide long-term predictions as well as answers to "How will a fire burn if ignited today?" Scientists want to create a model that can be used in both a fire behavior prediction system and a fire danger rating system.

Fuel Moisture

Whether in a laboratory test or in a forest, the moisture content of a fuel is the most important factor in flammability. During the Yellowstone fires, the fuel moisture of dead logs in the area fell to 7 percent. (There is no standard moisture content for kiln-dried lumber, so statements comparing this and other percentages to that of kiln-dried lumber are inaccurate.) *Fuel moisture content* is the amount of water a fuel contains as a percentage of its oven-dry weight. Fire managers can calculate this percentage by using calibrated wooden dowels. After exposing the sticks to the air, they weigh them and compare that weight with the oven-dry weight to arrive at the percentage of moisture. Or they can estimate fuel moisture from weather forecasts, using tables or charts.

The moisture of both dead and live fuels helps determine the ignition and spread of fires. Usually live trees contain from 80 to 250 percent moisture, with the highest in spring. Herbaceous fuels have the most moisture in spring and the least after they dry out in the summer. Live fuels are divided into woody and herbaceous. *Herbaceous* fuels are the grasses and other plants, which are called *forbs*. When herbaceous fuels dry, they *cure*, a process most noticeable in annual plants because they die. With evergreens, a little of the older foliage dies and the rest loses some of its moisture, whereas deciduous perennials lose their foliage and the stems lose moisture.

Moisture slows burning because it must be driven off before fuels can burn, and this process requires heat. But when dead trees hold little moisture, the surrounding live trees burn easily. Once cured, however, fuels can hold any amount of moisture from almost zero up to the 300 percent of water-soaked rotten logs. A sound log will not contain more than 30 to 40 percent moisture, unless it is submerged.

Not all vegetation will burn, however. The amount of living and dead fuel that will burn in the driest possible conditions is called the *total fuel*, and the amount that will burn at a particular time is called the *available fuel*. Dead fuels burn more easily than live ones do, because they usually are drier. The chemical content and other factors affect the flammability of live fuels, so that the more live fuels a forest contains, the less flammable it will be, unless the live fuels also contain volatile chemicals.

The volatile chemicals—oils and resins—in some live shrubs and trees make them burn as easily as a kitchen grease fire. Chaparral shrubs share this characteristic with conifers, which also contain large amounts of fine fuels. Fine fuels are those, like pine needles, that are thin and threadlike. They burn more easily than do larger fuels because they have more surface area in contact with the air and so they carry the fire.

Fuels and their moisture content can also be described according to their size, because smaller fuels dry out and absorb moisture faster than larger ones do. After a rain, the percentage of moisture in a fuel falls rapidly at first and then levels out, eventually reaching equilibrium with its surroundings. It will dry no more and will absorb no more moisture until the weather changes. In the real world, however, fuels never reach equilibrium because their moisture levels are always changing, owing to changes in temperature, humidity, and solar radiation.

The time required for a fuel to reach equilibrium is divided into *time-lag periods*, during which a fuel gains or loses 63 percent of the moisture it contains. Fuels that are less than one-quarter inch in diameter are known as *1-hour time-lag fuels*, or *fine fuels*. These include mosses, lichens, dry grasses and herbs, dry needles, and dead twigs. These fuels can gain or lose 63 percent of their moisture in only 1 hour. Accordingly, one-quarter- to 1-inch dead twigs and branches are called *10-hour time-lag fuels*. Dead branches 1 to 3 inches in diameter, or *100-hour time-lag fuels*, usually change moisture levels significantly only as the weather changes, because it takes four days for them to lose 63 percent of their moisture, and the weather usually changes within three or four days. Further up the scale, *1000-hour time-lag fuels* are dead branches and logs 3 to 8 inches in diameter. Because 1000 hours is 44 days, these fuels change their moisture level mainly with the season. Changes in weather do affect all these fuels but affect fine fuels much faster.

Because they respond to moisture changes similarly to the way that live fuels do, 1000-hour time-lag fuels are used by fire managers as a standard to describe seasonal moisture trends and thus seasonal fire predictions. The reason is that when these logs finally dry out in the summer, live trees and shrubs have dried as much as they can and so will burn easily.

Several other factors besides precipitation help determine the moisture of dead fuels. The effect of humidity resembles that of precipitation but changes constantly because it normally falls in the heat of the afternoon and rises at night. It also varies seasonally and with the weather.

Differences in temperature between sun and shade and day and night alter the moisture content of fuels. Night and the reduction in sunlight as the days shorten in the fall and winter raise the moisture content. Day length has a great effect. For example, on an average day in July, fuels in the sun receive twice as much heat as they do on an average day in March.

Wind dries or moistens fuels by moving the dry or moist air next to them. Wind also cools fuels in direct sunlight. As already mentioned, the direction in which a slope faces determines the hours and intensity of sunlight. Shaded soil stays wet longer than unshaded soil does. The soil's texture also affects a fuel's moisture because it affects its drying rate, with porous soils drying out faster than clay soils. The species of fuel influences its moisture as well; thus deciduous foliage holds much more moisture than evergreen foliage does. A fuel's moisture also changes with its elevation. Because snow melts and grasses cure later, fuels are dry for fewer weeks at higher elevations, and therefore the fire season there is shorter.

Researchers at the Intermountain Fire Sciences Laboratory in Missoula, Montana, are using satellite images to observe seasonal changes in vegetation across the United States. To obtain the relevant data, instruments on the satellite measure the reflectance in the red and infrared wavelengths, and computers then figure the ratios between the various wavelengths for different areas of the earth's surface. A high ratio indicates large amounts of growing green plants, and a lower ratio means less vegetation or plants that are curing. These ratios are then assembled into maps. The researchers have noticed a seasonal change in greenness in coniferous forests that is unrelated to changes in the trees' moisture content, leading them to believe that the satellite may be sensing changes in the understory through the foliage of the trees, or in small openings between them.

The Fuel Bed _____

In addition to moisture content, several other characteristics of fuels help spread fires, such as the fuel's chemistry. Live fuels can burn vigorously if they contain enough oils and resins to increase the rate of combustion and its intensity. Interestingly, ecologists think that plants, shrubs, and trees may have evolved flammable chemicals in order to encourage fires that burn competing plants.

The amount of fuel also determines how vigorously a fire will burn. The oven-dry weight of all the fuel in an area is called the *fuel load* or *loading* (see Figure 4.1). Total fuel loads vary from 1 to 5 tons per acre for some grasses and can reach 100 to 600 tons per acre in slash created by timber harvesting. Varying amounts of fuel load cause the main differences in fire behavior among fuel types. That is, even if an area contains huge amount of large fuels, a fire will not burn unless it contains a sufficient amount of dry fine fuel to carry the fire.

The spacing, or *compactness*, between the particles of a fuel, as well as how much it is divided, influences the spread of fire because it determines how well air circulates within the fuel and whether the particles are close enough to ignite one another readily. If the air cannot circulate easily around it, a fuel will

Figure 4.1
Fifty to 100 years after a fire, there is little danger of fire in lodge-pole forests.

burn less easily. For example, duff is so tightly packed that it cannot hold enough oxygen to sustain flames, and it burns only with glowing combustion. Usually, however, the particles of most fuels are too far apart to burn as quickly as they would if they were closer. Another example is the lodgepole pines killed by pine beetles in Yellowstone. Fire managers believe that because these trees were dry, they helped the fires advance faster and burn more easily. Because their needles had fallen and their twigs were too far apart to carry the fire, when the crown fires reached these forests decimated by beetles, they became surface fires.

The percentage of dead material in a forest contributes to fire spread. This percentage depends on the age of the stand of fuel and its history. Older stands may contain more dead material, but not necessarily. After 20 years, much dead material collects in chaparral shrubs, but forests often do not accumulate a great deal of dead fuel until they are 100 to 300 years old, the exact amount varying with the types of trees, their growth rate, the climate, and other factors (see Figure 4.2).

Figure 4.2
After 200 to 300 years, lodgepole forests accumulate so much dead material that when fires do come, they are large and intense.

Any breaks in fuels tend to stop a fire, and so both the horizontal and the vertical continuity of fuels are important to fire spread. Rock outcrops, bare areas, streams, meadows, and lakes interrupt the horizontal continuity of fuel. A forest without ladder fuels—shrubs or saplings or lower branches—to carry a fire to the tree crowns lacks vertical continuity, which usually means that a fire will be limited to the surface or ground fuels.

As fuels change over time, their flammability also changes, varying with their stage of growth and with differences in weather and the snowpack. In some years a dry summer following a wet spring can cause a bad fire season because the grasses will grow tall before they dry out or cure. With fire and regrowth, the forest itself also changes. For example, after a young lodgepole forest crowds out all the vegetation on the forest floor and the dead wood from the earlier fire has decayed, it seldom burns. But mature lodgepole forests, full of shrubs, saplings, and dead logs, can support intense crown fires. These changes over time are termed the *fuel cycle*, but unless the fuel is brush or a single species of conifer, this cycle has no average length.

The National Fire Danger Rating System

Fire danger refers to the chance of a fire occurring, based on weather, fuel moisture, and other factors. Fire managers usually use the fuel models of the National Fire Danger Rating System (NFDRS), completed in 1972 and extensively revised in 1978. They use models to predict fire danger because the danger depends largely on the fuels' condition. The National Fire Danger Rating System specifies sizes and the amount of fuel per unit area so that managers can use the models mathematically. Because meteorologists cannot forecast the weather for more than a few days, the system can predict future fire danger only as well as it can compare this year's trend with past years' trends.

In addition, the NFDRS makes predictions only for surface fires, not for crown or ground fires and only for a general area, not for specific sites. For site predictions managers use the fire behavior system developed by Richard Rothermel and described in Chapter 2. The fire behavior and fire danger systems use different fuel models that are not interchangeable.

Today fire managers can run the NFDRS with a computer program called AFFIRMS to produce four predictions, called *indexes*. The burning index of the NFDRS is most familiar to the public because it is often translated into the low, moderate, high, very high, and extreme fire danger ratings that appear on USDA Forest Service and other signs.

The NFDRS divides fuels into stylized classes, or fuel models, which describe the type and sizes of the vegetation, the depth of the fuel bed, the fuel load, the fuel chemistry, and the amount of dead fuels. To obtain the current fire danger ratings, managers feed in weather data collected in mid-afternoon each day. The data include current and maximum and minimum temperatures and relative humidities, amount and length of precipitation, average wind speed, and fuel moisture. To make sure that the system will operate as intended, fire managers must select the correct fuel model for their area, that is, the fuel with the worst fire problem in the area or with the largest risk of loss, not necessarily the predominant fuel type.

The names of the current NFDRS models, expanded

Snags like these on Big Baldy Ridge in the Frank Church–River of No Return Wilderness can fall and injure passersby as long as 25 years after a fire.

from 9 to 20 in 1978, refer to fuel types found in only one area of the country, but each model can also fit vegetation types found elsewhere. The sizes and arrangement of the fuels, rather than species, distinguish each model. For example, the short-needle pine type can refer to both old-growth Douglas fir and old-growth lodgepole. Each model specifies how much of each of the four types of fuel—trees, brush, herbaceous plants, and slash—covers the area, as well as other characteristics of the fuels, such as the height of the trees or shrubs, the diameter of their stems, the kind of foliage, and the amount of dead material.

Choosing a fuel model and running the NFDRS system are not enough, however. For fire managers to understand the fire situation in a particular area, they also must consider that area's history of fire activity and its seasonal changes. With this information, computer programs can produce maps of fuels, climate, and topography that show that area's fire danger.

Just as with the fire behavior prediction system, fire managers can use different methods to operate the NFDRS system.

First, they can use a hand-held calculator plus the weather or fuel moisture data; second, they can use charts and graphs called *nomograms*; and third, they can have computer programs calculate the indexes for them.

Canada, Australia, and the Soviet Union have also developed forest fire danger rating systems. The two subsystems in operation in the Canadian system are the Fire Weather Index and the Fire Behavior Prediction System. The Fire Weather Index gives numerical ratings of fire potential based only on weather, whereas the Fire Behavior Prediction System predicts the rates of spread and the intensity of the fire front for different fuel types.

Plant Communities

Vegetation Types   In addition to being classified by fuel models, fuels also are distinguished by plant communities, although plant communities do not tell fire managers as much about potential fire behavior as fuel models do. The reason is that when classifying plant communities, it is difficult to obtain exact data and to make sure that a certain fuel type covers the whole area under consideration. But each plant community does have a pattern of fire frequency, severity, and season.

According to Steve Arno, a researcher at the Intermountain Fire Sciences Laboratory, vegetation is the most important factor influencing fire frequency and intensity. For example, fires in grasslands can cover huge areas rapidly, but because the grass provides a low quantity of fuel per acre, they are easy to suppress and seldom spot embers ahead of themselves. Furthermore, fires in sagebrush grassland burn 100 times more intensely than plain grass does, but sagebrush does not catch fire as easily as grass does. And because sagebrush fires spot more effectively, they are more threatening. Fire easily kills sagebrush, but in the American West, increased grazing and lack of fire have allowed the sagebrush to spread into many former grasslands.

Another vegetation type that has extended into grasslands is the pinyon–juniper woodlands. If these ecosystems contain enough grasses and sagebrush, they can carry fire into the crowns of the junipers. The grass-killing chemicals produced by junipers mean that the older stands contain few surface fuels;

nonetheless, intense crown fires can break out during hot, dry, and windy weather.

Ponderosa pine stands naturally contain few surface fuels, owing to frequent understory fires. Such fires favor thick bark and large buds, which are what these trees develop. Ponderosa pines also grow far apart and usually lose their lower limbs, thereby preventing fire from climbing to the crowns. Because many ponderosa stands have had few fires this century, the old needles and understory trees and shrubs have built up, enabling fires to crown when they occur.

In forests containing a mixture of Douglas fir, other firs, and pines, the fuels build up naturally. In such forests, the fire frequency and intensity vary but fire is infrequent, and so fuels build up and, in hot, dry conditions, may lead to intense fires. The best example of forests with a record of infrequent fires is lodgepole pine, which has stand-replacing fires only every 200 to 400 years. But the tendency of mountain pine beetles to kill lodgepole pines adds to the likelihood of intense fires, which favor lodgepoles over other trees because lodgepoles produce many seeds, some enclosed in cones that open only when fire heats them.

Fire Climates   Each plant community grows in a region with a particular *fire climate*, the long-term weather pattern that determines the fire weather and the length of the fire season. The Forest Service has listed 15 fire climates in the United States and Canada. Summers in the *Interior Alaska and the Yukon* are short and warm, and the winters are very cold. The 10 to 15 inches of precipitation falls mostly in summer; spruce and aspen are the most common trees. The fire season here lasts from May to September.

Patches of the dwarfed spruce called *taiga* dot the *Sub-Arctic and Tundra* area of Canada in the south, and tundra covers the north. Only 10 inches of precipitation falls in the northwest and 25 inches in the east, most of it in summer. There are a few midsummer fires. Birch, aspen, and spruce grow in Alaska, with arctic tundra at higher elevations and in the north. Most fires blaze in the dwarfed black spruce forests, which easily support a crown fire.

The temperate rain forest of the *Northern Pacific Coast*, from Alaska to central California, receives up to 240 inches of precipitation, mostly in winter. Sitka spruce and western hemlock grow close to the coast, with Douglas fir inland. Douglas fir also grows with Pacific silver fir. Farther south, coastal redwood and California coastal pine replace the Douglas fir. In this moist, mild climate, vegetation grows quickly but it also decays quickly, so the volume of fuel may not be as large as expected from the growth rate. In late summer, foehn winds, usually from the north or east, can cause fires to exhibit extreme behavior.

Along the *Southern Pacific Coast*, 10 to 20 inches of precipitation falls at lower elevations and 60 inches at higher elevations. Chaparral grows on lower slopes and conifers on the mountains. The ocean keeps the temperatures moderate all year. Usually no rain falls in summer, drought is common in the south, and dry summer lightning storms frequent the northern mountains. In the north, the fire season lasts from June through September, but in the south it is year-round. Foehn winds, called Mono winds in the Sierra and coast ranges and Santa Ana winds in Southern California, often blow.

Sagebrush and grass cover most of the *Great Basin*, where pinyon and juniper grow at mid-elevations, and aspen, spruce, pine, and fir are found near the mountaintops. Summers are hot, winters cold, and the growing season short. Precipitation varies from 10 to 40 inches, depending on elevation, but most of it falls in winter. Because of the dryness, fuel loads are low, and so fires put out little heat. Dry grass and the oils and resins found in bitterbrush, pinyon, and juniper make fires spread rapidly. In summer, the temperatures are high, and dry thunderstorms are frequent. The fire season lasts from June through October.

The *Northern Rocky Mountains* in Canada and the United States have moderate summers, cold winters, and 10 to 60 inches of precipitation. In the southern part, precipitation mainly falls in winter and spring, but farther north it occurs evenly throughout the year. At the higher elevations the trees include white pine, lodgepole, ponderosa, grand fir, and spruce. Juniper, sagebrush, and mountain mahogany grow at lower elevations. Dry thunderstorms are common during July, August, and September.

In the *Southern Rocky Mountains* sagebrush, pinyon, juniper, and Gambel oak grow at lower elevations, and spruce, fir, and lodgepole pine are found higher up. Winters are cold and summers moderate. According to the elevation, precipitation varies from 10 to 40 inches. Frequent summer thunderstorms bring light rain. Foehn winds called chinook winds blow on the east side in spring and fall. The fire season lasts from June through September, with high pressure aloft and dry cold fronts bringing high fire danger.

The Rockies of southern Colorado also have the characteristics of the next category, the *Southwest*. Chaparral, grass, sagebrush, pinyon, juniper, and ponderosa pine make up the typical vegetation. The precipitation is scant, the days are warm, and the nights are cool all year-round. Late summer thunderstorms with heavy rains limit the fire season to May and June.

Except for grassland and forest remnants, farm fields cover most of the *Great Plains*. The temperatures are high in summer and low in winter. The precipitation varies from 10 to 40 inches, with a maximum in early summer caused by thunderstorms. In spring and fall, Chinook winds blowing from the Rockies can spread fires. Even though the fire season lasts from April through October, fires seldom occur.

Spruce, fir, poplar, and aspen grow in *Central and Northwestern Canada*. The long summer days in the high latitudes dry out fuels rapidly. Precipitation varies from 10 inches in the northwest to 30 inches in the east, more than half of it falling in summer thunderstorms. The length of the fire season varies with the area.

The *Great Lakes* fire climate region supports aspen, fir, pine, spruce, and hardwoods like oak and hickory. The lakes moderate the weather, so even though the winters are cold, the summers may be warm or cool, depending on the particular year. The 30 inches of precipitation falls evenly through the year. Strong winds and intense storms arrive in the fall, winter, and spring, with thunderstorms in the summer. Because deciduous trees sustain fire best when they have no leaves, the fire season peaks in spring. High-pressure areas from the north or west bring high fire danger.

In the *Central States*, hardwoods cover low rolling hills like the Ozarks and western Appalachians where maples, birches, oaks, ash, and hickory often mix with pines. Precipitation of 20 to 45 inches falling in the summer discourages lightning fires, leaving two fire seasons, spring and fall.

Spruce grows in the north part of the *North Atlantic* region, with hardwoods in the south. The 50 inches of precipitation falls throughout the year, but the fire season runs from April through October, peaking in the spring and fall. The New Jersey pine barrens, with their large areas of short-needle and pitch pines, attract fire.

Many flammable fuels, especially pines, grow in the *Southern States*. Oaks, cypress, and gums cover the coast together with an evergreen brush called *pocosin*, whose leaves contain oil. Warm and humid summers follow moderate winters. Most of the 60 inches of precipitation falls in summer and winter, and so the fire seasons are in spring and fall. Dry cold fronts and drought cause the highest fire danger.

Brush, grass, and pines grow on the *Mexican Central Plateau*. The summers are warm, with frequent thunderstorms, and the winters are cool and dry.

Although these fire climates cover only North America, fire ecologists have identified many others around the world, by vegetation types they call *biomes*. Each biome maintains its own broad relationship to fire, with subdivisions into fire climates.

One biome important to fires is the boreal or northern coniferous forest that ranges across North America and Eurasia and extends in fingers south down the mountain ranges. Where it grows on mountains, it is often called *subalpine coniferous forest*. Although fewer fires per unit area burn in the boreal forest than in another widespread type called the *Mediterranean* forest, vast areas of the boreal forest do burn in times of drought and wind, accounting for a large percentage of the world's forest fires.

The Mediterranean forest consists of fire-prone brush and trees that have small leathery leaves that conserve moisture. Chaparral, common in California and around the Mediterranean, is of this type. Long summer droughts and strong winds are common, leading to frequent fires except in cultivated areas.

Fire Frequencies

Fuel types can also be divided by their fire frequency. In the first type fires are rare or absent. Examples in the United States are coastal Alaska, the western side of the Olympic peninsula, and the subalpine zone in New England, such as Baxter State Park in Maine.

The second fuel type is typified by eastern deciduous forest and pinyon–juniper woodlands, where low-intensity small fires occur more often than every 25 years.

In the third fuel type, surface fires burn every 5 to 25 years, and crown fires of a few thousand acres blaze at long intervals, as in ponderosa pine forests and giant sequoia groves.

The fourth fuel type covers moderately severe surface fires that burn every 15 to 30 years, with large crown fires coming less often. Examples are white and red pine in the Great Lakes region and jack pine in the East. In the West, coastal redwoods and some lodgepole, spruce, and aspen belong to this group.

Stand-replacing crown fires roar across the fifth fuel type every 50 to 200 years, covering 5000 to 200,000 acres per fire. California chaparral is typical but usually burns more often. Others of this type are spruce–fir in Alberta, spruce in Alaska and Ontario, and lodgepole in Yellowstone.

In the sixth fuel type, fires of high intensity occur every 100 to 400 years. Western red cedar and western hemlock in the United States and Canada, as well as the trees of most subalpine zones in the Cascades, Sierra, and Rockies, show this long interval and high intensity.

Chapter Five

■ ■ ■

The Effects of Fire on Ecosystems

At the top of the ridge above Goat Lake in Idaho's Frank Church Wilderness, a hillside of wildflowers and whitebark pines overlooked a blackened canyon. In 1981, two years after the Ship Island Fire overran this area, the trees remained only as gray and black snags. The blackened soil is pocked with the holes of burned roots. Little vegetation covers this blackness, except a few grouse whortleberry, whose light green leaves and miniature red berries intensify the black.

Regrowth

Landscapes like this one show that two years is only a short time in the growth of high-mountain forests, that after a fire it takes many years for all the trees and shrubs to grow back to their former levels—up to 300 years in the northern Rockies. Many years after most fires, a burned forest still shows the effects. For example, Mosquito Ridge, also in the Frank Church Wilderness, burned 15 years earlier. Although here a cloak of green grasses, lupine, paintbrush, and small shrubs covers the ground between the dead trees and lodgepole pines 2 and 3 feet tall stand among the shrubs, you can still see the snags, from which wind has stripped the charcoal, transforming them into sculptures of silver wood.

Forests at lower elevations grow faster than do those at high elevations, such as Mosquito Ridge. Along the Middle Fork of the Salmon River in the same wilderness, for instance, two years after the 1979 Mortar Creek Fire, grass and small shrubs already carpet the slopes between the burned trees.

Fire and regrowth, as seen here on Mosquito Ridge in the Frank Church–River of No Return Wilderness, are part of a cyclic process like that of the seasons.

Plants begin growing again so quickly that in Yellowstone only a year after the big fires, grass and inch-tall lodgepole seedlings were coming up between the burned trees. In other, less devastated areas, grass and plants already covered the ground, accented by the magenta spikes of fireweed. Regrowth does not mean that fire has caused the death of the forest but only that it is at a different stage, as natural as that of an old-growth forest.

The Northern Range in Yellowstone also recovered rapidly. Grasses, plants, and big sagebrush prevailed before the fire. Each sagebrush burned at such a hot temperature that all the organic matter and plant seeds underneath it also burned. The grasses and other herbs here have not yet grown back in the spots where the sagebrush grew. But these black spots have created a place for new sagebrush seedlings to start growing without interference from grasses and other herbaceous plants. Don Despain, an ecologist for Yellowstone National Park, discovered in the black spots rings of sagebrush seedlings each 2 to 5 inches high, and he predicted that within 30 years one or more of the seedlings would be as big as the sagebrush was before the fire.

Mosaic Pattern of Fires

Forest fires create varied and broken patterns, called *mosaics*, that are typical of forest ecosystems. Because of this variation, usually only a third of the vegetation within the perimeter of a large fire actually burns. Bert Strom, a fire management officer, observed that the 1987 Deadwood Fire in the Boise National Forest showed this pattern: Of the 51,646 acres that the fire covered, 16 percent burned at high intensity, 18 percent at moderate intensity, and the remaining 66 percent either burned at low intensity or did not burn at all.

On Bunsen Peak above Mammoth in Yellowstone, ecology professor Jay Anderson pointed out an area of shorter trees on the bottom half of the peak that marks the site of a fire in 1882 and called attention to the black patches rimmed with strips of red brown that indicate those parts of the peak burned in the 1988 North Fork Fire. The brown needles are the result of surface fires plus the heat from adjacent crown fires. (Within two years after a fire, the brown needles usually have fallen to

Bunsen Peak in Yellowstone National Park, above Mammoth, Wyoming, shows the typical mosaic pattern of both new and old fires.

the forest floor.) Less than a third of the 1988 Ladder Creek Fire in the Nez Perce National Forest in Idaho burned hot enough to resemble the dramatic newspaper pictures of fires. Another third of the fire consumed ground fuels, killed or scorched the small trees and a few large trees, but left many green patches. And the remaining third of the fire area was left green.

Reasons for Mosaic Patterns   Fires cause mosaic patterns by burning at different intensities in different places and by burning different areas in different years. (Each area or "piece" of the mosaic is called a *patch*; the study of these is called *patch dynamics*.) There are several reasons for the varying intensity. First, because the night temperature inversions reduce the wind, fires burn less vigorously at night than during the day. As a result, crown fires may drop to the surface at night, where they usually kill only the understory of the trees.

Second, fuel moisture varies with the location. Because the sun shines on south slopes for more hours each day, they dry out more than do north slopes and also burn better. And a forest of older trees has a large percentage of dead material, so that fire will kill more of its trees.

Third, fires do not normally pass through areas that have been burned recently; that is, old burns tend to stop fires. In 1988 in Yellowstone, however, the extreme dryness and strong winds drove the fires right through some young trees on old burns, demonstrating that weather affects fire spread more than the mosaic pattern does.

Fourth, fires burning in strong winds sometimes damage trees less because the wind blows the flames and hot gases to the lee side of the tree, where the trunk of the tree acts like a chimney to channel them upward.

Fifth, mosaics also result from differences among tree species in how easily their foliage burns. For example, foliage that contains oils, resins, or other flammable liquids burns quickly and intensely.

Fire Damage Among Trees

Fire damages trees by a combination of crown, root, and cambium damage. Trees can lose 20 to 30 percent of their crown to fire before the loss will affect their growth rate. The cambium, just inside the bark, is a formative layer that produces new plant tissue. It is damaged more by the duration of a fire than by its intensity.

How different tree species grow also helps determine a fire's intensity. Thick bark, like that of ponderosa pine and western larch, protects against fire because fire can penetrate it deeply without injuring the cambium.

A tree's roots will be damaged only if the insulating layer of duff burns away. Thick duff and deep roots are good protection. Trees with thick trunks resist fire because their larger size prevents them from heating as fast, and trees with all their branches high up also resist fire. The giant sequoia of the California Sierra Nevada, for instance, has deep roots, a thick trunk, and high branches. Ponderosa pines have thick bark, deep roots, a high and open crown, fire-resistant needles, and a habit of growing far apart from one another. Their seedlings and saplings also can withstand low-intensity fires. Thick bark and deep roots seem to go together in the Northwest, as do the characteristics that make trees susceptible to fire. For example, subalpine fir has thin bark with resin blisters, shallow roots, a low and dense crown, flammable needles, and a habit of growing close together.

Deciduous trees resist fires better than evergreen trees do, because their foliage contains more moisture and fewer organic compounds than the foliage of most evergreens does. And of course, deciduous trees can grow new leaves each year.

The effects of fire on trees also depend on their stage of growth. Thus dormant plants resist heat better because their tissue moisture is low, but they also burn better when they have little moisture. Conifers are most flammable in the spring, when the old needles reach their lowest annual moisture level and the new needles have not yet grown, and in the fall when all the foliage has dried out and the older needles have died.

Succession _____

The term *succession* refers to the order in which plants return to an area after a fire or other disturbance (such as a volcano). After a fire, herbaceous plants, shrubs, and trees return in a sequence, with the herbaceous plants arriving first, then the shrubs, and last the trees. The trees and other shrubs start to grow at the same time as the herbaceous plants do but are not seen until later because the plants hide them.

The plants that return have survived the fire, either by sprouting or from seeds that are already at the site or were carried in. Indeed, some seeds wait for years for fire to give them a chance to sprout—the ceanothus seeds that one researcher found in a forest had waited for 200 years. Plants like the magenta-flowered, aptly named fireweed that are first seen after a fire usually grow on a particular burn for only a few years.

All species present before a fire start growing within five years, according to a study of the 1984 Rosie Creek Fire in Alaska. On sites where aspen grew before the Rosie Creek Fire, that tree appeared again first, and all the species returned within a year. On sites where white spruce dominated, its seedlings began growing first, even though meadow horsetail was dominant a year after the fire. On black spruce sites, its seedlings and grasses shared dominance a year later on upland sites, but black spruce seedlings were not common in the bottom-lands.

Sun-loving species dominate shade-loving ones because they grow faster and can resist the drought of open areas. Researchers studying a pinyon–juniper woodland in south-western Utah documented this succession. On this site, pinyon pine and juniper were present in equal numbers before the fire, and afterward the juniper returned before the pinyon did be-cause its seedlings can grow in dry open areas, and pinyon seedlings need the extra moisture found in partly shaded areas.

Climax Forests   To traditional botanists, the early and middle stages of succession are *seral stages*, which theoretically lead to a stable forest known as a *climax forest*. A climax forest maintains itself until a fire, an insect attack, a windstorm, a landslide, or the like disturbs it. But today many botanists regard the term *climax forest* as deceptive because in most climax forests fire suppression allows species that usually do not do well after fire to take over.

For a forest to be a climax forest, seedlings of its dominant trees must be able to grow in it so that it can perpetuate itself. But in real forests disturbances occur often enough that species seldom reach the climax stage and if they do, the stage lasts for only a short time. Because a climax forest contains much dead material, which at high elevations decays slowly, fire often burns it and the older trees, and a young, vigorous forest grows up to replace them.

Disturbances like fires cause gaps in the forest canopy, creating a mosaic with different stages of succession. The first plants that come in are called *pioneer plants*. They often are weeds, that is, tall plants that grow fast, flower early, and die soon. Some of their many seeds stay dormant for many years, so are always ready to grow when the conditions are right.

After them come shrubs and then trees of various sizes, which traditional botanists named *seral-stage plants*. Today, in-stead of seral stages and climax forest, some botanists call the stages *gap*, *building*, and *mature* stages. The first, the gap stage, corresponds to the seral stage in which pioneer plants dominate and full sunlight reaches the ground. The building stages are the intermediate stages in traditional succession, and the mature stage is equivalent to the climax forest.

Because the natural regrowth of vegetation on a severe burn like this one in Yellowstone takes a long time on a human time scale, we tend to regard such an area as destroyed, but it is really just in a different stage of its life.

T. C. Whitmore, writing in *Ecology*, explained the gap, building, and mature stage theory. He believes that there are two types of trees, those that colonize small gaps and those that colonize large gaps. He calls the two types *pioneer* and *climax* (or nonpioneer). Pioneer species have seeds that can germinate only in gaps in the forest canopy that are large enough to permit sunlight to reach the ground for part of the day. Climax species are those whose seeds can grow in the forest shade and thus are able to colonize small gaps, although the species have different abilities to grow in shade. Lodgepole pine is an example of a pioneer species that colonizes large gaps.

Succession or regrowth may follow different courses at different times within the same area. For example, a fire following an earlier fire—a double burn or a reburn—in the same area may produce a varying mix of species. Many botanists believe that what grows depends on what species happens to get a head start and crowd out any competitors. The pioneer species, however, which produce many small well-dispersed seeds, have an advantage, as do species whose underground parts, like roots or rhizomes, can survive a fire and send up sprouts.

When the climate changes, the path of succession changes. New kinds of plants and trees grow, and the fire frequency is altered. Some trees may not regrow after a fire if the climate change has made conditions poor for them, and instead meadows or grassland may replace them. Usually, however, even though the climate is changing on either a small or a large scale, most of the species present before a fire begin to grow back immediately. The speed of regrowth depends partly on the location of the site—whether it is on a north or south slope, in a valley, or on a ridge top. It also depends on the intensity of the fire, the moisture content of the soil, its pH (acid–alkaline balance), the nutrients present before the fire, and the length of the growing season. Because a high altitude shortens the growing season, increasing elevation usually slows down regrowth. The timing of a fire in relation to the growing season also affects what plants return and how fast they do so. Researchers in the Black Hills of South Dakota found that spring and fall fires thinned currants and young ponderosa pines without affecting the mature ponderosas. But summer fires in the same area became crown fires, killing all the pines and leading to an increase in currants.

Plant Adaptations to Fire

Natural selection favors plants with characteristics that enable them to avoid or resist fire. Where fire occurs only once in a plant's lifetime, such adaptations enable them to reproduce rapidly after a fire rather than resist it. Where fires occur often, trees have evolved thick bark: The giant sequoia can produce bark 2 feet thick, and besides being thick, it lacks the resins typical of the bark of many conifers and so resists fire better than they do. In contrast, some species thrive on infrequent intense fire, which burns their shade-loving competitors and kills their insect pests or plant disease cohosts. For example, a hot fire cleanses lodgepole pine of dwarf mistletoe and gives it an advantage over competing subalpine fir.

After a fire some plants sprout from their roots rather than from seeds. Where fires are frequent, plants that have this ability have an advantage. To allow for sprouting after a fire, chaparral shrubs, for instance, produce such large root systems that in 3 months the taproot of a seedling can grow to be 3½ feet long. Plants may also produce more flowers after a fire, as prairie grasses do, or they may disperse more seeds, as lodgepole pines do, or more of their seeds may germinate. Fire increases the germination rate of seeds by opening the site to sunlight and removing seed coatings that inhibit germination. Indeed, the seeds of many chaparral shrubs like ceanothus can sprout only after the heat of a fire cracks their coats. By rupturing the seed coats or melting the waxes in them and by providing charcoal, fire helps the seeds of chaparral germinate. Severe fires also destroy the compounds in the duff that inhibit germination. Because these toxins, produced by the shrubs and by the soil microorganisms living under them, prevent annual plants and new chaparral shrubs from sprouting, the seeds must stay in the soil for many years waiting for another fire to enable them to sprout.

Fire-Dependent Ecosystems

Chaparral   Vegetation types like chaparral, which invite frequent fires, are referred to as *fire-dependent ecosystems* because their health depends on frequent fire. (The term *ecosystem* means a group of interdependent plants and animals together with their environment.) A common chaparral genus, a ceanothus, snowbrush, is typical. Flammable resins coat its leaves. To germinate, its seeds require heat of at least 113° F for 8 minutes, but they can survive temperatures of up to 300° F. The nitrogen-fixing bacteria in its roots also help it invade a burned area without waiting for nitrogen bacteria to regenerate in the soil.

   Chaparral shrubs like chamise and manzanita burn often, even though they have adapted to surviving 6 months of annual drought. To reduce moisture loss via transpiration, wax covers their leathery leaves, and their stomata—tiny openings in the leaves that take in carbon dioxide and give off oxygen and water vapor—are recessed in pits. To gather the scarce water, these shrubs also have either a long tap root or extensive surface roots. Because of the dry climate in which they live, some branches and strips of bark die each year, so after about 30 years, half of each shrub has died, making it more likely to ignite. In addition, the leaves contain many flammable substances that burn easily: oils, fats, waxes, resins, ethers, terpenes, benzene, and alcohols. The small size of the leaves and twigs also adds to their flammability.

In California's moist, warm winters and dry, hot summers, chaparral shrubs grow fast, and so they soon lock up the nutrients in their foliage. Fire recycles many of these nutrients into the soil, and after a fire, when chaparral shrubs sprout again from their roots, they grow much faster than before. This increase in the growth rate is apparently due to the presence of charcoal, for in an experiment, adding charcoal to the soil caused them to increase sprouting by 25 percent.

Aspen   Two tree species in Yellowstone, aspen and lodgepole pine, are strongly dependent on fire. That is, fires make aspens sprout because they contain a growth enzyme that remains dormant until the heat of a fire destroys a chemical that keeps it inactive. A severe fire can stimulate aspens to produce as many as the 1 million sprouts per acre found in Yellowstone after the 1988 fires. Because of this sprouting ability, after a fire, aspens regrow more rapidly than conifers do. The roots of one aspen can send out hundreds of sprouts called suckers, which can grow to be 10 feet tall in only 6 years. Most groups of aspens all begin from one tree.

Fire also induces plants like aspen to produce large quantities of seeds as well as shoots. In 1989 in one spot in Yellowstone, Don Despain found 1000 aspen seedlings per square meter, next to a clump of sprouting aspens: This translates into 4 million seedlings per acre. Despain noted that earlier researchers had seldom found aspen seedlings in the western United States because they do not look like aspen seedlings. Instead, they resemble narrowleaf cottonwood, with narrow leaves and gray bark.[1]

---

[1]Aspen sprouts provide important food for elk and moose, and aspens of any size are a favorite food of beavers. Black furrowed spots mark the slender white trunks of these trees. Because the flattened stems of the small round leaves join the leaves at right angles, the leaves tremble in the slightest breeze, hence the name "quaking aspen." The boles of young trees are pale green because the bark conducts photosynthesis.

A 1982 study concluded that aspen and willow declined, and con-

Lodgepole Pine   Lodgepole pines maintain such an intense relationship to fire it led Donald Culross Peattie to remark in his book on western trees: "This is one of the most curious and significant of all western trees—It is at the same time a forest weed and a commercial timber crop, a tinder box in case of fire and a phoenix after it." (Egyptian mythology describes the phoenix as a bird which rose again from the ashes after it burned itself up every 500 or 600 years.)

Lodgepole pines produce short needles, about 2 inches long, short branches, and miniature cones, less than 2 inches across. Their reddish brown bark, only one-quarter inch thick, is arranged in flakes shaped like jigsaw puzzle pieces.

High-elevation lodgepole forests, such as those on the central plateau of Yellowstone National Park, display several growth stages after a fire. Each stage differs in its reaction to fire, and lodgepole forests in various areas differ in the length of each stage. The following times in the cycle apply only to the Yellowstone plateau; more productive forests have shorter cycles:

The old snags fall after 20 to 35 years, but for the first 40 or 50 years after a stand-replacing fire in Yellowstone, herbaceous plants and lodgepole seedlings up to 20 feet tall grow between the snags and the logs killed by the fires. Perhaps the forest resists fire at this stage because the only dead fuel is large logs that do not catch fire easily.

For a period of from 50 to 150 years the lodgepole seedlings grow 50 feet tall, forming stands so dense that sunlight cannot reach the forest floor. The undergrowth thus is sparse. Because the old logs have decayed, the forest floor cannot support a fire, and therefore the forest resists fire at this stage. Because the lack of sunlight kills the lower branches, the trees resemble a forest of poles. On dry forest sites the old logs decay

---

ifers and sagebrush increased, in Yellowstone from fire suppression rather than from browsing by the large number of elk. Other researchers have showed that grazing helps cause these effects. Any failure of aspens to regenerate well after the Yellowstone fires will show that elk grazing has contributed to the aspen decline and conifer advance. However, in the summer of 1989 Don Despain found the Yellowstone elk eating fireweed as much as they did aspen.

slowly, and therefore, many dense lodgepole stands that have no dead logs must have suffered an early reburn.

Then for a period of 150 to 300 years some of the lodge-poles die from overcrowding, thereby making room for sub-alpine fir, Engelmann spruce, lodgepole seedlings, and shrubs like grouse whortleberry. Now the forest becomes vulnerable to fire again, and nearly all stands burn before the Engelmann spruce and subalpine firs become dominant. But before a lodge-pole forest reaches this stage, it will stop fires except in drought conditions.

After 300 years the original trees die, leaving much dead material. Because the invading seedlings have grown large enough to act as ladder fuels carrying fire to the crowns, the forest is susceptible to fire. In 1988 a third of the lodgepole stands in Yellowstone were 250 to 350 years old.

After a fire, lodgepole pine often grows so fast other trees find it difficult to invade. Jack Lyon, who studied the 1961 Sleeping Child Fire in a Montana lodgepole forest, found that in the first few years after the fire as many as 159,000 lodgepole seedlings per acre were growing on some slopes. Half of these died in the first 12 years, but at the end of 21 years 3500 to 8000 of these trees were still growing. Because crowding kills some of them, the resulting dead material can encourage an-other big fire.

In the summer of 1989, Jay Anderson and his wife, Phyl-lis, counted lodgepole seedlings in seven severe- and moderate-burn areas in Yellowstone. In all cases, the most seedlings grew on the moderate burns where the trees still had rust-colored needles. They found the highest number of seedlings per square meter was 79 and the lowest was 0.4. These counts trans-late to 316,000 and 1600 seedlings per acre. Mature lodgepole forests in Yellowstone have 325 trees per acre, so even the lowest seedling frequency is more than 5 times as many seedlings as needed to regenerate the forest.

Lodgepole pines produce many cones of two types. First, its *serotinous* cones stay closed until fire melts the resin that holds their scales together. These cones can remain unopened on the trees as long as 25 years, and lodgepoles do not begin producing serotinous cones until they are 20 to 50 years old. Lodgepoles also produce *nonserotinous* cones, which open each year. When the pines regenerate after light surface fires or other disturb-

In this lodgepole forest, grass has begun to grow between the trees.
Courtesy of the Boise Interagency Fire Center.

ances, more of their cones open annually, as in Idaho's Sawtooth
Mountains where young lodgepoles are growing on ground
disturbed by road building.

Young lodgepoles grow poorly in shade and thus usually
cannot grow in the typically dense stands. On sites with poor
soil, lodgepoles grow less densely, allowing their own seedlings
to regenerate.

Don Despain, an ecologist at Yellowstone, and William
Romme, a professor of biology at Fort Lewis College in Dur-
ango, Colorado, who studied succession in lodgepole pines after
stand-replacing fires, observed that succession and fire frequency varied with the location within an area. In three of their
four study areas in the Medicine Bow Mountains of southeastern Wyoming, they found that the spruce–fir forests along
streams in the valleys were older than the lodgepole pine forests
above them. Among the lodgepole stands on the north slopes,
there were no lodgepole saplings, and on the driest south slopes,
there were no spruce and fir saplings. Therefore, they estimated
that a spruce–fir forest that would take 250 years to develop
on a valley site would require 400 years on an upland north

slope, and on the upland south slopes, their calculation was more than 400 years. Because the spruce and fir grew so slowly on these slopes, the forest usually burned again before they could take over.

From his studies of lodgepole pine in Montana Steve Arno of the Fire Sciences Laboratory in Missoula concluded that the frequency and intensity of fires in lodgepole forests varied with the summer climate, that low- to medium-severity surface fires burned every 25 to 50 years in lodgepole forests with dry summers. In lodgepole forests with moist summers, fires were less common, but when they did occur, they often were stand replacing.

Fire's Effect on Soil

One day in Yellowstone in 1989 it rained 4 inches in 20 minutes, triggering landslides. The removal of vegetation by the 1988 fires also contributed to the slides. Because stand-replacing fires like the Yellowstone fires are so intense, they affect the soil more than moderate fires do. Nonetheless, thick duff is common in forests with stand-replacing fire regimes, and it protects the soil from heating up too much unless it catches fire, and so fire does not usually burn all the duff, or the top layer of soil. But in severe fires, only ashes remain on the surface, and the upper mineral soil is "cooked" and discolored by a chemical change. In 1988 less than 1 percent of Yellowstone burned that severely, however, according to Park Service soil scientist Henry Shovic.

What temperature does the soil have to reach for this to happen? Studies of fires in California chaparral show that if the soil surface reaches 1000° F and 1 inch underground reaches 400° F, the chemical change will occur. Because fire blackens the soil surface and removes the shade of the trees, it raises surface temperatures in the postfire environment as much as 25° F. This rise in temperature causes snow to melt earlier, especially on south and west slopes, and so the grass and plants come up earlier in the spring.

Nitrogen, phosphorus, potassium, and calcium can vaporize in a severe fire. One laboratory researcher found that 738° F was enough to vaporize nitrogen in a ponderosa pine

The media in Yellowstone frequently filmed the area of this earlier blowdown to illustrate, falsely, the severity of the fires. Courtesy of the Boise Interagency Fire Center.

forest, but most nitrogen is lost after a fire through leaching, by water percolating into the lower layers of the soil.

Counteracting this loss, the ash and charcoal from the burned trees add minerals to the soil, which act as fertilizer. Some studies show that after a fire the level of these minerals in shrubs increases, but others show no increase because the fertilizer effect varies with how much nitrogen vaporizes, compared with how much ash and charcoal is deposited plus the effect of the fire on soil microorganisms.

Intense fires can kill the soil microorganisms to a depth of as much as 3 inches, but they soon recover. A lack of soil microorganisms may account for some of the increased plant growth seen after fires; that is, the plants may grow better because they do not have to compete with soil microorganisms for nutrients. Important soil microorganisms are the nitrogen-fixing bacteria, which are more sensitive to fire than other soil bacteria are, dying at only 167° F in moist soil. By means of a process called *nitrogen fixation*, these bacteria turn the nitrogen in the air into the nitrogen compounds needed by plants. Because the few bacteria left after a fire multiply rapidly, they can quickly overcome the loss of nitrogen compounds in all except severe fires.

Because some of the plants that grow prolifically after a fire already contain nitrogen-fixing bacteria in nodules on their roots, these plants do not have to depend on the nitrogen bacteria in the soil, which in any case may have been killed by the fire. Plants with such root nodules include lupine, most legume-family plants, and the shrubs alder, bitterbrush, and ceanothus. A study showed that ceanothus can fix 600 pounds of nitrogen per acre in 10 years. According to some ecologists, those plants that grow right after a fire require little nitrogen, so that the nitrogen lost in a fire presents no hardship. The presence of nitrogen-fixing bacteria on its roots thus may have enabled purple lupine to cover the northern range in Yellowstone by 1989. Don Despain noticed that most of the lupine grew where the range had burned but that much of the plants like lupine in Yellowstone in 1989 responded in this way because the trees that formerly dominated the site had burned, and moisture from winter snows had alleviated the drought.

Fire can also kill the symbiotic fungi called *mycorrhizae* that grow on the roots of many shrubs and trees. Mycorrhizae get their food from their host shrubs or trees and in turn act as auxiliary root hairs for the host plant. Normally, mycorrhizae recover rapidly after a fire. They need moisture more than the shrubs and trees do, and because most trees and shrubs depend on the mycorrhizae to help them absorb nutrients, drought will hinder their regrowth by preventing the mycorrhizae, and the trees and shrubs themselves, from growing.

Erosion After Fire

Fire can damage the soil by burning the roots and the humus that hold back the runoff and by burning the trees and shrubs that formerly took up water. Such damage makes erosion more likely. Fire also can cloud streams with sediment, which may harm spawning fish. For these reasons, intense fires usually damage the watershed. Because humus can hold five times its weight in water, a study of California chaparral showed the runoff increased fivefold after fire. The additional runoff and resulting erosion vary with the type of the forest, the steepness of the slope, and the amount of precipitation soon after the fires.

When heavy rains fall right after fires, California chaparral slopes erode easily, and huge debris slides can pour down mountains and into houses. A fire the summer before and 12 inches of rain in 24 hours caused a debris slide in February 1978 in the San Gabriel Mountains that carried away most of the settlement of Hidden Springs. Floods and slides like this one often occur in Southern California after a big fire. Accordingly, fire managers worry about flooding, erosion, and landslides when the bare soil after a fire on steep slopes exceeds 15 percent.

Areas of intense precipitation, areas with unstable soils or geology, and areas already disturbed by logging equipment, road building, or mining have the worst erosion after fires. Steep slopes with loose soil erode easily, especially where plants and duff have burned. Because the plants no longer hold back the soil, water can erode it more easily, and even when dry, the soil can slide downhill in a process called *dry ravel*. And where fire has removed trees on steep slopes, snow can avalanche more easily.

The amount of erosion after a fire also depends on how rapidly plants cover the ground. In some cases, it takes years. On the site of the Sleeping Child Fire, for example, a high-elevation site, it took 2 years for plants to cover 1 to 2 percent of the ground and 6 years for them to cover 25 percent of the ground. This study also showed that planting nonnative species did not help reduce erosion, and it also inhibited the regrowth of native species. Therefore, seeding to rehabilitate burned sites is seldom needed and can be undesirable.

Erosion is worse where fire has deposited water-repellant layers in the soil. Such layers form when fires distill the oils and resins from the leaves and needles. The oils and resins migrate downward, condense on the cooler particles underground, and bond to them. The layers often form in chaparral and in dry, sandy soils. A study of Yellowstone after the 1988 fires found water repellency in all areas, burned and unburned, except for one unburned range site. The forest soils repelled water more than the range soils did. Other researchers have also found these layers after fires in lodgepole forests. In one lodgepole forest in Oregon a 9-inch-thick water repellant layer lasted for 5 years, but often the layers do not survive for more than 1 year.

Because it increases soil and water temperatures, fire changes streams and the life in and along them. The lack of tree and shrub cover also causes more fluctuation in water temperatures daily and seasonally. The ash and charcoal raise the pH of the stream, making the water more alkaline. Fire-retardant chemicals also can pollute the streams, but the effects are minor, and researchers are continuing to improve the retardants to reduce their effects on water. Because the retardants are phosphates, they act as a fertilizer for the plants and trees. In areas undergoing salvage logging, roads add sediment, which can deposit mid-channel bars and silt up spawning beds. Burned logs and branches that fall into and across streams change the movement of sand and gravel in the streams and create new pools. Nutrients washed into the streams can cause blooms of algae.

G. Wayne Minshall, a professor of ecology at Idaho State University, made several predictions of the effects of the fires on the life in Yellowstone's streams, based on streams' response in other areas to logging and disturbances: Until the forest in Yellowstone grows back to its prefire levels, the streams will host different amounts of invertebrates and fish than they did before the fires.

Fire and Wildlife Nutrition

The number of aspens and willows rises after a fire because it removes competing conifers and, where the minerals have not been vaporized, adds minerals to the soil. Animals benefit from the additional minerals when they eat the new plant growth; they may even eat the charcoal and ashes. Researchers in Canada found that snowshoe hares ate the charred bark of black spruce, probably because the fire had destroyed bitter resins. Other researchers, who had seen whitetailed deer eating charcoal and even ashes after a fire, concluded that the minerals attracted them as blocks of salt do.

The additional minerals also stimulate the growth of grasses, thereby providing better nutrition for grass-eating wildlife. A three-year study in British Columbia found that Stone sheep grazing on recently burned areas in winter produced more lambs, showed more horn growth, and had lower counts of lungworm. The researchers thought that this happened because the grasses on the recent burns grew more abundantly and contained more nutrition than did those on unburned slopes.

The additional minerals also stimulate the growth of shrubs. The number of berry-producing shrubs increases following fire, as does the number of animals like the black bears that eat the berries and the deer, elk, and moose that eat the leaves of the berry bushes and other shrubs. But this increase also causes the number of cougar, which prey on deer and elk, to rise, too. Because trees and shrubs that resprout after fire—like aspen, alder, and willow—are favorite foods of beaver, the number of beaver rises after a fire.

Studies have found that the amount of protein in shrubs rises after a fire and remains higher for 5 years, thereby benefiting animals. One researcher found that twice as many female blacktailed deer living in a recent burn in northern Idaho ovulated as did those in an unburned area. According to another study, the better nutrition caused the deer population to increase from 30 per square mile to 98 per square mile by the summer after the burn. The greater flowering and fruiting and nutrients of herbaceous plants and shrubs attract wildlife to recently burned areas, but on the other hand, frequent severe fires may reduce grasses, forbs, and shrubs, which in turn lead to fewer animals that can graze or browse on them.

The Effect of Fire on Animals

The effects of fire on animals change over time, but the biggest impact is the modification of their habitat. Few studies have examined the adaptation of animals to fire, but biologists believe that animals with flexible habits and diets thrive after fires and that those animals that eat foods found only in mature forests seldom survive.

In the long term, fire creates more forest "edge," which provides habitat for a wider variety of animals than the forest did before the fire. The reason is that in the absence of fire, dense forests develop that reduce the amount of grasses and shrubs, resulting in a decline in the populations of elk, deer, and other large herbivores. In the short term, fire destroys the lichens woodland caribou eat, but in the long term, over 50 years, fire rejuvenates forests in which lichen production is declining.

Of the herd of 30,000 elk in Yellowstone in the summer of 1988, only 246 died inside the park and 89 outside the park in the fires, or only about 1 percent. Over the winter after the fire 25 percent of the northern herd of 20,000 died from the lack of forage, which was caused more by drought than fire. Since 1968 when the public outcry ended annual hunting, natural regulation like this winterkill has taken care of any excess of the park's large animals. Before the fires there were so many elk in the park that observers could find places where the trunks of aspens were covered with gray scars as high as an elk could reach, and even the bark of some lodgepole pines was scarred to a similar height.

Only a few bison died in the Yellowstone fires, but when they left the park to find unburned winter forage, 540 of the herd of 900 were killed by hunters. According to the Park Service, however, the hunting benefited the remaining animals because the bison herd also was overpopulated for the available range. Other large animals that died in the fires were 2 moose and 4 mule deer inside the park and 10 moose, 6 black bear, and 32 mule deer outside the park.

Scientists believe that the reason so many large animals died in the fire was that high winds caused the fires to speed up to as much as 10 miles a day. As proof, most of the animal carcasses were found in areas burned by crown fires when dry cold fronts brought high winds and kept the resulting smoke close to the ground; an examination of the tracheas of several dead elk showed that most had died of smoke inhalation.

The surviving elk, bison, pronghorn, deer, and similar animals will find that the fires have opened new pathways for moving to and from water, calving areas, and summer and winter ranges. Outside Yellowstone, in some rangelands lacking trees and dominated by sagebrush and bitterbrush, fire is detrimental to wildlife, especially deer. Because these shrubs do not sprout from their roots, fire removes both cover and forage for many years.

Some Yellowstone animals took immediate advantage of

the fires. Grizzlies, black bears, coyotes, ravens, and bald eagles scavenged the carcasses of animals killed by the fire. In fact, the smoke columns attracted raptors from many miles around to catch the voles, pocket gophers, and other small animals fleeing the fires. Observers even saw 40 ferruginous hawks, a prairie species that rarely comes to Yellowstone. The hawks were hunting in the Hayden Valley, probably attracted by the smoke.

Because fires have occurred every 250 to 400 years in Yellowstone for over 1000 years, park scientists have concluded that the kinds of animals present today have been the same for at least that long, even though their proportions may have changed. Indeed, they think that the animals here now have adapted to Yellowstone's large, intense fires.

The effect of fire on animals and vegetation depends on the type of fire and the type of vegetation. Fires in California chaparral, which are usually crown fires, kill more animals than do fires in most other vegetation types, because the fuel loading is high and escape is difficult from the tangled shrubs. Smaller animals suffer more from fire than larger ones do. Even though their burrows insulate them from fire, they can suffocate. A study of Yellowstone and elsewhere showed that many small animals can survive if their burrows are at least 3 inches deep. In a stand-replacing burn, the hot temperature of the fire kills all the voles, shrews, and mice, and as a result many of the animals whose diets depend on them, such as marten, will also die. Because a fire burns the seed-filled cones that red squirrels eat, the squirrels may disappear for as much as 25 years. Other rodents, like deer mice and ground squirrels, that thrive in open areas may multiply after a fire. Birds that depend on pine seeds, like pine siskins and Clark's nutcrackers, come to the blackened areas to eat the lodgepole seeds scattered by the fires.

Because fire destroys the sap that keeps bark insects away, these insects soon move into a burned forest, followed by the woodpeckers and other birds. The woodpeckers increase, but species requiring old-growth forest, like the great gray owl, decrease. Birds that nest in cavities in trees proliferate because fire-killed snags provide more nesting sites, especially after the woodpeckers have been there.

Burned forests offer immediate food for some insect pests, whereas others depend on the food that fire provides in the long run. For example, in lodgepole forests, mountain pine beetles kill the trees, and the dead material makes the forest more susceptible to severe fire, which kills most of the beetles but creates gaps in which the lodgepole can reseed. Fire also helps control other forest pests, like spruce budworm, which thrives in Douglas and subalpine fir forests: If the shrubs and understory trees in these forests burn, the number of budworms decreases.

The Effect of Smoke on Animals—and Humans   The smoke of wildland fires contains carbon monoxide, particles of charcoal and ash, and as many as 60 different chemicals including hydrocarbons from the burning oils and resins, and the tiny particles of ash, charcoal, and chemicals are what make smoke black. When they penetrate deep into the lungs, they remain there. A researcher estimated that working on a fire line for one day equals smoking four packs of cigarettes, and so firefighters who smoke put themselves at double risk. The smoke must also irritate the lungs of the animals that remain close to the fire, although most of these live relatively short lives, and so lung damage is less likely to matter.

Fire Suppression and Ecology

As we have seen, fire affects what grows, but so does the suppression of fire. Suppression plus the grazing of domestic animals favors trees and shrubs over grasses. A study of Zion National Park documented this tendency. Here researchers studied a plateau and two mesas isolated by cliffs where no fires had occurred for decades. They found that the number of shrubs had increased on the plateau but not on the isolated mesas, which cattle and sheep could not reach. The researchers theorized that on the plateau, grazing killed enough of the perennial grasses to give shrubs an advantage. If lack of fire had been the only cause, the numbers of shrubs would probably have risen on all three areas.

A lack of fire has also helped lead to the near extinction of the California condor. As the surrounding chaparral thickened without the intervention of fire, the number of rabbits dropped, on which the condors depended for calcium as well as for food. Because they could not eat the bones of bigger animals, the condors developed a calcium deficiency. In addition, the overgrowth of the chaparral shrank clearings enough that the birds found it difficult to spot rabbits and, when they did find them, had no room to take off after eating them.

Fire and Ecosystems   Many people think that fire is detrimental. Because it blackens the landscape and burns the trees, people emphasize its negative aspects. But biologists know that ecosystems need fire because plants and animals evolved with it.

Those who recognize the importance of fire to ecosystems worry that in the last 60 to 80 years many wildland fires have been suppressed, and they blame the advance of trees into grassland on this suppression, rather than grazing. The reason is that in forests adapted to frequent fires, suppression has caused pine needles, underbrush, and dead trees and branches to build up to much higher levels than they did before, whereas in the past, small fires that burned the understory fuels often kept the forests open.

On the other hand, in forests where fires naturally occur only every 400 to 500 years—like the cedar–hemlock forests of the Pacific Northwest or the lodgepole forests of the Rockies—fuel would have built up anyway. By delaying large natural fires, fire suppression has caused the fuel to build up only a little more than it normally would. It also has enlarged the unburned areas, so that if a big fire starts, there will be fewer old burns to stop or slow it down. But in the drought years when these big fires usually break out, old burns seldom stop them, anyway. Some old burns in Yellowstone, however, like the Mt. Washburn Fire of 1979, did slow a few of the 1988 fires. Now in Yellowstone and elsewhere there is a patchwork of forests, alternating between those with infrequent fires and those with frequent fires but now clogged with underbrush and other unnatural fuels, which allow fire to cover larger areas. Both types of forests are engraved with the smaller scale pattern of mosaics.

The size of the areas burned by the Yellowstone fires made this quick change even more upsetting. But because the forest is always changing anyway, fire is just a quicker change.

Whether large or small, forest fires stimulate plants and animals to grow and to adapt to fire. They also stimulate humans to worry about fire and to think of new ways to deal with it. The traditional way of handling wildland fire is to prevent it if possible and, if not, to suppress it.

Chapter Six

■ ■ ■

Fire Prevention

F rom 1941 onward, the number of lightning fires in the United States has stayed about the same, but the number of fires caused by humans has risen every year, because as population grows, more and more people live closer to the wildlands or go into the backcountry. John Russell, a fire management specialist at the Boise Interagency Fire Center (BIFC), feels that because of population growth, the number of wildfires everywhere will continue to rise, and therefore, the need for fire prevention and education also will keep growing. Fire can kill in several different ways. First, it can burn the lungs or enough of the skin and flesh to cause death. Or carbon monoxide, instead of oxygen, can combine with the hemoglobin in the blood, thereby depriving the body of oxygen. Because of its heat, fire can upset the body's cooling mechanism enough to cause a heat stroke. And fire can also cause a kind of chemically induced pneumonia through smoke inhalation.

Fire Precautions for Backcountry Travelers

What can you do to protect yourself from fire in the back-country? Consulting with a ranger immediately before a trip will help you avoid fires. When lightning is striking, in addition to taking the usual precautions, you should camp next to a green meadow or large rocky area. In case a strike starts a fire, this open area will provide a refuge. Also, when winds, additional thunderstorms, or hotter temperatures follow lightning strikes a day or two later, be sure to watch for fires.

To avoid fires, take care not to start one. Feel a campfire

to be sure it is cool before leaving it. Place backpacking or camp stoves where they cannot ignite anything, and if you must smoke, do it only in rocky areas.

If you spend several days in the backcountry, you can find out whether the fire danger has changed by testing how easily pine needles break. To do this, hold a dead pine needle with your thumbs and forefingers 2 inches apart and bend it. If it breaks before it bends a quarter circle, the fuel moisture is low and the fire danger is high. If the needle bends more than a half circle without breaking, the fuel moisture is high and the fire danger is low. Note that because pine needles' humidity rapidly changes throughout the day, a needle that bends in the morning may break in the afternoon.

Despite your precautions, if you do encounter a forest fire, keep calm. It is easier to stay calm if you remember that forest fires often look much closer than they really are. But when in doubt, leave the backcountry in daylight by the route that you took in or another that seems farther from the fire. If you see spotting, torching, crowning, multiple areas of fire, dark and massive smoke columns, or flames more than 4 feet tall, evacuate the area immediately. Before leaving, plan an alternative route in case the fire blocks your first escape.

If you are overtaken by a forest fire, the National Fire Protection Association recommends that you not panic or run, unless your path of escape is clear and smooth. Try to travel downhill. Put on clothing to protect the body from the heat, being sure to cover your legs and arms. Wear cotton or wool, as synthetic fabrics melt. Sweltering in wool clothes is better than being burned. If possible, take refuge in a rocky area, trench, vehicle, building, pond, or stream. Cover any exposed skin with dry clothing or dirt, as wet clothing exposed to fire will scald you. Avoid caves or wells, as the fire quickly uses up the oxygen in them. Lie flat with your head on an area that will not burn. If possible, lie in a depression in the ground containing only sparse or no fuel. If none of these refuges is available, try to reach an area that has already burned. If tall flames prevent entering the burned area, create a burned area by burning the grass and the fine fuels between you and the fire edge. As a last resort, enter the burned area through the flames, but only if they are less than 3 feet high. To do this, cover exposed skin, take several rapid breaths, and dash through the flames while holding your breath.

Once in a place of refuge, to avoid breathing dense smoke, breathe shallowly through your nose with it as close to the ground as possible. If possible, breathe through a dry towel or bandanna. The towel must be dry, because breathing through wet cloth will damage your lungs at lower temperatures than breathing through dry cloth will.

Remember that fires travel upslope three to four times faster than they travel on level ground. And even after a forest fire is out, snags still may fall. The Sleeping Child Fire study showed that after 21 years, 7 percent of the old snags still stood. These snags can injure or kill because they blow down so easily in wind. In 1988 falling snags killed two firefighters in the northern Rockies. Indeed, firefighters have a saying, "When you hear a snag is when it hits you," so avoid burned forests on windy days.

If you are in a vehicle when you encounter a fire, stop if the smoke becomes dense. Narrow canyons are dangerous, so if you are in a canyon, keep driving. If you cannot, park away from the heaviest vegetation, and turn off the ignition. Then turn on the lights, roll up the windows, and close the air vents. Get down on the floor and cover up with extra clothes or blankets. The Country Fire Authority in Victoria, Australia, recommends keeping wool, not synthetic, blankets in the car for this purpose. Stay in the vehicle until the main flame front passes. It will become hot and smoky, and winds may rock the car, but the gas tank probably will not explode. In a few minutes you can leave the vehicle and walk through the burned area.

What to Do When Fire Is Advancing on Your Home _____

If the fire is threatening your home, the authorities will probably evacuate the area. But if the fire arrives first, stay in the house rather than out in the open because the house will protect you from the heat. The flames will probably pass in 5 to 20 minutes. A concrete refuge area inside the house is the safest place.

Before the fire arrives, bring flammable items indoors. Then close the doors, including those between rooms; close the windows, shutters, and vents; and turn on the lights. Turn off any pilot lights and turn off the gas or oil. Attach garden hoses, equipped with spray nozzles, to the outdoor faucets. These faucets should have gate valves because they let more water though at one time than other valves do. If you have a portable pump, attach it to your swimming pool or water tank. Fill with water as many containers in the house as possible, and soak small rugs, sacks, and mops to use to beat out flames. Put valuables into the car, back it into the garage, shut the door, and disconnect the automatic opener if you have one. Open the damper on the fireplace to let air into the house, but close the screen to keep out sparks. Put on long pants and a long-sleeved shirt—of 100 percent cotton or wool—and gloves, goggles, and a helmet. If the roof is combustible, wet it down just before the fire arrives. This is easier to do if you put a lawn sprinkler on the roof. After the main fire front has passed, check for fires indoors and out, and put them out if you can.

Making Your Home Fire Resistant

What can you do ahead of time to protect your home? The USDA Forest Service recommends the following: First, choose a fire-safe location. Second, design and build a fire-safe house. Third, landscape it with fire-resistant plants, and maintain the yard with fire safety in mind. These steps are especially important in "wildland–urban interface" areas, those at the edges of towns where people have built homes in the woods or chaparral, or where city boundaries or suburbs press against wildland vegetation.

What is a fire-safe location? The bottoms of slopes, level areas, and places with few trees are good examples, but the best of all is an area away from wildlands. Avoid saddles, narrow ridges, and narrow or steep canyons. Choose an area where power lines run underground and there is a loop road or more than one wide access road with at least a 45-foot radius turning area. Any access road or driveway should rise less than 12 feet per 100 feet. On a ridge top, the house should be set back at least 30 feet from the side of the ridge. A firebreak at least 200 feet wide—wider on slopes—should enclose the perimeter of the subdivision.

What is a fire-safe house? How much risk does a house located in woods, brush, or dry grass have of burning in a wildland fire? Dennis Simmerman and Bill Fischer of the Intermountain Fire Sciences Laboratory in Missoula developed a

This house uses fire-resistant landscaping and materials, which will help it resist the hazards of its location in the wildland–urban interface. Courtesy of J. Smalley/NFPA.

simple risk meter that allows homeowners to determine that risk for an average year. In a drought year the risk will be higher. You can obtain a copy of this meter as well as information on fire safety and prevention from your local forest service or Bureau of Land Management office, as the meter has now been published by the National Wildfire Coordinating Group.

The meter is a concentric series of three cardboard wheels on a 5-by-8-inch card (see Figure 6.1). When using the meter, first sight along the slope of your yard to get the angle or percentage of slope and turn the inner wheel to that percentage. Next, choose one of the ten descriptions of vegetation on the back of the meter that best fits your area, and turn the next wheel to that number. Then turn the outer wheel to the type of roof: wood, composition, or noncombustible. An arrow on that wheel will point to the risk of wildfire to your home: low, medium, high, or extreme. Even a house in an area of dry grass on only a 5 percent slope will have a risk on the line between medium and high if it has wood siding and a wood-shake roof.

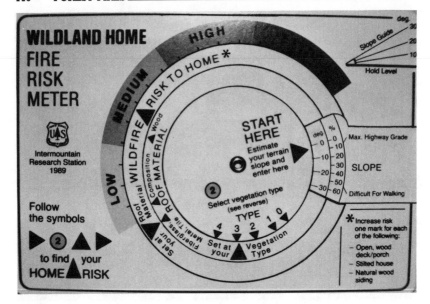

Figure 6.1
This simple cardboard risk meter can show homeowners the risks of living in forests and in homes with wood shingles. Courtesy of Bill Fischer, Intermountain Fire Sciences Laboratory.

Putting a metal roof on the same house will lower the risk to the line between low and medium.

Firebreaks will not save a wood-shingle roof or wood walls. So use fire-resistant materials. The roof should be metal, tile, asphalt, gravel, or fiber-impregnated cement, and the walls should be made of stone, cement, adobe, stucco, aluminum siding, or brick. For 60 years, the National Fire Protection Association has been trying to ban wood shingles nationally. As fire effects researcher Steve Arno stated, "Cedar shakes are the most incredibly inflammable building material ever concocted. Movies of Southern California fires show the cedar shake roofs spotting embers from one roof to the next, with the main fire burning along in the chaparral well behind." Studies show that a wood-shingle roof is 21 times more likely to burn than is one made of fire-resistant materials.

Treated shingles and wood siding—even with an Underwriter's Laboratory approval seal on them—lose the effects of the treatment over time. In fact, most such treatments prevent ignition only for an hour. Roof sprinklers cannot guarantee safety as water pressure and electricity may fail during a fire, halting the pump that draws the water. But even if they are running, the sprinklers may not put out water fast enough.

Therefore, if you cannot replace your wood roof immediately, put rainbird sprinklers on it, or use a new spray that will help it resist fire. This spray, a liquid polyphosphate fertilizer, was recently developed by the Texas Forest Service, which asserts that it can prevent fires until 30 inches of rain have fallen. It can be sprayed on roofs and siding with the agricultural spray guns used by lawn care and tree service companies. One gallon of fertilizer mixed with 1 gallon of water covers 100 square feet. In tests, 2-inch blocks of wood placed on the joints between treated shingles burned out without setting the shingles on fire, but noncombustible roofs are still safer. You do not need to give up the beauty of shakes, as some noncombustible shakes of metal and even cement look like wooden ones.

Build your home with doors and ceilings between rooms to shut off fires before they engulf the whole house. Two-story living rooms may look elegant, but they can carry fire to the second story. Put only small windows on the side of the house facing the forest. Install fire-resistant curtains indoors to protect your house from heat coming through windows and glass doors. To protect the outside of the windows and doors, install shutters or solid core doors, or prepare temporary wood covers that you can attach in a hurry. Make sure that windows are tempered safety glass, so that they will not break in the heat.

To keep out sparks, screen with metal mesh all vents, attic openings, and areas under porches, and box in the eaves and roof overhangs. Either screen decks and porches next to the house so that embers cannot land and start a fire on them, or build them of stone, brick, or cement. A brick or stone fence around the house will reflect heat away from it.

To provide water for firefighting, even when the power fails, install a swimming pool or water tank, equipped with a pump powered by a generator.

Arrange a firefighting water system separate from that supplying domestic water. The Insurance Services Office calculated that putting out a fire in a typical residence requires 1000 gallons of water per minute for 2 hours at 20 pounds per square inch. House fires caused by wildland fires may require more water. To be sure of having enough water, the water should flow from your pump at 50 pounds or more per square inch.

Put in a sprinkler system, for both the yard and the exterior of the house, and use metal, not plastic, pipes, so that they will not melt in a fire.

Buy buckets, shovels and rakes, and a ladder long enough to reach the roof. Buy 100-foot hoses with a ⅝-inch inside diameter, also long enough to reach the roof. You may wish to keep a backpack water pump on hand.

Bury power lines or see that trees do not touch them even in a high wind. If they do, ask the power company to cut them back.

These provisions will make your home relatively easy to defend in case of wildfire in the area. The California Department of Forestry stated that when firefighters first arrive at the fire, they decide which homes are likely to win and which ones are likely to lose in a battle with fire. The department thus suggests checking your house for five important features:

1. Thirty to 100 feet of clearance separate the house and forest or brush.
2. In the presence of flammable fuels and on steep slopes, the homeowner has cleared a wider strip of land, double on a 30 percent slope, and four times larger on a 55 percent slope.
3. A fire can't move uphill in the direction of the house.
4. The street or drive contains enough turnaround space for fire engines.
5. The roof does not have wood shingles.

Remember that Forest Service, National Park, and BLM firefighters are equipped to fight wildland fires, and so they often do not wear protective clothing or carry breathing apparatus that will allow them safely to enter a burning house to put out a fire. Likewise, the heavy protective clothing that city firefighters wear makes them inefficient at wildland firefighting, and so they cannot easily chase a fire into a forest or up a hill. All of these precautions also apply to summer homes among the trees, which people often build of readily combustible materials. The procedures taken to safeguard a home from fire should include landscaping.

Fire-Resistant Landscaping

A 30- to 100-foot greenbelt of nonflammable vegetation and landscaping should surround your home. A greenbelt is expensive, but not compared with the cost of replacing your house. Kent McAtee, a fire management officer for the Sawtooth National Forest in Idaho, pointed out that tree professionals charge about $100 (in 1990) to cut and remove one average-sized tree. At this rate, if you needed to have 25 trees removed, it would add only $2500 to the price of your home.

The greenbelt needs to be wider below your house than above it. Except perhaps for a few ornamental shrubs, single trees, and ground-cover plants, the greenbelt should contain no flammable vegetation. Water it to keep it green. The information on the risk meter advises creating a 3-foot strip of noncombustible material all around your house, with no shrubs and no landscaping bark or wood chips. The risk meter also suggests that all plants within 30 feet of the house, except isolated trees, be less than 3 inches high.

A green lawn makes the least flammable ground cover, but to remain nonflammable, the dead grass needs to be raked out of it periodically. Making a greenbelt includes removing tree limbs within 20 feet of the ground and any that hang over the roof. It also means clearing leaves and needles from the roof and the rain gutters and not allowing trees to grow up through decks.

When clearing a greenbelt, also move all firewood at least 30 feet from the house. Most people do not seem to realize the hazard of storing firewood close to a house. Sparks can ignite firewood easily, and once ignited, it burns hot and long and provides a ladder for the fire to reach the roof.

In addition to constructing a greenbelt, thin out the forest beyond it for at least 100 feet around the house, removing all dead material, including dry grass and needles. Removing all the dry grass is important because at 80 degrees and 15 percent humidity the probability of dry grass's igniting approaches 100 percent. Thin and prune the shrubs and trees, making sure to

This house has features that put it at a high risk of fire in its location in the wildland–urban interface. Courtesy of J. Smalley/ NFPA.

remove all lower branches up to 10 feet from the ground. Also, see that at least 10 feet separates the tree canopies. These measures will help prevent a fire from crowning.

When a fire is burning on the next ridge, there will not be time enough to clear and thin your yard, so do it every year before the fire season. The plants, shrubs, and trees in the yard should be fire resistant. Hardwood trees and shrubs are safer than conifers because they are less flammable. A study in Taiwan showed this variation in fire resistance: Fires burned only 16 percent of the hardwoods, but 55 percent of the pines.

Studies have shown that in 6-foot-high chaparral, a 10-mile-an-hour wind can send the flames to a 30-foot, out-of-control length. In 2-foot chaparral, it may take as much as a 50-mile-per-hour wind to do this, so select landscaping plants and shrubs that grow low to the ground.

Booklets on low-flammability plants are available from regional forest service offices and other sources. Suitable plants and shrubs vary with the climate, but some of those suggested are creeping sage, saltbush, rockrose, ice plant, Oregon grape, chokecherry, shrubby cinquefoil, squaw carpet, snowberry, buf-faloberry, raspberry, and rose. For greater protection, mix plantings with paths, concrete or gravel walkways, circle drives, and rock gardens.

Avoid activities that may start a wildfire. For example, place barbecues on a noncombustible surface, and clear all flammable material for 10 feet around them. It is safer not to burn trash, but if you do, burn it at least 50 feet from the house and 25 feet from woods, brush, or dry grass, in an approved incinerator covered with metal mesh.

The cover is important. Years ago a burning piece of paper escaped from an open barrel and ignited the dry grass in our yard in Los Altos Hills, California. Before the woman who lived upstairs and I could put out the fire, it had traveled beyond reach of the garden hose. By the time we beat the fire out with wet rugs, it had traveled the length of the yard. Ten more feet and it would have caught the chaparral on fire and threatened the entire neighborhood.

Community Planning for Wildland Fire

Neighbors can band together in associations or can work informally to make sure that everyone uses approved trash-burning methods and takes other steps to prevent fires. An association can more easily bring fire protection needs to the attention of local governments, builders, developers, and the media than individual homeowners can. A project to reduce fire hazards in the Berkeley Hills area belonging to the University of California offers an example of shared responsibilities. The project includes prescribed burning and thinning by hand and, in areas difficult to clear, a herd of 600 goats. The University Office of Environmental Health and Safety started the program with the help of homeowner groups and a fire prevention committee. The California (youth) Conservation Corps provides the hand labor, and local fire departments help with the prescribed burns.

To inspire similar projects, city and county officials need to include the danger of wildland fires in their land use planning. That is, fire hazard areas should be marked on land use maps, and fire protection measures should be part of plans for new developments. Some states already have laws requiring these measures. Citizens can urge local officials to decide on growth boundaries for urban areas, to cluster developments, and to preserve space between them. Clustering developments also helps protect them from fire and retains undeveloped areas for recreation and wildlife.

In addition, the federal and state governments should recognize that some areas have such great fire danger that no one should ever build on them. Such areas include those with little water, poor road access, steep slopes, heavy fuels, narrow canyons, and ridge tops. George Wuerthner, author of *Yellowstone and the Fires of Change*, stated: "In some parts of the west, we should zone certain areas off limits to houses due to high fire danger, just as flood plains are zoned so no one can build on them. Insurance companies don't insure houses built on flood plains and they shouldn't insure houses built in fire hazard areas."

Citizens should see that subdivision plans specify fire safety measures like access roads, adequate turnarounds, water supplies, underground power lines, density of housing, setbacks, and the position of houses on slopes. Plans should also specify adequate fire hydrants, fuel breaks around the subdivision, and the thinning or clearing of trees and brush. Fire-resistant building materials, landscaping with fire-resistant plants, and roof and yard sprinkling systems should be required.

Developers can base their subdivision plans on a set of model guidelines published by the Colorado State Forest Service. These suggest prohibiting building on slopes of over 30 percent or in gullies or areas of heavy fuels and advocate requiring thinning, fuel breaks, and other fire safety measures. Such measures may include requiring existing homes to change to fire-resistant roofs and siding within a certain number of years, to spray houses with fire-retardant chemicals, and to assess the costs of spraying them at regular intervals.

Local and state governments can buy conservation easements to limit land uses or to force landowners to keep the trees and brush thinned, or they can buy the land and lease it back to the owner with restrictions. They can also arrange land exchanges. Inducements for local governments to take these fire prevention measures can come from national tax incentives and technical and financial help. In return for training agency firefighters in structural firefighting, local governments can work with state and federal agencies to train city fire departments in wildland firefighting. Local governments can work to convince state and federal agencies that where national forests adjoin homes, the agencies should reduce the fuels in them.

Private enterprise can also help. A "private fire consultant" could advise homeowners what they should do and then provide the services, such as tree and brush trimming and removal, dead-fuel cleanup and burning, prescribed burning, and landscaping with species of low flammability. A consultant could also work with developers and community planners.

Insurance companies could provide additional incentives for fire protection. In figuring premiums they already consider building materials, sprinklers, and distance from and the quality of the fire department, and average fire losses in the area. They could also expand the number of fire protection measures influencing premiums and raise premiums for houses built in areas of high fire risk or refuse to insure them. If they raised premiums high enough for houses with wood-shake roofs, homeowners might stop wanting them. The companies could do this if they set rates that reflected the true risk of living in these areas. At present, because they average high-risk situations with urban homes to arrive at their rates, urban policyholders subsidize wildland homeowners.

The power of the insurance lobby will make these ideas difficult to carry out. As long as premiums are higher than the claims money paid to replace homes, only new laws will force the insurance companies to change their premium structures. In the meantime, publicity for the need to protect homes in wooded areas could help create national pressure for legislation. At the 1988 Symposium on Protecting People and Homes from Wildfire in the Interior West, architect Albert Comly stated that the media could help solve the interface fire problem by publicizing developments that use good wildfire design. He suggested that home design and improvement magazines take the lead in this.

The various forest and park services could help by changing the requirements for their administrative buildings to emphasize fire safety. In the past they have been concerned more with blending their buildings into the landscape. In Yellowstone, wood roofs covered many ranger stations and park headquarters, and many of the roofs touched the trees.

The interface problem is partly one of attitude. When

homes expand into wildlands, people's attitudes often prevent them from minimizing wildfire hazards. When they choose to live out in the hills, they want to live close to the trees and want the land to look "natural." They also love wood shakes. In their thinking, wildfires will destroy someone else's home, not theirs, and they do not want the government telling them what they have to do.

Fire Prevention

In 1988 the Westberry Fire burned 48 homes and other buildings on the outskirts of Rapid City, South Dakota. As a result, a committee of the Chamber of Commerce worked with the state department of forestry and the Forest Service to survey for fire danger 896 parcels of city land and 22 subdivisions outside the city on or adjacent to forested land. The survey is intended to guide fire departments and the agencies in helping homeowners reduce their hazards. Eleven percent of the city lots surveyed had extreme fire danger, 26 percent high fire danger, 9 percent moderate, and 54 percent low fire danger. Richard Botto of the South Dakota Division of Forestry said the survey determined that 11 of the 22 subdivisions surveyed outside the city had high risk needing immediate corrective action. Some of the high risk conditions found were lots of dead wood and litter, little or no thinning of trees, inadequate water, poor access, and homes with wood shingles.

Programs like that in Rapid City can prevent the need for fire suppression. Such programs are called fire prevention. Fire prevention programs consist of personal contact, public education, and law enforcement. Public education includes the specific steps that residents can take to prevent fires. In times of high fire danger, agencies close areas of high fire hazard and restrict activities likely to start a fire, such as logging, welding, campfires, and smoking.

Fire managers may write letters to those with a special interest in the area or talk to local officials or organizations, start a forestry or ecology club at the local high school, or arrange for annual programs at all grade levels. They may encourage teachers to use fire prevention materials in the classroom, especially in the elementary grades. Field trips and demonstrations help inform the public and the news media and alert the public to times of extreme fire danger.

The ever-present danger of old snags can be seen at Lake Creek
Lakes in the Frank Church–River of No Return Wilderness.

Fire prevention programs also publicize the penalties for starting wildland fires. On Forest Service land, setting a fire is considered arson, a felony with penalties of up to 5 years in prison and up to $250,000 in fines. Negligence that causes a fire is a misdemeanor punishable by a $5000 fine and up to 6 months in jail. The person starting the fire is also liable for damages and suppression costs, which may add up to several million dollars. Negligent acts include leaving a fire unattended, building a fire on a windy day, and setting off fireworks. Penalties on other federal lands and on state lands are similar.

The most famous theme in fire prevention is Smokey the Bear. The Wartime Advertising Council (World War II) invented him to counteract the threat of the Japanese setting U.S. forests on fire with incendiary balloons and shelling the Southern California coast. In 1944 the council really wanted to use Bambi, of the Walt Disney movie, but could not get a license to use him permanently, and so in 1945 it hired Albert Staehle, a commercial agency artist, to design the council's own symbol, the original Smokey emblem. In 1948 Rudy Wendelin updated it for the Forest Service. In 1950 a burned bear cub found after a fire in the Lincoln National Forest, New Mexico, became the "real" Smokey in the (Washington, D.C.) National Zoo. Another bear from the same forest succeeded him when the first one died of old age. Smokey's message is not outdated. People still cause wildfires, which seldom benefit forests and often threaten human life and property. Because of this, since 1987 the Smokey campaign has included material on the dangers of wildland fire to homes. A 1989 survey showed that only 71 percent of the children 5 to 13 years old that it polled recognized Smokey and his message. As a result, Elsie Cunningham, the Smokey program director, decided to return to a basic fire prevention campaign aimed at elementary school children. Part of it focuses on classroom presentations by fire officials, at which someone may appear dressed in a Smokey Bear suit.

During the 1980s, two additions, financed by private industry, were made to the traditional Smokey approach. The first is the Smokey sports program, which uses Smokey promotions at college and professional athletic events. Smokey appears; an award is usually made to the home team; and cards or posters are handed out to the fans. The second is the Smokey and the American cowboy program, aimed at rodeo enthusiasts.

It uses rodeos, from the local to the national finals, to give fire prevention messages. The rodeo announcer spotlights fire prevention, and Smokey signs autographs and rides in the parade and the grand entry.

Smokey is the best known, but he is not the only forest animal used as a fire prevention symbol. The National Fire Protection Association created another fire prevention emblem, Sparky the fire dog, to help prevent fires in the home. Other countries have adopted a wide variety of animals as fire prevention symbols, from the rabbit of Spain to the moose of the Soviet Union. Perhaps the most unusual is the Italian symbol, Sophie, a ladybug who is married to a computer.

Many states sponsor another fire prevention program, called Keep Green, which was started in Washington, the Evergreen State, during World War II, by the American Forest Products Institute (now the American Forest Institute), because it fitted so well with Washington's nickname. In 1944 the American Forest Institute made the program a national one. The most noticeable part of this program is the Keep (your state) Green signs painted on highways throughout the country.

Other programs aim at a particular fire problem such as fireworks, arson, or the wildland–urban interface. For example, the Central Oregon Fire Prevention Cooperative wrote a pamphlet entitled "Planning for Survival: How to Protect Your Home from Wildfire." "Wildfire Strikes Home," issued by the National Fire Protection Association, reports on the threat to forested lands from the growing number of homes in rural and suburban areas. The Sierra Front Wildfire Cooperators put out a booklet called "Wildfire Protection: A Guide for Homeowners and Developers." The National Fire Protection Association publishes fire code books, and the National Wildfire Coordinating Group writes guides, some of which list fire standards for mechanical equipment and structures, to try to prevent wildland fires.

In 1909, the National Fire Protection Association (NFPA) began campaigning for state laws prohibiting fireworks, and many states passed laws making most kinds illegal. In the 1960s the United States Consumer Product Safety Commission took over regulating Class C fireworks and setting standards for them; this has resulted in Class C fireworks being permitted in states where state laws had previously banned them. Since then, annual injuries number 10,000, and fires started by fireworks have risen to 50,000 a year, so the NFPA still campaigns against fireworks.

Another fire prevention program is sponsored by the International Association of Arson Investigators, which trains and educates law enforcement officers about arson fires, in structures and in wildlands.

Other countries also conduct fire prevention programs. In 1972 the Canadian province of Quebec set up seven non-profit Societiés de Conservation, which prevent and fight fires in their own regions. The members are the timber industry, landowners who own large tracts of land, and representatives of the provincial government. They pay annual dues to fund fire prevention campaigns and firefighting. At the end of each fiscal year, the government refunds to the societies part of the costs of putting out fires, thus giving the societies an incentive to prevent fires. Some of these measures are making annual school visits, meeting with forest user groups, and supervising berry picking and logging.

Presuppression

In addition to prevention, before the fire season, the USDA Forest Service, Bureau of Land Management, and state forestry departments prepare for fire by means of presuppression. *Presuppression* includes reducing fuel hazards, building and maintaining roads and lookouts, setting up caches of firefighting supplies, and adding crews and patrols during times of high fire danger.

These agencies reduce fuels by preparing fuel breaks and firebreaks. They construct fuel breaks by removing or changing the native vegetation on a wide strip of land, to leave only grass or ground cover. The 100- to 300-foot width of these strips allows firefighters to use them as a safety zone or an anchor for a fire line. To construct a firebreak, crews clear away all vegetation in a strip as wide as half the height of the tallest trees or shrubs, and they dig a path along the center of this strip down to the mineral soil. The vegetation in fuel breaks must be cut back every 5 or 10 years, but it must be cleared from firebreaks every year. Neither type of break, however, will stop intense fires because such fires can spot across them.

Fire management officers write plans for detecting and fighting fires on their lands. They find good places to build fire lines, get water, land helicopters, and set up fire camps, and they mark these on maps. In addition, from data on the area, including fuel types, the location of natural firebreaks, and information on past fires, officers map the hazards in their area and plan what they need to do before the fire season.

Fire management agencies also hire and train seasonal employees to be firefighters. Each forest holds a "fire school" for a week at the beginning of the season. For example, working on a fire line requires 40 hours of training. More advanced training is usually given on a regional, interregional, or national level, examples being training as airbase managers or as "mix masters" (those who mix the fire retardant). Agencies may also move firefighters and equipment close to possible fires at the beginning of the season. In 1983 the Alberta (Canada) Department of Forestry and Lands started a program of pre-suppression preparedness in which it prepositions in high-risk areas 500 firefighters and 100 helicopters with crews and then moves the crews around in response to changes in weather and fire danger. How many firefighters the agencies hire depends on the fire potential. The position of each crew is recorded on large maps at the Provincial Forest Fire Centre. As the fire danger increases, the centre transforms more forest offices into fire centers and bases additional crews at these centers.

The United States also prepositions initial attack crews and resources. One way is by attaching 20-person crews, engine crews, and helitack crews to ranger districts; and another is by training district employees in firefighting.

The combination of individual, local government, and fire prevention agency programs lessens the need for the fire suppression methods discussed in the next chapter, but they still are needed, as both lightning and people still start many fires.

Chapter Seven

■ ■ ■

Firefighting Methods

A Fire Camp

Wood chips and semitrailer rigs covered the green grass of one half of the airstrip. Below the ponderosa pine and Douglas fir that softened the canyon walls, helicopters clattered in and out of the other, roped-off half of the strip. Smoke sharpened the mountain air. Wall tents, an olive-drab circus-style tent, and fenced-off piles of cardboard cartons gave the impression of a set for "MASH." Two men were sharpening tools inside another enclosure, next to a stack of lumber. On the entry road a national guardsman checked incoming vehicles to see whether they belonged there. In the camp stood a row of turquoise and tan plastic portable outhouses. Washers and dryers hummed in a semitrailer open to the sky, and a line of yellow-shirted men and women filed past another trailer from which they carried trays of food.

This was not a battlefield but a fire camp, now called an *incident base*, the one for the 1989 Lowman, Idaho, fire. A green wall tent floored with wood chips served as an office for Marsha Karle, the information officer for the second team in charge of the fire. A wooden table, a folding chair, a Coleman lantern, one electric light, and two big cardboard boxes for files furnished the tent. She told me that the incident bases have information officers like herself to protect the reporters. The information officer not only helps them report on the fire safely but also informs the firefighters about the fire and about safety precautions. For large fires, the information officer has a staff of several people.

The Boise Interagency Fire Center (BIFC) contracts for

During the Lowman Fire in 1989, firefighters lined up for food provided by a contract caterer for the Warm Springs fire camp.

the food service, the washers and dryers, the sinks and showers, and other services for the incident base in advance of the fire season, so that it need only call these contractors when a fire breaks out. The center also may allow concessionaires to sell toothpaste and shampoo and even T-shirts and other souvenirs of the particular fire. In a large tent, videos are shown. If an item such as Marsha's table can be quickly and easily built, a team of carpenters builds it from lumber kept on hand. And a team of emergency medical technicians and an ambulance provide medical service.

The overhead team—the management team sent in by BIFC to manage the fire—keeps track of everything at the base and at the fire. Fire policy allows no drugs or alcohol and prohibits the firefighters from leaving the camp without authorization. The Logistics Section of the team stockpiles supplies inside a fence and sees that people sign for the things they check out. They keep track of all vehicles with big numbers on their windshields. In the bigger bases like this one, the National Guard helps out, often with transportation.

National Guard troops are often used on large fires to supplement other resources, especially to provide security for fire camps. Courtesy of the USDA Forest Service.

The official in charge of the fire, called the incident commander, and the rest of the overhead team run the operation. Their offices may be in travel trailers as they were in Lowman. For a big fire they set up locations called fire camps and spike camps to provide services for some crews closer to the fires. But crews sent into the backcountry for a few days manage without a camp, by using "coyote tactics," which means that they stay at or near the fire line with the equipment they have brought with them. More often though, helicopters, planes, or pack trains resupply them.

Fire Detection

A fire will not need a fire camp unless it becomes a large fire of 200 or more acres. Most fires are put out when small because they are found at an early stage by means of fire detection, and firefighters and resources are sent to them right away. Most countries today use lookout towers as the main method of fire detection. In Alberta, Canada, which is known for its up-to-date fire suppression, its 142 lookouts still report half the fires. Although lookout towers are expensive to build and run, they cost little compared with the value of the forest. A company in Brazil that makes lookout towers figures the cost of one tower equals the commercial value of 35 acres of forest. This company's elaborate metal towers, up to 250 feet tall and supported by guy wire cables, come equipped with little elevators.

The USDA Forest Service has experimented with using television cameras instead of people in lookout towers, but in a TV picture, an observer back at the base cannot easily distinguish smoke from mist. TV cameras also are expensive and cannot be serviced easily in remote locations. Even so, Poland has a system of over 90 TV cameras with 500-millimeter lenses, which it claims can detect fires as much as 30 miles away.

U.S. fire managers prefer using live observers, who more often detect fires from planes rather than from fixed lookouts. From the air an observer can tell more about the exact location of a fire than is possible from a lookout. A World War I pilot, Henry Arnold, who began aerial detection in California in 1919, discovered over 400 fires from the air that summer.

In the United States, most people who love the outdoors have at one time been inside a standard Forest Service lookout, which is a 14-foot-square wooden building, usually painted white. In 1983 my son Doug ran the lookout at Sleeping Deer, 45 miles northwest of Challis, Idaho. The lookout is 2 miles by trail from the end of a rocky dirt road. When another son, Stuart, and I hiked the 2 miles of rocks to the lookout, cotton-ball clouds were beginning to build up into towers over the peaks.

Doug had just finished showing us around the lookout when thunder cracked nearby. He told us to sit on the floor and not reach out and touch anything metal. So we stayed away from the bed, wood stove, and fire finder. He explained how the fire finder, invented by W. B. Osborne, lets an observer find the compass reading of a fire by sighting through a window containing crosshairs. He explained that with the information from two lookouts and a topographic map, the dispatcher can pinpoint the location of a fire.

Hail crackled on the roof, but within half an hour the sun again shone through the clouds. We could move around again. As the clouds drifted on or evaporated, Doug began to look for smoke. Many blobs and tendrils of mist rose from the dark green of the ridges. We found several grayer wisps, which looked like smoke, but Doug examined each with the binoculars and said, "Nope, that's just a water dog." He also told us that a lot of lightning strikes do not flare up into a fire until the next afternoon.

That summer, when Doug found fires, he reported them by radio. But in earlier days, lookouts used telephones, helio-graphs, and even carrier pigeons. Heliographs communicate in Morse code by covering and uncovering mirrors that reflect the sunlight.

Infrared Scanning Systems   Infrared scanning systems also help with detection. Although they can see through smoke, they cannot penetrate dense foliage. Since 1962 the Forest Service has used infrared line scanners, mainly to map fires and locate their hot spots. In 1974, the infrared mapping system was transferred to the Boise Interagency Fire Center.

At first the operators had to take the film to the ground for processing, but now they can process it on board the planes. After processing, they can drop the film at a fire camp via a drop tube or arrange to deliver it by ground transportation.

Fire managers can use scanners for fire detection, but they cost too much to use for routine detection except at times of critical fire danger. Line scanners employ infrared wavelengths that are farther from visible light than are the wavelengths used in infrared photography. Line scanners do not take infrared photographs but, rather, draw a map or thermogram of the thermal differences they record; therefore they can operate in total darkness. Those with dual bands, like the ones at BIFC, can detect smaller hot spots and more easily reject false hot spots than single-band scanners can. Fog, cloud, smoke, exhaust, fireplaces, generating plants, and warm rocks can cause false readings.

Because the outer edges of the scan blur, the planes fly an overlapping pattern. The width of the scan varies with the height of the plane. At 1000 feet it is 0.66 mile, but at 15,000 feet it is 9.83 miles. From 15,000 feet a line scanner can detect a 9-inch hot spot.

A second type of infrared unit called FLIR ("forward-looking infrared") is used to map smaller fires and to take close-up looks at big fires. The Forest Service sometimes mounts these units in helicopters to check to see whether lightning strikes reported by ALDS (aerial lookout and detection system) units have actually started fires and to map hot spots for ground crews and helicopter water drops.

In 1984 researchers developed a more advanced system of FLIR, called Fire Mouse Trap, because the plane with the camera acts as the mouse for the computer. It uses a forward-looking infrared unit in a helicopter or small plane with a monitor that the pilot can see. Sometimes a video camera is added. A navigation unit called a Loran-C gathers data on the plane's position via satellite and stores them in a laptop computer, which feeds the data into a computer back on the ground. A pen plotter attached to the ground computer draws a map of the fire perimeter and its hot spots.

One of the first times the Fire Mouse Trap was used was on the 1987 Yellow Fire in California's Klamath Mountains. Because thick smoke prohibited aerial reconnaissance, at times those on the ground could not tell the location of the fire. But using only an infrared VCR tape, the Mouse Trap completed maps of the fire within half an hour after a flight. It also mapped hot spots near houses in the area.

Now a new system called Firefly is scheduled to be working in 1992. It will draw a map and transmit it to those at the fire without the need for landing and hand delivery. The system will use a satellite and a dual-band infrared line scanner, and a VHF data link will transmit the thermal information gathered, along with comments, to a ground computer. This system will enable maps to reach fire camps within 30 minutes of the time the data arrive.

Initial Attack

Luckily, few fires grow large enough to need an infrared scanner or a fire camp. Small crews from local districts can fight most fires by reaching them right away with what is called *initial attack*.

Roy Inskeep, a fire management officer for the Challis National Forest, explained that when a fire is detected, the report goes to the dispatcher at the local ranger district. When the dispatcher calls Inskeep, he orders a plane and sends a helitack crew on its way. By the time Inskeep reaches the fire, the helicopter is usually already there. Inskeep looks at how thick and how continuous the fuels are and at the topography. Then he decides what additional resources are needed and radios the dispatcher to order them.

The leader of the crew who reaches the fire first confirms that the crew can handle it and then decides how to attack it. This crew leader becomes the incident commander (IC) for that fire, unless it requires an overhead team to manage it.

The first firefighters and equipment at a fire—the initial attack crews—may be ground crews with an engine from the local ranger station, or they may be helitack crews. The local district can also order fire-retardant planes or smoke-jumpers for the initial attack. Usually only one 2-person crew goes out on initial attack, but if the fire is running, 10 to 20 people may go.

Sue Douglas of the Payette National Forest, Idaho, commented that she finds the initial attack the most satisfying kind of job on a fire because she knows it is up to her and her partner to put out the fire, and she feels a sense of accomplishment when they have done so. For example, one Sunday afternoon in mid-July 1989 when she was on standby at the ranger district office, multiple lightning strikes were hitting the forest. When a call came, she and her partner jumped in their pickup and drove to a spot above the fire. They hiked down to the fire, put a scratch line around it, and radioed for a fire engine to come to wet it down. Just then the dispatcher asked them to go to another fire nearby, but they could not find it. After several minutes of searching, when Sue sat down to tie her bootlace, she saw the fire on the other side of a draw. She and her partner chain-sawed all night to build a line around the fire and then slept for 2 hours before starting mop-up. Sue's experience is typical. The usual fire is small and putting it out means hard work without glamour.

When the initial attack crews cannot contain a fire in a day, it is designated as an *escaped fire*. At that time fire managers make an escaped fire situation analysis to decide what suppression response to take. If an escaped fire grows larger than about 200 acres, it will become a *project fire* with an incident base (fire camp), and an overhead team will be sent in from outside the area.

Firefighting Strategies

Once they detect a fire, fire managers use one of three different strategies of fire suppression: confinement, containment, or control. Fire suppression is the science and art of fighting wildfire. Fire managers used to call the strategies the three C's, but they are trying to get away from these terms today because they can be confused with the results of the strategies, that is, a contained or controlled fire.

To control a fire, crews build a control line all the way around it to stop it from spreading. This break in the continuity of fuel usually contains a strip of mineral soil in the center, called a *fire line*, although most people call the whole control line the fire line. The length of a fire line in the United States is usually measured in chains of 66 feet.

To control a fire, firefighters also surround any spots outside the fire line and unburned islands within it, by means of additional fire line. They burn out the fire line and any unburned area between it and the fire. Then they cool down any hot spots within 300 feet of the edge of the fire. When they have done all this, they say that the fire is controlled. Usually a controlled fire will not escape past the fire line, even though it may flare up inside it. When containing a fire, crews stop it from spreading by means of a fire line or natural barriers, but they do not bother to cool the hot spots. Once they complete the fire line, managers say that the fire is contained, which means that its fire line is expected to check the fire's spread, although the fire still may escape.

When confining a fire, crews watch or monitor it and, if necessary, prevent it from escaping past barriers or boundaries. Confinement differs from containment because crews build no fire line. It differs little from the monitoring of prescribed natural fires in the wilderness, except that in monitoring fire managers consider fire behavior as well as boundaries. Managers do not consider monitoring a fire to be a suppression method.

Fire crews use two main methods of attacking fires, direct and indirect. In a direct attack they cool the edge of the fire with water, dirt, or chemicals, and then they scrape a fire line around the edge of the fire down to mineral soil. Because of the need to work at the edge of the fire, direct attack works only on small fires of low intensity, although it also is used on the flanks or rear of large fires where the wind is blowing the fire into the burned area. Crews with engines also directly attack most grass fires.

In an indirect attack, fire crews build the fire line at a distance from the fire, using natural firebreaks where possible and then burn out the area between it and the fire. Crews use an indirect attack when the fire is too intense for them or bulldozers to work close to the fire perimeter. Because they must construct a fire line wider than that used in a direct attack, in nonwilderness areas bulldozers often are used. Indirect attack is more risky because the fire set to burn out the fuel may jump the fire line instead of burning toward the main fire.

Crews burn out the fuel in one of three ways. In the first, they build the fire line 2 feet or so from the edge of the fire and burn out that narrow strip as they build the line. In the second, the *parallel* method, they construct the line up to 50 feet from the fire and set fire to the intervening area as they move along. Firefighters often use this method, with care, on the sides (flanks) of a large fire.

In the third method, *backfiring*, crews construct the line first and then set the fire along it, planning to have it sucked forward into the convection column of the main fire. This is dangerous for firefighters because they must start the fire in front of the head or front flanks of the fire, which can speed up any time and overtake them. And if the crews start a backfire too late, it may intensify the main fire. Backfires work best in light fuels, such as grasses. Crews use them only on large, hot fires and only as a last resort. They set a backfire so that it will burn an area twice as wide as the distance that the main fire is spotting or throwing embers. In both burning out and backfiring, firefighters may use *fusees*, similar to highway flares, to ignite the fire; they may use *drip torches*, large cans of an oil–gasoline mixture with a nozzle and wick attached; or they may arrange to have the area ignited by a helicopter using aerial incendiaries or a helitorch. *Aerial incendiaries* are pingpong balls filled with magnesium and ethylene glycol, which ignite when they hit the ground. A *helitorch* is a barrel on a platform suspended by cables 20 feet below the helicopter. The barrel is filled with a mixture of gasoline and *alumagel*, an aluminum compound. An automatic igniter powered either by electricity or a mechanical device drips the burning mixture onto the fuels. The reason that the barrel is suspended below the helicopter is so that it can be dropped if it malfunctions.

Building a Fire Line   If it is possible, the crew members build only a minimum fire line that they call a *scratch line*, by cooling the fire with water or by mixing dirt with it. Only when the fire is too large for them to do this do they build a true fire line. Joel Pomeroy, a member of the Angeles National Forest hotshot crew, explained: "When building a fire line you have to make a clear corridor going up to the sky, so you drop everything [trees and shrubs] out of the way." His crew leader has them build the line where the fuels are the lightest, usually on the back side of a ridge top in order to take advantage of the fire's slowing down at the top of the ridge.

As the crew builds a fire line, tree fellers walk ahead and fell the trees in the strip that will become the fire line. They try to keep the line as close to the fire and as straight as possible. This means that if the fire has fingers where it has advanced farther, they will not attempt to build a line that follows all the indentations but make a straight line instead. They also avoid steep slopes and take advantage of natural barriers. Sawyers follow the tree fellers, cutting up the trees, moving them out of the way, and clearing logs, branches, and brush. As they follow, the crew members burn out that corridor, grubbing out all the roots and brush and making sure to cut out a section of each root that crosses the line. Then shovelers rake or shovel away all that has been grubbed out and dig down to mineral soil in a narrow strip. But all this work does not make a fire line effective; it only prevents a fire from advancing if it is not spotting ahead.

The crew leader always starts a fire line from a cleared area called an *anchor point* or *safety zone* and ensures that his or her crew can complete the line before the fire reaches it. When it is windy or the fire is burning on a slope, crews build the fire line along the flanks or sides of the fire, rather than at the head of the fire, for safety reasons. A fire line across a steep slope must resemble a ditch with an earthen berm on the lower side. The berm catches any burning material that might fall or roll downhill.

When constructing a fire line the firefighter's main tool is the Pulaski, a combination of axe and hoe named after its inventor, Ed Pulaski, the hero of the 1910 Idaho fire.

Crews use brush hooks and single- and double-bit axes to reach and chop off branches and the stems of shrubs, shovels and McLeods (combination rakes and hoes) to clear the line of litter and duff down to mineral soil, swatters or wet burlap to beat out the flames of small fires, council rakes to build line in deciduous forest and also to mop up, and finally a combination tool that has a pick on one side and a shovellike hoe on the other to dig efficiently.

Bulldozers often are used to build fire lines in nonwilderness areas, but not in heavily timbered or rocky areas or on slopes over 45 degrees. Crews must use them with care because bulldozers can leave scars that last for many years. Usually bulldozers are used to construct fire lines along ridges or valley bottoms, working well away from the edge of the fire and pushing debris to the outside, so that it will not add fuel to the fire. A crew member called a *swamper* works with the bulldozer operator to saw off branches that may damage the bulldozer or hit the operator. In jack-strawed timber, a saw crew goes in first to cut room for the bulldozer.

Water applied by hose or backpack pump, foam, and fire retardants also are sometimes used to create fire lines. Crews can even construct fire lines with explosives; indeed, the Soviet Union uses them as their main method. First, they drill 3-foot-deep holes every 6 feet in the peaty soil. Then they place charges of ammonium nitrate in each hole and connect them with detonating cord. In the United States, however, explosives are used only occasionally.

For the Lowman Fire BIFC smokejumper Lynn Flock and his crew acted as a fire-line explosives team and were trucked in as far as possible to complete the fire line on a 45-degree slope. After they had hiked the rest of the way in to the site, a helicopter brought the explosive in a net. The explosive was a continuous tube of plastic explosive covered with an orange coating that made it resemble a telephone cable. The crew taped together the 86-foot lengths of the explosive, each weighing 50 pounds. Then they attached a 500-foot wire and blasting cap and set off 1000 to 1500 feet of the explosive at a time.

Mop-Up and Rehabilitation _____

After a fire is controlled, firefighters must mop it up. A *mop-up*, which completely extinguishes the fire or prevents it from escaping, may take weeks and may not be done for all fires. Firefighters do not always bury the hot spots they find because the fire could smolder underneath the litter, travel along in the duff, and ignite fuels at a distance days later. Instead, the firefighters feel for hot spots, dig them out, and cool them with water or dirt.

A crew mopping up the 1989 King Gulch Fire at Idaho City used water delivered to the site by hose from an engine and by helicopter. So that the helicopter water drops could be more effective, professional tree sawyers first cut down the smoldering snags. The biggest hazard for firefighters in a mop-up is that snags may fall on them.

Once a mop-up has been completed, fire crews or special rehabilitation or rehab crews begin to rehabilitate the land by means of antierosion measures. They construct miniature earthen dams called *water bars* along the sections of fire line that run downhill, and they often seed the fire lines with grasses. The methods they use in nonwilderness areas depend on the intensity of the fire, the condition of the soil, and the steepness of the slopes.

Outside parks and wildernesses, rehabilitation may in-

Two members of Louis Yazzi's hotshot crew from the Angeles
National Forest work on mop-up on the walls of the South Fork of
the Salmon River canyon, in the 1989 Dollar Fire in the Payette
National Forest.

clude salvage logging. Foresters want to log so that the timber will not be wasted, but conservationists believe that nature never wastes burned trees. For example, old-standing snags provide nesting sites for birds and homes for squirrels. Then, when the trees fall and decay, they release nutrients into the soil. The trees also hold water like sponges, giving new plants places to start growing.

At Lowman, Idahos Boise National Forest officials conducted the most extensive postfire rehabilitation ever conducted in a national forest in the United States. This fire was a moderate- to high-severity burn on 40,000 of the fire's 47,000 acres. According to Paul Moroz, the team leader of the project, the forest undertook the project to hurry the recovery process because the burned slopes of the narrow canyon presented several threats: Because the soil on the steep slopes of the canyon is shallow and sandy, without trees, rains and snow melt could cause landslides and flooding, which in turn could destroy more homes, close the highway, silt up the fishery and an irrigation reservoir, and damage the watershed.

Officials of the Boise Forest thus decided that the situation called for aggressive measures. Lynn Reinig, a hydrologist for the project, recalled that on 15,000 acres they first had crews cut down standing burned trees along the contour lines and stake them on the downhill side. They filled in any gaps underneath the trees to help hold back the soil. Additional culverts were installed where streams went under roads. The crew also placed bales of straw along streams, in gullies, and along the riverbanks to divert the water. Helicopters bombed the steepest slopes with opened bales of straw to act as mulch. To break up the water-repellant layers formed by the fire, helicopters sprayed the slopes with a natural soil stabilizer. Then the helicopters seeded 30,000 acres with nonnative grasses. Finally, the crew planted thousands of acres of ponderosa pine and Douglas fir and a few hundred acres of bitterbrush. The planting of bitterbrush for deer and elk forage will help achieve another goal: to reduce the effects of the fire on the wildlife. According to Marilyn Hemker, a wildlife biologist for the project, the fire had destroyed most of the winter range of the area's elk and deer and thwarted the bald eagles who use the river in winter. The team also plans to erect nesting boxes and leave standing old snags for smaller birds within the salvage timber sales.

Before they could complete the rehabilitation, the team had to write an environmental impact statement. Under its strict guidelines, timber companies must conduct salvage logging of about 135 million board feet by helicopter, according to Cyd Wieland, the project director.

Fortunately, right after the fire the rains were gentle and the winter snows light, and so the erosion measures largely succeeded in the short run. The continuing drought, however, has stressed the trees, causing more than usual to die from the effects of the fire.

A similar rehabilitation effort was conducted on Squaw Butte near Emmett, Idaho. A fire in 1985 had burned 218,000 acres of winter range covered with sagebrush and bitterbrush, which are important browse shrubs for mule deer. These shrubs recover slowly from fire, because neither sprouts from its roots. Because the fire had left no sagebrush or bitterbrush seed, Mary Dudley, a lookout on the butte, started a planting project in 1986 in which over 1000 volunteers planted bitterbrush and sagebrush seeds. And when rodents ate the seeds, they later planted 20,000 seedlings.

Minimum-Impact Wilderness Firefighting

In wilderness, however, to preserve its naturalness, rehabilitation after fire is avoided. Furthermore, because erasing the scars caused by firefighting is difficult, crews use minimum-impact methods of firefighting. These new methods are in keeping with the Wilderness Act, which defines wilderness as an area "to be affected primarily by the forces of nature with man's work substantially unnoticeable." Such methods—which have become the standard for fighting wilderness fires—require firefighters to leave "no trace." If they feel that a scraped fire line is essential, they make it as narrow and irregular as practical. Where possible, crews use natural areas like streams, rocks, meadows, or bogs as part of the fire line, and they cut down as few trees and branches as possible, and cover any stumps with soil and debris. They leave no sign of their campsites.

After crews have controlled a wilderness fire, using a no-trace mop-up, they restore the land to its former appearance: They roll over logs rather than cut them up. They fill in fire lines, build water bars across them, and scatter the logs and

After a 1986 fire, volunteers planted bitterbrush seedlings on Squaw Butte near Emmett, Idaho, to restore range critical to mule deer. Courtesy of Mary Dudley.

branches they have cut. And they do not reseed, replant, or terrace except to prevent landslides, because reseeding may bring in weeds.

Fire Crews

The crews used to fight fires in the wilderness are usually helitack crews, smokejumpers, or hotshot crews, because they are the most professional and highly trained. The United States has 60 hotshot or Class 1 crews, each with 19 professional firefighters and a crew boss. A few of the crew members work year-round, but all are experienced firefighters who have received additional training to become hotshots. These crews can be sent out of their own region or even out of the country on assignments.

One of these crews, Louis Yazzi's crew from the Angeles Forest in Southern California, saw action on the 1989 Dollar Fire near McCall, Idaho. According to Joel Pomeroy, one of the two assistant foremen for this crew, he and the others on the crew came to relieve another crew who had worked on the fire for 21 days. When they (Pomeroy's crew) arrived, they had already worked 9 days elsewhere. One day in late August, the crew was mopping up on the steep sides of the South Fork of the Salmon River canyon. They reached the site by plunging down a 50-foot bank and crossing the 100-foot-wide river on a Douglas fir they had felled. Hotshot crews rarely mop up, but Pomeroy explained that they had been scheduled to return home the night before because the fire had been contained, but no flights were available. Because the canyon is so rugged, the operations chief used the remaining hotshot crews for the mop-up there. As Pomeroy pointed out, "A fire is actually more dangerous in the mop-up stage than it is earlier. When you don't see flames, if you're not careful, you may let your guard down."

Hotshot crews in the winter sometimes serve as work crews for their forests, doing building maintenance and other tasks. In summer the Angeles crew goes to project fires in other areas. When the Santa Ana winds blow, crew members often fight fires in their own forest. When not fighting fires, they spend 1½ hours a day in physical training before going to work. They do calisthenics, take a run or hike, and finish with cool-down stretching. Pomeroy stated that the crew can stay on a fire at least 12 hours, and usually 24, with just the gear in their packs, in which they carry 5 or 6 quarts of water, warm clothes, and a little food. If they are resupplied, they can stay on the line indefinitely. But the incident commanders now try to restrict the firefighters' workday to 16 hours or less. Pomeroy remembered that for a couple of days when they were burning out the river bottom, he and his crew had to wait until the burn was finished, and so they did not get back to camp until after midnight; they still had to get up at 6 A.M. the next day.

There are several kinds of fire crews in the United States besides hotshots: engine crews, helitack, smokejumpers, and Class 2 and Class 3 ground crews. When the crews include a set number of resources of the same kind and type, they are called *strike teams*. The particular forest, park, or BLM district hires ground and helitack crews for the fire season. When the distance to the fire exceeds 50 miles, the district calls for smoke-jumpers from one of the regional bases, and for project fires it obtains additional organized crews from elsewhere. Each district's crews of seasonal employees supplement the highly trained hotshot, helitack, and smokejumper crews. Except during fires, these Class 2 crews have nonfire duties, and during fires, managers try to assign them to the less difficult and less dangerous tasks.

Helitack Crews

For the initial attack, fire management agencies try to use ground crews and air tankers if possible, rather than helitack crews and smokejumpers, which they rely on for fires in rough and remote terrain. A *helitack crew* is a special fire crew that is supported by helicopter.

In the United States the helicopters land to let out the helitack crews, but the Forest Service has also experimented with helirappelling. In Canada and the Soviet Union helicopter crews descend by rappelling, a technique for sliding down a rope.

While the helicopter hovers, the crew can rappel down at 20 feet a second into a forest opening only 7 feet across, except when high winds are blowing. In most cases the terrain is too steep, rocky, or forested for a helicopter to land. Rappelling thus allows firefighters to get to a fire faster. By 1989 the USDA Forest Service employed seven rappel crews in two regions. Most of the helicopters used in firefighting belong to private industries and are contracted by the forest, park, or BIFC for the fire season. A helitack crew from the agency employing the helicopter manages the helicopter and helps its pilot for the season.

Anna Marie Jehle, of the Challis National Forest helitack crew, described going to a fire: She always goes out on helitack with a partner, usually to a fire not too big for the two of them to handle. The pilot lands at the top of a ridge well above the fire, and they hike down to it. Usually the fires they work on are burning in only one to three trees because a fire bigger than that requires more than two people. Jehle takes three packs with her. In her initial attack pack she carries what she calls web gear: drinking water, high-energy food, survival gear, tape for the handles of her tools, and a fire shelter. The second pack contains tools, and the third pack has a sleeping bag and tube tent or tarp. The tools for the two consist of a Pulaski, a shovel, and a chain saw with a tank of gas for it. Usually Jehle stays on a fire overnight, working from 12 to 24 hours. She and her partner cut brush and branches to keep the fire from spreading, and they mix the fire with dirt to put it out because they cannot carry enough water with them to put out the fire. Jehle finds that the most difficult part of the job is the steep hike down to the fire and back. On project fires, Jehle helps set up and run a helibase for the fire. She also assists the pilots and briefs passengers on the safety procedures in the helicopters.

When there are no fires the helitack crew does other tasks such as taking in wildlife fencing in sling loads under the helicopter. Because the crew is on call from 9 A.M. to 6 P.M. each day, crew members bring along their fire packs and wear their firefighting clothes every day so that they are always ready to go to a fire.

Smokejumpers

The third kind of crew used in an initial attack, *smokejumpers*, reaches the fire by parachute, and so they can reach fires in remote areas in minutes. The Soviet Union, with 2600 jumpers, has the largest smokejumping operation in the world. In the United States, fire managers used smokejumpers more often right after World War II than they do now that their budgets have been cut, because smokejumpers cost three times as much as do other firefighting crews. They are called only when other types of crews cannot get to the fire quickly.

The United States' smokejumper program was started in 1939, and the first two jumpers parachuted to a fire in the Nez Perce Forest in northern Idaho in 1940. The United States now employs about 360 smokejumpers each year and maintains 12 smokejumper bases.

The Bureau of Land Management jumpers use rectangular chutes that they open themselves, and the Forest Service jumpers use round chutes that open automatically. With both types of jumper, a spotter determines when each jumps. Before anyone jumps, the spotter throws down weighted crepe paper streamers to test the wind to determine the best spot. Wind can blow the jumper into a tree or blow the chute sideways so fast that the jumper can sprain an ankle when landing. It also makes the chute difficult to keep upright in the air. Thus in order for

With a rectangular chute like this, the smokejumper first releases a small chute called a drogue chute, seen here, which both pulls up the jumper into a vertical position and pulls the main chute out of its pack. Courtesy of Wayne Williams, Region 1 Smokejumper Base, Missoula, Montana.

jumpers to be able to jump, in mountains the wind must be blowing less than 15 miles an hour. Because rectangular chutes are smaller, jumpers can maneuver them more easily than they can the round chutes. With rectangular chutes, jumpers can jump from 3000 feet, but with round chutes, they can jump from only 1500 feet.

The two kinds of chutes are connected to the plane differently. With the rectangular chute, one end of a line called a *static line* is attached to a hook on the plane, and the other end is connected to a stuff sack called a *(deployment) d-bag*. Inside the d-bag is a small chute called a *drogue chute*, which is attached to a ring on the jumper's pack but not to the d-bag. After jumping from the plane, the jumper waits 5 seconds and pulls the ring. The drogue chute comes out of the d-bag, and the plane flies away with the bag and the line. As the drogue chute opens, it pulls the jumper's head up and pulls the main chute out of its pack so it can open. After the main chute opens, the jumper pulls a handle on its pack to collapse the drogue chute, which descends with the big chute and the jumper.

With the round chutes, the Forest Service jumper is attached to the main chute in the same way that the BLM jumper is attached to the drogue chute. Both use the d-bag and the static-line temporary attachment to the plane, and both carry a reserve chute. After all the jumpers are on the ground, the plane drops—from only 200 feet above the ground—tools, food, sleeping bags, drinking water, and tarps in a big cardboard carton attached to a 20-foot cargo chute. Chute packers must make sure to attach the static line correctly to the cargo chute, for if they do it wrong, the airplane will take the place of the cargo, and the chute will open attached to the plane.

At a BLM smokejumper base visitors can see the giant size of the rectangular chutes: 300 to 375 square feet. They are big because they must support a jumper, 35 pounds of gear, and their own weight and that of the reserve chutes.

Lynn Flock, the training supervisor at the BIFC smokejumpers' loft, stated that new jumpers take 4 weeks of instruction, which includes at least 12 practice jumps as well as simulated jumps from a training tower. In the first week the jumpers must pass physical fitness tests in order to continue the program. One of these tests is carrying 110 pounds for 3 miles on level ground in 90 minutes. Although Flock himself has jumped more than 1100 times (350 of them to fires) and no longer worries about jumping, he still worries about landing safely.

At the end of a fire the jumpers usually walk out, carrying their gear in a 110-pound backpack topped with the crosscut saw bent over it in a curve and tied to the outside. If the jumpers are lucky, a helicopter may come in with a net to haul away their gear. In remote mountainous country or if they are needed right away at another fire, a helicopter will come for the jumpers as well as the gear.

At the Missoula, Montana, smokejumper visitor center, Wayne Williams explained that the jumpers rely on the Twin Otter, which can hold ten jumpers and requires very little take-off and landing space. Taxiways connect the "ramp," the area where they load the planes, to the Missoula airport. The smokejumpers who pack the chutes must be certified by the FAA as parachute riggers. Packing a chute takes 30 to 45 minutes. Before the riggers pack the chutes they check them and let them dry by hanging them in a high-ceilinged room called the Tower. The main Forest Service chutes are even larger than the BLM chutes, 875 square feet (32 feet across).

The building for repairing and packing the chutes is named the Loft. When a chute needs repair, a jumper takes it to one of the repair tables that resemble giant ironing boards. Williams stopped the tour of the smokejumper base at a mending table, where a smokejumper was carefully basting on a patch. Using old industrial sewing machines, the jumpers themselves manufacture and repair all their own gear except for their chutes and design and sew gear for other types of crews.

The senior jumper checks the smokejumpers' equipment before they get in the plane. Williams commented that jumpers based at Missoula have made over 300,000 jumps with only two chute-related deaths, and no chutes have malfunctioned since 1976.

The 4-week smokejumper training is so rigorous that 50 percent of the applicants drop out during the first week, which is surprising because many of the candidates come from the Class 1 or hotshot crews. The first week of training involves much physical effort, including building fire lines for 14 hours and then hiking out with a pack. During the rest of the training the crew members learn how to exit the plane at the let-down unit and also practice landing on the landing simulator and retrieving the chutes and themselves from poles called *stirrup poles*. Then the would-be smokejumpers make nine succeedingly harder jumps, including one into unbroken timber. For jumping, each Forest Service smokejumper wears a nylon flame-proof suit made of Kevlar, the same material as that in bulletproof vests. They stuff some of their gear in the pockets on the outside of their lower pant legs. A rappel ring is sewed into the suits to make it easier for the jumpers to rappel out of trees if they get hung up. They put their reserve chute on their chests and a bag of personal gear on their stomachs.

Safety

Firefighters wear clothes made of Nomex, a brand of fire-resistant fabric. All those who go to fires wear these outfits, whether they are crew members, officials, or observers. The pants are made of a greenish-brown fabric, treated with chemicals to resist fire, and the shirts are bright yellow. Nomex, which has the texture of thick, woven polyester, can resist burning up to temperatures of 480° F, and when it does burn it only chars. Because synthetics can melt onto skin in a fire, under these clothes firefighters wear all-cotton underwear. A hardhat, gloves, and a fire shelter complete the outfit. Although these special clothes help protect firefighters from burning embers, firefighting is still a dangerous job.

Most of the people who die in a fire die in truck or helicopter accidents or from being hit by falling snags, rather than by the fire itself. But fighting fire can give firefighters heat-related health problems, such as heat stroke, heat exhaustion, and dehydration. Heat stroke, caused by the body temperature's rising to over 103°F, can cause death or brain damage, with the danger coming from the total amount of heat absorbed. Carbon monoxide is also a threat, especially in smoldering fires. In one test researchers found that the blood of 62 of 293 firefighters after 8 hours on a fire line contained more than 5 percent carbon monoxide. Five percent is considered the maximum level safe for firefighters; it takes about 8 hours for carbon monoxide to be purged from the body if the amount breathed is 5 percent or less.

Because of the danger and the mental and physical stress, current policy requires fire managers to limit to 21 days the length of time that a crew can work on one fire. During these 21 days, firefighters must have 1 day off for each 7 days or 2 days off in 14.

To reinforce the importance of safety, firefighters learn the eight firefighting commandments, the ten standard firefighting orders, and the 21 situations that "shout" watch out. The commandments include planning safety routes, keeping in communication, watching for hazards, keeping track of the weather, making sure of directions, and acting before a situation becomes critical.

The standard firefighting orders emphasize knowing what the fire is doing, posting lookouts, and giving clear instructions that are also understood. One example of a watch-out situation is nighttime in a country you have not seen even in daylight. Another is feeling like taking a nap near the fire line. A third is getting frequent spot fires over the fire line.

After the summer of 1988 when the USDA Forest Service reviewed all these rules and other aspects of firefighting safety, the review committee found that the USDA Forest Service needed to improve driver training and vehicle safety for transporting crews to fires. The committee also learned that it should improve the physical fitness of the fire crews, train the crew leaders more thoroughly in fire behavior, and clarify their responsibility in wildland–urban interface fires.

Fire Shelters   The most important safety precaution for firefighters is carrying a personal fire shelter. The shelter, introduced in Chapter 1, was invented in 1960. The shelter is made of aluminum foil stuck to fiberglass cloth with glue that will still adhere at high temperatures. Even with tiny holes and cracks, the shelter will still give protection, but it does not make a person immune to fire. Even in a shelter, a firefighter can still suffer burns, so he or she should use the shelter only in an emergency. The shelter's main function is to protect the lungs and airways by maintaining a pocket of cooler air to breathe.

A meadow, rockslide, burned area, or creek bed provides the best place to set up a fire shelter. Before using the shelter, firefighters scrape away flammable litter and duff to clear a 4-by-8-foot area down to mineral soil for each person. Each firefighter opens up the shelter but keeps hold of it so that it will not blow away. Then he or she gets into the shelter while still standing up, wearing gloves to hold down the edges of the shelter when it becomes hot. The firefighter lies face down, holding down the front and rear flaps with head and feet, and keeping the sides spread out wide with the hands. To avoid injuring the lungs from breathing hot air, which may be 150° F even inside the shelter, the firefighter takes shallow breaths through a dry bandanna.

Training Courses   To learn safety procedures like deploying a fire shelter and suppressing fires, all crews take training and annual refresher courses. Each forest holds "fire school" at the beginning of the summer for its own employees. The Boise Interagency Fire Center and the forest regions offer specialized training, for both technical specialists and overhead teams in managing fires. The National Advanced Resource Technology Center at Marana, Arizona, offers advanced fire courses, but students must be recommended in order to attend this center.

Putting Out Fires

Water   Firefighters find water to be the single most useful tool for fighting a fire. They can make a fire line with water but usually use it only to slow the progress of the fire while they complete the line in the normal fashion. Firefighters try to spray water over as large an area of the fire as possible, because a spray has much more surface area than a stream of water does and so cools the fire faster. The nozzles they use can be adjusted to deliver any pattern of spray. Firefighters also try to use the lowest volume of water per minute and the lowest pressure that will put out the fire. They also spray the water off and on to make it last longer.

"Water is a cooling agent," Clarence Grady, a technical engineer for the Odin Corporation, remarked. "It has an annoying ability to form droplets. A detergent thus makes it spread better because it gets rid of the surface tension that makes the drops." Therefore, if possible, firefighters mix water with detergent to increase its wetting capacity. Adding the detergent can result in either "wet" water or firefighting foam. Foam penetrates wood three times better than water alone does.

Water is delivered to a fire in hoses, foam generators, backpack pumps, fire-retardant bombers, and helicopter buckets. The source may be a creek, lake, or tank. Under the direction of Bob Webber of BIFC, a horse trailer company manufactures, under contract, fiberglass water tanks to fit on the backs of trucks. BIFC buys the trucks as cab and wheels attached to a frame, and then technicians attach the tanks and other fittings. Some companies manufacture fiberglass water tank, pump, and hose units that can quickly be put in the bed of a pickup or utility trailer when needed. Others make fabric tanks resembling giant orange air mattresses or children's wading pools.

To get the water to the fire from a river, lake, or tank firefighters use portable fire pumps, which can ride on a truck, sit on the ground, or even float. Fire managers must plan around the pump's capacity and the slope because the faster a pump delivers water, and the more uphill it must pump water, the lower the water pressure it can maintain.

Firefighters use two kinds of hose, all-cloth (often linen or cotton with a Dacron filling) and synthetic or rubber lined and some combinations of these materials. The small amount of water leaking through cloth hose cools it enough to prevent its burning. Cloth hose also weighs less than do other types. Firefighters can lay hoses singly or progressively. In the progressive method they attach Y-shaped connections with shutoff valves at intervals and run side hoses from the connections to the edge of the fire. When laying hose they sometimes use special boxes attached to backpacks containing the coiled hose. The way the hose is coiled allows the operator to get it out easily by pulling one end. Once used, hoses resemble dirty spaghetti with a permanent wave, but they can be cleaned, repacked, and reused.

Foams Firefighters recently added detergent foam to their basic equipment. The foam is usually delivered by foam generators attached to truck-mounted water tanks. Foam works better than water alone because it smothers a fire as well as cools it. That is, foam excludes air from the fuel longer and more completely than water does and makes more water adhere to the fuel. Because the air in the bubbles has a high humidity, foam increases the humidity of the air next to the fuel, and the air in the bubbles insulates the fuel from heat and its white color reflects heat. The Texas Forest Service first used foam on wildland fires in 1971, but until compressed-air foam generators were invented in 1977, few agencies used foam. An air-aspirating nozzle—one with an air hole in its side—can also deliver foam, but it cannot shoot it as far. Another way to deliver foam is with a conventional water pump, with which a device called an *eductor* or *proportioner* must be used to draw the foam concentrate from a tank while the pump is pumping water.

For many years, structural firefighters have used air-aspirating nozzles and special foams for petroleum fires. The aspirating nozzles produce wetter, more rapidly draining foams than compressed air does, and they cost less but use more foam concentrate in proportion to water. To work, these nozzles need a large flow of water and concentrate, and the quantities needed

At the Boise Interagency Fire Center, this used fire hose will be cleaned, straightened, and rewound to use again. Courtesy of the Boise Interagency Fire Center.

mean that fire engines cannot carry enough to fight wildland fires. Not until 1985 did companies begin to manufacture foams especially designed for fighting wildland fires. These foams contain no phosphates and are biodegradable and nontoxic when applied. They have better wetting ability and more stable bubbles than do the pine soap and dishwashing soaps first tried.

A compressed-air system for generating foam that combines the energy of a water pump with that of an air compressor enables firefighters to apply foam from as far away as 150 feet. Because they can send out 35 gallons per minute, this system allows firefighters to attack directly fires of higher intensity than before. They can also use foam to make fire lines and to put out structural fires without entering the building. Foam can extinguish a fire in a 1000-square-foot house from outside it in less than 10 seconds with as little as 100 gallons of water. (The water-to-foam ratio is such that 500 gallons of water mixed with 1 gallon of foam concentrate can yield 5000 to 10,000 gallons of foam.) At the Lowman Fire, Ron Rochna put out the fires in the burning homes with about 250 gallons of water per house, plus one-half gallon of foam concentrate. It took more water than for a house alone because the vegetation around them also was burning. Rochna, who does research at BIFC on compressed-air foam systems, noted that on a hot dry day, foam will stick for an hour. After two applications the moisture from the foam extends one-half to three-quarters of an inch into the wood. Another advantage of foam is that hoses filled with foam weigh much less than do hoses full of water.

Foams do have a few disadvantages: They can blow away. They do not wet the ground much, and so surface fires may continue to spread. They also can interfere with the ability of fish to obtain oxygen. And crews must apply foam just before the fire arrives. For these reasons, wildland fire crews mainly use foam to protect buildings, campgrounds, and other developments. If homeowners want to do the same, they can buy a portable foam-generating tank on a handcart.

Helibuckets   Foam can also be delivered by helicopter, either from tanks or *helibuckets*, buckets that are attached to the helicopter by a cable. A bag full of buckshot sewed inside the front of the bucket tips it forward so that the helicopter can dip up water in the bucket from a lake, river, or ground tank. The pilot can inject the foam concentrate into the bucket and dump the resulting foam on the fire. Helicopters usually, however, drop water containing detergent additives rather than foam. The bucket under the helicopter is really a bag of reinforced vinyl held open by metal ribs that fold up like an umbrella. Attached to a retractable wire, a sleeve sewed to the bottom of the bucket holds the water in the bucket when pulled up inside it by the wire. Then when the pilot releases the wire, the water falls out through the sleeve, in a great plume of spray.

A new type of helicopter system called LADS, for Light Aircraft Delivery System, delivers foam. The system consists of tanks for water and foam concentrate plus a snorkel hose that allows the helicopter to fill its water tank in 21 seconds, even while hovering. By pressing a button, the pilot injects the foam concentrate into the water tank and with another button releases the foam onto the fire. Whenever a LADS helicopter is hovering and filling, it resembles a giant mosquito.

A LADS system helicopter can fill its water tank while hovering and then deliver foam to a fire. Courtesy of the Boise Interagency Fire Center.

Air Tankers and Fire Retardant   Tanker planes also deliver water containing additives, usually a type of fire retardant. The retardant absorbs more heat than plain water does. Technicians pipe water and the fire-retardant chemicals into the planes that drop the mixture on the fire. To enable the operator to see what the drops have already covered, the retardant or slurry is colored bright red with iron oxide, and thickening agents prevent it from washing off. Fire managers send retardant planes out on the initial attack to drop retardant just ahead of—but not on top of—large fires. Pilots cannot drop retardant right on large fires because it is dangerous to fly over them and, in any case, the retardant would not be effective.

Retardants work by lowering the temperature of the fuel so that it will burn only by charring, not by flaming. The most common fire retardants, ammonium sulphate and diammonium phosphate, keep on slowing the fire even after they dry out. Another additive, bentonite, a clay, turns the water into a thin mud. The first additive to be used, borate, has been shelved because it is corrosive and prevents plants from growing back.

Project or Campaign Fires

If the initial attack fails and the crews have not been able to put a fire line around the fire, they deem it an *escaped* fire, and the crew leader notifies the dispatch office of this development. Then the dispatcher can send for more resources, and the fire management agency can decide whether the fire should be designated a *project* or *campaign* (Canadian term) fire with an incident base or fire camp. Only 1 to 2 percent of fires become large enough to qualify, which is about 200 acres.

The designation of a project fire activates an elaborate support system, which in the United States is called an *Incident Command System* (ICS). The incident base may be located at a ranger station, Forest Service airstrip, private ranch, or even a local high school's playing field. The base becomes home for the firefighting crews while they are working on the fire, usually a maximum of 21 days. They bring their own small tents and set them up in the trees or on any level ground. The camp provides them with food, toilets, sinks, showers, washers, dryers, and other services. Living in a fire camp, according to Richard Pine, information officer for the 1989 Dollar Fire in the Payette Forest in Idaho, is like being in an encounter group because it is so intense. "It's not like you go to the office and work with other people but go home and eat with your family. For that period you eat with them, sleep in the same tent, work with them, and tempers may flare. The people who are cheerful and willing to help and cooperate with one another are the ones the fire bosses want on their fire teams."

The Incident Command System

The Incident Command System helps ensure that everything runs so smoothly that people will be cooperative. The second incident commander for the Lowman Fire, Steve Gauger from the Kootenai National Forest in Montana, explained that every fire start is an incident. "So whether it is two people or a thousand people, it is called an incident. Even where there are only

Firefighters bring their own tents and tarps to a fire camp, to be ready for a much-needed rest after workdays of 16 hours or more. Courtesy of the USDA Forest Service.

two people, one person is in charge, the incident commander." The system expands from the top down with four main sections and several subsections called *units*, added as needed. A manager has only three to seven persons under him or her. Even the 20-person fire crews are divided into squads of six, each under a squad leader, who answers to the crew leader or boss.

If a district cannot manage a fire by itself, the district ranger will send for an *overhead team*. Overhead teams are classified by experience into Class 1 and 2 teams which usually stay at a fire for only 14 to 21 days; if a fire lasts longer, another team will replace the first. There are 17 highly trained Class 1 teams in the United States.

For an especially large fire or several fires in an area, supervisors place the Incident Command System for each fire under the administration of an Area Command or Complex. An Area Command distributes the firefighting resources among fires or among divisions of a large fire. An Area Command was established, for example, for the Yellowstone fires by the Greater Yellowstone Coordinating Committee, which is composed of representatives of the surrounding national parks, national forests, and national forest regions.

The Incident Command System was established by the Riverside Laboratory of the USDA Forest Service in 1975 as the result of a 5-year project called FIRESCOPE. The project was launched after fires in Southern California in 1970 burned 500,000 acres and 700 structures in 13 days. It attempted to improve the way in which information is collected and communicated during a fire. The resulting Incident Command System was incorporated into a larger system called the National Interagency Management System (NIMS), which manages training, certification, publications, and technology. All federal agencies and many states have adopted the Incident Command System.

Under this system, for a small fire, one incident commander may direct an engine, a crew of firefighters, and a bulldozer. In contrast, for a major fire the incident commander is responsible for four sections: Operations, Planning, Logistics, and Finance plus information, safety and liaison officers, and their staffs.

The Operations Section, consisting of two main divisions, Tactical Resources (ground crews) and Air Operations (air attack and air support), runs the actual fighting of the fire. Air Attack covers air tankers and helicopters with buckets, and Air Support takes care of the fixed-wing air base and the helibase. Tactical Resources include the firefighting crews, the fire engines and their crews, and the bulldozers and their crews.

The Planning Section consists of the Resources, Situation, Documentation, Demobilization, and Technical Specialists units. The Resources Unit, in charge of the human resources on the fire, helps solve interpersonal problems. The Situation Unit collects, processes, and organizes the information and forecasts regarding the fire. At daily briefing meetings each division receives written instructions for the day for each crew. The Documentation Unit keeps a history of the fire and all actions taken on it and collects the daily reports for each of the other units in the ICS system. The Demobilization Unit arranges transportation home or to other fires for all crews when they are no longer needed. The Technical Specialists Unit includes experts in fire weather, fire behavior, and other related problems.

The Logistics Section, under two branches, Service and Support, handles the services provided to the crews while they are living at the base. Under Service, the Communications Unit handles all the radios and the outside phone lines. The Food Unit arranges for the food to be prepared by local caterers or to be trucked in from a catering firm outside the area. The Support Branch includes the Supply Unit, which orders equipment from BIFC and elsewhere; the Facilities Unit, which is in charge of the showers, washers, dryers, tents; and the Ground Support Unit, which oversees all the vehicles at the base and provides the transportation to and from the base from the nearest airport. It also transports crews and supplies to and from the fire if trucks can reach it. To help the drivers, Ground Support sets up numbered staging areas called *drop points* where the drivers unload food, tools, and crews. Finally, the Finance Section keeps track of the hours everyone worked, pays the contractors who provide the services, and keeps track of how much it all costs.

The Incident Command System cannot solve all the problems of fighting a large fire, but to be effective at all, it must

At the Lowman Fire, the Situation Unit of the Planning Section runs a daily briefing meeting for the crew bosses and overhead team. Courtesy of the USDA Forest Service.

be well organized. According to Clinton Phillips, a California fire consultant, in *Fire Management Notes*, managers should use trained firefighters in the Operations Section and on the line and train other personnel to fill less dangerous positions. But the problem is that those overseeing the fire suppression will do a better job if they have had direct experience with fires. That is, experience will prevent them from sending firefighters or equipment into dangerous areas, although crew leaders can always refuse to enter an area if they think it is too dangerous. The ICS also cannot control all fires: Most large fires can be controlled only by nature.

Chapter Eight

∎ ∎ ∎

Prescribed Fire

Agencies and landowners use prescribed fire—both natural fires and planned ignitions—to improve and restore ecosystems and to prevent devastating wildfires. They also use fire to control brush and to improve the quantity and nutrition of the grasses on rangelands. For 20 years, the members of the Santa Barbara County (California) Range Improvement Association have conducted prescribed burns on one another's land to control the chaparral (brush). If not treated, the chaparral will build up into a fire hazard, and fires in chaparral often burn explosively and defy easy control. Chaparral also absorbs so much of the sparse rainfall in this area that the reservoirs begin to empty. And by invading the grassland, chaparral reduces the growth of grasses for grazing.

Michael Galvin, one of the ranchers in this association, described the process. Each year the association meets to decide which areas to burn and to plan the burns in cooperation with the county, the California State Forestry Department, and the USDA Forest Service. The ranchers usually burn 2000 to 4000 acres at a time. First they construct firebreaks with bulldozers, usually along the bases of the slopes. In normal fuel they make the firebreaks the width of a one-lane road, but in brush they make the firebreaks three or four lanes wide. On north slopes the chaparral is so thick that they cut some of it ahead of time and let it dry. Before a burn they have county fire personnel check their preparations.

They burn in September but wait until the wind, fuel moisture, and humidity reach the desired range, called a *prescription window*, a term referring to the range of acceptable conditions that will allow the fire to accomplish its goal. Galvin observed that fire managers call this range a prescription window because if someone graphs two of the factors, say wind and humidity, and draws a line on the graph around the allowable amounts, it will form a rectangle. The prescribed fire needs some wind; otherwise trying to burn is "like trying to ride a bicycle that's not moving." In drought years, the association does not burn because a fire might escape and the grasses grow so little that fire would only injure them. Normally after a fire it takes 2 to 3 years for the grasses to grow enough for good grazing.

When they burn, the ranchers drive along the firebreak with pickup trucks equipped with water tanks and pumps. After the first pickup in the line ignites the fire with a drip torch, the following trucks spray water outside the firebreak to keep the fire inside the desired burn area and to control spot fires. Sometimes in narrow canyons or on exceptionally steep slopes they contract with state or national forest fire managers to ignite the fire by helitorch.

Galvin and his neighbors usually start a burn at the firebreak at the bottom of the hill about 9 A.M. when the temperature is low and the humidity is still high from its usual nighttime rise. They divide into two teams and drive slowly around the fire in a circle, spraying water and eventually meeting on the far side of the fire about 3 P.M. When burning a large area, they start in the evening so that the lower night temperature and higher humidity will help control the fire. In this case they ignite the most difficult parts first so that they will finish burning at night and then they burn the easier parts the next morning.

Types of Fires

A *wildfire* does not meet a fire management agency's prescription and so must be suppressed. A *prescribed fire* meets the agency's goals without threatening human life, property, or resources. A prescribed fire that has been intentionally set is a *planned ignition* or a *control burn*. A prescribed fire ignited by lightning and allowed to burn out is a *prescribed natural fire*. It will be allowed to burn only if it does not spread into certain areas, threaten human life or property, or become too intense.

These restrictions are specified in an approved fire management plan and in a prescription for the particular fire, which is made by the fire management officer for the unit conducting the burn. A fire management plan is made by the forest, Bureau of Land Management (BLM) office, or national park after a long-term study of the conditions in the area affecting fires.

The *fire prescription* is the acceptable range of temperature, relative humidity, fuel moisture, and wind direction and speed. It also outlines the procedures for burning, from ignition to mop-up, and includes a description of the vegetation and its species, the slope and the direction it faces, the topography, and the purpose of the burn. A fire management officer must prepare an environmental assessment as well as a prescribed fire plan or prescription, with maps and cost estimates, the objectives and limits of the fire, a description of the area, and a plan for managing the smoke.

The managers determine what kind of fire is needed for the results they want according to the predicted effects of fire on the species present. They must specify the rate of spread and the maximum flame length, flame height, and scorch height. The fire management plan requires that they not light the fire if it exceeds the limits and that they suppress the fire if it escapes. The managers must specify the length of the fire line and firebreaks they will construct, how many acres they will burn at one time, what firing pattern and ignition method they will use, and how many people they will need to conduct the burn.

Bill Fischer of the USDA Forest Service's Intermountain Fire Sciences Laboratory describes fire prescriptions as follows: "Medical doctors write prescriptions to treat the illnesses they diagnose. Similarly, a land manager writes a prescription to treat a piece of land that is 'ill or needs fixing.' A fire prescription specifies fire as the treatment and sets the conditions for conducting it."

Both planned ignition and natural fire programs can help prevent large, disastrous fires. But these programs are often hard to use effectively and safely in some fuels and some topography. Prescribed natural fires and planned ignition prescribed fires cost money, which must come from regular budgets, not from emergency firefighting funds. The money for fire suppression on federal land comes from emergency funds appropriated by Congress, and the money for prescribed fires comes from a variety of funds in the individual budgets of the national forests, such as fuel management, slash disposal, and wildlife management.

Prescribed Burning

History Scientists and historians believe that before the Europeans arrived, Native Americans intentionally set many fires: The accounts of early explorers mention the Native Americans' using fire to improve hunting, to make signals, and, in New England, even to encourage the growth of blueberries. Later settlers used fire to clear land for farming.

Timber growers in the South set fires to prepare seedbeds for longleaf pine and to prevent the pine from being taken over by hardwoods and brush. In 1907 H. H. Chapman of Yale University began a study of this burning of southern pine in the Ozarks and Alabama, which led him to champion prescribed burning around the world. Even though experiments by the USDA Forest Service in the 1920s and 1930s showed that this pine grew better with annual burning than with no burning, most federal agencies at the time omitted from their publications any mention of the good uses of fire. Today, however, the South leads the nation in the use of prescribed fire to reduce fuels and encourage the growth of certain species.

Fire was officially excluded from the national forests in 1924 after a controversy in which one group thought burning in spring and fall, called *light burning*, would prevent fuel buildup and improve the range, but others disagreed. After three meetings but no research, a committee of the Society of American Foresters decided that light burning was destructive, and it was not until 1943 that the Forest Service, under Lyle Watts, again encouraged the use of prescribed burning.

Professor Harold Biswell of the University of California at Berkeley was one of very few researching prescribed burning in the late 1940s and early 1950s. As a result, he almost lost his job because his dean feared that the University of California School of Forestry would get a bad name if it were associated with prescribed fire. Biswell first studied prescribed fire in ponderosa pine and then in giant sequoia. By 1965, his studies of sequoia forests showed that giant sequoias depend on fire to kill the seedlings of competing tree species. Without fire, shrubs and young firs shade the sequoia seedlings and prevent them from growing, and the sequoia was in danger of becoming extinct. In 1951 and 1952 William Robertson studied fire effects in the Florida Everglades, which led to experiments there with prescribed burning; about the same time Harold Weaver experimented with prescribed fire in the Rockies. Also in the 1950s Ed Komarek of the private Tall Timbers Research Station in Florida advocated prescribed fire worldwide based on studies the station made. In the 1970s foresters began to use planned-ignition prescribed fires. But these fires sometimes caused controversy because some escaped and caused damage, injury, or large wildfires. For example, in Ontario, Canada, in 1979 the Geraldton Fire killed the seven members of the ignition crew in 10 minutes.

Benefits   Prescribed fires prevent wildfires by reducing the amount of fuels and removing the small trees and shrubs that act as ladders to carry fire to the tree crowns. Decreasing the amount of vegetation near buildings, campgrounds, and other facilities means that managers can allow lightning fires to burn without as much hazard. Reducing fuels also diminishes the intensity of wildfires and weakens their resistance to control. Forest Service researchers studying southern pine plantations found that the largest wildfires occurred in areas that had not recently been intentionally burned.

Prescribed fires benefit ecosystems in several ways. Because the fires increase the number and size of forest openings where browse shrubs and grasses grow, foresters can use prescribed burns to improve wildlife habitat and forage for livestock and to help control insects and diseases like dwarf mistletoe. In addition, prescribed burns kill some shrubs and stimulate others, depending on whether or not the species are dependent on fire. For example, fire stimulates the growth of spirea, ninebark, and ceanothus, but not of sagebrush and bitterbrush. Therefore, when prescribing fire, managers consider what trees, shrubs, and plants they want to encourage. For example, when they burn grasslands to stimulate the growth of grasses, they burn in late spring when the perennial grasses hold enough moisture to prevent the fire from killing the roots.

Prescribed burning can also improve access and views for

tourists, remove dead trees, and thin out forests where trees grow so close together that none is healthy. Because burning returns nutrients to the ground, it spurs growth of the remaining trees. In some regions, such as the Pacific Northwest, foresters also use fire to prepare seedbeds for planting trees after logging, but they probably ignite more prescribed burns to remove logging slash than for any other reason.

Most prescribed fires burn less intensely than wildfires do, and so fire managers can achieve benefits with them that they cannot with natural fires. Low-intensity prescribed fires seldom cause erosion or affect the soil's ability to absorb water. Fast-spreading prescribed fires usually do not damage soils in light to medium fuels because most of the heat rises and is carried off by the wind. Only fires in large piles of fuel like logging slash burn the organic matter in the soil or vaporize the nitrogen. By removing some of the vegetation taking up water, prescribed burning can increase stream flows. For example, in the Sierra foothills, even though no rain had fallen, a dry creek filled with water within 3 weeks after a prescribed burn.

Planning Prescribed Burns _____

Before beginning the burning, fire managers must consider the safety as well as the results of prescribed fires. They can use a computer program to help them figure when the conditions for a prescribed fire are best. The National Fire Danger Rating System is not specific enough in regard to site, and so managers use the BEHAVE system, which helps them determine the conditions allowing them to achieve the goals of a burn without danger of its escaping.

Merrill Saleen, a fire management officer for the Payette National Forest in Idaho, says that his district conducts burns when humidity is from 15 to 25 percent and eye-level wind is 7 to 15 miles an hour. When the conditions approach the limits for humidity, wind, or fuel moisture, the permitted amounts of the other factors must then be lower. For example, on a day with 15 percent humidity, the wind must be near 7 miles an hour in order to conduct a safe burn.

Successful prescribed burns require enough fine fuels—like dry grass, leaves, or needles—to carry the fire, and they require larger fuels to be in the right condition to produce the desired results. Some fuels may need pretreatment. To change the effects of the fire, managers can increase the fuel moisture content by covering the fuel, adding water or foam, or burning in spring or fall or after a rain. Before the burn they can also change the fuel chemistry with retardants or reduce the amount of fuel by means of grazing or harvesting. By removing the dead fuels under the trees, burning when the trees are least sensitive to fire, and burning when the large dead fuels and duff have a high water content, fire managers can control the damage to trees.

In some forests, prescribed fire can accomplish the same goals as natural fires used to do. But in other forests, like lodgepole pine, prescribed fire is difficult or hazardous and therefore expensive. Other methods are even more expensive, and some are at least as hazardous. Chemical or mechanical treatment usually costs more than does prescribed burning, and chemical treatment has been suspended on public lands for environmental reasons. When planning prescribed burns, the Forest Service first looks at the possibility of using the forest products instead. For example, they may be able to arrange for companies to make wood chips and pellets for pellet stoves out of logging slash, so that less slash burning will be required.

The weather suitable for prescribed burning varies in different regions because of the differences in fuel types. In most areas fire managers seldom conduct prescribed burning in hot weather because the heat dries out the fuels and causes them to ignite too easily. The fuel moisture and wind speed are the most important variables in predicting the fire behavior of a prescribed burn. Humidity is also important. In most areas, the timber's humidity must remain between 30 and 55 percent, for below 30 percent the fire may escape and above 60 percent the fire does not burn well. Fire managers cannot burn grass when the humidity is above 35 percent, because it will not burn. And there must be enough soil moisture to protect the roots, seeds, and soil organisms.

Because south, west, and southwest slopes dry out early, they can be burned in the spring while the north slopes are wet enough to prevent the fire from escaping. Indeed, north slopes are so wet in the spring that managers can use them as firebreaks. But in the spring in most regions, the insides of the larger fuels hold too much moisture to burn well. Also, because the fire may linger under the duff until the fire season and then rekindle and cause a wildfire, managers usually burn in the fall if enough rain has fallen to moisten the soil. In addition, timing fires for spring and fall allows sprouting plants to recover easily and allows managers to control the smoke of the fire.

Prescribed Burning and Smoke

The effect of smoke on humans also limits the use of prescribed fire. In dry fuels, low humidity, and high wind, an intense fire usually gives off thick white smoke; in green resinous material, an intense fire burns with gray and yellow smoke; and with too little oxygen for complete combustion, a fire makes black smoke. The proper precautions can ensure that prescribed fires make little smoke. First, managers should avoid burning during temperature inversions but instead burn in unstable air when the wind blows in the right direction to carry away the smoke. They should make sure, however, that the air is not too unstable, because if it is, the fire may form a convection column and even escape.

The way that managers conduct the fire can reduce the amount of smoke: A fire burning against the wind gives off much less smoke than does one being blown along by the wind. Because it moves more slowly, more of the fuel burns and more of it burns hotter, and so the fire smokes less. Waiting to burn until the fuels have dried out also cuts down on smoke, and burning only a small area at a time diminishes the amount of smoke that the air holds at any one time.

Another problem is the lingering smoke at the end of a fire. This smoke has a high particulate level because it is the result of incomplete combustion. To get rid of it, fire crews mop up the fire and extinguish any big logs that are still burning.

Fire managers classify areas according to how important the absence of smoke is to them; that is, they try to keep smoke away from Class 1 areas, which are hospitals, airports, populated areas, highways, recreation areas, parks, and wildernesses.

Preparing to Burn

In preparing for a planned ignition, fire managers consider two things that can affect fire behavior. First, they consider local wind patterns and make sure that the wind speed is just enough to move the fire along and carry smoke away. They can burn with a very low wind speed, as the convection of the fire will disperse some of the smoke. The desired speed depends on the type of burn. If they are doing an underburn to get rid of brush, they will need more wind to move the fire along fast enough to keep it from killing the trees. Second, they allow for the topography. Remember that fire spreads faster on a slope and spreads uphill more often than down, so they prefer a slope for a prescribed burn. Burn areas, however, may be on the level or on steep slopes. On a slope fire managers can set the fire at the top of a ridge in such a way that it will "back" downhill so that they can control it more easily. On level ground they must set prescribed fires so they back against the wind to help with control. They can use fusees, drip torches, helitorches, flame throwers, or aerial incendiaries to ignite the fire.

Because fire managers must also consider possible damage to structures, rare plants, or archaeological resources, they often inventory these things before a burn and may arrange for their removal or protection. To ensure safety and to prevent misunderstanding, they have to specify how they will inform the public about the fire. Afterward, they must report how the burn turned out.

Prescribed burning crews are selected for their patience, training, and experience with prescribed burns. Today, schools of forestry in colleges and universities offer courses in prescribed fire, including practice on actual fires. Courses given at BIFC also provide the knowledge needed for prescribed burning, including monitoring prescribed natural fires in the wilderness. In addition, many fire management agencies train personnel: The California State Park system began a training program in prescribed burning in the early 1970s.

A Sample Burn

To give you an idea of how managers conduct prescribed burns, Fire Manager Merrill Saleen described a control burn that the Weiser Ranger District conducted. First, they set the fire on land for which a private landowner had signed an agreement with the state and the Forest Service for fire management. Ranger district personnel conducted the 800-acre burn of sagebrush grassland in two sections, one in the spring of 1988 and

The BLM uses prescribed burning for sagebrush, which is often ignited with a drip torch, as shown here, to give the grasses an advantage, thereby improving the range. Courtesy of the Boise Interagency Fire Center.

one in the spring of 1989. Saleen planned the burn to reduce the sagebrush and timber invasion of grassland, in order to prevent wildfires and to improve grazing and wildlife habitat. Saleen pointed out that removing the shade of sagebrush from grassland can increase grass production from 200 pounds per acre to 1000 pounds per acre. After determining that the relative humidity was between 15 and 30 percent and the wind between 8 and 15 miles an hour, Saleen decided to go ahead with the burn. Because it was spring, they did not put in any firebreaks or fire lines or use any fire crews. Instead, they relied on the north slopes acting as firebreaks and on the humidity rising to above 30 percent as night fell. To ignite the burn, they hired a helicopter. On that day, the operator used a helitorch, which meant that Saleen had to remain on the ground, because the Forest Service's safety policy for the intermountain region prohibits personnel from riding in a helicopter that has something hanging from it, such as a helitorch. So on that day Saleen could tell whether the operator had ignited the right places only by talking to him on the radio. For the next burn Saleen ordered a helicopter with a dispenser for Ping-Pong balls filled with magnesium and ethylene glycol. With these Saleen could ride in the helicopter and control the ignition pattern and timing.

Prescribed Natural Fire

Since 1968 fire managers have allowed lightning fires to burn in a wilderness if they stay within prescription. The fire plan for wilderness fires states this prescription and how far and how fast the fires will be permitted to spread and requires them to be put out if they exceed these limits. In national forest wilderness a prescribed natural fire must meet four criteria: (1) The wilderness must have a fire management plan approved by the regional forester; (2) the weather forecast must show that weather factors like wind and humidity will stay within certain limits; (3) the forest must have enough money and personnel on hand to monitor the fire; and (4) firefighters must be available to suppress the fire if it escapes prescription.

When fire managers designate a lightning fire as a prescribed natural fire, they arrange for people to monitor it. Those monitoring the fire keep track of the weather conditions; the fire's size, rate and direction of spread, and smoke plume; and the fuel types. They also watch for any threats to life, property, or administrative boundaries. Every day they measure the temperature, humidity, fuel moisture, and wind speed and direction and watch the progress of the fire. And they protect wilderness users by putting up signs, closing trails and areas when needed, and contacting the news media.

The USDA Forest Service classifies fires for monitoring as Situation 1 through 3 fires, based on the size of the fire, the fire danger, and the number of visitors to the area. For a small Situation 1 fire, one person collects data, usually by air and not necessarily every day. Personnel may instead monitor a fire from the ground near it, especially when they need fuel moisture samples. To obtain fuel moisture readings in the field, observers can push small battery-powered probes into the bark of trees. For a Situation 3 fire (one over 500 acres), several people, including a qualified fire behavior analyst, monitor the fire daily. They analyze the relevant data and make recommendations to the forest supervisor, who takes direct responsibility for the fire.

Helicopters have many uses in firefighting today, such as for transporting initial attack crews to the fire, dropping water on the fire, and igniting prescribed burns. Courtesy of the USDA Forest Service.

Monitoring gives managers the information they need to make decisions about the fire and provides records in case the fire later needs suppression. Keeping watch over the effects of a fire also enables managers to tell whether it has achieved its goals. They sometimes calculate the long-term effects of wildfires by studying index plots set up before the fire. Monitoring is now the usual method for dealing with fires in wildernesses, but some wilderness fires are still suppressed using the minimum action that will be effective, often the confinement strategy.

The 1989 Fires in the Frank Church Wilderness

One example of dealing with wilderness fires is that of the 1989 fires in Idaho's Frank Church–River of No Return Wilderness. That summer all forests and national parks were required to put out all fires until they had prepared new fire policies and had had them approved. On July 25 and 26, 1989, however, when a barrage of lightning ignited hundreds of fires in the

Northwest, the initial attack forces could not cover all the fires. Consequently, many of these fires grew so large that when the forest supervisors sent for crews, there were not enough to go around, and the managers had to decide which fires were important enough to suppress.

Gene Benedict, the fire management officer for the Payette Forest, recalled that in the Payette Forest they gave first priority to life-threatening fires, second priority to property-threatening fires, and third priority to fires threatening high-value resources, like timber.

There were so many starts that several of the fires in the Payette Forest burned together. Two that threatened the major resort areas of Warm Lake and Warren drew most of the attention and resources. Eventually, in late August, when the nonwilderness fires neared control, the Payette Forest managers were able to attend to the fires in the Frank Church–River of No Return Wilderness. They had tried to send smokejumpers to some of them during the initial attack, but high winds had prevented the jumps.

Because of the 1989 government directive to put out all fires, Merrill Saleen, the planning specialist for the 1989 fires in this wilderness, observed that the fire management team felt nervous about deciding to use the least aggressive strategy of suppression, confinement. Saleen outlined the decision process the team used for the fires. They used decision analysis, a formal procedure for choosing among alternatives. The district ranger, Earl Kimball, first showed them an escaped fire situation analysis he had made, which listed the facts about the fires and the values at risk. When conducting this analysis, Kimball had considered safety, effects of the fires, cost, and public sentiment. He also provided the team with objectives for dealing with the fires. Then using the decision analysis process and this information, the team drew up their strategies and tactics.

When conducting their analysis the team used the National Fire Danger Rating System to predict the fires' future. By late August, the days had already shortened and the temperatures had dropped. Once the temperatures fall in late summer, the fire danger seldom returns to its earlier levels, even with a return of hot, dry weather, and so the team decided that these fires would probably not cause any more problems. They therefore recommended that the forest take direct action on only one fire and limit that action to confinement, a decision that saved the taxpayers $6 million to $10 million over full suppression.

This fire—the Game Creek Fire mentioned in the introduction—threatened the ranger station and two ranches. To preserve wilderness values, the crews used minimum-impact methods to keep the fire confined, but the fire management officer gave them authority for more drastic measures if needed. To ensure that the firefighters knew what methods were essential, he assigned wilderness-trained hotshot crews to fight the fire. At the end of September the fire still smoldered but had not escaped from its predetermined area. When the forest service chief, Dale Robertson, visited the Payette Forest in mid-August, he approved the plan to use confinement with monitoring.

Prescribed Burns in Lodgepole Pines _____

It is difficult to allow prescribed natural fire in wildernesses whose fire regime favors intense, infrequent fires like that of lodgepole pine which may threaten nearby developments.

Jim Brown of the Fire Sciences Lab in Missoula, Montana, figured out fire prescriptions for planned ignition fires that would safeguard developments in Yellowstone National Park. He believes that fire scientists must do more research because few foresters have experience with prescribed burns in lodgepole and there are no studies of them. Brown estimated that a prescribed fire in Yellowstone National Park's lodgepole should ideally treat 2000 to 5000 acres at a time with aerial ingnition. To avoid spotting, managers should set the fire 1 mile wide and several miles long and burn only after August 15 and after the 1000-hour time-lag fuel moisture falls below 16 percent. To prevent future high-intensity fires, the burn needs to kill 60 percent of the understory and remove 70 percent of the litter and duff and at least 50 percent of the downed dead wood over 3 inches in diameter. To burn safely near developments, Brown recommended first mechanically thinning the forest, at a probable cost of $400 per acre. Fire managers should then surround the burn with one-quarter-mile-wide fuel breaks bordered with wider strips where the crowns of the trees do not touch.

Because in "safe" weather, fires in lodgepole tend to go

out, Brown calculated that acceptable conditions for the prescribed burning of lodgepole in Yellowstone would occur only
once in 3 years. To burn lodgepole successfully, managers must
set the fires in conditions close to those in which such fires are
uncontrollable. Because only every third summer would have
even 3 days suitable for burning, this system might take 50
years to reduce fuels to a safe level, just around developments.
And such a prescribed burning operation would conflict with
the national parks' philosophy of allowing natural processes to
take place unhindered and might reduce Yellowstone's value
as a natural laboratory.

Brown feels that because lodgepole favors large stand-
replacing fires, a prescribed burning plan could not have prevented the 1988 fires. Because the extreme dryness and wind
made the fires burn all ages of trees, old prescribed burns would
not have stopped them. Don Despain, an ecologist for Yellowstone, added that he also does not believe that prescribed burning would help prevent large fires in Yellowstone because most
fires in lodgepole are crown fires and because Yellowstone
lodgepole contains so little understory that burning it would
not help prevent future crown fires.

Even though no researchers have yet published studies
of prescribed burning in lodgepole, some fire managers have
had practical experience with it. Ron Pierce, a fire management
officer for the Three Rivers District in the Kootenai National
Forest, conducted planned burns in lodgepole, using stand-
replacing burns to convert decadent lodgepole into shrubs for
wildlife habitat. In order to get the lodgepole to burn in conditions in which the fire will not escape (that is, spring or fall),
he and his crews first bulldoze down all the trees and let them
dry for 2 years before burning. In areas where heavy snows
have broken many of the trees, they burn them without bull-
dozing first. In mixed Douglas fir and lodgepole forests, they
have also done some understory burning using low-intensity
backing fires to prevent the fire from killing the thin-barked
lodgepoles. According to Pierce, because many pure lodgepole
stands have no understory, understory burning in these stands
is impossible. He thinks that two fires within a few years of each
other create such stands. He noticed that so many snags had
fallen 10 to 15 years after burning a lodgepole forest that the
forest could burn again, and so after 6 or 8 years he often burns

stands like these a second time. But because Pierce's area does not rise much above 5000 feet, lodgepole may act differently in Yellowstone, at 8000 feet. In Yellowstone, 150-year-old trees reach only the size of 70-year-old trees in his area.

Personnel in the Gunnison National Forest in southwestern Colorado burned a large acreage of lodgepole in stand-replacing burns. Jerry Chonka of the Cebolla Ranger District in that forest scoffed, saying, "It's all bogus about not being able to do prescribed burns in lodgepole." In his ranger district Chonka has conducted prescribed burns in lodgepole since 1981 to get rid of lodgepole stands infested with dwarf mistletoe and to reopen the bighorn sheep's traditional summer migration routes, which have been overgrown by lodgepole. Building roads in the rocky, steep terrain was too expensive, and so burning seemed the best choice for eliminating the dwarf mistletoe. Chonka made only stand-replacing burns, which are designed to kill all the trees. The stands varied from young "pole forests" to old growth mixed with spruce and lodgepole seedlings. Perhaps the lodgepole here is easier to burn safely than it is elsewhere because it grows at 9500 to 12,000 feet and alpine tundra borders it on the upper side. Chonka did not pretreat the sites or use any crew except two or three ignition specialists who lit the fires with a driptorch. He and his staff take care not to ignite a fire unless the probability of ignition stays below 70 percent, and they also keep the probable spotting distance under one-half mile.

Because of the drought, in 1988, Chonka and his staff could not do any burning. In 1989 when they tried it, their first burn escaped at 30 acres, and so they had to suppress it and did not try any more that summer. In 1990 because of the continuing drought, they planned no burning. In the years that they could burn, they burned always during the warmer months, from April through November. When they work on a fire, they herd it like cowboys herding cattle. They plan the ignitions to make sure that the fire burns in the directions they want it to go. Then they monitor it each day and burn out additional areas to keep the fire away from houses and out of steep canyons. Both Pierce and Chonka conducted mainly stand-replacing burns. Pierce found when doing understory burns in mixed Douglas fir and lodgepole that he had to use low-intensity fires to prevent killing the lodgepole. But so far, no one has done much understory burning in lodgepole, even though some Yellowstone lodgepole does have understory.

Future Use of Prescribed Fire

Reducing fuel hazards by means of planned ignitions and allowing natural fires to restore wildlands to their pre-European appearance can conflict with recreation. But if a wildfire is put out today, the unburned area will catch fire sometime in the future. John Russell, a fire management specialist at BIFC, stated that even if we could have put out all the natural Yellowstone fires early in the 1988 season, those areas would burn in large uncontrollable fires sometime in the future anyway.

History professor and author Stephen Pyne, who studied the history of wildland fire, believes that including human-caused fire in forests will preserve the natural forest landscape. In his book *Fire in America*, he writes that human-caused fire is the natural state of wildland fire because humans belong to the ecology. Fire effects expert Steve Arno put it more strongly: "There isn't any rational choice about the use of fire, unless you want to convert wildlands to intensively managed croplands, tree farms, or urban landscapes."

Chapter Nine

■ ■ ■

Fire Management, Fire Policy, and Yellowstone

A tour of the Boise Interagency Fire Center gives one an idea of U.S. wildland fire policy and technology. As we mentioned earlier, this center, BIFC ("Biff-see"), serves as the national center for coordinating firefighting among federal and state agencies and assists in other types of emergencies. When a forest, national park, state or county forestry department, or even another country needs more firefighters, equipment, or supplies, it can order them through this center.

Five federal agencies, the USDA Forest Service, U.S. National Park Service, U.S. Bureau of Land Management, U.S. Bureau of Indian Affairs, and U.S. Fish and Wildlife Service, run BIFC cooperatively. Each agency has its own director. Because it owns and operates the center's buildings and land, the Bureau of Land Management serves as the host agency, but there is no overall director. In addition, BIFC houses the Idaho office of the National Weather Service. At the center, rectangular buildings and trailers cluster around a two-story main building topped with an air traffic control room. Green lawns, a few shrubs and pines, and acres of asphalt parking lots separate the buildings. Arriving and departing firefighters may notice how fireproof it looks.

The Boise Interagency Fire Center _____

In the Logistics Center on the top floor of the main building, BIFC keeps track of all the fire crews and planes; a big wall map of the United States with cutouts of the available planes shows their locations. The center keeps the names of the fire crews and resources available from all over the United States on cards in rows of metal pockets that cover the walls. On one wall are the cards of crews still available, and on another wall are the cards of crews that have been sent to fires. Data on individual crew members are kept in a computer, but the pocket system allows those running the Logistics Center to tell at a glance the locations of all the crews. Another section of the Logistics Center houses the information on fire weather and on the status of fires and shows on a chalkboard the major fires in the country and their status. Information on fires is sent in daily reports by the incident commanders.

The Idaho office of the National Weather Service at BIFC receives weather information from the national office of the weather service in Washington, D.C. In Washington, meteorologists feed data from the twice-a-day launching of 300 weather balloons all over the United States into a computer that plots the weather maps and makes the forecasts. Fire weather specialists at the Idaho weather office make daily forecasts for BIFC, and when requested by the incident commanders BIFC sends these meteorologists and mobile weather stations to the fires. Other buildings hold the headquarters for two advanced weather techniques, RAWS, the remote automatic weather stations, and ALDS, the automatic lightning detection system, which were described in Chapter 3.

Equipment needed at the fires is sent out from the warehouse, located at the edge of the airfield. At the beginning of the fire season, supplies like pumps, batteries, sleeping bags, and shirts stuff the warehouse shelves from the floor to the 60-foot ceiling. Photos of the supplies on the ends of the shelves show their location. Forklifts raise the operator along with the fork so that he or she can see to load and unload the supplies and remove them when needed. At the height of the fire season, the forklifts buzz around constantly, and the warehouse is only half full. The warehouse employees do not have time to put things away before sending them on to the fires, and so they just mark them with their destination and group them under clear plastic tarps. Out on the front lawn and on the asphalt next to the airfield stand huge piles of cartons sent here by other equipment caches for transport to current fires.

This fire crew from Alaska is arriving at the Boise Interagency Fire Center to work on one of the hundreds of 1989 Idaho fires.

Wayne Dawson, the warehouse manager, explained that eight regional fire caches and two warehouses in the United States store the equipment. This warehouse orders items as well as keeps the standard set of supplies found in all caches. The warehouse employees organize many of the supplies into kits. For example, the chain-saw kits contain saws, chaps to wear when using them, and parts for repairing them. According to Dawson, the General Services Administration (GSA) supplies more than half the items found in the warehouse and standardizes them to BIFC's specifications. Warehouse employees keep track of the stock of each item, so that they can order almost anything that a fire organization may request from other caches or outside sources. But those in the field making the request must plan ahead. As Dawson commented, "If they order an elephant, they better have a bale of peanuts to feed it, because it's on its way."

The warehouse adjoins the airfield where BIFC acts as an air base for planes bringing in fire crews and for tanker planes carrying retardant taking off for fires in southern Idaho.

These supplies sent by BIFC to the Lowman Fire are ready for distribution at the Warm Springs fire camp. Courtesy of the USDA Forest Service.

Because the airfield is connected to the Boise airport, its control tower also directs BIFC's traffic.

The managers at a fire order by radio the tanker planes and other resources. BIFC operates a special department, the Radio Cache, to provide and maintain the radios. Here technicians design, install, and repair two types of radio systems, one to enable the firefighters and the overhead teams staffing a fire to talk to each other, and the other to enable them to talk to the outside world. All the radio systems come in kits consisting of a base station and hand-held radios. Just before the staff sends out the radios, they retrieve the batteries from the cold storage room in the warehouse and put them in the kits. During a fire, the radio cache supplies personnel to manage the radio system. For example, in a trailer at the Lowman fire camp, technicians repaired the hand-held radio units and sent those they could not fix back to BIFC. When the radios come back to BIFC, the staff uses computers to determine which ones need repair. The infrared mapping system, discussed in Chapter 6, also occupies a corner of the Radio Cache building.

At one end of BIFC's grounds, in the maintenance and equipment building, the staff designs and assembles pump and tank units to install on truck bodies. Under contract, a private horse trailer plant makes the tank units, which are constructed of fiberglass because it lasts twice as long as metal does.

The staff also conducts research, such as on the foam used in wildland firefighting.

Another low building serves as a training center, where the staff members conduct and develop training courses. The courses cover varied skills from basic firefighting to those needed by the incident commanders of major fires. The center's staff also teaches courses elsewhere. In 1988, Dick Terry went to Fort Lewis, Washington, to train 5000 soldiers in basic firefighting so that they could be sent to Yellowstone to replace the firefighters needed elsewhere. To help the center staff and students and those doing research on wildland fire, the center maintains a library, run by Rozella Hopkins, which includes training courses, videos, slides, books, and articles on fire-related topics.

History of BIFC

The idea for BIFC began before 1963 when the Boise National Forest proposed a fire center at its air tanker site at the Boise airport, to bring together its various air, helicopter, smoke-jumper, dispatch, and warehouse operations at one location. When the Boise National Forest invited the Boise District of the Bureau of Land Management to locate its fire dispatch office at the center, the invitation coincided with the BLM's desire for a coordinating center, and the idea for the Boise Interagency Fire Center started taking shape.

The formal idea for BIFC came from a BLM task force that in 1963 proposed a center for coordinating the Interior Department agencies' firefighting. By 1965 the BLM had set up a Great Basin fire center in old military buildings at Gowen Field in Boise. Roger Robinson was the first director of the center. After large fires near Elko, Nevada, in 1964 showed the need for interagency coordination, the Forest Service joined the BLM in the Boise Center, renaming it the Western Inter-agency Fire Coordination Center. In 1968, construction of the buildings for BIFC began, and in 1969 the BLM, Forest Service, and Weather Bureau signed an agreement for the joint operation of the center.

In 1974 the National Wildfire Coordinating Group (NWCG) was organized to set up multiagency fire planning for the five agencies managing federal funds: the Park Service, Bureau of Indian Affairs (BIA), Fish and Wildlife Service, BLM, and Forest Service. In 1977 the BIA moved its fire management headquarters to BIFC, and in 1979 the Fish and Wildlife Service did the same. By 1987 BIFC could mobilize more than 22,500 personnel in less than 10 days. The current director of the BLM at BIFC, Jack Wilson, hopes to make BIFC the national center for technical knowledge of fire. How did we get to the point where we needed BIFC to manage wildland firefighting?

History of Fire Policy

Scientists study fire history in two ways. The first is by examining the location of fire scars in tree rings. From the fire scars, scientists can tell the fire history of a forest before recorded history; they can even date fires as far back as the age of the oldest tree trunk that has not rotted away. To date fires, the scientists drill into the trees at the edges of the fire scars, sometimes called *cat faces*, although they have a hard time deciding where to drill, as some trees display many fire scars, with a fold of healing tissue marking each one. By counting the rings in the coring inward from the cambium to an abrupt color change, researchers can pinpoint which year a fire occurred. Changes in the ring's width or slant, pitch deposits, or crumbled areas in the coring are other ways to determine the year of a fire. In stands with no fire scars, the researchers average the ages of the trees. Fires may also be dated by means of the charcoal layers in lakes and ponds.

The second method of studying early fires is through the accounts of early travelers like Lewis and Clark, whose journals reported ten fires they suspected as caused by humans. Another early traveler, Warren Ferris, wrote about the Shoshone tribe in the Lemhi Valley setting fire to the forest as a signal to call its bands together. The Native Americans sometimes used fire in war. In the 1878 Sheepeater war in Idaho's Frank Church–River of No Return Wilderness the Native Americans sur-

One way in which fire ecologists determine a forest's fire history is by dating the fire scars on the trees, both surface scars, like this one, and internal scars that the bark has grown over.

rounded the U.S. soldiers, set fire to the hillside, and kept the men trapped there for 14 hours. Because the early explorers in Yellowstone, however, described dense forests, the Native Americans may not have set fires there. The early accounts also described the Native Americans' setting fires to drive game, to clean their campsites, and to protect them from enemies. But did they set fires, or merely live in areas of frequent lightning fires? A study of northeastern Wisconsin showed that oak savanna—usually found only much farther south—had been recorded in a public land survey in 1834. At that time this area of scattered oaks in grassland grew only on land near the sites of Native American villages. But the researchers found that the oak savanna has now disappeared except for one small forest.

Studies using interviews, historical journals, and fire scar samples show that before 1860 the areas where the Native Americans lived had more frequent fires than did the uninhabited areas. Steve Arno stated that the studies that he and his colleagues at the fire sciences laboratory did found that the Native Americans' fires probably equaled lightning fires in shaping the vegetation of the northern Rockies. Because the Native Americans often lived in grasslands where lightning seldom starts fires, most researchers think the lack of intentionally set fires after the Native Americans were moved to reservations caused the observed increase in the shrubs and trees in the grasslands. For example, photographs of the Bitterroot Valley, Montana, show that the trees and shrubs have become denser and have moved into areas that were grassland in 1860. Some researchers believe that grazing and overgrazing rather than the absence of intentional fires caused this invasion, that by cutting growing grasses, grazing gives sunlight and added water to tree seedlings.

The fires abated after the European settlement for two other reasons. Land clearing, which broke up the large tracts of forest and continuous fuels, meant that fires could not spread across the valleys as easily. And by the late 1800s, vast herds of cattle and sheep grazing the West had greatly reduced the amount of fine fuels, the grasses.

However, at the same time timber cutting in the lake states left slash that fueled disastrous fires, one of which was the great Peshtigo, Wisconsin, fire of 1871, which killed 1500 people. This fire was the worst in terms of lives lost that the United States has ever suffered. About then, people also began to worry about exhausting the timber supply. In 1873, a committee of the American Association for the Advancement of Science lobbied for laws to preserve timber, their interest coming from the European tradition of managing forest for timber rather than for other uses. That year Congress passed the Timber Culture Act, which promoted tree planting.

Drought, land clearing, and logging continued to cause large fires. One of the worst of these, the Hinckley, Minnesota, fire of 1894, killed 418 people. In 1891 the continuing concern for timber and fires led Congress to give the president the power to create Forest Reserves by withdrawing public lands from settlement. Accordingly, in 1898 President Theodore Roosevelt created the Division of Forestry, headed by Gifford Pinchot, one of the first men in the United States to receive a college degree in forestry. Pinchot advocated multiple use of the forest, and under his direction the U.S. Forest Service began a policy of fire prevention and total fire suppression. Rangers made fire control a main goal, but they had leeway in deciding which fires to attack and how much effort to spend. This policy emphasized saving valuable resources like timber, and so foresters put little effort into saving forests with noncommercial timber.

In 1905 the Forest Reserves were transferred from the General Land Office to the Bureau of Forestry. Passed in 1908, the Forest Fire Emergency Fund Act allowed those agencies responsible for fighting fires to be reimbursed for their costs without budgeting for firefighting. The Weeks Act of 1911 allowed the Forest Service to make cooperative agreements with the states for firefighting, authorized acquiring private lands for national forests, recognized the importance of forests as watersheds, and permitted the Forest Service to acquire forests in the eastern United States.

As the federal control of timber grew, so did the goal of organized fire suppression. The national forests let rangers allow fires in remote areas to burn, but the U.S. National Park Service, established in 1916, maintained a strict suppression policy. By 1919 the U.S. Forest Service had also adopted a policy of intensive fire suppression, and the 1921 Mather Field Conference, organized by Horace Greeley, the chief of the U.S. Forest Service, standardized its ideas about suppression.

Greeley's leadership helped pass the Clarke–McNary Act of 1924 which expanded the Weeks Act, and Greeley also lobbied for the McSweeney–McNary Act of 1928, which made the Forest Service responsible for forestry and fire research. The New Deal of the 1930s, which set up the CCC and WPA, made workers available for forest projects, such as fire roads and lookouts.

During the 1930s three bad fires persuaded the U.S. Forest Service in 1935 to adopt the 10 A.M. policy of fire control. According to the 10 A.M. policy—the first attempt at total fire suppression—foresters would try to contain all fires by 10 A.M the day after they started. The worst of these fires, the Tillamook Fire of 1933, which burned 300,000 acres, was started by a logger who was illegally running a steam donkey engine after the forest had been closed for fire danger. Because many fires start small and remain small for much of the summer even if they are not suppressed, crews succeeded in suppressing fires often enough that the 10 A.M policy became the standard. Even so, prescribed fire was still being used in southern pine plan-

This helicopter is making a water drop during the mop-up of the 1989 King Gulch Fire near Idaho City, Idaho.

tations, and in other parts of the country, prescribed fire was used to remove logging slash and to prepare sites for new trees.

After 1945 the aircraft skills gained in World War II enabled aerial firefighting to become a major method of controlling fires. Operation Firestop tested aerial water drops: First it tried dropping weather balloons full of water and then experimented with crop-dusting planes and borate. In 1955, using old navy planes, Joseph Healy set up the first squadron of borate bombers. As firefighting began to use technical methods like aircraft, the U.S. Forest Service recognized the need for technical fire research, and in 1948 it began a fire research program that in the 1960s expanded into the fire labs it operates today.

The Value of Fire to Forests

Formal recognition of the usefulness of fire in forest management began with the Leopold Report. In 1963 the Interior Department set up an advisory board on wildlife management, with A. Starker Leopold of the University of California at Berkeley as its chair. In its report, the Leopold Report, the board proposed that each park make as its highest goal maintaining or recreating its original flora and fauna. The department had told the board only to make recommendations on wildlife management, but it ended up expanding on this. For example, the report advised planned ignition burns rather than natural fires, but fire managers have used this recommendation to justify natural fires.

By 1967 controlled burning was already being encouraged in 2.9 million acres of private and government forests. As a result of the Leopold Report, in 1968 the U.S. National Park Service began to stop suppressing some fires in certain areas in the parks. By 1972 Yellowstone had adopted a program of natural fire. Originally it had permitted natural fire in only two areas east of the park roads, but by 1976 it had extended this area to most of the park.

At about this time, the Forest Service also began a natural fire program that required the forests to include fire plans in the management plans they had to make, under the National Forest Management Act of 1976. This act requires both fire control and fire use. Under the resulting plans, in 1978 the first forests began to allow natural fires in wilderness areas. (The media nicknamed both of these programs the "Let Burn" program or policy, but this book uses the terms *prescribed natural fire* or *natural fire* instead.)

To help the public and its fire managers keep up with the natural fire policy, in 1978 the Park Service rewrote its fire management policies and revised them in 1983. The revision emphasizes prevention and suppression as well as natural fire. By 1978 the parks and forests had made agreements with one another that allow managers in a park or forest to "accept" a fire approaching from another park or forest.

During the 1960s and 1970s, the Park Service and the Forest Service standardized their firefighting equipment, training, and procedures. In the 1970s the National Wildfire Coordinating Group (NWCG, consisting of the five federal agencies that run BIFC, plus the National Association of State Foresters and advisers from the U.S. Fire Administration and the National Fire Protection Association) standardized the supplies in the national fire caches and developed a series of training courses. In the 1980s the NWCG established the Incident

Command System, and as part of it, it set up the Fire Equipment Working Team, which studies and dispenses information about new fire equipment and chemicals.

The Fire Policies of the U.S. National Park Service, the USDA Forest Service, and the Bureau of Land Management

From the beginning, the different purposes of the Forest and Park services affected their fire policies. The purpose of the Park Service was to preserve the parks, provide public enjoyment, and let natural processes unfold without interference. The Organic Act that established the national parks specified public enjoyment as one of the parks' purposes and instructed the Park Service to "conserve the scenery and the wildlife" and "provide for the enjoyment of the same." Russell Dickenson, speaking at the 1985 Symposium on Wilderness Fire, compared the visitors who enjoy the parks with sport fans who support their team. He observed that the loss of visitor support could threaten the parks' existence, and so to gain greater public support for the parks he advocated more interpretive programs explaining fire management in national parks.

In contrast, the USDA Forest Service tries to manage the forests for several uses, including timber, grazing, mining, oil and gas, watershed, wildlife, recreation, and wilderness. Such management differences between national parks and wildernesses mean that, for example, hunting is permitted in wildernesses but not in national parks. The Forest Service's economists figure the cost of fighting forest fires in two ways, one for wilderness fires and the other for nonwilderness fires. Because they believe wilderness fires do minimal damage, putting them out would not be cost effective. For nonwilderness fires, the money earned from logging companies for hauling away the timber can be subtracted from the cost of fighting the fire, greatly reducing the final bill.

In contrast, the Bureau of Land Management suppresses all fires in its 800 wilderness study areas (WSAs) because of the threat to surrounding developments, but these areas may become wilderness when the BLM completes its study and legislation in the 1990s. The BLM's policy allows planned ignitions in wilderness study areas, but so far there have been none.

When suppressing fires, BLM firefighters use methods that leave little trace on the land, such as hand lines and burnout rather than bulldozers. Outside the WSAs the BLM conducts many prescribed burns to increase the growth of grasses for domestic livestock. The BLM's guidelines for prescribed burns are strict, to prevent the fires from escaping and to help land managers achieve their objectives in using them. Knowing how agency policies differ may help clarify the problems that developed in the Yellowstone fires.

Causes of the Yellowstone Fires

Fire scientists concluded that drought and wind caused the immense sizes and extreme behavior of the Yellowstone fires. The extreme fire behavior prevented much of the firefighting from being effective and showed that crown fires are probably uncontrollable in extreme conditions. For example, on one day the fires crossed all but 20 of 400 miles of fire line. Of the 249 fires in the Greater Yellowstone Area, 13 became major blazes. Yellowstone Park and the neighboring forests designated 31 of the fires as prescribed natural fires when they started. In the park, 12 of the natural fires went out by themselves. The Park Service later declared 16 of the other natural fires to be wildfires. The 3 other natural fires occurred in adjacent management areas, 1 in the Custer National Forest, 1 in Grand Teton National Park, and 1 in the Bridger–Teton Wilderness.

Of the acres burned in the Greater Yellowstone Area, 60.6 percent suffered canopy fire, 33.7 percent surface fire, and 5.7 percent burned grassland; 95 percent of the area burned in the park was burned by only seven fires. Of those, five fires started outside the park, and people caused three of them. The fires that started outside the park consumed 60 percent of the acreage burned inside it. Of the 13 large fires, the 8 largest were Storm Creek, Hellroaring, Fan, Clover–Mist, Snake River Complex (Red and Shoshone), Huck, Mink, and North Fork. Crews fought the North Fork, Huck, Shoshone, and Hellroaring fires from the beginning, but the Park Service allowed the other 4 to burn until July 21. Before July 21 the fires had left many patches of unburned and lightly burned areas, but after that time, when the winds blew hard for many days, they burned large contiguous areas of canopy.

During the summer 25,000 firefighters fought the fires, including 4000 troops, but only 1 firefighter died—when a snag fell on him in the Shoshone National Forest. During the summer more than 4 dozen firefighters were trapped and had to resort to their fire shelters.

Fighting the Yellowstone fires cost $120 million, more than any other firefighting effort in U.S. history. According to an editorial in the *Washington Post*, the political need to respond to the news stories led to the great expense. To try to put out the fires, fire managers used at least 77 helicopters, each costing $1700 or more per flying hour. The aircraft flew 18,000 hours; air tankers dropped 1.4 million gallons of fire retardant; and helicopters dropped 10 million gallons of water. Indeed, there were so many big fires that a shortage of radios, helicopters, infrared scanners, and trained firefighting personnel hindered the operations.

Scientists say that Yellowstone has burned like this before. William Romme and Don Despain found that large fires had swept Yellowstone at three different times in the last 300 years: 9 percent burned sometime between 1850 and 1869, 15 percent between 1730 and 1749, and 19 percent between 1690 and 1709. In comparison, in 1988, 26 percent of the park burned. The 1988 fires grew so large because four factors were occurring at the same time: drought, large areas of old-growth forests, multiple lightning strikes, and strong winds. The winds blew so hard that in those 4 days, half of the acreage burned that summer was consumed, but the wind moving the fires that fast actually reduced the amount burned.

Because much of the area burned lies along the park roads rather than in the backcountry, tourists notice many burned trees, especially along the road from the Tetons into the park and along the road from Old Faithful to Madison. The burned trees also are visible along the road in from West Yellowstone and around the northern loop road to Mammoth. Because so much less burned in the backcountry, driving on these roads gives a misleading impression of the amount that burned.

The Fuel Buildup Issue   Did the fuel built up from all those years of suppressing fires make Yellowstone more likely to burn? Depending on the age of the forests, the fuel could have built up no more than 20 to 25 percent as a result of fire suppression, according to the calculations of Don Despain and William Romme. Lodgepole forests rarely burn more often than every 200 to 400 years, and firefighting really did not become effective in remote areas like Yellowstone until after World War II. Not until then did fire managers begin to use planes and helicopters. Since World War II the fuel could have built up only 10 to 20 percent compared with what it would have done during the 200 to 400 years of the natural fire interval. Despain estimated that on Yellowstone's northern range, which is only 20 percent of the park, fires have been suppressed for 80 years, and because the fire interval here is only 25 years, the suppression did cause a significant fuel buildup in this area.

Yellowstone's lodgepole forests share a long fire-interval with the western hemlock, red cedar, and other trees and also the tendency toward fuel buildup and stand-replacing fires. Forests with long-interval fire regimes differ from those like ponderosa pine with short-interval fire regimes. Not all evergreen forests need frequent fires to keep down fuel buildup, and not all forests with the same types of trees will react to fire in the same way. For example, different lodgepole pine forests have different growth rates and kinds and quantities of understory plants, and so they will vary in the way they react to fire.

Some people believe that the Yellowstone fires could have been prevented by planned ignitions. This would have made the patches of same-aged trees smaller, but in August and September 1988 the fires burned through stands that had burned since 1945, which in a normal, nondrought year would have stopped the fires. Earlier fires in Yellowstone in 1976, 1979, and 1981 burned as intensely as did the 1988 fires and spread rapidly, but they soon cooled off and slowed down because the trees contained a normal amount of moisture. In its 1988 wildland fire report the Park Service emphasized that the Yellowstone fires showed fire behavior not seen since the Great Idaho Fire of 1910. Such behavior included spotting over one-half mile, 150-foot flames, and a rate of spread of 2 miles an hour and 10 miles a day.

The Early Suppression Issue   Some feel that it was not just the drought that caused the large fires, that if the Park Service had put out the natural fires right away, much less of the park would have burned. And if the natural fires had not combined with human-caused ones, would much less acreage have burned? To try to settle questions like this, Congress directed the Agriculture and Interior departments to appoint a Fire Policy Review Committee.

The Fire Policy Review Committee believed that the park officials could have stopped any of the earlier fires in their first 5 days, but back in July no one predicted that the usual summer rains would not come. In addition, early in the summer, because of the drought, some of the surrounding forests were suppressing lightning fires while at the same time the Park Service was allowing fires in Yellowstone to burn. These differing practices confused the public and helped foster controversy over the fires.

Report of the Fire Policy Review Committee

In the summer 1989 issue of *Western Wildlands*, Ron Wakimoto, a professor of wildland fire management at the University of Montana and a member of the Fire Policy Review Committee, discussed its work. At public meetings held by the committee in towns just outside Yellowstone the committee found that the public did not understand fire terminology or policy and were bothered that few park service officials participated in community activities. Most of the people supported the prescribed natural fire program, but many criticized the Park Service's actions at the time of the fires. Several disliked the firefighting tactics, and some thought that suppression should have begun earlier, because of the topography, fuels, and extreme fire weather.

Based on the information it gathered from the meetings and other sources, the committee made several recommendations. First, it suggested that prescribed natural fire policies be reaffirmed and strengthened and that planned ignitions be used more often to reduce the amount of hazardous fuels. The report also said that fire management plans should be reviewed to ensure that current policy requirements were being met and were being expanded to include interagency planning and stronger prescriptions. Another recommendation was that fire management officers certify every day that adequate resources were available to keep prescribed fires within prescription. Plans to limit the use of prescribed fire in unfavorable weather or fire conditions or to balance the demands for resources should be implemented. Finally, additional research and analysis on weather, fire behavior, fire history, fire effects, and the use of stand-replacing burns was needed.

The committee members found that Yellowstone's fire plan lacked prescription criteria for deciding which fires to declare as natural and that the only fire plans not meeting current policy were those of the national parks, including Yellowstone. Yellowstone's original plan, approved in 1972 and in use at the time of the 1988 fires, specifies only that the park would allow natural fires to burn if they did not threaten human life, property, or endangered species or burn close to the park's borders. That plan contained no formal procedure for deciding when to suppress a natural fire. In contrast, at that time the fire plans of the national forests around Yellowstone and of Grand Teton National Park all contained specific guidelines for natural fires.

The report of the Fire Policy Review Committee suggested that even when management plans do offer prescriptions for natural fire, managers should add more criteria, such as fuel moisture content, drought indicators, and the number of fires burning elsewhere in the nation. The report recommended that fire prescriptions include the impacts of fires on visitors and communities, and it also suggested limiting the size and number of natural fires in one unit at one time. Furthermore, Congress should fund firefighting in the same way for all agencies. At present only the Park Service can use emergency funds for prescribed natural fire. Because all other agencies must use budgeted funds to monitor natural fires, they usually designate few as prescribed natural fires. In closing, the committee found that the public and some incident commanders did not understand minimum-impact suppression tactics. Indeed, the committee members themselves disagreed about whether planned fires in lodgepole could reduce fuels without causing control problems. But they warned of an increasing risk of similar immense fires elsewhere.

The Park and Forest Services' Reactions to the Fires

The report by the Fire Policy Review Committee was not the only one. The U.S. National Park Service also convened its own committee, chaired by Norman Christensen of Duke University.

This committee, called the Greater Yellowstone Area Postfire Ecological Assessment Panel, consisted of 15 teams, mostly made up of college professors. Its report, issued in March 1989, supported the wisdom of a natural fire program.

According to the Burned Area Survey made by the park's Division of Research, of the 793,880 acres burned inside Yellowstone Park, 323,291 was canopy burn, 281,098 acres was mixed burn, and 51,301 acres was nonforested burn. The survey also listed 37,202 acres as undifferentiated (miscellaneous) and 100,988 acres as undelineated. This last category—surface burns under dense, unburned canopies—was impossible to map from the air, and so in the complex process of arriving at these figures, the research division used satellite images and aerial photographs. The resulting detailed Burned Area Survey map, obtainable from the park headquarters, resembles a sprinkling of multicolored pepper.

Except on steep slopes, Christensen's ecological panel expected the fires to have little effect on runoff. Because the shade of the canyon walls dominates the temperatures in the tributaries of the main drainages, there should be little change in water temperature and thus little effect on fish and aquatic life.

The panel noted that researchers documented as many as 1 million lodgepole seeds per acre in the Greater Yellowstone Area. Researchers also concluded that 335 elk, 36 mule deer, 12 moose, 6 black bear, 9 bison, and 5 osprey died in the fires. By examining the tracheas of some of the dead elk, research ecologist Francis Singer determined that most of the elk died of smoke inhalation. Teams of various agencies conducting post-fire surveys did not find any dead grizzlies. The panel, however, was more concerned about the 800 miles of fire lines and other human scars on the landscape than about the direct effects of the fires. Nonetheless, it did not advocate reforestation, seeding of nonnative plants, soil stabilization, and the artificial feeding of the elk, deer, bison, and moose. Rather, the panel's report emphasized that the Park Service must monitor Yellowstone to see whether any of these procedures will be needed in the future.

Also as a result of the fires, the Park Service drew up new guidelines for monitoring prescribed fires. In January 1990, it announced that the Kings Canyon and Sequoia national parks would resume their very successful natural fire policy as a model for other parks. The park managers in these parks must follow strict new guidelines for natural fires, permitting natural fires only within specific ranges of temperature, wind speed, humidity and fuel moisture level, and only above certain elevations.

The USDA Forest Service also recommended much stricter requirements for prescribed natural fires. Concern over the Yellowstone fires led the Forest Service to set up a task force in September 1988 to review the prescribed fire program. The new requirements pertain to deciding when to allow a burn, training for managers, and coordinating plans with other agencies. The task force also advised planned ignitions to reduce fuels along wilderness boundaries and around developments within wildernesses. In June 1989 the Forest Service sent directions based on the report to the forests to guide the revision of their fire plans and to help in the management of fires until the revised plans have been completed.

According to Superintendent Bob Barbee, the Yellowstone officials will make two changes in that park's particular policy. First, they will try to coordinate and communicate better with the public and the surrounding forests. Second, they will set up uniform guidelines for the park and surrounding forests to determine when fires need to be extinguished.

The Media's Response to the Yellowstone Fires

Most people in the United States will never learn about these recommendations. Indeed, from the media reports during the fires, they already have formed opinions of the fires and that someone was at fault. John Varley, chief of research at Yellowstone, pointed out that whatever position one held on national park topics when the fires began, the fires only reinforced it. In his article in *Western Wildlands* Ron Wakimoto wrote that the information given to the media at the time of the fires seemed to have been inconsistent. That is, at the same time the United States was spending $1 million a day to fight the fires, television reports emphasized their ecological benefits.

Yellowstone superintendent Bob Barbee worried that the emphasis of the news stories on the destruction of the park had upset the residents of the surrounding towns. In addition, the news stories played up some of the disagreements over firefighting tactics, when in reality there were only two. Finally, the reporters asked ordinary citizens and firefighters for their opinions when they should have asked people like the incident commanders, who really knew what was going on.

Barbee feels that the media unfairly blamed the fires on the Park Service's natural fire policy, even though two of the main fires, the Storm Creek and Mink, started outside the park and the national forests themselves declared them prescribed natural fires. Barbee believes that the fires were a natural event beyond human control, like the San Andreas (earthquake) fault, and that when the conditions of drought, high temperatures, forests with lots of dead material, and high winds come together again, such fires will break out again. In fact both Barbee and John Russell, a fire management specialist for the BLM at BIFC, believe that the lodgepole forests surrounding the Colorado towns along the Front Range above Boulder and Denver can easily burn in large intense fires. Indeed, in June 1989, a 2500-acre fire destroyed 49 homes above Boulder.

The Yellowstone media problems have been examined by Conrad Smith, a professor of journalism at Ohio State University, who studied the print coverage by analyzing the stories and sending questionnaires to reporters and their sources. He also analyzed the television coverage with the aid of a panel of 18 journalists and fire experts involved in the fires. Smith found that in both print and television, many stories were factually accurate but most were exaggerated in urgency. Most stories also lacked the background needed to understand the fires and fire policies. In addition, many of the stories implied that Yellowstone had "burned down," that this was a disaster, and that the Park Service was at fault for their "let burn" policy. As a result of his findings, Smith suggested that to be well-informed, news consumers need to be aware of the limitations of daily news media and seek additional, objective information sources. John Varley, chief ecologist at Yellowstone, concluded that the media response to the fires taught us that we cannot convey complex ideas on television. Its 10-second sound bites allow only enough time to say something colorful rather than meaningful. As a result, many Americans did not hear the whole story or even the correct story, and Yellowstone may suffer because of it.

The Effects of Wildland Fires on Businesses _____

Businesses in gateway communities like West Yellowstone claimed that they suffered from the fires, that they lost 30 to 40 percent of their business while the fires burned. Such claims only added to the controversy over the fires, but ironically, later these businesses more than made up for the loss: In October 1988 business rose 40 percent over an average October, and in 1989 visits to the park increased 9 percent, to an all-time high.

In parks and in and near wildernesses less well known than Yellowstone, the effects of fires on economic interests last longer. Stanley Potts, a big-game outfitter in the Frank Church –River of No Return Wilderness, lost $8700 in equipment and supplies to the Golden Fire of 1988, which burned his Cradle Creek camp and threatened three other hunting camps. As a result, most of his clients canceled their trips that fall, and so he lost about $17,500 in income. At first Potts blamed the Forest Service, especially when it denied his claim for the equipment, but then he remembered that rangers had warned him the fire was showing extreme behavior when he left the area to guide a bighorn sheep hunt elsewhere, 3 days before the camps burned. Also, when the fire neared his camps, the USDA Forest Service sent smokejumpers to one camp and firefighters to another to try to save his equipment. After the fire, the USDA Forest Service helped him with his special-use permits to guide sheep hunts.

An outfitter in the Selway–Bitterroot Wilderness, Dave Hettinger, had a similar experience in the fires of 1988. In the third week of August, when the Forest Service finally decided to fight the multiple lightning fires in the Selway–Bitterroot Wilderness, it was too late to stop them. One of these fires consumed 40 to 60 percent of Hettinger's hunting area, 7 tons of his hay, and a hunting camp. Hettinger hopes only that during drought conditions in the future, the government agencies will be a little more cautious with the "let burn" policy, even though he also believes that "Fire is as natural as the mountains themselves and should be used as a management tool for both the land and wildlife."

Chapter Ten

■ ■ ■

Solving Global Wildland Fire Problems

T he Yellowstone fires may cause debates for years over natural fire and the use of fire, but the agencies responsible had to start dealing with fire again the next summer. The USDA Forest Service Research Laboratories help them by providing technical knowledge. Two such labs, one in Missoula, Montana, and the other in Riverside, California, devote their research entirely to fire. The regional experiment stations also conduct some fire research.

Fire Research

One of the Missoula lab's projects was to film the first video ever taken from inside a fire. It was made by Wayne Adkins at a planned fire in Ontario, Canada. To do this he constructed a metal container shaped like a chimney and filled with insulation. Then he made a double-glass window for it with the space between the pieces of glass filled with water. At the site he put the container up on a tower. As the container heated, the video recorded bubbles appearing in the water and cracking noises as the chimney expanded with the heat, but the heat did not ruin the tape or the camera.

Other projects, such as testing fire retardants, are conducted in the lab's two wind tunnels and a combustion chamber. For fuel to use in these tests the lab workers gather pine needles each fall and buy shredded aspen excelsior to simulate grass. Researcher Merlin Brown can make the wind blow up to 7 miles

Using fire in this combustion chamber at the Intermountain Fire Sciences Laboratory, researchers study the effectiveness of fire retardants. Courtesy of the USDA Forest Service.

an hour in the wind tunnel with a 10-foot diameter, and in the tunnel with a 3-foot diameter he can turn up the wind speed to 47 miles an hour. The control panel enables him to change the humidity in the chamber from 0 to 100 percent and the temperature from 40° F to 130° F.

The U.S. National Park Service also conducts research, but only on the history, geology, and ecology of particular parks. The Yellowstone fires, however, have drawn many scientists to the park for postfire research. As of October 1989, 81 scientists representing 35 different institutions were working on 103 fire-related research projects.

Fire Management Goals

In order to try to solve wildfire problems, whether by means of research or other methods, fire managers need to look at them in the larger context of world environmental problems. One of these problems is the need for more land for agriculture and other social needs versus the preservation of ecosystems.

Another is the excess production of carbon dioxide and other gases that may lead to global warming called the greenhouse effect. And a third problem is deforestation and the consequent desertification.

Fire Management and the Need for Land   The conflict between the preservation of the ecosystem and the fulfillment of human needs is especially acute in India. Because the rural inhabitants depend on the forest and adjacent grasslands for their animals to graze, said A. G. Oka—of India's Ministry of Environment and Forests in a speech to the 1989 Global Conference on Wild-land Fire in Boston—the challenge is to find a fire program that can help meet the expectations of the growing numbers of people. The greater numbers of people drive the grazing land into the forest, as the villagers burn the forest to increase the amount of grassland; then their animals overgraze the grass-land. Oka stated that the government must deal with the hunger and need for land before it can think about stopping the fires.

In the United States, the need for agricultural land and fuel wood has only begun to affect the forests. Here, foresters usually deal instead with conflicts between the need for wood products and the need for recreation and wildlife areas. People do not want fires in camping or hiking areas even when they realize that fire has shaped the landscape as they like it. Fire managers must try to figure out how to use prescribed fire to reduce hazards and maintain fire in the ecology of forests while keeping homes and developments safe from it.

Fire Management and the Greenhouse Effect   When considering the effects of fire, fire managers need to plan for the probable climate warming caused by excess carbon dioxide. In 1896 scientists first determined that the increasing proportion of carbon dioxide and other gases in the atmosphere from industries and automobiles would cause the atmosphere to trap more of the sun's heat. In the 1970s scientists began calling this process the greenhouse effect because the gases act in the same way as the glass in a greenhouse does. Some of the other gases damaging the earth's atmosphere are methane, nitrous oxide, and chlorofluorocarbons (gases used in spray cans and refrigeration). Scientists disagree on how fast the greenhouse effect will cause the temperature to rise, but most agree that even though

1988 was the hottest year worldwide for many centuries, the greenhouse effect did not bring 1988's drought. Instead, it was the result of a short-term northward displacement of the jet stream, described in Chapter 1. James Hansen of NASA's Goddard Institute of Space Studies testified in 1988 before a Senate committee that the greenhouse effect had caused the temperature increases of the last 10 years, including the 1988 drought, but Stephen Schneider, of the National Center for Atmospheric Research and the author of *Global Warming*, disagreed, asserting that it is too soon to know. The reason that it is too soon is that when scientists use computer models, they may omit data affecting the outcome because they do not yet know all of the factors affecting it. Accordingly, the output is flawed. Some of the areas about which data are lacking are the role of the oceans, cloud cover, and forest in the atmosphere's temperature changes. But if we wait for more evidence to show that the greenhouse effect has arrived, it may be too late to do anything about it. Some scientists have already obtained evidence for the presence of the greenhouse effect from analyzing the air trapped in ancient Greenland and Antarctic ice. One of these researchers, Hans Urscher, found the amount of carbon dioxide to have increased by 25 percent and methane, by 200 percent since the start of the Industrial Revolution. The climate has been warmer and the amount of carbon dioxide higher than it is now, but the temperature and the proportion of carbon dioxide are rising today much more quickly. By the middle of the next century the rise in temperature may extend the growing season, in some parts of the world, by 1 or 2 months. Some computer models predict that the greenhouse effect will lead to less rainfall and hotter summers in the continental interiors, which in turn may result in more wildfires.

James S. Clark of the New York State Museum in Albany studied the relationship between fire frequency and climate warming during the last 750 years. To do this he measured the amount of charcoal in sediment layers at the bottom of a Minnesota lake. He found that during the warm, dry fifteenth and sixteenth centuries, his sample forest averaged 9 years between fires. But during the Little Ice Age in the seventeenth, eighteenth, and nineteenth centuries, there were fires only every 14 years and they were less intense. After reviewing the literature on fire and climate change, fuels researcher Kevin Ryan speculated in *Wilderness & Wildfire* that the extension of the growing season alone could result in a longer, more severe fire season. Stephen Schneider also predicts that the greenhouse effect could worsen fires. In his book *Global Warming* he wrote, "When it is hotter and drier there is a much greater chance of forest fires." Our present forest communities are recent associations; the boreal or northern coniferous forest is only 6000 years old. Existing theories on how vegetation relates to climate suggest that any fluctuation will change the distribution of vegetation, Schneider believes, but researchers have not yet substantiated this. A warmer climate may allow Douglas fir, grand fir, and western larch to grow higher in the northern Rockies and crowd out Engelmann spruce, subalpine fir, and whitebark pine.

Have you ever visited the Great Basin and noticed the double timberline on the ranges? Cold causes the upper one, and dryness the lower one. Both timberlines may move up as the climate warms. Because there is a limited amount of mountaintop, the warming could shrink the high-elevation forests into smaller biological islands.

In their 1967 study of islands, Robert McArthur and Edward Wilson found a higher rate of extinction there, and the smaller and more isolated the island was, the higher the rate would be. Other researchers have discovered that the isolation of one mountaintop from the others affects the extinction rate as though it were an island. Thus as mountain forests shrink, the extinction rate may climb. Similarly, as urban development and subdivisions divide forests into islands, their extinction rate may rise. A study of 37 canyons in Southern California isolated by residential developments showed that the smaller the canyon was, the faster the rate of extinction would be. In suburban islands like these, regular moderate fire is also becoming extinct as a natural ecosystem process. Instead, there either are no fires or there are intense wildfires, and the disappearance of moderate natural fires affects ecosystems more than does the extinction of any one species. And this is what has prompted foresters to try to preserve the natural process of fire rather than certain species.

Fire and Deforestation   Deforestation and desertification are most acute in the tropics where the rainforests also are shrinking into islands as land cleared for agriculture divides them up. In a speech at the Global Conference on Wildland Fire, Jean Paul Lanly, director of the United Nations' Food and Agriculture Organization, revealed that since 1900, half of the world's tropical forests have been burned or cut down, mostly by developers, and half of that deforestation has occurred since 1980. According to Lanly, a square of tropical rainforest measuring 190 miles by 190 miles, or 36,000 square miles, is cleared each year, mostly by foreign investors. In one state of Brazil, Rondonia, 14,000 square miles has burned in the last 10 years.

Scientists think that losing so much forest could change the world's weather. In fact, a study of a tropical rainforest showed that 10 to 20 percent less water evaporated from cleared land than from the forest. Clearing tropical forest also makes the remaining forest more flammable by letting in sunlight that allows the understory vegetation to grow and letting in wind that dries out the forest. Then large, intense wildfires can result during drought.

In some areas, cutting and burning the forest result not only in deforestation but also in desertification, which leads to famine. *Desertification* is the spread of a desert environment into arid or semiarid regions. It can come about through drought, climate change, and degradation of the land by humans. People degrade the land by damaging the soil, using up the surface water or groundwater, and removing the vegetation. As much as 23,000 square miles of land in the world becomes desert each year. Overcutting of timber plus more and larger wildfires caused by the greenhouse effect could lead to forest loss and desertification even in the United States. The World Watch Institute recommended that 321 million acres of trees be planted by the year 2000 to stop desertification and meet the need for fuel, fertile soil, and water.

Global Cooperation in Fire Management _____

By sharing fire management information and resources, the countries of the world can help avoid some of these problems. One group working on global cooperation in fire management is the Northwest Forestry Commission established by the Food and Agriculture Organization. One of its study groups is the Fire Management Study Group, which promotes the exchange of ideas, information, and aid among the participating nations and sponsors tours for fire professionals from many countries. Group projects have included translating fire courses into Spanish and installing joint remote sensing stations. In addition, organizations such as the International Geosphere–Biosphere Program try to prevent deforestation and land degradation and promote international cooperation in fire research. The National Fire Protection Association also encourages global cooperation. Founded to prevent structure fires, today this group also attempts to prevent wildland fires from threatening homes through the publication and distribution of the National Fire Codes and through public education and training. In 1987 it published the booklet "Wildfire Strikes Home," which outlines the threat of wildland fires to homes, and in 1989, it cosponsored the Global Conference on Wildland Fire in Boston.

An example of international cooperation is the joint Jiapro project of Canada and China, completed in 1989, which developed a modern fire management system in the Daxinganling Forest in China. Between 1974 and 1981 a series of exchange visits led to the idea for the program, in which the Canadians, directed by the Ontario Ministry of Natural Resources, trained the Chinese and gave them equipment for a new forest fire center at Jiagedagi, the region's largest city.

The United States is also working with other countries on fire management training. With the help of the USDA Forest Service's National Advance Resource Training Center at Marana, Arizona, the International Forestry and Disaster Assistance office of the U.S. Department of Agriculture arranges for courses in wildfire suppression for fire officials of other countries. At first the center gave the courses in the United States, but in 1985 it conducted a course in Chile, in 1988 in Mexico, and in 1990 in Spain. These courses include safety, fire behavior, fire prevention, firefighting tactics and strategy, aircraft use, and prescribed fire.

Another example of international cooperation is the agreement between the United States and Canada to share firefighting resources. This agreement was drawn up in 1982, but until September 9, 1988, the United States was unable to receive resources from Canada because its government had no provision to pay for them. But on that day Congress passed Law 100–428, which permits the United States to pay Canada for any resources it sends. After that Canada sent the United States

At a global conference on wildland fire in Boston, fire experts from many countries share ideas for improving fire management. Courtesy of J. Smalley/NFPA.

resources to help with the Yellowstone and other 1988 fires, including 12 air tankers, 12 lead planes (the ones that tell the tankers where to drop the retardant), 125 helicopter personnel, 200 pumps, and nearly 4000 Pulaskis.

Worldwide conferences like the one held in Boston in 1989, at which 300 fire experts from around the world heard speeches and participated in workshops, help solve fire problems. At a workshop at the conference, fire managers advanced their ideas for improving fire management around the world. They recommended that nations share more information and exchange fire management personnel at all levels, from suppression crews to leaders. They should also develop regional cooperative fire agreements. Training in wildland fire suppression, equipment, and communication should be standardized around the world. And finally, nations should recognize that technology and firefighting resources will be of no help if economic or social conditions have caused the fire problem.

The United Nations Disaster Relief Organization has set up a goal not to erase but to reduce the effects of disasters like wildfires. As the U.S. part of this project, the federal government appointed the National Committee for Disaster Reduction, which has developed ideas for reducing losses in disasters. One idea is for local governments to provide effective warnings and forecasts and to improve emergency preparedness. In order to do this, they must first map out the various hazards in their area, assess the risks, and prohibit building in high-risk areas. To reduce some of the hazards, technical help may be needed in such projects as remodeling existing structures for fire safety.

Issues Concerning Wildland Fires

Besides the global environmental problems affected by wildland fire, specific issues concerning wildland fire are who should be responsible for protecting homes in wildlands, who should bear the escalating costs of fire protection programs, and whether fire can be preserved as an ecosystem process. Should land-managing agencies, local governments, or homeowners be responsible for protecting homes in wildlands from fire? As a citizen you have a duty to let those responsible for fire management know your opinions. If you do not like the policies, you should try to change them. You can publicize what is wrong and work with fire managers, or you can elect new government officials who will change the policies or the managers, or both. But you must be willing as a taxpayer to pay for policy changes and be willing as a homeowner to submit to fire safety regulations and limits on home sites.

In *Wilderness and Wildfire*, Tom Power suggested that cost effectiveness requires people who build homes in areas of fire risk to pay for controlling wildland fires in those areas, although fire researcher Bill Fischer sees the issue differently. He asked "But should wildland homeowners be at the mercy of adjoining federal landowners that let fire come at them?" If a private landowner allows a fire on his or her land to spread into a national forest or park, that landowner should be liable to the federal government for damages and firefighting costs. And to prevent fires burning in the opposite direction, from federal to private land, Fischer stated that agencies need to minimize fuels along the boundaries where public lands meet residential areas.

In Chapter 6 we discussed how homeowners can work individually, in neighborhood associations, and with local governments for fire prevention and protection. Homeowners' groups, local governments, and state and federal agencies all must cooperate and coordinate their efforts. The consequence of not doing so is clear. For example, many homes burned in the summer of 1981 on the east side of the Sierra near Lake Tahoe because fire crews from different agencies were not able to talk to one another on their radios: The frequencies were different. After these fires the Sierra Front organization was formed to prevent this type of problem, and in 1986 this or-

Radio communications
are vital to modern
firefighting. Courtesy of
the USDA Forest Service.

ganization enabled 1200 firefighters from various agencies to
work together to suppress the 1986 Fredericksburg Fire without
losing a single home.

Australia provides another example of shared responsibility. Australians believe people who live in bushfire areas
should live there at their own risk, but they combine personal
and government responsibility. In Australia, the ubiquitous eucalyptus trees burn explosively, and drought often parches the
land, so that bushfires occur frequently. Australia has accordingly developed a disaster plan for aid from the national government, and regional and municipal fire prevention committees
emphasize public awareness of home protection and a general
warning system. In the state of South Australia, the Country
Fire Authority maintains a 24-hour hotline to answer the public's questions about fire regulations. It also gives out a free
information kit that helps homeowners take personal responsibility for their own fire safety, and, beginning in the 1960s,
the Australian forest service has ignited 6.7 million acres per
year to help ensure their safety. Using aerial ignition, fire man-

agers burn 2 to 4 percent of the land in most states each year, because they cannot control bushfires unless fuels are regularly reduced.

Costs of Fire Suppression

What about the increasing costs of fire suppression? Who should pay, and how can we keep costs down? Ron Wakimoto wrote in *Western Wildlands* that if we try to put out every fire, we will end up spending millions of dollars putting out fires that would have gone out by themselves. And in dry, hot, and windy weather like that during 1988, some fires are impossible to put out; in such conditions firefighters can only steer fires around developments and try to keep the buildings from burning.

Although fire benefits many forests, it also destroys timber that people consider valuable. Tom McCloskey, in *Wilderness and Wildfire*, stated that the costs and benefits of fires are difficult for fire managers to calculate. How can they put a price tag on the scenic, ecological, and recreational values of an area? What is the value of a nongame animal or bird? How much money does a forest add to the local economy? Since 1983, a computer system has helped the Forest Service calculate both the costs and the benefits of fires. This National Fire Management Analysis System has figured the cost effectiveness and efficiency of the fire programs for the Forest Service, other federal agencies, and many states, and the system tests programs and strategies in various fire weather conditions under different budgets to find the most efficient one.

How can fire suppression costs be cut? The costs of fire suppression and management will be difficult to keep down in drought years. Education programs regarding fire safety measures for those who live in the interface and laws requiring fire-safe structures and fuel reduction on private and federal lands around buildings may help reduce the number and size of fires in the long run. In some forests, the greater use of natural fire may help prevent large wildfires that would threaten residential areas.

How can fire be preserved as an ecosystem process? This goal becomes increasingly difficult as wildland areas shrink in size and populations increase. Owing to long-term fire suppression, national forests and parks in the United States now have a new problem: the end of fire at natural intervals. Some wild areas are too small to allow natural fires to burn without endangering nearby developed areas. Should managers suppress fire to preserve existing vegetation in the short run, when doing this will allow new species that are not adapted to fire to take over in the long run? Or should they allow the natural process of fire to remove the existing vegetation in the short run, so that those species will continue to prevail in the long run? How large an area must be set aside to preserve all the natural species and processes, including fire?

Fire management agencies have not yet resolved these difficult policy questions. To do so, the definition of a park or preserve may need to be expanded. For example, by incorporating villages into reserves and parks Nepal is beginning to help make the economic well-being of its people compatible with the purposes of its reserves. The programs in the Annapurna Conservation area demonstrate compatibility of nature conservation with human needs, with the income of tourist user fees going to the villagers.

Yellowstone Park also is used extensively by humans. To maintain enough undeveloped area to keep species from becoming extinct and to allow natural processes like fire to continue, conservationists want managers to consider the Yellowstone ecosystem as one with the surrounding forests and to prohibit certain uses of these forests, so that they will remain essentially undeveloped. They have banded together in the Greater Yellowstone Coalition to try to achieve this goal.

Looking at this idea from a similar viewpoint, Roderick Nash, author of *Wilderness Is a State of Mind*, suggested at the 1983 Symposium on Wilderness Fire that wildfire belongs to an uncontrolled environment called wilderness. In this context, fire needs preserving as much as does any other part of the wilderness. To restore fire to its rightful place, Nash believes that humans must set prescribed fires if they are necessary, and to accept fire in wild areas, they need to see its need, harmony, and beauty.

Remember that as part of the uncontrolled wilderness, fire is a wild force and that wild forces like fire cannot always be controlled by humans. Resource managers need to consider what fire policies will preserve the wild force of fire without endangering human beings. The public needs to recognize that natural conditions, not fire policy, caused the Yellowstone fires and to prepare for that scale of fire recurring. If fires of that size and frequency are natural and cannot be controlled by humans, then people should live elsewhere or expect to have to leave and possibly lose their homes when the fires come.

It is important to preserve wildland fire because it maintains and renews ecosystems, but if it occurs too frequently, too intensely, or over unnaturally large areas, it can change ecosystems and cause deforestation and desertification. If wildland fire occurs too seldom, its absence can result in an unnatural fuel buildup that can contribute to wildfires that can change or damage the ecosystems in which they burn.

The frequency of fire that is most beneficial depends on the kind of fire and the kind of ecosystem. In undisturbed tropical forests, where for generations relatively few farmers have caused small fires by practicing slash-and-burn agriculture, large fires are rare, and therefore the large fires of today's developers, and the many small fires of the increasing number of new farmers who have migrated from cities, damage the forest. In contrast, in temperate forests, large fires naturally occur often, and so large human-caused fires are not as likely to devastate the forest. Therefore, to return the frequency of fire to a natural level, some countries need to try to lengthen the intervals between them, and others, like the United States and Canada, need to shorten them in some areas.

Reducing fire intervals will be difficult in areas where development and recreation conflict with any use of fire. Natural frequency will be difficult in forests like lodgepole that have a fire regime of large, intense fires every 200 to 400 years. It will also be difficult in regimes of rare or absent fire, like tropical rainforests. As John Varley, the chief of research at Yellowstone, pointed out, the conflict is whether we want humans as the primary manager of wildlands or whether we want nature as the primary manager. But it is not necessary that we manage all wildland areas in the same way. In wildernesses and certain parks, nature can be the primary manager, but in other areas nature may need help. In still others, humans may need to be the primary manager to protect communities. The way in which humans will change world ecosystems the least is to respect all the processes of nature, including fire, which means that we must manage fire so that it does not ruin ecosystems but instead renews them, as nature intended.

Bibliography

Abrahamson, Warren. "Post-fire Recovery of Florida Lake Wales Ridge Vegetation." *American Journal of Botany* 71(1984): 9–21.

Administrative Fire Review: Deadwood Fire. Ogden, Utah: USDA Forest Service, Intermountain Region, 1987.

Advisory Committee on the International Decade for Disaster Reduction. *Reducing Disasters' Toll: The United States Decade for Natural Disaster Reduction*. Washington, D.C.: National Academy Press, 1989.

Agee, James, and Larry Smith. "Subalpine Tree Reestablishment After Fire in the Olympic Mountains, Washington." *Ecology* 65(1984): 810–819.

Albini, Frank. "Wildland Fires." *American Scientist* 72(1984): 590–597.

American Forestry Association. "Amending the Let-Burn Policy on Public Forest Lands." Washington, D.C.: American Forestry Association Policy Paper, 1988.

Anderson, Hal E. *Aids to Determining Fuel Models for Estimating Fire Behavior*. USDA Forest Service General Technical Report INT-122. Ogden, Utah: Intermountain Forest and Range Experiment Station, 1986.

———, *Sundance Fire*. USDA Forest Service Research Paper INT-56. Ogden, Utah: Intermountain Forest and Range Experiment Station, 1968.

Andrews, Patricia. "Methods for Predicting Fire Behavior— You Do Have a Choice." *Fire Management Notes* 47(1986): 6–10.

Arno, Stephen, and Ramona Hammerly. *Timberline: Mountain and Arctic Forest Frontiers.* Seattle: The Mountaineers, 1984.

Barrett, S. W., and Stephen Arno. "Indian Fires as an Ecological Influence in the Northern Rockies." *Journal of Forestry* 80(1982): 647–651.

Barro, Susan, and Susan Conard. *Use of Ryegrass Seeding as an Emergency Revegetation Measure in Chaparral Ecosystems.* USDA Forest Service General Technical Report PSW-102. Berkeley, Calif.: Pacific Southwest Forest and Range Experiment Station, 1987.

BioScience 39 (November 1989). Issue devoted to the Yellowstone fires contains the following:

Christensen, Norman, James Agee, Peter Brussard, Jay Hughes, Dennis Knight, G. Wayne Minshall, James Peek, Stephen Pyne, Frederick Swanson, Jack W. Thomas, Stephen Wells, Stephen Williams, and Henry Wright. "Interpreting the Yellowstone Fires of 1988," pp. 678–685.

Elfring, Chris. "Yellowstone: Fire Storm over Fire Management," pp. 667–672.

Knight, Dennis, and Linda Wallace. "The Yellowstone Fires: Issues in Landscape Ecology," pp. 700–706.

Minshall, G. Wayne, James T. Brock, and John Varley. "Wildfires and Yellowstone's Stream Ecosystems," pp. 707–715.

Romme, William, and Don Despain. "Historical Perspective on the Yellowstone Fires of 1988," pp. 695–699.

Schullery, Paul. "The Fires and Fire Policy," pp. 686–694.

Singer, Francis, William Schreier, Jill Oppenheim, and Edward Garten. "Drought, Fires, and Large Mammals," pp. 716–722.

Biswell, Harold H. "Man and Fire in the Ponderosa Pine in the Sierra Nevada of California." *Sierra Club Bulletin* 44(1959): 44–53.

———, *Prescribed Burning.* Berkeley and Los Angeles: University of California Press, 1989.

Bock, Jane, and Carl Bock. "Effect of Fires on Woody Vegetation in the Pine–Grassland Ecotone of the Southern

Black Hills." *American Midland Naturalist* 112(1984): 35–42.

Branch of Fire Management, National Park Service. *National Park Service Wildland Fire Report 1988.* Boise, Idaho: Boise Interagency Fire Center, 1989.

Brown, A. A., and K. P. Davis. *Forest Fire Control and Use.* 2nd ed. New York: McGraw-Hill, 1973.

Brown, James K. "Could the 1988 Fires in Yellowstone Have Been Avoided with a Program of Prescribed Burning?" Paper presented at the annual meeting of the American Association for the Advancement of Science, San Francisco, 1989.

————, *Handbook for Inventorying Downed Woody Material.* USDA Forest Service General Technical Report INT-16. Ogden, Utah: Intermountain Forest and Range Experiment Station, 1974.

Brown, James K., Rick Oberheu, and Cameron Johnston. *Handbook for Inventorying Surface Fuels and Biomass in the Interior West.* USDA Forest Service General Technical Report INT-129. Ogden, Utah: Intermountain Forest and Range Experiment Station, 1974.

Bunting, Stephen, Bruce Kilgore, and Charles Bushey. *Guidelines for Prescribed Burning in Sagebrush–Grasslands.* USDA Forest Service General Technical Report INT-231. Ogden, Utah: Intermountain Forest and Range Experiment Station, 1987.

Byram, George M. *Atmospheric Conditions Related to Blowup Fires.* USDA Forest Service Station Paper 35. Ashville, N.C.: Southeast Forest and Range Experiment Station, 1954.

Caplinger, Larry. *Happy Complex Fire Narrative.* Ureka, Calif.: Klamath National Forest, 1987.

Carey, Alan, and Sandy Carey. *Yellowstone's Red Summer.* Flagstaff, Ariz.: Northland Publishing, 1989.

Carrier, Jim. *Summer of Fire.* Salt Lake City: Peregrine Smith, 1989.

Central Oregon Fire Prevention Cooperative. *Planning for Survival: How to Protect Your Home from Wildfire.* Salem: Oregon State Department of Forestry, 1988.

Chambers, John. "The Evolution of Wildland Fire Management and Policy." *Fire Management Notes* 48(1987): 5–8.

Chandler, Craig, Phillip Cheney, Phillip Thomas, Louis Trabaud, and David Williams. *Fire in Forestry*. New York: Wiley, 1983.

Chapman, H. H. "Fire and Pines." *American Forests* 50(1944): 62–64, 91–93.

Chase, Alston. *Playing God in Yellowstone*. Boston: Atlantic Monthly Press, 1986.

Christensen, Norman, James Agee, Peter Brussard, Jay Hughes, Dennis Knight, G. Wayne Minshall, James Peek, Stephen Pyne, Frederick Swanson, Stephen Wells, Jack W. Thomas, Stephen Williams, and Henry Wright. *Ecological Consequences of the 1988 Fires in the Greater Yellowstone Area*. Yellowstone National Park, Wyo.: Greater Yellowstone Postfire Ecological Assessment Workshop, 1989.

Clark, James S. "Effect of Climate Change on Fire Regimes in Northwestern Minnesota." *Nature* 334(1988): 233–235.

Clark, James S. "The Forest Is for Burning." *Natural History*, January 1989, pp. 51–52.

Cohn, Jeffrey. "Gauging the Biological Impacts of the Greenhouse Effect." *BioScience* 39(1989): 142–146.

Colorado State Forest Service. *Wildfire Hazards: Guidelines for Their Prevention in Subdivisions and Developments*. Fort Collins, Colo.: Colorado State University, 1987.

Cottrell, William H., Jr. *The Book of Fire*. Missoula, Mont.: Mountain Press, 1989.

Country Fire Authority. *Bushfire Survival*. Victoria, Australia: Country Fire Authority, 1987.

Cwynar, Les. "Fire and the Forest History of the North Cascade Range." *Ecology* 68(1987): 791–800.

Davis, Kathleen, and Robert Mutch. "Wildland Fire Hazards: Safety and Survival Guidelines for Recreationists and Homeowners." *Fire Management Notes* 48(1987): 18–20.

Despain, Don. "Nonpyrogeneous Climax Lodgepole Pine Communities in Yellowstone National Park." *Ecology* 64(1983): 231–234.

Despain, Don, Ann Rodman, and Paul Schullery. *Burned Area*

Survey of Yellowstone National Park: The Fires of 1988. Yellowstone National Park, Wyo.: Division of Research and Geographic Information Systems Laboratory, 1989.

Dipert, Duane, and John Warren. "Mapping Fires with the Fire Mouse Trap." *Fire Management Notes* 49(1988): 28–30.

Dorney, Cheryl, and John R. Dorney. "An Unusual Oak Savanna in Northeastern Wisconsin: The Effect of Indian-caused Fire." *American Midland Naturalist* 122(1989): 103–113.

Drysdale, Dougal. *An Introduction to Fire Dynamics.* New York: Wiley, 1985.

Ehorn, William, and Neil Paulson. *Yellowstone Fire Management Review: North Fork and Wolf Lake Fires.* Yellowstone National Park, Wyo.: USDA Forest Service and U.S. Park Service, 1988.

Fahey, Timothy, and Dennis Knight. "Lodgepole Pine Ecosystems." *BioScience* 36(1986): 610–617.

Fire and Fuel Management Problems in Mediterranean-Climate Ecosystems: Research Priorities and Programmes. MAB Technical Notes. Paris: Man and the Biosphere Program, UNESCO, 1978.

Fire Information Officers Guide. Washington, D.C.: National Wildfire Coordinating Group, 1982.

Fire Management Policy Review Team. *Final Report on Fire Management Policy.* Washington, D.C.: USDA and Department of Interior, 1989.

"Fireworks: Spectacular but Dangerous." Reprinted from National Fire Protection Association paper, in *Fire Command,* July 1989, pp. 11–14, 31–34.

Fischer, William C. *Photo Guides (3) for Appraising Downed Woody Fuels in Montana Forests.* USDA Forest Service General Technical Reports 96, 97, and 98. Ogden, Utah: Intermountain Forest and Range Experiment Station, 1981.

Fischer, William C., and Stephen Arno, eds. *Protecting People and Homes from Wildfire in the Interior West: Proceedings of the Symposium and Workshop, Missoula, Montana, 1987.* USDA Forest Service General Technical Report 251. Ogden, Utah: Intermountain Research Station, 1988. Includes the following:

Anderson, Hal, and James K. Brown. "Fuel Characteristics and Fire Behavior Considerations in the Wildlands," pp. 124–130.

Arno, Stephen, and Ronald Wakimoto. "Fire Ecology of Vegetation Common to Wildland Homesites," pp. 118–123.

Bugbee, Bruce. "Creative Techniques for Fire Hazard Planning," pp. 84–89.

Bushey, Charles, and Sonny Stiger. "The Role of the Private Fire Consultant in Assessing, Reducing, and Mitigating Wildfire Danger to Rural Home Sites," pp. 157–159.

Chappell, Gregg. "The Federal Government's Role in Major Disasters: An Overview of National, State, and Local Government Relationships," pp. 22–26.

Comly, Albert. "Guidelines for Wildland Residential Subdivision Development—An Architect's Perspective," pp. 97–99.

Davis, James B. "The Wildland–Urban Interface: What It Is, Where It Is, and Its Fire Management Problems," pp. 160–165.

Foster, Jerry A. "How Are Insurance Premiums for Homes Located in Wildland Areas Developed?" pp. 19–21.

Groves, Guy. "County Land Use Planning: How Can Planners Help the Fire Services in Protecting Homes from Wildfire," pp. 90–96.

Jekel, Louis. "Private Enterprise and Fire Protection Services: A Look to the Future," pp. 46–47.

Lee, Bob. "Helping Homeowners and Developers Understand Wildland Residential Development Programs," pp. 57–59.

Montague, Dick. "Turf Battles—How Do We Minimize These Struggles in Emergency Management?" pp. 43–45.

O'Neill, Anthony. "A National Crisis," pp. 7–9.

Schlobolm, Paul, and Ron Rochna. "Relationships of Water, Wet Water, and Foam to Wildland–Urban Interface Fire Suppression," pp. 185–188.

Schmidt, Wyman, and Ronald Wakimoto. "Cultural Practices That Can Reduce Fire Hazards to Homes in the Interior West," pp. 131–140.

Smith, Brooke. "The Wildland Residential Fire Problem: A Fire Engineer's Perspective," pp. 105–111.

Tokle, Gary. "Using Wildland Residential Standards, Laws, and Regulations for Protecting Now and in the Future," pp. 68–70.

Forest Fire Management in Alberta. Alberta, Canada: Forest Protection Branch, Forest Service, n.d.

Forestier, Katharine. "The Degreening of China." *New Scientist,* July 1989, pp. 52–55.

Fosberg, Michael, and Francis Fujioka. "Medium and Extended-Range Fire Severity Forecasting: A National Research Plan." From Preprint Volume, Ninth Conference on Fire & Forest Meteorology. Boston: American Meteorological Society, 1987.

Fuchs, Fred. "Fire Protection Project in China." *Fire Management Notes* 49(1988): 3–7.

Gaylor, Harry P. *Wildfires: Prevention and Control.* New York: Robert J. Brady, 1974.

Geiman, Stephen. "Initial Attack Management System (IAMS) Information Package." U.S. Department of Interior, Bureau of Land Management. Boise, Idaho: Boise Interagency Fire Center, 1987.

Great Basin Type 1 Overhead Team. *Lowman Complex: July 26, 1989 Through August 18, 1989.* Boise, Idaho: Boise National Forest, 1989.

Gregersen, Hans. "People, Trees, and Rural Developments: The Role of Social Forestry." *Journal of Forestry,* October 1988, pp. 22–29.

Gruell, George E. "Fire on the Early Western Landscape: An Annotated Record of Wildland Fires 1776–1900." *Northwest Science* 59(1985): 97–104.

———, *Fire and Vegetative Trends in the Northern Rockies: Interpretations from 1871–1982.* USDA Forest Service General Technical Report INT-158. Ogden, Utah: Intermountain Forest and Range Experiment Station, 1983.

Hackett, Thomas. "A Reporter at Large: Fire." *New Yorker*, October 2, 1989, pp. 50–73.

Haines, Donald. "A Lower Atmosphere Severity Index for Wildland Fires." *National Weather Digest* 13(1982): 23–26.

Hamilton, M. P., L. A. Salazar, and K. E. Palmer. "Geographic Information Systems: Providing Information for Wildland Fire Planning." *Fire Technology* 25(1989): 5–23.

History of BIFC. Boise, Idaho: Boise Interagency Fire Center, 1989.

Hummel, Mark. *Wildfire Protection: A Guide for Homeowners and Developers*. Carson City, Nev.: Sierra Front Wildfire Cooperators, 1987.

Jeffery, David. "Yellowstone: The Great Fires of 1988." *National Geographic*, February, 1989, pp. 255–273.

Juday, Glenn. "The Rosie Creek Fire." *Agroborealis* 17(1985): 11–20.

Juday, Glenn, and C. Theodore Dyrness, eds. "Early Results of the Rosie Creek Fire Research Project." Fairbanks: University of Alaska, Agricultural and Forestry Experiment Station, 1984.

Keeley, Jon E. "Fire-dependent Reproductive Strategies in Arctostaphylos and Ceanothus," pp. 391–396. In *Proceedings of the Symposium on the Environmental Consequences of Fire and Fuel Management in Mediterranean Ecosystems*. USDA Forest Service General Technical Report WO-3. Washington, D.C.: USDA Forest Service, 1977.

———, "Role of Fire in Seed Germination of Woody Taxa in California Chaparral." *Ecology* 68(1987): 434–443.

Kercher, J. R., and M. C. Axelrod. "A Process Model of Fire Ecology and Succession in a Mixed Conifer Forest." *Ecology* 65(1984): 17–42.

Kilgore, Bruce, and Dan Taylor. "Fire History of a Sequoia–Mixed Conifer Forest." *Ecology* 60(1979): 129–142.

Komarek, E. V. "Effects of Fire on Temperate Forests and Related Ecosystems: Southeastern United States." In T. T. Kozlowski and C. E. Ahlgren, eds., *Fire and Ecosystems*, pp. 251–277. New York: Academic Press, 1972.

Kozlowski, T. T., and C. E. Ahlgren, eds. *Fire and Ecosystems.* New York: Academic Press, 1972.

Leopold, A. Starker, S. A. Cain, C. M. Cottam, I. N. Gabrielson, and T. L. Kimbal. "The Leopold Committee Report: Wildlife Management in the National Parks." *American Forests* 69(1963): 32–35, 61–63.

Le Van, Susan, and Carlton Holmes. *Effectiveness of Fire-retardant Treatments for Shingles After 10 Years of Outdoor Weathering.* USDA Forest Service Research Paper FPL-474. Madison, Wis.: Forest Products Laboratory, 1985.

Lotan, James E. *Effects of Fire on Flora.* USDA Forest Service General Technical Report WO-16. Washington, D.C.: USDA Forest Service, 1981.

Lotan, James E., and James K. Brown. *Fire's Effects on Wildlife Habitat.* USDA Forest Service General Technical Report INT-186. Ogden, Utah: Intermountain Research Station.

Lyon, L. Jack. *Effects of Fire on Fauna.* USDA Forest Service General Technical Report WO-6. Washington, D.C.: USDA Forest Service, 1978.

———, "The Sleeping Child Burn—21 Years of Postfire Change." Research Paper INT-330. Ogden, Utah: Intermountain Forest and Range Experiment Station, 1984.

Lyons, John W. *Fire.* New York: Freeman, 1987.

MacArthur, Robert, and Edward Wilson. *The Theory of Island Biogeography.* Princeton, N.J.: Princeton University Press, 1967.

Madany, Michael H., and Neil West. "Livestock Grazing—Fire Regime Interactions Within Montane Forests of Zion National Park, Utah." *Ecology* 64(1983): 661–667.

Malanson, George, and Louis Trabaud. "Vigour of Post-fire Resprouting by Quercus Coccifera L." *Journal of Ecology* 76(1988): 351–365.

Martin, George C. "Fuels Treatment Assessment—1985 Fire Season in Region 8. *Fire Management Notes* 49(1988): 21–24.

McCloskey, Richard. *Conceptual Framework for Fire in the Forest: Influences on the Landscape and Management Decisions in the*

West. Ogden, Utah: USDA Forest Service Intermountain Region, 1989.

McConnell, Chris. "Legendary Bear Gets His Paws Back into Fire Prevention," *Chicago Tribune,* September 25, 1989.

McLean, Herbert. "Standoff in the Stanislaus." *American Forests,* January–February 1988, pp. 21–75.

McPhee, John. *The Control of Nature.* New York: Farrar, Straus & Giroux, 1989.

Mead, Mark, John D. Mann, and David Yarrow. "The Fate of the Earth Depends on the Fate of the Trees." From *Solstice: Perspectives on Health and the Environment* and reprinted in *Utne Reader,* May–June 1989, pp. 49–57.

Merrill, E. H., H. F. Mayland, and J. M. Peek. "Shrub Responses After Fire in an Idaho Ponderosa Pine Community." *Journal of Wildland Management* 46(1982): 496–501.

Milstein, Michael. "The Long, Hot Summer: Rare Conditions Spark an Inferno at Yellowstone and Test Park Fire Policy." *National Parks,* November–December 1988, pp. 26–28.

Ming-Yih, Chen, and Lu King-Cherng. "Effect of Wildfires on the Main Forest Ecosystems in Taiwan." Paper presented at Meeting Global Wildland Fire Challenges, Boston, July 23–26, 1989.

Mohr, Francis. "Light-Hand Suppression Tactics: A Fire Management Challenge." *Fire Management Notes* 50(1989): 21–23.

Moore, John. "Firestorm!" *Readers Digest,* March 1989, pp. 77–82.

Morrison, Ellen. *Guardian of the Forest: A History of the Smokey Bear Program.* Alexandria, Va.: Morielle Press, 1989.

Mott, William Penn, Jr. "Federal Fire Policy in National Parks." *Renewable Resources Journal,* Winter 1989, pp. 5–7.

Muir, Patricia, and James Lotan. "Disturbance History and Serotiny of Pinus Contorta in Western Montana." *Ecology* 50(1985): 1865–1868.

Nash, Roderick. *Wilderness and the American Mind.* 3rd ed. New Haven, Conn.: Yale University Press, 1983.

National Fire Policy Review Team. *Final Report on Fire Man-*

agement Policy. Washington, D.C.: U.S. Departments of Agriculture and Interior, 1989.

National Fire Protection Association. *Building Interagency Co-operation.* Quincy, Mass.: NFPA, 1988.

———, *Protecting Your Home from Wildfire.* Quincy, Mass.: NFPA, 1988.

———, *Wildfire Strikes Home.* Quincy, Mass.: NFPA, 1987.

National Service-wide Activity Review of Firefighter Safety, Welfare, and Productivity. Washington, D.C.: USDA Forest Service, 1988.

National Wildfire Coordinating Group. *Firefighters Guide.* Boise, Idaho: Boise Interagency Fire Center, 1986.

———, *Foam Project Issue Paper.* Boise, Idaho: Boise Interagency Fire Center. 1988.

———, *S-390 Fire Behavior: A Student Guide and Text.* Boise, Idaho: Boise Interagency Fire Center, 1981.

Newell, Marvin. "Fire Resistant Species for Wildland Residential Areas." Memo to regional foresters, July 11, 1987.

Nordwall, Bruce D. "Airborne Surveillance Will Give Forest Service Real-Time Fire Maps." *Aviation Week and Space Technology,* May 29, 1989, pp. 105–107.

O'Gara, Geoffrey. "Beyond the Burn." *Sierra* 74(1989): 40–42.

Peattie, Donald Culross. *A Natural History of Western Trees.* Boston: Houghton Mifflin, 1953.

Perkins, James, and George Roby. "Fire Management Training in International Forestry." *Fire Management Notes* 48(1987): 18–20.

Phillips, Clinton. "An Evaluation of the Incident Command System." *Fire Management Notes* 48(1987): 6–7.

Postel, Sandra. "Global View of a Tropical Disaster." *American Forests,* November–December 1988, pp. 26–36.

Proceedings of International Wildfire Conference: Meeting Global Wildland Fire Challenges, Boston, July 23–26, 1989. Quincy, Mass.: National Fire Protection Association, 1990.

Proceedings—Symposium and Workshop on Wilderness Fire, Missoula, Mont., November 15–18, 1983. USDA Forest Service General Technical Report INT-182. Ogden, Utah: Intermountain Forest and Range Experiment Station. Includes the following:

Arno, Stephen. "Ecological Effects and Management Implications of Indian Fires," pp. 81–86.

Bancroft, Larry, Thomas Nichols, David Parsons, David Graber, Boyd Evison, and Jan van Wagtendonk. "Evolution of the Natural Fire Management Program at Sequoia and Kings Canyon National Parks," pp. 174–180.

Cheney, N. Phil, and Charles George. "Australia's 1983 Ash Wednesday Fires," pp. 232–324.

Dickenson, Russell. "Environment for Fire and Wilderness Management in the National Parks," pp. 4–8.

Fields, Arlene. "Firebase" (computerized bibliography of wildland fire), p. 270.

Gaidula, Peter. "Training in Support of Park and Wilderness Fire Management Programs," pp. 220–224.

Gruell, George. "Indian Fires in the Interior West: A Widespread Influence," pp. 68–74.

Habeck, James. "Impact of Fire Suppression on Forest Succession and Fuel Accumulations in Long-Fire Interval Wilderness Habitat Types," pp. 110–118.

Heinselman, Miron. "Fire Regimes and Management Options in Ecosystems with Large High-Intensity Fires," pp. 101–109.

Lewis, Henry T. "Why Indians Burned: Specific Versus General Reasons," pp. 75–80.

Mutch, Robert, and Kathleen Davis. "Visitor Protection in Parks and Wildernesses: Preventing Fire-related Accidents and Disaster," pp. 149–158.

Nash, Roderick. "Sorry, Bambi, but Man Must Enter the Forest: Perspectives on the Old Wilderness and the New," pp. 264–268.

van Wagtendonk, Jan. "Fire Suppression Effects on Fuels and Succession in Short-Fire Interval Wilderness Ecosystems," pp. 119–126.

Pyne, Stephen. *Fire in America*. Princeton, N.J.: Princeton University Press, 1982.

———, *Introduction to Wildland Fire*. New York: Wiley, 1984.

———, "The Summer We Let Wild Fire Loose." *Natural History*, August 1989, pp. 44–51.

Radtke, Klaus. *Living More Safely in the Chaparral–Urban Interface*. USDA Forest Service General Technical Report PSW-67. Berkeley, Calif.: Pacific Southwest Forest and Range Experiment Station, 1983.

RAWS Support Facility. *Remote Automatic Weather Station (RAWS) Standards*. Boise, Idaho: Boise Interagency Fire Center, 1987.

Report of the Task Force on Prescribed Fire Management Criteria. Washington, D.C.: USDA Forest Service, 1989.

Rice, Carol. "Fire Management in the Berkeley Hills." *Fire Management Notes* 50(1989): 19–20.

Rice, Carol, and James Davis. "Minimizing Fire Damage Through Local Land Use Planning." Paper presented at Meeting Global Wildland Fire Challenges, Boston, July 23–26, 1989.

Riggan, Phillip, Suzanne Goode, Paula Jacks, and Robert Lockwood. "Interaction of Fire and Community Development in Chaparral of Southern California." *Ecological Monographs* 58(1988): 155–176.

Robertson, W. B., Jr. "A Survey of the Effects of Fire in the Everglades National Park." Washington, D.C.: U.S. Department of Interior, National Park Service, 1953.

Romme, William, and Don Despain. "The Yellowstone Fires." *Scientific American*, November 1989, pp. 37–46.

Romme, William, and Dennis Knight. "Fire Frequency and Subalpine Forest Succession Along a Topographic Gradient in Wyoming." *Ecology* 62(1981): 319–325.

Rothermel, Richard. *How to Predict the Spread and Intensity of Range Fires*. USDA Forest Service General Technical Report INT-43. Ogden, Utah: Intermountain Forest and Range Experiment Station, 1983.

Rothermel, Richard, and George Rinehart. *Field Procedures for Verification and Adjustment of Fire Behavior Predictions*. USDA Forest Service General Technical Report INT-142. Ogden, Utah: Intermountain Forest and Range Experiment Station, 1983.

Russakoff, Dale. "Letting Smokey Be Smokey." *Washington Post*, August 24, 1989.

Ryan, Kevin. "Lesson Plan Outline for Section on Effects of Fire on Fuels in Course 'Fire Effects on Public Lands'." Boise, Idaho: National Wildfire Coordinating Group, Boise Interagency Fire Center, 1989.

Salisbury, Harrison. *The Great Black Dragon Fire: A Chinese Inferno*. Boston: Little, Brown, 1989.

Schneider, Stephen. *Global Warming: Are We Entering the Greenhouse Century?* San Francisco: Sierra Club Books, 1989.

————, "The Changing Climate." *Scientific American*, September 1989, pp. 70–79.

Schroeder, Mark, and Charles Buck. *Fire Weather*. Agricultural Handbook 360. Washington, D.C.: USDA Forest Service, 1970.

Sedjo, Roger. "Forests to Offset the Greenhouse Effect." *Journal of Forestry*, July 1989, pp. 12–15.

Seip, D. R., and F. L. Bunnell. "Nutrition of Stone's Sheep on Burned and Unburned Ranges." *Journal of Wildlife Management* 49(1985): 397–405.

Sielaff, Phillip. "Initial Attack Management System Information Package." Paper presented at Weather Information Conference, Reno, Nev., 1989.

Simpson, Ross. *The Fires of '88: Yellowstone and Montana in Flames*. Helena, Mont.: American Geographic Publishing, 1989.

Smith, Conrad. "Flames, Firefighters, and Moonscapes: Network Television Pictures of the Yellowstone Forest Fires." Paper presented at Third Annual Visual Communications Conference, Park City, Utah, 1989.

————, "Gonzo Flame Video in Yellowstone: How the Media Covered a Natural Catastrophe." Draft of chapter for Philip S. Cook, Douglas Gomery, and Lawrence Lichty, eds., *The Future of News*. Washington, D.C.: Wilson Center Press, forthcoming.

————, "Reporters, News Accuracy, and the Yellowstone Forest Fires." Paper presented to International Communications Association, San Francisco, 1989.

Sorensen, James. *Twenty-Five Years of Progress Through Interna-*

tional Cooperation 1962–1988. Quincy, Mass.: National Fire Protection Association/North American Forestry Commission, 1988.

Staff of the Billings, Montana, *Gazette. Yellowstone on Fire.* Missoula, Mont.: Falcon Press, 1989.

Starkey, Edward. "Impact of Fire on Nongame Wildlife." In *Rangeland Fire Effects: A Symposium (1984).* Boise, Idaho: Bureau of Land Management, 1985.

State of the Environment: A View Toward the Nineties. Washington, D.C.: Conservation Foundation, 1987.

Stephenson, David. "The Use of Charred Black Spruce Bark by Snowshoe Hare." *Journal of Wildlife Management* 49(1985): 296–300.

Summary of Public Comments on the Fire Management Policy Report. Yellowstone National Park, Wyo.: USDA Forest Service/. U.S. National Park Service, 1989.

"Sunnyside/Black Tiger Fire (Colorado) Individual Fire Report." Boulder, Colo.: USDA Forest Service, 1989.

Tausch, Robin, and Neil West. "Differential Establishment of Pinyon and Juniper Following Fire." *American Midland Naturalist* 199(1988): 174–184.

Tiedemann, Arthur. *Effects of Fire on Water.* General Technical Report WO-10, Washington, D.C.: USDA Forest Service, 1978.

Trenberth, Kevin, Grant Branstator, and Phillip Arkin. "Origins of the 1988 North American Drought." *Science* 242(1988): 1640–1645.

Turbak, Gary. "To Hell and Back in a Pup Tent." *American Forests*, September 1986, pp. 29–48.

Using Meteorology to Forecast Fires' Severity. Berkeley, Calif.: Pacific Southwest Forest and Range Experiment Station, n.d.

VanNao, T., ed. *Forest Fire Prevention and Control.* The Hague: Dr. W. Junk, 1982.

Wade, Dale, and James Lunsford. *A Guide for Prescribed Burning in Southern Forests.* Atlanta: USDA Forest Service, Southern Region, 1989.

Walsh, Tom, ed. *Wilderness and Wildfire.* Miscellaneous publication 50. Missoula: University of Montana School of Forestry, 1989. Includes the following:

Ohler, David. "John Q. Public Versus Smokey the Bear: Liability and Natural Fire Policy," pp. 8–10.

Power, Tom. "The Economics of 'Let It Burn'," p. 7.

Ryan, Kevin. "Climate Change, Wildfire and Wilderness," pp. 18–21.

Wakimoto, Ronald. "Let It What?" pp. 4–6.

Warren, John. *Fire Mapping with the Fire Mouse Trap.* Boise, Idaho: USDA Forest Service Advanced Electronics Systems Development Group, 1986.

————, *Thermal Infrared Users Manual.* Boise, Idaho: USDA Forest Service, Boise Interagency Fire Center, 1984.

Warren, John, and Ralph Wilson. *Airborne Infrared Forest Fire Surveillance—A Chronology of USDA Forest Service Research and Development.* USDA Forest Service General Technical Report INT-115. Ogden, Utah: Intermountain Forest and Range Experiment Station, 1981.

Weaver, Harold. "Fire and Its Relationship to Ponderosa Pine," pp. 147–149. In *Proceedings of the Seventh Annual Tall Timbers Fire Ecology Conference, 1968.*

Webster, Henry. "Urban Development in Forests: Sources of American Difficulties and Possible Approaches." *Renewable Resources Journal,* Summer 1989, pp. 8–11.

Wells, Carol. *Effects of Fire on Soil.* General Technical Report WO-7. Washington, D.C.: USDA Forest Service, 1978.

Wells, Wade G., II. "The Effects of Fire on the Generation of Debris Flows in Southern California." *Reviews in Engineering Geology* 7(1987): 105–114.

Western Wildlands. Missoula: University of Montana School of Forestry, Summer 1989. Issue devoted to the Yellowstone fires. Includes the following:

Davis, Kathleen, and Robert Mutch. "The Fires of the Greater Yellowstone Area: The Saga of a Long Hot Summer," pp. 2–9.

Romme, William, and Don Despain. "The Long History of Fire in the Greater Yellowstone Ecosystem," pp. 10–17.

Schullery, Paul, and Don Despain. "Prescribed Burning in Yellowstone National Park: A Doubtful Proposition," pp. 30–34.

Singer, Francis, and Paul Schullery. "Yellowstone Wildlife: Populations in Progress," pp. 18–22.

Wakimoto, Ronald. "National Fire Management Policy: A Look at the Need for Change," pp. 35–39.

White, R. A., and M. F. Rush. "An Example of International Assistance: The Jiagedagi Fire Management Project." Paper presented at Meeting Global Wildland Fire Challenges, Boston, July 23–26, 1989.

Whitmore, T. C. "Canopy Gaps and the Two Major Groups of Forest Trees." *Ecology* 703(1989): 538–541.

Whitney, Stephen. *Western Forests.* New York: Knopf, 1985.

Williams, Edward, and Archer Smith. "Case History of the Brasstown Fire." Paper presented at the National Fire Behavior School, San Dimas, Calif., 1962.

Williams, T. "Incineration of Yellowstone." *Audubon* 91(1989): 38–85.

Wood, Wilbur. "Political Fires Still Smoulder." *The Nation,* August 7–14, 1989, pp. 162–164.

Wright, Henry, and Arthur Bailey. *Fire Ecology: U.S. and Southern Canada.* New York: Wiley, 1982.

Wuerthner, George. *Yellowstone and the Fires of Change.* Salt Lake City: Dream Garden Press, 1988.

Zuckert, Judi. *National Park Service Wildland Fire Report, 1988.* Boise, Idaho: National Park Service, Branch of Fire Management.

INDEX

810006

S0-BCY-793

3 1230 0091 1 0004

"[These essays] explore isolation, weaving together the intangible and material touchstones of life periods with remarkable ease . . . Beneath an eternal-boy persona, a surprising tenderness reveals the struggle for human connection . . . *Everything We Don't Know* demonstrates the pain of sometimes misguided perceptions, and the many routes an insatiable mind can take."

—*Foreword Reviews*

"What a great read! Aaron Gilbreath has put together as fine a book of essays as you're likely to find these days. At times I felt as if I could be reading a John Jeremiah Sullivan collection. Aaron Gilbreath's strong, candid yet insightful first-person narrative is compelling, clearly honest, and frankly, it reminded me of many things I'd prefer to forget, yet did so powerfully enough to keep me coming back for more."

—James Williamson, guitarist of Iggy and the Stooges

"I've been jonesing for the nex~~~~~~~~~~~
Aaron Gilbreath's *Everything W(~~~~~
failed relationships, poverty, kn~~~~~~
recovery—it's like a primer on~~~~~~
American living, written with h~~~~~~
loved this collection."

The Urbana Free Library

To renew: call 217-367-4057
or go to urbanafreelibrary.org
and select **My Account**

—George Singleton, author of *Calloustown*

"Aaron Gilbreath's first collection of essays, *Everything We Don't Know*, is a rowdy, exuberant, obsessive, and often hilarious examination of the ennui and energy of a youth spent rambling through the wild west and other meaningful landscapes. Combining a novelist's understanding of narrative structure and pacing with the essayist's digressive talents, Gilbreath creates a voice that embodies the best journalistic qualities of Hunter S. Thompson, Mary Karr, and Joan Didion. Gilbreath's essays combine humorous, unsentimental, unflinching prose with rigorous research, harrowing drama, and confessional moments of deep reflection. *Everything We Don't Know* is a testament to the adage that the greatest gift any writer possesses is a curious mind; and the abundant fruits of Gilbreath's curiosity end up being the greatest gift of this book."

—Steven Church, founding editor of *The Normal School*
and author of *One with the Tiger*

"*Everything We Don't Know* is an electric, funny, and far-reaching collection about Gilbreath's early loves and misadventures growing up out west. Sometimes ecstatic, sometimes angst-filled, he follows where curiosity leads, anchoring himself in resiliency and feeling, intelligence and humility. The essay "It's Really Something You Should Have Examined," about his girlfriend Abby and his ferret Wiggy, highlights Gilbreath at his quirky and tender best."

—Marcia Aldrich, author of *Girl Rearing* and
Companion to an Untold Story

"Aaron Gilbreath writes the kind of essays I'm always crossing my fingers for when I open a new collection. He grabs the threads of history, nature, pop culture, geography, and travel, and weaves a kind of wild web around the personal essay. Honest, open, deft, and able to turn a phrase like a bad ass—Gilbreath is now on my shortlist of go-to essayists."

—Amber Sparks, author of *The Unfinished World* and
May We Shed These Human Bodies

"Gilbreath is among that rare breed of writer with both a journalist's keen eye for observation and discovery, and a memoirist's skill for shining a light on our human foibles, mistakes, and thwarted ambitions. His brilliant examinations expand and contract seamlessly between the outer world and his own inner life—from Googie architecture to the Redwood Forest to his harrowing efforts to kick heroin. Gripping, honest, and endlessly intelligent, *Everything We Don't Know* marks the debut of a major literary talent."

—Justin Hocking, author of *The Great Floodgates of the Wonderworld*

"Aaron Gilbreath's new collection of essays shatters the tenets of memoir, and leaves the shards out in the sun to stew, before putting them back together in ways more frazzled, distressed, hilarious, scarred, and thereby more human, and true. Along the way, Gilbreath's exhilaratingly cockeyed meditations on the seemingly mundane detritus of our world—when leashed to engagements of friends, jobs, lovers, family, strange music, and stranger architecture—are allowed to dovetail with (in his words), "these mythic notions [that] colonize your head." I, for one, am grateful to have had my head colonized by these wonderful essays."

—Matthew Gavin Frank, author of *The Mad Feast* and *Preparing the Ghost*

EVERY THING WE DON'T KNOW

ESSAYS
AARON
GILBREATH

CURBSIDE SPLENDOR

CURBSIDE SPLENDOR

All rights reserved. No part of this book may be reproduced in any form or by any electronic or mechanical means, including information storage and retrieval systems, without permission in writing from the publisher, except in the case of short passages quoted in reviews.

Published by Curbside Splendor Publishing, Inc., Chicago, Illinois in 2016.

First Edition
Copyright © 2016 by Aaron Gilbreath
Library of Congress Control Number: 2016949234

ISBN 978-1-940430-83-6
Edited by Alison True and Naomi Huffman
Book design by Alban Fischer

Manufactured in the United States of America.

www.curbsidesplendor.com

CONTENTS

EVERYTHING WE DON'T KNOW

DREAMS OF THE ATOMIC ERA

By the time I recognized their gaudy beauty in 1995, the 1950s and '60s motels along Van Buren Street had largely turned into rent-by-the-hour sex dens and the haunts of junkies and crack smokers. Those buildings that had ceased operation sat fenced and boarded up, colonized by squatters and pigeons, pending future demolition. In the thirty years since its heyday, Phoenix, Arizona's "Motel Row" had degenerated from class to kitsch, and finally into one of my hometown's most crime-ridden corridors, a parched vacation-land graveyard desiccating in the same desert sunlight that once drew its customers. I wanted to photograph the vernacular architecture before the 'dozers arrived: the funky fonts, Polynesian huts, upswept flying-to-the-moon roofs and signs that said "Coffee Shop" in baby blue. I'd already shot the fronts of maybe ten motels, both functioning and condemned, and had collected from local antique stores all the vintage postcards featuring their images. The time had come to venture inside. So I jumped the fence one morning at the condemned Newton's Inn and Prime Rib.

I was cornered by the time I heard claws on the pool deck. I spun around from the boarded office window I was about to photograph, and there it was: a Dalmatian crouched seven feet in front of me, ready to pounce. The dog inched closer, barking and growling and showing its teeth. It trapped me by what used to be the door to the front desk. Weathered boards covered the windows behind me. A cyan and orange row of rooms stretched to my right. In front of me the kidney-shaped pool, black water stiffening in the bottom, palm fronds and pigeon parts floating atop its skin. To escape, I'd have to hustle past the pool toward the gap in the brick fence where I'd entered—some sixty feet away—then cross the forty feet of naked dirt between it and the two fences I'd jumped. This dog would overtake me in the open. I imagined its jaws clamping on my ankles, lashing its head from

11

side-to-side like a feeding crocodile while gnawing them to a grizzly pâté of bloody socks and tendons. I shifted to the right to put the pool between us. It scrambled to meet me on the other side, snarling.

Garbage littered the pool deck: gravel, cinder blocks, roofing material, beer bottles. I picked up the long metal base of what might have once been a stop sign. Banging it against the ground I yelled, "Go! Get out of here!" The dog crouched, barking louder. The thought of hurting an animal nauseated me, but if this one charged, was there a choice? Head down and snout out, its arched back echoed the shape of the sweeping roof at the neighboring Sun Dancer Hotel, a Googie parabola poised for launch.

Brittle chips of gunite flew as I pounded the rod over and over. Puffs of dust drifted between us. People once vacationed here, I thought. Families en route to California swam, sunbathed, and digested big steak dinners while watching Ed Sullivan in their refrigerated rooms. Newton's original yellow brochure said, "Modern as tomorrow . . . Yet based on a proven reputation for hospitality."

When the dog made quick steps forward, I stomped my feet and stood my ground.

* * *

The forces that draw hobbyists to their favorite things are often inexplicable. Whether the hobby is golf, porcelain angels, or chopper bicycles, why these and not something else? Even when I was twenty my interests were eclectic. Throughout childhood and adolescence I'd gone through what my parents accurately called phases. "Aaron's going through another phase," they'd say without a hint of disapproval. As a kindergartener I'd fixated on trains. Mom and Dad took me to the Burlington Northern Santa Fe tracks in Flagstaff to search for rusty ties. They hung reproduction oil lamps in my room back in Phoenix, bought me a model electric train set to play with, conductor's overalls to wear. Then it was *Star Wars*. Everything had to be *Star Wars*: toys, t-shirts, sleeping bag, sheets, shampoo, birthday cakes, Pez dispensers, silverware. Then I went gaga for GI Joe toys, then comic books, then anime, skateboarding, southern California beach culture, Vintage Hang Ten shirts culled from thrift stores, European beer, surf instrumental music, antique A&W root beer mugs, loose leaf tea. One year I wanted to replace my brown bedroom carpet with beach sand and sleep in a hammock between two fake palm trees; the next year that bedroom was decorated with Depeche Mode posters and bootleg vinyl. The world was new and fascinating. Everything held potential interest, yet my attention focused intensely on one thing at a time. Obsessions were how I processed information.

Sometime in 1995 I discovered architect Alan Hess' book *Googie: Fifties Coffee Shop Architecture*. I found the title in the index of another book, or maybe I spotted it on a bookstore shelf. I can't recall, but the effect was profound. It wed my eyes to the pastel majesty of the fifties and early-sixties, catalyzing a reaction as mysterious as the chemistry of pheromones yet as binding as marriage, a love affair that outlasted all future phases.

Googie was a bold, innovative style of commercial architecture born in post-WWII Los Angeles. Often called Coffee Shop Modern, sometimes Populuxe, Jet Age, Space Age, and Doo-Wop, Googie can be traced to a coffee shop architect John Lautner designed in 1949. The shop was called Googie's. It stood on the corner of Sunset Boulevard and Crescent Heights, a dissenter in a sea of Art Deco and Streamline Moderne. When Yale Professor Douglas Haskell was driving north on Crescent Heights with an architectural photographer in 1952, they came upon Lautner's creation. "Stop the car!" Haskell yelled. "This is Googie architecture." While Haskell was uneasy about what seemed its flamboyance, he did recognize the design's uniqueness and acknowledged experimentation's role in birthing new architectural forms. To him, Lautner's coffee shop epitomized a new style, which he called "Googie architecture" in an article in *House and Home* magazine. No longer referring simply to the coffee shop but to Lautner's pioneering work, the term Googie spread though architectural circles nationwide. So-called serious architects dismissed it as garish, using Googie as a slur for design excess, sloppy workmanship and lack of discipline. But others soon refined and reinterpreted Lautner's concept, most notably the LA firm of Louis Armét and Eldon Davis. During the fifties and mid-sixties, Googie spread throughout California and the US, not only in coffee shops but bowling alleys, diners, motels, car washes, and car dealerships.

While difficult to define, Googie was highly recognizable. Its landscapes were tropical and lush. Buildings frequently contained indoor gardens. Other architects later mixed in idealized Polynesian elements such as coconut palms, thatched huts and Tiki heads and torches. Buildings were composed of organic forms, highly abstracted, that seemed to defy gravity. Boomerang shapes infused every aspect of the design, from the roof to the corners, including Formica countertop decorations, steel beams and butterfly chairs. Amoebas were also popular motifs, found in logos, signage, pools' shapes and menus, as were with the intertwined loops of the stylized atom. This was the Atomic Era, the Jet Age, later the Space Age. As scientists explored the inner space of the atom, astronauts explored outer space, and UFOs held America's attention. Googie incorporated simplified visual elements from both space exploration and molecular science. Concrete dome-shaped buildings took the form of flying saucers. Others more subtly evoked the Martian cities and space stations then appearing in movies and on the covers of sci-fi books and magazines. Spiky starburst decorations resembled Sputnik. Twinkling asterisks looked like stars.

Another architectural signature was the parabolic, boomerang-shaped roof. These gave the impression of movement, suspended animation, a building preparing for takeoff. Sweeping roofs announced the building's presence to approaching motorists from a great distance—a necessity since car travel had become a key component of commerce. The added room these roofs created accommodated large sheet glass windows in the front and sides of buildings. This broke down the barrier between inside and outside, allowed sunlight to pour into a bright, festive interior, and gave passing drivers a view of all the fun they could be having if they stopped in for a meal.

Part Jetson's, part Disney Tomorrowland, Googie's aim, as with most vernacular architecture, was to efficiently utilize roadside commercial locations while capturing consumers' attention in a highly competitive marketplace. Unlike other designs, Googie embodied the era's vision of a utopian future, the promise of atomic science, space exploration, a booming economy. It pointed the way to progress.

The Googie aesthetic appealed to my sensibility. The fonts. The cheeky allure of pink next to yellow next to powder blue. Red and white Terrazzo flooring infused with gold flecks and the gaudiness of flagcrete. It gripped my attention as vigorously as the face of a beautiful woman, yet it embodied what, in his song with that title, Thelonious Monk called an "ugly beauty."

I had long been a sucker for the nostalgic. I went through a Medieval period as a kid, reading everything I could about knights and castles, followed by a WWII period filled with tanks, grenades, and the Western Front. I watched *Happy Days*, *Leave It To Beaver*, *The Andy Griffith Show*, and *The Brady Bunch*. Clichéd as it sounds, the fifties and early-sixties seemed so quaint, so contented. It was an impression my father confirmed. Dad called it "a wonderful time to live." He described how girls on roller skates delivered burgers at the Phoenix carhops he and his buddies frequented. He talked about the now demolished drive-in theaters where they took dates. "There was something about reaching in to a sliding top cooler at a fruit stand and pulling out an ice cold bottle of Coke," he said. "Everything seemed colder in those days." My parents were kids then, entertaining big dreams like everyone else about the big houses, families, and careers they'd have. Dad wanted to play boogie woogie piano in a country swing band like Bob Wills' Texas Playboys. Mom wanted to do social work or join the Peace Corps. I wanted to experience the Eisenhower Era's culture. The post-war optimism. A world where everyone shimmied 'n' shaked, did the hop, then the bop, then they swapped and did the stroll. A time when milk was still wholesome, bacon wasn't bad for you, and root beer arrived in thick frosted mugs.

Once I saw the black and white photos in Hess' book, these notions gripped me with an evangelical force. I fantasized about walking into a coffee shop, waving to the waitress and saying, "Hey Peggy, howya doin'? Cup of coffee when you get a minute," and having her wink and say, "Sure thing, sugar," as I seated myself at the Formica counter between a guy in a checked fedora and a woman in cat eye glasses and a rhinestone cardigan. There, in view of a parking lot filled with finned cars, I would read the paper. I was twenty years old. I never read the paper, not even for school work. But planted in that shiny metal swiveling chair I would feed myself pieces of fried eggs and ham without taking my eyes off the newsprint.

This was the other part of Googie's allure: I associated the aesthetic with my parents, and the older I got, the harder I clung to them against the ravaging current of time. Even though I wasn't aware of it back when I was taking photos, I seemed to think that by experiencing old drive-ins and diners, I could experience my parents as they were at my age. I'm glad I never realized this back then, because it seems more delusional than romantic: thinking that the taste of a lime Ricky, or even knowing what one was, could facilitate such intimacy. Yet that's exactly what I wanted.

The movie *Short Cuts* came out in 1993, *Pulp Fiction* and *Reality Bites* in 1994. When I watched them again sometime in '95, I noticed certain scenes were set in Googie coffee shops. In *Pulp Fiction*, Travolta sits opposite Samuel L. Jackson in a pink vinyl booth and offers him bacon. "Pigs are filthy animals," Jackson says. "I ain't eat nothin' that ain't got enough sense to disregard its own feces." I did some research. The shop was called the Hawthorne Grill, originally named Holly's. Armét and Davis designed it. And it sent my mind racing: if these places were still open, my little dream was doable. I had to find them.

* * *

With my native Phoenix a mere three hundred and seventy-five miles from Los Angeles, Googie had spilled easily into the city. Once I started searching, I found numerous examples: Christown Lanes bowling alley on 19th Avenue and Bethany Home Road; the Herman & Sons Pianos store on 20th Street and Camelback; a Methodist church behind Los Arcos Mall; a Tiki Dairy Queen on 70th Street and McDowell. There were scattered Googie car washes and car dealerships too, and a tall white building on Central Avenue that resembled a giant punch card. But it was East Van Buren that housed the densest cluster.

Named after the eighth US President, the street runs east and west through downtown Phoenix. City founder Jack Swilling built his farm between 32nd and 36th streets south of Van Buren in 1867. From those early days until the 1920s, it remained a quiet rural road on the northern edge of town connecting Phoenix to adjacent Mesa and Tempe. As the automobile grew in popularity, the road's location made it such an important corridor that, after WWII, four highways converged on it: highways 60, 70, 80, and 89. People traveling between the East Coast and southern California, Sonora, Mexico, and Alberta, Canada traversed Swilling's old road.

During the twenties and thirties, locals built auto camps, huts, and cottages to capitalize on the traffic. These places more closely resembled campgrounds than motels, bearing such names as Camp Phoenix, Camp Montezuma, and Autopia. Camp Joy, one of the first, sat on 22nd Street in what was then the country beyond the city's eastern boundary. "Rates $1.00 a Day and Up," its postcard advertised. "Present this card to manager and he will do his best to please you." As auto-travelers became more sophisticated, so did their demands, and the trend soon shifted from camps to autocourts, to hotels and motor hotels—later shortened to motels. Soon motels and their ilk stood side-by-side, one after the other, competing with each other and numerous souvenir stands for tourist dollars. Piano bars and dance halls popped up, then coffee shops, steak houses, even a boxing and wrestling arena. Signs lined the highways coming in to the Valley, announcing the bargains and services that awaited travelers.

Van Buren became known as Motel Row. "The Pyramid Motel," one postcard said, located "in the heart of Motel Row." Businesses advertised: Kitchenettes. Baby cribs. Telephone in each room. Singles, doubles, family suites. Texas length Queen size twin bed. Filtered and heated pool. Hi-fi, radio, free color TV. Hot water in winter, refrigeration in summer. Thermostatic heat. Panel ray heat. Steam heat. Central forced air heat. Electronic baseboard heat. Refrigerated cooling. Florescent lights. Private patios. Private sun deck. Shuffleboard. Putting green. Newsstand. Dining room, banquet room, cocktail lounge, excellent café. Wall to wall carpeting. Ceramic tile baths. Modern lobby. Coffee served at no charge. Car-ports. Near airport. Minutes from downtown. Bus stop at door. Spacious, beautifully landscaped grounds. Informal resort atmosphere. Designed with an accent on vacation luxury. All major credit cards honored.

By the mid-fifties, competition grew fierce. Pools and free breakfast became outdated weapons in the commercial arms race. To differentiate themselves from the pack, businesses erected bright Googie signage, sweeping boomerang lobby roofs and devised various gimmicks to lure customers. The Ramada Inn on 38th Street built a trolley on a track to shuttle guests to their rooms. Not to be outdone, the Hiway House on 32nd installed a miniature train for kids to ride. As in Las Vegas, Van Buren motels decked themselves in exotic themes to wow visitors. There were the Western themed motels like the Stagecoach and Frontier. There were the early Americana themed motels like the Log Cabin and Old Faithful, the Arabian-themed Bagdad, Caravan and Pyramid motels, and the Mexican-themed Sombrero, El Rancho, Mission, and Montezuma. Some upscale resort hotels left large areas relatively vacant in their center so they could build casinos in case the state legalized gambling; it never did. Googie fell out of fashion in the mid-sixties, replaced by less gaudy architectural styles, but new motels went up on Van Buren reflecting the Polynesian fad sweeping the nation: the Tropics, Tahiti, Coconut Grove, Samoan Village, and the crème de la crème, the grand Kon Tiki Hotel, where celebrities like James Brown stayed while passing through town. There were over 150 tourist lodges on east Van Buren between the mid-thirties and mid-sixties, making it arguably Phoenix's best known and most traveled street. With its reputation for charm and class, citizens considered it the pride of the city, and Newton's Prime Rib was one of the best restaurants.

During my seven years living out of state, I occasionally thought of Newton's. Hearing the term "steak house" reminded me of it. An ugly bar in Oregon reminded me of it too—a tan box with a neon red Schlitz sign mounted on off-white flagcrete. For some reason, the tiki bar scene in *Goodfellas* also reminded me of it. Although Newton's restaurant wasn't Googie—no parabolic roof or starburst motifs—it exhibited all of the grand gaudiness of the era: grey cinder block walls traced with thick iron accents and light fixtures; a brightly colored interior and bright outdoor signage; and cylindrical metal lighting that hung outside, the matted surfaces of which were perforated with holes like those on a diner's heat lamp. Newton's was Atomic Era-meets-Excalibur. Sometimes I'd see old advertisements in print magazines—tinted photos of beehived women and men with skinny ties eating inside dim restaurants with red velvet walls—and I'd wonder: what state was the building in now? How much more decrepit, if it was even there at all? I Googled the name Newton's but found nothing.

I vowed that the next time I visited family in Phoenix, I'd drive by and see. Then I forgot to when I made the trip home. When I got back to Oregon I told myself: next time. But I did mention the place to my parents while visiting them.

The three of us were standing around their kitchen that day. Like many longtime Phoenicians, both my parents had eaten at Newton's. During my days photographing Van Buren, I didn't tell them about jumping the fence to enter the property, but when I mentioned Newton's in passing, Mom said, "Oh yeah, that used to be the place to eat in town. Everyone went there, all the city's bigwigs and chief muckety-mucks." Back in its heyday, the general consensus was that there were two places for great steaks in Phoenix: Durant's on Central Avenue (where patrons entered through the back door and kitchen), and Newton's. Mom pointed to Dad and said, "He used to go there on business all the time."

In the corner of the kitchen, leaning against the counter, Dad smiled. "Business was an excuse to eat," he said. "Prime rib. I loved their prime rib." Dad's eyes grew distant as he described his meal: the thick red meat marbled with fat; the rich sour cream horseradish sauce; baked potato on the side.

I said, "Well what did the interior look like?" Neither Mom nor Dad could remember details, only that it was garish.

"But the food," Dad said, nodding his head. "Phenomenal." He crossed his arms across his chest and stared into the distance.

Mom looked at him in his culinary rapture, then looked at me with her brows scrunched. She said, "Whatever happened to that place?"

During the sixties, increasing numbers of travelers began flying rather than driving. Cheap desert and a demand for housing pushed the burgeoning population to Phoenix's edges, transferring business from downtown to the burbs. The more chic, affluent districts of the newly decentralized metropolis migrated northward, leaving once classy downtown joints like Newton's and Durant's wanting for business. It was a pattern repeating itself across the United States. The new interstates delivered the lethal blows.

First the Feds built I-17 in 1969. Faster, more modern, it featured its own set of services. And as in so many cities, as the interstate siphoned away traffic, the old commercial strip fell into disrepair. Fewer vacationers rented rooms. Few stopped for dinner or recharged at coffee shops. They didn't even drive the road. The Caravan Inn once touted its Oasis restaurant as "one of Phoenix's most popular dining places." By the time the Feds finished their piecemeal construction of Phoenix's I-10 in the eighties, the Oasis no longer existed. Approximately twenty functioning motels remained, and Phoenix's version of the Vegas Strip, our Great White Way, had become what the locals called the Boulevard of Blowjobs.

Desperate for customers, motels installed mirrored ceilings, waterbeds and closed-circuit pornography. Signs advertised adult movies and hourly rates. A few places featured Magic Fingers vibrating beds. In turn, innkeepers facilitated the street's transformation from nationally renowned vacation destination to locally feared red light district. Crime rates soared.

On the street and in police blotters, Van Buren became known as VB, and related news stories centered largely on drug deals, robbery, murder and prostitution. As a kid, it was the butt of all my friends' and my drug jokes. "Let's go score some crack on VB," we'd say, or, "Hey, I saw your mom the other night. She was strutting VB." The name seemed close to VD for a reason.

When I discovered the street's architectural splendors, the Sun Dancer was closed. The Kon Tiki was closed. The Tropics Motor Hotel's coffee shop no longer served coffee or had functioning doors. Same with the cafes at the Sands and Desert Rose. Newton's Inn and its prime rib restaurant had been condemned for four years.

Friends I told this to asked me, "Who cares?" I played Esquivel's "Mucha Muchacha" on my stereo and wondered how they couldn't recognize the grandeur of gaudiness. They also failed to appreciate Esquivel's space age lounge music, so eventually I quit discussing Googie and explored the street alone.

* * *

Although this might sound like a line from a B-movie, in the Atomic Era, nuclear energy was touted as the future source of the entire world's power. Many scientists, boosters, and business people said that one day, not only would automobiles be atomic, but also appliances, medicine, weapons, food preservation techniques, and the entire urban grid. Fanciful as it sounds to our modern ears, back then, nuclear applications seemed limitless, and the American public was enthralled. Thirty-five million people watched the live television broadcast of the 1952 atomic test at Yucca Flat, Nevada. Just as that mushroom cloud had lifted into the heavens, so too would the imagined luxuries and conveniences awaiting the average citizen. People actually believed that large nuclear power stations would soon make electricity so abundant that it would be too cheap to meter. They believed that nuclear energy would do for civilization what coal and oil could never do, and that history would recognize this period as a milestone in human technological and cultural development on par with the first smelting of bronze and the Industrial Revolution.

Like the music on the radio, people were jazzed. Ford Motor Company unveiled its nuclear concept car in 1958. Named the Nucleon, it included a small nuclear reactor in the vehicle's rear in place of the traditional internal combustion engine. Two booms suspended a power capsule which held the radioactive core. Depending on the size of the core, Ford said cars such as the Nucleon would be capable of traveling some 5,000 miles without recharging. Once the core expired, owners would just take it to a conveniently located charging station, which designers imagined would eventually take the place of gas pumps.

In 1963, the California state and federal governments proposed detonating small nuclear explosives to cut a section of I-40 through southern California's Bristol Mountains. As unsafe as that sounds now, the idea was one of many proposed by Project Plowshare, a scientific organization investigating civilian applications of atomic energy. Part of the US's larger Peaceful Nuclear Explosions program, or PNE, one of the group's principal selling points, was nuclear technology's low-cost compared to conventional construction methods. A 1964 *Time* article recorded Plowshare scientists at a Livermore, California laboratory expounding on nuclear devises' potential use in canal-digging, specifically in widening the Panama Canal and cutting a new Isthmian channel through Nicaragua along what was nicknamed the Pan-Atomic Canal. "Ploughshare men," the article reported, "are sure that if modern, 'clean' explosives are used, the radioactivity that escapes will be of little significance."

Nuclear medicine remains an active branch of medicine. Companies still irradiate food to preserve it. But, like the Nucleon, the idea of nuclear commercial engineering died on the drawing table, and by the late seventies, atomic energy had assumed a more sinister reputation. Nuclear weapons proliferation increased public fear of cataclysmic war. In 1979, one of Three Mile Island's reactors suffered a partial meltdown, making it the worst civilian nuclear accident in US history. Chernobyl's reactor exploded in 1986. Both of these incidents effectively crippled the nuclear power industry and extinguished the last rosy embers of the Atomic Era's consuming optimism. The audacious names, the heroic plans, the frequent use of the term "modern"—it all sounds so over-the-top now, like society temporarily went nuts. But maybe it's no different than our world now. Maybe a nuclear utopia is no more outlandish than the modern idea that fast internet connections and shared information will somehow improve all human life, giving voice to the voiceless, eradicating ignorance, and erasing humanity's religious and political divisiveness so that people across the world all see that we're far more alike than we are different. Every age has its grand delusions, and every era, like every person, is defined as much by its accomplishments as by its fantasies, the ones we dream and the ones we fail to achieve. As we age, our own dreams wither and our vision of all possible futures narrows. If we live in the same place long enough, the streets we drive, the buildings we pass, will bear the markings of our lives, and sometimes carry painful reminders of our youth, our thwarted ambitions, and people who have died, along with the condemned husks of our former selves. Maybe that's just the cynic in me talking, the hardened aging realist who has seen the street of dystopian dreams, the place where the future once imagined now lays in ruin, because the future finally arrived.

* * *

In the *Phoenix New Times* article "Tough Row to Ho," reporter Susy Buchanan accompanied police on a 2004 roundup of Van Buren prostitutes. In a group of handcuffed sex workers, one named "The Troll" sobbed beside a blonde, giving the cops a story about wanting to straighten up her life, pleading with them that, if they'd just let her go, she'd return to school in Colorado and become a beautician. The blonde eyeballed her disapprovingly and said, "You a ho! It ain't never gonna be straightened up. Once a ho, always a ho. Get used to it."

East VB was such a fertile dump that sex workers from cities across the county traveled there to work. Just as it had in its days as a resort destination, it had earned a local and national reputation. On a typical night in the 1990s, a driver could spot twenty to fifty girls, women and men dressed as women pacing the cracked sidewalks. Black, white, heavy, thin, all the clichés were true: they wore short skirts, high heels, big hair, gaudy make-up and tight, low-cut tops that revealed deep cleavage and fatty midriffs. While most were middle-aged, some of the women cops arrested were in their sixties and seventies, old enough to have vacationed there with their parents as children.

In people's minds, the street came to symbolize the boundary between the "safe" and the "dangerous," meaning the white and non-white, the privileged and non-privileged, sides of town. And most people I knew would away from it. Except for one excursion.

Three friends and I once drove there on a Friday night during our senior year of high school. We were bored. It was late. We'd been drinking. Someone suggested we "yell at the hookers." Friend 1 found the idea amusing. Friend 2 found it titillating. Being a reliable risk-taker who had yet to develop a more inclusive sense of empathy, the prospect of a dangerous adventure thrilled me. The lackadaisical Friend 3 went along for the ride.

It might have taken ten minutes to drive from Friend 1's affluent north Phoenix neighborhood. There, as one car in a series of slow cruisers, we drifted past figures shuffling in front of the neon signs. Men slouched at bus stops waiting for customers, not buses. Women stood beside payphones engaged in pretend conversations. We started yelling out the windows. "What's up honey?" "Looking for a good time?" I knew it was cruel. We were mocking the unfortunate. It makes me cringe to think how a bunch of us white kids thought this was exciting: the danger, the grime, the empowering knowing that we'd sleep that night on the safe side of town. Knowing it didn't change my behavior, but every day these women faced actual danger and survived in a culture that perpetually demeaned and repressed them. Whenever some stranger grunted on top of them, whenever they got arrested on Van Buren, they faced the fact of their limited means and thwarted aspirations, sacrificing part of the youthful visions of their future selves in order to make a living. These women probably grew up wanting to do something rewarding or different with their lives. Now they were here, enduring the added insult of high school boys' callous curiosity.

For some reason, Friend 1 stopped his Bronco beside a tall woman in a miniskirt. The gray spandex terminated along the seam of her butt cheeks. She leaned toward the passenger window and said something about a ride. Then she climbed into the back seat and scooted between me and Friend 2.

"Who's going first?" she said. She looked at me, then at Friend 2. Friend 3 wouldn't turn around. The smell of cigarette smoke and perfume filled the car. I caught Friend 1's terrified eyes in the rearview.

Friend 2 said he'd go and the rest of us said no thanks, we'd changed our mind and will let you out right here. "Oh no," the woman said. "My time is precious. You think you can go wasting it with this shit?" We apologized in whiney voices and told her we'd drop her off wherever she wanted. When I turned to check her out, I noticed the bony cheeks, pronounced Adam's apple and thin over-treated hair.

Someone started arguing with her, and soon our overlapping chatter reached a furious pitch: we aren't paying, we don't want anything, no something for nothing, get out, please get out now.

She said, "I got a pistol in my purse, honey, so don't you sass me."

Adrenaline flooded my insignificant body. Her right thigh pressed against mine. I looked at her purse. It sat on her lap. I wondered, was she bluffing? Who would she shoot first: us in back or them in the front? I kept my eyes on her long veiny hands. If she reached for that purse, I vowed to grab her wrists and wrestle it from her. Instead of a struggle, someone said okay and handed her some bills. We pulled into a side street where she lifted her towering frame from the seat, leaning so far over that her square ass passed inches from my face before it slipped into the night.

We deserved much worse. Her time was precious. And you can't go around treating people like that. My parents had taught me better, yet driving away from Van Buren that night, my friends and I didn't discuss our failure to respect these women's humanity. Instead, we laughed about the incident because, terrifying as it was, it made us feel like survivors, tough and triumphantly returning from this imagined battlefield. Like most teenagers, we loathed our hometown for its asphyxiating boredom, and we refused to see ourselves as anything more than victims of tedium, searching for excitement. This is why discovering Googie on Van Buren years later felt like a revelation: finally there was something interesting to do in Phoenix.

Like most twenty-somethings, I wanted nothing more than to escape to some place cool like San Francisco or San Diego. Googie transformed Van Buren from the skuzziest to the most interesting place in town, which transformed Phoenix into someplace bearable. Granted, VB offered none of the innovative eateries captured in Hess' book—no Coffee Dan's to photograph, no bright, verdant interiors like Pann's or Ship's. But in Phoenix, looking at the burned out skeletons of vacation destinations seemed better than getting stoned at a friend's house, watching TV, or going to the mall, which were my usual entertainment options. I imagined a local newspaper headline: "Kid Finds Something Interesting in Capital's Most Notorious Crime Zone."

So I'd park, and men in baggy uniform pants and white tees would change direction to walk toward my car. "What's up man?" they'd say. If I passed them while driving at my slow investigative pace, they'd spot me peering and think I was interested in them rather than the motels behind them. They'd say, "Whadyou need?" I'd shake my head, say, "No thanks man, I'm good."

When I came back with the camera, I photographed the buildings from the sidewalk. Stepping from my car felt dangerous. The whole act felt invasive. It attracted attention. People watched me from motel windows and the steps of nearby trailers. I kept a two-inch knife in my pocket, but the sidewalk offered the red light's main form of protection: exposure. Cars whizzed past. Sometimes pedestrians: a teen in a wife-beater with a tattooed neck; a grown man riding a child's BMX. I'd nod. A few nodded back. Eye contact seemed bold enough to double as a warning: I see you, so don't mess with me. Some people eyeballed my 35mm. It was my grandpa's. Mom had given it to me when he passed away that summer.

Other locals greeted the camera with suspicion. They peered from behind curtains, crouched smoking on porches and squinting at me. Since I wasn't there to make a purchase, I assumed they thought I was a NARC or some unwelcome source of trouble. When one East Indian man stepped from a motel office and into the frame, he waved me off. "No photo, no photo," he said. I apologized, explaining I was interested only in the architecture. He shook his head and yelled louder, but the sidewalk was public property, so there was nothing he could do about it.

A skinny shirtless man once leaned out of his unit at the Arizona Motel. "Whata'you up to?" he said. His body was a tangle of sinewy muscle, skin pulled taught across stomach, arms and neck. A large mattress set on the side of his wall beside a few wooden boards. I told him I was photographing the architecture. When he asked if I was with the paper, I said no, and he said he was a scrapper. Not like a fighter, he explained. He owned a pickup and kept regular routes collecting any spare parts or metal he could sell to a dealer. "You want to see something worth takin' pictures of," he said, "man, scrapping is it." Still convinced I was a reporter, he offered to let me ride with him for an article he said I should write. His life intrigued me. I told him I might take him up on that later.

If motel units' doors were open I could sometimes see into the rooms. Usually an unmade bed was the most visible detail, the corner of a mattress exposed below ruffled sheets. Other times people sat on the bed's edge, staring at a TV. Like the prostitutes, these residents were someone's children. At some point they had recognized how luck determines one's chances in childhood, and the way circumstance unwittingly narrows one's options in adulthood, squashing our innocence as we accept the fact that some of our dreams are either no longer feasible, or require too much effort to work for. I recognized this, too, but I'd benefited the other way. When I told the scrapper that I might take him up on his offer, I meant it. I wish I'd meant it more. Now that I see how empty buildings are without people, it's too late to tell their stories. But back then I didn't come for the people. I came for Googie, and I favored the details.

If I snuck inside the old kitchens, I wondered, would I find plates bearing the Tropics Motor Hotel logo? Would there be a box of old Hyatt Chalet matchbooks under the reservation desk? A dusty stack of Newton's brochures in a storage closet? I coveted what I could use: glasses imprinted with the Old Faithful Inn logo. Sun Dancer Hotel mugs, silverware, stationary, pens.

I considered bringing a set of screwdrivers and a battery-powered drill to steal the signs but feared getting caught. Even though I thought of it more as an architectural salvage operation, cops would disagree. If not me, though, who would save them? Phoenix didn't have a Mid-Century Modern preservation league back then. Unlike golf and sun-tanning, Googie didn't rouse sufficient local interest. Bulldozers kept busy clearing the way for new buildings. Without me, I knew the signs, fixtures and décor would end up in a landfill, more scrap to be melted down for material. This stuff belonged in a museum. But to rescue it, I'd have to come at night when the illicit economy thrived.

To avoid the dangers of peak hours, I only explored in the morning: eight, nine, ten a.m. Even then cops drove by. It wasn't a crime to walk with a camera, but somehow it felt like it. Because it required such fruitless and intense explanation, I never told friends about my explorations. I never even told my parents. What would they say? They wouldn't confiscate my car keys, but they would likely lecture me on the dangers of my interests. When I went to Newton's that morning, I was scheduled to be in a college class. No one knew where I was. If something happened, I hoped someone would piece the story together.

* * *

Jumping Newton's fence was easy. I parked my truck on a side street. On the Inn's more secluded west side, a cinderblock wall abutted a chain link fence topped with unruly spirals of razor wire, creating a double, back-to-back fortification.

I pulled myself up the cinderblock, found a gap in the barbs wide enough to place my feet then jumped. A forty foot dirt lot separated the street from the property. I leaned through a gap in the motel wall to study the wild garden of untended plants. It was silent, appeared empty. In case the homeless had encamped there, I walked softly atop the gravel. Raising my 35mm to my eye made me nervous, as if by lending one of my senses I forfeited the others. I hung the camera around my neck and listened for voices, breathing, shuffling feet. When fantasies rot, they smell like anything else: hot garbage cans, algae water.

Palm trees loaded with brown fronds rustled in the breeze. Pigeons flapped from the roof. I tiptoed across a patch of what was once the central lawn—four years worth of brittle die-off and blooms of Bermuda. A pair of blackened jeans laid matted to the ground, splayed as if their owner had fallen and evaporated.

In 1966 at the neighboring Travelodge, a robber once carved out the manager's eye to prove how serious he was when he demanded money. In 1974, a thief shot another manager there; he later died at St Luke's Hospital down the street.

I scanned the lot again, checking and rechecking. Icy fingers seemed to keep tickling my back. Occasionally the hiss of a passing car blew by on Van Buren, but tattered tarps blocked all views through the fence to the outside world. And that silence—it was more still than other mornings.

Amid a stand of derelict palms sat a dented white trailer. The dark arm of its tow hitch stood propped on cinder blocks. Aluminum foil covered its windows. Slowly I crept past it to the southern row of rooms. Pigeon shit splattered the walkway. Instead of boards, curtains covered the windows. When I tugged on the knobs, the doors didn't budge. I was simultaneously disappointed and relieved.

One room's door was open. I stopped and heard no movement. The silence emboldened me, so I pushed the door further to peer inside. It appeared lived-in. Mismatched blankets were heaped atop the bed. A small nightstand stood by a leather belt amid scattered tins of cat food that I hoped people hadn't eaten. And beer cans everywhere, littering the orangish-brown carpet. I wanted a photo. I'd been too nervous to snap any. But fearing the occupant might be inside, I eased the door partially closed and stepped quickly across the lot. That was when the Dalmatian came galloping.

I pulled my socks as far up my calves as they'd go, as if cotton could protect me from canines, and I kept my eyes on the dog as I bent down. When I stomped my feet he retreated slightly. When I charged a few steps forward, he stood his ground. So I kept my back straight, waved my arms and yelled. Nothing happened. He stood there growling. I stood there yelling. We could have stood there forever. Finally I started throwing garbage at him. Cardboard. Beer bottles. Rock after rock. When he backed deeper into the yard I did what my body demanded and what my mind told me not to do. I ran.

Gripping the long metal base of the sign I'd picked up, I sprinted across the pool deck. Sprinted past the row of rooms, sprinted and knew how stupid I was for doing it. If guard dogs were like cougars, running would only trigger its predatory response.

At the building's end I slipped through the fence. I kept expecting to feel teeth latch onto my ankle, to hear the sound of scrambling paws. I twirled and jogged backwards, looking for the dog, but he wasn't there. I dropped the pole. Climbed the fence. Slipped between the barbed wire and snagged my shirt, shorts and forearm on the dusty razors. As I lifted myself onto the cinder block, the Dalmatian stepped through the hole and started at me from across the lot. He just stared.

For thirteen years I wished I'd snapped a few good photos, but in my haste, I hadn't taken a single one.

* * *

When I moved back to Phoenix in June 2007, one of the first things I did was drive to VB. A lot had changed in the seven years I'd lived away. Used car lot replaced countless motel properties. Naked dirt stood in place of others. Some, like the old Arizona Palms, offered deals to airport travelers: "Two for $35.99," the sign said. "Daily • Weekly • Kitchenettes • Pool." Most had transformed into inexpensive apartments and transitional living facilities. Like the upscale Sands Hotel on 33rd, which became the United Methodist Outreach Ministry's New Day Center, the largest family homeless shelter in Phoenix.

In April 2007, the city's last three motels to offer hourly rates ceded their "Sexually Oriented Business" licenses, meaning no more hourly rates, no more signs advertising adult movies. The Log Cabin, the Classic Inn, and the Copa Motel, which, in an interesting twist, had been demolished the previous month—all three stood on VB. Police had built a case after a year-long investigation, and the City concluded what seemed obvious to all: that they were linked with prostitution.

The street was changing. Local groups unveiled plans to revitalize Van Buren by encouraging local business to open shop. As downtown gentrification crept east of Central Avenue along Motel Row, new attitudes came with it. The street fell within Phoenix Mayor Gordon's "Opportunity Corridor," a name he coined for an area filled with vacant lots, industrial sites and other under-utilized properties. It was ripe for redevelopment, what some commercial brokers called an emerging market. Redevelopment had long been waiting for a catalyst to ignite it here. That catalyst arrived in 2008 in the form of the city's new light rail system, which travels down Washington Street, a quarter mile below VB.

Before the economic slump, Van Buren redevelopment had already started. In 2006, the 178-unit Escala Central City apartments began construction on the empty Phoenix Drive-In property, the Valley's first drive-in movie theater. Escala was the first new housing project on east Van Buren in countless years, and some predicted it would be the first of many to come.

Once the motels surrendered their licenses, violent crime fell nearly forty-eight percent, and prostitution arrests decreased by more than seventy-one percent. In 2006, there were 203 prostitution arrests in the area around Van Buren and 24th. Between February 2006 and February 2007, cops made only eight prostitution arrests. And not a single homicide was reported in 2007; the previous year there were five.

I know, I know, I could hear my dad saying: "Things change—cities, people, fashion. Nothing to get sad about." I studied ecology in college, so I understand that we live in a dynamic world, that we need to adapt, because if we're not changing we're dying. Curbing crime meant East Van Buren's hard-working residents might soon enjoy a safer, more agreeable neighborhood with streets they could walk on, and new business to patronize. It also meant many of the lower income residents would get priced out. This was the start of the area's gentrification cycle, and that and the erasing of history made me wistful. Unlike hourly rates at the Log Cabin, nostalgia turned out not to be a passing fancy.

I drove west on VB, through the decreasing addresses toward downtown. In the bright sunlight, ancient images raced through my mind: the Dalmatian, the barbed wire, Newton's weedy lay out. Familiar buildings flashed on the roadside: the city's first Denny's, the drug-dealer Circle K, an old liquor store with a neon sign. Finally, I thought, I get to see Newton's again, and this time I was going to capture it on film. My heart thumped in anticipation. My fingers drummed the steering wheel, but as I sped up VB, I saw an increasing number of vacant lots, and my fingers drummed less from excitement than fear. Where motels once stood, there was now bare dirt, and weedy squares littered with beer cans and broken glass. Dry, bent palm trees and partial cement foundations broke their desolate monotony, and a deep part of me knew what I would find at 917 East.

Expecting what I found on 9th Street didn't make it any less wrenching. Newton's was gone. My camera lay on the passenger seat, and in the Inn's place stood Camden Copper Square, a high-end, two-story, gated condo complex. Trimmed palm trees decorated the property, standing sentry along the black metal fence and tan, stucco walls. The copper-colored letters on the sign called it "An Apartment Community." I knew what it was: the new face of redevelopment, designed to attract the young executives and well-to-dos who'd started frequenting the bars and restaurants popping up throughout downtown as part of the city's coordinated revitalization project—"infill" and "mixed-used" urban planners call it, "gentrification" to others.

I turned into the Camden on what was still labeled 9th. A callbox hung from a stucco island dividing incoming and outgoing traffic. When the man in front of me waved an ID before a sensor, an automated security gate entrance opened and his white Acura slipped inside. Rather than follow my natural impulse to sneak in, I turned into the adjacent visitor lot. What was there to see? These kinds of condos were a dime-a-dozen in Phoenix. They'd surrounded me my whole life.

I parked in a narrow space by the front office. Two white teenage girls sprinted down the sidewalk laughing, trying to make the light. In the park across the street, Hispanic kids in red shorts and tank tops kicked soccer balls back and forth. Three young urbanites in tight black jeans strutted toward Central Avenue and some vision of a downtown night life beyond, maybe a bar, maybe a tour of the galleries in the nearby arts district.

The Hyatt Chalet Motel across the street, renamed the 7 Motel and fenced for as long as I could remember, was gone too. It was now a dirt lot. Something upscale would soon stand there—a sushi restaurant, a wine bar with polished concrete floors and exposed duct work. The Googie starburst, asterisk, sputnik—whatever name you assign that signature ornamentation for what looks like a fizzing sparkler—were, as Hess described, a symbol of "energy caught in the act of explosive release, like a coruscating diamond." Yet Van Buren's energetic vernacular decayed so quickly that it seems never to have existed. Wildwood, New Jersey of all places has the Doo Wop Preservation League, a 501(c)3 nonprofit founded in 1997 to preserve and increase awareness of the area's Googie architecture. LA has the Los Angeles Conservancy's Modern Committee. Since 1984, they've saved priceless Googie structures like Ship's coffee shop, Pann's and the Wich Stand. Phoenix lacked any comparable mobilization.

I locked the car and walked across the street. I had always told myself that I'd sneak into the 7 Motel to photograph it from the inside. I never did. After the dog cornered me, I quit visiting VB all together, yet I kept telling myself I'd try again next weekend, next month, sometime soon. At least with my camera, I could have fixed local preservationists' error by filling the historical gap. I was ideally positioned to document it. Now here I was, another thirty-something carrying childhood regrets, a man in a lot staring at a new condo building, trying to stare the past back to life.

A SECONDARY LANDSCAPE

We reached the Canadian border at two a.m. with the PCP hidden in Dean's insulin syringes and the weed buried in the peanut butter.

During the previous three weeks that July, Dean and I had driven my dad's minivan from Phoenix up the Pacific Coast. Unshaven, studded with mosquito bites, and stinking of alder wood smoke, we hiked and camped in Redwood, Mt. Rainier, and Olympic national parks. There, far from humanity, we scaled precipitous sea stacks, touched orange sea stars in tide pools, and watched seals watch us from the breakers. While tripping on mushrooms near what was then the world's tallest tree, I perched atop an enormous fallen redwood log whose upturned trunk stood ten feet off the ground and studied a deer browsing the tangled understory. When I slipped on the mossy bark coming down, I fell face-first into ferns. Dean crouched on a nearby log, snickering maniacally. "I am tripping so hard," he said.

We were close friends, in our early twenties and halfway through college. This was precisely why we'd come: debauchery and comic misadventure. But also, the more time I spent outdoors, the more I realized that nature was more than scenic beauty and the physical challenges of rugged topography. As strange as it sounded even to me, being in wilderness awoke me to something woven into the fabric of the universe. The air in natural areas like Redwood National Park felt threaded by an enigmatic buzzing, not a measurable force like wind or gravity, but the nagging, low-frequency suggestion of scenery within the scenery, a secondary landscape. I told no one about this sensation other than Dean, and even then I struggled to describe it.

"It's the sense that there is more to reality than what we see," I kept saying during the trip. "That some meaning lurks behind the obvious phenomenological level." Dean nodded and asked questions, but my explanations failed to clarify. "It's like peripheral vision in the mind's eye," I explained, "out there on the cusp of perception. Like shadows. Rustling leaves."

Hearing myself say this aloud, I feared it sounded nuts. Back in Phoenix, I'd sometimes wondered if thoughts like these signaled the onset of a psychiatric disorder such as schizophrenia. But when I stepped back into a moist old-growth forest, the sensation returned and dispelled my concern. This perception of a nonphysical component of the physical world was real. Was it God? Heaven? Parallel dimensions? Had I been gifted with the powers of a seer?

As a friend, Dean tolerated my incessant yammering. As a fellow outdoorsman, he was attuned enough to nature to entertain challenging cosmological possibilities. "I don't believe in God per se," he said. "I do believe that things have a spirit, a life force, if that makes sense." His mom attended church every Sunday but didn't raise him Catholic. Yet, he was adamant: "There is definitely a larger force in the universe. I just don't know if it's a Christian-type god."

Whatever it was, I wanted a direct encounter with it. So when the people we were staying with in Vancouver came home with PCP on our last night in British Columbia, Dean and I bought some.

Twenty Canadian dollars got us two gelatin capsules of white powder. My friend Christie's roommates sold it to us. They'd let us sleep for three nights in their white weathered bungalow. It had tilted front columns and a warped, creaky porch. They listened exclusively to techno music by day, hit after-hours clubs at night. Dean and I could do without the techno, but Vancouver was beautiful, our hosts friendly, and we didn't want to leave. But with seven days to drive back to Phoenix and funds evaporating, we had no choice. We devised a plan. That night we would travel as far south of Bellingham, Washington as our weary bodies would allow and then sleep in the van in a hotel parking lot. We'd been doing this the whole trip to save money: sleep in the van, "shower" in gas station bathroom sinks, cook food on our camp stove. After three weeks on the road, we'd paid for only two motel rooms.

We bought the PCP after midnight and started the long drive south. The van's wheel wells, spare tire, and carpeting seemed the most obvious hiding places. Dean figured the last place border agents would look was inside his insulin syringes. At a gas station along the highway, he removed the needles from two of them, placed the inch-long capsules at their tips, then slid the orange caps over the capsules. Positioned in the center of a bag among a hundred other syringes, chances of discovery seemed slim. It was genius. I reciprocated by scooping a space in the center of our peanut butter jar, stuffing the bag of weed inside and smoothing a lid of leguminous brown over top.

A type one diabetic, Dean tested his blood sugars every few hours and gave himself shots throughout the day. On hikes, he refrigerated the glass vials in a specially fitted ice pack which he carried in his blue daypack with the bag of syringes. We were walking down the vacant shore of Washington's Olympic Coast one day, dark water lapping to our right, when he spotted a huge raven hunched over his daypack, picking through the spilled contents by our tent. At our approach, the bird leapt into flight with Dean's only bag of syringes in its beak. Waving his arms and screaming profanities, Dean ran after him. Some twenty vertical feet up, the raven dropped the bag on the gravel, cawing as he went. We retrieved them unharmed.

Dean wasn't scared of death. He'd accepted mortality while I was still playing with *Star Wars* figures. He had no choice. If his diabetes didn't kill him in his youth, it would likely get him before he got old. The injection of insulin caused spikes in blood sugar levels that often led, more than the diabetes, to debilitating complications: blindness, kidney failure, heart disease, impotence, stroke, reduced circulation, numbness in extremities, infection, gangrene, amputation. Maybe that was why he wasn't afraid of catching rattlesnakes. On weekends he scooped them up with hooked poles in the desert outside Phoenix and slipped them into gossamer nets to get a closer look. He once caught a Gila monster, North America's only venomous lizard, with his bare hands; he pinned its head with four fingers so it couldn't turn and bite him. Bad dates, boring weekends, living his whole life in Phoenix—those things worried Dean, not death.

The previous week on Mt. Rainier, I'd asked him if he thought death was the end or if something followed after. "I don't know," he said. "I'm suspicious of heaven, but reincarnation seems possible. It's an ancient tradition." I nodded my head, staring into the forest.

I didn't know what I believed. Some days I was a deist, others an atheist, most days an animist. My mom's side of the family was Jewish. When I was a kid, Mom wanted me to appreciate the basic aspects of our heritage. So I attended a Jewish elementary school, and Mom and I lit the annual Chanukah candles, but she and I never went to synagogue, and I abandoned my bar mitzvah study halfway through. Age thirteen seemed too arbitrary a number to signify anything, and tradition didn't require I know the English translation of the Hebrew I was supposed to recite. How could mindless repetition of a cryptic language make me "a man," especially when the only hair on my body was a blonde peach fuzz? Clearly I had become spiritual by age eighteen, but what sort of spirituality wasn't clear. I had no plans to practice yoga, or study Kabbalah, or read Buddhist texts. I knew only one thing: I needed a sign.

"God is a mystery," my Grandma Silvia always said. "That was Einstein's view. Maybe God is a man, and maybe a being, but to us down here, he's first and foremost a mystery." I didn't want to be worrying about God on a decadent roadtrip, but I couldn't help it. Wilderness made me think about design, which made me think about cosmology, which made me wonder if we were alone in the universe and if human existence had any purpose or not. Life and death were everywhere in the lush coastal forests. Young hemlocks grew from the soft innards of rotting tree trunks. Green shoots poked from the furry remains of decomposing animals. Death and its fertility were as in your face as trail-markers, and it all led back to questions concerning creation and meaning: why were we here? What would become of us when we were gone?

When I looked around, I found distressing potential answers: a soaring hawk carrying a wriggling snake in its claws; spawning salmon with tattered gray skin dying in streams after laying their eggs, and the way ravens and raccoons tugged at their flesh when the fish washed ashore. Was this the heartless universe that God fashioned for us? Part of me loathed any divinity who built us this way, able to question our own existence but access no answers, just carbon machines blind to our purpose, built to lay eggs, eat each other and die. It seemed cruel.

When the Peace Arch at the Canadian border came into view, Dean said, "Here goes nothing." Darkness spilled like Alaskan crude around the brightly lit station, a darkness so thick it gummed the edges of my peripheral vision.

I checked my eyes in the mirror for redness, and wiped my palms on my shorts. Canadian and US flags flew side-by-side atop the arch's crown, with the words "Children of a Common Mother" etched in the gray cement. A rattling in the van's tired engine mixed with the drone of crickets, and I'd wondered about the condition of prisons that drug smugglers were sent to, and whether we'd pay bail in American or Canadian currency. Dean cleared his throat.

The agent rattled off questions with a surprising indifference:

"Where are you coming from?"

"What was the purpose of your trip?"

"What is your destination?"

They seemed the sort of questions a spiritual leader would pose, which made me want to ask him the same things. I also wanted to blurt: that's it? All that preparation, the digging and stashing and answers Dean and I had rehearsed, for that? The agent didn't request ID. He didn't look in the van, the interior of which was stacked floor-to-ceiling with plastic bins full of clothes, canned food, river rocks, and camping gear. He simply stared puffy-eyed and dangled his arms out the station window, then he said, "Safe trip guys." We were the only car in line.

* * *

Sometime in my late teens, I'd started my wondering. All our struggles, accomplishments, heartbreak—for what? What was the point? I didn't understand where we as human beings came from, where we were going or why we were here. Where was here anyway? If the universe sat within another universe, where did that sit? Nothing made sense. When I started taking weekly hikes by myself at age eighteen, it was because the wilderness seemed to offer a more direct, unbiased source of existential information.

The outdoors had always been a presence in my life. My parents didn't hunt or fish, but as a kid they sent me to sleep-away camp in northern Arizona and Colorado, and back home, we hiked. Phoenix contains numerous desert mountain parks, and we visited many of them. We picnicked at South Mountain Park, climbed Squaw Peak, saw petroglyphs on A-mountain. Mountains piled upon jagged mountains along the brown horizon. My dad, who was raised in a small town in southern Arizona, taught me the names of rivers, mountain ranges, and plants, and about regional history. "See that?" he'd say on family outings. "That's a palo verde tree. It means 'green wood' in Spanish." And: "That there's Picacho Peak. It's the sight of the only Civil War battle fought on Arizona soil." My dad was a diehard Arizonan, enchanted by the desert, proud of his state, and he imparted this passion to me. But it was an entry-level college geology class that got me fixated.

Geo 101 was mind-blowing. Caldera-complexes, plate-tectonics, fossilization—the field's fundamentals forced me to look at landscapes as not just scenic backdrops, but as the result of the earth's dynamic physical processes. Concepts like volcanism, hydrology, ecology, and decay also brought to life the great sweep of time preceding my brief existence. Our planet was 4.5-billion-years-old, the universe 13.7. Six thousand years of recorded human history didn't register as a blip on that grand a scale. And if the mundane components of my daily life—term papers, unreciprocated crushes, which scent of detergent to buy—meant nothing measured against epochs and millennia, what was I?

When the geology professor described the Superstition Mountains east of town as "a collapsed volcano," I drove out to see them. I'd lived in Phoenix my whole life yet had never thought of those mountains as anything but the home of the storied Lost Dutchman's Mine. I parked in a lot and took a National Forest trail. The fall air was warm, the sun bright but comfortable. Native creosote bushes scented the air with a clean, medicinal fragrance, and tall saguaro cacti towered around me as I navigated the rocky slopes.

I started hiking a new local mountain range almost every week: the Goldfields, Sacatons, White Tanks, Usery Mountain. Yellow brittlebush flowers bloomed, sweetening the air with pollen. Coyotes darted between bushes and hummingbirds buzzed my head. Obsessing in a way drug counselors might describe as typical of the addictive personality, I started reading natural history, biogeography, and field guides to learn the names of local plants and animals. In turn, this led me to nature writers such as John Muir, Thoreau, Terry Tempest Williams, and Edward Abbey, which led me to introductory texts on Native American culture, and to Western existential and moral philosophers such as Hegel, Heidegger, Sartre, and Hume, and later, to mysticism.

As a budding mystic, I had long been attracted to certain oddball terms: "astral glow," "dark arts," "the seventh son," "spirited away." Certain movies, too: *Journey to the Center of the Earth*, *Planet of the Apes*, *Willy Wonka and the Chocolate Factory*. Here kids turned into blueberries. Giant lizards filled the frame. Colors flared to artificial shades of near solar-intensity then smeared across the screen, leaving tracers. Watching them as an adult, I could almost feel the tab of lysergic acid on my tongue.

After I'd started smoking pot at seventeen, I noticed a warping of my sonic predilections. The long, hypnotically repetitive instrumental end of the Butthole Surfers' song "Pepper" mesmerized me. So did the trailing echo-effect on Perry Farrell's voice in early Jane's Addiction. And Jimi Hendrix's guitar. Many Meat Puppets lyrics expressed an acute awareness of nature, like the chorus on "Leaves" where the lead singer, Curt Kirkwood, sings: "Something that's been around for so long . . . Every minute on the calendar is wrong." And lines like in the song "Things": "Ancient things' design." Whatever that did or didn't mean to the band, I knew what it meant to me: nature was big, human life small, the scope of time too great to comprehend.

As my THC-intake increased, so did my reading of anything that sounded remotely "mind-expanding": Aldous Huxley's *The Doors of Perception*, the Tao Te Ching, Castaneda's *Teachings of Don Juan*, William Burroughs. When I stumbled on the term mysticism somewhere around 1995, it confirmed what I'd secretly hoped: that potheads weren't the only ones who sensed the supernatural. People around the world from all cultures had apparently been seeking insight into their surroundings for centuries. Loosely defined, mysticism was the awareness of, and attempted union with, an ultimate reality or spiritual truth through heightened awareness and direct experience. Mystic sub-traditions existed within many popular religions: Vedanta within Hinduism, Kabbalah within Judaism, Sufism within Islam. Even Christianity had Christian mystics. While I wasn't concerned with the complex historical details, I was interested in the tradition's accessibility: regardless of your religious affiliation, the experiences of enlightenment, divine consciousness and union with God were available to anyone willing to practice a specific mystical discipline. This was a huge relief. I already practiced my own system of psycho-pharmacology. Rather than doing yoga or meditating, I continued on the lazy route of self-medication.

In one of my many surveys of Native American culture, I'd read that Native peoples had used certain psychoactives, particularly hallucinogens, for religious purposes since prehistoric times. Peyote use dated as far back as 5700 years. Yokut and Chumash Indians shamans in California had administered parts of a flowering plant called sacred datura to induce visions. The Mazatec of Oaxaca used morning glory seeds and psilocybin mushrooms for divination. The Urarina of Peruvian Amazonia used the drug Ayahuasca for ceremonial rites, same way prehistoric Europeans used the amanita mushroom. It worked for them. Couldn't it work for me?

I started small. After college classes ended for the day, I frequently climbed atop one of Phoenix's desert mountains, like Camelback or Papago, smoked a bowl of weed and stared into space. High above the city, my mind was flooded with abstract thoughts. Bright geometric patterns appeared and shifted into glorious abstractions at speeds so fast they were difficult to track. I filled spiral notebooks with environmental diatribes, seasonal observations, ideas for books I should write, digressions on ecological principles I'd just read about in Aldo Leopold's *Sand County Almanac*, and hummed the melodies of music I didn't know I could compose. Seated in the sunlight on pink granite outcroppings, these moments were monumental. When I reviewed my notes later in my bedroom, I mostly found cryptic ramblings: "Values, morals, ethics, belief system," and "Life exists → evolves to fill niches & utilize available life sustaining properties." What the hell did that mean? Trying not to despair, I would flip the

40

journal page, light a joint and start a new entry. I did this for nearly two years. By the time Dean and I took our trip in the summer of ninety-five, I had begun suffering the law of diminishing returns: the more I smoked, the less I felt, and what I felt when I felt anything was confused, numb, and unenlightened.

Every drug I took failed to deliver mystic insight.

Mushrooms amplified colors and produced amusing tracers, but portals never opened inside bedroom closets as in the film *Poltergeist*.

Acid made wallpaper patterns swim like living MC Escher prints, but whatever world it hurled my friends and I into, I wasn't disembodied enough not to feel the strychnine in my achy spinal column, and police still left tickets on the windshield of my Volkswagen that I illegally parked on a busy commercial street while we stumbled around high.

The mescaline I once ate while camping near Sedona made me see red eyes in the forest all night. But the mythic creatures I hoped they were attached to never emerged to deliver wise messages, and the one other person who thought they saw those eyes was tripping on acid. Still, I always stayed on the lookout for new interdimensional transport.

* * *

After crossing the border, Dean and I drove through the darkness past Bellingham, looking unsuccessfully for places to sleep. The air was cool and moist, the night still. Vast networks of tiny country roads filled the woods, but we found no overnight options. The trick, we discovered, was to locate a hotel in a relatively safe neighborhood whose lot was filled with enough cars for ours to blend in. We needed to roll in, park between paying customers' cars and rearrange the luggage to make room for our beds without attracting security guards' and other patrons' attention; otherwise, guards tapped on the window and kicked us out.

That night nothing felt right. What chain hotels we found along I-5 were largely empty. Gas station parking lots were either too small, too vacant or too exposed to truckers, travelers and highway patrol. The forest roads we found outside small towns had gates on them, preventing access to the secluded spots deep in the woods. Sleeping on the shoulder wasn't an option. Two summers before, Michael Jordan's father had been shot to death while he napped in his car at an Interstate rest area. We kept driving.

The serrated points of evergreens loomed on the roadside. The tops of firs, cedars and spruce were black silhouetted against black. My eyes itched from fatigue and my calves ached. Dean drank Diet Coke to stay awake. I slumped in the passenger seat.

I hadn't stayed up all night since I was a kid, and even then it was only to consume countless sodas and watch horror movies until my middle school friends and I passed out on the living room sofas at dawn. This was different. Here we moved in a hushed, eerie realm of limited-visibility populated by truckers, druggies, coyotes, and those damned to the graveyard shift. Who else walked the earth at this hour? In European folklore, this was the witching hour, the period after midnight when supernatural creatures were thought to be at their most powerful. Tearing down the highway as the rest of Skagit and Snohomish counties slept, I felt like an undercover operative, someone with a mission and an accumulation of secrets. I savored the feeling.

I needed to feel this. Already my routine was: eat, sleep, watch TV, go to school, drink on weekends, week after week. I could see the writing on the wall: two more years of college and it was off to the work force. A nine-to-five job. A cubicle. Florescent bulbs hanging from the office ceiling. Then what: marriage? Mortgages? Kids? Then cancer treatments, bladder control issues, erectile dysfunction?

There had to be more to life. We weren't tadpoles, we were humans. Yet even something as atypical as a roadtrip got mired in the mundane: find food, get sleep, pump gas, brush your teeth. I wasn't sure what I expected, only that I expected more.

Thin clouds formed a sheet over the highway, blocking the stars. Dean said, "I bet there are tons of bats out tonight."

With all the farms in those fertile volcanic lowlands, I said he was probably right. What else was out there? I stared into the darkness. A semi's headlights passed. A large tractor sat dormant in a field. I said, "You ever wish there were goblins and griffins and all those mythical beasts?"

Dean looked over smirking, scrunching his brow. "Are you high?" he said.

Tarantulas, hawks, Gila monsters—was a horde of natural wonders enough to satisfy him? I turned to the window and rubbed my red eyes. "I just think the world must have been a whole lot more magical in ancient times."

In Medieval Europe, common people suffered the black plague, Inquisition and poor sanitation. But they also believed in elves, luminous fairies and nymphs. I'd explored caves, soaked in springs, slipped inside the dank cavities of hollow trees, and I had never seen any of these creatures.

I imagined forest hovels, warlocks tending wood fires, concocting potions, casting spells. Roots, herbs, and berries. A broth filled with charms. Bats flapped overhead on the night of the full moon while knotted hands stirred iron caldrons.

Round about the cauldron go;
In the poison'd entrails throw.

I thought of the witches of *Macbeth*:

Double, double toil and trouble.
Fire burn, and caldron bubble.

I unrolled the window and hung my hand outside. Chilly wind battered my palm, sweeping the sweat aside. At seventy miles per hour, momentum resembled time speeding forward, hurtling us toward the smothering repetition of home. My dry eyes searched the sky for the moon but couldn't find it.

Adder's fork, and blind-worm's sting,
Lizard's leg, and owlet's wing,
For a charm of powerful trouble,
Like a hell-broth boil and bubble.

I set my head on the window sill and let the wind ruffle my hair. It seemed the world's magic lessened with each year we aged. Childhood had been filled with it.

When I was nine, I woke up every Saturday morning to watch the

Dungeons & Dragons cartoon. Based loosely on the role-playing game—which, at the time, had a harmful, occult reputation among parents—the cartoon series aired on a local TV station from 1983 to 1985. The premise was fascinating. During a casual day at the fair, a group of young friends got pulled from their rollercoaster ride into an alternate dimension: the "Realm of Dungeons and Dragons." Without reason or warning, the rollercoaster broke free from its track, disintegrated, and hurled the kids into an alien land where a longhaired elfin man named the Dungeon Master assigned them each weapons suited to their talents and temperament. One was a Ranger who shot magic arrows; one a teen wizard who pulled items from a hat; the eight-year old barbarian had a club that produced shockwaves when it hit the ground. Like most kids, all they wanted to do was return home. As they searched for a way back, they stumbled from adventure to adventure, rescuing the unfortunate and battling the dimension's many evil forces: swine-faced soldiers named Orcs, skeleton warriors, and a demon named Vengar. The show had true bottom-of-the-barrel geek appeal, and I ate it up, because beneath the mundane setting of these ordinary kids' lives lurked an exciting ulterior world, a world where they had superpowers, a purpose, a chance to be heroes and no clue about any of it until a portal spirited them away.

In Episode 11, "The Box," the mythological Greek character Pandora appeared in the altered form of Zandora. In Greek mythology, Pandora's box—originally a jar—wasn't a force of liberation, it was the source of the world's troubles. Zeus gave Pandora the jar and instructed her to keep it shut. Since she had also been given the gift of curiosity, she inevitably opened it, and out rushed ills the world had not previously known: various evils, disease, burdensome labor. The story goes that Pandora hadn't acted out of malice, only curiosity, and when she saw what she'd unleashed, she quickly closed it. Hope, apparently, also laid at the bottom of the jar. I felt the same way at age twenty while out in the woods. And watching Episode 11 as a kid, I knew that, had I found a box in a canyon, I would have opened it, too.

"Let's not go back," I told Dean. We could ditch everything, live in the van, get crappy jobs, sleep in National Forests, travel city to city, park to park, and be free.

"I agree," he said. "I could do this forever."

He steered the van between the straight yellow lines. I looked at my watch. We were well past the witching hour.

* * *

By the time we reached the town of Everett, the dark eastern sky was turning light blue. We wanted to see Possession Sound, that narrow stretch of water between the mainland and Whidbey Island. Instead, we watched the sun rise behind the Cascades from a window seat at McDonald's.

Pink. Lilac. Shades of ghostly lupine.

Four sausage and egg breakfast sandwiches.

As enchanting a sight as sunrise was, I wanted nothing more than to find a place to curl up in the passenger seat. Dean assured me we would sleep soon, and drove us to a nearby convenience store. We looked disheveled. Mud splattered Dean's hiking boots and socks, and the hole in the bottom of my black Converse All-Stars kept letting in tiny pebbles. Blearily, we pulled caffeinated sodas from the store cooler as a frantic woman in her mid-twenties begged the clerk to use his phone. "Please," she said. "I don't have any money." The clerk refused.

When we found the women by the gas pumps, pacing in the yellow dawn, Dean asked if she needed help. She said she was trying to get home, then tailed us to our van and climbed into the passenger seat. "Hurry," she said, "they're following me."

Her long brown hair twirled as she scanned the perimeter. I didn't see anybody. A single car sat in the lot. It was probably the clerk's.

Dean took the seat behind her and unfolded his pocket knife, in case she tried something.

She directed me down the street. "Go left." I steered the van down a two-lane road. Her long nails dug into the arm rest, and I wondered how we'd ended up entangled in a stranger's drama.

"Turn there," she said. We veered into a residential neighborhood. White, manicured houses lined the green, narrow streets.

I studied our passenger sidelong. Trim waist, small nose, pink lips—had Dean and I seen her in a bar, we would have both wanted to talk to her.

But in this frenzied state, she could have just robbed a store, fled the scene of an accident or had a pistol in her shirt.

Eyes bulging, she said, "They're right behind us!"

I glanced in the rearview. There weren't any headlights. Was she hallucinating?

Dean's aunt was schizophrenic. She refused assistance, quit taking her medication, and lived on the Phoenix streets in and out of homeless shelters.

My stomach knotted from adrenaline.

"Hurry," the woman said. "They're right down that street."

I looked out. The street was empty. Just rows of unlit houses, rose bushes and parked cars.

I tried to think up ways to get rid of her. Yet another part of me feared she might really need our help. Her behavior, as strange as it was unsettling, mixed with the adrenaline and sleep-deprivation, awoke something in me that all the weed and shrooms could not.

Dean tried to extract information, but the woman only screamed, "They're catching up."

No one knew Dean's aunt's exact location day-to-day. Sometimes she called the family house to berate Dean's mother, claiming she'd hired people to kill her. Other times she called to rant about demons who were pursuing her. Demons—that was a recurring obsession. As we sped through Everett, Dean's aunt was somewhere lost in Phoenix.

I repeated Dean's question. "Who's following you?"

"Some people," the woman said in a loud, labored voice. "They're jealous. They always are." She looked around but wouldn't make eye-contact. "Keep going straight."

Dean caught my eye in the rear view. The dull two-inch blade hung by his knee.

I floored it, as much to calm her as myself. Was this a lesson the spirits were trying to teach Dean and I? Keep doing drugs and you could end up losing your mind. If there were spirits, maybe this was a warning, their way of asking if I was prepared for the answers that I sought. Could I handle the truth? I'd never previously considered it. Maybe I would fall apart and want my ignorance back—too much fruit from the Tree of Knowledge. Or maybe I would melt like the Germans in *Raiders of the Lost Ark* when they laid eyes on the contents of the Ark of the Covenant. Then again, maybe I had it backwards: couldn't Dean and I be winning karmic points by helping a troubled stranger?

I steered our crowded van. Wasn't I doing the same dumb thing that I always did: looking for meaning where there wasn't any? Why did my mind always go for these outlandish supernatural explanations, rather than the most reasonable? Maybe I had tripped one too many times. One day I might take a trip and never come back, go over the deep end, like her. But it wasn't just me; it was a generalized problem with the human mind, the downside of cognition: the need to find order in disorder, to make sense out of the inexplicable, even if we imagined it.

As my mind buzzed with debate, the woman motioned with one hand. "Right here."

I parked in front of a large home set back on a verdant yard, expecting her to dart from the car and run to safety. Instead, she hung her right leg out the car door and paused. "Okay thanks," she said. "We should hang out sometime." She scribbled her number on a scrap of paper that she fished from our ashtray. "Call me."

Dean climbed into the passenger seat as she sauntered up the front steps. He pocketed his knife. "My God," I muttered. "What a trip." I began mulling over theories as to what we'd just experienced: was she running from a rapist? An abusive boyfriend who threatened her? Was she suffering from amphetamine psychosis?

"You know there was nobody following us," Dean said, "right?" I nodded then admitted I wasn't entirely sure. He snickered at my naiveté. "She's totally schizophrenic."

I trusted he was right, but I didn't want him to be. While the empirical side of me favored scientific thinking, the whimsical side resisted the idea that medical science could classify and explain away the complex and sometimes troubling nature of human behavior. I thought I'd read somewhere that certain scholars believed many of the great Biblical prophets' visions resulted from seizures. What modern doctors would diagnose as epilepsy was, back then, perceived as the frightening ability to channel divine messages. When prophets spoke, ancient people listened. Now prophets and believers got tranquilizing prescriptions.

We debated calling the number to see if the woman was alright, then we stored the paper in the ashtray and headed out of town.

I steered us down the winding roads and onto the interstate, merging with the stream of morning commuters. The sun rose over the Cascades, blinding my tired eyes. Dean sipped his soda.

"I can't believe you thought she was serious," he said further down the road.

"Hey, what do I know?" I shrugged and put on my sunglasses. "She was scared. I mean, anything's possible."

Dean shook his head, sucking on his straw.

* * *

We slept in a south Seattle motel that morning: checked in during rush hour, checked out at 6:30 p.m. For the next two days we drove through Washington and Oregon into Northern California. As exhaustion set in not long after sunset, we agreed to sleep in the next town we hit. Twenty-nine miles northwest of the town of Weed, and several hours before bedtime, we arrived in Yreka.

Next to a pasture beyond the glow of lights, we emptied the capsules onto a CD case and cut the PCP into lines with a credit card. Unsure of the proper dosage, we did it all, snorting it through a rolled dollar bill until our eyes teared up and noses stung. I wanted to sneeze but feared expelling the precious powder.

We sat in the van wiping our eyes. I cut the engine and rolled down the windows. The smell of dry grass mixed with the glue-like odor caking my nostrils. Crickets chirped in the field. Our arms rested on the warm metal frame.

"This stuff sucks," I said. Knowing we'd be too many hundreds of miles away to complain, our Canadian hosts had probably cut the drug with something to keep the bulk for themselves.

"Maybe it takes a while," Dean said. We decided to drive around.

Searching for a safe place, still hoping to lose our minds without

48

attracting police, we headed west. Like the rollercoaster in *D&D*, the narrow country road buckled, lifting free of the golden valley and hurling us into the mountains. Thin pines crowded around, deepening the already deep night. On a curve in the road, I eased the van into a dirt pullout tucked against a hillside. We stepped outside. A fine patina of stars dusted the heavens. I looked up and my head spun so fast I thought I was going to puke. Dean said he felt the same. I looked down, hoping to dull the motion sickness, but the dizziness remained. Squinting didn't help, or drawing breath.

One of us said, "I need to lie down." For some reason we chose the middle of the road.

Stepping from the shoulder, we laid on our backs on the warm blacktop. Feet to the east, heads to the west, Dean sprawled on one side of the lane line, I on the other. We folded our hands across our chests like mummies and set our shoulders a foot apart.

The chirping crickets grew louder and warmth rose through the back of my shirt. Following teenage drinking protocol, I focused my eyes on something fixed: the stars. They glowed between the dark treetops but were not staying still. They seemed to be slowly rolling over, the night sky's entire surface slewing to the right. I watched the celestial film drift southward as if atop a body of water, pulling me with it as it spilled over the trees. I pinched my eyes shut, trying to halt the world, but it revolved within the darkness under my eyelids.

"I'm getting sick standing still," I said. Dean too. We were in the foothills of the Klamath Mountains, in one of the West Coast's most Eden-like and least populated areas, and we couldn't do anything but close our eyes.

The hills were quiet enough that we assumed we would hear a car approaching. Or, with our eyes open, at least see the headlights reflected on the pines. We wouldn't be able to test this theory until a car drove up from either direction, and it didn't matter. I thought I was going to have a heart attack. My chest pounded and pulse thumped in my neck. Pressing my fingers to my temples, I awaited the pang of expiration.

I had long wished I shared Dean's quiet acceptance of death. Heaven sounded wonderful, reincarnation better. I wanted to imagine that, upon dying, our spirits were ferried into another dimension where our minds lived on—our conscious selves, with all our memories, personality, and sense of humor intact—so that, even if reincarnated as a Skagit Valley farm cat or a Snoqualmie Pass huckleberry bush, we would forever remain ourselves. Aaron, always Aaron. I just kept thinking of what my dad believed. "When you die," he'd said on numerous occasions, "you die. That's it." He'd been raised Baptist but later forsook it as "Fear of fire and brimstone." Many people, some in our own family, spent their whole lives preparing for the afterlife—penance, church services, no drinking, no dancing, frequently giving alms. But what if, as I feared, their conception was wrong and my father's was right? That we were doomed to lie in the dirt until we became indistinguishable from it? Lying on that mountain road, I thought we were resting in our graves, that if a car didn't kill us the PCP would, leaving us for the animals to pick apart. Foxes would emerge from the forest to tug at our flesh. Coyotes would drag an arm in one direction, a rib in another.

During my elementary school, a recurring sensation often washed over me. For that brief moment right before sleep, I drifted through space in a universe without planets. Nothing in the distance, nothing in every direction. For one overwhelming second my primate brain grasped the elusive notion of death as a long, black, empty forever. That's what awaits us, I'd think: eternal nothing, infinite blackness. The sensation never lasted more than two seconds. Then my eyes jolted open, and I pressed my face into the pillow to silence my sobs.

I opened my eyes while lying on the road and felt sick.

After untold dizzying minutes, Dean and I decided it was best to try to get some rest. We had a full day of driving the next day, and staying in the hills wasn't easing our discomfort. With wobbly legs and dilated pupils, we stood up and drove down the mountain.

None of the town's few gas station and grocery store parking lots felt safe, so we parked on the dirt shoulder of a rural road. Neither of us knew if angel dust precluded sleep, but we lowered the front seats anyway, spread blankets over our partially dressed bodies, drank a beer, and closed our eyes.

Right as I started to doze, Dean nudged my shoulder. "Did you feel that?" he said.

I looked out from under the pillow, said, "What?"

"The car move." He sat up. Blankets fell around him. "It felt like something rammed the car, like another car."

We cupped our hands on the cool glass and stared through the windows without unrolling them. Darkness spilled around us. Cows. Fences. "The whole van moved," he said. "You didn't feel that?"

I hadn't felt a thing.

THE STONED AGE

It started just as I'd feared. I had to say, "Hi, my name is Aaron and I'm in here for weed." The idea sounded so ridiculous I wanted to dive out the window. The most harmful side effects some stoners suffered were short-term memory lapses and Cheeto-stained fingers. Other people smoked pot and just fell asleep. Yet here I was, in a mixed drug recovery group for smoking dope every day, all day, for three straight years.

I sat with my back against a white painted wall, facing five other people in a tiny room lined with drab industrial carpeting and ringed with foldout chairs. Ted the group leader said, "Welcome Aaron." The other members muttered the same. I was twenty-one years old.

Why I ended up in this mixed group rather than Marijuana Anonymous I cannot recall; my mind was still hazy in those early days. Group met at night once a week, on the second-story of an ugly-as-hell white office building lined with palm trees and mirrored glass in Tucson, Arizona. Unlike AA, NA, or CA, our group represented a potpourri of chemical agents; all vices were welcome. My mom found the group after I asked her and my dad for help.

I'd moved from Phoenix to Tucson in January 1996, partly to study ecology, partly to sober up. What I told everyone, including my closest friends JT, Chris, and Jason, was that I was moving because Arizona State University, where I'd spent the last five semesters, didn't offer the ecology degree I wanted, only the University of Arizona did. The primary truth was that I had to remove myself from my social circle in order to change my behavior. My theory was that the hundred miles between the cities would put my drug contacts at too far a distance to be useful, and without easy access to weed, I'd be forced to spend my free time doing things other than slumping on couches getting baked in front of televisions. I would start reading all the books I owned but was too lazy to get through. I would further my studies of natural history, improve my photography skills and pursue my dream of writing about nature and culture. And then, as the final component of my personal reconstruction, I would make new, less intoxicated friends, friends without breathy, space-case snickers, friends with huge, imposing, identity-defining interests. People like me.

After five or six months nothing had changed. Rather than strangling my supply, I frequently got lonely and drove the two hundred mile roundtrip on weekends to get stoned with my friends and buy a bag for the month. Eventually I found new sources in Tucson: a brother of a childhood friend; my elementary school buddy Brett who I'd spotted on campus. He was funny, chatty and smart, and we'd been close as kids. Now we had little in common but his pot supply. We'd get stoned and sit around with his roommates and I'd listen to them talk about U of A sports. I'd often go outside and skate while he and his roommates played video games, then we'd smoke a little more and I'd pay for my bag and split. He usually had fragrant, fluffy buds—not overpriced California hydro, but not the ammonia-scented Mexican dirt weed so common in Arizona either. A nap of fine fuzz often coated Brett's weed. Sometimes its tacky, crystallized edges stuck to your fingers, and like fresh truffles to a cook, I savored my purchases. I stored the buds in small plastic film canisters to keep them plump and moist. The few times that my stash ran out before I could re-up, I scraped and re-scraped resin from my filthy pipe stem at home and waited for Brett to answer his phone, and then all the resin did was fog my head. This wasn't why I'd moved.

One morning when I should have been in class, I found my canisters empty. I called Brett to restock but he didn't pick up. He was probably in class. Without even the crumbs of a desiccated bud to tide me over, I didn't know what to do with myself. Though I preferred a red-eyed, glazed-over, completely crippled high, just the idea that there was shake in my canister could have comforted me until I got more. I put on a surf CD and waited a few minutes before redialing Brett. Again, no answer. I called my other connection but he didn't pick up either. Oh shit, I thought, double shit. What the hell am I going to do? I'd waited too long, hadn't planned ahead, and now—well, I didn't know what now. In three years I'd never endured an entire day with a break in my supply. I scraped my bong stem clean of resin, scraped and re-scraped my pipe until I had to pluck tiny metal shavings from the dark, gooey tar, and I studied the debris in the bottom of my bong. What had once been green was now blackened sediment, as bloated and dank as swamp muck. I poured the brackish bong water through a paper towel to filter any smokeable bits and then microwaved them dry, and with the tip of my pocket knife, I smeared the tiny resin mass across my pipe's screen. Watching the clock, I put the flame to the goo and inhaled until the wad glowed orange then faded white, releasing the last of its bitter toxic ghost. I exhaled a pale wisp, not enough to call a hit. The microwaved bits disintegrated when I handled them and slipped through the screen. I cursed out loud and wanted to kick something and wondered: should I drive to Phoenix? Maybe cruise side streets in sketchy South Tucson and try to buy weed from loitering strangers? Dealers down there were mostly crack addicts and junkies, not at all safe. I slumped in my living room chair and waited a while before redialing my connections. My chest tightened while the phone rang. When they didn't answer, I threw my head back and lit a cigarette to calm down. What felt like a pool of acid gurgled in my stomach. With my eyes closed I could feel my angry heart pound and I faced a whirlpool of swirling thoughts—the facts, the ugly truth, options. Sober or not, my mind was not clear, but the next step was obvious. When I opened my eyes, I called my parents.

They'd always said that I could tell them anything no matter how bad it was. So I told them: "I'm a pothead and I can't quit." Dad was shocked. Mom said she "kind of suspected" but didn't know how to broach the subject without running me off. I was hardly around as it was. Since turning sixteen I'd mainly come home to shower and sleep. I spent the bulk of my time at my friend Chris's house, at school or hiking the desert, and even then I arrived home at hours where my parents and I rarely crossed paths, because I was either stoned or hungover, and I didn't want to hear their suggestions about doing "extracurricular school activities" or attending family functions that infringed on my social time. "I feel so guilty," Mom said, as if confronting me earlier would have convinced me to act responsibly.

Now, humbled before them, we forged a plan: quit using drugs and go to support groups or a counselor. I suggested I take the semester off to dry out in what I called a "stress-free environment," maybe read some things about addiction, or maybe just my Edward Abbey and desert ecology books.

"We think this requires a professional," my parents said. They suggested someone to help me learn to deal with stress, reacquaint myself with my emotions and explore the sources of my compulsion. From the tension in their hushed voices I could tell they were nervous. They spoke in short sentences, listened more than spoke. Mom was a loud New Yorker, a born talker, yet as I unloaded, she mostly said, "Mmhmm. Yes, mmhmm." There was a restraint there, timidity, as if by not acting heavy-handedly, she might successfully direct me to help without making me defensive enough to squeeze them out of the equation.

After I'd detailed the situation, they agreed to let me reduce my course load to one class—just to keep my toe in the pond, Dad said—but I had to promise to abstain and use my free time constructively. If I didn't get it together that semester, I would still have to take the full five-class load the next semester. They didn't chastise me. They didn't say "We told you so" or ask how I could be so stupid as to get myself into this mess the way I asked myself how I could be that stupid over and over again. They offered only encouragement: you're strong; you can do it; thanks for being honest; we love you. I felt relieved as we talked, relieved to have the burden of secrecy lifted from my conscious, relieved that my parents hadn't scolded, judged, or rejected me. We had once been so close, but I had long feared that if they learned of my problem, it would be such a crushing disappointment to them that I would take on the stigma of "the ruined son," and that they might love me less. To prove to myself and to them that their faith in me was justified, I got off the phone, laid my foot-long, blue plastic bong on the kitchen floor, and crushed it beneath my shoe. The scratched, dirty cylinder shattered underfoot, sending shards skidding across the linoleum. It was hard to see my old companion go, worse to have to be its executioner, but the violence of its end, and the hollow pop its expiration made, only reminded me of the shallowness of our relationship. I kneeled to collect the pieces, dumping them into a plastic grocery bag, then shuffled out of my apartment into the alley behind the building. I clutched my small metal pipe in my other hand. Its compact weight in my palm felt as comforting as it had hundreds of times before. These, my constant companions, two empty fetid tubes. I slid back the side-latch on the dumpster and out rushed the stink of festering garbage. Holding my breath, I took one final look at the pipe and bag of shards and tossed them in. They disappeared into the squalid mound forever, and I went back inside. To make sure I followed through with our agreement, Mom found me the group.

When I walked into group the first night, I eyeballed the room, partly to see what I expected would be a pitiful assemblage of shriveled barflies and burnouts in stained sweatpants, partly to measure my condition against theirs. I arrived scowling. I didn't want to be there and I didn't care who knew it. But as soon as I entered the room and the other members looked at me, my gaze dropped to the drab carpet, and I flopped into an empty seat by the door.

Our group consisted of five people. There was Carolina, a beautiful, cocaine ravaged Latina in her early twenties, newly impoverished without her drug dealer ex-boyfriend's income. There was Ben, a plump late-forties pain-pill-popper with feathered hair and a cigarette-rasp. The other two were quiet, early-forties, male alcoholics. One was a middle class executive in dark slacks and crisp collared shirts who I loathed on site, the other an effeminate prep cook who primarily drank but also smoked pot and gobbled pills once intoxicated. He generally sat with his thin legs and arms crossed, head down, blonde hair parted so a sheet of it hung over one side of his dour face. He drank first thing upon waking, and in group, he always sat beside me.

I was the group's only "marijuana dependent," a more ludicrous title to me than "chronic masturbator" or "shopaholic." Saying it aloud felt as cool as getting high and telling people you were "on weed." I might as well have been saying I was addicted to Taquería Guadalajara's bean burritos, because I ate those three or four times a week and thought constantly of the small mom and pop restaurant's homemade horchata. Did that habit require professional assistance? Maybe I should put on a gaudy Hawaiian shirt and grow a mustache and start asking kids on high school campuses if they had "a dime bag of grass" to sell, then my new persona as the out-of-touch NARC would be complete. Thinking all this, I'd sat in my car in the parking lot that first night during break, and considered ditching the whole thing. I could lie to my parents and tell them I'd attended, make up stories about the people in there who were worse off than me. Tell them how much it was helping to purge myself of the dark, antisocial longings I carried inside me. Then I could sit comfortably at home and read.

* * *

The ravages of hard drugs and alcohol have been thoroughly depicted in books and film. *Trainspotting*, *Requiem for a Dream*, and *The Basketball Diaries* deal with heroin. *Bright Lights, Big City* and *Boogie Nights* involve coke. *Barfly* and *Leaving Las Vegas* portray the horrors of consumptive boozing. The list goes on. Yet most modern American marijuana flicks depict the lives of daily dope-smokers as comic, light-hearted affairs.

Take The Dude in *The Big Lebowski*. The Dude, aptly named of course, is a peaceful, beloved bungler who, when he isn't bowling and tucking back his long hair, stumbles from dramatic event to dramatic event, alternately clueless or baffled by the complexity of his situation. Cheech and Chong, whether parked on a median or trailing plumes of smoke, experience more adventures than problems. The 1990s saw a string of stoner movies—*Dazed and Confused*, *The Stöned Age*, and *Half Baked*—where snickering characters decked in tie-dye and vintage clothing get high, search for parties in their old V-dubs, and live blissed lives to the tune of "Slow Ride." Despite the contraband on their persons and the THC clogging their synapses, no real harm befalls any of these stoners. Even Shaggy from *Scooby-Doo* speaks with the telltale pothead's affect—that, like, uh, total spacey drawl—and he solves crimes!

Although some Americans worry that pot-smoking can lead to the use of harder drugs—or at least signal a young person's increased interest in chemical experimentation—many others don't take weed all that seriously. The general consensus on marijuana's dangers might best be summarized by one telling and hilarious line from *Half Baked*. When the character Mary Jane says, "Marijuana is terrible. It's a gateway drug. I mean, everybody knows that it leads to other stuff," Dave Chappelle's character says, "Yeah, mostly junk food."

Another example of the hapless, loveable toker is Jeff Spicoli, from *Fast Times at Ridgemont High*. A perma-baked high school surfer, Spicoli is the archetype American pothead: bumbling yet witty, laid back yet subversive, and largely harmless despite his antics. He orders pizza during class, butts heads with the uptight history teacher Mr. Hand, and even crashes a football player's car. He's always out of work and short on cash. But when Brad Hamilton, the movie's popular male lead, asks him why he doesn't have a job, Spicoli says, "All I need are some tasty waves, a cool buzz, an' I'm fine." In real life, such a statement would widely be seen as tragically adolescent, but on screen, the magic of humor makes the inherent tragedy of his limited ambition lovable. Spicoli functions as the film's comic relief. He's the foil to the stiff Mr. Hand, who represents boredom, old age and oppression in all its forms. Who doesn't watch a movie like *Fast Times* and find himself rooting for the underdog? Don't most people enjoy seeing authority figures get punked? Spicoli's not just a comic stoner, he's the drowsy antihero who represents all of our suppressed rebellion and hedonistic lust. While we slave away at boring jobs, he coasts through life and hits the beach. While we tell our overbearing bosses, "Yes ma'am, no sir," Spicoli laughs in authority's face. As we try to monitor our diets to stay fit, Spicoli inhales slice after greasy pizza slice and innumerable bong hits.

And because Hollywood has immortalized him during his prime years, Spicoli is destined to remain eternally young and free in our eyes, forever the high school joker, perched on the edge of self-destruction, yet never having to face the ramifications of his intoxication, or the way teenage lifestyles constrict adult career options. If there was a Spicoli biopic which followed his life after high school, it would probably be called *Still High in Ridgemont*, and it would show him living in his parents' basement, working the night shift at a suburban convenience store where he chain-smokes Pall Malls and keeps his thinning hair in one of those embarrassing adult ponytails. "Mom bums me out when she gets on my case," I imagine him telling the camera. "That's why I stash my buds in the shed out back. Every time she changes my sheets she finds and takes my stuff!"

I might sound like a buzzkill overanalyzing one of Hollywood's most memorable creations, but, as much as I still love it, *Fast Times* reminds me of my own recklessness. In high school and early college, I wore vintage Hang Ten shirts that I'd found at thrift stores, and a few buddies started calling me Spicoli. "Hey Spicoli," they'd say at parties. "Where's the pizza?" Or they'd just call out "No way!" in a gassy drawl. I didn't know whether to be flattered or offended. The characterization worried me partly because, in addition to my long blonde hair, I knew I'd become as spacey as *Fast Times'* stoner prince. Also, paranoia had set in. I was having trouble separating irrational thoughts from reality, and I kept worrying what people were thinking when they looked at me. And even in Tucson, after I quit smoking pot and had long since cut my hair, the anxiety wouldn't go away.

After three years awash in THC, the chemical residue of abuse had reduced me from a confident, conversational extrovert to a fretful wad of trembling Chihuahua energy. I'd assumed sobriety would return me to the previous era of clarity and calm; instead, it felt like someone had yanked back the shower curtain while I stood there naked and sudsy. My natural inclination had always been to get out of the house as much as possible—eat out, go to bookstores, meet friends, ride bikes, see bands play; the world was too interesting to stay at home. Yet I winced now under other people's gazes, or even the idea of gazes, and for the first time in my life, the looming specter of an observing public made me want to hide indoors.

Part of the problem might have been that my detoxifying body started behaving as strangely as my brain. Everything that required piloting presented a monumental challenge: crossing streets; stepping off curbs; maneuvering between chairs at a café or in class. Walking unaccompanied across open spaces made my shoulders hunch and neck arc as I scurried toward the next bit of cover. I was hyperaware of my movements—how my arms swayed and legs swung—because some internal force seemed to be hampering their control. My pace felt either too fast or too slow, which made my muscles tense and increased my uncomfortable perception of how I looked to other people. So I wore a low-set baseball cap to reduce my awareness of others. To steady my awkward appendages, I kept my hands in my coat pockets on cold days, and clutched my backpack straps on warm ones. I quickly learned all the spots around town and on campus that offered the greatest amount of shelter and required the least amount of maneuvering: sidewalks lined with trees; street crossings with low curbs; back routes between U of A buildings traversed more by groundskeepers than students. And I avoided the streets, creeping to class through the alleys instead, favoring the station of the city's detritus, the fetid garbage bins and tossed sofa cushions, feasting pigeons and feral cats, the unseen and unwanted, my fellow outcasts.

* * *

"You don't know what he's like," Carolina said. Her brown eyes scanned the room then settled on the carpet. She and the drug dealer ex-boyfriend she was discussing had abused cocaine to the point of psychosis. They would snort coke mostly, but sometimes freebase. Then she'd undo the screws on the electrical outlet covers to search for the cameras and microphones she insisted were recording her. She blamed the police but sometimes "the government," as if they needed audio archives of her talking for hours about invisible surveillance. Ted, the support group leader, usually said, "Did you find any cameras or microphones, Carolina?" She admitted she had not. But on certain days she still assumed, even fourteen, thirty, sixty days sober, that it was only because she hadn't looked deep enough inside her walls.

"They have technologies," she said, "high tech thingies you don't even know are there." None of the group members challenged her. We nodded, stared at our shoes. She removed the electrical covers so frequently that her ex eventually stopped screwing them back on. When he refused to quit coke, she left him to get clean. Now she existed in a state of terrified anticipation, telling us how she expected him to break down her apartment door and beat her for her abandonment, how she owned a gun, frequently peered through the curtains looking for his car and had nightmares about their inevitable confrontation. She was strong. I envied her resolve. I also felt horrible for her. No person should have to live with those fears, especially after making the wise decision to get clean. Her stories also made me grateful that I hadn't gotten strung out on hard drugs. I kept that to myself.

During my first weeks in group, a routine "Hi, my name is Aaron" was about all I offered. I'd never been in a clinical environment before, never confessed my sins to priests or a shrink, and I didn't want to. I assumed I could do this on my own. I couldn't imagine how the presence of out-of-control strangers would bolster the willpower I believed necessary to resist temptation. Sobriety to me depended on a person's level of self-control, not talking about our feelings or whatever people did in these bullshit settings. So I mostly just sat there, listening.

The bitter prep cook usually kicked off our sessions by inventorying his previous week's woes: he slipped and drank a beer when he woke up the other day; he drank a Near Beer before that and it made him want a real one; his boss didn't appreciate his work or his efforts to get clean, and his coworkers snorting coke in the refrigerator made him want to drink.

Ted would ask, "How's the sleeping issues? Getting more solid rest through the night?"

Bitter would shake his head. "Not good," he'd say, squeezing his crossed-arms tighter. If tallying our grievances was all group was about, I told myself I wouldn't stick around. Ben talked about gaining weight after giving up the opiates, how the added pounds made breathing difficult. One night he talked for ten minutes about gout. When my parents called about my progress, I told them these people were the reason support groups were useless: just a bunch of sad sacks who needed coddling and thrived on other peoples' pity. It had only been two weeks.

When Bitter talked, he rarely looked up from the floor. He'd relapsed numerous times over his decade-plus of abuse, ruined his marriage, lost jobs, then ended up back in group half-expecting to relapse again. As much as I tried not to, I thought that, as the group's youngest member, I was stronger than him, stronger than Ben and the executive, too. Having lived that sad cycle for so long, those three seemed unlikely to ever clean up for good.

Carolina was their opposite. She didn't discuss her headaches or stubbed toe, didn't complain about various restaurants' rip-off lunch prices or the frustration of finding a good paying job with large gaps in her résumé. She told and retold her cocaine horror stories as if to remind herself why she needed to stay straight, and I listened with a twisted fascination. She described how she'd pulled the electrical wires from one apartment's walls, even tugging them through the cheap dry wall of a motel room. She followed the white trench with her dry, bugged-out eyes as it moved toward the ceiling, the crumbling material dusting the carpet and her arms powder white. Fearing someone who knew their address might rob them, she and her ex frequently rented motel rooms to binge. She'd spend large portions of those days in a chair in the room's corner, legs pressed against her chest, arms wrapped around her knees, peeking beneath the curtains for cops and federal agents. She thought the military aircraft that flew over town—jets and bombers from Davis-Monthan Air Force Base—were some sort of urban reconnaissance involved with the war on drugs. She misidentified other motel patrons as possible assailants, and sat ready for them to knock on the door all night.

To get me more engaged in group, Ted asked me a series of questions one night: "Does your family have a history of addiction?" "How old were you when you first used?" "How did you get into marijuana?" "What made you decide to quit now?" I told the short version:

No one on either side of my family had been a hardcore addict. My dad's youngest brother was a pianist who smoked cigarettes and might have dabbled with coke when he toured with Waylon Jennings, but I heard nothing of the road seeping into his regular life, or at least he'd been too broke to support a habit. Two of my dad's other brothers had spent many years smoking dope. Wake-and-bakers like me, they'd smoke from the time they woke up to the time they went to sleep; age and heart problems had put an end to that, though. My folks weren't drinkers. They didn't frequent bars, never took acid in the sixties. My mom had smoked pot exactly three times, and my dad never developed a taste for it either. So minute was marijuana's presence in my parents' lives that they hadn't even thought to tell me about my uncles or their own scant history until I was in my late-twenties. Between these regular Joe, straight-and-narrow parents, somehow I ended up the wild one.

I first got drunk when I was thirteen. After guzzling a bunch of my parent's gin on a school night for no reason, I called a girl I had a crush on and babbled for a while, then fell face-first down our carpeted stairs and woke up the next morning in a bed covered in what I thought were crumbs but turned out to be vomit. I started drinking beer with friends on weekends at age sixteen, but for some reason, a year passed before I smoked dope. Chris, JT, and Jason—those guys were my brothers. We'd known each other for nearly a decade, went to movies, parties, concerts, camping, traveling, spent all our free time and reached various milestones together. Initially we smoked a little here, a little there, always on the weekends, usually at night. After a year of casual toking we were getting stoned together—and also alone—every night, seven days a week, in one to ten sessions a day. On weekends we'd also get drunk. Then we'd stay up late getting rowdy, sleep late the next day, load the bong upon waking, eat a very stoned lunch, then go back to sleep. By the time night hit, it was time to get stoned again and open the first of many beers. It seemed amusing at first. Being perpetually baked became our new comic character: Laughy, Dopey, Mumbly, and Forgetful, the Four Stooges of Fun in our own imagined Cheech and Chong movie. Lunch time? Load some bong hits. Seeing a movie? Roll a joint. Doing a shift at work or getting ready for bed? One quick toke.

Before JT and Jason got their own apartment, our loitering centered around Chris' place. He lived in a cinder block addition on the side of his mother's house. Spent Coke cans, flattened Ben & Jerry's containers, and Reese's Peanut Butter cup wrappers covered the floor. Every weekend, Jason and JT and I swept the trash aside and cleared enough carpet space on which to spend the night. We awoke next to overflowing ashtrays, and spray-painted cryptic messages on the walls such as "our friends the ants," referring to a brief infestation. Clothes both dirty and clean mixed with the trash; only Chris could tell them apart, though when selecting an outfit the distinction hardly mattered. He'd come in from the laundry room holding a plastic bin and there, feet from his dresser, dump the laundry on the floor. The dresser was for weed.

We were seventeen, eighteen, nineteen. By the time I turned twenty, my brain started to misfire. I couldn't remember things: what commercial had just played on TV, the dates of doctors' appointments, points that professors made in class. I couldn't concentrate on conversations and had trouble staying engaged in groups, preferring to slouch in a chair and grin into space while the socializing occurred without me. Three years of this passed and all I had to show for it was an increasingly blank stare and a memory so badly failing that I hardly remembered a time when I had the energy to pursue my goals. That and, two and a half years into college, I needed to pick a major.

I tried to control myself but never could for long. I kept that foot-long plastic bong in my car when I drove to the university. I took it everywhere. I'd slip into the parking garage after classes—a parking spot that my parents paid exorbitant prices to get me—and smoke a little before going for a solo hike, or before driving to Chris' to smoke more with him and whoever else was there. I smoked before going to work at a dull office job on campus, and to my other job at a sandwich shop. My friends and I packed bowls while driving city streets and learned to smoke pinch-hitters in crowded shopping centers without getting caught. We took bong hits around campfires and in the backyard at parties. I also started ditching class more frequently to hike and smoke alone. No matter what I did, I couldn't resist getting high. I had no will power, and I hadn't yet learned that it wasn't will power that got you sober.

As much as I tried not to, the urge frequently proved overwhelming and I smoked before school. One morning while driving stoned over the Rural Road bridge, I slammed into the back of a pickup truck at fifteen miles-per-hour. I'd been going forty, looking east at the morning light illuminating the Superstition Mountains. When I returned my attention to the road, all three lanes of traffic had stopped. I hit the brakes and skid into the truck. It stood so high off the ground that the rear bumper cut right across my VW Bug's hood, bending the flimsy metal outwards and upwards in an aluminum tulip. The truck didn't suffer a scratch, but my forehead bled from banging against the windshield, which now had a vast spider web of fractures stretching across it. The driver stepped from his truck and glared at me through my open passenger window. He said, "What the fuck are you doing, dummy?" I apologized, dabbing a rag on my forehead. I suggested we swap information on the nearby side street where there was a bus pullout. He called me a few other names before the cop arrived. I agreed with them all.

Another time I hit an old man on a bike at five miles-per-hour. I'd just smoked an enormous bowl in a lot behind a grocery store at about seven a.m. While I coasted toward the exit, the man darted from the right, where a bike path exited a park and entered the lot. My lids hung heavy and low but still open enough to see his eyes bulge and mouth expand in a pitiful O as he tipped over sideways, disappearing over my now-fixed hood like a paper target at a shooting range.

I jumped out, muttering apologies and asking if he was okay. He grabbed his left thigh and dragged it across the blacktop toward the curb. I was terrified. Had I broken his leg or damaged his spine?

"Sir," I said as I approached, "let me—"

He held up his hand. "Get away from me!" he yelled. "Murderer, get away!" My heart thudded so violently that I could hear the blood pumping in my ears. I had better hope he could walk again, he said, or he was suing me, yet he refused my offers to call an ambulance, preferring to rock on the curb and moan like a wailing widow at an Italian funeral. Bodies might get frail in their early sixties, but I'd tapped him at most. He didn't seem hurt, though maybe I was too high to tell. As he clutched his thigh and said he might never walk again, I took it as a warning. What if I hit a pedestrian at fifteen miles an hour, or forty? Then what? After countless apologies, I told him he was a horrible actor and drove off. I moved to Tucson four months later.

My friends thought that what I was doing was laughable. When I told Chris on the phone that I attended group he said, "That's kind of extreme." I'd heard other stoners echo that sentiment. "Find me one documented case of weed killing anyone," they said. Marijuana was just a plant, like mint or basil, a fragrant, resinous mass of tiny flowers. "What's the worst that can happen if you smoke too much? You eat a lot and fall asleep." Countless armchair-advocates declared pot's harmlessness. They said "science" had never established THC—aka, Δ^9-tetrahydrocannabinol, Cannabis sativa's major psychoactive compound—as an addictive substance, instead characterizing weed as medicine, the healing herb that increased appetite in chemo patients and made many artists more creative under its influence. I agreed when they said the war on drugs was a flawed approach, because

66

the core issue was one of demand not supply. But it felt overly simplistic to call the concept of marijuana dependence another phony condition whose treatment was "big business." These stoners pointed fingers at Washington's hypocrisy conferring legal status on certain profitable drugs like tobacco and alcohol, while big pharmaceutical companies—or "Big Pharma," as they referred to it—got our citizenry addicted to prescriptions. Then they'd mention the 12,000 or so Americans who died in alcohol-related car accidents every year and conclude, "Which is worse for you: cigarettes, pills, coffee, or weed?"

To these people I wasn't addicted to marijuana, only "habituated," psychologically dependent on not so much the drug as the routine. Because if cannabis didn't cause agonizing physical withdrawals the way heroin and alcohol did, and people couldn't overdose on it, what else could I be?

* * *

My route to school ran between University Boulevard and 1st Street. Four east-west alleys divided that section of what was blandly called the West University neighborhood. Three times a week I shuffled east along 2nd Street from my ugly, cinder-block apartment, past the Craftsman and other bungalows that dominated the area. Built between 1900 and the 1940s, some of these houses were restored, painted tan or bright pastels. Others featured second and third room additions rented as apartments. At this point, there were three interesting alleys to choose from. I preferred the southern route, though none were boring. Something new always presented itself, not simply a pile of antique bricks recently dumped there, or a taxidermied trout set for a few days atop a fence, or the words "Whistle Stop Snitches" newly spray painted on a trash bin, but details revealing the pulse of local life, an aspect of the community's character that required patience and repeat visits to notice.

I met a friendly stray cat with no left ear who lived near a certain aluminum shed. He was gray-and white with clean fur and no tag. Unlike the other feral cats who scattered at my approach, this one rushed from the shadows to get pet, affectionately nibbling on my fingers as he turned to brush his cheek against them. I started feeding him. Through a wire fence

I saw an elderly man sweeping the packed dirt of his small backyard. He wore a tan cowboy hat, brown polyester trousers and an off-white pearl button shirt. The broom was a ragged, permanently bent arc of bristles, and the dirt he swept only drifted to settle on another part of the yard. I saw a young man painting a portrait of his house on a large canvas, saw a Hispanic woman whose tiny, backyard guest house doubled as a hair salon. I didn't know people re-tarred their swamp coolers until I spotted a man doing it on the side of a house. I awoke every morning excited for my next stroll, invigorated in a way I hadn't been in years. Beyond Googie, I'd rarely taken an interest in my urban surroundings or the lives of city residents.

During my free time, I started exploring other alleys on my bike. Historic central Tucson was threaded with them. Often fortified with motion-sensitive security lights and "Beware of Dog" signs, they ran north-south or east-west on every block, often both directions, packed two or three to a block. As in other cities, Tucson's alleys provided garbage trucks access to bins and residents to rear garages. But here, tall candelabras of prickly pear cactus grew against fences, their plump green pads thrust into the air. Native creosote bushes released a clean, medicinal fragrance during winter rains. Hummingbirds perched in mesquite branches. Most of the city's primary building blocks were visible as well: adobe, red brick, corrugated aluminum, sheets of tin, stucco, cement, ocotillo fence posts, large volcanic rocks, rotting wooden boards, and barbed wire. One wrought iron security door had been shaped into the silhouette of a saguaro cactus.

As if the city actively denied their existence, many of these routes didn't have names, and the anonymity imparted a comforting, otherworldly atmosphere that felt far off the urban grid. Many weren't paved either, or they had been until the old asphalt returned to dirt.

Some of the artists and college students who rented these units accessed them through the alley. I sometimes passed them: hipsters on bikes; a hippie with died pink hair in a flowing tie-dyed dress. Yet the people I encountered most were just passing through. The Union Pacific railroad tracks ran a few blocks from my apartment, lined with the sorts of vacant warehouses and boarded up buildings where transients spent their days in the shifting shade. Leathery-skinned men walked past me lugging heavy backpacks and drank beer by dumpsters. Native Americans from various Southwestern reservations traveled the alleys to and from the parks where they sat in little covens. Filthy train-hopping kids with full face-tattoos strolled by on the way to the spots they busked for change. I wanted to say hello to them all, or at least nod, but I kept my head down, eyes shielded by the bill of my hat.

Even though Ted advised us not to place too much importance on the numbers, I recorded the days on my Canadian Rockies wall calendar. October 8: first day with no weed in three years. Not only weed, but no alcohol. I drew a black X stretching from each corner of the square. Every week or so I marked it: October 21: fourteen days sober. November 1: twenty-five days. November 18: forty-two days.

To reinforce my commitment, I scribbled the words "Weed = feel bad. Sobriety = feel good" on a thin ribbon of notebook paper and kept it in my wallet. It was a simple formula but difficult to follow. I slid it in the space in front of my IDs so that, even without reading the words, a glimpse of the clean white paper reminded me of what had at some point become a quest for purity.

* * *

In group, the bitter prep cook detailed his week's struggles: his ex-wife was bugging him for money; he felt old, hated his job; the stress made him want to drink. We offered encouraging messages which came out canned such as, "Hang in there man, you've made it so far." He wagged his leg, mumbled thanks.

Carolina seemed to be progressing. She wasn't using coke. Her boyfriend never called or came over, so she peered under the curtains less frequently. But she was lonely. She missed the company of a romantic companion and the bustle of so-called friends coming in and out of her old house. Ted discussed the necessity of staying single while adjusting to our new lives, recommending extreme caution when making new friends. To be safe, I decided to make no friends at all.

Years later, I saw that I failed to use group as a safe place to examine the forces that compelled me to use. Back then, I spoke only vaguely of my anxiety—how I'd once been the outgoing, congenial ham in my circle of friends, but had degenerated into the mercurial isolationist. I didn't describe how now, when I wasn't hiking or riding my bike, I spent my days in my small dark apartment with the blinds drawn. No one called. No one visited. I chain-smoked cigarettes and read natural history and watched *Pulp Fiction* over and over, savoring the surf music and coffee shop scenes, and envying the ease with which John Travolta's character plunged a needle into his arm. He seemed unburdened by guilt or repercussions. Aside from his murderous profession, he led a somewhat normal life despite his habit, or at least a social one. He danced with Uma Thurman, read books and talked food politics over breakfast. My envy of his character scared me. Part of me wished I'd enrolled in more than one college class that semester to get me socializing and out of the house and away from these unhealthy thoughts. The other part of me still winced at the prospect of going outside more than necessary. I'd started having pizzas delivered to lessen interactions.

Ted said he would check the literature, but he'd had marijuana dependents in previous groups and knew cessation could produce insomnia, agitation and anxiety. "Just stay committed to sobriety," he said with a smile. "I assure you the symptoms will pass."

Bitter didn't take my issues as seriously. While I talked, he sighed and tapped his foot. I could feel his disdain like heat from a radiator. While getting seated he'd once asked me, "Staying away from the herrrb?" Another time he muttered something like, "How's the big green battle?" I wanted to punch him in the face. Instead I taunted him, said, "How's the lettuce chopping? Probably prepping a lot faster now that you're not drunk."

"Okay," Ted said smiling. "Simmer down."

Simmer down? This motherfucker and countless others thought my problem was a joke. On their website, NORML, The National Organization for the Reform of Marijuana Laws, said, "Marijuana is the third most popular recreational drug in America (behind only alcohol and tobacco), and has been used by nearly 100 million Americans." Even though US Federal law outlawed the drug, NORML believed that public policy should reflect rather than deny pot's widespread popularity and its benign nature. "Marijuana is far less dangerous than alcohol or tobacco," the group said. Comparing it to the 400,000 annual tobacco-related deaths and the 50,000 people who died every year from alcohol poisoning, the group stated that marijuana "is non-toxic and cannot cause death by overdose." It even quoted the European medical journal, *The Lancet*, which claimed that "The smoking of cannabis, even long-term, is not harmful to health." In light of such sentiments, how else was I supposed to feel if not defensive? The message seemed to be that, unlike my groupmates' hardcore boozing and drugging, my problem was just another figment of my anxiety.

Like the built-up THC then draining from my body, the smothering residue of this line of thinking sometimes clouded my mind. "I've tried heroin, too," I blurted in group. "And coke and meth."

It was true. But the group smelled desperation. Ted said, "Does that mean you had a problem with those drugs?"

I said no, my friends and I had only tried them. I imagined Bitter rolling his eyes, but I didn't look. And I didn't take the opportunity to broach the subject that I knew I should have been exploring: that deep down, what I feared most about myself wasn't my relationship with pot, but the way I related to the world. I had what many laypeople called an "addictive personality." My life to that point had been composed of a series of passing fancies, phases so clearly defined that a historian could chart them like periods in European landscape painting. I didn't just like my favorite things, I structured my life around them. The way I was then obsessed with ecology and nature writing was the same way I'd been obsessed with *Star Wars*, bootleg records and the beach years before. And it was the same way I was becoming fixated on exploring Tucson's alleys.

I didn't mention how I'd enjoyed the heroin and had recently started thinking about doing more. I didn't complain about how it seemed like everyone I knew outside of group could, like Travolta, somehow function despite their use, and I didn't admit how, even though there was no short-cut to healing, part of me wanted to take the easy way out. And I didn't mention that I had finally started to see my problem for what it was: a deep-set change in mindset that had started during a period of hedonism and developed into a full-blown dependence on self-medication. No one is just a drug addict. We're escapists. Or avoiders. Or we're in pain because we've been traumatized, or self-loathing, or scared, the sum of our genetic disposition and the products of our primary relationships, always the children of people who can't raise kids perfectly.

When Ted asked why I used marijuana, the others stared at me and I shrugged, muttering something about having "gotten into the habit." What was the point of talking about it? This endless discussion hadn't kept Bitter from relapsing. I was doing everything I was supposed to. I'd quit visiting Brett. Quit going to Phoenix. Thrown out my paraphernalia. And in pot's place I read, hiked, explored my city on my bike, cooked healthy vegetarian meals, and at home I marked my calendar.

December 1: fifty-five days.

December 16: seventy days.

December 31, New Years Eve: eighty-five says.

January 26: one hundred and twelve days.

Wasn't that enough?

* * *

During our late teens, my friends and I watched *The Stöned Age* more times than I can count, not that I could remember how many times if pressed for a number. Although the movie was often considered the little low-budget brother to *Dazed and Confused*, we thought *The Stöned Age* a thousand times better. Its premise was simple and mirrored our own M.O.: the never ending quest to get "drunk, stoned, and laid." Random lines like "I don't want no chicks with zits, I want fine chicks!" were not only hilarious, they captured the unrequited longing and nonsensical nature of our average teenage lives. Plus, the soundtrack included Blue Öyster Cult's "(Don't Fear) The Reaper," and I loved that song.

As my own stoned age came to an end, I kept peddling around town. Through Iron Horse and Rincon Heights, Sam Hughes and Armory Park, Pie Allen and Barrio Viejo—through every available alley in all the historic neighborhoods, my Schwinn's plump, whitewall tires glided across the uneven dirt.

Things were unruly back there. Lacking the exposure and pruning of the streets, alleys are where people stashed their secrets: the car parts and chassis's residents hoarded in backyards; the racks of jars full of nails, screws and wires they stored beside their laundry room; the porn, soiled undies and yellowed sheets they stuffed in the dumpster at 11:00 p.m. so the neighbors wouldn't see.

Certain sections felt like a purgatory for castaways who had yet to make it to the grave, as if shed cells from the city's aging skin fell and settled there. Other sections felt like gardens where life thrived in the fertile bed of decay. Broken glass and a dented hubcap sat beside fragrant spring flowers and sapling trees. Lizards crawled across crumbling walls, living their entire lives around piles of yard debris that residents had left to desiccate beyond their fields of vision.

One morning I passed an old, very tan man lying on his back beside a ten-speed bike frame in the shade of a tamarisk. His eyes were closed. I thought he was asleep. But at the sound of my footsteps his lids parted to display bloodshot eyes. "Mornin'," he said, "You know anything about some food for some services?" I asked what kind of services. He said, "Me singing you a song." I gave him a cigarette, and he started making up lyrics to a formless melody as I sauntered by.

* * *

Carolina missed group one week, then the next. She hadn't called Ted to announce her absence. While he advised us not to assume anything, the rest of us speculated during smoke breaks: she'd relapsed; she'd returned to her boyfriend; he broke in to her apartment and did something horrible. I considered the possibility that I'd been wrong about her conviction, that maybe she rather than the others had been our weakest link. Bitter hadn't relapsed in months.

I'd started to regret my tensions with him. Surely he had some redeeming qualities that the confessional setting failed to bring out. Who knew what kind of troubled life he'd led before this—a rough childhood, mean parents. I needed to lighten up. One night, out of the blue, he told me: "Out of everyone here, you're the one I worry least about." I'd wished I felt the same.

I don't know if Carolina ever returned to group, because eventually I too quit attending. No personal triumph signaled it, no magic number on my calendar. I simply told myself I'd learned all I could from listening to other addicts and was tired of having the same conversations. I'd been sober for five months. I wanted to fill my time other ways.

Then an old friend came through town. She and her girlfriends were driving from Kansas to southern California for spring break, and they brought a few bags of Midwest dirt weed. To save them money I let them stay in my apartment. I took them hiking and out to Mexican food. They smoked during their one-night stay; I did not. They slept on my floor, all tan and excited for the beach, and when we awoke the next morning, I found myself thinking as much about their herb as their enviable trip. I knew better than to ask for weed. I should have also known better than to allow it in my apartment given my tenuous state, but there was nothing to do now except resist temptation. As they each took showers and I cooked them breakfast, I decided to ask for a little—just a little. I stopped short of asking and cursed myself for considering it. I had worked too hard at sobriety to throw it away. Six months, I told myself glancing at the calendar, six months. I poured them coffee and we ate in my living room. Then, as the girls stuffed their clothes into their bags and collected their toiletries, I blurted, "Think you can leave me with a little pinch?"

Of course, they said.

The moment they left, I fired it up in a pipe I made from a soda can. Confusion, isolation—the experience was as bad as I'd remembered it. Hiding in my apartment, the blinds drawn, time seemed to tick backwards. I couldn't remember why coffee beans sat on the kitchen counter. Had I made coffee already, or was I preparing to make a pot? I couldn't find my lighter, which had been in my hand what seemed like minutes before but could've been an hour or two. Too edgy to go outside, I sat in my living room chair listening to surf instrumentals at high volumes and lost myself in the melody until the effects subsided.

I still didn't return to group.

* * *

There's a scene in the movie *Half Baked* where Dave Chappelle's character gets up in front of a group of recovering addicts. It's a small room, lined with bench seats and filled with people. Chappelle stands at a lectern on a stage, a sign listing "rehab" hanging behind him, and he greets the crowd. "Hi. I'm here today because I'm addicted . . . to marijuana."

One infuriated rehab patient jumps to his feet. "You in here 'cuz of marijuana?" he says. "Marijuana? Man, this is some bullshit!"

Bob Saget, playing a fellow addict, stands up and tells Chappelle, "Marijuana is not a drug. I used to suck dick for coke."

The first patient mutters, "I seen him."

Saget says, "Now that's an addiction, man. You ever suck some dick for marijuana?"

Chappelle pauses. His eyes dart back and forth. His faces scrunches in concentration. "No," he says, shaking his head. "No, I can't say I have."

The first rehab patient screams, "Boo this man!" And the angry crowd pelts Dave with trash as he runs off stage.

A month after I quit group, a man stood in the alley, peeing behind the dumpster near my truck. I was taking out the trash. "Howsit going?" he said. I told him good and asked how he was. He zipped up and said, "Wudyougot going today?" He had on dark Levi's, a black t-shirt and a red bandana to absorb the sweat from his black hair. I gave him a cigarette and we sat on neighboring parking blocks along my building's rear wall. He laid a large green duffle bag beside us. When I asked where he was from he said, "From the other side." When I asked where he was headed he said, "Chasing that poon tang, dude, you know that's what it's all about." He smacked my shoulder with the back of his hand, and laughed until he coughed then spit on the asphalt.

Poon tang, I thought, have some respect. It sounded like a line from *The Stöned Age*. We sat and smoked in the shade, smoked and watched the spiraling forms of our exhalations rise into the scorching blue sky as sweat streamed down our temples.

LAND SPECULATION

By the time the nurses led Kari down the hall, the mushrooms had so scrambled her mind that she didn't realize it wasn't the drug causing her discomfort, it was the bees. Yellow-jackets actually, forty-nine stings we later counted.

I left my truck running in front of the ER, trying not to arouse Kari's suspicion by slamming to a halt. "I'm going to get your Sprite," I told her. "Just stay lying down and I'll be right back. Promise to keep your head down." Then I raced to the nurse's window and said, "My girlfriend and I just got swarmed by bees and she's allergic."

With the languid calm of a grazing elephant, the nurse said, "What are her symptoms?" I listed them: red eyes, blotchy skin, numb feet, shallow breathing.

Through the glass partition, the nurse studied my eyes and my breathing, making me think she had already diagnosed my condition: early-stage psilocybin toxicity, questionable character.

"And where is the patient?" the nurse said. As I pointed to my truck, Kari sat up, her bulging eyes and gaping mouth visible through the windshield.

I patted the counter. "I'll be right back." Then I rushed outside, swung open the car door and told Kari, "It's okay. Don't worry."

"What are we doing here?" she shrieked.

On the frantic drive down from the Redwoods to Eureka, I'd lied and told her we were going to a convenience store. "Just lay your head on my lap," I said, "stretch out, and I'll get you a Sprite. Does that sound good?"

She lifted her legs onto the passenger seat and lowered her head onto my lap. "It sounds great," she muttered. She liked Sprite. It calmed her stomach. Acting as if I was just massaging what she called her "itchy feet," I peeled back the cuffs of her jeans to inspect her ankles. They were swollen, growing puffier by the minute, and cloaked entirely in splotches of ghost white and pink. Same with her back. I lifted her shirt. Discoloration spread above and below her waistline, creeping all the way to her neck and spilling over her ears and onto her cheeks. And her eyes: the whites and hazel irises had darkened to scarlet. This was the mortal stain of spilled pig's blood, diseased liver crimson. Devil red.

My fear was that her throat would shut. That's what I heard happened to victims with bee allergies: their trachea constricts, then they suffocate. But how do you ask someone if they can breathe without implying that they might soon not be able to? While we had only eaten a few small caps, this was one of her first mushroom trips. I didn't want to throw her into a six hour nightmare of screaming panic by giving her terrifying news to fixate on. She was already a worrier. She worried about homework, worried about calories, worried about whether she would make a better school teacher or counselor. She worried if I thought she was a wimp because she preferred to hike on- rather than off-trail, worried if I loved her as much as she said she loved me. On shrooms, she would flip, and it would be my fault.

"Honey," I said, "do you hear that whistling? Is that you or the car?" As soon as I said it, I knew it made no sense. I laid my palm on her chest. "Take a deep breath for me." She took a deep breath. I said, "Everything feel normal in there?" She nodded an exhausted nod. Then I drove the forty-five miles to the closest hospital at ninety miles an hour.

Although the mushrooms hadn't hit me yet, that summer I was twenty-two years old. Driving on drugs was one of my few skills. Kari was more innocent.

She and I first met in high school in Phoenix, dated for a couple weeks, then she left me unexpectedly to return to her previous boyfriend. She came from a wealthy family. They lived in a historic neighborhood in the shadow of a large mountain my friends and I frequently hiked. When she and I later ran into each other during college in Tucson, we set a time to meet for coffee. Soon we were an item, and I could barely contain my excitement.

I fell for her this time as quickly as I had the first. She was smart, intuitive, joyful, and compassionate, and she was loyal to her friends. Short with light brown hair, she had a set of pink lips that arched in the shape of a heart when she smiled, and she smiled all the time. Her buoyant personality was so uplifting that my close friend Chris had once also developed an immediate crush. In high school he kept saying, "She's so cute, like, adorable, huggable, unbearable cute." In terms of mischievous experiences, she was also unseasoned.

Unlike me and the guys I hung out with, Kari had never taken acid and she rarely smoked weed. She drank beer on weekends but hardly to excess. This was college. Everyone drank beer to excess. Although she smoked cigarettes socially, she never woke up as I did and immediately reached for her pack. She'd cook breakfast, watch some TV, maybe have a smoke later just to socialize outside. She was stable that way, and normal. When I discovered the first signs of her profound maternal streak, I knew that eventually she was going to leave me. Though she never said it outright, the situation was clear: she planned to have children with someone in the not-too-distant future; did I feel the same?

She wanted it all: kids, a house, good job, a family, normal human goals that back then, with the exception of the house, I didn't share. She worked at a daycare, later a Montessori school. She studied Sociology with a special interest in child psych. With pride that stemmed from her innate feminism, her stated life goal was to be a mother. I found that enviable and attractive—an outwardly focused life and a tight family bond. I went so far as to consider her wholesome, the kind of woman my dad might have fallen for growing up in the fifties in small-town Arizona. Kari and I shared little besides our age, address, and interest in each other, but at least she had interests. I'd met so many people whose sole hobbies were sex, booze, and TV. Kari did watch lots of TV. She liked staying at home on weeknights and weekends watching talk shows and sitcoms and movies, but her passion for her college classes and her career goals were inspiring and unnerving. After her interest in child development led her to a job at Montessori, she'd return home from work and describe the accomplishments of her young students: this one drew a cool, complicated picture; that one cut-and-pasted a collage without eating the paste; the lessons she taught in vocabulary and art. Sitting together on the couch, I listened and asked questions. She loved her work with children in ways I couldn't understand. I tried, but I related more to Edward Abbey's memoir *Desert Solitaire* than to activities that involved nurturing anyone younger than myself. Kari was more advanced than me, and I wasn't ready to learn how to be.

This summer I'd driven up from Tucson alone, hiking and camping new parts of the Northwest. In Bellingham, Washington I parked my truck and took the B.C. ferry to Juneau where my mom met me and we explored southeast Alaska together. Two weeks later, after tons of hiking and sightseeing, Mom flew home, and I boated back to Bellingham. Innocent as it seemed, I recognized it then as clearly as I did now: I was trying to recreate the magic of that previous summer trip, that sense of newness, invincibility and freedom that Dean and I experienced while exploring the wild West Coast. But you only get one first hit. After that, you're always chasing something that you can't catch.

Kari had flown to Seattle to meet me. Now we were driving down the Coast together, hiking, sightseeing, and roadtripping for a week. I was excited. I was confused. I'd been sober for months but had started dabbling. Nothing daily, but my usual ritualistic consumption seemed inevitable. Against my better judgment, I'd brought a quarter ounce of mushrooms on this trip along with a tiny bit of weed that, after all the hard work in my drug recovery group, I knew I should not have been smoking. It was a bad sign. Anyone could see that, even through the haze of smoke and shrooms.

Racing down Highway 101 that July, I kept checking Kari's breathing: does your throat itch? Feel tight? Feel okay? Averting a sense of urgency with my hushed tone, I stroked her hair and kept calmly saying, "We're getting close to that soda sweetie. Almost there." She said the mushrooms made her body "feel all buzzy," a thought which I encouraged lest she think, as I did, that she might soon die in my truck among the dairy farms and redwoods. When we finally reached Eureka, I followed the hospital signs through unfamiliar neighborhoods and told her I'd spotted a convenience store.

Now she was sitting up shrieking, "What are we doing here?"

"Just dropping in for a visit," I said while lifting her from the cab. "We're visiting really quickly, to get cream for your stings. Don't worry. Everything's fine. You're fine." I carried her featherweight in my arms through the parking lot. Her feet hurt too much to walk. They were as puffed as rotting walruses. She stared at me with those pig's blood eyes. Then by the door I stopped, lowered my voice and said, "Just remember, we cannot let them know we're tripping. Okay? Don't say anything about drugs or how things look or sound weird or anything. Just keep it between us." She nodded. "Let me do the talking, and we'll get in and out of here and back on the road in a hurry. Okay?" She nodded. I kissed her lips.

The nurses hustled her down the hall, leaving me standing with a short man in a white lab coat and an out-of-date-looking pair of prescription glasses. He introduced himself as the doctor. He said, "So tell me what happened." I did my best.

We were in Redwood National Park. Kari and I had been seeing each other for over three months, and after weeks of gentle nudging, she finally agreed to try hiking off-trail—'bushwhacking,' it's called. While traipsing atop an enormous, downed redwood log—the thing must have been thirty-feet around—she stepped on a bee's nest—which we later found out were yellow-jackets—and they attacked. I didn't even see the nest; insects must have built it beneath a slab of peeling bark. They got inside her jeans, her shirt, her shoes. They tagged her arms, face, ankles, scalp and chest.

He nodded as I talked, scribbled notes. When he looked up he stared into my eyes in a way I considered suspicious.

I didn't mention how I had sustained an equally aggressive attack— fifty-one stings, we later counted. I didn't say how I'd been hiking, like an idiot, with no shirt or socks on, only black Converse All-Stars, shorts and a baseball cap. I didn't—I don't think—offer my hiking pedigree in order to show that, despite the current situation, I was more than some brazen, irresponsible John Muir wannabe who lured his girlfriend into danger to impress her, and that, in addition to and despite that, I had hiked, camped and traveled all over western North America, from Baja California to central Alaska, exploring parks and the rugged backcountry, and that in all my years of off-trail hiking—innumerable hours of it in my native Arizona's rattlesnake-rich deserts—I had never once been stung by a bee.

He might have been impressed, too. Lots of people I told the stories to were. In fact, if I thought about it, as unique experiences go, this bee sting incident was pretty interesting. It would fit nicely alongside my other memorable travel stories. Like the time I drank a beer with a Navajo man in Flagstaff who called me "Pee Wee" because of my beach cruiser, and who talked candidly with me about the daily effects of racism and white colonization on his people and his life. And the time a scorpion stung my foot inside a Texas state park shower. And of course the snarling Dalmatian in the boarded-up motel. Same with the drive down here: ninety miles an hour after eating mushrooms? Exciting stuff. Except that Kari was now suffering because of me.

To my knowledge I said none of this. I just stood there stiff and sweating, watching the pastel hallway glow more and more brightly and if I was making any sense. The whole place felt so blindingly bright and sterile that my stomach turned. Usually hospitals unnerved me. This one made me feel like a pollutant. My forearms were dusted with what I thought was fern pollen. Dark forest soil lined my fingernails. Brown bits of twig clung to my shoelaces. I pictured my body as a neon green virus molecule, part-cartoon, part electron microscope image, with all the bumpy, angry surfaces they display at 250,000 magnification. I saw my viral self drifting through the hospital, then into the cartoon mouth of a woman in one of those human body medical cross-section diagrams for asthma inhalers, me binding like a steroid to clean lung tissue. Whoa. Did that mean I was a toxin or medicine? Death or temporary relief for Kari's innocent, focused existence? Part of me wished I was a steroid. Then she wouldn't be sick among strangers in an unfamiliar town.

Either I spoke or the Doc read my mind. "She's going to be fine," he said and handed me paperwork. Great, I thought. Fantastic. But what about the two of us? This incident might reveal an unbridgeable rift, weakening or breaking our new bond. I tried not to think about that. Instead, I filled out the paperwork, repeatedly wiping my sweaty palms so the pen wouldn't slide out. I tried to be cool, sort of relaxed and jokey like, "Slow day at the office?" Checked my handwriting's legibility, trying to keep it free of weird squiggles and Dali-esque marginalia. All the dates seemed correct. Her name. Insurance. I'd dotted all the eyes, I mean I's. I was proud of my drugged-up composure, then immediately ashamed of my pride. No one should be skilled at feigning sobriety.

I handed him the clipboard and thought, He knows. Everyone knows. When you're messed up, bystanders always seem to recognize it. You become overly aware of your mannerisms but can't conceal your condition. You think, If I wasn't high, would I dangle my hands at my side like this? If I wasn't high, would I normally lean against a wall with one hand in my back pants pocket, nodding yes this aggressively? And am I walking weird? I feel like I'm walking weird. I barely feel my feet. They are touching the ground, aren't they? You look down, confirming gravity's hold, then think, Well, I definitely seem to be hunching over, and that's a giveaway. Better straighten up. But instead, you overcompensate. Then when people look at you, you think it's because they're privy to all this tortured interior monologue, as if a transcript were printed on your forehead like a weather report: "Dark skies inside Aaron today. Storm system moving in, perfect conditions for tornados. Chance of disintegration: 100 percent." Yep, you conclude, they know.

Or not.

My performance with that nurse was spectacular: articulated words, concise sentences, no bulging eyes. I hadn't said anything suspicious like, "That coat is friggin' whi-i-ite." Or, "Dang, love the retro glasses." I was just cruising through this doctor-patient interaction with the swiftness of whatever popular basketball stars regular people talked about whose names I didn't know because sports completely bored me, especially when compared to reading John Muir's journals.

Besides, I'd eaten these things tens of times before. Eaten them in the city and desert and forest. Eaten them with my best friends and alone, camping and at peoples' homes. Then I had motored through the sober world relying on the last turning gears of my gummed-up mind. In years past, my friends and I would eat shrooms and somehow manage to order burritos at twenty-four-hour Mexican food joints while hallucinating. Or buy sodas at convenience stores—counting out bills, chatting with clerks—when minutes before we'd been laughing uncontrollably at trimmed oleanders. Once I even picked up my paycheck at Subway sandwiches as the psilocybin giggles started to overtake me. Having to make sense when nothing made sense—that was my business. I needed that printed on a business card.

I looked through the front window at my truck—parked between the lines, all proper-like. I scanned the ER. An empty rolling bed sat against the wall far down the hall, which seemed to grow longer the longer I stared down it. A metal rolling table sat nearby too, close enough to see that some implements covered it. Shiny metal things, what I imagined were scissors and stitchers and folders and such, tools you'd use in reconstructive surgery. Or skin origami. And look at those crazy ass forceps or whatever those are, I thought. Wow. My mom used to pull her famous fried beef tacos out of a vat of boiling Crisco with tongs like that. These health care providers should go into the taco business. They could pull, like, ten tacos out of the grease at once.

Ahahahahaha, hahahahaha, hahahaha!

Ha.

Kari reappeared. The nurses seemed to eyeball me as they passed. I wondered if Kari had broken our agreement of psychedelic secrecy, blurting something like, "Your faces are melting!" They led her past me and into an adjacent room.

Doc said something like, "You can go in there now."

The nurses helped Kari onto a bed in the tiny room, which sat beside the front door and front desk, and then they left. We were alone. Alone with our thoughts and secrets.

The room fell silent. I stood by the bed, staring at Kari, wondering if my hands normally hung by my side this way. A single chair sat against the wall. Would it be weird to sit in that chair on the other side of the room? Would that make me seem callous or disinterested? I wasn't disinterested, I just wanted to sit. My feet hurt and whole body itched. But things looked so lonesome over there.

I slid my hands into my pockets. The nurses probably wouldn't mind if I dragged the chair closer. Or I could lift and carry it over. I stood by the bed thinking, staring at Kari and her pursed lips and the trouble I'd caused. Then I pulled the sheet up over her swollen, shoe-less feet, over the weak rise-and-fall of her familiar narrow chest, on up to her neck so just her face stuck out from the sheet. She looked like a puppet in a Jim Henson bit. She looked Muppetish. She smiled.

"Is that comfortable?" I said.

She whispered, "Yes."

Beside the chair ran a short counter lined with jars of bandages, Q-tips and tongue depressors. Above that hung a pastel cabinet filled, I assumed, with smocks and cotton balls and rubber gloves. "Look," I pictured myself saying to Kari while pulling on a pair. "Cow condoms."

"Why are the walls breathing?" Kari said.

"Ssshhhh!" I said, leaning close, my finger pressed to my lips. "Don't say that too loud, honey. We don't want the doctors to hear." Not that they'd throw us in jail. I just didn't want to be detained longer than her recovery required. These were the last days of our journey, the ones you wish would last forever, like melting ice cream and libidinous sunny weather, and we'd intended to drive three-hundred-twenty miles to Sacramento that afternoon. We'd only made it seventy.

Kari looked petrified then laughed. "Oh yeah."

We smirked at each other. The silence enclosed us.

Cold air moved across my skin. Her brown hair spread across the pillow like seaweed in the tide pools we'd visited in coastal Oregon. The filaments still shone in the harsh hospital light, but they seemed less healthy and luminous somehow, unnaturally limp, as if I had sucked the spirit from them.

I'd only wanted her to see the outdoors. Maybe she would come to love it the way I did, or at least see what I saw in it and understand my attraction. With such different visions for our respective futures, Kari and I needed a bond of some kind, a couple of strong common interests to solidify our union. Otherwise, what did we have? A relationship based on shared air space and a mutual need for emotional companionship. I'd hoped that we would find our bond in nature.

The room did seem to be breathing, the walls swelling and contracting, swelling and contracting—a giant lung. Ha, I thought, magic mushrooms, is that all you've got? I stood and considered it. Was the room actually breathing, or was it shrinking instead? Squeezing us together or pushing us apart? What if this was a new technology: rooms that changed dimensions to help treat the emotional connection of the people in it. If there was any town whose hospitals would have spatially adaptive rooms like that, it'd be Eureka. This was is a hippie-college-logging town. It had once been a major galaxy in the Dead Head universe. It was still loaded with fellow co-op-shopping tofu-eaters driving art cars and VW Things, the kind of longhairs who kept decomposing yellow school buses in overgrown backyards for parts and guest rooms, or in case Ken Kesey's ghost reunited the Merry Pranksters. Northern California was also home to an enormous network of backwoods marijuana-growing operations. Millions of dollars' worth of potent herb sprouted under the protection of the tall redwood forest canopy.

These were dinosaur forests, straight out of the Carboniferous. That's why I wanted Kari to hike off-trail here. "To truly experience the Redwoods," I kept saying, "you have to bushwhack in an old-growth forest. Tromp through the undergrowth, bushes up to your armpits, sword ferns over your head. Then walk along the mossy top of a downed tree, staring into the dark woods."

The idea unnerved her. "Aren't there bears and snakes out there?" she'd ask. "What if we get lost?" This had become the running theme of our relationship: off-trail versus on-trail; playing it safe versus playing it bold; the novel versus the familiar; how worn paths separate the rote from what's interesting. Maybe that's why she had always liked cats more than dogs: cats are content at home; dogs have to leave the house to run. No, that wasn't accurate either, just like my motives weren't so benevolent. I wanted her to experience the redwoods, yes, and I also wanted her to be more like me so I didn't have to think about my own wildness and deficiencies.

"We won't get lost," I told her over and over.

"Maybe at some point," she would say. I knew that meant never if I didn't facilitate it.

I might have pushed too far. "In the Redwoods," I'd said, "you expect a brontosaurus to peer out from behind a tree. It's that surreal." Mushrooms would "enhance" this quality.

"I don't know," she said. "I mean, what's going to happen?"

"You're going to go nuts for a few hours, and it's going to be fun," I said. "That's all." She nodded. Hallucinogens require you to relinquish control, which, I explained, is half their appeal. "Just completely losing your mind, because the thing is, you'll always get it back. It's temporary insanity, the only good kind."

Temporary insanity. In the ER, it all sounded like self-serving BS. Thinking you could eat mushrooms and a few hours later drive the chilling hairpin turns of the rugged Northern Coast Range? That was insanity. That and dating me.

If we made it back to Tucson, I assumed she would never hike again. That seemed tragic. It was just a few welts. Stings seemed a fair price for a memorable experience, and the point of taking roadtrips is having memorable experiences. This was college. I firmly believed that experience was the net sum of your youth, one of the few things that remained after time and your body betrayed you, the interest you accrued to survive the lean years beyond your forties. Like Christmas every year, I saw it coming: adulthood and responsibility, the twin headlights of death's approaching train. So like Nigel in *Spinal Tap*, I turned up my amp past ten, to eleven, believing that these were the last days—last days of fun, last days of freedom, last of the interesting stuff—believing that fun receded like a tide following graduation. That's how little I knew about anything. I thought that when our joints ached and blood pressure ran high, when we were tied to bleak office jobs to finance thankless offspring, all we would have to look forward to was what we could look back on. That to endure this grim future, all a person could do besides run away and start over was relive golden moments, moments like this, and find comfort that yes, we may be old, but the Earth is a big fascinating place, and we at least experienced a bit of it. What was the alternative: we sure watched some great television? Hell no. Go down the rabbit hole.

My ass felt wedged in that hole.

This made me think of Alice and the White Rabbit, of Alice and the Queen of Hearts. And that tea party scene, my God. All those characters with the big heads and exaggerated features. What colors! And why did the Mad Hatter keep that "10/6" card in his hat band anyway? 10/6 of what, his mind lost to mercury poisoning? Or was that just his little trademark?

It made me wish I had a trademark. Not rainbow suspenders over a shirtless chest. Definitely not a cane with a skull handle and fake ruby eyes.

But something, some signature look. I looked like a homeless skateboarder who just stumbled into town after three days lost eating bark in the woods, a total dirtbag. Or that's how I felt. How were you supposed to feel when you nearly kill the most important person in your life?

Kari laid in the bed without moving. With her eyes on the ceiling, she looked dead.

Tick.

I thought I heard the big black arm of the wall clock move.

Tick.

I was pretty sure that was it. What else in this morgue room had moving parts?

I held my breath and listened for the tick.

Nothing.

Maybe the nurses were standing outside our door listening, straining to hear what would confirm their suspicions. Or watching us through the gap between the frame and the door. Covertly, I redirected my gaze, as if it was a spontaneous act. Nothing.

Tick.

Maybe it was just the clock.

How long were we supposed to stay in here anyway? Ten minutes? Ten hours? No one told me. No one said, "Just wait here until the blotches fade and those Devil red eyes turn white again." No one said, "Notify us tomorrow if she still can't feel her big swollen feet." Or maybe they had and I'd forgotten.

Tick.

What if they were holding us until the cops arrived? Seriously. That wasn't beyond the realm of possibility. They could be stalling us while telling officers on the front desk phone, "Yes, they're in Room 6A, wearing cut-off green army shorts and Converse, no socks. No, the plates say Arizona. Oh yes, we'll keep them busy."

I stood there and planned my speech, how I'd talk to the police as calmly as I'd talked to so many convenience store clerks and all-night Mexican restaurant staff during my late-teens when my friends and I were perpetually stoned.

After a few seconds of thinking, I couldn't remember a word.

What?

I looked at Kari. Her mouth pinched shut, gaze fixed on the ceiling panels.

I mean, should we just expect that nurses will eventually come in and tell us when to go? Or were we waiting for some fancy medicine to counteract the bee venom? Someone should have told us how long that chemical reaction takes; we can't just putz around patchouli-stink Eureka all day. While Kari was clearly no longer in danger of death, my metabolic mushroom clock was ticking. In another hour, I'd be peaking like her, and then who knows what would happen. I might start hanging tongue depressors from my lips to impersonate a gopher, or find myself staring into a mirror cackling at the lunar landscape of pores on my face, wondering how I ever thought I looked like Luke Skywalker as a kid, with Mark Hamill's deep butt-chin. I'd probably end up composing lyrics to fictional songs about caveman bowlers to the tune of "Like a Rolling Stone," a song which I hated. I always told myself that I may eat mushrooms, but I'm no hippie. I pictured the nurses administering Kari a bee venom antidote via IV in some cold steel room down the hall—the "Insect Victim Wing."

"What medicine'd they give you in there?" I whispered.

Kari stared at me a moment then said, "I don't know."

Uh oh. If I asked somebody how long we should stay, they might tell me, "We already told you." Then I'd really look messed up. I stood there thinking, looking at my arms—all long and gangly, like human arms hanging from the furry shoulders of an orangutan. But it was also weird to just stand around here waiting. That seemed crazier than asking someone.

Kari stared into space, arms at her side. She looked as I had imagined she'd look at her funeral from the bee envenomanation or whatever, before my eyes swelled shut from the beating her brother, sister and parents would give me for killing her.

I glanced at the wall clock. We've only been here five minutes? That can't be right. I looked at my watch. It showed the same time.

To get a sense of how much time I had before the mushrooms kicked in, I considered asking a nurse to describe the stages of Kari's healing.

Then I remembered the nurses. They intimidated me. It felt like they were judging me. "Thinking he's Thoreau," their eyes seemed to say. "Getting this poor girl stung like that. If that was my man, I'd dump him faster than he could say 'don't go.'"

Dumped. That was my greatest fear. Not rattlesnakes or bear attacks. I had spent the bulk of those past four college years and most of high school single, yearning for connection, assuming love was reserved for other, more mature people. Finally I'd met Kari, this gentle, responsible, smart stable woman with the most loving, maternal streak I'd ever encountered, and when she inevitably found out that I couldn't give her the life she wanted, she was going to leave me. I knew she'd be happier if she did, but I wasn't going to admit that and hasten her departure. I needed her. I had long since soiled my innocence and thought it wise to absorb hers. I had convinced myself that opposites attract because people's differences complement each other, that a coupling of opposites creates two whole individuals. I'd even told myself that although I didn't want kids now, with enough time and Kari's example, I might grow to want some. Lies. The desperate pleas of a man thumbing rides on the highway: "Please take me with you," the hitchhiker screams, "I'm lost! There's nothing else out here!" Deep down I knew that I wouldn't care about infants or toddlers at this stage in life. Just the word toddler made me queasy. It sounded like an excretory function, or a verb: "The poop log toddled precariously from the tip of little Mikey's bottom." Why voluntarily invite that stuff into your life? Granted, as an outdoorsman, I believed that clean hands and sterile environments were hugely overrated, but so was parenting. Uninterrupted sleep, meals eaten without onesies and cribs crowding your kitchen table, doing whatever the hell you wanted whenever-the-hell, that was the good life.

It might be true what that hippie bumper-sticker says, that not all those who wander are lost, but some of them must get lonely. They have to. When I imagined the life Kari and I could have together, I imagined a lifetime of acting like I wanted it. It would be her life we'd be living. Why couldn't I tell her that? Just be honest and admit it? Instead, when I thought about this, I thought back to how single life felt before I met her, and I hoped that maybe if I hung in there long enough, select parts of her personality might still rub off on me. That maybe Kari's normalcy could envenom me, that her stability might attach itself like twigs on a shoelace, so that her visions of a future would become my visions. And if Kari wouldn't stay, then maybe she could fix me before she left.

She looked at me from the bed. Her eyes were still red, but slowly growing whiter. "Hey red eyes," I thought. "Can you see that I'm selfish?"

I looked away at the walls. Pastels. The kind of ice cream social colors you put in a baby's room. Which was another thing that made me queasy: the way people always probed into your parenting instincts. If you told them you don't have any, they thought probing deeper would reveal the truth.

"Don't you want to create life?" they'd say.

"I'm already creating one," I'd say, "my own. One free of pediatrician appointments and crying in the night."

"Come on," they'd say, "what about preserving your family lineage?"

And I'd say, "My four half-brothers are preserving it already."

"Okay," they'd say, "as a naturalist, what about preserving the species?"

"The earth does not need one more successful copulater."

What sort of parent would I make anyway? My girlfriend was covered in spots. Two shriveled house plants slumped in my apartment. I didn't have a credit card, couldn't balance my checkbook. Sometimes I turned in my school work late. When I was sixteen, I didn't know you had to put oil in your car, and one hungover morning after hearing some pings, my engine locked up. My first car, my first six months of driving, and I was already on my second engine. How many marriages would I have to ruin, how many times would I have to lose my kids in a national park, or get them stung by scorpions while camping, before people accepted what I told them?

I should have fessed up, told Kari right there: "You deserve a better man."

She would figure it out eventually. She could see how restless I often got watching TV with her on sunny Saturday afternoons, the way I suggested we do something other than see a movie each Friday night, my complete lack of parenting fantasies. She was smart. She noticed more than she let on. So why bring it up. I was a land speculator in the land of the lonely. I refused to rush back to my old vacant lot.

The wall clocked ticked.

My eyes burned and stings itched.

Where were those nurses? Waitresses at Denny's at least visit your table every few minutes to refill your water.

"Pssst," I said to Kari. "Hey." She looked over. "Onth you fleel up to it, we'll haul ath through the Coathst Range. It'th still early enough. We can make it to Thacramento, maybe flurther." Words wiggled like snakes from my mouth. My tongue stuck to the roof of it, lips stuck together. To speak, I had to peel my mouth apart, sealed as it was by what felt like plaster. Licking didn't help. Were they shellacked gooey white? I started to ask but thought better of it. We both needed to believe everything was under control.

I smeared my lips with Chapstick. It tasted like medicated surfboard wax, cherry plus preservatives plus plastic plus fat. I took a sniff. Took a lick. Then I ran my teeth across the top to shave off a bite. It tasted just as bad on my tongue.

"What are you doing?" Kari said.

"Oh just—I don't know. You feeling better?" Her skin was slowly darkening to its Sunbelt bronze. She said she was, though her feet still tingled and the welts itched and the room was really, really bright. I started to feel the countless points of pain on my body. They combined into one unbearable accumulating burn that throbbed like the walls of our room. For the first time I thoroughly surveyed my damage. Swollen red pyramids, tons of them, ran up and down my arms, ankles, wrists and legs. I poked them. Scratched them. Rubbed my shirt across them hoping the rough cotton would provide more relief than my nails. Nothing worked. I wanted to see the welts on my eyebrows and ears, but I feared things would spiral if I saw myself in a mirror.

I said, "Let me go get some Calamine for us."

"Wait," Kari said. "Don't leave me alone."

Leave her? This hadn't occurred to me. I was the one leaving our room's quiet shelter. I was the one who had to ask the staff questions then try to sift through the answers, or at least nod a lot. One time this kid in college told me how he took a leak while peaking on acid, and he made the mistake of peering into the bowl. "I flushed the toilet," he said, "and it was like my whole life went down with the pee. My sanity, my future, my—just everything, it all flushed down the bowl at once." He snickered when he said it, but the shock of acquired wisdom hadn't dulled through the years. "It scared me to death," he said. I felt the same way.

"I'll be right outside," I said. "Close your eyes and think happy things." I stepped into the hall.

We had been in that room nearly two hours.

A nurse stood by the front door, her arms crossed, staring through the glass at my red pickup and the green world beyond. When I asked about leaving, she fetched the doctor.

Words came out of my mouth, vocalizations. He looked carefully into my eyes. I imagined a kaleidoscope of color had replaced their natural brown, some swirling of tangerine trees and marmalade skies from a *Laugh In* set. I pictured my old eyes filled with new fire, bristling crematory flames crackling from the churning furnace of all my mixed intentions. Orange, yellow, red, flickering, and lashing against the expanded black canvas of my dilated pupils. He handed me a square of paper and said, "Get her Benadryl."

Benadryl? I thought, or said. Was he messing with me? You can get that stuff anywhere. It's so benign a compound Pfizer packages the pink pills in pink-and-white boxes. Benadryl. So we don't even have to be here right now?

"That's right," he said, sending adrenaline through my chest. "Same thing you buy at any drug store. Every time you and Kari go hiking, carry a box with you. That's all it takes."

He smiled. I smiled. He knew.

Or not.

"Thanks Doc," I said. "We'll go get some right now."

From Eureka, I drove us straight through the Coastal Mountains, turned south at Redding and aimed for Arizona, where for the next two and a half years we each carried secrets and secret intentions, holding our cards close to our chests, forever our eyes Devil red.

ANCIENT HISTORY

My Uncle Sheldon is infirm, though nobody knows why. Asperger's? Depression? Social anxiety disorder? "Socially awkward" is my family's own diagnosis.

Which of Sheldon's issues stem from biology, which from conditioning? It's the old nature versus nurture debate. Being raised in Flushing, Queens among loud-talking Jews might not be listed in the DSM as a medical condition, but it's certainly a strong enough force to shape personality.

At the dinner table his mother still tells him: "Slow down." "Chew your food." "Don't talk with your mouth full."

"Fine," Sheldon says, dropping his fork on the plate with a clink. He turns his head in a huff, his mouth ringed white in salad dressing, then slowly lifts the fork to resume eating. He's sixty-one years old.

This has been Sheldon and my grandma's routine for as long as I can remember. Apparently it's the same smothering dynamic they brought with them from New York City when they moved to Phoenix in 1969.

Ever since I was a kid, my mom and dad and I have joined my Grandma Silvia and her second, goyische husband Carol for dinner on Christmas, Easter, Chanukah, and Passover, plus regular Sunday meals. Sheldon always attended. He did laundry at their house on Sundays. During the wash cycle, he read my grandparents' newspaper and watched TV, which conveniently positioned him for free food. After Sheldon quit working at the clothing store his father, my Grandpa Shapiro, owned, his employment became erratic. He worked short stints at odd jobs—as a standardized test grader, a parking lot security guard—each separated by long gaps of unemployment, so he's always searching for ways to save money. No matter where we eat, a restaurant or someone's house, he always takes home a doggy bag.

At Grandma's we eat at a large rectangular table. It's a dark, black walnut table set atop the living room's avocado green carpet. Ever since Grandpa Carol passed, the seating arrangement has remained the same. Grandma sits at one end. Mom, Dad, and Sheldon and I sit along the sides, I'm at Grandma's right hand, and Sheldon is at her left. And when Sheldon howls his signature non sequiturs about Mexican day laborers, recent art films, and newspaper headlines, Grandma yells: "Sheldon, quiet down." "Lower your voice." "Ssshhhh, I'm talking."

"Alright already," Sheldon says, folding his arms. Depending on how much food remains on his plate, he often pushes back his chair and stares at the table. He's hard of hearing, but he always hears his mother.

He eats as if he has somewhere else to go. Without concern for courses or taste, he thrusts salad into his mouth, moves to the main dish, usually has more salad as the rest of us are starting the salmon, then he skips dessert. "I'm watching my girlish figure," he likes to joke before taking a single forkful of cake. He refuses to wear a hearing aid, opting instead to read lips. So I speak in simple sentences and try to enunciate my words. We all do. But he responds at such jarring decibels that everyone shooshes him, everyone but me. I could never shoosh him. It's too patronizing.

Nowadays, as she did when I was a kid, Grandma leans close to me after scolding Sheldon and says, "See? He doesn't listen." And I think, Neither would you after years of nagging.

* * *

Before moving to New York at age thirty-one, the furthest east I had ventured was the Alabama-Georgia border. For years I proudly proclaimed that if I died without ever visiting New York City, I wouldn't feel deprived. Only years later did I realize one source of my aversion. The East had come to represent failure to me. East was neurosis. East was the past.

My mother's family fled Queens for Arizona after my Uncle Howard killed himself. He was twenty-seven years old, a Chemistry PhD student at the University of Michigan Ann Arbor, and engaged to be married. One day, unprompted by any specific event anyone knows or will discuss, he downed a lethal cocktail in his school chem lab.

After Howard's suicide, my grandparents fell apart. They took off work.

They sought comfort in their neighbors. Had they been religious, they would have sat shiva. No one on that side of the family would ever discuss how else they endured the preceding months of mourning. All I know is that, to take their mind off of the tragedy, my grandparents vacationed in Phoenix in the spring of 1969. They moved the family there the following summer and never looked back. It took my mom thirty-four years to return to the Empire State, and that was for business, not pleasure. Everyone insisted that if I would've met Howard, I would've loved him. "Everyone loved him," Grandma says. The mantra seems to comfort her.

After a recent Thanksgiving meal, I joined Sheldon and Grandma in my parent's bedroom. They'd gathered around a black and white family photo from their years in New York. Arranged in a V according to height and age stood Howard, beside Sheldon, beside my mom and Grandma, then Grandpa holding my grinning Aunt Debbie.

Grandma put her finger on Howard's gray face. With his straight frame posed stiffly in a suit, he stood, half-smiling. "Here's the one I miss," she said. "I'll never understand." I used to think, How could she understand? He took his reasons with him. Now I think she knows more than she can bear to admit. I put my hand on her back. She looked up, her eyes clouded pink.

"He suffered from depression," Sheldon said. He lowered himself on the bed, and his lips tightened as our eyes met. "Manic depression." Maybe. My mother doesn't recall Howard being diagnosed, but years of psychotherapy have left Sheldon thinking in clinical terms. Sheldon recalled a weekend where Howard came home from college. The first day Howard was cheerful and happy to see the family. With each day he became increasingly quiet, "crabby" in Sheldon's words, and spent more time in his old room. To me, that seems more like Howard's frustration with his relations. Even consecutive years of such behavior hardly resembles mania.

To my surprise, Grandma offered her own theory. Howard got into a couple of heated arguments with his father around that time. Though they later reconciled, she suspects Howard knew things about my grandpa that she did not, dalliances he was having with other women, possibly more. "Howard tried something once before," she admitted, "and he said, 'Mom, I'll never do that again.'" After thirty-three years spent wondering about my fallen Uncle's suicide, this was the most openly I'd ever heard them discuss the possible cause. She repeated, "I'll never understand it." She and I left the room with our arms around each other's backs. Sheldon tailed behind. She said, "He would have been—"

"Sixty-five," said Sheldon.

Some of us need reminding. Mom gave me her brother's name as my middle name to keep his memory alive. Other people never forget.

* * *

In my family, Sheldon's memory is legendary. Wondering whether it was the Brooklyn or the Midtown location of the old E.J. Korvette department chain where Grandpa Shapiro first worked? Unclear about the configuration of the Flushing, Queens neighborhood near 48th Avenue and 190th Street in the late 1950s? Ask Sheldon. "Yah," he might say, "there was a deli next to that tailor." When Mom couldn't remember the names of her elementary school friends, he listed them without pause, completing the picture with their parents' names, ethnicity, and occupation.

If Grandma comments that Sheldon remembers everything, Sheldon shakes his head. "I do not," he says.

She says, "You do too."

The source of his retention might lie in the paucity of his current existence. In addition to his fleeting employment at relatively stress-free jobs, Sheldon isn't married, has no kids, few friends, and no mortgage. With so little to clutter his mind, it's as if life demands only a fraction of his cognitive capacity. That and he isn't creating the future memories that so often replace our old ones. He fills his time in other ways.

"Were you at Borders at the Biltmore last Saturday?" he recently asked me. We were at Grandmas' getting ready for dinner. Sheldon sat on the couch, legs crossed, reading Kafka's *The Metamorphosis*. We're both big readers, but as far as scope and variety, Sheldon has me beat. He reads *The New York Times*, classic novels, obscure Eastern philosophy and self-help. Last spring he gave me a dog-eared copy of philosopher Alan W. Watts' *The Wisdom of Insecurity*. I studied philosophy as an undergrad yet had never heard of Watts.

I admitted I'd been at Borders. I'd been sitting in a cushy pleather chair in the literature section that night, reading magazines in-store so I wouldn't have to buy them with my meager earnings. That's my standard relaxation routine. Sheldon has his own. During the week, he reads the paper in Fashion Square Mall in a certain brown leather chair located by the elevator near Crate & Barrel. Borders seems to be his nighttime spot. To be fair, I hadn't seen him, but if I had, I would've hidden. I accept that this makes me a callous person, but I go to Borders to read, not socialize. And as much as I am learning to love Sheldon despite his eccentricities, engaging him would have closed what brief window of opportunity I had to unwind. Besides, he still embarrasses me a little.

"Yah," he said, smiling, nodding. "I thought that was you."

For some reason he says "Yah" instead of "Yeah." I can't figure this out. Does his partial deafness cause this affect? Can he not hear the mispronunciation? Maybe it's an attempt at sophistication, the same way some people emphasize the Frenchness of the words memoir or chevre. "I absolutely love this chev-reh," these people say at parties, not "chev" or "chev cheese," but "chev-reh." But you wouldn't hear the host reply, "Yah, me too." "Yah" isn't a habit of the intellectual or refined. It's a Sheldonism.

Besides the voice, volume, and manners, he has many signature–isms. He doesn't accept handshakes, for instance, only bear hugs. As a kid, I recognized his hugs as unnaturally firm and lasting far longer than my aunts' and dad's brothers'. Wanting to avoid them, I tested a technique. I stood far back while shaking Sheldon's hand, leaving enough room between us to make an embrace impractical. That never worked. He simply used my hand to pull me into his grip where, with my diaphragm constricted and arms pinned to my sides, it became clear that I was one of the few human beings he had touched all week. You couldn't help but feel sorry for him, living a life of severe social deprivation, but sympathy is fleeting when you're gasping for breath.

Another tick: he communicates in erratic jolts, interjecting unprompted tangential commentary from the margin of the conversation. While my mom tells Grandma and me about her day at work or asks to pass the pepper, Sheldon will blurt:

"People are greedier than they used to be."

"I saw James Baldwin read once in the sixties, in New York."

"You know what movie you would like? *Love in the Time of Cholera*."

"Quiet," Grandma will say, "we're talking." Then Sheldon will look back down at his folded hands or return to reading the paper.

Once when I was twenty, Sheldon announced to everyone in Grandma's living room, "Wow, he has pimples."

I looked down at the coffee table beside me, shaking my head. Slowly I looked up, eyes squinted. Taunting him, I said, "Is that right? I hadn't noticed." I wondered if he had Tourette's. I'd recently heard him mention that he took medication, though he never said for what. These ticks became a liability as a teen.

When friends came to my house during family gatherings, I always warned them in a fake Jewish grandmother accent that Shelll-don would be there. Then I'd roll my eyes. Girlfriends required more delicate negotiation. With my fragile, questionable sex appeal at stake, I had to preserve whatever cache I imagined I was developing. So I'd fetch these girls sodas and potato chips, and make sure to pepper the conversation with stories about my harrowing skateboarding accidents, cool bands I saw perform, anything to establish deep personality differences between the relative with whom I shared increasing facial resemblances. With as few girlfriends as I had in my youth, I couldn't afford to lose a single one, and when the time came to introduce them to Sheldon, I always offered a blunt warning while walking over to him: "My uncle is loud and will say some strange things. Just ignore him."

Then he'd bear hug her and me and say something like, "Did you ever see that movie *Sixteen Candles*? You look a lot like Molly Ringwald." My knees would buckle.

Clearly whatever medication he took was not for Tourette's. It didn't matter. I was so petrified that looking like Sheldon meant I was fated to live his life of loneliness, ridicule, and introversion, that I failed to recognize how petrified he was in general all the time. He doesn't function well in groups. Too many people talk at once. Ambient noise muddies the dialogue. Since he can only concentrate on reading one person's lips at a time, the inherent back-and-forth of conversation frustrates him. So he ends up on a chair in the middle of the room reading, alone. Occasionally you'll look up and catch his eyes on you. Not awkwardly, leering. Only looking, reaching out.

* * *

The day Grandpa Shapiro died, Sheldon stole his jewelry. Grandpa had heart problems. When he failed to answer his phone, Sheldon raced over, ostensibly to check on him. After finding his father dead on the bedroom floor, he called my parents for help. When they and the police arrived, Sheldon shuffled through the living room, past the crowd. "I have an appointment," he muttered. His pockets were so swollen with bracelets, rings, and necklaces that he jingled on his way out the door.

Sheldon didn't care that his theft was obvious. He thought he deserved the loot as some sort of cosmic recompense for his unhappy existence. While the police jotted notes and Grandpa lay still, my parents watched Sheldon rush from the condo. They were furious, of course, disgusted and shocked, but they decided it was best to let him go. Yelling wouldn't have slowed Sheldon's escape. Confronting him wouldn't change his way of thinking. My mom loved her brother, and she felt sorry for him. She figured, let him have the jewelry; with no wife, no children, and no job, he had so little already. The valuables didn't concern my parents; it was the principle: my grandpa had done so much to help Sheldon.

At the E.J. Korvette department store in New York, Grandpa worked as a buyer and merchandiser of jewelry, crystal, fine china, and house wares. In Phoenix, he opened a clothing store called MR Menswear, on Adams Street downtown. He later owned another called the Habber Dasher in Chris-Town Mall. I spent a lot of time at MR as a kid. I ducked behind circular shirt racks, built long chains from the plastic clamps used to secure ties and collars on mannequins. At that child's elevation, the whole store smelled of powder-fresh carpet deodorizer. One day I pressed a black button under the tall register counter, and firemen in bright red suits soon stepped through the front door. Grandpa had to apologize, telling them false alarm, just the kid. He had me wave goodbye as they left. Then we laughed about it together and he patted my cheek.

Sheldon lived with his parents in New York until age twenty-two. When they moved to Arizona, Grandpa bought Sheldon a house in central Phoenix and employed him at the stores for twelve years. He made sure Sheldon had a car, insurance, and steady income. He never, to anyone's knowledge, made fun of him or called him names. This wasn't enough. Sheldon blamed his father for how he turned out, blamed Grandpa for somehow ruining him, Howard, Grandma, and the family.

Howard and my grandfather had a strained relationship. Howard was an intellectual, Grandpa a pragmatist. As the son of Russian immigrants, Grandpa developed a lofty opinion of hard work and an aversion to even the appearance of poverty. He wanted all the material comforts and security America offered its successes, and he forced that philosophy onto his son. Grandpa disapproved of science—what money was there to make? He wanted Howard to be a doctor, or a lawyer, or some clichéd lucrative profession that I can never get a straight answer about because what little info anyone offers often varies. Two facts are clear: Howard the intellectual was sensitive, and that fatherly disapproval burdened him with a weight that he couldn't shake. Sheldon wasn't close with Howard, but according to my mother, he privately blamed my grandpa for his brother's death.

Witnessing the candor that Thanksgiving Day, I asked a question I had never previously asked anyone: how many times did Grandpa stray? Sheldon immediately said, "Serial monogamist."

"Yeah," Grandma said, "he fooled around, more than once." She stiffened her slouching posture, holding her head high, back straight, hands on both hips. "I was young and stupid. Naïve. But—" She shook her head and shrugged as if to say, what're you gonna do? Grandpa—born William Shapiro, known to everyone else as Bill—regularly went out with his friend Henry to bars, dinners, and shows in the City. Sylvia Greissman, my grandmother, never discouraged him. "I figured, it's Friday," she said. "This man worked all week. We have the rest of the weekend together."

Once, after telling a longtime friend that Bill was out with Henry, the friend told Grandma, "You sure it's not Henrietta?" In Phoenix years later, when Bill's brother Irving learned that Bill was leaving Sylvia, Irving told her, "He'll get what he deserves."

Grandma always advised her children to never hold a grudge, to forgive and move on. "I had no trouble meeting men," she told me on Thanksgiving. "Even before Bill." But after the split, whenever Grandpa heard Grandma was seeing someone new, he appeared—at family functions, on the phone, even her home—often wanting her back. While attending a meal at my parent's house once, Grandpa met Grandma's new boyfriend. Feeling threatened, he offered what amounted to the extent of his decorum: he said, "He's a handsome man."

"He was very insecure," Grandma told me. "He had no confidence in himself." She said it came from his parents. They were matched up very young in life and were never really happy together. Grandpa even felt ashamed of them, partly from their poverty, partly from the way their character—immigrants with accents, unassimilated—affected people's perception of him.

"I once saw a photo of my father in Puerto Rico," Sheldon said, "standing beside a gorgeous, tan brunette."

My grandparents divorced four years after settling in Phoenix. Grandpa died when I was twenty years old. My last memory is of hugging him goodbye in his living room, the grit of his chin stubble rubbing against my cheek, the smell of his woodsy, spicy cologne in the air.

I wasn't present on the day of Grandpa's death. I was on vacation. My mother says Grandpa kept tons of cash lying around the house. No one knows how much. Sheldon found it, some or all. Mom insists it doesn't matter, which is why, a decade later, nobody has confronted Sheldon about the theft.

* * *

At a Christmas party when I was eighteen, my half-brother Scot mentioned how much I looked like Sheldon. "You asshole," I said. "Fuck you," and stormed out of the room.

As a teenager, I'd seen a black and white childhood photo of Sheldon riding a bike down his Flushing sidewalk, and adrenalinee filled my stomach. Similar eyes, similar nose, similar chin. The sight of these resemblances, the undeniable fact that certain bits of him lurked inside me, made me want to scald my face with acid and scrape my cells clean of DNA.

Some people look at their relatives—an abusive father, alcoholic mother—and vow never to become them. I looked at Sheldon and wondered if I had a choice. Watching him consume a slice of pizza in three bites as he shuffled across Grandma's living room was like standing on an icy Chicago sidewalk in a gale force wind: untethered, I feared I might start sliding toward the curb, directly into oncoming traffic. If his was a medical condition, what if it didn't skip my generation? Considering the way bipolar disorder can strike people in their early thirties—just as they thought they'd escaped the period of greatest risk—my worry seemed justified.

When Sheldon recently told me, "You look more like our side of the family the older you get," I didn't know what to say. I looked at him, nodded, and could only conjure a nervous "Thanks?"

He laughed. "We're the beauties." He said it with a self-deprecating flourish, then added, "Your grandfather was very handsome in his youth."

* * *

"An Indian came to my door with two containers of beer," Sheldon said at dinner not long ago, "asking for food. Navajo. Really nice." He shrugged between spoonfuls of turkey. "People think they're all drunks, but eighty percent of Indians aren't like that."

Sheldon identifies everyone in two ways: what they are and how they act. "A rude Jewish woman cut me off in line." Or, "I once spent a weekend in Mexico in the seventies, and the people there were very friendly. Not like some of the ones you meet around here. Gangbangers, they call them." The irony, as my mom points out, is that when the vote came up in the sixties about whether to integrate his Queens high school, Sheldon rallied for integration with local black activists and a few of the teachers in front of the school. He has long been hyper-liberal, a pacifist who quotes Gandhi and Martin Luther King Jr. He strictly votes Democratic and recounts recent Republican victories and environmental set-backs with visible disgust. "Jews have traditionally sided with social causes," he points out. "We know what it's like to be vilified." But what I point out to Mom is that, if you have to qualify any person or their comments with the caveat "not a racist," then the truth of that statement seems questionable. Sheldon I grant more leeway.

"When you're like him, everything is about how people treat you," Mom says. "He's either rejected or accepted. That's his whole social dynamic." To an outsider unfamiliar with these jarring non sequiturs, Sheldon likely sounds racist. He used to to me. "I spoke with a very nice black man," Sheldon said. "Some of the black men can be a little, shall we say, arrogant. But he was so kind, helping me find some things." Only when I started trying to understand my uncle's lonely life, did I start to hear his sweeping pronouncements not as a measure of human worth, but as a measure of human receptivity to him. His fixation was less a racial than a behavioral taxonomy. Like Braille or a blind person's cane, labeling people based on their demeanor helps him navigate the world. Are Mexicans welcoming or hostile? Are Jews more receptive to him than Koreans? If he can identify patterns, then he can avoid trouble and more efficiently find help. For Sheldon, saying Jews are this, Puerto Ricans are that, is the equivalent of saying, "The #9 bus always runs late, so take the #6. It's quicker."

"This one Mexican came to cut my palm tree last month," Sheldon said. "From Chiapas. He really appreciated being here. Some of them take advantage." Sheldon would know. After Howard passed, the family dynamic changed. Prevention became top priority. My grandparents lived in fear of losing another child, so they become overly protective. They didn't put bars on the windows or forbid their children from eating outside the home; instead, they became hyperaware of their children's frailty. They micro-managed, worried, and nagged their concern as if to fit the Jewish stereotypes I grew up believing. The brunt fell on Sheldon, the sole surviving son. He was already fragile enough to require coddling, but as the degree of coddling increased, he softened further. Instead of forcing him to toughen up and securing his independence, he became dependent.

Sheldon took advantage of this paradigm shift. He not only capitalized off the attention previously directed at Howard, he milked my grandparents' sympathies in order to feed his own laziness. When he didn't get what he wanted, he threw fits. A few times when he needed money they wouldn't give him, he threatened to kill himself. In a huff, he pushed over the cash register at the Haber Dasher once. No one commented when he blew a thousand dollars on a 35mm camera and equipment he never learned to use, or lectured him about the hundreds of dollars he spent on a seashell collection that now sits housed in a box in his garage.

Mom thinks his understanding of human behavior is lopsided because it's over-simplistic. She told him that peoples' response to us don't always reflect their feelings about us. Sometimes people are rude because they're just in bad moods: they lost their job that week; they're going through divorce; they quit smoking and are irritable. It could be anything.

Yet Mom also coddles him. To protect him, she types his résumés and proofreads each round of his job applications. His last job grading standardized tests was the longest he's held in years, and he quit. No one knows why. Mom suspects social sensitivity: he felt people were laughing at him, or he had a run-in with a single unfriendly employee and felt slighted. "My heart just bleeds for him," Mom says. My dad won't extend any sort of empathy.

"I'm done with him," Dad says. "I give him respect because he's your mother's brother, but that's all I will give him any more." Dad has given Sheldon countless second chances. Dad's tolerance for honest mistakes is huge—I crashed my first car, got cited for alcohol possession at age sixteen, done many stupid things—but Sheldon has exhausted it. He once banned Sheldon from our house after he caught him in their bedroom, rifling through their mail after Grandpa died. He was looking for financial info—assets, wills, checking and credit card records—for ways to get money, or news about what the rest of the family was hiding from him. Dad said, "It was the last straw."

Sheldon's savvier than Mom and I think. "My father was the type of salesman who would tell someone trying on a suit, 'Yah, it looks great,' even if it was a size or two too big," Sheldon once said. "I on the other hand would tell them it's large. Get another size. Why lie?" He shrugged, puckered his lips. "My father didn't think this was good for business, but people want that kind of assistance. They come back for it." We all do.

* * *

In *When Harry Met Sally*, Billy Crystal and Meg Ryan get food at a diner, and Crystal tells her, "No, you did not have great sex with Sheldon . . . A

Sheldon can do your income taxes. If you need a root canal, Sheldon's your man. But humpin' and pumpin' is not Sheldon's strong suit. It's the name." Then he shows her with an impression: "Do it to me Sheldon. You're an animal Sheldon. Ride me big Shelll-don. It doesn't work." No one I know ever did it to my Sheldon. He lived that part of his life in secret, however much he lived it at all. My heart still breaks for him that he hasn't enjoyed lasting or intense romantic relationships the way the rest of his family members have.

Sheldon asked me if my girlfriend still lived in North Carolina. When I told him that she and I had broken up, he released a mournful sigh. "I'm sorry to hear that," he said. "She was very beautiful. And you said you liked her very much." Unlike many people, he actually remembers what things you tell him.

"Mom tells me you're writing a lot," Sheldon said last month. "That's very good, Aaron."

If I had a girlfriend now, I'd bring her over to Grandma's house, let her meet him, talk about Mexicans and politics and his 1970s vacations. When I tell him I love him, I mean it. I don't want to feel burdened by our relationship anymore. It's not fair to either of us, especially if he's ill. So at dinner he and I discuss movies, books, the charms and difficulties of living in New York. I liked living there, I told him, cold or not. He asked, "Are the people there friendlier now?"

Last week I opened the copy of Watts' *The Wisdom of Insecurity* he gave me. Marginalia covered most of the 152 pages: black ink marks, frenzied dashes, enormous sloppy asterisks. Sheldon underlined sentences, bracketed whole paragraphs. On one page he underlined "the real world," on another "promises, hopes, and assurances." I flipped through the book front-to-back, reading the short phrases that he underlined with what, from the thickness and intermingling curves of the markings, seemed a visible excitement. I made a list:

"chronic insomnia;"

"man is basically selfish;"

"the quest for security;"

"we are not divided;"

"sorrow, and boredom;"

"unfair distribution of pleasure and pain;"

"intensity of joy;"

"you can get away;"

"the dead;"

"resisting the inevitable;"

"understanding;"

"There is no experience but present experience;"

"By letting it go he finds it."

Watts was a British thinker. He translated numerous volumes of Zen Buddhism and Chinese and Indian philosophy, and much of his own work tackles the subjects associated with those traditions: higher consciousness, the nature of God and reality, the non-material pursuit of happiness, personal identity. Watts' ambiguous language is plagued by what I consider the smoke-and-mirrors trickery of cheap, woo-woo, New Age metaphysics. But I kept reading, searching for clues to what my uncle was responding to in these passages: was it the insecurity parts? The lessons on living "in the present?" Forgiveness? " . . . but it is just the feeling of being an isolated 'I,'" one passage said, "which makes me feel lonely and afraid."

Thirteen of the twenty-nine lines on page seventy-nine were underlined. Seven asterisks coated the margins. Beside one paragraph sat a clot of scribbling so thick it resembled human hair. "The principle thing is to understand that there is no safety or security," it said, and, "the more you struggle to escape, the more you inflame your agony." But the sentence that struck me hardest was on page 104. Scored with black ink, it read: "Here life is alive, vibrant, and present, containing depths which we have hardly begun to explore." I slid the book in the middle of my bookshelf, beside some of my most cherished story collections and autographed volumes. As an heirloom, a family photo.

* * *

Mom keeps a large framed photo of her father on her dresser. Black and white, cropped from the shoulders up, it shows Grandpa wearing his white Navy uniform, a huge grin creasing his smooth, shaven cheeks. His eyes always pinched closed when he smiled, as if his mouth needed all the skin to express the joy contained within him. When I look at his face, I see my own. Everybody seems to. My friend Sarah saw the photo and stood straight up, turned around to my mom and me and said, "You two look just alike. Is that weird?" That might explain why Mom tucked a photo of me at age sixteen into the picture frame. I too am smiling wide, eyes squinted half shut, teeth showing just like Grandpa's.

Recently Sheldon blurted, "Oh my Aaron, you've lost so much hair."

No longer sensitive to such observations, I playfully said, "I know. It's matrilineal. I blame your Dad." I laughed extra hard to show that I was kidding, and when he noticed, he laughed back.

* * *

Sheldon was limping the other day at dinner, so I asked what happened. He said his new medication made him faint, and when he fell in the bathroom, he bruised his foot. Faint, I wondered, what's he on: mood stabilizers? Tranquilizers? Is he mixing alcohol and sedatives? No one asked the name of the medication, because when we had inquired before, he felt we were being nosy and changed the subject. That day we only offered advice on using frozen corn to reduce swelling.

I used to wonder if he exaggerated the severity of his deafness, using it as a way to distance himself from his nagging mother and the hostile world. As Dad says, "Wouldn't you lose your hearing too if someone was always correcting you?"

At my mom's fifty-eighth birthday dinner at Red Lobster, Sheldon started describing a Hawaiian vacation he took in 1973. Slumped low in the booth, Grandma gripped his bicep, leaned close to his ear and whispered, "Everyone can hear what you're saying."

"My mother," Sheldon later told me, "she unnerves me sometimes." Mom fears I have the wrong impression of Grandma. She says that growing up, when she got stressed from having too many things to do—high school homework, college term papers—and didn't know where to start, Grandma told her not to get overwhelmed. Then they would sit down together, make a list of everything that needed doing and check each item off as they completed it. "Grandma would stay up late with you," Mom said, "talking, if you had a problem. With anyone. Sleep—she didn't care. She'd stay up with me all the time, working through my lists."

And Sheldon? Last week, I finally asked Mom what I have been wondering for years: What's wrong with him? She folded her hands behind her back, leaned against the kitchen counter. "I don't really know," she said, tilting her head. "I'm sure if he was born today he would have a clear diagnosis. We just didn't have that back then." Unlike what I previously believed, his traits weren't the product of overprotective parental smothering following Howard's death. When Howard died, Sheldon was twenty-two. "He was always different," Mom said. That's the most detailed diagnosis any of us have come up with.

She described Sheldon as a good brother back in New York. Admittedly, when they were kids, she had to write "Loraine" on masking tape and affix it to her favorite yogurt or soda in the fridge so Sheldon wouldn't eat them. And he'd eat them anyway. She laughed when she said this, because he always took an interest in how she was doing. He would join her and her friends in the living room when they came over, ask her about school, what she was reading, if she had a boyfriend. My Aunt Debbie was embarrassed by him as a kid. "She still is," Mom said. Debbie joined us at Red Lobster that day.

While Grandma paid the bill, Sheldon dumped the remaining cheese biscuits into his doggy bag along with packets of Sweet 'N Low. Dad snickered. I shrugged. Debbie stood up and scurried into the lobby.

One recent Christmas Day, my family was sitting around my second cousin Marty's living room after lunch. Marty grew up in Queens and retired in Phoenix. Grandma and Marty sat beside each other on the couch. My mom, Sheldon, and I sat in chairs facing each other on opposite sides of the room. As he'd done before, Marty was complaining about his parents' unwillingness to rent a bigger apartment in Queens growing up. His parents made him share a bed with his older brother Harvey until he was sixteen, Harvey twenty-two. "They couldn't get a two-bedroom?" Marty said. "In the same fricking building?" He was facing Grandma but addressing the entire room. "They paid $52 a month," he said. "I still remember that numba."

"For your mother," Grandma explained, "it was about change. She didn't like change. For your father it was money."

Marty waved his hand. "The money is bullshit," he said.

From across the room, Sheldon looked at Mom and me. "Why harp on something that happened fifty years ago?" he said. "You're sixty-two years old. Get over it already." Mom and I looked at each other, shocked by his self-awareness. Sheldon laughed and waved his own dismissive hand. "I forgave my father for many things," he said in his booming voice. He nodded at me and grinned. His eyes squinted in narrow, gleeful slits, slits like mine, in an expression that to an outsider probably looked exactly like my grandfather's. Marty kept talking. Grandma didn't look at him. Only Mom and I seemed to hear Sheldon when he muttered, "That's ancient history."

THE BURDEN OF HOME

If you haven't seen the 1987 movie *North Shore*, take that as evidence of your refined palate. The movie came out when I was in sixth grade, and it was so corny that I refused to acknowledge how profoundly I connected with it. It's the story of Rick Kane, an eighteen-year-old surfer from Tempe, Arizona, who wants to earn the big, pro-circuit money that his idol, and the movie's antihero, Lance Burkhart, earns. When Rick wins a surf contest at a local artificial wave pool, he skips college and uses the five-hundred-dollar prize to move to Hawaii and tackle the epic waves of the legendary North Shore.

Once in Hawaii, Rick rides the waves alongside the locals. He falls for a native beauty named Kiani and clashes with a tough surf crew called the Hui. Nearly everyone discourages him: "This is our wave." "Leave local girls alone." But the line that always stayed with me came during a scene in which Rick is eating lunch with Kiani and her family. Kiani's three brothers corner him at the table. They mock his surfing and call him JOJ—short for "just off the jet." Then the oldest brother stares into Rick's eyes and says, "Go back to Arizona, haole," meaning outsider, white boy, non-Hawaiian native. It was as if he were speaking directly to me, a teenage kid desperate to leave Arizona.

Like Rick, I lived in Phoenix, was obsessed with the beach, and wanted out of the desert. I envied the lifestyle that coastal California afforded: the temperate weather, the scant clothing, the year-round range of outdoor activities. While southern Californians spent their summers riding bikes and hanging out on the boardwalk, we Phoenicians endured an average of a hundred or more days of one-hundred-degree heat. Touch a car door in July, and you'd burn your fingers. But that wasn't all. Arizona was completely uncool. It's associated with lame Hollywood westerns, golf and retirees. To coastal denizens, we were hicks.

Sometime in fifth grade, just before *North Shore* came out, I bought a bodyboard and learned to ride waves pretty well. At home, I covered my bedroom walls with images clipped from surf magazines: black sand and palm groves; bronze women in bikinis splashing through azure water. I stuck surf stickers on my door, corny ones that said "Body Glove" and "Mr. Zog's Sex Wax" in blinding pink and yellow fonts. When I lay in bed at night, I pictured myself sleeping in a thatched hut and drinking from coconuts. I taped a quote from an ad on my door: "Summer is an attitude, not a season." And I wore only shorts, even in winters that reached the low forties. When my parents dropped me off at middle school, I gathered with my friends on the playground before class. Condensation frosted the tetherball pole. Crystallized dew coated the brown winter grass. And I'd stand there shivering with my arms crossed, wearing shorts and a flannel and a hooded Vans sweater, watching my breath. At one point, I asked my parents if we could replace my bedroom's brown carpet with beach sand. They asked where the bed would go. "We'll build wooden boardwalks around the edges," I explained, "with one plank diagonally across the middle for the bed." And how would I avoid dragging sand into the rest of the house? "I'll wipe my feet every time I leave my room." The brown carpet stayed.

When I first saw *North Shore* I was shocked. The posters, the neon gear—my room was decorated just like Rick's. Rick was a dorky aspirant, and clearly, so was I. Worse, as wannabes playing dress up, we had no credibility next to real surfers. What was more embarrassing for a would-be surfer than never to have trained in the ocean? No matter how we dressed, how politely we acted, or how hard we tried to fit in, Rick and I would always be what we were: the guys from the desert wave pool.

Still, as much as I related to him, I knew I wasn't entirely like Rick. Not because I didn't surf. And not because I wasn't old enough to leave home like he was. It was because after all his struggles—being ostracized by locals, punched in the face, slammed into reefs—he successfully assimilated, went from outsider to insider, while I did not and never would. By the movie's end, the Hui let him ride their waves, Kiani falls in love with him, and Turtle, his one true friend, quits calling him barney. Although Rick doesn't win the professional surfing paycheck he initially hoped for, he does earn acceptance and respect, which, in the emotional formulations of ham-fisted screenplays, and in the hearts of angsty teenagers, is the real prize. I didn't fare as well.

Whenever my friends and I went to California, it was our clothes, our diction, and our license plates that betrayed us. Locals called us Zonies, their version of haole for Arizonan tourists. Zonies fed the local economy, but we also clogged the narrow streets, took the parking spots, made the wait at restaurants longer, and, worse, got in the way in the water.

During the beginning of *North Shore*, whenever people ask Rick where he's from, he searches for an honest yet sufficiently vague reply: "Oh, the mainland," he tells them, or, "Um, like, kinda outside LA—sorta." When faced with a similar situation in California, one of my close friends used to stammer, "Oh, well, uh," and eventually spit out, "San Diego." He hated driving around the beach with that maroon albatross of a license plate on our car, the word Arizona broadcast in bright white letters beside a saguaro cactus emblem.

One night, when I was sixteen, my friends and I were walking down a side street in Newport, California—a surfing town—when we came upon a party at a beach house. People filled the tiny yard. A keg sat in one corner near a stack of beach cruisers. Attractive girls in tiny shirts stood beside guys with sun-bleached hair and muscular forearms. As we walked past one guy called out, "Nice haircuts! What, you all get them cut at the same place?" A couple of dudes laughed, a girl sniggered. I tried to keep my head up, trying to maintain a modicum of dignity in the face of harassment, but when my eyes met this guy's, I couldn't scowl like I wanted to. I could only look away. The Rick I saw in me wasn't there. As we skulked by he yelled, "Go home!"

LEAVING TATOOINE

At age twenty-four, I sold my vintage *Star Wars* toys to buy a thousand dollar mountain bike that I barely rode for the next ten years. Purging my favorite action figures and spaceships felt like euthanizing the family pet, but at my age it seemed time to eliminate the anchors of childhood.

Although I was only dimly aware of it, that sale traded artifacts from the first part of my life for what resembled a harbinger of adulthood. Not the bicycle itself but the price tag: who but a grown-up could invest such an outrageous sum in a bike? What I didn't recognize was that, although bikes were commuter vehicles for many people, the one I planned to buy was just another toy. I already had a car that needed gas and insurance. I had cats to feed and rent to pay on an apartment that I shared with my-girlfriend, Kari, and I owned a perfectly functional vintage beach cruis-er. A thousand dollar off-road bike was an irresponsible indulgence, and dropping that much cash on a flashy plaything offered proof that I still thought like a kid, that and the fact that I began to miss my action figures even before I sold them. Greedo, Boba Fett, IG-88, three separate Jawas, one with the rare vinyl cape—trying to calculate the value of my collection while agonizing about the pending sale, I kept wondering: how was I going to live without them?

The figures lived in original *Star Wars* action figure cases under my parents' stairs. Wedged in a dark secondary enclosure in the back of a clos-et, my prized childhood possessions sat amid special occasion dishes, a short artificial Christmas tree, and other things my folks didn't frequently access. It wasn't the figures' absence from daily life that terrified me. It was the idea that, if I sold them, they would no longer be available. Granted, I'd stored them in the closet so no one would see that I still owned toys, but it always comforted me to know that my *Star Wars* toys were there, remain-ing their little droid and Jedi selves, their consistency and fidelity serving as bulwarks against the small, smothering landslides caused by the shifting substrates of adolescence.

Even if I no longer played with them, I did check on them. During my high school and early college years, whenever I got the urge, I would crawl under the stairwell, pry open the wooden hatch, and duck into the dark rear area. Inside the musty enclosure, my flashlight beam cut through dust that rose from the cardboard boxes. Stored in a black case shaped like Darth Vader, a gold case shaped like C-3PO, and a gray one shaped like a laser rifle, I'd carry the figures into the light aboveground, and I'd open the lid. The tiny latches clicked when you popped them. Even after a decade, the smell of plastic remained strong. Upstairs in the hallway or in my childhood room, I'd lay the cases on the carpet, pull out my favorite characters and study them: the fine striations on Darth Vader's pant legs; the yellow eyes of Jawas. I liked running my fingers across Death Star Droid's cold silver body, and squeezing the squishy foam on 4-LOM's robe. Other times I'd just stare. Locked in their assigned slots, labeled by name with a sticker that Kenner toys provided, the figures stood rigid and lifeless, their unbendable arms flat against their sides. Their faces registered nothing, yet to me their molded expressions and painted-on eyes resembled those of family. These characters, like my parents, had always shared this house with me.

* * *

I was born on May 25, 1975. *Star Wars* came out on May 25, 1977. When I first saw the movie, I fell asleep in the seat next to my parents in the theater. My dad didn't care for the film; he's never been into sci-fi. My mom liked it, though she wasn't initially as taken by it as she was *Close Encounters of the Third Kind* and, later, *9 to 5*. Only after repeat viewings transformed my affection into an obsession did she come to love the movie. *Star Wars* became our filial glue, one of many things that bound us together.

My mom liked to shop. When she went to the mall or a department store, she brought me with her, and we visited the toy department to check for new *Star Wars* figures. The Kenner toy company released action figures in waves, partly as a marketing ploy to maintain consumer interest. The tactic worked. Hunting for a new set of miniature plastic characters offered the sort of thrill that any Tusken Raider could appreciate. Even those of us not otherwise prone to that compulsive collector's condition called "completism" soon found ourselves stricken with it. Lando Calrissian's aid Lobot, Jaba the Hutt's henchman Klaatu, the Bespin Security Guard—I wanted them all, including the boring ones.

Stores used to stack their figures in enormous displays, multiple rows high and wide, so pawing through them took time. To streamline my hunt, I developed a technique. While flipping through the figures hanging on racks, I would tilt the cardboard backing to the side; that way I could see which characters hung in the rear and middle of each row. When I spotted figures that I didn't own, I'd swipe them from the rack, pile them in my arms, and rush over to my mom, where I presented them like a housecat delivering a dead bird.

Reminiscing about these moments now, I often picture myself jumping up and down like an electrocuted Jawa, yammering on about my discoveries while lobbying for their purchase. In fact, my displays were the standing still, eyes-bulging, head-going-to-explode-with-joy type. If Mom had enough money, she'd buy me a figure or two. Back in the late 1970s and early '80s, they cost two to three dollars, depending on the store. I'm sure that every time I found new characters, I begged to get them all, and my mom had to explain that, for whatever reason, we couldn't do that. These were lean years for us. I wasn't a crier. I didn't throw tantrums. Yet thanks to my parents, my collection expanded, figure by figure, until I owned so many that trips to the toy store presented me with the same figures over and over: Imperial Snowtrooper, Dengar the Bounty Hunter, Hoth Rebel Commander, Leia Organa in Bespin Gown. It seemed like whenever I started to worry that I'd have to wait for the release of a new movie in order to revitalize store stock, Kenner would release a few more figures, and the space in my storage cases shrunk.

During the first decade of my life, my family was pretty broke. We lived in a Phoenix apartment. Then we moved to Las Cruces, New Mexico. Later we rented a small, yellow, cinder block house on Phoenix's west side. Then a mixed neighborhood of lower to middle class white people, Native

Americans, and Latino families. Low riders trolled our streets. Metal heads with feathered hair circled the block in muscle cars. My parents drove a long, brown 1970's Cadillac which they bought from an elderly couple in Sun City. It was the archetypal "old lady grocery store car," where the paint was faded but the ashtrays and trunk had never been used. My father quickly stained the tray with his Benson & Hedges 100s, and my clambering feet helped wear the bench seats' brown fabric. The neighborhood muscle cars always reminded me of cockroaches. With their fronts dropped and rears raised on large, racing tires, their upturned butts seemed ready to squirt enemies with some noxious chemical. The comparison was easy. Our backyard was infested with roaches. Dad went out back most nights and smashed them with a flyswatter. He was struggling to find work. Mom had a job, but to generate additional income, she renovated and resold antique furniture and glassware that she culled from yard sales. Seeing our need, my mom's father offered my dad a job at his men's clothing store.

The Haber Dasher was located in Chris-Town Mall. Built in 1961, Chris-Town was Phoenix's third mall, and Arizona's first enclosed one. Many mid-century malls used flashy design elements to lure shoppers: fountains, glittery Terrazzo flooring, strange Space Age lamps and light fixtures. When I started hanging out there, Chris-Town was still noticeably Space Age in its architectural accents—the flagstone, some slipper-shaped stairs by a fountain, even Woolworth's logo font—but it had outlived its elegant heyday by over a decade. The pink and powder blue air of its early-1960s origins had long since given way to an '80s brown, yellow, and orange schema. Everything in the early Regan Era seemed to have the sickly tint of used cigarette butts. The Mall's floor tiles were marbled browns. A faux wood pattern coated the trashcans and ashtrays. Brass poles and fixtures were common, most visibly the ones holding up the navy blue ropes at the UA Cinema 6 box office.

My grandfather's store stood near the food court and movie theater, an echoey hall enlivened by the greasy orange aroma of Pizza D'Amore and the sweet froth of Orange Julius. While Dad worked, I wandered. I spent hours playing Tron and Galaga at the Red Baron video game arcade. I made frequent stops at a tiny gyro stall to eat free samples of slow-cooked meat, and I hid inside department stores' circular shirt racks where I eaves-dropped on conversations. Crouched inside, I debated whether to jump out and scare people. I always chose more subtle things to confuse them: tapping the toes of their shoes, scratching their leg with a hanger, whisper-ing "pssst, over here" and watching them turn around. I spent a lot of my time looking at the *Star Wars* figures.

The mall had a Mervyns and Woolworth with sizeable toy departments, but Kay Bee Toys was closer to Grandpa's store. It stood underneath the tall escalator that led into UA Cinema, and, looking up from below, the the-ater's geometric light fixtures seemed a mix of disco club and *Empire Strikes Back*. Its long light beams resembled those in the scene where Darth Vader and Luke Skywalker fight in the carbonite encasing room in Cloud City.

Once, Mom and I were in Kay Bee, and a man started talking to us. My mother is attractive and fit, so I imagine the guy was flirting with her. That happened a lot. One time at a department store cash register, I stepped out from behind her leg and told a man, "She's married." I don't recall him saying anything vulgar or pushy, only that he stuck around after paying his bill and wouldn't stop talking to her during her transaction. The man in Kay Bee walked past us and commented on the *Star Wars* toys we had in our hands. "I love those movies," he said. "You can see a few continu-ity issues, but the movies are too good for them to matter." Continuity issues, my mom explained to me, were mistakes. I thought, Mistakes? I never noticed any. The man mentioned the way Darth Vader's chest plate faces two different directions in the same scene, and the way the shoulder pad on Luke Skywalker's Stormtrooper outfit disappears in one scene in the Death Star, then reappears later. I looked up at him as he spoke. Was this true? He smiled at me, but he seemed serious. His words were a reve-lation: if there were errors in the films, then the worlds they depicted were make-believe. My mom must have understood that make-believe worlds often meant more to people than the world in which they lived. Here she was, feeding my fascination with Dagoba and Tatooine, while we drove a hand-me-down.

I was an only child. Without siblings to filter any of the affection or finances, all my parents' love arrived directly to me. They bought me *Star*

Wars sheets, a *Star Wars* toothbrush and *Star Wars* shampoo. A few of my birthdays were *Star Wars* themed, as were my lunchboxes, t-shirts and shoes. Between 1978 and 1985, Kenner released around one hundred and fifteen different *Star Wars* action figures. I ended up with nearly every one. I was a fanatic. Under most definitions, I was also spoiled, though by all accounts I didn't act like it. I now often wonder how my parents afforded this bounty. "We were struggling," Mom once told me, "but we tried to live beyond our means and enjoy nice things." They also cut corners. During the months preceding *Return of the Jedi*'s release, she stopped at Burger Kings and other stores to ask if she could have one of the promotional posters for her obsessed son. She framed the poster and hung it in my bedroom: "*Revenge of the Jedi* Coming May 25, 1983 to your galaxy." Nearby stood a life-size cardboard standee of C-3PO. He held a box of C-3PO Cereal. "New! Kellogg's C-3PO's," the motto said. "A New Force at Breakfast." Mom got it from a grocery store.

As with so many aspects of childhood, I only noticed the self-sacrifice of parenting later: the way our parents labor to improve our station and, in giving us a better life, they drain themselves of their own through fatigue, credit card debt, heart disease, and emotional overeating. Here my parents were, in the prime of their lives, working long days at jobs and collecting antiques at yard sales on weekends to resell, so that they could buy me toys and eventually move into a nicer house. I didn't think we were poor. I didn't think I was spoiled. I only thought we were a family that had an ugly car and an ugly house, and so did most everyone around us, and life was great. This simple perception is as much the product of the child's limited vision as it is the imperfect nature of memory.

Childhood is strange pabulum. It's nonfiction partially fermented into fiction by the passing of time, and its effervescent strength makes us woozy and prone to swooning. Our vision of it is equal parts illusion and delusion, yet it's as real as the joy we felt, the scars we carry, the photographic proof. Because it's an incomplete portrait, for those adults who survived it, childhood is as much a feeling as it is a bundle of facts. It's dates, events, anecdotes, names, fused together by questionable emulsifiers and stretched into what is often the thinnest of narratives. As a whole, it's as impressionistic as a Jackson Pollock, its splatters suggesting patterns that aren't necessarily there, and it often resembles a mess of colors, emotionally charged fragrances, and feelings. What it felt like to be a kid in a certain place in time. What it feels like to remember it. For me, that era felt and looked like *Star Wars*.

Even though the films take place in a distant galaxy, *Star Wars* is a product of 1970s and '80s Earth. Beneath the moisture farm sets and costumes of Cloud City lay the same Chris-Town Mall universe I grew up in: the garish earth-tone color schemes of Montgomery Ward clothing; men's hairy chests showing through unbuttoned shirts. I recognize my own life in the Mos Eisley Cantina. Greedo's vest, worn over a green turtleneck track suit, resembled something my New York relatives would have worn. Snaggletooth could have purchased his maroon jumper at the same store as Evil Knievel. I had a sixth grade music teacher who owned an aquamarine velour top with ruffled neckline similar to Hammerhead's. No matter the lengths George Lucas went to disguise his stories' origins, my childhood had the same desert sky, the same orange and brown clothes, the same feathered hair, as the people of Tatooine.

As the details of even our strongest memories fade, it's easy to wonder if any of it ever really happened. My action figures held clear imprints. No hazy edges, no conflicting accounts, the chiseled plastic stood as unyielding evidence of my early years. Look, Greedo and the Jawas seemed to say, it was real, just as you remember it. Like a moon rock proving an astronaut's visit, when I looked at my toys, I not only had confirmation, I felt my childhood again—a rush of sensations, colors, smells. I could see and feel what it was like when my dad drove me to school, and how it felt when he would slip into my bedroom most weekday mornings and sing "Reveley" through cupped hands, like a trumpet, then rub my back and whisper, "Time to get up." I could picture how Mom sat on my bed and pet my hair when I screamed from a nightmare: "It's okay," she'd say. "It's just a dream." And remember the way it felt to scout yard sales with her on Sunday mornings, and then sit at a yellow table to share breakfast at McDonald's. It wasn't that I couldn't part with my toys or that I refused to grow up. It was that I couldn't accept that those days were done, and that my parents, once so youthful and energetic, now faced memory problems and biopsies, heart problems and diabetes. And I, nearly a quarter century old, feared severing the most powerful link to our shared past: the action figures which stood on my shelves as witness to so many of these formative moments. Liquidating them felt akin to burning family photos. Considering my parents' struggle, eliminating my collection seemed no different than throwing away the fruits of their labor, the evidence of their striving and upward mobility. As an adult, seeing those toys brought up dismal thoughts: I want to go back there. We can never go back there. We will never know those days again. Which might have been the best reason to get rid of them.

* * *

This story shocks most people for practical reasons: "You made a thousand dollars selling toys?" I had a lot of them, and they were in great shape. No scratches, no sun-fading, no animal chew marks—had I sold each toy individually myself, I would have made a lot more. To save time and effort, I sold them to a store that specialized in collectible, vintage toys. The first prequel, *The Phantom Menace*, had just come out, and I wanted to cash in on America's renewed interest. Had I held on to them longer, their value would have increased, but half the issue was that I'd held onto them long enough.

Kari and I carried the boxes into the toy store. The owner was expecting me. I'd visited a few weeks earlier to let him know I had things for sale. After some obligatory chit-chat, he started arranging the boxes' contents atop his long, glass display cases. Another employee, a teenager, took various items to a different counter and flipped through price guides, jotting notes and tabulating their value. In one case under my stuff, *Star Trek the Next Generation* figures stood in sealed packs. Kari looked over at me and offered a supportive smile.

The previous week, I'd driven to my parents' house when they weren't home. Alone, I crawled under the stairwell one last time. I pried open the wooden hatch and ducked into the dark warm womb of an enclosure. My flashlight beam cut through dust as I pushed aside the Christmas tree and started dragging boxes into the hall. Box after box of playsets, spaceships and tiny accessories collected in Ziploc bags. The black Darth Vader case, the gold C-3PO—I set them on the carpet in my old upstairs bedroom and sat down in the light. The latches clicked when I popped them, and I inhaled the smell of plastic, finding comfort in a scent my body registered as toxic.

One by one, I pulled out my favorites: Boba Fett, Jawas, R2. I peeled back one Jawa's hood. Uncovered, his face looked like a withered fig, the ends twisted and front incised with the striations of a desiccated ancient. Without his cover, he seemed tense. I replaced the cape and looked around. There was the naked wall where my *Revenge of the Jedi* poster had hung. There was the corner where my cardboard C-3PO cut-out had stood. Continuity issues, my mom had explained, were mistakes. I squeezed the foam on 4-LOM's robe and a strange indignity filled me, a mix of regret and offense, as if I had ignored my moral compass and done something taboo.

In 1999, my mother was in great physical condition from years of jogging and aerobics, but she worried about her mind: would it fail her? She'd started to forget things, and she wondered how much worse it would get. My dad was sixty. He had heart problems, the beginnings of diabetes, and he would soon have stints installed, an angioplasty, and suffer a cancer scare. My Grandpa Shapiro had died years earlier, leaving my mother devastated and forced to straighten out his disorganized finances. And the usually sharp comic mind of my dad's dad, Granddad Gilbreath, was starting to show signs of age. Not long after the sale, doctors diagnosed him with Alzheimer's.

Alone in my room, Death Star Droid's limbs felt cold in my hand. No matter the air-temperature, the Droid's limbs always felt cold. I set him on the carpet, as if he needed a rest. Looming above him like an uncaring god, I tried to find something in his blank bug eyes, some life or warmth or recognition, but those large unseeing lenses only absorbed light, their black paint applied by a Chinese factory worker to a small, helpless body unaware of how dwarfed it was by the world in which it lived.

TILLAGE

"I love you," Kari said, steadying her voice from across the table. "But I'm no longer in love with you."

She sat with folded hands, sushi spread in a colorful row across her plate, and deposited the news with a mechanical efficiency.

I tossed my napkin on the table and stomped out the door.

She slid into the passenger seat of her own car and broke my brooding silence.

"I'm sorry I stormed out."

"It's okay," she said, and clutched my hand. I couldn't look over. Labored exhalations and a pounding heart. "So." She stared straight forward. "What do we do now?"

"Drive," I said and started the car.

* * *

From room 210 of the Buttonwillow Motel 6, you can hear the sighs of sleeping semis returning to life. Surrounded by saltbush scrub and Interstate 5's hum, feral dogs patrol the parking lot as I draft an application for a $2000 grant.

"I've been hiking and writing about California's Central Valley for a decade," I type, the fifth version of my project proposal since arriving yesterday. Calexico's song "Windjammer" plays on my computer, a live version recorded June 21, 1998 at an in-store performance I'd attended. "Your generous funding would allow me to trace Frank Latta's historic boat-trip from Bakersfield to Frisco Bay and pen the accompanying piece, which I have always imagined as part of a larger collection of literary nonfiction, travel pieces and environmental reportage."

I replay the song and type the biographical statement: "Thirty-two, native of Phoenix, Arizona, studied Philosophy and Ecology." Thirty-two, I think. Thirty-two and, should I add, living rent-free with his parents in order to write full-time after six years book-selling in Oregon and two internships in New York? Would the darker truth evince instability or determination? I get up from the table and open the door. A manurey compost smell rushes in, the rural aroma of nearby stockyards and tilled black earth. It's the smell of promise, the smell of death, which itself smells of new life.

Latta's story demands narrative devices and the impressionistic chop of a dissected Monet. How should I phrase this? "Latta's route details an extinct, ghost landscape, illuminates the altered hydrology of the Valley's vanished hydro- and ecological condition, provides the opportunity to educate folks about the beautiful necessity of remembering the past, and the avoidable dangers of forgetting."

I slide my hands in my pocket and lean against the open door.

* * *

"I could live here," Kari said in Sacramento one fall. We coasted the sycamore-lined streets in her Acura, with me navigating the historic Midtown neighborhood around 21st and G, and all its pruned rosebushes and clean white Victorians. She squeezed my knee. Low morning fog draped the yuccas and picket fences, creating a serene urban dreamscape I knew she would like.

It'd be easier to collect material, I figured, from the Central Valley's center.

* * *

The aching neck roused me. My whole body, originally upright on the Bakersfield motel bed, had wilted like an iris, head folded over neck folded over chest folded over waist. I pulled myself back upright and leaned against the headboard, my heavy lids peeling apart from brown, pinprick eyes.

Slick with sweat, my fingers lifted the cut straw from my lap and set it beside the lighter and spoon atop *The Great Central Valley: California's Heartland*. This book was my bible. When I bought it, I'd protected the dust jacket with some super strong Mylar. I'd read the whole thing, all 264 pages, without creasing a single one. Strung out, I couldn't keep awake long enough to read it again.

Local news flickered on TV, and I smelled my moist fingers. It wasn't sweat, but drool.

* * *

"And close along the water's edge," it said, "there was a fine jungle of tropical luxuriance, composed of wild-rose and bramble bushes and a great variety of climbing vines, wreathing and interlacing the branches of willows and alders, and swinging across from summit to summit in heavy festoons." Upon first reading Muir's passage, from *The Mountains of California*, in 1996, it confounded me. 'Tropical luxuriance,' I thought, in the place where, driving I-5 from Oregon to LA the previous year, Dean and I could only say "This place is a dump." A basin now rank with manure and edges so hazy they erase the Sierras had presented scenes powerful enough to move Muir? It couldn't be true. I read on.

"The Great Central Plain of California," Muir wrote, "during the months of March, April, and May, was one smooth, continuous bed of honey-bloom so marvelously rich that, in walking from one end of it to the other, a distance of 400 miles, your foot would press about a hundred flowers at every step."

Honey-bloom, it said.

Honey-bloom.

* * *

Kari walked in holding two bags of groceries. "Still there, huh?" She stepped around my spot on the living room floor, dropping the bags on the kitchen counter with an intentional thunk.

"Been working on this essay for *Sierra* magazine's contest," I said, awaiting the applause.

Heavy paper crinkled from behind the wall.

Unshowered and unshaven, dressed only in boxers with a chest licked with sweat, I sat as still as a yoga instructor: back straight, muscular legs outstretched in a V. The California atlas sprawled before me, the routes of my four previous Valley explorations outlined and dated in thick black ink. Beside it, a ringed notebook filled with journal entries and drafts of "What if John Muir Had Fallen in Love with the Central Valley Instead of the Sierras?" After two weeks of work, Kari never asked to see it or what it was about, and I never submitted it. The essay seemed frozen in perpetual draft, all unfulfilled promise with no definite direction and only scattered hints of beauty. Who cares about what could have been? I thought. All that matters is what was.

I couldn't figure out what she saw in me. Maybe my caring side attracted her, the side that pressed wildflowers in journals and saved spiders from the shower when she alerted me to their presence. Or maybe it was the side of me that served her perfect pots of oolong tea and could make silken tofu taste like scrambled eggs. My natural history knowledge might have appeared to hold the potential for a future profession, but I rarely talked about potential professions with any specificity, and she had to sense my instability. Who looked at a soiled hiker sleeping in his truck on a roadtrip and saw husband material?

"How was work?"

"Tiring," Kair said, "but good." Teaching rambunctious school kids was always "tiring," her days spent working toward the release of nighttime TV. "I'd like you to come in soon and give an ecology lesson," she said.

"That would be fun."

Sweated coffee fumes rose from my skin. Calexico's early song "Wash" played on the stereo: "Slip away the night/While the whole town's asleep/ Caught between the space/Where you wanted to be."

Paper bags crinkled behind the wall.

As Kari slid onto the couch and lifted the remote, I put on the headphones.

* * *

The performance was intense. Calexico's two members set up in the corner of Stinkweeds Records, atop a short wooden platform beside the magazine rack and wall of glass: four-piece drum set, mini-xylophone, tan vintage amp, cheapo mic. June 21, 1998—I'll never forget that day.

Kari and I sat on the cement floor, backs against the store's seven-inch record rack, feet against the stage. They played "Windjammer," "Sanchez," and "Fake Fur," songs that accompanied me on all my Valley trips. Joey Burns' guitar carried enough surf-tone and fuzz to tear a hole in the cosmos. His singing had feeling, and John Convertino's jazzy brushwork—filamentaceous rolls and spins in soulful time signatures—synced perfectly, intuitively, with Joey's playing. To my ears, they created true artistry, a spontaneous creative moment of undiluted self-expression. New musical directions, I thought, art that paid the bills.

One of the ten audience members plugged his four-track recorder into the band's equipment. They were cool enough to let him, and as he rolled up his chords after the show, I offered to trade a copy of a recording I'd made for a copy of this one. "Sure," he said and gave me his phone number. I called four times over the next two months. Left messages. Planned to attend one of his own band's performances to prod him in person. But he never called back, and I finally gave up.

* * *

I'd practiced the lines out loud: "We want different things in life. I love you but we're too different."

TV played on mute on the Fresno motel television. I cleared my throat, finally released from its opiate croak, and revised my current draft: "What we want in life is just too different." I was going to be the one to say what we both knew, me, the one who planned to somehow write books, who thrashed through miles of Arizona cactus flats and steely shrubs every weekend only to see how it felt to be in the middle of roadless heatstroke nowhere, to feel the thrill of accomplishment, the burn of exertion, and worry if I was lost. Plus, the sense that in nature the palpable cosmos' mystifying riddles bore down on my over-thinking mind. "We hike to test death and slate desire and stare down the looming darkness," I'd read somewhere, or maybe imagined in one of those vivid nod dreams. So a couple loaded months had clouded my memory, binding fantasy with reality in a Frankenstinian reconstruction. I'd been strong enough to kick heroin once. I could be strong enough to say it. Who was it, after all, who told tailgaters to fuck themselves with a tap of the breaks, rather than a demure shift into the slowest, furthest lane? The one who fell from that oak trying to photograph a birds-eye view of the Cosumnes River bottom? One who wanted to move to Sacramento to write a book? To Oregon? To anywhere?

Kari didn't understand why I was so heartbroken about the live Calexico CD. "Because once something like this slips away," I'd explained, "you're likely never to get it back."

"Aren't studio recordings just as good?" she said.

I revised my speech further: "I'm not a nurturer. I don't want kids. I hate sitting home on Saturdays. I get bored watching TV. I'm happiest outdoors, on the road, far from home. Happier than during most other activities, more than sleeping or eating, being with friends or family or even in love." But you can't say this stuff to people. Their feelings get crushed. You look inhuman. Because maybe, you are.

* * *

Sunlight poured through the towering oak canopy. My backpack, filled with trail food and bottled water, scraped against the wild grape vines as I pushed through the brush to the languid slough. The Cosumnes River Preserve was a flooded backwater that contained the Valley's largest protected riparian forest. This was Muir's tropical luxuriance, thankfully preserved, just as he'd described.

Spring trip, 1997: three nature preserves in two days. In the arid southern portions I jumped over arroyos, skirted mirrored vernal pools, laid like a drunk in fields of luminous poppies and perfumed purple lupines. Fresh-picked flowers decorated the inside of my truck as I drove back to Phoenix, the stems in the air-conditioning vents, petals hanging like garters from the dash.

When poppies were just flowers.

* * *

"Nothing turns me on more than a beautiful woman appreciating my brain." It came out so much more fluidly in my 2004 journal than from my clumsy mouth. Writing it down, though, the painful awareness that I'd never had stung worse than the idea that I never would. Worse than the loneliness, the break-ups, the five years sobriety.

The ultimate idea: romance planted in a mutual appreciation of each other's intellect and creativity. "I don't want to be sexy," I scribbled, "I want to be smart." Then added, "No, I want a woman who thinks smart is sexy. Same way I do."

* * *

The homeless man leaned toward our window from the median. I dropped change in his cup before the light turned green.

"That's probably what you do on your trips," Kari said, serious.

I wanted to scream, wanted to yell, wanted to cry my correction about the nature of research, the necessity of patience, the writer's long haul, the staggering volume of material and experience I'd so far collected and hoped one day my brain would spit out in some beautiful form after this lengthy gestation, but how, then again, would she know a thing about that when I knew so little about her?

Instead, I laughed. "No, I'm not that clean."

* * *

Stuffy, sterilized by chlorine, nightstands bearing brown melted divots from myriad smoking strangers, the universal mark of shared property, disposable moments, careless occupation, intoxication. I'd rented the same room—number 113—that I'd rented the previous year at the Merced Motel 6. Merced, far and away the middle San Joaquin's ugliest "big" town.

The Gerald Haslam books I'd just bought—*The Other California, Coming of Age in California*, and *Voices of a Place: Social and Literary Essays from the Other California*—sat on the nightstand. I'd finished *Voices of a Place*, most of *The Other California*, read and reread *The Great Central Valley* four or five times and, now that I could keep awake while reading since I was off dope, made nearly as many notes as that thing had pages. Intending to start my new books, I instead sat there on the bed, leaning against the same wall, staring as I had the previous year out the same open door, trying to remember what it felt like that day. To be young, hopeful, naively optimistic, thinking I'd have my own book by now, a soulmate, a life.

The days when the Valley remained a vast unmapped notion felt then in 1999 a lifetime away. My future had been a block of wet clay to be sculpted, a series of cryptograms yet defined. During my first solo expedition in 1997, this land was the future: an immeasurable emptiness, sprawling and complex, filled with excitement and promise, adventure and discovery. A festooned canopy. A vernal pool.

It seemed to have slowly evaporated somehow.

Sitting upright, absorbing the pastel morning and view of Highway 99, I read the previous year's journal entry, written right there leaning against that wall: "Morning light, powder blue and rosebush pink, streaks the eastern sky." Pointless observations and atmospheric impressions—the lazy muted moans of a narcotized mind. A wasted mind. Wasted time.

I closed my eyes, recalling the way I once set the spoon, straw and balloons back into the Altoids tin where I kept them. How lone drops draining from my nostrils often landed on my knee below the hem of my favorite hiking shorts. How I'd stared out the window, heard the woosh of passing semis and wing beats of crows pecking the lot for crumbs, how songbirds lined up along electric lines silhouetted against that powder blue and rosebush light, as if it all meant something.

I wanted so badly to be high, loaded and dreamy. I could smell the heroin, feel the sour burn hanging like a gathering raindrop in my nose, lingering before draining down my inflamed throat. That Thai dressing smell, that caramel bile mixed with melted plastic and engine fluids. No one ever knew I'd once suffered withdrawal to kick the brief habit. Not my friends, my parents, and somehow, not Kari.

I should call Kari, I thought, tell her I made it okay, that the trip's going well.

Instead I leaned against the headboard and scribbled in my journal: "Chemistry as artificial transcendence. Mistook this for living, for feeling, for progress."

* * *

Sweat slid through my sideburns as I watched Kari and her mom carry boxes to their cars. Clothes, appliances, photo albums and dishes—carted silently to our apartment building parking lot, mother moving daughter back into her home, past the wallflower fixture, the crumb in the carpet fiber.

Love blooms, love dies. What else was there to say? Should I have asked if she remembered the time during our Sacramento trip where I drove her to the Cosumnes Preserve to show her Muir's tropical luxuriance, what all my excitement was about, and how she never got out of the car? How she just sat in the passenger seat—"No," she said, "you go"—because we'd gotten swarmed by yellow-jackets, and so I left her and cut through the dense undergrowth along the slough? How I rushed, not for fear of getting caught by preserve staff in an off-limits area, but out of consideration of her boredom? Did she remember that? I did. She was doing the right thing leaving me and moving on. She could do better. She, the persistent worrier, self-described homebody, lover of sitcoms, and someone so terrified of hurting people's feelings she routinely avoided conflict until the backed-up vitriol burst forth volcanically, the person who had raced back to Phoenix weeks into her freshman semester at University of Oregon because she felt isolated. We didn't align. Yet I couldn't help but wonder: how was I not moving out?

* * *

At least I'd never passed out in the John. Bookstores, yes. In philosophy class, yes. But never in a bathroom. At least I'd never shot up, never stole anything. Nodding's never the plan, just where it all sort of leads regardless of intent.

Intent. I said it aloud. Such a philosophical concept, part animal psychology (ie: if preference implies intent, is it proof of decision-making in animals?), part conceptual hair-splitting moral theory. A quick sniff drew the drug back into my nose. I never intended this. You'd rather have a millionaire's bed, something plush and downy, full of feathers and flannel that puffs around in a tender hug as you sink in to its soothing folds. Something akin to loving arms. I only wanted something to own, something my own. A house, a pickup, 401-K—big property like my own book by now, birthed of hard work.

Motel beds are so hard.

A drop leaked from my nostril and landed on my knee. I should be out in the field, I thought, making notes in natural areas, finishing reading, taking as many photos as my camera will allow. Instead, a talking head announced the weather in New York City. Two hosts covered the newest child protective seats and spoke to some aging Southern cook over a crackling skillet. My body slowly tilted to the side.

* * *

A surprise email arrived in my work email inbox one day. "I learned so much from you," Kari said, "not only about myself but the world around me. To this day, when I go on road trips, I always make sure to check out the view and note the riparian (sp?) areas as I pass by them."

She lives in Phoenix still, with her husband now and two kids.

I wrote back but labored over the wording. How do you say "I work at a retail bookstore" and "I'm still working on the Valley thing at age thirty," without sounding like a loser? I mentioned the bookstore and my writing and maybe that was the difference: I no longer cared what people thought. I was no longer scared of making impressions. "I'm on a mission," I told her. Too bad part of my mission wasn't apologizing for my mistakes.

* * *

"Studying?" the waitress asked. "Writing an essay?"

"Studying," I said, "so I can write an essay," and described Latta's 1938 boat trip from Bakersfield to San Francisco Bay. "I'm going to retrace the exact course, campsite-to-campsite, by car and foot—since most of those waterways aren't there to boat on anymore—and then tell the story of the land itself as well as the people."

Her hand on her hip, she leaned over my packet of Xeroxed newspaper clippings and the map I'd drawn of his journey and smiled. "Hmm. So you can ride a boat from there to there?"

"No, not anymore," I said. "Those rivers and wetlands are all gone now. It's like that old Valley is dead, never to return. And that's what I want to show."

* * *

The CD-R arrived at my New York apartment in a thin white envelope, the stranger's careful handwriting along the disk's edge. Hearing those songs for the first time flooded me with enough memories to fill the Kern River. You can hear my joyous "woo-hoos" during the applause, my voice calling out song requests: "Spokes." Desperate. Envious. Hungry. Enchanted.

The show played on a loop that freezing winter. My then-girlfriend Abby liked the music and was excited for me. "I waited nine years for this," I explained.

"Turn it down a bit," she said the night it arrived. "They're sleeping below us."

"Who cares what the neighbors can hear." I moved the boom box into our office and studied the German postmark. World tours, big tour buses, bands who opened for them—Calexico had come a long way since those days. A long way from Arizona.

* * *

I lean against the frame and stare at the semis a couple more minutes before closing the motel door. Back at the desk, I replay "Windjammer" and finish the proposal: "On Saturday June 18, 1938, San Joaquin Valley historian Frank Latta and three high school kids embarked on an unprecedented, and now largely forgotten, expedition. Starting on the Kern River in Bakersfield, California, the crew maneuvered their fifteen-foot skiff 455 water miles through a maze of flooded sloughs, primitive ditches, and rivers swollen with snowmelt, finally reaching Treasure Island in San Francisco Bay on July 1. It was the first and only recorded float trip from Kern County to the sea."

I type another draft but know I can do better. How should I phrase this? "The wild San Joaquin Valley's agricultural conversion is a human story of lands mapped, lives lost, fortunes squandered, and the cumulative facade of what history calls 'progress.' I hope my piece can sit alongside Gerald Haslam's essays, David Mas Masumoto's *Letters to the Valley*, and Gary Soto's stories, that in capturing this oft-ignored landscape's character, I can paint a worthy portrait of Mr. Latta, a man whose passions and professional contributions centered fully on this Valley. As a land of superlatives, paradoxes, and surprises, where tarantulas coincided with cranes, marshes met barrens, summer drought followed spring floods, I believe Haslam's "other California" shines best in a layered, multifaceted narrative."

"Multifaceted" is good. But I haven't yet worked in "honey-bloom."

TRAGEDY OF THE COMMONS

Why would neighbors want to know each other? Look at us.

In my second apartment building in Portland, Oregon, there was Dave, the balding, grey-eyed introvert who, when not in his apartment, could be found browsing the sci-fi/fantasy section at the bookstore where I worked. Elliot was the shy forty-something musician in Converse All-Stars who practiced the same chord progression on his acoustic guitar over and over for the first ten months of my residence. There was Tom or Tim or Todd—I never got it straight—who, when you made a joke, simply bulged his eyes instead of smiling, as if forty years of repressed laughter threatened to launch them from their sockets. Louise's cooking mishaps required frequent visits from the fire department. Then there was Chad.

Chad wanted you to know that it was he who'd crafted that art in the hall—yes, the cut section of green garden hose set on his welcome mat, previously the Tab soda can, before that the single yellow brick—and that he'd done so with items fished entirely from the trash. "Pretty cool what you can find in there," he'd say if, like me, you encountered him nearly every night while reading a book after work on the building's communal front bench. It didn't matter what you were doing. When he encountered you, he interrupted.

"A friend of mine just sent me these," he said one night. I was walking toward my unit, lugging two huge laundry bags. He was standing in the hall, closer to my apartment than his own three doors down, just waiting for me or Tom/Tim/Todd or any one of our neighbors to walk up so he could share photos of himself. "I was a dirty fifteen-year-old punk," he said, lifting a photo from the stack in his hand. "Man, it's crazy."

I didn't look. I spent my eight-hour workdays in retail satisfying the demands of demanding strangers; at home, I told myself, I needed invisibility.

So I said "Huh," then slipped inside my apartment to separate my shirts and socks.

I'd left Arizona for Portland, Oregon, four years earlier after landing a job at Powell's Books. Phoenix bored me. It felt stiflingly familiar, too spread out, and dug up a lot of dark memories from my past. I needed out. It seemed to me at the time that the best place for a bibliophile to work was the world's largest new and used bookstore, so I staffed the registers at Powell's Books, maintained the inventory on its towering shelves and hosted weekly author events. And just months earlier I'd moved into this second-floor walkup in Northwest Portland from my previous dump in the city's Northeast quadrant—partly to be free of the stink of ferret urine that had, thanks to a sweet but undisciplined pet who didn't always find the litter box, suffused the unit with a farmhouse odor, partly to enjoy a historic, more heavily wooded neighborhood closer to work. Memories of my old life reeked. My new life, I vowed, would radiate fresh air and flowers.

The air was fresh when I opened the windows, but my new digs suffered the usual drawbacks of dense urban living. Portland State University students ruled the adjacent building. It loomed on the other side of a narrow wooded green strip, and its windows faced mine. Theirs was the kind of building where off-key twenty-something karaoke singers yelled "More vomiting!" when you tried to end their session with fake gagging and coyote howls. Mine was the kind where raccoons climbed tall trees then plunged ten feet to fight over the trail mix you threw them. The kind of complex where the pixelated witch's laugh of a neighbor's alarm regularly jarred you awake at 6am, going "eh, eh, eh, eh, eh" for an hour a few times a month, then, after you yell, "Kill your fucking alarm!" for thirty minutes only to realize no one was home, forced you to slide a gently worded note under their door requesting he or she (you never once saw the person) shut it off when not home, thanks. Still, on the inside, this was hands-down the greenest, oldest, most beautiful and comfortable apartment I'd ever had. That you could call this residential collective an apartment "complex" was just a comic bonus. I certainly had one.

So there, in my new studio with the large picture window and antique wooden floors, I settled into a stimulating routine: work all day, read on the porch at night. I consumed countless books on the bench this way, everything from Marc Reisner's *Cadillac Desert* to Joan Didion's *Slouching Toward Bethlehem*.

Finding me out front, my face inches from the print, Chad stopped, leaned over and read the title on my book's spine aloud. "*Normal*. What's that about?" I told him it was a short story collection featuring people with problems, though that pretty much described all literary fiction. "Ah," he said. "I should be in there."

The next time he arrived holding a wine bottle filled with urine, which he planned to lean against his door in the hope that someone would steal it. "We used to do this at punk shows in the desert," he explained, holding the bottle out for inspection. "Some jerk thinks, 'Oh, cool,' takes it, then is like, 'Aah man, that's piss!'"

"Huh," I said. "Clever trap."

Since we lived on the same floor, I passed daily through his ever-changing hallway gallery on the way to the exit. He taped a rotating collection of fliers to his door: art exhibits, movie screenings, upcoming poetry slams, coffee shop ads which served, as I interpreted it, as both a to-do list for folks not reading the local weeklies and a public sampling of his personal tastes. The bulletin board approached identity the same way band t-shirts did for high school kids. It said, in no uncertain terms, "This is me, this is what I'm into." I'd stop at his door heading to and from work and read the new items, not seeking haiku competitions, just glimpses into his character that didn't involve conversation. He did pick some cool events. But judging from the consistently low-quality Xeroxes and eclectic business cards, he also seemed to display anything he found or was handed on the street.

The objects he set on his welcome mat seemed equally haphazard: a bird cage, a tattered straw hat, the colored bricks. Items changed weekly. One day you'd walk by and see a yellow brick. The next day you'd find it replaced by a plastic Halloween pumpkin, or a pile of fallen acorns, maple or elm branches thick enough to call logs, a copper gecko tied to a rope threaded under the door so that, like a fishing line, he knew when someone touched it. The thing is, the items didn't seem to carry any significance. They didn't possess inherent aesthetic qualities or ring with symbolism.

They didn't relate to current events or to each other in a way that, in gallery speak, could be called "of a piece." They just sat there on his door mat, inert, each receiving their own loosely measured week in the resident public's eye. It sounds mean, likely bitter and close-minded, but viewing those items, I saw bricks broadcasting to the world, "I am weird." A Tab can that screamed, "The person in this unit is unbearably interesting. Talk to him." Like nametags at a corporate team-building seminar, the logs and hose and hat weren't meant to be anything other than ice-breakers for their owner; they waited to bridge the silent divide between Chad and his neighbors, at least the neighbors who didn't put their ears to their doors to first listen for his footsteps before entering the hall. This was social media before social media: an expression of loneliness, neediness, vanity, hunger. At least that's how I took it. These qualities were easy to recognize since I carried them myself, me, who kept albums that I didn't like in my collection because visiting friends would think they were cool, me, who displayed books on my shelf that I'd never read because they were part of the canon, advertising, "The person in this apartment is unbearably literary and rock and roll." But for myself I had more patience. Something about Chad triggered me that I couldn't initially figure out.

I didn't study visual art in college. I didn't read about art movements, periods or styles as an adult. Having ignored Portland's local gallery scene, the only art I came in contact with were the paintings in windows that I walked past while shuffling around town, yet I wondered if contemporary art could be this arbitrary. If I were a critic, my review of Chad's exhibit would've read: "Accidental, capricious, deliberately indiscriminate." The one art I knew intimately was literature. Honest essays and fiction were only accidental in that first drafts and opening paragraphs rarely foretold the shape of the finished piece. The creative process led the artist along a surprise course in unforeseen directions, a process akin to an early morning drive down an unfamiliar road that starts out dark and gradually grows lighter. But this welcome mat mélange was as accidental as tripping on a curb. It was a parent saying "Oops" as baby filled its diaper in the Walmart checkout line, then Chad adding, "Not oops: art."

In truth, his art wasn't my problem. My problem was that he irritated me for some reason, so I resented everything that sprung from him. Logs became lectures about pee at punk shows. Bricks continued conversations I'd tried ending on the porch. That's why I never asked his name. I figured, how friendly could a person get with someone who refused introductions? I knew the feral cat rule: if you don't want to hear constant meowing, don't feed feral cats. And isn't it Dracula who never leaves your home once invited in?

* * *

When I moved to Portland, the idea of living in a dense, walkable urban area sounded invigorating and socially progressive compared to the sprawling commuter conditions I grew up in, but the practical demands of density took some adjustment.

I was an only child. My childhood home consisted of my mom, dad, me and some hamsters. At one point we had a rabbit, but he lived in the backyard. My mom's New York family was talkative and loud, but our house was one that offered privacy and space when you needed it. I have four half-brothers, all of whom I love, but we didn't grow up in the same house. They were older than me. Without siblings to share with, I got my own room. If I wanted company, I invited friends over. When I wanted to be alone, I simply closed my door. Growing up this way, I got used to dictating the terms of my personal space and social interactions, and in the process, I grew overly accustomed to enjoying my hobbies with an intense, singular focus.

I used to draw. When I wanted to draw, I drew. When I wanted to read, I read. When I read as an adult, I remained the same way. I liked finishing an article in one sitting. I know that's a privilege, but it's what I was used to, because constant back and forth and interruptions frustrated me. There was something pathological about what was partly neurological. Maybe Chad wouldn't have bothered me if I had grown up with siblings in a big, noisy household. Granted, I could have set firmer boundaries with him, but that felt rude, and I was so used to being able to simply read a book or listen to music by closing a door, that I wanted him to read my closed-off body language without exchanging a word. I wanted him to go away by doing nothing at all. And after work, I often wanted to be alone.

While staffing one of my bookstore's customer information desks, a middle-age woman set two huge architecture books on the counter in front of me and asked, "Which one of these would my sister like more?"

"Well," I said, "what does your sister like?"

Clearly amazed by my failure to grasp the obvious, the woman puckered her lips, arched one brow and said, "She likes books."

I said, "You definitely came to the right place," and pointed to the book on the left. "That one. She'll like that much better." She agreed. It didn't matter that I'd only glanced at the covers.

As thrilling as it was for a bibliophile like myself to work with books and see daily proof that not all Americans had abandoned reading, customer demands wore me out.

"Will you watch my bag while I use the bathroom?"

"Tell me a good book for a ten-year-old who hates reading but loves army guys but isn't too violent?"

"What's the name of that one with the two brothers from Kentucky who embark on that adventure looking for their lost dog and meet that Indian shaman?"

"I'll just park my stroller here behind your chair."

"You're telling me you can't find the copy of *My Dog Skip* that your website says you have?"

Customers in the art department were some of the most challenging. Haughty, gruff, and demanding, they and their oversized rock-star sunglasses reinforced my feeling that the visual arts in Portland were too often a fashion accessory for people whose greatest talent was creatively dressing themselves. Take the dude wearing the brown derby, railroad suspenders, Ray-Ban Wayfarers and shiny slacks. He asked me to locate books about an artist named Tanahashi. "What's his first name?" I said.

Brown Derby said, "Could there be more than one?"

"We have an enormous database," I explained. "Over two million books in stock." Then I listed the first hits to illustrate the daunting scale of our search.

"Don't be so condescending," he said, turning sideways to face away from me. "Supercilious."

"Score," said Chad. I looked up from my book. A chipped, five-foot-tall particleboard shelf rested on one of Chad's shoulders and a full gallon water jug hung from a rope on his other. He set the shelf by the door and walked over to the bench. "Look what else I got." He pulled a copper gecko from his pocket and flipped a back panel, revealing a smudged inner chamber. It was an ashtray.

"Cool stuff," I said, wanting but resisting the rude urge to return my attention to my book. Judging from the deep lines incising his cheeks, he must've been nearly forty. He kept his thick auburn hair messy, cut to different lengths like fronds on a palm. I had to give him credit, though: he had more hair than I. I was twenty-nine and balding. And with all the digging and hauling involved in dumpster diving, at least he got exercise. All I did was sell books then sit on my butt reading all night.

He normally arrived clutching the night's score: a couple of unpainted wooden boards; a Mini Etch A Sketch which, for weeks after, hung on a rope from his doorknob, displaying the little pictures he'd drawn. "Aren't these crazy," he said once, holding a pair of antlers to his head.

The randomness of his commentary eventually became routine. "I just saw this guy," he said, holding two Trader Joes bags. "He makes his way through the neighborhood sometimes. I think he's crazy." Another time, carrying a halogen lamp: "You ever hear those animals out back? Once I looked out the window, and there was a raccoon staring me face-to-face." Portland was once a city filled with actual and phony freaks. Talented artists lived beside transparent posers, and the latter—immersed as they were in a legitimately thriving artist's community whose members included countless authors, zine-makers, and bands all living in Elliot Smith and Dead Moon's long shadows—refuse to be ignored. So they manufacture oddity. They dress loudly. Sport peculiar facial hair, glasses and hats. Where Tom/Tim/Todd and Dave were marked by the kind of charming natural oddity all of us imperfect humans could relate to, Chad's was the kind you painted on your face before a Swedish death metal concert, the kind teens in coffee shops tried to impart by reading *The Anarchist Cookbook* while wearing a top hat and cape. Which might have been the saddest part: he exhibited no evidence of intoxication. He seemed straight, and when the only influence you're under is what laymen call "an annoying personality," you can't just quit consuming the culpable agent.

"Hey," he said, coming off the street holding a scuffed record player. "You ever think about what it'd be like if this place had ten more floors and a rooftop thing you could look off of?"

That night I tipped over the gecko. The next morning, it was gone.

* * *

If you can accept the broadest definition and admirable lunacy of performance art, then you can accept what I came to call "display art." Display art—i.e., inanimate objects set alone or in seemingly random arrangements in ordinary, unlikely places like car hoods, welcome mats, and the tops of walls in grocery store parking lots—occupies the same creative genus as a Degas or hand-stitched sock-monkey.

Like Richard Brautigan's *Trout Fishing in America* and Ornette Coleman's music, this initially sounded nuts. But the chance to open an increasingly calcified mind to new ideas was one of Portland's most endearing qualities. It was one of the reasons I moved there from my then-heartless and artless suburban hometown of Phoenix in the first place. Despite my initial resistance, I couldn't undo the impact: if stuff in a dumpster was just ordinary trash, then stuff placed in select locations was neither trash nor ordinary. The mere selection of it—narrowing a bin full of options, recasting its fate—made it if not pretty, then at least special. It ceased being garbage when it resumed being wanted, which by extension made it meaningful. Then, when deposited somewhere glaringly bland, that stuff came to suggest just enough buried meaning to spark debate among viewers.

That could be the thing: if beauty is in the eye of the beholder, and art welcomes infinite interpretation, maybe the beguiling nature of Chad's items were their most affecting quality. They made visitors say "What the hell is this crap?" or text a photo to friends with the caption "WTF." Those who didn't conclude "random BS" searched for meaning in the mess. While I couldn't admit it then, I frequently found myself processing books at work or lying in bed wondering if I'd been fooled by the exhibit's simplicity. Was I too focused on the accidental appearance? The seeming randomness? Was this like tasting mediocre sashimi at a hyped sushi restaurant and wondering if your taste buds were the problem, not the food? If someone else had made these displays, I might have been more open to them, but their maker annoyed me too much to give them a chance. The problem wasn't him as much as it was me, the closed-minded viewer.

* * *

Of course I'd long considered reading somewhere else. Because I smoked, I used the porch. It offered greater comfort than reading while leaning out my high shower window, and dodging the rising plume while angling the pages to catch the dim bathroom light. But on nights when my need for solitude outweighed my tolerance for interruption, I experimented with alternatives: the spacious lawn of a nearby nonprofit; the picnic tables in Couch Park, the tiny, tucked away garden of an expensive condominium. An adjacent complex's front staircase proved the most practical. Sandwiched between handrails and a jungle of landscaped greenery, the narrow staircase was cozy. I'd plant myself on a step, throw my legs out, then lean against the iron railing. Unlike my bench, though, this spot sat directly in the path of incoming traffic. Every time a tenant went in or out, I had to scoot to the side to make room, which made me, despite all attempted courtesy, a pain in the ass. Confrontation was immediate.

On my first visit, a man stepped past me on his way to the door. The key clicked in the lock, the bolt disengaged. Instead of stepping inside, he turned around and said, "Excuse me, do you live here?"

"Uh, no," I said, exhibiting the sort of shame I wished my ferret exhibited when he missed his mark. "I live around the corner and needed a change of scenery. I can leave if you need me to." He arched his brows, studied my book, and said I could stay if I didn't make it a habit. I said, "Absolutely."

Turns out, I didn't make a habit of it, but only because I favored my bench. That was my porch, I figured. I paid to use it. I was comfortable there and refused to let one odiferous loudmouth run me off. In a building full of Flannery O'Conner characters, somehow only one posed a problem.

There was Richard the horny Hennesey-toting DJ who rolled a milk crate full of LPs into a cab a few times a week and wore so much cologne that if you didn't wrap your hand in something when touching the front door, you'd taste Richard in your food that night. There was Rey from level one, the mopey, unemployed clove-smoker permanently decked in black who spoke of Borges in a barely audible, undeniably depressed whisper. He'd pssst pssst about Argentina and *Ficciones* a while, then quit talking mid-sentence and slip back inside. Elliot darted by, head down, avoiding even the chance of accidental eye-contact. My exchanges with Dave consisted of me saying "Hey man" and him muttering "He-hello." Richard rarely stopped. He just rolled past with a "What up." Then there was Terry.

Terry lived on the second floor at the top of the stairs. Though only in his late-twenties, he wandered Irving and 21st streets and the building's halls with a profound sluggishness that suggested medication, and if he spotted you anywhere, even at the grocer, he stopped, stood directly in front of you as if to block escape. Seemingly oblivious to time, he talked about his bleak temp jobs and politics and tax laws. He'd lecture and leave no room for responses because he barely drew a breath. I watched his mouth closely but couldn't determine how or when he took in air. There was no huff, no quick nasal drag. I just had to assume that, like Mick Jagger running around clapping on stage, there was some system there. He never ended a conversation. You had to disengage by excusing yourself, but even then he'd follow you. For fear of getting drowned by his conversation, I ran inside and hid in the laundry room whenever I heard him approaching.

Chad walked too fast. By the time you heard footsteps, he was standing beside you.

"Oh, well," he says, "today I found a perfectly fine red bird cage next to two petit pan rolls in the trash by Ken's Artisan Bakery. I'm going to eat one roll buttered, make little bird legs out of bent paperclips for the other roll, and set it on the swing in the cage. I'll call it, 'Bun on a Wire.'"

* * *

DJ Richard stumbled onto the porch holding a beer. A woman wearing a red Chinese silk dress emerged behind him, four mini-chopsticks stuck in her bun. "What up," he said, checking the street for approaching headlights. "Waiting for a friend." Like me, Richard grew up in Phoenix, in a part of the city I knew intimately through parties and college. He'd even moved to Portland in August 2001, exactly one year after me. He held up three Pabst tallboys dangling from a plastic six-pack ring. "Wanna beer?"

"Ah, no thanks," I said. "I appreciate it though."

He patted his back pocket. "How 'bout a sip of some Hennesey?" As much as I once liked cognac, at the time, I rarely drank. I was trying to enjoy life clear-headed, and I no longer enjoyed a buzz. In college, booze had started turning my attention inward, pulling me out of the conversation and away from the socializing. At least it had when I'd quit eight or nine years before. Politely, I declined.

Richard said, "Suit yourself."

He and his friend lingered beside the bench, giggling and tickling and sipping their beers. I couldn't concentrate, and not solely due to envy. My attention kept drifting from the page to the details of their chatter. What were they saying? Something about a party, the names of people attending? It was New Year's Eve. I had laundry in the machine. Over the drunken lovers' flirting, I kept hearing the sound of my own voice saying, "Ah, no thanks." The somber weight of my resistance, that dedication to solitude, control, finishing books in silence—the very definition of "no fun." The phrase "no thanks" echoed in my mind.

"Hey Richard," I said, "I'll take you up on that beer."

He handed me one. "It's New Year's, bro. What the hell."

The can chilled my palm and fizzed when it opened. Then we raised our beers in unison and howled, "Happy New Year."

The woman offered her hand and slurred, "I'm Michelle." They'd been drinking since 3:00 p.m.

Once they sped off in their friend's car, I resumed reading. My beer rested beside the bench, only a few sips lighter.

After a few more sips I poured the beer in the planter.

* * *

There's this character Leon in Brock Clarke's short story "Accidents." He's a reporter. He drinks in the mornings and lies to his wife at night. He tells his editor boss "I need to be some kind of new man," then with one drunken slip up he gets the whole town gossiping about how the boss might be gay. When presented with opportunities for self-improvement, Leon routinely chooses the losing path: parking his car under a KFC exhaust fan which slicks it in grease; publishing unnecessary photos of a man's dead father; breaking simple promises; lying to his wife. He calls them all "accidents." I've read this story multiple times, and each time makes it harder to find legitimate accidents in the world around me.

A photocopy of four pieces of toast arranged in a grid hung from Chad's door. When I stopped to have a look, I noticed the door was open.

Cautiously, I listened, my ear to the crack for signs of activity. Once assured the place was empty, I eased the door open and peered inside. Junk coated the studio: stray notebook pages littered the floor. Fabric and paper banners sporting slogans like "Happy Birthday Carol!" and something about dentistry hung across the corners. Nails affixed other banners to the roof, and they all sagged in large arcs. Plastic milk crates sat wedged under the edges of everything and in between things, part structural supports, part storage spaces. A flattened futon mattress stretched atop cinder blocks and boards by the window, a window whose sill was covered with rugs. A pyramid of mismatched pillows towered atop blankets of competing colors and patterns. That free scuffed record player balanced atop a sleek modern CD player and stereo receiver. By the bed stood a beige eighties-era television with hand dials and a wire antennae. This was an empire of clutter, an amazing feat of urban recycling and domestic engineering, ugly but impressive.

Not long after, on my way to work, I left an empty tin of oolong tea on Chad's mat. Ti Kuan Yin, specifically. It looked ridiculous there: a purple and black label, a tiny metal square. It sat like dirty plates awaiting collection by room service. Or maybe it looked pretty, like tulip bulbs not yet buried in rich soil, like taped-up running shoes left on a curb after a marathon, or all possible future conditions of a growing baby boy.

The tin was gone that night after work, replaced by something else. I don't recall what.

IT'S REALLY SOMETHING YOU
SHOULD HAVE EXAMINED

It came to me one morning while racing to the train: Wiggy and I should ride the subway together all over New York City. It would be fun, sharing that singular New York experience with my favorite pet, the ferret who used to pee on my carpet and who, according to NYC Health Code Section 161.01, was a "dangerous wild animal" and "naturally inclined to do harm," too dangerous to enter the five boroughs. Clearly lawmakers had never met the guy.

Wiggy was a domestic loafer. The only thing he was naturally inclined to do was coil up in warm laundry and eat anything left within reach. Contrary to the Health Code description, I had so thoroughly cuddled the ferocity out of him that the only resemblance he bore to the wild members of his genera was in appearance. When my girlfriend Abby and I moved from Oregon to New York together, Wiggy flew from Portland to Cincinnati to Philly as a carry-on, overnighted in a Hampton's Inn, then drove with us up the Garden State Parkway in a rental car to our new apartment. While racing to the subway I pictured him—the lone weasel on the A Train. He would poke his snout out from my unzipped backpack to gaze at morning commuters, and passengers would ignore him the way they ignore everything but the overhead station signs.

When I told her about the plan, Abby said, "That would be hilarious." And it would have been.

We'd moved to New York to continue our relationship while she finished her final undergrad year. She was a bright, talented musician who loved to read and dance, I an aging bookstore clerk. She came into my bookstore one day, dressed in a black peacoat, a fragrant, delicately freckled beauty bearing a thick head of black lustrous hair. After a year together—a year of travel and romance and intense intellectual conversation—I thought, "She could be the one." Maybe what people said was true: that if

153

you waited patiently enough, love would find you. A few months in, something told me we weren't a match. I also doubted myself. I'd been wrong many times before, but she was too brilliant and passionate to let her get away. So I left my job and followed her east. There, at a incomprehensibly elite school, she felt like the lone Mississippian with student loans and parents who couldn't afford to pay her way. I was the thirty-one-year-old balding guy in skate shoes and flannels who used the school library computers for email. Wiggy was our mascot.

"I'll take photos of him and me posing in places we're not allowed to be," I told Abby. "It'll be a series: Wiggy and me in Times Square; Wiggy and me sharing red bean buns on Canal Street; Wiggy staring down a Central Park carriage horse." The photos as I imagined them would provide the images for that year's Christmas cards. "Wiggy salutes you!" the caption would read, above a picture of him peeing in a fancy Park Avenue residential planter.

"Just you?" Abby said. "Can't I go?"

"Of course. I didn't mean just me and him." And I hadn't. I was only thinking out loud.

Instead of pursuing the absurd "Project Ferret in the City," both Abby and I got swept away in the current of our new hectic lives. Fall's chill overtook our summer heat. Before we knew it, the maples' green leaves fell crisp and orange. Black squirrels raced across overhead power lines, crashing through treetops to stash nuts in limbs. This was my first East Coast winter. Already, the cold felt intense, and I could tell we had a dark long winter ahead.

* * *

"Aaron!" Abby howled. "Wiggy peed again. This has to stop."

"I know," I said, rushing into the kitchen where a yellow puddle spread from behind the radiator. I said, "I'm sorry," upset but not enough to prove I was a good disciplinarian. During the first few weeks of our residence, this became our routine. Wiggy would pee on the tile. Abby would find it. I'd race in holding paper towels and cleaning solution.

"There's always a learning curve," I explained; new smells and a break in routine caused confusion. "He'll know the rules soon." Then I'd grab him and say, "Bad Wiggy," in as firm a voice as I could muster for someone so cute, then thwack him on the nose. "Bad." It's what trainers recommended, and it worked in Portland.

We had a lot of fun back in Oregon, Wiggy and me. When he was young and I in my twenties, he clawed my feet in bed to wake me up, then I chased him around the apartment playing one of many games. We were always chasing each other around that apartment. Although I kept my tiny studio clean—dishes washed, papers organized—it bore all the signs of carefree bachelorhood. None of my silverware matched. The cupboard overflowed with vintage Tab, Seven-Up, and coffee shop glasses purchased at thrift stores over a decade. Shelves of books dominated the walls. Then there were his toys. Fuzzy balls, rubber chew toys, and fake mice lay scattered across the hardwood floor. Under my computer desk, not far from the bed, sat Wiggy's "litter box." It was just an endless series of disposable puppy pads made of diaper material that dogs-in-training use. I called it a litter box because saying "puppy pads" made it sound like I slept in view of yellow pee stains, which I did. He never took to my attempted box-training as a kit. Instead of being firmer or trying different techniques, I gave up, lazily setting the pads in a corner and changing them daily. That was a mistake.

Surprisingly, Abby tolerated the puppy pads and found it amusing that Wiggy's beds filled the apartment. His primary bed, a fleece lined sack, sat on the floor beside the couch. A down lap blanket he liked burrowing into lay bunched on the couch's opposite end. I kept the closet open so he could climb in at his discretion and sleep in a pile of clothes I no longer wore. When I showered, I left my pajamas on the bath mat; this provided a place to wait until I got out and placed him in the tub to lick the water off the basin. This was our morning routine. "Everyone likes having options," I told Abby, "even animals." Being accommodating seemed a hallmark of a good roommate, even a good relationship skill. Like when I went grocery shopping. I'd set the paper bag down by the fridge while unloading items, and if Wiggy crawled inside it, I just left the bag on the floor for him to play and sleep in for hours. These were harmless adjustments to my environment that reflected my philosophy on cohabitation: sometimes you have to alter your lifestyle to suit the nature of the people in your life.

It's also why I let him dig deep channels into the interior of my couch. It was a crap thrift store hand-me-down whose purplish velveteen fit more in a goth castle than my sunny studio. So it was no loss when Wiggy clawed through the armrest and started displacing the stuffing so he could sleep there in winter. When Abby came over and asked, "Where's Wiggy?" the answer was frequently, "In his hibernacula." He'd stick his nose out the hole, and we'd hand him nuts and dried mango. Abby loved that. "Breakfast in bed," she'd say. Bits of yellow foam drifted constantly across the floor as Abby and I made love on the bed and sofa. Because Wiggy enjoyed the exercise of excavation, allowing him to indulge his instinct seemed more important than preserving the structural integrity of the world's ugliest couch. It seemed unwise to expect anyone to live contrary to their nature.

In Oregon, Abby was a packrat. She squirreled receipts and photocopies and newspaper clippings away into cardboard boxes. When we moved in together in New York, all of that increased to smothering proportions. Boxes sat overflowing on the bedroom floor, where she frequently pawed through them in search of a Xerox or folder or sock that she needed immediately, or she'd be late for school. She kept nearly every *New York Times Book Review* and *Sunday Magazine* she bought. She let dishes and coffee cups and incense ashes pile up. Tables were usually coated with the papers and crumb-covered plates she insisted she would get to that day. Rather than folding them into dresser drawers, she draped many of her clothes over her tall IKEA shelf; pants and dresses hung as if deposited by a tidal surge. Granted, she had ADHD, but her legitimate medical condition created a source of static, as she struggled to deal with my stress, and I struggled to live comfortably amid clutter.

While we shared a passionate physical relationship, and talked endlessly about literature and music, in our approach to daily living, Abby and I were opposites. I used file cabinets and coat hangers and kept pens in plastic containers. I rarely left ashes in trays for fear a breeze might blow them on the floor. After a meal, I immediately scrubbed pots and pans. Somehow I was tolerant of Wiggy's accidents and muskiness, but only because, minus the prancing and weasel physiology, I recognized in Wiggy many of my own traits: the free spirit, the jester, the solitary adventurer. If

Abby had ADHD, I suffered from something else, some still unnamed psycho-emotional malady I was too frightened to research. The main symptom: I preferred living alone.

For a decade I had defined myself as a person who enjoyed solitude and inhabiting his own apartment. Whether my friends believed it or not, spending great stretches of time by myself never felt lonely, only liberating, and the fringe benefit was that no one else had to suffer the effects of me indulging my whims. Keeping my own hours, taking long road and hiking trips where and when I wanted, reading late into the night. With no one to worry about me, there was no one to neglect, miss or disappoint when I called to say, "I'm going to be home late tonight." Bachelorhood seemed my natural state. Then I met Abby. Loving her made me wonder how much I'd been fooling myself. Life was more satisfying with someone special in it. I didn't seem to want freedom so much as I wanted to meet my romantic companion, the love of all loves, my best friend and partner; if my apartment felt better empty, it was only because I had yet to meet the right person. Abby could be the one. Every time I walked through our messy apartment, I reminded myself: peace comes slowly; there's always a learning curve. I loved Abby, so I squirreled my frustrations away, told myself that I needed to learn to adapt. We'd reach a compromise soon.

Our two-bedroom apartment sat on the second floor of a hundred-year-old house. The Irish family who owned it lived on the first floor. Every morning, the scent of their cooking bacon permeated the halls. It took Abby five minutes to walk to school and me ten minutes to walk to the commuter train that led to Grand Central Station. I worked part-time in the City, the other time at home. Situated fifteen miles north of Manhattan, the "Village of Bronxville" was the poshest zip code I had ever inhabited, our apartment the largest I'd ever rented. Windows graced every room. Golden sunlight washed the interior. Views of our manicured streets could be had at any angle. We even had enough room for an office—our first separate work space. Wiggy liked it too.

As if he were the owner and we the renters, Wiggy pranced excitedly through his new home. He sniffed every square inch of the unfamiliar carpet, then scratched his back against the books Abby shelved on the bookshelf's lowest rung. I scattered his toys throughout the apartment, and he chewed the bloom right off the rose.

"Aaron," Abby frequently said, "Wiggy looks like he's getting ready to pee."

I'd rush in to pick him up, and when Abby wasn't looking, I'd take him aside for a pep talk. How could I get angry with him? I was the one who had failed to train him properly. When I lifted him to address him face-to-face, his body hung limp in my hand like a stole. "You're making me look bad," I said. This is how I talked to him, like a coconspirator, like he understood.

Abby eventually devised a new arrangement. I moved Wiggy's beds, toys and pads into the office and sealed the doorway between it and the kitchen with a tall piece of luggage. The knee-high suitcase blocked his exit without entirely shutting him off from our scents and sounds. It also sent a message. The office, bathroom and closet were his wing now. The kitchen, bedroom and living room were for humans. I made it as comfortable as possible: laid his fleece bed, my old pajamas, and the same blanket on the floor; kept the hall closet door open so he could sleep in my box of clothes. Neither he nor I liked the new arrangement, but I had Abby's comfort to consider now, so I voiced no complaints. He wasn't as accepting.

Some mornings Abby woke me saying, "Wiggy got out." She'd been drinking coffee at the kitchen table when he sauntered past her, trotted into the living room and started riffling through her piles of *New York Times*.

"All he wants is to be closer to us," I'd say. "He's lonely." While I always returned him to his room, I secretly cursed her messiness and applauded his resistance. "Good work," I'd whisper, alone in our office. "You can come out once she goes to school." And after Abby left, I'd remove the luggage, stretch out on the couch to work on my laptop, and Wiggy would join me to run around the living room before falling asleep on a blanket on my lap.

* * *

Putting things off isn't normally one of my problems. But that winter, procrastination assumed the form of mantras: "We'll take the subway ride next weekend," and "Once things calm down a bit, we'll take a Sunday to do the ride." Sundays passed. Garbage trucks collected bags of autumn leaves. By the time twenty degree temperatures froze water in the cracks in our street, I tallied a list of all the things Abbey and I hadn't done. We hadn't visited the Statue of Liberty. We hadn't visited my mother's childhood home in Queens. We hadn't openly discussed ways to lessen our rising domestic tensions. Time was part of the problem. There was never enough of it. And at age five and a half, Wiggy, it turns out, didn't have much left.

Abby enjoyed taking him for walks in the strips of woods lacing our neighborhood. His eyes brightened in the sunlight, fur fluffed as he sniffed dandelions and dug holes in moist dirt. Then, back home, we bathed him to combat flees and fluffed his hair further. "Look," Abby would say. "I gave him a Mohawk." Eventually the temperature dropped too low for walks. I bought a winter coat heavier than I'd ever owned. I never forgot about the planned subway trip, though.

Aside from his ferret rule, all I knew about Mayor Giuliani were the standard sound bites. He'd turned Times Square into the symbol of New Corporate York. He'd eliminated the squeegee guys. He'd so efficiently shrunk the homeless population that people wondered where upstate he'd shipped them all. Many locals considered Giuliani a weasel, but I had no clue about local politics. I'd never previously set foot in the city or state before moving there. All I knew was that, from day one, NYC Health Code Section 161.01 seemed to suggest that maybe moving was a bad idea.

Early on the morning of August 21, 2006, Abby and I were checking our luggage at the Portland airport. Everything we might need during our first week we had packed into our suitcases and carry-ons. Abby sipped coffee. Wiggy slept in his carrier. The airlines ticket agent told us, "I'm sorry, I'll be right back." She spoke for fifteen minutes on a phone at a distant counter. When she returned she said, "New York law prohibits ferrets within city limits." I told her I was aware of that but didn't see how that affected our flight into JFK. "It means commercial airlines are prohibited from even flying them into the city."

I'd spoken with three separate agents about pet-rules weeks before and had done everything they'd instructed: shots, pet carrier of specific dimensions, health certificate issued by a licensed vet within ten days of transport. Not one agent mentioned that this law banned us from airports. I said, "So what are our options?" Our flight was scheduled to depart in forty-five minutes. After investigating flights to White Plains, Boston and DC, she rebooked our flight to Philly with a layover in Cincinnati.

"You really love that ferret," she said, handing us new tickets.

"He's family," I said. Numerous other people said the same thing. The Portland airport gate security, the Cincinnati flight stewardess, the beefy Philly car rental guy, all of them said, "You really love that ferret."

My parents found this amusing when I recounted it on the phone. When they called me in Oregon, they always asked, "How's Abby?" Then, "How's our grandson?" They'd been married for thirty-five years. The joke was that, as long as I had Wiggy, he was the only grandkid they were likely to get. Now my Dad liked to ask, "Is he driving Abby nuts yet?"

Flying over Nebraska and Iowa, thoughts of Giuliani's law sparked an adolescent resistance in me that manifested as a plan. "We'll ride the F through Brooklyn," I later told Abby, "the 7 through Queens. Then the 1, the A or C, the B or D, the 4, 5 or 6, completely webbing Manhattan." In my mind, the ride took the form of a mock protest. With Wiggy dressed in a miniature sandwich board reading "Just another commuter," maybe our minor revolt would get Wiggy's picture in the New York Post, maybe the Village Voice. If anyone asked, "Is that a ferret in your backpack?" I'd say, "Why yes, in fact it is," and hand them a flier. A preliminary design scheme formed in my mind. The Xeroxed front would feature two side-by-side images: a dirty, goiter-faced, one-legged pigeon eating trash by a subway vent; then, a cute sleeping Wiggy, curled atop his fleece bed. Above the images the caption would read, "Who's the better neighbor?"

The breadth of Wiggy's and my travel itinerary broadened monthly. Soon I was planning to photograph him eating a knish at Katz's Deli and sipping borsht at Veselka's. "What if he wiggles out of his carrier?" Abby asked. "He could jump off the subway platform and be gone forever."

I said, "He won't." Back in Portland, he'd enjoyed walks in my neighborhood park, accompanied me a few times to the grocery store, once even to fetch Thai food take-out. He always traveled inside my roomy blue backpack, where he'd poke his head out and try to sniff things. Aside from the pandemonium of honking taxis and the extra eight million people, New York wasn't so different.

Abby said, "What if the cops catch you?"

"I'll say he's got a PetCo Christmas catalog photo shoot in Midtown.'"

Wiggy and I lived for adventure. That shared trait was one of the reasons we got along so well. He wanted to sniff and excavate new spaces wherever he went; I liked to read and learn new things and explore the furthest reaches of whatever region I was living in—especially this, our new home, one of the world's greatest cities. Some people call ferrets nosy. I call them the Lewis and Clark of the mammal world. Plus, in Manhattan, no one would even notice him. A homeless man can take a shit on a sidewalk there and not elicit more than a sidelong glance from pedestrians. Why would a three-pound weasel draw attention?

Like everyone else, Abby assumed I simply thought he was funny and cute. But in a deep, secret pocket of my psyche, I wanted to be Wiggy. He led the ideal life. Given a place to eat and sleep, the world became both his bedroom and frontier. Like John Muir in his Sierra Nevada sheep-herding days, Wiggy spent the night wherever he wanted, explored constantly, followed his curiosity wherever it led, and got to love people at his own discretion. Cats may symbolize aloofness, but ferrets perfected it. When he got lonely, he'd find you and coil up nearby. When he wanted to be alone, he crawled inside the couch and emerged when he was ready. Back in Oregon, I had perfected this lifestyle: read, hike, eat, try and fail to forge a romantic relationship, then go back to my cave to read, hike, and eat. All I could do now was supply Wiggy the essentials for continuing that life.

This left me in a strange situation. I was living vicariously through a weasel.

* * *

"Uch," Abby said. "Gross." She stepped into our bathroom as I stood in front of the sink, getting ready for work.

"What?"

"What do you mean what?" she said. "Using your toothbrush to scratch your back? Nasty."

I looked into her eyes not face-to-face, but in her reflection in the mirror. "It's not the brush end I'm using," I said. "It's the handle." She scrunched her nose in disapproval as she lifted her nightgown and lowered herself onto the toilet.

With Wiggy on lock-down, a trait-by-trait critique of my behavior had infiltrated our daily interactions, threatening to become the dominant thread of our conversations. Like when Abby told me, "Don't do that with your leg."

"Do what?" I asked.

She placed her hand on my knee to still its bouncing. "Tapping it all crazy." We were at a restaurant. I had to whisper an explanation.

"I'm a leg-tapper," I said. "I'm full of nervous energy." I stopped tapping to spare her the irritation, but when, unbeknownst to me, the tapping resumed, Abby shook her head, and I shrugged. "Sorry."

I kept tapping. The critiques continued. She disapproved of how I drank our green fruit smoothies straight from the container. "Get a glass," she suggested.

"Why waste the time getting a glass only to have to waste more time washing and putting it away?" I took a sip and returned the jug to the fridge.

Another morning when she heard a loud honking coming from the shower, she pulled back the curtain and asked, "Are you blowing your nose in there?"

Shampoo ran down my ears. "No," I said, though I had been seconds earlier.

She grinned. "Good, because that is nasty." Her sister's ex used to do that—she called it a "farmer blow"—and Abby said not only did the practice gross her out, it reminded her of that conniving, selfish dirtbag of a man who disrespected her sis. "Not even a man," she said. "A boy."

Don't drum your pen on the desk. The office smells like puppy pads. Being the target of intense reform makes you feel broken, insufficient. "Why are you nagging me?" I'd say. "I don't nitpick everything you do." Inevitably that deteriorated into, "If you don't like it, too bad." Why, I wondered, did she invite me to New York?

One night, overwhelmed, I stepped onto the street outside the house to call my dad. "Maybe I'm not built for relationships," I told him. It was scary to consider. Where does that leave you? Destined to spend the next forty-plus years alone and meeting brilliant, caring women you can never love or share experiences with?

"Maybe you are built for relationships," he said, "just not this one." He was right.

In Oregon, living apart, Abby and I had such passion, such chemistry. Now I sought consolation in what Abby was—intelligent, energetic, gentle, well-read—and what we had been.

In the chilly winter air, I tugged on my coat collar. "So what's wrong?" Dad asked.

"Everything."

"Everything, huh?"

I detailed my grievances. Distance had already replaced emotional intimacy. We were becoming what Abby called "just roommates," and poor ones at that. Dad asked for specifics, and in listing our maladies, it became clear that Abby wasn't the only one doing the critiquing. Constantly I told her, "You have to clean some of this stuff up. There's no room on our tables to put my work or breakfast."

"I know," she'd say, "I'm sorry. I'll get to it today." We'd have this conversation six or seven times before she'd actually clean it up.

The messes had gotten so bad that I took photos—just to prove to myself that I wasn't exaggerating. I wondered, how long is the world's longest learning curve? Dad had taught me that love starts a relationship, but making a marriage last requires a degree of work. What if Abby and I worked hard only to discover there was still no middle for us to meet in?

Sitting on the curb in the dark, only a few stars were noticeable overhead. I told Dad, "I love Abby, but I think I need to be alone." A column of exhaled breath snaked past my face. "You know? But here, it's the wrong kind of alone, it's more loneliness. This here is not enough."

"Well," Dad said, "what would be enough?" Before I could answer, he said, "Let me put it to you another way. If you need all this, why are you in a relationship?"

I saw my breath, a single plume. All the normal reasons came to mind: I loved Abby. She loved me. Coupling is human nature. You can't be a bachelor forever. I saw my breath, then the plume was gone. I said, "I don't know."

* * *

Abby spent Thanksgiving with her aunt in North Carolina. We needed to save money, so I suggested she go alone. "You have fun with your family," I said. "Wig and I will hold down the fort." I gave her the $100 gift check my parents sent that week, bought her snacks and magazines for the plane ride. When she asked how I would spend the holiday, I told her what I'd been telling friends back in Oregon: "Eat a cold turkey sandwich with the other loners at some down home West Side diner." Instead, I did better. I reserved a table at Jezebel's soul food restaurant on 45th and 9th on Thanksgiving Day, and walked there from Grand Central through Times Square.

"Just you?" the maitre d' asked.

"Just me," I said, trying to act as if I didn't feel awkward dining alone.

He delivered me to a small wooden table pressed against a far wall in the rear of the dining room. Large enough for two, he removed the second chair. I squeezed through the gap between tables and set my bag behind the man to my right. He was sharing a meal with a family of six.

"Peter is nothing like that," one woman at his table said, "and you know it."

"Know it?" the man said. "I know nothing!" and sent the others into a fit of laughter. They swirled glasses of red wine and later made a toast.

Rather than face the adjacent wall, I faced the whole restaurant and the crowd at the entrance. The view of 9th was better from this angle; plus, the wall behind me was mirrored. I couldn't hide. Everywhere I looked, there I was. I read magazines, ate my turkey, kept my head down. When I looked up, my eyes frequently caught the gaze of impatient patrons in trench coats and scarves. They squeezed into the vestibule like rush hour commuters, awaiting their turn at the greens and mashed potatoes. I looked away, covertly studying other diners.

A quiet, elderly couple sat to my left. He in a navy blazer, she in an emerald green dress, they whispered occasional conversation that, even from a foot and a half away, was too low to hear. Once, he touched her hand and she smiled. They spent the bulk of each course in silence, staring through the restaurant, their eyes tracing pedestrians passing on 9th.

After dessert, I ordered coffee to postpone my return home. I pictured my parents sharing a meal with my grandmother in their Phoenix living room, pictured Abby enjoying homemade biscuits and sweet tea in Raleigh. I missed her. I missed my family, my friends back in Oregon. Maybe I'd mistaken relationships for smothering and associated compromise with the end of individuality because I hadn't yet met the right person. Or had I mistaken bachelorhood for my natural state? I craved intimacy too much to really be a loner. I'd mixed it up. I think. It was confusing to crave love and autonomy at the same time. Confused or not, I knew one thing: my disdain for Giuliani was a blatant case of emotional transference.

I had done some research on the ferret-law's history and found a transcript online. On his WABC-AM radio call-in show in 1999, Giuliani told a ferret advocate from Oceanside, New York, that this "obsessive concern that you have for ferrets is something you should examine with a therapist." The advocate's name was David Guthartz, and he called to criticize Health Code Section 161.01. "There's something deranged about you," Giuliani told him.

Guthartz said, "No, there isn't, sir," and pleaded, "Don't go insulting me again."

"I'm not insulting you," said Giuliani. "I'm being honest with you. Maybe nobody in your life has ever been honest with you."

When Guthartz said, "I'm more sane than you," the Mayor said, "David, this conversation is over, David. Thank you." And hung up. In David's absence, Giuliani concluded: "This excessive concern with little weasels is a sickness."

Back home, I released Wiggy from his prison. He started scratching at the luggage when he heard me come in, and as I removed the partition, he came galloping out. He whizzed past my foot with a playful squeak, beckoning me to chase.

He slipped behind the bookshelf then sniffed the spines of all the books Abby had recently purchased and left stacked against the wall. When he darted behind the couch, I had to stop him from crapping on the carpet. I thwacked his nose but it felt mean. In place of punishment, I stacked puppy pads in that now-marked corner so he'd have a bathroom on each side of the house. It seemed more compassionate than banishing him to his solitary wing, but I knew it was counterproductive. He'd peed there before, and once ferrets establish their scent, they return to that spot. I was already six years too late.

After I went to bed that night, a scratching awoke me: Wiggy was trying to scale the corner of the comforter to climb into bed. I lifted him up and let him sleep with me like old times. Rather than coil on top of the sheets, he lifted the top blankets with his nose and slid underneath, settling in the warm pocket by my feet. When I woke up the next morning, he was snoozing on Abby's side.

When she called the next day to ask about Thanksgiving, I felt about as human as a sewer rat. On my first day alone, I had moved all of her papers and magazines into a single pile, pushed all her folders and books onto one side of the kitchen table, and spent subsequent days exploring new sections of Manhattan alone. I investigated cramped markets in Chinatown, walked unfamiliar streets in the East Village, SoHo, the Chelsea waterfront, and stunk up the fridge with pungent dishes from Korean restaurants. At night, I read. I'd grown fond of the quiet. Something in me seemed broken, maybe asleep—that nesting instinct and urge to couple up. When couples walked by holding hands in Central Park, I wondered, Which one sleeps on the couch after a fight? Does one resent the other? Couples passed and I imagined answers, and I always concluded how much more whole they likely were than I. Either something was wrong with me, or something was wrong with Abby and I. Or more likely, both.

Not long after Abby's return, we resumed the familiar pattern. "You've been saying you'll clean up the papers in the living room for over week," I said.

"I've been on vacation," she said. "Give me a break."

Finally, we came to a single compromise. She agreed to leave one half of the kitchen table free of her stuff. No newspapers, no books, no plates or coffee cups, or the French press filled with that morning's spent grounds, were to cross the center onto what became, in grade school parlance, "my side." This way, when I brought our breakfast over, my plate actually touched table, rather than her school work or papers. "Thank you for doing this," I'd say as I laid my plate and mug on the natural wood grain. There we would discuss the towns where we might move if she got into graduate school, but I wondered how I could last the six months until graduation. Although the table qualified as progress, I wished it mirrored the rest of our relationship.

* * *

Snow fell and collected in dirty black piles along the shady sides of buildings. The fantasy of a ferret subway ride didn't diminish. The crowning achievement, I decided, would be a visit to Central Park's Great Lawn. How cool it would be for him prance on the grass between the tall buildings? I studied a map, wondering which subway to catch. The B and C stopped at 81st. From there we could cut east through the woods to the Lawn. While I acted like I wasn't worried about the ride, I knew Abby was right: the city was riddled with the kind of crevices that ferrets could slip into. Once inside one, there'd be no retrieving him. Plus, if cops spotted us, Wiggy could legally be confiscated and destroyed. Ferrets live an average of seven to ten years. At age six, Wiggy had entered his golden years. Why risk it now?

* * *

One Easter morning, I found Wiggy coiled on the floor, retching and slinging spit all over himself and the carpet. "Holy shit," I said. "Abby." He pawed at his cheeks, foaming, as if trying to dislodge a blockage. "Abby," I yelled. "We have to go the hospital!" The only vet open was in White Plains, seven miles north.

When the cab arrived we said it was an emergency. The driver clicked his tongue and sped up the parkway. Abby held my hand. Wiggy lay motionless in a bed of fleece on my lap. I pet him, wiped his cheeks of saliva.

He was breathing but slowly. His eyes locked open, vacant and glassy. "It's going to be okay," I whispered to him, hoping he would find the tone comforting, hoping that saying it would make it true. I whispered and we wept.

The vet rushed him away, put him on IVs, said to call back in four hours. "We'll take good care of him," she said. After some convincing that it wasn't cruel to leave, Abby and I walked a couple miles to a diner. We ate eggs and cake and mashed potatoes drowned in gravy. We tried to read and make chitchat, but all I could think was whether we'd return to find Wiggy healing or dead.

"He'll be okay," Abby said.

Frigid air leaked beneath the adjacent window pane.

"Yeah," I said, spooning potatoes. "Thanks, sweetie. I hope so." I had to conceal my teary eyes.

That's the thing about pets. You know all this, even while they're young, that one day they're going to die, and it's going to break your heart. You comfort yourself by counting the numbers on their expected lifespans—seven, eight, nine years. You think, Man, that's so far off, think of all the fun we'll have from now until then. You tell yourself that if something should happen, you'll deal with it so they don't suffer, that you'll put them out of their misery if that's what mercy requires. But who puts you out of yours? Then, once you pay and sign the papers, and your pet is thoroughly sniffing their new home and learning how not to put their paws in your face while sleeping in your bed, you forget they're even mortal. Finishing my potatoes, I looked across the table and saw Abby outside of the house, apart from the mess. I saw Abby and thought, What an incredible human being. Why can't we be a match for each other? Why aren't we right?

Back at the clinic, a tech in bluish-green scrubs greeted us. "You're here for Wiggy Gilbreath?" She slipped into a back room and emerged with Wiggy, who she handed me, squirming, like a lost piece of luggage. "Aaah," Abby said. "Look. He's so happy to see us." He crawled up my chest and perched like a parrot on my shoulder, pressed against my neck. When Abby scooped him up to kiss him, a little green Band-Aid slipped off his wrist, revealing a square of shaved skin.

The vet took me aside to chat. "Wiggy's got big problems," she said.

Pressed for specifics, she said, "If you feel his side, you'll notice a lump." She placed my two fingers on his side, which pumped in and out in a frenzy of nervous breathing. A small but noticeable swelling of tissue rose above his haunch. It wasn't visible, but you could feel it. "Could be cancer," she said. "My guess is an enlarged pancreas from an insulinoma—diabetes, basically." Insulinoma, a condition common to aging ferrets, is a pancreatic ailment that often leads to increased insulin production and low blood sugar. When he arrived, she explained, Wiggy's blood sugar had dropped so low he'd nearly gone into shock. They'd revived him intravenously with fluids and stabilized his blood sugars. The only course now was maintenance: medicine, fluid, constant monitoring, which would be simple since I now mostly worked from home. The vet prescribed Prednisolone—a steroid widely given to cancer patients—administered orally in a dropper or baby "syringe." "If he won't eat solid foods," she said, "give him baby food, delivered the same way. And get Wiggy a regular vet." Unlike lawyers, cosmetic surgeons, and book publishers, the world's best ferret doctors were not found in Manhattan. The City was full of dog psychologists and cat surgeons but, thanks to the law, lacking ferret specialists. My vet back in Oregon advised finding a vet in Jersey or Westchester to hold him over until Abby moved to North Carolina for grad school and I moved to wherever I was going.

We hugged the vet and thanked the staff and took a cab to the train station. It was too cold to walk and expose our little patient to the winter air. The IVs had pumped him full of his youthful vigor. In the cab, he scratched at the carrier with the strength once reserved for my ugly couch. He pawed at my hand when I stuck it inside, nibbling on my thumb and beckoning me into a game of cat-and-mouse that made Abby and I laugh. "Let me see that Fuzzle," she said, taking him out. "Oh, Wiggy," she said, "you're back," and showered him with kisses.

Easter turned out to be the last day he possessed that level of strength. When the vet's fluids metabolized, Wiggy's energy waned. For the final two months of his life, he ate an exclusive diet of baby food—a gloppy, pungent stew of pureed poultry—and Prednisolone. I fed him by hand, every day, with a spoon. His fur lost its shine, and his spunk came in spurts as erratic as warmth in New York in April. No matter how gently I held the granules to his mouth, hard food never interested him again. He gummed and let them fall. The clutter in the house no longer mattered. Cover the whole bedroom with clothes, I figured, why squander what time we have left. But in the cab, as the fluids surged, that morning's horrors felt behind us, and nothing bad lay ahead.

Abby bought our tickets at the train station, and I found an empty bench to wait. Wiggy sat in his carrier on my lap, and a little girl and her mother stopped in front of us. Still holding her mother's hand, the girl leaned over, straining to see what oddity lurked behind the carrier's dark mesh. "Want to say hi?" I said. She nodded, and her mother told her, "Go up and see," giving me a grin that implied, "She's shy."

"He's a ferret," I said and scooped him from his fleece. I cradled Wiggy in my arms, showing he was friendly. Like a dozing king, he sprawled there and lifted his lazy head just enough to sniff and survey the scene. "He won't bite," I said. "I promise." She released her mother's hand and sauntered over. I ran my fingers across Wiggy's back, and held him out so she could try. She paused a moment, then stroked his back and giggled. I asked if he looked funny, and she nodded. Smiling, she looked back at her mom, and when she finally ran back over, I lifted Wiggy's shaven hand and made him wave. The mother mouthed back, "Thank you."

On the train to Bronxville, Wiggy was calm, so calm that he didn't need the carrier. Once we got a seat, I took him out and set on my lap. "What's out there?" I said, holding him up to the window. He stared at passing houses, passing trees, occupying a vinyl seat like any other commuter. Forested creeks threaded the neighborhoods, the maple boughs slowly leafing out, working to grow as thick as they were the summer we arrived. Squirrels darted beside the tracks, resuming life after winter. "Who's that?" I said. Wiggy's wet nose left little streaks on the glass. It tapped my chin, registering damp and cold, while to my right, Abby looked at us and smiled.

Soon she held out her hands, and when I'd deposited Wiggy in them, she cradled him in her seat, stroking him as she had this entire year, being so sweet to him, to me, to us, despite us all.

MY MANHATTAN MINUTE

I found out I didn't get Meredith's old job as a publicity assistant at Katz & Strayhorn Publicity the day of the company Christmas party. Meredith called it "keeping it in the family." I called it insulting.

That publicity assistant job was supposed to be my ticket in, the first paid step on the golden road to a publishing career. But I was still just another intern. And after the Christmas party, an ex-intern.

The previous fall, at age thirty-one, I'd followed my girlfriend Abby to New York so that she could finish school and I could further my fledgling career. I'd worked six years at Powell's Books—intelligent retail and customer service work, but retail all the same. My real aim was to write. So before her school year resumed in affluent Westchester, I boxed my deeply rooted life, stored my enormous library in Abby's Mom's basement in Portland along with half my clothes and all my records and CDs, and I moved to New York. I'd never been there before, but it seemed the right place for a writer to be.

* * *

Who knows how these mythic notions colonize your head. I suppose a youth among books suggests a career in books. But leaving quiet, arty, affordable Portland and casting myself from the repetitive retail bottom of the publishing food chain to work the production end, I held what I considered informed, but what were in fact vague, notions of that future career: work at a publishing house, a magazine, or an inspired combination where I worked in editorial and also wrote freelance. Meaning, I wanted to work in some sort of creative, editorial, literary capacity.

"Capacity," it turned out, was code for "I'm clueless."

My immediate objectives were to study the market, see which occupations fit, and fatten a dangerously thin résumé. At that age, anything, even appearing as the balding, lost-in-life intern, seemed better than "Curriculum vitae: Bachelors in Philosophy; six years retail." Other people confirmed my righteous path by explaining how connections from these gigs would foster further connections and generate job opportunities. How else to justify spending thousands of dollars of your savings and your girlfriend's student loans to do free labor in one of the country's most expensive cities? Two days a week I interned at a new literary magazine based in Brooklyn. There, in a gorgeously renovated one hundred sixty-year-old stable off the Atlantic Avenue stop, I read a few hundred fiction and nonfiction submissions, proofread pieces selected for publication, did copy-editing, fact-checking, and called numerous indie bookstores to encourage them to try a few copies. "We're a new quarterly out of Brooklyn," my sales pitch went. "Do you sell the *Paris Review*, *Granta*, *McSweeney's*? It's similar. I'll send a sample PDF." I loved it.

The other three days a week, I interned in Katz's Publicity Department. Initially I worked under the Senior Publicist. After a competing house lured her away, I worked under Meredith, the twenty-five year old assistant. She lived with three other recent college grads in a two-bedroom Brooklyn flat with a dog rarely attended to by its hungover owner. And while I suppressed my "likes" and "awesomes," she said "like," like, a lot, while laughing and reading media gossip sites during scattered sixty second breaks between phone calls, filing, and photocopying. But that didn't bother me. If anything, I figured I was smarter, more cunning, and more worldly than her. Having the advantage of age carried wisdom. Retail experience imparted a desperate, life-or-death thirst for career improvement that bordered on monomaniacal, and I've-seen-the-alternative-and-it-sucks hunger that her upper class New England upbringing could not likely match. At least that's what I told myself. She didn't seem tough enough to handle all the hurdles and gin-swilling, sexist, pat-your-bum pigs I assumed a publishing life would hurl at her. She may have held the chair, but I was taking it from her.

"Okay," she'd say each morning as I approached her desk. It sat square in the middle of the office's busy center, just out of view of the front door. "Today, I have a three hundred mailings for you for book-so-and-so. But first, if you could mail these review requests,"—she'd hand me a stack of month-old faxes she'd let pile up in lieu of more pressing tasks—"I'd love you forever." Really, Meredith was fine. The tasks were just boring.

To make Meredith seem like less formidable competition, I denigrated her in my mind. I frequently imagined her prepping for work each morning, how she might rouse her beleaguered consciousness with three cups of coffee, scoot a spent Cabernet bottle and cheap opener aside to make room for her yogurt-and-toast breakfast, an empty dog bowl by her sore slippered feet. I pictured four adults sharing two windowless bedrooms, Ylang-Ylang soap coated with hairs of varying colors, women breathing in each other's morning breath before tossing a distant hello to the then-boy-friend/problem-of-the-moment, himself dressing in the only bathroom, all above some noisy bar where the music permeated the floor until 2:00 a.m. and the party continued on the street until 4:00. I needed to elevate my ego to feel like I had a chance in this profession. The fact was, Meredith was smart, ambitious, and well-read, and she wouldn't have landed there otherwise.

"I'll get right on it," I'd say, and bound off toward the mailroom. First, though, I'd hit the kitchen, brew a stiff cup of free black tea, pocket four or five teabags, then guzzle half a cup of the perpetually brewing coffee—secretly, since I still told everyone I "don't really touch the stuff." That was true back in Oregon, but I'd given in now that my calves ached and red eyes itched from my late night habit of sending short stories to literary magazines that inevitably rejected them, researching my first freelance articles until midnight, and alienating Abby who sat at home studying, alone and irritated.

The coffee hit my brain while I was in the mailroom packaging review copies for National Book Critics Circle members and freelancers. With over fifty new books released each season, the gears of Katz & Strayhorn Inc.'s publicity machine never stop turning. In addition to their voluminous roster of regular reviewers, freeloaders, and special interest groups who inundated Meg the Department Head with requests. Like most publishing houses, Katz mailed so many books for potential coverage and jacket blurbs that they had their own FedEx and UPS machines to generate postage. Boxes of galleys, advance reading copies, and finished books lined the halls, often stacked four high. Evan, the twenty-three-year-old temp, and I emptied, moved, and consolidated the boxes constantly. We sent review copies and their glossy press releases one hundred to five hundred at a time during "push." Then we dragged thirty-plus pound mailbag after thirty-plus pound mailbag to the loading bay. The bay—a garbage can dressed as an alcove attached to a freight elevator—contained the kind of mysterious oily stains that stained well-dressed execs' shirts. It was where crushed cardboard awaited recycling.

After the first mailing, I'd return to Meredith's desk for new marching orders. She'd be hunched over stacks of paper, taking calls, or in Meg's office planning author tour itineraries ("First, San Francisco, then off to the conference . . . "). Other times she'd be eating a quick lunch while laughing at Katz's office manager Blake ("He is such a weirdo.") with another assistant.

Often, Meredith would ask, "Ready to do another mailing?"

I felt goofy walking the streets near youthful NYU in my office clothes. My parents had kindly equipped me with a new professional look—collared shirts tucked into slacks, leather dress-ups instead of skate shoes. In place of my well-traveled blue North Face daypack, I carried an oxblood leather attaché, the ultimate badge of successful execu-yuppieism. It was a look I'd long loathed on all but my favorite professors, but it now lent a confident, marketable, urban intellectualism, something my flannels and Levi's had long concealed.

The work may have been tedious, but I felt it was an investment. Even Chief Executive Officer Jesse Albright started somewhere at the bottom. If a job opened up, I wanted Meredith and Meg to think immediately of me.

While hosting a reading back at Powell's the previous year, a friendly young woman with bright, intense eyes and a down-to-earth potty humor gave me her card. Rene Welsh, it said, Katz Senior Publicist. "I'm on tour with the author," she said, motioning to the debut novelist at the lectern. She invited me to call if I ever needed anything. I called first thing upon landing in New York.

By late August, publications like *Slate* and *Time Out New York* had all declined my internship applications, and Rene, over lunch, repeatedly warned how there was "no glory" in the Katz gig. "It's a lot of physical labor, a lot of grunt work," she said, likely figuring it was better to scare me off now than have me suddenly quit showing up.

"My ego is not involved in this," I told her. "And I'm used to grunt work."

"Great," she said. "You'll be fine."

Strutting down 12th and University that day after lunch, Rene stepped to the end of the soiled sidewalk and said, "It sounds clichéd, but it's true: if you can make it here, you can make it anywhere." She gripped her cell phone. "I'll call you soon."

I watched her disappear into the throng of people on the sidewalk.

* * *

For years I claimed I didn't care if I never set foot in New York City. As a lifelong outdoorsman, it simply didn't interest me. Camping, hiking, exploring old-growth forests and sleeping in my truck on road trips—those, like writing, were unwavering passions. Any place where people can say "if you're not in New York, you're camping out," (New York Governor Thomas E. Dewey), call a pigeon wildlife (writer Nina Malkin) and the outdoors "what you have to pass through to get from your apartment to a taxicab" (writer Fran Lebowitz) wasn't for me. Plus, to my progressive environmental mindset, it seemed the ultimate blight, a polluted urban eyesore smothered in steel, garbage, and an unbearably compressed eight million people. Residents of Manhattan Island went from foraging thick hardwood forests and wild herring to living amid trash bags and miles of rusted security gates in some four hundred years. I didn't care to set foot there.

My Grandma Silvia always hocked me in chinik about New York. "You have to go," she'd say, smacking her palm on the closest surface. "Everybody has to experience it at least once."

When I did occasionally experience a desire to seek out high literary culture, it was never strong enough to lead me east. Western North America contained countless compelling destinations that all sat higher on my next-to-see list. I'd explored the Yukon, Alberta, Alaska, British Columbia, and nearly every state west of the Rockies intimately, with tent, truck, boots, and backpack. But necessity often overrides preference. New York City was where writers worked, the nerve center of American book and magazine publishing. If I wanted to write, I could no longer ignore it.

In addition to first dates and running out of weed, one of my greatest fears during college was spending my adult working life in a bleak, halogen-lit cubicle, pushing paper. It terrified me because it meant spending my life repressing rather than utilizing my creativity. Having abandoned drugs and everything mind-altering, I had entrenched myself in the noble grind of making an honest living selling books, but a new fear replaced the old one: neglecting my artistic abilities. Label books, shelve books, label books, day in and day out; surely there was more to life than retail. I needed some place that fed my mind, and New York had long offered refuge and employment for creative types. Maybe I'd been wrong about New York. A newer, countercultural Ellis Island seemed to await people like me, where Lady Liberty's silent lips cry: "Give me your tired, your poor,/Your huddled masses yearning to breathe free,/The refuse of your MFA programs./Send the couch-surfers and self-described artists to me." Or at least to Brooklyn.

Abby was leaving Portland for school whether I came or not. Through the fog of prejudicial dismissals, her impending departure forced me see this city for what it was: publishing's proverbial hub. Home to hundreds of glossies, four of the nation's ten largest dailies, and publishing houses from HarperCollins to Harcourt, never mind the storied history (Willie Morris' *Harper's*, George Plimpton's *Paris Review*, Dylan Thomas's White Horse Tavern, Joseph Mitchell's Bowery) and the litany of lit mags headquartered at its universities. The more I considered moving, the more New York resembled a creative's paradise, a restless cauldron of fellow artists and intellectuals paid for their wits, efforts, and imaginations. Now I needed to see if I fit into it.

My first subway rides to work seemed to confirm my decision. Perched behind novels, magazines, and the *Times*, New York's general commuter appeared more literate than even the Pacific Northwest's legendary bibliophiles. I'm home, I thought. Scowling or not, indifferent or not, these baggy-eyed New Yorkers felt like kin, united by our shared love of the written word.

Which is what I told friends in Portland when they asked how I was adjusting. "Is it what you expected?" they asked. "Do you love it?" Love was too strong a word. It was stressful, expensive, cold, and competitive. With a pricey apartment in Bronxville, a thirty-minute train ride to Grand Central, two internships, less than five nightly hours sleep, fifteen to twenty smokes a day, the deal was done. Yet I only needed to endure one year. Abby would be finished with school in May, and we could leave by August at the latest. I figured that, like a lot of things, maybe love grows on you. So when, two months in, the little voice in the back of my head began saying, "This is not my scene," I ignored it. I went on with my business.

So when news of the Junior Publicist's departure trickled down to me and Evan The Temp, I started sniffing around. Of course I phrased these inquiries in ways that buried my bloodhound motives in the sugary banter of water-cooler conversation. I'd start with, "Great news for Kay," followed days later by, "I bet you are inundated with applications." Then, "Any news on the job front?"

Meredith's poker face revealed nothing. "We've definitely received some interest," she said.

I never filled out an application. No one offered me one, though why would they? A thirty-one year old intern didn't seem like such a great prospect compared to a seasoned applicant they knew.

* * *

Evan The Temp slid a galley across Kay's old desk. "You read any of this stuff?"

He'd just finished undergrad at Duke and was ostensibly seeking paralegal work to get a feel for the profession before pursuing law school. When we met, he wore a ball cap and white Frank Zappa t-shirt. His voice carried the slow syrup of his native Virginia, and his exasperated comments evidenced all the impatience of an inexperienced teen. "No one reads this shit," he'd say while we did mailings. He'd toss one of the hundreds of folded publicity packets across our tabletop and shake his head. "You know this goes straight in the trash." More than once I'd told him how, while cobbling together introductory statements for those Powell's events, I'd mined these materials for lines like, "Lush with passion, humor, and ultimately hope," an "unforgettable collection by one of America's foremost fiction writers," "Gorgeous, vivid, and rife with ringing epiphany . . . " I'd also agreed that publicity materials were, by necessity, sales-pitches disguised as descriptions, but they were as vital to the literary arts as publishers and agents.

Evan loved novels, particularly lavish historical ones, but he was here for the money. Couch-surfing at his brother's place while seeking more steady work, he drank late into the night, smoked weed, and "jammed," by his own description, to Phish and Zappa. Working long days at Katz, he assembled wall units and moved boxes on dollies to make room for more boxes, and he snuck outside to smoke cigs under the scaffolding on the street. It was the same spot where one of the editors smoked. And a payroll lady. And previously the Junior Publicist. I chewed nicotine gum so my habit didn't diminish the appearance of a tireless work ethic. When Rene, Meredith, or Meg came looking, they always found me working in the office.

With Kay the Junior Publicist gone, Meredith allotted the vacant room to us. This arrangement made it easier for her to delegate projects and afforded us a shorter trip when dragging mailbags to the elevator. Evan and I frequently tackled large mailings together, and while I was officially an 'intern,' and he a 'temp,' we were both drifters here doing menial tasks. But this new setting, intimate and nestled inside the office's busy center, afforded an alternate glimpse into the publicist's daily life.

Meg, of course, walked by frequently, peering in to make sure we were working. When she went to lunch, and the sound of Meredith's soft phone-voice guaranteed she wouldn't be looking, I searched the computer's document folders, rummaged through the desk, and scanned shelves for anything interesting. One day Evan strolled into Kay's office bearing a mischievous grin. "Think it's time to do some Christmas shopping," he said, and started stuffing books into his coat. He winked. "Glad my family are big readers."

During that final month I wised up, too. Seeing my time at Katz diminishing, the idea that someone would invite me into the fold became an increasingly ridiculous hope. *Slate*, *TONY*, and *New York* magazine all declined my second round of internship applications, and instead of mailing applications to *Harper's* and *Audubon*, I decided to abandon interning altogether. Instead of menial labor, I spent the next six months writing. Sitting there at Kay's desk that day, watching Evan Christmas shop in the office that would soon belong to Meredith, I finally accepted myself for the cheap servant I was, and started collecting the practical information I assumed vital to the writing game.

I pocketed the business cards I found in Kay's desk drawer for a *Men's Journal*'s deputy editor, a page editor at the *Los Angeles Times*, a senior publicist at Farrar, Straus & Giroux. I asked Meredith for countless ARCs and finished books, which I stuffed into my blue backpack that I'd resumed wearing the previous week along with my skate shoes. I photocopied fifty pages of contacts from the Bacon's media guide: names of editors, email addresses, preferred methods of contact for pubs like *The Nation* and *Village Voice*, places I planned to pitch, and did, in the coming months. I'd long wanted to write reviews, and during my morning galley stuffing, I looked with envy at those freelancers on the postage labels, imagining a life spent in a Brooklyn brownstone reading books that simply arrived in the mail. I figured envy without ambition was as damning as complacency, so I filled a folder with the stuff I'd plundered.

It was there, in Kay's office on my last day interning, that I snuck onto Gmail while stuffing envelopes and found my first freelance assignment: two hundred dollars for a sixteen hundred-word profile of an obscure California author for Sacramento's alt-weekly. I was thrilled.

And when Blake asked me to bartend the Christmas party, I agreed.

"If you need some extra money," he said. He also promised free wine to drink and take home. "Albright orders lots of the good stuff."

Meredith overhead and leaned into the office. "You don't have to work that if you don't want to," she said. It was thoughtful, a compassionate gesture, but it wasn't about want anymore so much as need.

At that moment, I recognized myself for the conniving, career-obsessed hatchling I'd become. Looking at Meredith, I felt guilty for always micro-analyzing her. I was always wondering if her folks in Connecticut sent checks to help cover costs, wondering how, with sky-high Manhattan rent, she could afford plane tickets home, new clothes, good groceries, and pricey mixed drinks, let alone those expensive salads. She deserved credit for her efforts, not scrutiny. The ten-hour days, room-sharing, all the assistant's low-totemic struggle, I felt awful for belittling her in order to convince myself that I was a viable applicant. I just felt old and unemployable. It wasn't her fault that I wanted what she had. Pitted against her and plotting my ascent, I'd also failed to acknowledge her humanity. Maybe assisting Meg was her preferred route to financial stability. Maybe she was homesick, too, and still searching for her own career calling, or she only wanted the chance to work with books and have a cultured life in America's densest city, just as I did. People probably wondered about me, this thirty-something dude, and why I was there. I certainly asked myself everyday.

Life and passion were either getting away from me, or I was finding new ways to define them, leaning dangerously close to career advancement over harnessing my lifelong passions. Still, doubt nagged me. I wondered if I was taking full advantage of my New York opportunities. I wondered if my writing career would advance faster if I'd interned at Condé Nast rather than here. Wasn't it possible that I needed the Columbia Publishing Course too, or grad school at Columbia, or that my calling wasn't publicity or editing, but at a literary agency? Watching Meredith those months, it seemed fifty-hour weeks would inhibit rather than assist my artistic pursuits, unlike a life out West, where time was abundant, nature bold and rent cheap. Deep down, I knew this. My gut told me. And yet part of me worried that if I raced home that summer to write, rather than snagging a New York job, I had failed.

That last day at Katz, I had more pressing concerns. "I don't know how to make drinks," I told Blake. "Other than whiskey straight."

"Just fake it," he said. "Pour a little soda, then a little hooch. No one will know. They'll be drunk."

I imagined Graydon Carter—whom I'd mistake for just another guy in a suit—chastising me for pouring too little gin into too much tonic. Was "I'm a writer, not a bartender" a sufficient defense?

I told Blake, "I'll figure it out."

Journalist Simon Hoggart once said that living in New York is "like being at some terrible late-night party. You're tired, you've had a headache
since you arrived, but you can't leave because you'd miss the party."

My last day at work, the entire staff moved furniture. Like a good family, people from the art department, rights, and editorial helped Blake position the tables that held the cheeses and meats. Poinsettias stood in
various corners. A giant wreath hung by the door. As was tradition, Albright bought expensive caviar, served in a shiny silver dish, and at 5:00
p.m., gathered the staff for what Meg called the "Yeah, we made it another
year" toast.

"This is publishing the old fashioned way," Albright said, raising his
champagne flute. "When Europeans come in here, they say, 'Oh, now this
feels like a publishing house.'" He complimented everyone on a winning
year: five bestsellers, two Man Booker Prize nominees, and three runners
up for the National Book Critics Circle Award. Now a new book, a spiritual cooking memoir, promised to be next season's big success. Free copies
lay piled on tables by the entrance, intended for the agents, editors, and
reps that attended each year. Everyone raised their glasses. Blake rolled his
eyes. Before too long, the staff started stuffing bottles of wine into their
bags to take home.

As folks sipped bubbly, I filled a canoe-shaped bin with beer and ice.
Evan and I crafted an attractive display of beverage options at a separate
table, and we were soon joined by Nick, a hilarious, flamboyant, rail-thin
actor in black skintight jeans. He'd once interned there, too, and returned
for intermittent temp work between acting and other gigs. He'd brought
some weed that he promised to share with Evan later that night.

"So, what do you do?" Nick asked me.

"Oh, like everyone else in this city, I'm a writer," I said. "And you?"

Twisting an outstretched hand like a flame into the air, he said, "I am an
artiste." It was indomitable, pained, self-aware, and beautiful. I am artist,
his display intoned, watch me temp.

Nick painted and wrote, but was primarily an actor. He had a show soon opening off Broadway, and he lived in one of those highly coveted rent-controlled apartments allotted to Theater District actors. The established and the striving competed fiercely for these units, making lists long, waits longer, and chances slim. And here he was working for a hundred twenty cash. He snuck a sip of liquor and told Evan, "We'll smoke later, honey, relax."

For the next several hours, we poured drinks. And more drinks. Albright fetched numerous glasses with a warm "More red wine, please," but he didn't have a clue I'd been interning the last three months. I wasn't surprised.

On a break from the bar, I was surprised to spot Shane, the man who'd assisted with the interviews at that literary nonprofit. He'd failed to email me his final decision yesterday as he'd promised, and the course of the next six months, possibly my life, was riding on that undelivered message.

I weaved through the crowd to reach him. "So," I said, shaking his dry, nicotine-scented hand. "I never received word. Any news on the job front?"

He poked his straw into his drink. "Well," he said. "It was between you and this other person, and—" He tilted his head. "It was very close. Very, very close. I'll keep you posted about anything promising that comes across my desk. I have your email, so."

I returned to the bar thinking, *Please*. All these people will have jobs come Monday. After the holiday break they'll return to their desks, and I'll remember how it felt to have peered into publishing from the freight elevator.

* * *

The subway mariachis might have signaled the end. Decked in leather vests, singing a huapango, they'd boarded the 5 train one December day. Their exotic vitality moved indifferent commuters to actually look up from their papers, and that deep guitarrón seemed to point me home. Living far from my folks for the past seven years, far from my aging grandmother and the desert of my youth, I felt like I'd been missing the real party for ages. So after Abby and I split up, I moved back to Phoenix, moved in with my parents, rent free, no hassles, no judgment, no rush. With free snacks, free laundry, and boundless free time, the arrangement put me close to my parents for what would likely be the last time, and it allowed me to write as much as I could.

According to Pulitzer-winner Lucinda Franks, a writer in New York is "a little bit like a tree falling in the forest. You're never sure if somebody's going to hear you." Few hear me on my parent's back porch here in the desert, either.

Our cat Red brought home a cactus mouse tonight—still alive, scared stiff when he dropped it on the welcome mat. Two nights ago, during a chorus of particularly yappy coyotes (they enjoy howling by the neighboring horse corral), a shooting star asserted its brief, burning presence across the sky: bright light, blue as mercury, followed by yellow fizzle. Other than that, it's pretty quiet around here.

I spend a lot of time on this back porch. Overlooking a desert wash filled with palo verde and saguaros, I nestle into a cushioned chair with my legs up, write for hours and read anthologies and story collections like the remarkable ones coming from Katz & Strayhorn. The commute is short. Lines aren't long. Aside from June, July, and August, the weather's always nice. The yard's always quiet. Books surround me. The cat, though, is a killer.

With indiscriminate lust, he kills rodents, lizards, jackrabbits and snakes, consuming their meaty tops before dumping their hindquarters on the patio to rot.

Once I confirmed that tonight's mouse was not only alive, but uninjured, I locked Red inside to set the little guy free. But I never saw him go. I just turned around and he was gone.

\'ra-di-kəl\

Hearing teenagers in purple flannels call their soy mochas "rad" perfectly illustrates the mechanisms behind the regurgitating cow stomach that is American pop culture. Not that that's a bad thing—"nothing new under the sun" and all yields innovative hybrids—but the feedback loop of fashion really strikes a nerve when what was new in your youth becomes another generation's vintage clothing. One of the dominant aesthetics of the last few years has been the 1980s: Ray-Bans, short shorts, fanny packs, wrist warmers. Forget the old "friends don't let friends wear neon" maxim. The image of *Pretty in Pink* James Spader and his antagonistically feathered hair seems the most fitting mascot for our time, a time where we find eighties slang unwittingly coloring our conversations: dude; awesome; bummed; stoked; shred; balls out; this rules. And of course, the crown jewel, rad.

On the suggestion of a childhood friend who is also struggling with the difficult fact of our combined seventy years, I rented *Thrashin'*. It's a sports-sploitation flick that came out in 1986 when we were nine years old, and it features all the stomach-churning, Pepto-tinted vibrancy of the era, as well as a Circle Jerks song.

In the mid to late eighties, Hollywood spent much time and money trying to capitalize on then-underground sports and their associated subcultures: surfing (*North Shore*), breakdancing (*Breakin'*), BMX-biking (*Rad*), and skateboarding (*Thrashin'* and *Gleaming the Cube*). Along with the synthesizer soundtracks and presence of non-ironic moustaches, what unites most of these films is their reliance on the same dramatic formulation: small town kid and/or outsider competes in a high-stakes competition against nationally known surfers/skaters/BMXers in the hopes of not only winning the prize money, but also the respect—and heart—of a girl. As Powell-Peralta-era skaters ourselves, *Thrashin'* repelled my friends and me. A skate gang called The Daggers who wear dangly dagger earrings and paint their faces when they "joust" with their enemies in a drainage ditch? In the parlance of our childhood: it was redonculous. Listening to lines such as, "Well, what do you thrash?" "What'd'ya got?" felt as embarrassing as having your mom stand outside a skateshop dressing room, checking to see how your pants fit. In a narrative sense, the movie was bad. Not good bad, like retro seventies pimp-in-leather, gimme-some-skin bad, but awful. Worse yet, while rendering an innovative, subversive subculture as clownish stereotypes decked in sleeveless jean jackets and plaid shorts, Hollywood even failed to capture skateboarding's most obvious linguistic feature: the word rad. Not one character says it in the entire movie! At all!

During the entire hour and thirty-two minutes, the characters utter a litany of dated, often pungently cheddary terms that, unlike rad, have never come back into fashion: gnarly; studly; stylin'; tasty skate betties; acid rock; you're dead meat; I'm gonna cream that mother! But no rad. This registers as a particularly epic oversight. Not because the characters in that competing skateboard movie, *Gleaming the Cube*, say rad in the first five minutes. ("That was so rad," a kid tells Tony Hawk while skating an empty pool.) And not because the characters in that maudlin 1986 BMX movie *Rad* say rad (and dude, and awesome) constantly. It's tragic because skaters in the Venice Beach/Santa Monica area—the very area in which *Thrashin'* is set—seem to have coined the term.

Although I can't say for sure fer shur, the famous Z-Boys of Dogtown appear to have invented rad in the second half of the seventies. This was back in the days of sidewalk surfing, when shoeless shredders with bowl cuts balanced on the pointed tips of their skateboards to hang ten, a time when disco still shook the bubble booties of many a slick-haired New Yorker. The Z-Boys were surfer kids. Out of habit, they injected their aggressive surfing moves into the then softcore, ballerina sport of skating and, in the process, birthed modern vert skating and the sport as we know it today. They were inventive. To them, style was everything. Clothes and language and tricks mattered. No surprise, then, that it was they who sawed the tail end off the word radical, as if it were some constrictively low roof on an old Econoline van, and fashioned something new.

Only an old dude with parental leanings would have to tell you that rad is slang for cool. An adjective derived from the word "radical," rad also means good, great, awesome, okay! It's an expression of extreme enthusiasm which captures the joy you feel about something completely, overwhelmingly magnificent: a sunny day; a woman in a skirt; finding a twenty dollar bill on the ground. Rad is a smile you can say. It's also the highest form of flattery, a stronger qualifier than cool, more super in its superlativeness than awesome. There are no gradations of rad, no radder or raddest. Yes, people say "raddest," but the term is redundant, used more to fit a sentence's tense or texture than to imply a qualitative hierarchy. As with pregnancy, rad is an absolute: something is either rad or it is not. You are either pregnant or not. There is no kind of pregnant.

All of which should elicit a resounding: duh?

Okay, but how about this: according to Merriam-Webster, radical (\'ra-di-kəl\) is Middle English, derived from the Latin radicalis, meaning "of roots," and radix, meaning "root." As an adjective, it first appeared in the 14th century, after which it came to mean different, drastic, extreme, counter to tradition, a break from the ordinary. (A radical change in company policy.)

In early skateboarding vernacular, radical usually referenced tricks or someone's bravura (killer) performance—"a radical air," "a radical session"—or meant crazy, wild, edgy, unplanned, a precursor to modern skateboarding's "sick." In retrospect, the connotation might be extended to those pioneering skaters' lifestyles in general: not having long hair, which most anyone can grow, but the Z-Boys' fundamental shift away from accepted skateboarding tradition. As a noun, a radical is someone who stands in extreme opposition to accepted norms and customs, a person of revolutionary ideas or one who calls for drastic social, political, or economic reforms. (This was before Mountain Dew commercials made the term extreme as unpalatable as a frat party.) So Z-Boys like Tony Alva and Stacy Peralta weren't only radical sportsmen, they were revolutionaries, because they essentially said, "No more hanging ten, fools, it's time to tear up some pools," and their new style turned a stick with wheels into a distinctive breed of clothing and speech that swept through global culture and changed human history. They did the same to words.

Viewed through an anthropological lens, it's no surprise that rad would have originated in southern California, the land of free-thinking and invention that gave the world tons of great things (rad shit) like Vans, surf instrumental music, Korean tacos, and The Minutemen. I mean, could rad have originated in the Midwest, that flat kingdom of soybeans and corn? All northern California seemed able to deliver was the term "hella," a contraction of "hell of" used in place of "very" (That VW is hella fine) which arose in San Francisco's Hunters Point neighborhood in the late 1970s, spread through Berkley and the Deadhead ranks like fleas, and still lingers in crunchy places like Eugene, Oregon and Flagstaff, Arizona. It's a term I still begrudge northern California for. But if rad is a kind of lyric chopper bicycle, one can't help but try to picture the exact moment the welder hit the frame. I picture kids being lazy. Summer in LA. It's hot. Everything gets sluggish when you're stoned and full of burritos or just fried from skating for miles through that toxic bus exhaust heat. You look for shortcuts: cutting through alleys to bypass a block; cutting across lawns to bypass forty-five degree angle sidewalks; jaywalking to get a Slurpee. Shortening words seems an obvious extension. Laconic lips inadvertently turn radical into rad, the same way they truncated "totally" into "totes." Consider the convenient, Smart Car portability of totes versus the many-sectioned centipede of totally. Or abbreviating "whatever" as "whatevs." Such sonic ingenuity is proof that stiffs like Mr. Hand in *Fast Times at Ridgemont High* are wrong for thinking that stoned bums like Spicoli never contribute anything to society. (Um, how about the phrase "tasty waves," Mr. Hand?) It's also nothing new. You can hear whatevs' earlier incarnation in the 1987 movie *North Shore*. When the bad boy native surf gang spots clueless mainlanders in their lineup, one of them tells Vince, their leader: "Plenty'a haole surfers, but we'll blow them away, bra." Vince growls: "Whatevahs."

So convenience and style, the twin mothers of invention. But also, whether the Z-Boys knew it or not, abbreviating radical was a way of claiming a bit of the dominant culture as their own. Like spray-painting drunken geometries on the sides of the station wagon your mom gave you when you turned sixteen, removing the "-ical" removed the whole word from the standard lexicon—a radical move, in the literal sense—tearing away its

Latin roots so they could refurbish this bit of fourteenth century Middle English into a full-on American original, as wholly ours as jazz and Blues and hamburgers. As with all popular inventions, though, the words got away from them.

When the 1970s turned into the '80s, rad entered what would be its golden age. Everyone said it, every teased-hair mall rat from Reseda to North Carolina, thanks to the vehicle of its popularity: Valley Girl talk, aka Valspeak. Valspeak emerged in the late 1970s in California's San Fernando Valley. Built from bits of surf and skater slang from nearby beaches and fused together with some sort of pink chewing gum, this bubbly pastiche was characterized by its rising terminal intonation—which, like so many Canadians I know, made declarative sentences sound like questions—and its overuse of terms like like, totally, you know, sooo, whatever, radical, duh, as if! Frank Zappa wrote a song about Valspeak, after which the nearby Hollywood media machine pushed the local Valley phenom into national visibility. There was the 1983 movie *Valley Girl*, the TV show *Square Pegs* (1982-1983), then later *Bill & Ted's Excellent Adventure*, *Buffy the Vampire Slayer*, *Clueless*, recently *The Hills* and whatever, whatever, whatever—the familiar feedback loop of culture. (Soooo over it, btw.) Despite its initial underground origins and the subsequent Valspeak craze, it was the *Teenage Mutant Ninja Turtles* cartoon that gave radical its final push through the blood/brain barrier of popular consciousness and into wider use. "Radical!" screamed Donatello, Leonardo, Michelangelo and Raphael in seemingly every episode during the late 1980s and early '90s. Suddenly, the kids in your high school marching band were saying radical. Your little cousin with the big-rimmed glasses was saying it. The boy down the street who always had snot caking his nostrils was saying it—people who'd never touched a skateboard, let alone heard the *Repo Man* soundtrack. Which is probably part of the reason nobody wanted to touch the word for so many years. It was tainted. But America has a short memory. Time makes old leprosies appear fresh again.

Every generation goes through this, with each decade defined as much by its music and the cut of its pants (bellbottom vs. baggy vs. super skinny) as by its slang. The 1920s were the era of the "bee's knees" and "the cat's meow." The late '40s were "so reet." The be-bop '50s had its Beat "cool cats" and "daddy-o." The "groovy" '60s were "far out." The disco '70s were "dynamite" and "out of sight." People were "buggin' out" in early '90s hip hop, had "bling" in the late '90s. Rad came to prominence during the Valspeak era alongside other hokey, surfy terms such as "bogus" and "gnarly," yet somehow, rad outlasted them all. It's always baffling how certain words stay relevant while others die out. The dueling processes of cementation and erosion seem arbitrary. I don't hear people saying "hot dogger" or "tubular." (Then again, I never heard anyone in the late '80s say "I'm gonna cream that mother!" the way The Dagger's leader in *Thrashin'* did.) Yet "right on" never died out. "Killer" never did either. Or maybe I've been saying both for so long that I failed to notice how dated I sounded. Theoretically, "golly gee" and "far out" could come back into fashion, but more likely these sayings, like MC Hammer pants and Kid 'n Play haircuts, will forever remain artifacts of their respective times, sunk in the murky bottom of that cultural La Brea Tar Pit where all the VHS tapes, "jive turkeys" and giant, old school mobile phones go, props for period pieces, too dated for even future scenesters to touch. (After all, before there was the pejorative hipster, there was the pejorative scenester.) While "as if!" sleeps on memory's casting couch, waiting to see if irony will ever call it back to duty, people say rad. A lot. Maybe because its appeal mirrors its definition: as a word that means cooler than cool, it will likely always remain the epitome of cool.

When wisemen say "everything comes in cycles," I have to keep my eyes from rolling. That canned phrase is so vague as to be almost meaningless, and it reeks of such woo-woo New Ageyness that I can almost smell the BO at Burning Man. But as a saying, it too has never fallen out of favor, no matter how much I wish it would (and wish it would take "everything happens for a reason" with it). Also, I have to admit, in some sense the line is true: what is old often becomes new again. Trendy, yes, but not in an annoying way. Some things are evergreen, like Son House's 1941 "Depot Blues," which will never sound anything but stirring and heartfelt, and Link Wray's driving instrumentals such as "Ace of Spades," and a thick strawberry milkshake shared with your soul mate at a mom and pop roadside stand in the coming summer heat. Maybe The Chiffons' "He's So Fine" sounds "of an era" as they say (now that's a great phrase), but age has reduced none of the melody's potency. My mom was a kid when that song ruled the airwaves in the spring of 1963. I was born in 1975. Yet when it plays, we both sing along and sway our heads. You have to. The song is contagiousness. Maybe all great cultural artifacts work the same way. If it's good, it's good, built of marble, never to erode. Like the word cool. Like Bob Dylan's visage in most any early black and white photo where he's smoking a cigarette with his sunglasses on. Like a blue and white, 1956 Ford Fairlane. Not like the movies *Thrashin'* or *North Shore* or *Rad*, which will age more like wet wooden wine barrels than the sturdy vintages they contained—unraveling, rather than improving—and endure as entertainment for future drunken teenagers going through an ironic phase, as well as commentary on the Hollywood mindset at a certain point in history. Definitely not like the word rad.

Frankly, the word never really went away. Like headbangers who love Iron Maiden, and cockroaches who will survive nuclear apocalypse, rad was always there, lurking in the margins while we all did something else, like watch the rise and fall of nü-metal and Creed and American Idol winners. Will hair-metal ever come back? Hopefully not. I spent enough of my childhood surrounded by dirtheads in torn acid washed jeans and those brown tasseled moccasins to repeat that nightmare. But as long as there is air to breathe, somewhere a hesher will play air guitar to Ratt, just as other slang words will lay in wait after their generation has finished playing with them, letting the dust of decades settle upon their dormant husks before the new kids on the block (NKOTB) rise from their (vintage, refurbished) playpen to pick them up again and naively, like all previous generations, think they invented what was never really new to begin with. Because as Carl Sagan said, "You have to know the past to understand the present." And Confucius before him: "Study the past if you would divine the future," which resembles in content but not origin that famous line in Ecclesiastes 1:9, "There is no new thing under the sun," which bears witness in today's contempo garage bands who ape Thee Headcoats who aped The Kinks, just as The Kinks aped rhythm and blues, for homo erectus is descended from apes, and so too will future thirty-somethings with receding hair-lines spend way too much time dissecting the films and vernacular of their now retro youth while begrudging the cruel nature of time and, in turn, reveal their own uncoolness (not a word) by completely draining the ca-chet from an actual word by thinking too much about it, which is somehow antithetical to cool, even though to appear cool you have to think a lot about what you're going to wear and what you're going to say and how to style your hair. For as The Dude in *The Big Lebowski* said, "Yeah? Well, you know, that's just like, uh, your opinion, man," so too did Stanley "Stoney" Brown (Pauly Shore) in *Encino Man* say, "Don't harsh my mellow," a phrase I quote here for the first and last time, and will never utter again.

BETWEEN DISAPPEARANCES

Moore Street, York Street, Edgar Street, Gay Street—there are a number of little streets in Manhattan that few people have heard of. The only one that matters to me is Cannon.

Like the children of so many European Jewish immigrants, my Grandma Silvia Greissman was born in 1919 in a Lower East Side tenement. "Cannon Street," she said over and over throughout my life. "96 Cannon Street. I can still picture it in my mind." When she was two or three, her family moved to Brownsville, Brooklyn, on the other side of the East River. By the 1910s, Brownsville had acquired a reputation as a notorious Jewish slum rife with organized crime, yet in the words of my Grandma Sylvia, "It was as an upgrade."

I wouldn't know. The closest I'd ever been to Brownsville is Alfred Kazin's memoir *A Walker in the City*, partly about growing up in Brownsville in the decades before the Great Depression. But my grandmother's childhood secured her and my place in the great, ongoing story of the Jewish-American diaspora, the saga of migration, alienation, aspiration, and assimilation, which is itself a quintessential New York story. Tenements, the Williamsburg Bridge, upward social mobility via eastward borough mobility—the touchstones of her early life are now the easy symbols of the immortal Gotham tale, elements so familiar that they have become clichés. Yet for someone like me, born in the American West, her cultural DNA once seemed to provide just enough of a pedigree that I, no matter how little I really knew about the City, could always counter my ignorance and insecurity in front of other people with the sense that, "Hey, you might have lived in New York in the late nineties, but my family is from here." Only in my early thirties did I start to reevaluate this.

Cannon Street formed one locus in the triad of sacred places that defined my family's mythology. There was Cannon Street. There was

Flatbush, Brooklyn, where my mom's aunt, uncle, and cousins lived. And there was my mother's childhood home in Flushing, Queens, the house where her family lived until they decided to finally leave New York for the Southwest in 1969.

Growing up Phoenix, I heard about the Flushing house all my life. It was a five-bedroom stand-alone with a yard at 48-40 190th Street. Even in scorching, cactus-covered Phoenix, my grandma and Uncle Sheldon referenced the house as if it were down the street. The talk was always about how Flushing was partially rural when the family moved there from Canarsie, Brooklyn in 1950, the year after my mom was born. There was talk about the area's large Jewish and Italian populations, about how Flushing hosted the World's Fair in 1939–40 and 1964–65, how the state pavilion, observation towers and twelve-story tall Unisphere still stood in Fresh Meadows-Corona Park, a tidal marsh which had, before the World's Fair, served as a dump. "When we moved there," Grandma liked to say, "it was the country, and we were moving up in the world."

Although I only lived in New York for one year, the Flushing house, like my family's loud voices and Yiddish sayings, formed part of my mythology and identity: if not by birth, then by bloodline, I was a New Yorker. Yet I'd never seen the house.

In her late eighties, my grandmother got dementia. As her memory failed, the details of her life began to fade. Important dates, our family history, the stories she'd always told, they were all disappearing. After I moved back to Arizona, Grandma repeatedly asked, "Did you visit Flushing?" I told her I hadn't. When she asked why, I didn't have a good reason.

* * *

A few months after leaving New York in the summer of 2007, I flew back to see jazz saxophonist Sonny Rollins play a historic concert at Carnegie Hall, celebrating the fiftieth anniversary of a landmark gig he did there in 1957. During my free time, I made a family pilgrimage. Since I didn't have time to travel all the way to Flushing, I focused my attention on the Lower East Side.

Unfortunately, Cannon Street didn't appear on the maps I found in local bookstores. Everyone I asked gave the same response: "No, never heard of it." Some cursory web research revealed the street's location. It was down by the Williamsburg Bridge, not far from the East River. My grandma had always said she was born by the Williamsburg Bridge. On a slip of paper I drew a simple map and set out from the YMCA where I was staying near Columbus Circle.

Cannon Street sits in that easternmost corner of the City where the great curve of lower Manhattan Island—the tip of which was known as Corlears Hook during Dutch and British times—breaks SoHo and Chinatown's orderly grid into a wedge of sideways streets. The FDR winds by like some grey buoyant boom keeping the neighborhood's innards from spilling into the East River, while Delancey Street funnels traffic over the Williamsburg Bridge into Brooklyn. Delancey is one of the main filaments that holds together this edge space of triangles and trapezoids. Other than residents, few people had reason to venture this far on it. There was no good Chinese food there at that time, no row of art galleries or boutiques to draw the yupster or shopping set. All of the Lower East Side's remaining ethnic landmarks—Guss' Pickles off Broome, Yonah Shimmel's Knish Bakery on Houston, Kossar's Bialys on Grand—were further west. But I had a reason to come. This sense of purpose and provenance filled me with an almost smug privilege as the B train rattled down its tracks toward Houston.

I took the B to Broadway-Lafayette and walked to Katz's Delicatessen. Katz's may be a culinary landmark, but it's also a symbol of the neighborhood's Jewish history. Since I'd only eaten there once before, and eaten only pie, I ordered a ridiculously oversized brisket sandwich heaped with mustard and sauerkraut, and three fat pickles. Even this lunch, I told myself, was part of my heritage.

The story of the Lower East Side is well documented. It was one of the main neighborhoods where immigrants lived after arriving in New York. During its heyday between the 1880s and 1930s, the Lower East Side, or LES, housed a dense, rambunctious mix of Germans, Italians, Irish and Eastern Europeans. This was the portal into America. For Jewish Americans, though, the LES maintains a particularly powerful grip on the imagination as a symbol of new beginnings. It was ground zero of the Jewish diaspora, a homeland before Israel, for it was here that many of the Jews who fled Europe's late 19th century and early 20th century anti-Semitism started their new lives.

In 1825, New York was still populated primarily by native-born citizens, but people from all over Europe soon started pouring in, intent on improving their economic station. Between 1820 and 1870, approximately seventy percent of the more than seven million immigrants who entered the US entered through New York State's various immigration stations. Naturally, this influx altered the composition of the City. Awash with Czechs, Poles, Hungarians, Bulgarians, Austrians, Latvians, Rumanians, Lithuanians, Greeks, Turks, Arabs and Lebanese, New York became the multicultural mélange that it would forever remain. By the 1880s, immigrants' motives expanded. In addition to financial improvement, most of those who arrived were fleeing political and religious persecution. Chief among these were the Jews.

New York's first Jewish resident was Jacob Bersimon. He arrived from Holland on July 8, 1654, when New York was still called New Amsterdam. A month later, a group of twenty-seven people arrived from Brazil, escaping the Inquisition which had swept through the country after Portugal captured Brazil's last Dutch stronghold. Their move set the standard for the majority of those who came after.

In 1846, New York City housed 10,000 Jews, in 1880, 80,000, most of them German. In 1881, Czar Alexander III began a formal campaign of persecution by establishing pogroms and forbidding Russian Jews from owning land. Jews streamed out of Russia. It was the largest mass exodus since their flight from Egypt. Some of these exiles were my grandfather's parents. Another Russian pogrom in 1882 caused 81,000 more Jews to flee to New York. According to Edward Robb Ellis' book *The Epic of New York City: A Narrative History*: "Between 1881 and 1910 a total of 1,562,000 Jews came to America. A majority stayed in New York, and a majority of this majority settled in the Lower East Side, converting it into the world's largest Jewish community. By 1910 there were 1,252,000 Jews living there. Irishmen and Germans hastily left for other parts of the city, leaving New York's oldest dwellings to the newcomers."

Despite their numbers and the Statue of Liberty's "bring us your tired" dictum, the old prejudices existed in New York, and many residents worked to exclude Jews from various neighborhoods, schools, clubs and jobs. Numerous LES Jews became peddlers, since so little capital was required to sell merchandise from a pushcart. Street peddlers sold everything from hats to toys, jewelry to sweet potatoes. In her book *Lower East Side Memories*, Hasia R. Diner paints a vivid portrait of the neighborhood: "Heaped high with merchandise, [the pushcarts] stretched in endless lines up and down the main streets . . . They were edged up close to the curb and wedged together so tightly that one could not cross anywhere except at the corners. The pushcart peddlers, usually bearded men in long overcoats or old women in heavy sweaters and shawls outdid each other in their loud cries to the passers-by." LES residents made maximum use of limited space, creating a noisy, bustling commercial life that resembled nothing else in America. The arrangement had its problems.

As most new immigrants did, Jews associated largely with fellow Jews, acclimating to their new home by seeking the food, language and customs of the old country. The Lower East Side became a neighborhood where, in the words of Hasia R. Diner, "Jews lived in a universe of almost total Jewishness." Here, Yiddish was primarily spoken, because the hybrid language helped bridge the communication gaps between those who spoke Russian, German or Polish. It also helped created "a foreign land right in the midst of America."

In addition to its cultural isolation, the LES suffered sanitation problems. In his book *American Metropolis: A History of New York City*, author George J. Lankevich described the tenements' medieval conditions as "crowded and loathsome," a place where the incidence of tuberculosis soared. "In 1900," Lankevich wrote, "the population density of the Jewish East Side ghetto reached 640,000 persons in a square mile, the highest such figure in world history."

From Katz's I walked down various side streets south on Essex, once a major local thoroughfare, and turned east on Delancey. The Katz's cashier who I asked hadn't heard of Cannon Street either, and because my grandma's dementia was gradually worsening, I started to wonder if she might have mixed up details. The further I walked, the less hopeful I became. The neighborhood was depressing, an industrial ecosystem of brown, brick housing projects and a few small trees, hardly a historic or visibly distinguished area.

In the shadow of one project, I asked a young Latino man the direction of Cannon Street. "Cannon Street?" He squinted his eyes. "Cannon Street." His dark, baggy jeans hung low on his waist. He chewed his lip, tipped his black ball cap and glanced east and west, then he said, "Nah man. And I've lived here pretty much my whole life."

I continued east, toward the thick scent of river water blowing between buildings and the Williamsburg Bridge. Then it appeared: a tiny green sign to my right listing Cannon Street. I turned to face it. Cannon was less than half a block long. Sandwiched between a parking garage and an elementary school, there were no tenement buildings here, no historic residences of any kind, only rows of projects rising in every direction, indisputably Soviet in their bleak utilitarianism.

I straightened my posture and walked south along Cannon. Craning my neck in search of an address, I scanned the garage's weathered back side, staring as if the building would suddenly fade into a tenement the longer I looked. In a matter of steps the street ended at Broome, and I turned back around. I must have appeared confused, because a man standing on the front stairs of the school asked if I was looking for something. "Yeah," I said, "Ninety-six Cannon Street. My grandma was born there in 1919, and I wanted to see the building, take a picture for her. Know where ninety-six would be?"

He descended the steps and stood beside me, shaking his head. "This is all the Cannon Street there is." He waved his arm north to south. "From that to that." He introduced himself as Norris, the superintendent of Florence Nightingale Elementary, PS110. He offered what he knew of the street's history: PS110 was built in 1903; the projects at the southern end likely went up in the 1950s, as most of them had. "Most likely they tore yours down to build that," he said, pointing to the closest brown tower. "Ninety-six probably was right there. Or maybe over on the other side of Broome, if it ran all that way. Hard to say."

"Any idea about the origin of the name Cannon?"

"No," he said. "Maybe a battle or something?"

He offered to show me the blueprints and old area photos that the school kept on file. "We've got 'em upstairs," he said. "Any other day, just tell me the next time you're coming." He liked the idea that I'd come to take photos for my grandma and to understand our family history. "My grandmother," he said, "lived to be one hundred and four. And my son— he's thirty now—went to school right here." After we shook hands, he went inside and I didn't know what to do. So I photographed the street and the school, even photographed the projects and garage, all of it and its meaning dwarfed by the soaring steel mass of the Bridge. I stood and stared. Cannon was a weird little street.

Unlike nearby Pitt and Columbia streets, Cannon had no counterpart on the Bridge's north side, no extension that shed its name and become one of the main channels aerating Alphabet City. Instead, it stopped at a wire fence on Delancey. Behind the fence, an empty lot, its rough black asphalt streaked with the late-day shadows of the Bridge's support beams and a pigeon's dry corpse.

Cannon was as long as PS110 was wide. It wasn't Manhattan's shortest street. That title often went to Weehawken in the West Village, though some argued that Moore Street, in Battery Park, was shorter. Others said Edgar Street downtown was the shortest, though thanks to its size and configuration, Edgar hardly resembled a street, more just the lanes coming in and out of a parking structure. There were many short streets below 14th: Mill Lane in the West Village; Gay Street, between Stonewall and Waverly Place; Minetta Street, just beyond Bleecker. But those obscure names weren't part of my city. They were bits of someone else's mythology.

Hoping for more info, I looped down Broome to Lewis Street and asked the security guard at the closest project if the building's address used to be 96. "I don't know," he said in a Caribbean accent. "Could be." Dressed in black slacks and a black button-up, he stood in a cramped, rectangular structure on the building's front steps.

I glanced behind him for an address: 550 Grand Street. "No idea?"

"No idea." He suggested I come back when his supervisor was on the property.

"When will that be?"

"Maybe an hour or two."

I shuffled back down Lewis, feeling thwarted in a way well beyond defeat. What had I expected? To walk past Essex and find a preserved tenement building etched with a large bronze 96, in a streetscape like those described in Joseph Mitchell's *McSorley's Wonderful Saloon*? This wasn't a Martin Scorsese film set. This was the other quintessential New York story, the story of New York the recycler, New York the perpetually reborn.

The opening lines of Cynthia Ozick's *New Yorker* essay, "The Synthetic Sublime" read, "More than any other metropolis of the Western world, New York disappears. It disappears and then it disappears again; or say that it metamorphoses between disappearances, so that every seventy-five years or so another city bursts out, as if against nature—new shapes, new pursuits, new immigrants with their unfamiliar tongues and worried uneasy bustle." In *Through the Children's Gate*, Adam Gopnik expressed this phenomenon another way: "There is always a new New York coming into being as the old one disappears." Which is also true of ideas: hundreds of writers and thinkers have stated this same simple fact in their own way countless times before, because my sense of loss, and the City's fundamental dynamism, exists on a continuum of loss and gain stretching back through the modern waves of immigration, to the Indians who lost their land to the Dutch. I shouldn't have needed to traipse all the way down Delancey to discover this, the obvious truth of countless New York books and movies. But it wasn't truth that I was after.

I'd assumed I was trying to educate myself about my origins, yet only after circumstance deprived me did I realize my true goal. I wanted to feel that I finally belonged to this city, to relate as something other than a fleeting, one-time commuter who forged his own fabricated rootedness from other peoples' stories. I wanted to feel that there was more to my connection here than an aging bloodline. If I could touch some part of the old metropolis—a house, a street, a brick—just one iconic building like the ones on nearby Pitt Street—I could truly inhabit the triptych of my family mythology and tell myself, and everyone thereafter, "That is where I'm from." Instead, all I had was another clichéd Gotham story—the failed pilgrimage—as well as the old one: my grandmother, daughter of immigrants.

I left Cannon and walked toward Kossar's Bialys, past rows of drab projects, determined to flush the disappointment from my mind with some traditional baked bread.

* * *

I never mentioned the trip to my grandmother. Instead, when I got back to Arizona, I started writing down everything she said about her New York years. Dates, place names, surnames of relatives she couldn't remember anything more about. During lunch in the food court of Fashion Square Mall one afternoon, she mentioned a few streets she'd lived on in Canarsie and Brownsville, so I handed her a napkin from Panda Express and had her write them down.

As she aged and dementia further eroded her memory, every bit of information seemed increasingly important. Personal history has an ugly myopic side: details that mean everything to you mean nothing to others. Fine, you think during someone's longwinded story of third grade show and tell, I'm glad that happened to you, but what does that have to do with me? Even I, invested in my grandmother's history, found a few of her stories too personal to relate to, others full of narrative dead ends and incomplete details. Yet I clung to them. These fragments were now my mementoes of her, no different than photographs, and my interest in them only partially derived from what they reflected about our family. I also liked to magnify their importance, to think that her stories contributed in some small way to a larger historic portrait of the city I now wanted to belong to.

Memories such as this:

"My mother used to take me and [my younger sister] Helen shopping on Pitkin Avenue [in Brownsville]. Pitkin was where the shops were. We would browse the windows and my mother would ask, 'Okay, what would you like?' And I'd tell her, 'I like the dress but not the top,' and she would remember. She didn't take any notes. She'd buy material—'remnants,' it was called; they were cheaper than material sold by the yard—and recreate them from memory. I would get to high school and girls would say, 'Oh, did your mother make that too?' She was a beautiful seamstress."

And this:

"My father worked for a company called American Home Equipment, as a collector. They sold silverware, plates, pots, and most people bought on an installment plan. His job was to collect the money. He would go all over the city and collect the twenty-five cents in buildings in the Lower East Side, in Brooklyn, Manhattan." Many of his customers were poor. "He always felt bad for these poor people. They apologized for not having enough money to make the payment. He would give them more time, then come back. He learned Italian from working with the many Italians that lived in the neighborhood." After work, the family would meet him at the trolley two blocks away. "Mom said, 'Bring an umbrella.' No one had cars in those days—the average person—except my friend Rita. They had a house, not an apartment, which was a big thing back then."

And this:

"My father was an intellectual. He could have been a teacher, worked for a bank. He was self-educated. He helped us with our homework—composition, history. He would sit down when I was having trouble with a problem or something and say, 'Okay, Silvia, now what's the trouble?' and have a look." Even though he lacked a formal education, he was well-read. "He knew history, geography, math, especially geography." This innate curiosity led him to vagabonding. "He wanted to see the world. So he would go off for weeks at a time. My mom called him a hobo." When asked what specifically her father was doing, where he slept and where he traveled, my grandmother shrugged. "He was just traveling around—hitchhiking, riding different trains. He would write frequently to say hi and tell his whereabouts."

And:

"My mother always called him a hobo, but he was very smart. He always read the paper," especially the local Jewish paper, probably *The Forward*. "I can still picture him in his chair, reading the paper. Or at night, sitting at a table doing the numbers from his job." Grandma and her sister Helen slept in the same bedroom. "We would often talk and goof around at night while he was downstairs trying to do paperwork. He'd come into our room with a strap and say, 'Okay, keep it down or you're going to get it.' He never hit us, but when he spoke, you know he meant it." There were few residential elevators in those days, so, "My father had to climb up stairs, in these old apartment buildings. He was out in all sorts of weather." He died at age forty-nine from cancer of the larynx, but he first got sick at age forty-seven. "Lost his voice, from the smoking. He was never sick a day in his life until that."

I reread these stories and feel like I know my grandmother not just as a grandmother, but as a person. But would anybody else care about these details besides me?

Granted, her family's move from the Lower East Side to Brooklyn is the classic story of immigrant upward mobility. Aside from enjoying a life with more comforts, moving across the River was the first step toward becoming middle-class Americans, to becoming "assimilated." Brownsville was a noisy place, but it was better than Cannon Street. Such was the immigrant's eternal hope, that the next neighborhood, however loud or crime ridden, wouldn't be as bad as the previous one. You could see this arc in the numbering of addresses in the note she scribbled, a qualitative improvement outlined 1 to 4:

1.—Sterling Pl.
2. 438? Saratoga Ave
3. Park Pl 1800?
4. Sterling Pl. => Eastern Parkway => Canarsi—Quonset huts

The arrows in the last line suggest the larger pattern: movement away from slums, toward some vision of Eden: from Cannon to various apartments in Brooklyn, to a two-story house in semi-rural Flushing, and eventually, to a mid-century ranch house with a large xeriscaped yard, swimming pool and orange trees in Arizona. She'd forged a comfortable life. Somehow I'd become intent on tracing our lineage back.

* * *

A year passed in Arizona, then two. In the winter of 2009, I booked another trip to the City. I wanted to spend a few days there before heading up to grad school in Vermont. This, I decided, would be my time to visit Flushing. At dinner one night, I told my family the news.

"The house in Flushing?" Grandma said.

"In January?" said Sheldon.

My mother was excited. "Take pictures for me. I haven't seen it since, well, since 1969."

"Flushing?" said my mom's cousin Marty. He'd recently moved to Phoenix from Brooklyn after retiring from teaching math, and he came to my grandma's to spend time with the family and read her paper. "Now it's all Chinese. You wouldn't even recognize it."

On a yellow stickie, my mother drew me directions: a cross showing 188th Street running south from its junction with the L.I.E. Above it she wrote "near the Fresh Meadows Shopping Center," though we both doubted that it was still there. "From the end of the subway line," she said, "you take the bus to Utopia Parkway. Then you walk to 190th Street and 48th. It's pretty easy."

"The 7 train will take you right there from 42nd street or Jackson Heights," Sheldon said. "The old IRT. Your grandfather used to ride it from work in Manhattan every day."

Instead of directions, Grandma said that in high school, she'd befriended a girl named Gurty. Gurty was also Jewish, but she'd fallen in love with an Italian kid. Grandma eventually got married, had kids and moved to Flushing. She and Gurty kept in touch but saw little of each other. One day she was walking around the neighborhood and ran into Gurty. They asked each other: "Do you live around here?" They both said: "Right down the street." It turns out Gurty lived on 190th, too. She still lived there.

"You should visit her," Grandma told me. "You can stay there if you like."

* * *

Even though I arrived in January lacking adequate winter clothing, I set out on the 7 train toward Flushing. I'd researched the area. It was a diner's dream.

During the 1970s and '80s, Koreans and the Taiwanese composed the bulk of Flushing's population. Its few Chinese restaurants were Cantonese. Thanks to immigration from all parts of Mainland China, Flushing now housed the second largest Chinatown in the City, second only to the one in lower Manhattan. Among its many restaurants and food stalls, visitors could find items from most areas of China, including dishes that were difficult or impossible to find in the rest of the US. It had cuisine from Fujian, on the southeast coast, food from Qingdao, on the northeast coast, from Wuxi near Shanghai and Harbin in the northeast. So diverse were the neighborhood's offerings that *The New York Times* called Flushing "the best neighborhood in New York for tasting the true and dazzling flavors of China." I wanted to taste them all, even if it meant stuffing myself with multiple, gratuitous meals and carrying take-out boxes back on the subway. Here was another reason I had come to love dense Eastern cities over the spacious, suburban monoculture of my native West: learning about new cultures without leaving the continent.

As the subway car shook atop the elevated tracks, I thought of all the dishes I would eat. A few websites claimed that the basement food court in the Golden Shopping Mall sold Flushing's best dumplings, Sichuanese street food, and hand-pulled noodles. How any place as blandly named as the Golden Mall could boast such incredible food confounded me, but that was where I headed.

When I exited the 7, I stepped into a bustling streetscape. Bright banners overhung cluttered storefront windows, their Chinese characters trailing vertically alongside melting sleet. The sidewalks were packed, the skies grey and brooding. I pulled my jacket collar up and scanned the shops for the Golden Mall's address. After circling the block multiple times, I still couldn't find it.

Everyone I asked for directions either shook their heads without speaking or answered in broken English. I finally found a post office where the beleaguered clerk pointed me back to 41st. There, under a nondescript canvas overhang, a small set of stairs led into the basement. A hive of hallways unfolded before me. Stacked boxes of produce lined the walls. Doorways, corridors, a woman in a paper hat laying pastries in a bakery case—I navigated the maze until I found the food court.

Despite its name, the court was not a spacious room ringed with restaurants. This was a cramped den loaded with plastic folding tables. People sat shoulder to shoulder, hunched over steaming bowls. The food stalls were shallow aromatic brood cells, fronted by a counter and a couple people tending stoves. I was the only Caucasian there.

After a few passes, I found what I hoped was the stall I'd read about in *The Times*. It sold liangpi, a cold noodle dish from Xi'an that included four separate sauces and came topped with cilantro, sliced cucumber and bean sprouts. A man stood pounding noodles on a table coated with flour. A woman wearing an apron nodded in a way that suggested she was ready for my order. I said "Liangpi" as well as I could, but she stared back. I smiled. She smiled. She pointed her pen to the list of menu items and said a few word in Chinese. The entire menu was written in Chinese, though in which of the country's seven recognized dialects, I couldn't say. I pointed to a nearby photo of what I hoped was liangpi and said, "Qǐng," "please," one of the two Mandarin words I knew. Then I added "Xièxiè," "thank you," the other word I knew. The clerk scribbled my order with a smirk.

I sat beside a man eating noodles. All around me, people slurped noodles and sipped tea. Something about the sound and intensity of their movements lacked the neurotic quality of my Uncle Sheldon's eating habits, a quality I always associated with neurotic, Jewish New York. Were this my grandmother's dinner table, such behavior would have embarrassed me; here, I relished it. It was novel, and I respected any culture that recognized the way slurping improved a food's flavor by aerating each bite.

When my dish arrived, it didn't look like the way I expected. It was soup. I'd clearly ordered the wrong thing. In fact, I probably never found the right stall. But no matter. The broth was some of the most complex and flavorful I'd ever tasted, better than most phō, and just as delicious as the guay tiew Thai soups I'd discovered on my last New York trip. I slurped and slurped, sprinkling my shirt with tiny fat globules, then lifted the bowl to drink the broth. "Xièxiè," I said before leaving. The clerk waved. I weaved between tables and went back above ground to consider my options.

It was late. The bus route I'd mapped to the Flushing house was too convoluted to be useful at this hour. The distance was too far to walk, the air too frigid. My best bet was a cab, although in rush hour traffic, a ride would be expensive. It seemed wasteful to come this far and not visit the house, even tragic, yet part of me didn't want to go.

After the disappointment at Cannon Street, I wasn't eager for another letdown. And really, what was there to see? My grandmother's birthplace was gone, and even though my mother's childhood home still stood, what did I expect it to show me? The Jewish-Italian Flushing wasn't the Flushing of these Chinese residents any more than modern Flushing was my mother's.

The winter air stung my face. Yellow cabs lined the street. Instead of walking towards them, I walked the other way, away from 190th and an idea which would remain, like so much of this city to those of us who never really lived here, a myth. Maybe one day I would move back east. Maybe I would actually live in one of the five boroughs. But whatever happened, Cannon, unlike Weehawken and York and all those other little obscure streets, would forever remain the center of my New York, shrunken, immaterial Cannon, a half block that even lifelong residents have never heard of, the one with a lifespan as short as its acreage, its face changing year to year, like my own.

HEY COWBOY

The first time I saw him he was sleeping in the post office, face down under the counter with the shipping slips and red, TYVEK Priority Mail envelopes. He had on brown snakeskin cowboy boots, blue jeans, and a yellow pearl button shirt.

I dropped my letters in the slot then whispered, "Hey man, you okay?"

He sat up, set his cowboy hat on his head. His thin, silver, shoulder-length hair hung crispy, his angular face gaunt. "Yeah," he said. "Yeah, I'm okay." His front top teeth were missing. He smoothed his blue sleeping bag out and laid back down. He must have been fifty years old.

I spotted him next when I was walking from the library to my car. He was dancing on the street, one block south of the PO. That was Friday night. He was wearing the same hat, boots, and shirt. Hordes of college kids streamed past, drunk and loud, smoking and laughing. The women wore tight skirts and short summer dresses. The guys texted as they walked, high-fived each other and eyeballed the women. A bluesy R&B band played on the sidewalk, two men hunkered beside amps, one on bass, one on electric guitar.

The cowboy twirled in a fevered counterclockwise circle opposite the band, spinning on the sidewalk's edge between foot traffic and the curb. He would shimmy a few steps, spin, then his right arm would rise upwards like a broken wing, where it flapped half-extended, palm back as if reaching for the guitar licks, flapped as if that meant something. Then he spun, shimmied, turned and flapped, over and over again. Pedestrians shuffled by. The guitarist sang, "I'm a soul man."

I considered dancing with him. At age thirty-three it was time I learned. I watch dancers with envy—at concerts and weddings. Even the sloppiest, most shameless squirmers have gallons more guts than I do. I stand there watching but have never willfully entered a dance floor. When I tell people this, they ask why not.

"I'm self-conscious," I say. "I know I'll look like an idiot."

"Women like a man who makes an effort," they say, "more than his moves."

Recently I started making an effort, secretly, in my bedroom. I close the door, put on some juke joint blues, something like T-Model Ford with a bump and a shuffle, and I cut loose. I feel my legs wiggle, feel my feet stomp, let my hips float wherever the rhythm takes them and feel how my shoulders follow in an unconscious drift. I stand far from the full-size mirror so I can't catch glimpses of my uninhibited self, which I fear resembles a beached, gasping carp.

Dancers tell me that the trick is to not think about it. You just move.

I stood on the street that night watching him move. A kid in baggy jean shorts howled, "Hey, cowboy!" Cowboy didn't hear. His right outstretched arm wobbled as he spun, lifting as a sermonizing preacher's would at the call of the Divine. The music played. Cowboy spun. Spun, like the wheels on my car as I drove away, round and round in the same dumb direction, going the opposite way that I needed to go for nights turned to decades, spinning, another stifled spirit too scared to do what it needed to do.

EVERY SUPPER THE LAST

It's tempting to assume that my father didn't want to celebrate his seventieth birthday because he felt old and fragile and wanted to conceal his decline. But Dad never liked birthdays. He dislikes being the center of attention, prefers not to have anyone make a fuss over him, and he's never found one's day of birth worth celebrating.

As he said the day before he turned seventy: "You know me, a birthday is just a birthday. Every day that I wake up is a birthday." Which is exactly the problem: I live in fear of the day when he won't wake up.

My dad grew up in the country—first in rural southeastern Oklahoma, then small-town southeastern Arizona. Thanks to a lifetime eating hash browns, white bread, mashed potatoes, and biscuits smothered in thick sausage gravy, he now has three stents placed in his arteries, uses nitroglycerin spray for angina, and takes seven separate medications for high blood pressure, cholesterol, diabetes, and related cardiovascular problems. He was on eleven meds a few years before. He acts like this means that his health has improved. The fact is, he can rarely carry groceries without suffering an angina attack, his diabetes leaves him so tired he naps throughout the day, and his blood pressure continues to rise.

As if he needed another problem, Dad's primary diabetes medication recently quit working. Now his blood sugar level spikes somewhere between 125 and 230 milligrams per deciliter. The healthy level is 100. At the end of the month his doctor is going to start him on insulin shots. This is upsetting news, not only because injections will leave my father's fragile, pale skin poked full of tiny holes and put him at an increased risk of kidney failure, heart attack, and stroke. It's upsetting because, regardless of insulin's potential effectiveness, it's another sign that he is going to die, and soon. Possibly within the decade.

Maybe I'm being morbid. Maybe Dad will live into his eighties the way his father did, but I'm not getting my hopes up. Dad's mother died when she was sixty-five during triple bypass surgery following her third heart attack, and as Dad once told me at lunch: "I never expected to live past sixty-five." His mother had diabetes too. Her glass insulin vials rattled whenever Dad opened the refrigerator as a kid. She stored them on the top shelf of the door, by the butter.

Ever since Dad's health soured over a decade ago, no matter what operations he's endured and what treatment he's received, he has only acquired new ailments, never cured any. His doctor described insulin shots as "the last tool" in modern medicine's "kit." To me, insulin injections seem like a morphine drip for a terminal cancer patient, a way to manage the condition of someone beyond recovery.

People with both diabetes and heart conditions are extremely susceptible to strokes. Many times I have imagined scenarios where I'm helping Dad walk from my car to his house. In the most common scenario, he leans against my shoulder for support as he drags a limp leg beside him, the foot twisted inward and tipped on its side. Other times I picture Dad trying to speak through a set of palsied lips. Spit glistens in the corner of his mouth. His lips slant in what resembles a permanent frown, a frown being the one expression I've rarely seen on the ever-jolly Joe Gilbreath. He mumbles something and I say, "What's that now Daddy-o?" and a frustrated glint flashes in his eyes as he struggles to make the words sound as clear to me as they sound in his head. When I'm able to imagine him avoiding a stroke, I picture a slow deterioration: Dad slumped in a wheelchair, parked in a white corridor in a nursing home with a blanket on his lap. That's how my granddad looked the last time I saw him alive. During these darker moments, I often wonder how Dad imagines the way he'll spend the coming years. I hope it involves he and Mom somewhere resplendent, like in a second country home in the pines of northern Arizona. It's too loaded a subject to broach, though, so I don't. Even if I did ask, Dad wouldn't tell me the truth. As my father, he's committed to protecting me from life's more agonizing elements. But as his son, shouldn't I be committed to protecting him from harm?

I wish I could say that I am his greatest ally in the fight against his wasting, claim that I show my love for him by telling him precisely what the doctor did not: that he wouldn't need so many medications if he'd just improve his diet. I used to tell him that, but no more. He won't listen to dietary advice. Now, instead of discussing it, I secretly fret.

* * *

Dad's "a birthday is just a birthday" line is his standard birthday preamble. He says it every year, partly because he believes it, partly because he hopes it will keep his family from forcing him to celebrate. Having heard this preamble for thirty-four years, I know what he means by it. Rather than designating a special day to commemorate someone's existence—the day when people express their gratitude for your birth because, the idea goes, life would be empty without you—Dad thinks we should let people know that we love and appreciate them throughout the entire year. Tell them you love them. Call them out of the blue. Send them a surprise email. Be friendly. I agree with his sentiment and try to put it into practice. What caught me off guard about this year's preamble was the way Dad added a startling new layer of sincerity. "I don't need anything," he said to me in the kitchen. "I have been truly blessed. When you have friends and family, you are a rich man—that's wealth. At least I think it is, anyway."

I nodded and thought, Have been? How about I am blessed? Maybe he was feeling morbid too, because his comments sounded like the sort of thing a person says when they think they're going somewhere.

What he didn't know at the time was that he was going somewhere, whether he liked it or not. My mom and I told him it would be fun to have dinner, just the three of us. "Nothing fancy," Mom said. The next day she suggested a new restaurant that he'd never heard of, and when the three of us drove into a part of Phoenix where we rarely ventured, Dad saw through the ruse. "You two," he said smirking. "I thought I smelled an ambush."

My three half-brothers, kids from Dad's first marriage, had reserved tables for a celebratory meal at Manuel's Mexican Restaurant. When my parents and I arrived, Dad's youngest brother Mike, and my brothers Scot, Todd, and Mark, and their wives and kids were all there—nearly twenty people total. During dinner Dad played with all his grandkids. He joked and laughed with the adults. He even admitted that he was glad we "forced dinner" on him. "Like anyone needs to force you to eat," Scot said. But toward the end of the night, after nearly two hours, Dad's energy waned. He's a good performer, so unless you know what signs, as I do, you might not notice his fatigue. He becomes less active in what had previously been an energetic conversation. If they come at all, his witty retorts come at slower speeds, and he stumbles over the setup of even his favorite jokes. Socializing, especially with big groups, requires more energy than his diabetes allows.

Yet, as usual, Dad ate crap: a green chile burrito beside a mound of refried beans whose lid of leaking cheddar stained the plate with orange grease. Pork and beans are protein, he would have said had Mom or I critiqued his selections. And what would I have said? You should have ordered a taco salad made of iceberg lettuce served in a fried bowl? There weren't many healthy options at this Mexican restaurant, and Mom and I booked it.

Dad drank a diet soda, though, as if that made much difference.

While the waiter removed our empty dishes, my uncle Mike leaned over and whispered to Dad, "You have the best family." Hearing this made me wonder how good of a son I was if I wasn't trying harder to save Dad from his bad habits. Between sips of ice water, I read Mike's birthday card. "Joe," he wrote, "as my older brother, you have always been my idol." A few of the grandkids ran around the table. Dad smiled and drank his soda while everyone chatted around him. Maybe this was why he avoided birthday parties: the unavoidable realization that eventually, on your birthday, you become closer to death than to birth.

Scot turned to Dad with a mischievous grin. "Hey," he said, "you know what the good thing about turning seventy is?" Dad shook his head and Scot snickered. "There is none."

"In that case," Dad told him, "I'm going to live to a hundred just to piss you off." They both laughed at that. Even when they were younger, they've always been like two old men, ribbing each other for sport. I laughed too, envious of their ability to take it all so lightly.

* * *

My dad retired five years ago. Now, every weekday, he eats breakfast and lunch at an old cowboy bar and restaurant called Harold's. It sits in the desert outskirts of Phoenix not far from our house, a dark-stained wooden building like a Wild West saloon. Between meals Dad comes home and tries to read; usually he ends up falling asleep in his living room chair. With his head tilted back, his mouth falls open, and the book comes to rest atop his domed belly. This is how he spends a large portion of each weekday. After a couple of drowsy hours, he drives back to Harold's for lunch, jokes around with the other patrons, then comes home and naps for the rest of the afternoon. When Mom gets home they eat dinner and talk. So much of his life now revolves around food. Maybe that's because, with no business to run or kids left to raise, one of the last pleasures he has in life is sensory. Yet, the more food he puts in his mouth, the more of his time it seems to steal.

Most of his friends from Harold's are fully or semiretired. These regulars compose what wait staff calls "the breakfast club." They drink coffee, eat burgers and steak and barbecue brisket, and gab about politics and the day's news. Long before receiving the news about the insulin, Dad swore to Mom and me that he'd quit eating biscuits, white toast and hash browns for breakfast. He claimed he only ate ham and eggs now. "Protein," he said, "lean and good for your blood sugar." But the way he always falls asleep in his chair, who knows what really goes on at that bar. Part of me feels guilty about my lack of involvement, especially since I'm in the ideal position to monitor him since I'm back living at home. Another part of me knows he wants to enjoy himself in peace, so I now grant him that. It's his life. Why should I tell him how to spend it? I wouldn't be too pleased if people told me how to live my life: get a normal job; quit this writing thing; wear loafers instead of Vans; get married and have kids; settle down already. As much as it hurts to see him age, I think it'd be worse to see him deprived.

One night, not long after moving back in with my parents, I found Dad standing over the kitchen sink eating Oreo cookies. In a nonthreatening tone I asked if his doctor would think that was a wise idea. Dad said the doctor didn't know he ate cookies. I didn't mention how that wasn't my point. Instead, I asked if he'd considered altering his diet in order to combat his diabetes and heart disease. He swallowed a sip of 2% milk and said, "I have." Then he told me about that questionable no toast, biscuits, or hash brown policy, and added that he no longer drank cold buttermilk, only 2%.

Another time Dad asked if I wanted to get a hamburger for lunch. I declined. I'm concerned about developing his health problems, so I rarely eat burgers. I also don't eat fried food, and I eat as many whole grains and vegetables as possible. I drink green tea instead of soda. Also, as much as I enjoy spending time with him, accepting his offer felt akin to endorsing his diet.

"But have you ever eaten a Whataburger burger?" he said. Whataburger is a fast food chain in Texas and the Southwest.

"Not since I was a kid."

Knowing it was what I wanted to hear, he said he didn't eat Whataburger very often, and he didn't eat their fries, but when he has one of their burgers for a snack between meals, man, he cooed, he cannot believe how delicious they are. Feeling like he might still be giving too much away, he added: "It's like a salad, they put so much lettuce, tomato and onion on it."

"You don't have to sell your snacking as healthy to me," I said smiling. "I'm through bothering you about any of it."

A friend once commented that living at home must be great. "You get to see your parents every day," she said. I told her it was great. After living outside my home state for seven years, it was refreshing to spend so much time with my folks, and to enjoy each other's company as adults free of the occasional disciplinary static that so often colors parental relationships. But living there was also emotionally trying. No one wants to watch their parents age, just as I assume that parents don't want their kids to see the unflattering side of the aging process.

Over the last few years, Dad's hair has gone completely gray. Where it used to be thick up front, it's now wispy thin, and little moles and purplish spots show through on his scalp. The skin on his arms and hands has lost its elasticity and taken on a slack, wrinkled texture that bruises easily. Thanks to his blood-thinning medication, his blood runs easily when he cuts or bumps himself even slightly, and he has to dab the cut with paper towel to help the blood clot. His hands, the hands that once held mine and still hold Mom's, are colonized by liver spots, and a single, dark mark lingers behind his right knuckles. Of course I know age changes bodies; what startles me is the way he only partially resembles the man who raised me. His personality is the same. His sense of humor is the same. His characteristic laugh, the laugh that people who meet him usually remember, is as warm and loud as ever. The bright green light in his eyes still shines. But his body is someone else's, and the force within it is fading.

My mother, at sixty-one, is more fit than all of the thirty-somethings I know. Mom eats a stellar diet, exercises daily, and has the trim, muscular build of an athlete half her age. Twice a year she hikes the Grand Canyon from the South Rim to the North Rim and back in one day. I've never once hiked the Canyon, let alone made that fifty-mile roundtrip. Her health might explain why Dad gets especially evasive when she tries to discuss his.

"What'd you have for lunch today?" she asks.

He says, "Hamburger, no fries, and a salad."

Mom's brows furrow and she says, "What salad?" He never orders salad. At this he laughs and winks at me, knowing that I know he went to Whataburger. "Well," she says, "I don't think hamburgers are the sort of thing you should be eating."

He has never been a man controlled by pride. He never used to embarrass easily and has never once, in my memory, even mentioned feeling embarrassed at all. But part of me wonders if the lessening of a person's independence also simultaneously increases a person's pride.

At comments like Mom's, Dad will simply nod and make claims such as, "I only ate half the bun." Or he'll make some pseudo-scientific statement like "a burger is high-quality protein," or say how it's okay to eat a hamburger because at breakfast he eats ham instead of sausage, and ham is "leaner than sausage." Mom will then roll her eyes or shake her head, and before she can point out the ridiculousness of his comments, he'll simply say, "Loraine, I'm fine," and change the subject.

Even if he won't heed her, at least she confronts him. I respect her doggedness. Whereas my silence still makes me feel as culpable an enabler as someone shoving buttered white toast into his mouth, Mom won't buy Dad the foods he wants. "I'm not contributing to your problems," she's said more than once while watching him eat Oreos that he bought at the store himself. He just chews his cookies and smiles. I used to wonder if he interpreted my lack of effort as comradery or lack of interest, but when he shoots me a wink during one of Mom's small lectures, I know he believes I'm on his side. I am, but not in the way that he thinks.

Then again, can you really save someone from themselves? Dad couldn't save me from my own dark urges during my adolescence. Even if he'd known that I'd smoked pot every day for three straight years, he still couldn't have stopped me. I would have found a way to get high. Just like he couldn't keep me from trying all those other drugs back then. And the way that, no matter how much he loathed cigarette smoking, and no matter how many times he advised I never start, he couldn't get me to quit smoking cigarettes until I was ready to quit on my own after many false stops. So is he, as my father, accountable for my poor choices? Is it his fault I got into drugs and cigarettes? No. When I asked for help when time came to quit smoking dope, he was there to help. People relinquish their habits when they want to, if they ever want to at all. All we friends and family members can do is offer a few choice words of encouragement, directives from the heart, and hope that they act upon them; if they don't, then we have to be there to support them when they're ready to stop.

Of course, some will never stop. Like all people determined to indulge despite sensible critiques, Dad sneaks around my mom's back. While she's at work, he eats miniature yellow donuts coated in waxy chocolate frosting. He buys sticky glazed cinnamon rolls and eats them after lunch. And when Mom goes to sleep, he stands at the kitchen counter, eating his new favorite creation, what he calls a "roll-up." It's a piece of deli ham rolled around a slice of Swiss cheese. He assembles each roll-up from a stack of meat and cheese, and eats it along with white, buttered toast that he dips into a container of creamy potato salad. When I find him at night indulging like this, I say nothing about it. I no longer even shake my head. I come home from work, chat with him for a few minutes and have some laughs and then go to bed. What would I say that I haven't said already? Bad Dad, you're very, very bad. Eat some of the tofu and curried lentils I have in the fridge.

Mom knows about his snacks; she has the deep knowledge that comes from nearly four decades of marriage. That and she looks in the trash for evidence. He hides the cellophane wrappers from his Twinkies and cinnamon rolls deep inside the trash, and whether in the kitchen garbage can or the big bin in the garage, Mom finds them.

"He's having an affair with a Twinkie," she said in the kitchen once. She held up the torn cellophane. "Here are her panties!" We all laughed. There seemed nothing else to do.

I laugh to counter the effect of brooding over that common, universal question that I am only now frequently asking: what will my life be like when my mother and father are gone? I can imagine a day when I myself am dead. I can imagine a world without me in it, but somehow I can't imagine my life without my parents. A life where Dad isn't here to retell our family history and make jokes and call me son? Where Mom isn't here to laugh and describe her Grand Canyon hikes and to say out of the blue that she loves me? That hardly seems like a life at all, but it's going to have to be.

Sometimes I find myself composing Dad's eulogy while driving around town or lying down to sleep. I'll rest my cheek against the pillow, or turn a corner onto a familiar street, and I'll suddenly become aware that I'm wondering what exactly I'll say at his funeral. To prepare for an event that has yet to happen seems masochistic, but maybe I'm being practical. Once Dad passes, I tell myself, I might so completely fall apart that I won't be able to write anything coherent, let alone speak without crying, so I better write the eulogy now. When I think that logic over, though, I realize that I'm not composing the eulogy to be practical. I'm doing it as a way to prepare myself for the moment that has had me bracing for years, the moment when my phone will ring, and I'll answer it, and Mom will say, "Aaron, I'm at the hospital. Dad died," and all the breath will leave me as fast as it left him.

After Dad's birthday dinner, my parents and I drove back to the house and spent some time chatting. The three of us went into their bedroom. Mom sat on the bed, skimming the paper. Dad settled into his recliner, leaning back and propping up his feet. I sat by the door, petting Red the cat. All the revelry had left Dad subdued, and he seemed happy to be home where he could rest.

Somehow we got onto the subject of my parents' courtship and they lapsed quickly into reminiscence. My parents met at a sandwich shop. Mom was Dad's waitress. She was twenty-two years old, a student at Arizona State University, and had just arrived in the desert West with her family from New York. She spilled soup in his lap, but they disagree about who wiped it up. He says she did. She says no, he cleaned it himself. Dad was thirty-three and still technically married. After a number of dates and countless expressions of his affection, Dad took Mom to meet his parents for the first time. They lived in Tucson two hours away. That night, the four of them talked, and when Mom left the room for a moment, Dad's mother—my granny—got up from her chair, sat down next to Dad on the couch and said, "Is this love or lust?"

Dad said, "It's love, Mom."

"That's good," she said.

Hearing this, my mom laughed. "I didn't know Granny said that." Mom remembered Granny playing gospel music on a record player for her. "She said, 'This is what I grew up to.' I sometimes wondered, Was she testing me?"

From his leather recliner Dad said, "She was sharing with you." As if sensing her self-doubt he paused then added, "She thought you were a lovely, wonderful person."

Mom said, "Did she?" seemingly relieved to hear this forty-year-old information. "It was hard. I felt like such an outsider: this Jewish young girl from New York." She pointed to Dad across the room and laughed. "He was older, divorced, had four kids. I still had an accent."

Theirs was a collision of cultures. Dad's mother was a heavy set, half-

French woman who smoked cigarettes and cooked constantly. She grew up among Christian farmers in rural southeastern Oklahoma, and she died when I was six months old. By all accounts, she cooked the best cream gravy you have ever tasted. When Dad was a kid, she'd call him and his brothers in for supper and the house would smell like fried chicken, buttermilk biscuits, mashed potatoes, and gravy.

Mom described the breakfast Granny and Granddad cooked the next morning. It was the usual big country Gilbreath feast. "Granddad always made the biscuits," Mom said, "and Granny made the gravy." Normally this sort of discussion would have grabbed Dad's attention, but he was still thinking about the first night they all spent together.

"She played you The Happy Goodman Family," Dad said. His mother loved Southern gospel music. She owned numerous records—The Statler Brothers, The Blackwood Brothers—but The Happy Goodman Family was her favorite at that time.

I'd never even heard of any of these performers.

Mom looked up at me from bed. "I wish you could have met Granny," she said, "and seen Dad back then. He lived on fumes. He would stay up late, get up early on a few hours sleep, and go right back to work." Dad sat smirking in his chair, neither adding nor contesting anything she said, only smiling. "He was the first person I ever saw use Visine." She pantomimed the act of applying drops to red morning eyes. "Then," she said, her gaze fixed on Dad, "he'd do it all again at night—partying with coworkers, going to the bar."

He laughed. "In those days it was called 'a conference.'"

At 9:30, after Mom went to sleep, Dad led me into his office and said, "Let's Google The Happy Goodmans." I sat in the black rolling chair in front of the computer while Dad leaned against the desk beside me, and we scrolled through live clips on YouTube. The Happy Goodman Family were arguably the most popular and famous gospel group of all. Founded in the 1940s by pianist and vocalist Howard "Happy" Goodman, the group consisted of a number of Howard's brothers, as well as his wife Vestal. Howard was a large man with sagging jowls and a broad face. Vestal was a woman with a body like an obelisk and a voice like a racecar engine. Later in her career, she had a towering column of black hair composed of two hair pieces stacked atop one another, kind of like Elvira's. Vestal and Howard passed away, but during their heyday between the 1960s and '80s, they sang gorgeous harmonies.

Dad and I watched clips of the band performing in settings ranging from Arlington, Texas in 1969 to the Grand Ole Opry in the 1980s. We stared at the screen in silence, listening to songs that were now considered classics, such as "God Walks the Dark Hills" and "I Wouldn't Take Nothing For My Journey Now." Then he directed my attention to the search engine and told me to type in "Bill Gaither." Nearly 800 YouTube hits appeared.

Gaither is a Southern gospel and Christian musician who also organized a series of worldwide concerts called the *Gaither Homecoming*. The concerts took place in enormous venues filled with Christian music fans. Performers included both legendary gospel singers and younger, up-and-comers. The shows were frequently recorded, and Gaither broadcasted them on religious-oriented cable channels and sold the shows on DVD and VHS.

"We used to always watch this," Dad said. He leaned closer in order to see the screen. "Your mom and I would race home on Saturday night to watch it."

This surprised me. Officially, Dad's family was Baptist. Many Okie families were. His parents had occasionally attended church, but they weren't religious, and by the time Dad was in his twenties he considered himself an atheist. Religion always seemed to him a means of control—"fire and brimstone," he's always called it, "all about fear." The idea of a single creator keeping tabs on peoples' behavior never seemed plausible to him, and he didn't believe that the only way a universe this well-ordered could come into being was from a single deity. The Bible was written by people, he'd told me when I was a kid, not God. "God is the Supreme Politician that human beings use to keep us in line." Instead of scripture, he reads Einstein and Tesla, turning to science to understand nature. Surprisingly, the mystery of existence didn't interest him.

When the subject of life after death came up during my adolescence, Dad occasionally said, "You live once, you die, that's it." According to

Dad's belief system, what we have at this moment is as good as it gets. He'd echoed this sentiment one night in the kitchen. He and Mom and I had just eaten barbecued spare ribs, and Dad and I were doing dishes. "Why spend all this time worrying about what you can't control: why am I here? What's the purpose of living? What if an airplane falls on me? You die. You can't change any of that." He toweled off the knife he'd used to cut the ribs. "I'm here because I'm here. I try to get the most of the best things of life, live a good life. And then, you die." He slid the knife into the drawer and glanced at me over his shoulder. "It is what it is." That was the same line he used when describing the doctor's decision to put him on insulin. Mom said that sounded too resigned for her taste. I agreed, but Dad only smiled and gave me a wink. "The golden years aren't so golden."

Recalling this, I watched the screen. Dad directed my attention to a video displayed in the sidebar. "Click that," he said. It was a clip of two bickering bass singers named J.D. Sumner and George Younce trading insults about the other's career. J.D. was a rail-thin man of six feet, six inches who'd made his name singing for the The Blackwood Brothers and The Stamps. Younce had sung with a number of gospel groups. J.D. towered over the short, squat Younce. George grabbed the microphone out of J.D.'s hand in order to finish J.D.'s singing part, and J.D. smacked the side of George's bald head. Dad explained that in real life the two singers were close friends, but on stage they played the part of embittered rivals. Their differing heights imparted an Abbot and Costello quality that was nearly as funny as their banter.

Another clip showed J.D. seated on a couch in what appeared to be the backroom of a concert venue. "George spent forty-five minutes fixin' his hair," he said. "Then forgot it and left it at the hotel."

George responded: "J.D. said to me the other night, said, 'Did you hear how my voice filled the room tonight?' I said, 'Yeah, I seen a bunch of people leavin' to make room for it.'"

Dad pointed at the screen and said, "Try that one." It was titled "George Younce's Final Appearance Part 1." Dad leaned close and studied the footage. "Mom and I watched this particular concert when it first aired," he said.

Younce, the same man whose body had filled out his suit in previous videos, now stood withered in this black sport coat, thin as a skeleton. He was seventy-four years old when it was filmed and on dialysis. Young back-up singers had to help him onto the stage. Then, when he stood to sing, the singers watched closely to make sure he didn't fall. His hair was thin and gray. His skin had a bleached, sickly pallor. "I don't have a lot of strength anymore," Younce told the crowd, "not much voice even anymore." The close-up shots revealed a large lump and scratch on his forehead and eyes tinted a yellowish red. Despite his frailty, he still possessed his legendary warmth and wit, and he frequently laughed when speaking between songs.

Introducing the next number, George said that many people had asked to hear it, and so, "One more time, on this marvelous stage, let me see if I can get through this song once again." The song was called "Suppertime," and in a soft voice George sang: "Many years ago in days of childhood, I used to play when evening shadows come." He reached for the arm of one of his fellow singers and, gripping it, a young man fetched a chair for George to sit in. "Then winding down that old familiar pathway," George sang, "I heard my mother call at set of sun:

Come home, come home, it's suppertime
The shadows lengthen fast.
Come home, come home, it's suppertime.
We're going home at last."

I mentioned that it must have been hard for George to be there. "I don't know how he keeps from crying."

Dad said, "Well, he didn't know it was his last concert." Of course, "George Younce's Final Appearance Part 1" was only the title given by the person who posted the footage on YouTube. Bill Gaither marketed the video as *A Tribute to George Younce*, the year after Younce passed. "That's also how Southern Baptists are," Dad said. "Death isn't a tragedy, because they believe they're going somewhere better when they die."

Like Dad, I'm an atheist. "It would be great to believe that," I said.

Dad said nothing.

Watching Younce's last concert, I couldn't help but feel that this might be the last quiet moment Dad and I would ever spend together. I feel that about most of our shared moments lately. A simple chat, a Sunday drive, a birthday dinner. Now everything takes on a weighty significance. It becomes: The last conversation. The last concert. The last supper. And nervously I savor these moments and then write about them in my journal, as if by preserving the details the event's participants will endure off the page, the way Jesus' followers endure in heaven.

After letting Younce finish his song, Dad and I stood in the kitchen eating sliced strawberries from a bowl and talking about gospel. "There were lots of crazy hairdos in those videos," I said. I told him that the music was alright, but I preferred blues and rock and roll.

"Gospel, rock and roll—all those styles are connected down there," Dad said. He rummaged through the cupboard for something sweeter. He was out of Oreos.

We ate and talked a few minutes, stared into space, then he said, "Alright son, I'll see you in the morning." As always, I hoped that would be the case.

* * *

The next morning I found Dad in the kitchen. He wasn't eating, only counting out his pills. He plucks each pill from the collection of bottles in the cupboard, places the pill in a shot glass then washes down the mix with a gulp of diet soda. It's his morning ritual.

I looked around. The kitchen counter was bare. Not one birthday card remained. "What'd you do with them all?" I asked.

With his back to me he said, "Threw them away."

"Already? It's been twenty-four hours."

"You know," he said snickering, "you and Mom are just alike." He was referring to the plastic bag I have full of notes and holiday, birthday, and Valentine's cards from all my grade, middle and high school friends and ex-girlfriends, as well as from my parents and grandparents. The bag is in a box in the garage behind the trash bin. The contents date back nearly twenty-five years.

The pills made little clinking sounds as they fell into the shot glass. I explained that I wouldn't feel so weird about getting rid of the older cards if they ended up somewhere other than dumped atop old spare rib bones and yellowed Q-tips.

"Okay," he said, "but where else is it going to go?"

I had no answer for that, only, "I'm sentimental."

"Well, there's nothing wrong with that." He gulped a soda and swallowed his pills. "Mom is worse than you. She shoves everything in a drawer in her bathroom—every card, note, postage stamp." The collection had recently become such a mess that he'd moved it all into a box and stored it in the garage.

"Alright," he said, "I'm off to breakfast." He grabbed his cell phone and car keys from the counter and, as always, I wondered whether to tell him to stay away from the hash browns and biscuits, to only eat the ham and not drown it in gravy. But I said nothing. I leaned against the kitchen counter, watching Dad collect his things. He patted my shoulder as he walked by and I thought: Like believers to their religion, let Dad heed his own call. Go home, I now think, go to the place where your mother calls to you when it's suppertime, go to her in your mind the way I can still go to you now.

EVERYTHING WE DON'T KNOW

On Friday March 23, 2012, a year after Japan's Fukushima nuclear disaster, a Canadian patrol aircraft spotted a rusty vessel floating toward the British Columbia coast. It was the Ryou-Un Maru, a Hokkaido shrimping ship, and it was unmanned.

The 9.0 Tōhoku earthquake that struck Japan's east coast killed nearly 16,000 people and unleashed a tsunami that decimated towns and washed between four and eight million tons of debris into the Pacific Ocean. A splintered, foaming mess containing cars and cables, houses, lumber, and human beings surged as far as six miles inland before spilling into the sea. About 70 percent of the debris sank, but a year later, 1.5 million tons, what the *Los Angeles Times* said amounted to "roughly 100,000 garbage trucks' worth," were still floating on the open ocean.

The Ryou-Un Maru was the first large piece of tsunami debris to cross the Pacific. The press called it a "ghost ship." The Canadian transport ministry monitored to make sure it didn't leak fuel or block commercial passage. After a month drifting north, the US Coast Guard blasted the ship with cannon fire 180 miles off the Alaskan coast and let it sink 6,000 feet.

Three months later, a sixty-six foot long cement dock beached itself in a scenic cove north of Newport, Oregon. People climbed atop it, posed, and took photos. The dock had floated 4,700 miles from the town of Misawa on northern Honshu, Japan's main island. The seven foot tall structure's Styrofoam filling kept it afloat, and a metal plaque identified its origins. As Hirofumi Murabayashi of the Japanese Consulate in Portland told the news, "The owner of this dock is Aomori Prefecture, and they told us that they do not wish to have it returned." Authorities sawed off a section to display in a tsunami awareness exhibit at Newport's Hatfield Marine Science Visitor Center, and Oregon Governor John Kitzhaber created a hotline to report tsunami debris.

People on the Oregon coast are used to picking up trash. Everything from lighters and plastic bags to huge swollen logs wash ashore, but this trans-oceanic debris was different. Debris hunters came to photograph and collect it. Some sold their finds on eBay. Tsunami treasure hunting became sport, and the town of Seaside, Oregon even used it to attract tourists. But coastal trash is neither fun nor attractive. It strangles birds, poisons fish, and damages fisheries, and it can carry invasive species. After Fukushima, debris provided powerful evidence of decreasing oceanic health, and it served as an undeniable symbol of ecological connectivity. If the trash made it this far, people reasoned, what about the radiation?

The massive tsunami that pounded Japan's Fukushima Daiichi nuclear complex in 2011 caused a triple meltdown, multiple reactor explosions, and released large but still unknown amounts of radioactive cesium-137, cesium-134, strontium-90, neptunium-237, uranium-236, plutonium-239 and -240, iodine-131 and -129, ruthenium, tritium, and radium into the air, groundwater, and ocean. The French Institute for Radiological Protection and Nuclear Safety's report called the plant's initial breakdown "the largest single contribution of radionuclides to the marine environment ever observed." People named the radioactive material "the plume" and watched as it dispersed on various Pacific currents. With all the debris hitting the West Coast, the distance between Japan and the US no longer felt so vast.

As the California naturalist John Muir famously said, "When we try to pick out anything by itself, we find it hitched to everything else in the Universe." Americans wanted to think of Fukushima as Japan's problem. We were here and Japan was there. So we sent our condolences and donated to relief efforts and got back to watering our gardens and eating sushi—myself included. The question many scientists were asking on everyone's behalf was whether Japan's problem was poisoning the plankton that larger fish ate. If so, it would poison us.

Scientists didn't initially know how the radiation was moving through the marine ecosystem, or what it would do to marine life over time, but a few, like oceanographer Ken Buesseler, immediately started studying it, and many activists and conspiratorial bloggers knew they had to cut through the governmental rhetoric and Tokyo Electric Power Company cover-ups to find the truth. One truth was as clear as it had always been: everything is connected. If you thought you were safe, you were wrong.

* * *

I first visited the Oregon coast as a tourist in 1995. My parents and I came on vacation. We'd visited Seattle the previous summer, and western Oregon looked like an equally beautiful destination. By the time I graduated from college in Arizona, return trips had left me so in love with the Northwest that I moved to Portland in 2000, intent on sustaining myself on its moist air, clean tap water, and abundant local food. I was a co-op person. I ate ancient grains, organic produce, and lots and lots of seafood. I still do.

Most of the protein in my diet comes from Pacific fish. I prefer the small silver oily species: sardines, anchovies, saury, and herring. Small fish are rich sources of calcium, phosphorus, vitamins A and D, and omega-3 fatty acids. Protein sustains your energy. Certain omega-3s, like DHA and EPA, may reduce the growth of breast, colon, and prostate cancer, lower blood pressure, prevent hardening of the arteries and heart disease, and possibly lessen the cognitive degeneration associated with Alzheimer's. Americans take supplemental cod liver oil for omega-3, but my beloved little fish are naturally loaded with it. The general wisdom is that eating fish a few times a week is part of a healthy diet. It's one explanation why so many Okinawans live to be centenarians. Seaweed, tofu, and tea are other reasons. I consume those foods every week.

We Jews eat lots of fish. I eat it for breakfast, for lunch and for dinner—it doesn't matter what season. After high school I vowed not to suffer my father's health problems. I loved country food, but I refused to suffer health problems caused by diet. So I went vegetarian for a while, later vegan. Now, I eat a more balanced healthy diet.

To cut down on our water and carbon footprints, my wife Rebekah and I became weekday vegetarians: no beef, chicken, or pork Monday through Friday. At a time when the overfished Pacific bluefin tuna faces extinction, and farm-raised salmon's nutritional and environmental costs are hotly debated, shifting my eating habits from livestock and large fish to durable "bait" fish felt like smart environmental stewardship. It's called eating lower on the food chain. Many of those small fish sit low enough on the trophic ladder, and live short enough lives, that they aren't as polluted with mercury and PCBs as higher order, top predators like tuna, sea bass, and swordfish. Many reproduce quickly, so they've rebounded from past overfishing and can be responsibly managed as a sustainable, healthy food.

To further lower my footprint, I usually buy Pacific fish, rather than fish imported from the Mediterranean and North Atlantic. The Pacific is less than 100 miles west of our home in Portland. It's the world's largest ocean, and one of the most productive. But after Fukushima, I no longer feel safe eating from it. When I buy my monthly stash of Japanese, South Korean, and Thai canned fish, I wonder whether I should buy sardines and anchovies from Spain, Portugal, or North Africa instead.

Since moving to Oregon, I've visited the coast countless times. I've swam. I've boogie-boarded. I've been sprayed by waves crashing at the base of tall lighthouses, and I plan to hike and camp on the coast for the rest of my life. Rebekah and I just bought a house and want to raise a child. The blue water looks as true as it always has. But now when I visit places like Seaside and Newport, I look out over the ocean and wonder what's coming for us next.

* * *

In March 2013, a fourteen foot long, black and red wooden beam was found on the beach near Oceanside, Oregon. It was a kasagi, the horizontal crossbeam that connects the two side beams on a Japanese torii temple gate. The following month, another kasagi beached itself near the Siuslaw River in Florence, a hundred twenty miles to the south. Locals rightly wondered if the kasagi were radioactive.

Cesium-137 can burn or sicken you on contact. When ingested, it accumulates in your muscles and other soft tissues, where it gives off the gamma and beta radiation that can cause cancer. Other Fukushima and Chernobyl nucleotides, like strontium-90, are easily ingested when they get in food and water. "Once in the body," says the Centers for Disease Control and Prevention, "Sr-90 acts like calcium and is readily incorporated into bones and teeth, where it can cause cancers of the bone, bone marrow, and soft tissues around the bone." As coastal Oregonians photographed and sold debris on eBay, others questioned the wisdom of handling trash from the world's second worst nuclear disaster. Fortunately, authorities concluded that the kasagi were not radioactive.

Shinto temple arches are sacred, but no one knew where these originated until Sadafumi Uchiyama, curator of the Portland Japanese Garden, saw the beams in the news and tracked down the eighty-five-year-old man who'd dedicated the shrine in the town of Hachinohe. Uchiyama flew to Japan, met the man—who cried at the meeting—and helped ship the beams back for free.

Following the Daiichi nuclear meltdown, the Japanese government evacuated some 160,000 people from the contaminated area that officials deemed the "Fukushima exclusion zone." Residents, utility, and emergency workers and US sailors onboard the USS Reagan suffered radiation sickness while securing the reactors, offering humanitarian support, and cleaning up after the tsunami. Many Fukushima residents left their homes wondering what illness they would later contract; over four years later, only a fraction have returned home.

Home to 330,000 people, the city of Koriyama sits in central Fukushima Prefecture, about thirty-five miles away from the Daiichi nuclear facility; this places it fifteen miles beyond the shifting boundaries of the exclusion zone, at most. Fukushima Prefecture once produced peaches, tomatoes, rice, and beef. After the accident, farmers let irradiated crops rot in the fields, animals had to fend for themselves, and the city of Koriyama recommended that children between ages three and five play outside for no more than thirty minutes a day. Children up to age two were not supposed to spend more than fifteen minutes outside. In one Reuters article I read, the reporter overheard a mother at an indoor playground tell her kid, "Try to avoid touching the outside air." I read a lot of articles.

Articles say that in Koriyama, three year olds know the word "radiation." Before eating, they ask adults if their food is safe. According to Reuters, the city's radiation levels have dropped since 2011, but its children continue to play indoors, and fear of exposure dictates many peoples' behavior. At first, parents preferred strong preventative measures. Staying inside seemed wise. Over time, many started to worry about the long-term effects of an indoor life. Surveys found that Koriyama children were noticeably sluggish, had increased stress responses, and decreased grip strength and physical coordination. Many have never learned to ride a bike. The threat of radiation on land is real, but another disturbing health risk is psychological.

* * *

Since the nuclear accident, blogs have been filling with predictions. Websites with names like Freedom Outpost and The Truth expose what they consider the real Fukushima story beneath the bureaucratic cover ups. They run color-coded maps showing the plume's dispersal. They claim that "The west coast of the United States is being absolutely fried by radiation from the Fukushima nuclear disaster" and declare "Dangerous levels of cesium-137 have been discovered in mushrooms and berries grown along the west coast." Many of these sites dabble in other topics, such as voting fraud, IRS scams and how the film *Noah*, in one post's words, "Promotes The Luciferian Gnostic Belief That The Creator Of This World Is Evil."

Scientists counter such claims, dismissing them as pseudoscience, and pointing out how their authors misinterpreted the data or took it out of context. Not every bluefin tuna tested in California waters is contaminated with radiation, said the voices of reason. Every one of the fifteen bluefin that one study examined contained Fukushima radiation. But never mind the facts. Conspiracy theorists have banner ads to sell and self-published books to promote. Other people in positions of influence swung the opposite direction, away from apocalyptic end-times declarations, and made wild claims about safety that were just as irresponsible.

In March 2015, *Forbes* magazine ran an article claiming that, "Contrary to all the hype and fear, Fukushima is basically a large Superfund site. No one will die from Fukushima radiation, there will be no increased cancer rates, the food supply is not contaminated, the ocean nearby is not contaminated, most of the people can move back into their homes, and most of the other nuclear plants in Japan can start up just fine." When I read that I thought, Just fine? Not contaminated? The author's flippant dismissal was as devoid of sympathy as it was of evidence.

The conspiracy theorists respond to such claims with their own weapons of fantasy. Why do you think sea lions are dying by the thousands in Alaska and California, they say? Why do you think the polar bears are losing their hair? They cite newspaper reports that show sardines bleeding from their eyes and gills, and they describe the California coast as a dead zone. "Have you seen as many seagulls as you did fifteen years ago?" one blog said. The rocks at California beaches are "unnaturally CLEAN," warned Planet Infowars, "there's hardly any kelp, barnacles, sea urchins, etc. anymore and the tide pools are similarly eerily devoid of crabs, snails and other scurrying signs of life . . ." The cause wasn't warming waters or oceanic cycles, the bloggers assured us. It was radiation. And the worst was yet to come.

* * *

Saury are one of my favorite fish, and they only live in the Pacific. I keep stacks of canned Japanese saury in our basement so I can easily heat them in a skillet to serve over rice. This is one of my standard healthy breakfasts. None of the research I've found says saury are contaminated, but I still can't decide whether to give them up. I've been debating for two years.

Known to biologists as Cololabis saira, Pacific saury also go by the name "mackerel pike." Koreans call it kongchi (꽁치). Russians call it saira (сайра), the Chinese qiu dao yu (秋刀魚). In Japan it's called sanma (サンマ).

Translating as "fall swordfish," sanma is one of Japan's most popular fish, which is no small feat in an island nation whose citizens each consume over one hundred and twenty pounds of seafood per year. Not to be confused with the Japanese comedian Sanma Akashiya, saury is a serious-looking, long slender swimmer related to the needlefish, and its appearance in Japanese markets and on sushi menus marks the beginning of autumn. The fish is so abundant, beloved, and easy to prepare, that the Japanese throw annual festivals celebrating its arrival. In 2012, the Meguro Saury Festival in Tokyo attracted 35,000 people. Here in the US, few gaijin have heard of saury.

The Edo Emperor ate saury pickled, raw, and salt-grilled. The most popular way to cook it now is sanma no shioyaki. 'Shio' means salt, and 'yaki' means grilled. This simple broiled preparation unleashes rather than masks the fish's rich natural flavor—just fire and salt. Most Japanese homes have an electric, stovetop fish broiler, or one built into the oven; they're like electric kettles in England, there by default. In Japan, restaurants usually serve sanma no shioyaki with grated daikon radish, sometimes a lemon or sudachi wedge. To bring out the flavor, you squeeze on the citrus, maybe drizzle on some shoyu, and place a bit of diakon on each bite. If the fish is longer than the grill, some cooks cut the fish in half. Most regular sanma cooks have a grill big enough to accommodate the fish whole—head on, guts in. The guts contain oil that keeps the fish moist, but they taste bitter. Some people eat the guts because they're nutritious. Some people eat the guts to remind them of hardship, that life is a mixture of the bitter and sweet.

* * *

I discovered saury by accident. I was shopping at a Japanese grocery store in the suburbs, browsing aisles of seaweed and savory soup stocks in search of old favorites and new foods to try, when I found tall blue cans of a fish called mackerel pike. Mackerel pike, I thought, which is it: mackerel or pike? Could a fish be both? Was this a translation error? Unlike the straightforward cod, sole, snapper, shrimp, I didn't know what flavor to expect. Since the label was written in Hangul, I didn't understand what this fish was or how to prepare it, but lower on the shelves, I found a Japanese version in small orange tins for $2.69 labeled "Sanma kabayaki."

Unlike the first Korean cans, which were packed in salt water, this Japanese version was roasted and basted with a thick, savory, semi-sweet glaze made from soy sauce and sugar cane, a preparation called kabayaki. The seafood you'll most frequently find kabayaki is freshwater eel, or unagi. Canned sanma kabayaki arrives similarly: filleted, headed, partially boned, broiled and basted, and to me, the flavor is even more delicious. Once I opened that first tin, I fell so hard that I now live off the stuff, buying ten to twenty tins at a time and stacking them in our basement.

Cans are small and easy to store. I cook the tiny fillets on a skillet, letting the heat further char their soft edges and caramelize the sauce. Sometimes I put the heated sauries on a salad. Usually, I serve them over warm white rice and eat them with a bowl of miso soup. This is my take on a traditional Japanese breakfast. One 100 gram can of my go-to sanma kabayaki contains 17 grams of protein and 22 grams of unsaturated fat. Total calories: 340. Like saba mackerel, saury is oily and rich, but the meat is lighter, whiter, and cleaner tasting. The mix of salt, fat, and umami satisfies in a way that lasts long after breakfast. Something about the fish-rice combination flips off the crave switch in my brain and drastically reduces my snacking urge, letting me work a long time and concentrate deeply. Sauries have become an integral part of my idea of healthy living. I was born in a nation of hot dogs and sausage patties, but I learned to take a cue from the Japanese and Koreans: eat more fish, drink more tea, and start eating saury.

In their 2008 song "Fish Heaven," the Japanese band Gyoko—meaning "Fishing Port"—sings: "Fish. Fish. Fish. You get smart when you eat fish. Smart Smart Smart. Fish Fish Fish. You get healthy when you eat fish. Healthy. Healthy. Healthy."

All the Fukushima books and articles I've been reading—not the conspiratorial blogs, but credible outlets like *The New York Times*, *Atlantic*, and *Scientific American*—have helped me sort out some of what's happening in the Pacific Ocean, but I'm still not confident that science knows enough to predict what's still going to happen to Japan and America's seafood supply over time. There's so much information, so little understanding. All these conflicting sources—I can't make sense of them, can't synthesize.

Although we know that oceans are large and dynamic enough to dilute many poisonous materials, all that we don't know could fill thousands of oceans. In the meantime, I keep reading more sources, and cans of sanma stack up in our basement. Nearly every week, I serve the little fish over rice. When it's cold out, I crave their flavor. The weeks I resist feel emptier without them, but I resist because I can't decide if I need to stop.

* * *

In 2013, South Korean banned all imports of fish from eight Japanese prefectures: Fukushima, Iwate, Miyagi, Aomori, Ibaraki, Gunma, Chiba, and Tochigi. South Korea found the Japanese government's response to the disaster too weak to instill confidence in its seafood. Japan didn't have a clear enough plan about how to contain the radioactive water that the Daiichi plant was leaking into the ocean. They still don't. Japan contested the ban with the World Trade Organization, claiming a lack of scientific evidence. Korea hasn't lifted the ban.

The phrase "Made in Japan" used to signify high quality. After WWII, the nation built itself into one of the most innovative, technologically advanced, and wealthy nations in history. By the 1980s, Japan's prosperity and industrial efficiency was the envy of the developed world. Consumers trusted Japanese products. Japanese automobile manufacturing systems were so sophisticated and efficient that American car companies tried to replicate them. Decimated by the War, Japan had something to prove. It labored for decades to claim its place in the world economy, and to repair its pride. It succeeded. Nuclear energy helped power its ascent.

Since China's rise into a world power, the phrase "Made in China" started to make Americans worry about the quality of Chinese exports: was this dog food laced with melamine? Was there lead in this plastic toy's paint that would poison my kid? Ours became an era of counterfeit Chinese mutton and honey products that contained no pollen, and "Made in China" became shorthand for cheap and questionable. As time passed after Fukushima and the sad Pacific swirled, some people started seeing the phrase "Made in Japan" the same way, casting its famed white rice and green tea into doubt, and left some of us wondering if Fukushima's radiation would ever reach American shores.

* * *

On a remote beach on Graham Island, British Columbia in 2012, a Canadian man found Ikuo Yokoyama's rusty Harley Davidson motorcycle. Yokoyama had stored his bike in a white cube container in his backyard in Miyagi Prefecture. The tsunami swept it away and killed three members of the twenty-nine-year-old's family.

In Washington's Olympia National Park, another Misawa dock landed on a rugged stretch of coast between the Hoh River and the town of La Push.

In the Gulf of Alaska, radar technician David Baxter found a soccer ball near the FAA's radar station on Middleton Island. The teenage owner, Misaki Murakami, had written his name on it, so Baxter and his wife shipped Murakami's ball back to him in Iwate Prefecture.

Throughout coastal Alaska, spray cans, building insulation, plastic bottles, Styrofoam, and oyster farm buoys were washing ashore and worrying locals. "Whatever happens in the ground or air or sea," Tlingit Tribal President Victoria Demmert told CNN, "will end up in our bodies." Wildlife eat the plastic, and people eat the wildlife—not just subsistence hunters like the Tlingit, but anyone who buys Alaskan salmon, which is a lot of people. Alaska produces approximately 80 percent of North America's commercial wild salmon.

At the time of the Ryou-Un Maru, some experts predicted that the mass of debris would hit the US coastline in either March 2013 or March 2014. Eight months after the tsunami, one conspiracy-minded website warned, "The largest pieces of radioactive tsunami debris could arrive on [the] West Coast of US and Canada 'within days.'" No mass ever hit. The material that hadn't sunk had dispersed across a 4,500 mile long area so that, five weeks after the tsunami, the National Oceanic and Atmospheric Administration could no longer see the debris fields by satellite. But it wasn't just visible debris that concerned people.

According to one color-coded map that went viral online, the imperceptible menace that author William Vollmann calls "invisible and insidious" in his 2015 Harper's article was still out there, swirling and churning and making its radioactive way closer to Hawaii and America, and presumably moving up the trophic ladders from plankton to tuna and salmon.

Scientists had a good grasp of the impact of Fukushima radiation on land. In the ocean, the scale of the disaster was too great for even experts to fully decode, its location too complex. Oceans are mysterious. We only understand a fraction of what occurs in them. We understand very little about where and what salmon do when they leave rivers to feed in the ocean. We don't know much about young Pacific albacore tuna's migration routes before age three, only that they swim back and forth across the Pacific to feed and spawn. In fact, as Oregon State University research assistant Delvan Neville said, the small safe traces of the "Fukushima fingerprint" isotope cesium-134 that his team found in Oregon albacore between 2008 and 2012 provided additional details into the fish's migration route between Japan and the West Coast that science didn't previously have. The cesium levels in those tuna were safe, but the concern was about what would happen in coming years.

A few months after Fukushima, Ken Buesseler, an oceanographer at the Woods Hole Oceanographic Institution in Massachusetts, assembled a research team of seventeen scientists to sample the seawater, plankton, and fish near the Fukushima Daiichi facility. Buesseler knew someone had to measure the disaster's marine impact in order to establish a baseline for coming changes. So in 2011, for fourteen days and nights, his team labored out on the ocean collecting samples, which were later tested by sixteen different international laboratories.

Plutonium-239 has a half-life of 24,000 years. Strontium-90 has a half-life around 29.1 years. Cesium-137's half-life is 30.17 years, cesium-134's is two years, and tritium's is 12.3 years. That means that ten half lives must pass—about 123 years—before tritium's radiation levels fall to something close to pre-contamination level. In that time, nucleotides like cesium and strontium accumulate in your bones and decimate your thyroid.

At the end of the research trip, Ken Buesseler wrote in his web journal:

"We've been out here 24/7 on a specialized research ship for almost two weeks with millions of dollars in equipment gathering more than 1,500 samples and thousands of gallons of seawater and the only thing we can say for certain is that, yes, there is radiation in the water and some of it came from Fukushima. Not exactly a stop-the-presses story. That will come later, but will anyone care at that point?

...It's easy to see how the public could become frustrated with science and the scientific process. People want to know if it's safe to eat the fish or drink the milk. Decision-makers want to know what they should decide. Everyone wants the truth.

Scientists, though, cannot always arrive at definitive answers. There are error bars on data points and uncertainty clouding answers to even the most basic questions. There's a reason for that. We live in a complex world that does not always lend itself to simple answers or definitive yes-or-no responses. Science is not about the pithy sound bite—it's about reasoned responses and careful analysis of hard-won data."

Meaning: we had to get used to not knowing everything so quickly.

* * *

As I sat outside in the shade on my lunch break recently, a man walked up and started talking. "You're sitting outside in this heat," he said, "working on your computer. I should buy you dinner for not sitting in your car running the air conditioning. I mean, come on! This is Portland. Do something." He stared at me expectantly, waiting for agreement, affirmation, a response, anything, but I only gave him a glance before looking back down at my computer.

I only had six minutes left on my break. I was working on this essay when he approached, editing this sentence: "But the truth is as true as it was when the Native People fished the Northwest Coast, and when John Muir articulated it in his journals: everything is connected. If you thought you were safe, you were wrong."

The man kept talking. "I mean, do something. Right? Everyone's in their cars on their computers, staring at their computers and talking."

He held a nice leather attaché in his right hand. His blue and white Hawaiian shirt and tan cargo shorts were as clean and unwrinkled as the clothes of the other business people who walked by on lunch. He seemed manic, but he arrived like a prophet of doom.

"Here we are now," he said, "and everyone's just sitting in their car running the air conditioning, looking at Facebook, like everything's going to be fine tomorrow."

I wanted him to leave.

He stood there and stared.

I didn't engage. With my head down I said, "Have a good day, man."

He waved his hands as he walked off, saying, "There is not going to be a tomorrow."

* * *

At room temperature, cesium-137 occurs as a liquid. When it bonds with chlorides, it forms a powder. Besides nuclear reactors, the isotope is used in Geiger counters and medical and industrial devices.

In 1989, in apartment number 85, Building 7, on Gvardeytsiv Kantemirovtsiv Street in Kramatorsk, Ukraine, authorities found a small capsule containing cesium-137 embedded inside the concrete wall. The radioactive capsule probably originated in an industrial instrument, somehow ended up mixed with the cement before or during construction, possibly when the instrument was improperly disposed of, and scrappers resold the scavenged material. Nobody knows. Two separate families lived in the apartment during the nine years between the building's construction and the radiation's discovery. Leukemia killed six of them. Seventeen got sick and survived. The incident is known as the Kramatorsk radiological accident.

Two scrap metal collectors in Goiânia, Brazil broke into an abandoned hospital in 1985 and found a teletherapy unit. The private Institute Goiano de Radioterapia performed radiotherapy, a medical treatment that uses beams of radiation to kill localized cancer cells. When the hospital relocated, it partially demolished its former building and took its cobalt-60 teletherapy unit, but it failed to properly dispose of its caesium-137 unit. The scrappers heard that the site might contain valuables. In one of the derelict treatment rooms, the men found a 1950s model Cesapan F-3000 designed by Italy's Barazetti and Company. The sealed radioactive capsule was encased inside a heavy, rotating stainless steel and lead wheel. Assuming they could sell the metal, they carried the teletherapy unit's rotating assembly home in a wheelbarrow, laid it under a mango tree in one of their yards, and disassembled it, releasing the cesium. Over the course of days, the men vomited, felt dizzy, and had diarrhea. When one of the men's hands swelled up, he visited a doctor; the doctor attributed his symptoms to food allergies. It was the hand he'd gripped the machinery with. By then, they sold the parts to a neighboring junkyard. Exposed to the air in his garage, the junkyard owner noticed that the rice-sized particles glowed blue at night. The material mystified the man's friends and family, so he gave them some. Five days later, many came down with gastrointestinal issues, including his wife. After his wife linked the symptoms to the material, she took it in a bag on a bus to a doctor, and authorities later secured the compromised sites and treated twenty infirmed people in the hospital. Four weeks later, the junkyard owner's wife and three other people died. The remaining sixteen survived. The International Atomic Energy Agency called the incident "one of the most serious radiological accidents ever to have occurred." The house with the mango tree, and its topsoil, were destroyed.

The 1983 Chernobyl nuclear power plant disaster released huge amounts of cesium-137 into the Russian air and countryside. Winds carried it throughout Europe, with the greatest levels detected in Belarus, Austria, Ukraine, Sweden, and Finland. Domestic animals suffered mutations. Radiation appeared in alpine plants, and some European countries temporarily banned Russian imports.

The study of human knowledge is called Epistemology. This branch of philosophy addresses the nature of knowledge, its dispersal, acquisition, and reliability. This includes the ways information spreads throughout the human population. Sometimes information stays were it begins. Most times it travels from its source, morphing and accruing or diluting as its radius expands. Epistemologists want to know how much we can trust information, and how we can know what we know.

During the 1940s, '50s, and '60s, the US military tested nuclear weapons at sites throughout the Marshall Islands in the North Pacific, in what's called the Pacific Proving Grounds. These sub-surface detonations released cesium-137 and strontium-90 into the ocean, air, and soil, and small quantities of both radioisotopes still circulate in the Pacific.

* * *

When sanma migrate from the tropics to Russia's cold coastal waters, Japanese, Korean, and Chinese fisherman lay out their nets. Around Japan's north island of Hokkaido, commercial saury season starts on August 15, and at the end of September for the other islands, but the meat is richest in fall. Between September and October, when the southbound fish pass back by Japan's west coast, fat from their Russian feeding, they contain the highest oil content—up to 20 percent. During this peak period, the sauries caught along Japan's Sanriku Coast, on the northwest corner of the main island of Honshu, are the most prized off all.

Sanriku lies on the opposite side of the island from Fukushima, but it's also high on the north side, and its proximity to Fukushima makes me wonder if the ocean currents might somehow spread the poison in the fish's direction. I haven't researched the currents on nautical maps, so I shouldn't draw paranoid conclusions. But sometimes I picture the sanma swimming through blue toxic water on their way up the Japanese coast, and I wonder if I have a death wish.

Beyond currents, what if the migrating sanma enter the plume as they travel between the south and the north to feed, consuming nucleotides as they head toward the warmer waters of Southeast Asia? Maybe it doesn't work that way. I've searched the web and books and can't find details. Together, all this information doesn't necessarily add up to anything, but the severity and weight of the information somehow feels conclusive. I still haven't quit.

This summer, we bought a grill. Sanma was the second thing I cooked on it. I bought two frozen fish from a Japanese grocer and dusted them with salt. That night, the air filled with the thick marine scent of charred flesh. Fat crackled as it dripped into the flames. Our dog came sniffing around for scraps. This is how people have cooked sanma for hundreds of years.

At the kitchen table, I pinned the fish's head with my finger, sliced off the tail and ran my chopsticks along the length of its belly, creating two fillets. With the fish splayed open, I picked out as many of the tiny, numerous ribs as I could and used my chopsticks to pluck nice thick bites right off the spine. Bones, heads, spines, fins—to me, the flavor and nutrition far outweigh the effort. I also ate the guts. I'd been wondering about their bitterness. How bitter was bitter? The sharp, mineraly bite of the dark organs filled my mouth, and I quickly washed it down with water.

The Japanese are an island nation defined by their relationship with the ocean. If I have to stop eating sanma, I only lose one dish and the idea of a healthy meal. If the Japanese have to stop eating it, they not only lose their food, they lose one connection to their history, and part of their identity with it.

* * *

On February 19, 2015, trace amounts of radioactive cesium-134 and cesium-137 were found in samples gathered from a dock in Ucluelet, a small town in Pacific Rim National Park Reserve, on Vancouver Island, BC. The levels registered below Canada's safe legal limit. A seawater sample taken about 745 miles west of Vancouver had already tested positive for cesium-134 in October, but this February sample was the first time Fukushima radiation had been identified on North America's western shore. Ken Buesseler tested it.

Irritated that the US government had steadily reduced, rather than increased, its Fukushima monitoring and research efforts, Buesseler crowd-founded his own citizen-science monitoring agency in 2014, called the Center for Marine and Environmental Radioactivity (CMER). He installed four monitoring stations off the Oregon coast, and he began analyzing seawater samples that researchers and volunteers sent to his Massachusetts laboratory. In conjunction with a Canadian-funded program called InFORM, led by University of Victoria scientist Jay Cullen, CMER planned to add a dozen more stations along coastal British Columbia, with the Scripps Institution of Oceanography adding another ten. Anyone concerned about Fukushima and public safety knows that only fools trust the government, and Buesseler's work provided qualitative evidence of the government's disregard: an independent researcher was the first to discover Fukushima radiation on the West Coast, not a government agency.

The sample contained 1.4 becquerels of cesium-134 per cubic meter (Bq/m3), and around 5 Bq/m3 of cesium-137. A becquerel is a unit of radioactivity. For comparison, Japanese waters contained 50 million Bq/m3 following the meltdown, and they contain 1,000 Bq/m3 now. Canada considers 10,000

Bq/m3 of cesium-137 the safe legal limit. "Even if the levels were twice as high [as 1.4 Bq/m3], you could still swim in the ocean for six hours every day for a year and receive a dose more than a thousand times less than a single dental X-ray," Buesseler wrote. "While that's not zero, that's a very low risk."

That seemed like good news. But I no longer know what to think.

I'm worried. My wife's worried. Some of our friends are worried, though some of them are inclined to neurotic anxiety. Still, the threat is real. The other threat: the unknown. The human mind likes what talk shows call "closure." It tries to make full circles. It prefers completed puzzles to pieces. We struggle to live with enduring mystery, because lingering questions physiologically disturb our minds. God, cosmic meaning, the afterlife, the "truth" about Fukushima—the unsettling effect of such knowledge gaps linger in the mind, circulating like nucleotides until we resolve them with answers from science or religion. The ocean still feels too big to instill confidence in me. The scientific method is objective, but it still requires belief; you have to trust the methods. I trust science. When it comes to discerning truth, we have devised no better system. But when it comes to disasters that involve top-heavy governments, I'm also a cynic.

* * *

"No one will die from Fukushima radiation," *Forbes* wrote in March 2015, "there will be no increased cancer rates, the food supply is not contaminated, the ocean nearby is not contaminated, most of the people can move back into their homes, and most of the other nuclear plants in Japan can start up just fine."

Eight months after that article, in October, a study linked Fukushima radiation with increased rates of thyroid cancer in local children. Of 370,000 kids tested in Fukushima Prefecture, 137 had confirmed or suspected cases of thyroid cancer—a rate twenty to fifty times higher than kids outside the Prefecture.

That same month, researchers Ken Buesseler and Jay Cullen announced that their monitoring efforts show that, despite the damage to

Japan, North America's West Coast remains unaffected by Fukushima radiation. As PBS reported:

"'To be very direct about it . . . at the levels that we're seeing, if one were to consume 20 kilos [over 40 pounds] of salmon in a year, the dose that one experiences from consuming that fish is about 300-fold less significant than if you're a pack-a-day cigarette smoker,' said Jay Cullen, an associate professor of ocean sciences at the University of Victoria, at a recent presentation of his latest data."

Cullen and Ken Buesseler, a senior scientist at the Woods Hole Oceanographic Institute, found no trace of radioactivity from the meltdown of the Fukushima Dai-ichi nuclear reactor in fish collected off British Columbia. Rather, the faint traces of radioactivity they found can be traced to weapons testing done over the Pacific in the 1960s and '70s.

* * *

Four and a half years have passed since Fukushima, and here's what I know for sure: I moved to Oregon in 2000. I've visited the coast countless times. The water still looks clean, the blue still true. It's always been too cold for me to swim in without a full wetsuit. I like to dip my toes. Sometimes I get in to my knees. Sometimes I submerge my ankles. Mostly, I stand on the rough sand shivering, gazing at the horizon, and I let the frigid waves wash over my feet with consecutive lines of foam. It's the same foam that washed away entire Japanese villages.

During the week, the fish keep sizzling in my skillet, and cans tower on my shelves. With the way I eat, I've put the ocean inside me. This water composes part of my cells. Its protein has become my protein, its trouble my trouble, while its little fish carry me toward a future I don't yet know.

As forty-two-year-old Koriyama resident Ritsuko Kamino told *The Japan Times* in 2015, "It's better not to live in fear." Eight months after the Fukushima meltdown, she left Koriyama and moved to the city of Naha nearly 1,300 miles to the south, on the Japanese island chain of Okinawa. Thanks to its clean environment and diet, Okinawa has one of the densest populations of centenarians in the world. As Kamino spoke to the reporter, she checked radiation levels on her own meter and advised her seven-year-old son not play outdoors.

A RECKLESS AUTONOMY

The thud of slamming car doors jolted me awake. Car doors had been slamming in the underground parking lot for what felt like the entire night, but when I pulled back the thin sheet to check my phone, I realized they'd probably only been slamming for part of the morning. It was 7:31 a.m. I'd gone to sleep just after 2:30.

I stretched my legs as far as the back seat of my truck would allow. Right outside my window, hotel guests dragged wheeled luggage toward the lobby, letting their big oblivious footsteps pound atop the pavement. One of the slammed doors set off a car alarm, and now a high-pitched squeal was echoing through the parking structure like the angry call of a predatory bird. With the sheet back over my head, I squeezed my eyes tight and took a deep breath. When I awoke later it was almost 8:15. In forty-five minutes the hotel would stop serving its complimentary breakfast.

This was my vacation. I had driven to Tucson from Phoenix to see a Bay Area band play. Countless bands were returning home from South By Southwest, and most had booked shows along the way. Since I'd missed this particular band the last time they played Phoenix, I drove the two hours south to Tucson, caught the show, slept in my truck in some chain hotel parking lot, then drove straight to Los Angeles the morning before to see another band perform that night. Seven hours one way, four hundred eighty miles, burning ninety dollars worth of gas, without enough money to sleep anywhere but my truck. It wasn't even my truck. I'd borrowed it from my dad. My dented, fifteen-year-old Toyota Corolla had tiny cracked tires and a grimy, rattling engine that was liable to die somewhere in the desert. Also, the Corolla wasn't a suitable place to sleep. Dad's pickup stood high off the ground. Its back seat was long and wide, and the windows were tinted enough to conceal its contents—factors, when combined, that make ideal sleeping quarters.

As strange as it sounded, I'd been sleeping in cars on roadtrips since I was twenty, so long that I even had a name for it: car-camping. I'd car-camped alone on both extended trips and weekend excursions, had car-camped with an ex-girlfriend and car-camped with friends. I'd slept in the camper shell of my old Toyota pickup, in a rented Subaru station wagon, in the back of a mini-van, back seat of a sedan, and in the back of a rented SUV, not just in my home state of Arizona, but throughout California, Oregon, Washington, Texas, and British Columbia. Many people found the practice dangerous. "Just get a room," they'd say. "Spend the money to be safe." They were missing the point. If I spent money on rooms every night, I couldn't afford the trip. I only rented rooms if I needed a full-body wash and couldn't find a free shower at a public beach or a pay one at a truck stop. I could wash my face, hair, arms, and teeth in gas station bathroom sinks—not as thorough as what's called a "bird bath," but clean enough that I looked presentable in public. What little money I had went to food and gas.

Anyway, back in my twenties, sleeping in the car was part of a trip's appeal. It was adventurous, and adventure was fun. And car-camping not only freed you from having to pay exorbitant prices at chain motels, it let you overnight in towns that were too tiny to have motels, and in landscapes too wild to contain much infrastructure. With the right car, properly equipped, you could park on old national forest logging roads, on public beaches, or on residential side streets in beach towns. You could park in cul-de-sacs overlooking pastures and in state parks' developed campsites. Then, you could wake up to gorgeous views of beaches, mountains, and lakes—just lower your truck's tailgate and be greeted by a cool breeze and the sort of scenery travelers paid big money to see from their hotel balcony. I'd cooked many breakfasts on my Coleman stove in front of such scenes. Granted, sleeping on a side street in Mission Beach or a dirt road in the backcountry posed certain threats that you had to prepare for, but if you could successfully avoid getting robbed, killed, or kicked out by security guards, then what you experienced was a pure type of freedom, an invigorating autonomy, too rare in everyday life. Most people didn't understand this.

Sixteen years and a lifetime later, I was still doing this.

The upscale Residence Inn I'd found in Burbank was shaded and safe. It stood along I-5, a few feet from perpetually roaring traffic, on the edge of the city's tiny downtown. If I had company, we would have split a cheap room, but none of my closest friends could join me on this trip. Dean had just lost his job, moved back in with his parents and was scouring the city for work. Chris had an eight-month-old baby to care for, was back in school finally earning his bachelor's, and he and his wife were struggling to pay their mortgage. JT managed a big copy center and mostly stayed at home with his girlfriend and her kid. Alex had a kid too, a demanding job, and a crazy ex whose joint custody gave him constant headaches. Somehow all the crap we'd once dismissed as the bleak concerns of geezers had caught up with us. Well, not with me. I might not have had enough disposable income to fund many trips like this, but I hadn't committed myself to kids or mortgages, either. I was single, self-employed, subsisted off of taco carts and ham sandwiches, and only rented apartments. Such concessions guaranteed that my time was mine to fill. I could stay up till 2:00 a.m. reading if I wanted to, or hike in the mountains on a whim, with no fear of abandoning or disappointing anyone else. I had no one to account for but myself. I was also at that age where you started to wonder if the life you'd fashioned in youth could nourish your adult heart.

But this band was one of my favorites—still underground but on the verge of blowing up—and they were playing three consecutive LA shows. Last night's took place inside some guy's apartment in an old warehouse east of downtown. Marketing types called it a "live/work space," but it was really a long brick rectangle where he could fit both his VW Bug and a bed. Tonight's show was on the UC Irvine campus, seventy-five freeway miles to the south, inside a trailer that doubled as a classroom. I refused to let age or finances interfere with my enjoying life. So I left everyone to their regular lives and drove west alone. It made me think of that Stooges song "No Fun," where Iggy sings: "No fun, my babe, no fun/No fun to be alone/Walking by myself/No fun to be alone/In love with nobody else." Admittedly, Iggy was sixty-something years old then, his slack, wrinkled skin draped atop his ribs like a Shar Pei's, but he still played shows, still climbed atop amps and flung around the microphone, and when he spoke, he spoke with the same intelligence and wit. He'd lived his life on his terms and succeeded, financially and personally, and wrote some of the world's most timeless songs and seemed to have fun doing it. I envied that. In my teens I had vowed never to spend my best years enslaved to some mind-numbing office job just to earn a check, squandering my decades in a florescent-lit cubicle rather than out doing what satisfied me. And, here I was.

Inside the truck, trapped breath and body heat turned the cool spring air into a furnace, slicking my chest with sweat. The car alarm had finally stopped, though. Guests were no longer chattering loudly or dragging luggage. The hush made me want to go back to sleep. But I knew I needed to take advantage of that breakfast—and steal as many teabags and packets of instant oatmeal as my pockets could hold—so I could put the money I saved on food into my gas fund. With a yawn I pushed off the covers, rubbed my itchy eyes and felt around for my clothes. I'd find a place to shower later.

My clothes lay under the passenger seat and stunk of other peoples' cigarettes and beer. Keeping my head down, I dug through my backpack and pulled out a wrinkled black collared button-up and dark Levi's from the box on the floor. Since I wanted to sleep here again tomorrow night, I had to follow the prime directive of my car-camping system: remain undetected. So, lying on my back, I pulled on my pants and shirt, careful not to shake the truck, and before sitting up to tie my shoes, I made sure there was no bright light source that would cast me in silhouette. Understandably, people tend to get suspicious of people in the back of parked cars.

Another car-camping technique I'd developed over the years: be cautious when stepping out of the car in the morning. You don't want anyone to notice that you slept in it. When you open the back door, people will be able to see in, and the more observant few might notice the pillow and blankets on the seat, and the luggage on the floor. It's not hard putting two and two together. Also, to anyone watching, it will look weird seeing you step out of the back seat rather than the front. To avoid this you have to climb over the armrest and exit from the driver's door, as any normal person would. The thing is, to anyone who's been standing there long enough to notice that you didn't just pull into that spot, but had been parked there for eight hours, any exit might look strange. So, if anyone has been lingering nearby long enough to notice, I always let them gather their luggage and go inside first. If there are security cameras with their lenses aimed my direction, all I can do is hope that the person watching the security footage is as oblivious as most Americans and won't notice that I parked and never got out the entire night.

With my clothes on, I scanned the garage for cameras and onlookers, then climbed over the armrest and out the driver's side. Blood rushed to my feet. My knees didn't pop, though, and my neck didn't ache. It felt good to stand upright, released from that fetal position. I couldn't resist prolonging the sensation of normal circulation, so I pulled my foot behind my back to stretch my thigh muscles, thankful that, even at thirty-four, I needed no medications or special sleeping conditions to get by, suffered no health issues, like high cholesterol, back problems, or adult-onset diabetes brought on by lifestyle. I took moderately good care of myself: besides the temporary taco and sandwich diet, I ate salads, drank water, and no longer smoked. I had friends with migraines, permanent back pain, high blood pressure, therapeutic mattresses, special shoe inserts, hair plugs, slipped discs, carpel tunnel, sciatica, insomnia, acid reflux, bad knees, and others who constantly complained: "Oh, my allergies have been killing me;" "Oh my God, I've had a cough all month." I stretched my other leg and complimented myself on being able to sleep anywhere that I needed to. When I was twenty-two, I'd slept under a chair for three nights on the ferry from Bellingham to Alaska. I could still do that if necessary. It made me proud that I was old yet didn't act like it. Then I wondered if it was the other way around: maybe I was old and needed to act my age.

While the fog started to lift from my fatigued head, I noticed a white metal sign hanging on a cement column beside my truck:

Parking Only
for Hotel Guests
$15.00/Day

Please See Front
Desk for
Parking Permit

It was pitiful to think that, on my current budget, the amount of money many thirty-somethings dropped on two cocktails was what I tried to spend over the course of two days. The show last night was five bucks. Tonight's would likely be the same. If I parceled my resources correctly, I could spend fifteen dollars on food over the course of two days, but not all at once, and definitely not for parking.

Instead of making me feel savvy and industrious, this all made me question my lifestyle: no girlfriend, no money, no health insurance. Were music and fun all I wanted out of life? I leaned into the side mirror to fix what was left of my hair. It was thin up top, thick around the sides. I flattened a few rogue strands and studied my tired eyes—red slits ringed by dark bags. I rubbed them and stood up straight. Then I walked toward the lobby.

* * *

Counter to the usual progression of things, the older I got, the deeper my musical appreciations grew. I got into Blues in my late-twenties, got into mid-century hard bop jazz soon after. I went through a classical music period where I listened to Handel's Water Music and Bach's Brandenburg Concertos so frequently that a friend asked if I was going to start wearing white shirts with ruffles. Although my tastes kept expanding, music had always been one of my central preoccupations. My dad got me into it.

When I was a kid, we played a game. While he drove me to elementary school, we would listen to jazz or country on the radio, and I had to guess the musician. "Who's that?" Dad would say.

I'd tilt my ear toward the speaker. "Duke Ellington."

Then during the next song Dad would smile and glance at me sideways. "Who's that?"

"Sachmo," I'd say. And Count Basie, Bennie Goodman, Bob Wills, and Buck Owens. After a few years, I could name scores of them.

Most kids in middle and high school had their favorite bands. I had mine, too. Like most teenagers, my attachment to music was fierce and devoted.

When I was fourteen, some friends and I camped in front of a department store box office at the mall to get concert tickets. This was before the Internet. Tickets sometimes sold out so quickly that in order to secure them, you had to physically stake your claim. We did this multiple times. We would have our parents drop us off on the edge of the mall parking lot, where no one could see this embarrassing transaction. Then we would ignore their heartfelt goodbyes as we carried our blankets and pillows up the stairs to the store's outdoor entrance. Other kids usually beat us to the best spot right against the door: a birdlike boy with dyed-black hair and smeared mascara; two goth girls lounging on their backs, smoking cloves. My friends and I would lay our bedding down on the cement and try to make the next thirteen tedious hours as bearable as possible. This was before iPods or good portable video games. We had to talk to pass the time.

As the night wore on, other kids would show up. They'd lie atop their sleeping bags, open bags of chips and chatter about the band: I love the guitarist; I love this album; I saw them play in Albuquerque; I've wanted to see them for years. Despite the fear of losing our place in line, my friends and I would sometimes walk to a nearby convenience store and get candy and giant forty-four ounce sodas—anything to kill an hour. When the rising sun would start to brighten the eastern horizon, everyone would get excited, not just about the tickets, but about the impending release from our boredom. The sky is glowing orange! It must be nearing 9:00 a.m.! Then we'd look at our watches: nope, only 7:00. We ate more chips and sucked soda, and when an employee finally unlocked the doors she would warn us, "No running," and everyone would run toward the box office, weaving through the home furnishings department, past displays of coffee makers and saucepan sets, frenzied fans treating each other like enemies on a battlefield rather than kindred spirits who had just spent the night in bed together sharing their deepest musical obsessions.

By the time my friends and I turned sixteen, few shows required these extreme measures. The bands we listened to played small clubs who sold tickets through local record stores, which also sold zines and seven-inches and books of tattooed pinup girls, all of which made us feel part of an elite group of insiders privy to a shadow universe that existed under the surface of the larger, dumber, consumer-droid culture.

Punk, surf, rockabilly, psychedelic—throughout our teens and twenties we saw hundreds of shows, from Bad Brains to The Mermen to The Cramps. We saw bands that were nobodies that later became legendary, saw bands that were legendary and whose members are now dead. I stored all of the tickets and flyers in a box in my closet.

Friends and I still talked about certain moments over a decade later. "Remember when the sax player in the Nixon mask blew fire over our heads?" "Remember when they pushed their amps over and left mid-set?" "Remember when the drummer nodded out and his cigarette fell and lit the set list on fire?" These excited reminiscences were often followed by the refrain: "That's still one of my favorite shows ever."

Even now, I craved such rogue exhibitions, the wildness and spontaneity. What I also craved was the camaraderie. Being sandwiched between hundreds of sweaty strangers in a crowd right up against the stage, your shoulders unnaturally bent, stomach pressed against someone's pudgy back while someone else's forearm pressed against your ass, all that flesh squished together in a bizarre, malodorous union, and for that one hour of music, that brief moment in your otherwise routine life, you were family. You weren't cutting each other off on the freeway. You weren't vying for the last parking spot or grumbling to yourself in the grocery store line about how long they took to swipe their credit card and step aside, because really, my God, how fucking hard was it to turn the card's magnetic strip in the direction shown on the keypad and move on already? No. You were kin. Brothers and sisters united in a bloodline of shared passion: to hear loud music and collectively unhinge. Cups of beer whizzed past your face. Elbows occasionally speared your temple. But if someone fell down in the crowd, you picked them up. If someone turned pale green, you asked if they wanted out. If they said yes, you lifted them up and gently passed them to guards over the security partition. And when you danced, your body moved with theirs.

I would never be able to carry on without these moments. People who didn't enjoy live music confounded me, the same way certain asymmetrical sea creatures who moved through water without fins or visible appendages confounded me. Life was visceral experience, not just the pursuit of security and the avoidance of discomfort. As I texted Chris after last night's warehouse show: "I'd sleep in twenty gutters to see that again."

I'd told him about this band months ago. "You have to hear them," I said. Within weeks he was playing their songs as compulsively as I was.

Chris was my age. We'd known each other for eighteen years, when he was thin and I wasn't half bald, and he was the last people in our group of guys who remained equally consumed by music: always up on new bands, constantly suggesting records to check out. Most of the best shows we'd seen as kids, we'd seen together. And for the past few years—while everyone else went to bed early, or stayed home watching TV, complaining how loud guitars hurt their ears—he and I still went to shows, weekdays or weekends, no matter how late.

But things had changed. Where previously we would email with news that so-and-so was playing next Thursday, his common response to such emails now was: "Sorry, can't go. It's my turn to feed the baby." Feeding time was 5:00 a.m. He and his wife Sasha took turns. They were trying to get their eight-month-old daughter Liv on a set sleep schedule, but she still woke up crying in the middle of the night. He got up four times one night last week. The average number was three. He and Sasha also took turns getting up to check on her at night. When Chris and I did go to shows, he asked Sasha for what he half-jokingly called "permission"—permission to stay out late, permission to drink too much beer. It really wasn't a request so much as a pre-apology for how tired, hungover, and useless he was going to be the next day. Sasha didn't make him ask permission. She didn't guilt him about wanting to go out, and she loathed the term permission for all it implied about the balance of power and the nature of married life. He just felt guilty about making her carry all the responsibility.

They traded feeding morning duties when she could, and he would text her from the show: "How's Liv? You two okay? Love you." But when work or fatigue meant Sasha couldn't trade, Chris ended up on his couch at home

255

trying not to pout, and I ended up standing in the audience alone, milling around between sets and sending him texts: "Man, you would've loved this." I wasn't rubbing it in. I was just excited, and he was one of the few people who understood why. What I couldn't tell him—and what I hope he didn't sense in my messages—was that I preferred this to parenting, preferred it to most anything really—to date nights spent watching movies on couches, to waking up early to have breakfast with my parents, to the comforts and security of a good job, and increasingly, it seemed, to adulthood itself.

Unlike regular life, live music was rarely dull or predictable. It also elevated my existence without committing me to the sort of job required to finance the eighteen-plus year task of parenting. I felt self-absorbed thinking this, even immature. So many of my friends who had kids constantly extolled parenting's virtues: "You can't imagine how much joy kids bring you," they'd say, "that you could love another human being so deeply." Baby's first steps, baby's first day of school, the quiet moments at home alone when they looked up at you and said, I love you dad—"It's so rewarding. I would throw myself in front of a car for that kid." I believed them. I felt that way about my parents. Yet these were the same people who admitted: I'm always tired; I'm buried in chores; I have no time to myself; I worry I'm doing it all wrong; sometimes I can't breathe; I'm stuck at my job at least until she starts middle school; I wish I could just jump in the car and drive to the beach and talk to no one. At night they drank too much wine to cope, or smoked occasional cigarettes even though they'd officially quit. And they warned me to be careful on this trip, to rent a motel room or not go at all, all while insisting that "Fun doesn't end once you have a kid." Maybe my thoughts on parenting would change. "Once you meet the right person," Sasha told me, "you'll feel differently." Part of me believed her. I felt a parental instinct. Their baby Liv was a grinning, crawling, gurgling bundle of chubby pinchable dough, and I turned mushy every time I saw her: got on the ground to play, showed her how to pet the cat, lapsed into a ridiculous goo-goo voice. But between the fatigue, bills and lack of free time, I doubted I could handle all aspects of parenting, and despite Sasha's wisdom that meeting your mate changes things, I'd given up hope that I'd ever meet the right person. So I turned my attention elsewhere.

The history of music was marked by a few, fleeting, magical junctures: 1957 in New York jazz, 1962 in Liverpool, 1967 in San Francisco, 1970 in Detroit, 1990 in Seattle, the mid-'70s at CBGB's. Stars had aligned to produce so-called local "scenes" whose underground bands ended up transforming music throughout the world. Whatever it was that caused such things, that mysterious convergence of talent, timing, and personalities, it was happening again right now on the West Coast, and somehow—by good luck and staying up on new music—I'd found out about it.

If the musical eras that Chris and I had lived through in our teens were any indication of future patterns of history, then I knew that this moment would pass as quickly as the rest. The underground bands would one day be discovered by the larger culture. They'd start playing big cavernous venues with higher ticket prices and higher percentages of meatheads in the crowd. They'd tour constantly to spread the word, put out numerous singles and albums to feed the furnace of popular demand while it was hot, and as the musicians aged and tired of the road, they'd likely tire of their own musical ideas, abandon their previous style, and their song-writing would change—suffer, possibly. And as they played the same songs over and over for years and years and things became as routine as a job, their shows would lose the power and purity that once made them monumental. Read any book on music history. This was often the pattern. But right now, these particular West Coast bands were young and energetic, their music fresh and unprecedented, and their intimate shows still overlooked enough to feel like a dirty little secret. Future fans would look back on this year in awe and wish they could have experienced it. And we, the informed obsessives, would know that we did experience it—that we were there—not to brag or feel superior, but to relish the fullness that comes from devouring something of substance, be it food, foreign lands, or a whole era at the height of its artistic potency. It was rare that you were aware that something culturally significant was happening while it was happening. Usually such appreciations occurred in hindsight. But I was aware of it. Chris was too. He had a different life now.

I wasn't going to miss it.

* * *

I arrived at the venue around 5:30 last night to scope it out. The band's website listed no start time, no place name, only an address followed by the letters "LA." It was seductively cryptic. I figured the location was either an art gallery or some crumbling bungalow where people drank beer on the dead lawn and the band set up in the living room. Either would be sufficiently rowdy and intimate.

Before I found a safe hotel lot to sleep in, I drove to the venue, to make sure I had the right place so I wouldn't miss the music. The place was in the old warehouse district, a gritty industrial section ringed by freeways, southeast of downtown, where the city's famous Art Deco bridges crossed the empty cement channel of the Los Angeles River. My friends and I had passed this area countless times as teenagers while driving to the beach. It appeared solely as a sea of shabby roofs on the other side of the elevated freeway. Having watched movies like *Repo Man* and *Boyz in the Hood*, I imagined the world down there as a post-apocalyptic no-man's land where the homeless cannibalized each other, gang members carjacked you, and every fence was barbed and covered in shredded plastic bags. Turns out, the area wasn't so bad.

West of Alameda ran a number of streets where trash tumbled past parking meters that no cars parked in front of, and where people built shanties out of cardboard and sat on the curb drinking from bottles. But on the other side of Alameda, the area had been repackaged as the Downtown LA Arts District, and many of the old warehouses were being transformed into fancy lofts for people who wanted some idealized experience of urban living. In the coming years, the area gentrified. Back then, the process was only beginning. It still had grit. It didn't have many coffee shops. There was a gun club in one building, a sound stage in another. One was being repainted, another torn down. Some of the old buildings were still skuzzy, though, like the off-white one at the end of 6th that had a sign painted on it that read "Global Farms Enterprises, Inc. Garlic & Ginger Wholesale Distributors." And the one that I assumed was the venue.

A large banner ad stretched across the front. "Downtown Artist Spae .com," it said, misspelled:

RENT WORK SPACE w/ TOOLS

Fabrication Creation Location

I parked and studied the row of metal security grates that ran along its pale grey front, a shade as lifeless as old bologna. A young guy in jeans and a white tank top shuffled into one of the units. It was the only unit whose open door wasn't covered by a grate. I got out of the truck and approached it. A white, late-'60s VW Bug sat parked in the opening. Beyond that stretched a long rectangular corridor. The floor was cracked cement, the walls exposed brick, painted white in places, tan in others. A few pipes ran up the sides alongside some wires. "Hey," I said. "This where the show is tonight?"

The kid in the tank-top sat in a chair against the wall. "Yeah," he said.

"How much is it?"

"I think five." He scratched his shaved head and yelled, "Troy!" Then, "He'll know. He lives here."

The guy at the other end of the unit dropped the huge rug he was dragging and looked up. He was over six feet tall and wore the same outfit as the first guy: tight blue jeans, heavy black work boots, a white tank top, and suspenders hanging from his waistband. They looked like skinheads, but no Nazi punks would be listening to the sort of psychedelic garage bands that were playing tonight.

"Is this your work space?" I said.

"Yeah," he said, stepping beside me. "I mean, I live here too. It's live/ work." He said he was a musician. Then he stopped talking and stared at me, suspicious of my presence. He seemed to contemplate my motives. I complimented his place to disarm him and said I'd driven all the way from Phoenix for the show. "Whoa," he said. "Phoenix?"

I didn't mention Tucson. For some reason, standing there with these strangers, all the clothes and bedding stuffed in my car, my enthusiasm for music suddenly embarrassed me. All I said was, "I just love this band. They're like no other." It was the truth, but there was the detailed truth, and then there was the simple truth you told people.

He offered his hand. "Troy."

"Nice to meet you. Aaron."

The other guy stood up and shook my hand. "I'm Robbie." He lived in a unit a few doors down.

I asked when the show started, and Troy ran his hand across his head, wagging it side to side. "Well, I dunno, nine? Eight? There's four bands. My band opens."

A young brunette woman emerged from the rear. To Troy she said, "You want me to work the door?" He shrugged. She sat down on a stool and started texting.

When the phone in Robbie's hand rang, he checked the number and handed it to Troy. "Excuse me a second," Troy said, holding it to his hear. "Hey, what's up. Yeah." I gave him a wave, told Robbie that I'd see him tonight. Then I drove past downtown and up the I-5 in search of a place to sleep. The Residence Inn was the first nice hotel I saw from the freeway, and when I exited to investigate, I spotted the underground lot, with its many parking spaces sheltered from the sun, and pulled in.

* * *

Once on a roadtrip when I was twenty-one, I woke up in my truck's camper shell, in the middle of the night, and thought I was in a grave. I was lying on my back. Everything was black. Something pinned my arms against my sides and pressed my legs together. The voice in my head said: I think I'm dead.

Filled with terror, I sat up and drew a breath and tried to get my bearings. I wiggled free of what turned out to be a sleeping bag and rubbed condensation off the window with a dirty sock. I peered through the glass. Nothing. Where was I? When I opened the back hatch, the familiar smell of forest rushed in: rich soil, moist air, plant life. As my eyes adjusted, the shapes of sword ferns came into focus, a deep blue light backlit trunks of trees. Then I remembered: I was in the coastal Redwoods. Alone, on vacation.

When I lay back down I was relieved, but I kept thinking, That's what it's like to be buried alive. You can't breathe underground.

* * *

I made one quick circle through the underground lot, confident that I would have no trouble parking there after the show let out. I got dinner, spent some time in a bookstore. Then I drove back to the warehouse district and parked on 6th near the bridge.

The street was empty. There were a few stars in the sky. Cars passed somewhere nearby, but no headlights shone. This wasn't the frenzied, traffic-choked LA I was used to. It felt peaceful, like a tiny desert town, comfortably decaying and happily forsaken.

When I reached Troy's place, two white wooden boards filled the entryway, spray-painted with the words "Happy birthday" in black. A cover, Troy later explained, to throw off police and dampen the sound. I slipped inside, paid my five bucks, and cut through the crowd to the side of the apartment that was functioning as the stage. People mingled all around. Men wearing dark sunglasses leaned against walls, chatting up women. Women in dark skirts and tight t-shirts sipped cans of Pabst. Nearby, the headlining band's bassist smoked and laughed at someone's joke. This felt more like a house party than a show. They'd even turned Troy's kitchen into a bar. A cloth screen enclosed one side of it, with a hole cut for drink orders. A hand-written sign said: $4 vodka, $4 whiskey, $1 beer. I looked around. There were only about sixty people.

I had missed Troy's band but caught the next two openers. The first was high energy, so good that I bought the cassette they had for sale. The second tore through a fuzzed out set of dark, sixties pop that had the crowd transfixed and swaying into each other. But when the music stopped, the crowd dispersed and left me exposed. I felt like an idiot standing by myself, killing time between sets with no one to talk to. There were only so many times you could look at your phone. As the band dismantled their equipment, I got some water at the bar. Most everyone around me was young and chic. The way they held their beers, the way they leaned in to each other, hands in their pockets, flirting, laughing. I took a sip of water then slipped outside.

The spring air relaxed me. Across the street stood an enormous warehouse where eighteen wheelers filled their cargo trailers with produce by day. East down 6th was quiet and dark. The road stretched outward, blank and flat until it reared in an arc like the back of a hissing cat into the bridge over the river. The street, skeleton warehouses, the dry riverbed—the world was halted and austere, a hollow carapace of unfulfilled potential awaiting redevelopment, not unlike how I felt.

I leaned against the wall and thought of Iggy Pop singing to an imagined woman: "Come on. Well, come on. No fun to be alone. No fun to be alone. Hang on, don't you let me go. No fun to be alone. Said to be alone." I twirled my phone and looked frequently at the time. I didn't want to go back inside until the headliners started. It was easier to hide, catch the show, then split, even though I knew it only drew my aimlessness into sharper relief.

Two members of one opening band stumbled outside to smoke. They were drunk, fumbling with a lighter. An empty beer bottle fell from the guitarist's hand and nearly shattered on the cement. He looked down at it in shock, then up at me, his mouth a huge O. "That was close," he said snickering.

I debated texting Chris. I wanted to at least tell him the basics, that the bands were stellar, the venue an apartment. I didn't want to make him feel bad about missing it, but I was so excited I had to tell someone, and I wanted him here.

An airplane passed overhead, its wingtips blinking like some sort of beacon to the lost. I listened to the hum of excited chatter indoors. "Happy birthday" said the words on the board. Happy, happy, happy. After a few more minutes, I slipped my phone in my pocket and went back inside.

A crowd had gathered in the far end of the apartment. The headliners were setting up. I weaved between people to the front. The four members adjusted knobs on amps, plugged in guitar pedals, checked mics with a tap. The lead singer pulled a worn green electric guitar from a case and spun it around twice by its neck, then rapidly spun it back in the opposite direction before draping it across his tattooed chest in one swift movement. A guy next to me to whispered to his friend, "That motherfucker is bad ass and all coked up." The singer took a long pull from a beer and set the can atop his amp. The audience watched in silence. Smoke from a joint wafted into the rafters.

In a spray of words as rapid as a hummingbird's heart, the singer spoke into the microphone: "Hey hey, we're The Terrierists from San Francisco. Thanks for coming out tonight, and thanks to Troy for having us." He hit a note on his guitar, sending a wave of distortion rumbling through the building, and with the words "One, two, three, four," the bass and drums kicked in, and the crowd flew into a frenzy.

Bodies jumped up and down. Bobbed side to side. Swung their heads and arms and hair like windmills. Sweaty skin slid against mine, soaking my clothes as the crowd jerked and swayed with the jittery volatility of kelp in a tide. There was no separation between audience and band. When the guitarist screamed, his face hung inches from ours. I stood beside the second vocalist. Her keyboard's plastic edge poked my leg. As much as everyone tried not to, it was hard not to bump her, let alone to stay upright. Kids kept getting thrown onto the drum set. One knocked over a cymbal. Most fell atop the bass drum, barely laying there a second before another dancer picked them up.

While tearing through a bunch of my favorite songs, the singer hopped in place, spit into the air and dragged the tip of his guitar across the rug while soloing, as if to gather sound from the static. Veins bulged in his neck. He tapped pedals that sent warped echoes through the air, and he and the keyboardist sang harmonies over them. When someone knocked over his microphone, he popped the stand upright with a flick of his shoe and gripped the tip in his teeth to steer it towards him.

Seconds passed between songs. One, two, three, then the next one. One, two, three, then another fast one, all fast ones.

Beer splashed my face. Empties were crushed at my feet. At one point the crowd surged and knocked the keyboardist to the ground. Arms went out and lifted her, and when she righted her mic, she sang her lines right on time.

I kept thinking, This band is going to be huge, completely explosively huge.

Despite all our frantic tossing, one short, chubby punk girl and I kept bumping into each other. She wore a jean jacket and dark pants, red lipstick and blonde bobbed hair. When her beer got bumped from her hand, it soaked my pant leg. She smiled and mouthed "sorry," and we waved our arms in sync for a moment until the crowd shifted and threw her sidelong. I caught her on her way down and stood her back up.

And then, as quickly as it started, the show ended. "Thank you warehouse," the singer said. Sweat poured from his chin.

The audience stood still. People wiped their faces. Eyes darted around, filled with energy and anxious for an encore, and when the band started packing up, the crowd dispersed. I stood there and texted Chris: "I'd sleep in twenty gutters to see that again." He didn't text back.

As people streamed out the front door, others stood around talking and finishing their beers. I spotted a guy by the merch table, slipping a digital recorder into his pocket. He wore a dark jean jacket, roomy jeans and black Converse All-stars. He looked older; his hair was white. And he, like me, was alone. "Hey," I said, "is there any chance I could get a copy of that recording?"

"Of course," he said. I fished a pen from my pocket so I could give him my email address. Neither of us had any paper, so he tore a piece off the brown paper bag that held the many records he'd just bought. "That was amazing," he said, "wasn't it?"

"Seriously unreal." I leaned the paper against the flimsy particleboard wall and scribbled my information. "I've seen a lot of shows, and that was no doubt one of the all-time best." He agreed. I handed him the scrap. "I'm Aaron, by the way."

"Mark." We shook hands.

Upon closer inspection, his clothes revealed more about him than he probably would have liked. Where other kids wore tight Levi's jean jackets, bright flannels, and worn Vans, Mark's jacket had a "Nightmare Before Christmas" logo above the front pocket. It appeared to be a promotional jacket, something people gave you at a premier maybe, or you mailed away for. His Converse were too clean to be anything but brand new, or maybe he only wore them when he went out. I felt guilty scrutinizing him from his clothes, especially since he'd offered to share his recording for free. But something about his demeanor made me self-conscious and uncomfortable.

He tucked the records under his arm. "Where do you live?"

"Phoenix. I drove out just to see them play."

"Wow," he said. "Phoenix. That's a long drive." I considered mentioning Tucson but stopped short. He sensed some hesitation and smiled; then he stole the words from my mouth: "But worth it."

"Worth every second."

The band had only played for fifty minutes.

"You going to the show at UC Irvine tomorrow?"

"Absolutely," I said. "And the third show after that. That's why I came."

Mark said, "Where are you staying?" My eyes darted to the side and I paused before answering. When I car-camped in my twenties, I announced it to everyone as if it were a badge of honor.

I looked up at Mark. "At a friend's in Santa Monica," I said. He nodded. His expression suggested that he didn't entirely believe me.

I did have friends in LA. The one in Santa Monica was getting ready to move to San Diego with his wife. The other two—one in the Valley, one near Venice—always insisted I call when I visited. "You always have a bed," they said, and they meant it. But I was busy ignoring the shifting horizon of middle age, busy chasing the same fading dream, so I didn't call.

"How about you?" I said. "You live nearby?"

"Redlands," he said. Even though my eyes registered no judgment, once the words left his mouth, he seemed anxious to take them back. I knew Redlands. It was a landlocked town of shaggy palms and toxic smog some fifty miles east of downtown. "It's really not so bad," he said, "maybe fifty or sixty minutes." He smiled dismissively, as if a fifty mile drive after 1:00 a.m. was no big deal, but I suspected the drive took longer. He had to go back tonight, he explained. He'd left his teenage daughter alone at home, and he had to work in the morning. It was Thursday night.

It wasn't difficult to understand how he, like me, was trying to disguise the consumptive intensity of his musical attachments, trying to look like less of a freak and avoid being typecast as the old guy who refused to grow up. And despite the differences in our clothing and the gray of his hair, there was no denying what he was: not only a kindred spirit, but precisely the person I might one day be if I kept living the way I was living.

I still couldn't tell if that was a bad thing or not.

In the awkward silence he held up a red twelve-inch record. "Have you seen this?" A flying dragon graced the front, its sinuous body drawn in a thin, black line. "It's a ten minute song. It takes up both sides of the record."

It hadn't seen it. It sounded awesome. "If I have any money left by Sunday, I'll have to get a copy."

We smiled again, nodded. Looked away. Then I said, "Alright, I'll see you in Irvine."

I got in line to use the bathroom and spotted a soiled-looking man pulling empty beer cans from the trash. His skin was leathery and brown. Dark swatches of dirt stained his jeans. With people all around him, he put the cans in a huge, swollen garbage bag and dragged it through the apartment and out the front door. Before I could figure out what I'd just witnessed, I heard "Oh my god!" It was the chubby punk girl.

She threw her arm around me and squealed, "My dancing partner!" I threw my arm around her and leaned in. "You totally caught me when I fell. And you totally shook your shit. You and me—" She pointed her fingers between me and herself "—friends for life. You know." With that she bumped her big hip into my butt, so I spun her around like a country waltzer and bumped my hip back into hers. She held up her beer and went, "Ha ha ha." Her breath reeked of booze.

I said, "How much fun was that show?"

She giggled. "Too much. And not enough." One of the pins on her jean jacket fell off, and when she went to pick it up, her beer spilled on the ground. Her friend appeared in the entryway and waved her over. "I have to go," she said, and gazed up at me with a disarming earnest. Strands of wet hair stuck to her temples. I felt the overwhelming need to ask her for her phone number, not to try to sleep with her, but to stay in touch and somehow be friends, maybe long distance email-buddies who occasionally met at shows. We'd shared something tonight that seemed too powerful, too personal, for us to just part ways and never see each other again.

Her green drunken eyes swam in their whites. Then she high-fived me and slipped out the door.

Ah, fuck it, I thought. I ducked into the dirty bathroom and suppressed my regrets.

Speeding up I-5 toward Burbank, I lowered all the windows and hung my arm outside. The wind cooled my face. Cars raced beside me in neighboring lanes, more cars than I expected for 2:00 in the morning. We swerved and weaved past each other as the eastern edge of the Santa Monica Mountains opened before us. A carload of teenagers darted by. All I could see were heads silhouetted in the back seat, a cigarette ember glowing inside the cabin. The sight made me wish I had someone here to share this with, but even alone, I was glad I had come. I wondered why I had ever questioned my enthusiasm, all the while knowing that I would question myself again the next time.

* * *

Muddy Waters once said that the daily life of a touring musician amounted to one hour of ecstasy and twenty-three hours of misery. Although I could play drums, I didn't consider myself a musician, but I did understand what he meant.

The next morning I walked through the parking garage toward the hotel lobby. My hair was greasy, my armpits damp. Beyond the sliding glass doors, the concierge clerk stood behind the front desk. The sight of his clean white collared shirt made my heart race a little. Every time I did this, I hoped my technique worked as well as it used to.

The theory was simple: project confidence, look like you belong there. Don't avoid everyone's eyes, but don't try to make eye contact with everyone either. Look neither eager nor guilty. Oblivious was best, so I always looked straight ahead and walked in like I'd been there a thousand times.

The glass doors slid open and I strolled in. The clerk looked up, and I nodded as I passed. From the corner of my eye I quickly assessed the layout: lobby in front, food to my right, bathroom to my left. Without missing a step, I turned left toward the men's room and stepped to the sink to quickly rinse my oily face. I stared in the mirror for a moment: eyes still red and puffy, ringed in black. I splashed my face with water and patted it dry with paper towel. They had nice paper towels, as thick and soft as cotton. Everything here was nice: faux marble countertops, potted plants beside each sink, the wicker basket of towels. I took another towel and shoved it in my pocket for later, then followed the scent of bacon and eggs down the hall.

A large crowd filled the dining room. Business people mostly, Indian or Pakistani, in their early thirties, all chattering about some ongoing conference. The men wore dark slacks and shiny collared shirts. The women also wore dark slacks and reflective, solid-colored button ups. They carried leather attachés and canvas computer bags, shoveled waffles, toast and sausage into their mouths, and guzzled coffee, lots of coffee.

I sauntered across the cushioned carpet, past a sign warning that breakfast was reserved for guests and that no one else was "allowed past this point," and I stepped into the small U-shaped room crowded with steam trays and tubs of cereal. Fellow diners swarmed around me as I filled a Styrofoam bowl with oatmeal and sprinkled it with crushed walnuts and cinnamon. On a plate I piled fluffy scrambled eggs, skillet potatoes, and a few strips of bacon, a greasy monument to American abundance and the ongoing feast of our good fortune. When no one was looking, I stuffed five bags of mint tea into my pants pocket, along with four packets of instant oatmeal, and I filled a cup of coffee for later.

I sat at a small window table behind a young woman with a baby in a highchair. The baby smacked its hands on her table. The woman took bites of a muffin then spooned applesauce into her child's mouth. Its mouth was ringed with food. Muffin littered the floor.

A teenage boy with obtrusive bangs walked by drinking orange juice. He sat down, brushed his bangs from his eyes, then tilted his head so the bangs flopped back in place. When I'd had long hair, I used to do the same thing. Now my head was colonized by the wispy sort of fuzz that ended up all over your bathroom sink rather than blocking your vision.

Maybe it wasn't parenting that bothered me so much as the mundane. Too much of life was just so earthly. If you broke down the activities that composed our daily existence, it didn't amount to much: which size garbage bag should I get? What's the difference between spearmint and wintermint? Did the cashier actually give me my 10 percent discount? Always scrub the counter so food particles don't stick. I needed something transcendent to counteract the blandness, even if it only lasted a few minutes. Which was the problem: it only lasted a few minutes. Then it was back to, Is fluoride healthier than fluoride-free? Back to this.

A flatscreen TV hung on the wall, playing CNN. The President was in Afghanistan, making a surprise visit to Karzai. Below the screen sat five older men, conducting some sort of meeting. They spoke in low solemn tones, and when they spoke, they often looked at the ceiling, as if there were important bits of information to gather there, or maybe looking for release. One had a yellow legal pad that he never wrote on. He just rubbed his palm across it, slowly moving it side-to-side.

Without warning, adrenalinee surged through me. I didn't understand why. I'd done this exact thing countless times before. I'd even stolen hotels' newspapers and read them by their pools. When I was younger I was so cocky that I would spend twenty minutes showering in a gas station bathroom. Paying customers would knock on the door, rattling the doorknob and getting impatient, and I'd wipe the water off the floor, put my toothbrush away and eventually strut out past them, carrying a small towel and toiletries bag, unaffected by their stares. But as I looked at my oatmeal, my heart raced and I thought, At market value, this stuff costs nothing, but if I get caught, it will be the most expensive starch I have ever eaten. If the clerk came over and asked what room I was in, would I just make up a number? What if I did and he said, "There is no 237 here, sir," and called the cops? I could bolt. I could get to my truck and onto the freeway before police arrived. But what if he summoned them without first confronting me? What would I say? "Oh, I'm just traveling on a budget, officer. Sorry." "You know better," police would say, "you're old enough to have kids. Act your age." And I would tell them: "Yes, I am."

Silverware clanked against plates. The din of adjacent conversations rose above the chatter in my mind. Slowly, I looked up. The businessman conducted their meeting. The teenager flicked his bangs. No one paid me any attention. On TV, the President stepped out of a helicopter and waved, and somewhere near Redlands, Mark was doing whatever it was he did for a living, and likely passing his day thinking about tonight's show in Irvine. Maybe he was wondering whether I would make it as I'd promised. Maybe he was wondering whether to leave his daughter at home alone again or to bring her along. If I was him, I'd bring my daughter along. He was probably thinking about the distance, too, calculating mileage, the drive time, and plotting the best route to take to avoid peak traffic, all the while comparing the real story to the fake story he would tell to anyone who asked where he lived. I had already done my calculation.

It was seventy-five miles from here to Irvine, a short drive if I went right now, a two hour drive during Friday rush hour traffic, which is what I would contend with because I wasn't going right now. I was going to walk out that door with my cup of coffee, and after I stored my stolen provisions in the cardboard box in the backseat of my truck, I was going to find a gas station bathroom to shower in, spend a few relaxing hours in a bookstore, maybe go to the beach or find a sunny park bench to lounge on and eat a decadent slice of coconut cream from Los Feliz's famous House Of Pies, then I would drive those seventy-five miles, traffic, high gas prices, and appearances be damned.

(BE)COMING CLEAN

I was riding the light rail to my second day of work, hours after visiting my new methadone clinic in Portland, Oregon, when I noticed the visual details of the Skidmore Fountain station. Solitary men in army surplus jackets leaned against the Burnside Bridge's support beams. Women with gaunt faces huddled together smoking. Like an angler trained to spot the promising fishing holes, I could tell a dope zone from a non-dope zone. It wasn't hard.

This was October, 2000. When I'd left my native Phoenix the previous week, I was twenty-five-years old, fresh off probation for felony heroin possession, and my fiancé Kari who I'd been living with had just abruptly dumped me with no more explanation than "I love you but I'm not in love with you." I interpreted that as "You're a loser," and at that point I was. She hadn't discovered my habit. She had only accepted what we'd both intuited for most of our three years: that we were a poor match. Yet as I watched my would-be mother-in-law help move Kari's belongings from our apartment, the loss of her stabilizing presence left me all the more aware of how adrift I'd become. Rather than sulk, I ran to Portland to work at a bookstore. How else could I fail? I'd so clearly hit rock bottom that any future catastrophes would surely seem like improvements in comparison. Aside from the staff at my clinic, nobody knew I was on methadone.

The Skidmore Fountain station sat under the Burnside Bridge, two blocks up from the Willamette River. There was a large antique store and restaurant beside the station, an outdoor sporting goods store down the block. Unlike the grid of one-way streets surrounding it, only the light rail tracks ran under this part of the Bridge, so every weekend artists and vendors used the space for the bustling, family-friendly Portland Saturday Market. Yet busy missions and homeless shelters stood overhead on Burnside Street, their front lined with people waiting for rooms and food.

Some people slept on the sidewalk, their bodies wrapped in soiled blankets and sleeping bags that smelled of wet flannel and ashtrays; others stood outside in the rain smoking for most of the day. And because its location sheltered dealers from the leering eyes of passing car traffic, Skidmore Fountain station was then one of the easiest places to buy heroin in town. I tried to ignore the fact that it was a five minute walk from work. I'd been clean for barely one year.

From the stop near my apartment, the train cruised silently station to station: NE 7th Avenue, Convention Center, Rose Quarter. Locals called the light rail system MAX, short for Metropolitan Area Express. I stared out the window and watched grey light flash through gaps in the Steel Bridge's frame as we shuttled over the River and into downtown. When the train doors opened, an automated voice announced "Skidmore Fountain," and cool damp air rushed inside, carrying with it the dirty smell of damp cement. The doors seemed to stay open forever. Each second felt like a taunt. When the train finally pulled away, I turned up the music in my headphones.

Originally the idea had been to get off methadone and begin my new life in Portland completely substance-free. I'd started my first program the previous year in Phoenix after my arrest, the details of which I'd also concealed from Kari and friends. The clinic stabilized me on a moderately high dose. Because I wanted to free myself from methadone before anyone discovered I was on it, I had the nurse start gradually reducing it to one milligram shortly after my enrollment. Before I left Arizona, the clinic gave me enough take-out doses to last my first week in Oregon, advising I drink half the contents of each tiny bottle—so half a milligram—in order to complete the tapering process. With my new job looming, and the pressure to perform while making favorable first impressions on coworkers, I decided I wasn't ready for that. Was there a worse time to detox from opiates than during the start of a career? Due to its high fat solubility, methadone metabolizes slowly. Its longer half-life means it has greater therapeutic effects than morphine-based drugs; it also means that methadone withdrawal can span anywhere from two weeks to six months, much longer than heroin. Even though the nurse insisted discomfort would be negligible, I ignored her, drank the full milligram each morning and signed up with a new clinic.

I rented a small apartment in a wooded residential neighborhood. I started my new job at Powell's. And with minimal research I found CODA. CODA was Portland's oldest nonprofit methadone clinic and one of its most reputable. It was also the closest to my apartment. Set off Burnside Street in an ugly white building disfigured by mismatched materials and unflattering lines, CODA's front door sat on 10th and NE Couch streets. Enrollment was anonymous. The clinic never disclosed its patients' names if someone called asking. It even sheltered its entrance on a side street so patients wouldn't be spotted by Burnside's passing car and bus traffic. Methadone is one of the world's most controversial forms of addiction treatment. CODA understood the need to keep our identities hidden from the family, friends, and coworkers who might disapprove of our method of recovery.

CODA's methadone dispensary, as it's known in clinical parlance, opened at 6:30 a.m. Monday through Saturday, and closed at 1:30 in the afternoon. When I arrived just after 7:00 the first time, the line of patients waiting to dose stretched from the dispensing window halfway to the front door, maybe twenty feet. Most of them looked to have just rolled out of bed: pajamas, fuzzy slippers, baggy Portland Beavers sweatshirts. The place smelled of morning breath and floor disinfectant. Between people besot with bed-head stood a solitary businessman in black slacks and a white collared shirt. I stepped in line behind the other patients and played music on my headphones, hoping to ease the tedium of waiting ten to twenty minutes for a sip of liquid.

My Phoenix clinic resembled a deli—a tiny counter, no glass partition, brief wait in a short line. CODA's dispensary seemed as guarded as a bank teller's drawer. Two side-by-side windows stood in a small alcove walled on three sides, and the windows were only accessible through a narrow doorway which staff could close and lock if necessary. A nurse sat at each computer terminal behind a thick pane of glass and a big, white, plastic bottle of methadone. A thin tube ran from the bottle into a contraption that administered the quantity designated by the patient's computer profile. Protocol was strict and explicit. Patients had to wait behind a line of black magnetic tape until the patient in front of them left the dispensary. We had to drink the dose then throw the paper cup in the trash before leaving, while the nurse watched, so no one could share or sell their meds. On Saturdays, everyone received one take-home dose for Sunday. Those patients who had earned weekly take-out privileges carried a lockbox—meaning, any container fitted with a lockable lid—to store their week's six bottles. The rest of us took our medicine at the window every morning, one dose at a time.

The list of brand and generic names for methadone reads like a list of aliens in a sci-fi movie: Adanon, Adolan, Althose, AN-148, Biodone, Dolamid, Eptadone, Heptadon, Heptalgin, Heptanal, Heptanon, Mephenon, Metasedin, Miadone, Pallidone, Pentalgin, Phenadone, Physeptone, Sedo-Rapide, Symoron, Tussol.

Methadone is available in various forms: a traditional pill, a sublingual tablet, a ready-to-dispense liquid oral concentrate, and a dissolvable "disket" which disperses in water just like an Alka-Seltzer tablet. The pre-mix liquid is the most common form, as it allows clinics to adjust a patient's dose milligram by milligram. CODA used a pre-mix, colored red to distinguish it from water. Not that I ever asked the name of it. I just drank what they poured in the cup.

I never injected heroin regularly. I snorted it for a year, but everyone from high-level executive pill-poppers to people living in halfway houses enrolled here. My Phoenix clinic called their service "methadone maintenance." Back then, CODA called theirs "opioid medication assisted outpatient treatment." Now they call it "medication-assisted treatment." Their purposes were the same: to relieve narcotic cravings and alleviate withdrawal symptoms so that addicts could stop using illicit substances long enough to rebuild their lives. Unfortunately, my original motivation for enrolling was not so noble. I simply wanted to avoid the physical torment of withdrawal. Methadone would get me off the heroin without inflicting dope sickness, and then, I thought, like magic, I'd live a sober life again.

In addition to its slow metabolism, methadone is a physically addictive chemical, so depending on your dosage it takes months to taper off of it, and often years before you're psychologically ready to begin tapering. While there exist what are called "juice bars"—profit-driven businesses where patients can take their dose and keep using drugs if they want to, as long as they pay their money—reputable clinics are designed to help addicts transition from a dysfunctional dependent life to a productive sober one, and that requires a long-term commitment.

When I first enrolled in Phoenix I thought nothing about long-term investment or the daily irritations of such a routine. I was scared and hasty. By the time I arrived in Portland over a year later, I understood the complex nature of my chosen treatment and the fragility of my sobriety. At one milligram, I could either schedule my last day with CODA in advance, or I could simply quit visiting the clinic when I felt like it and detox on my own. Instead, I figured it was best to stay with CODA for a little while—a few weeks maybe, a few months at most, just feel it out.

I stared at CODA's scuffed white linoleum while inching toward the front of the line. When the patient before me departed, I stepped through the door. "Hi," I said, "my name's Aaron Gilbreath. I'm a new patient." The pale nurse welcomed me and searched the computer for my info. I'd called the previous week, scheduled an appointment with a staff member, and been granted "guest privileges."

After a few moments reading the screen, the nurse hit a button and a mechanism clicked. The tube released a tiny drop of red fluid into a cup: one milligram. She peered into it and smirked. "Not much in there," she said. The average patient took between eighty and one hundred and twenty milligrams. She slid the cup under the glass and I emptied the contents into my mouth, placing the drop on the back of my tongue to make sure every bit slid down my throat. I had an unscientific idea of the process. I imagined that if those precious methadone molecules got caught on any surface other than my tongue, they would spread across my cheeks, dissipate in saliva and end up somewhere outside of my bloodstream. This is why I always brushed my tongue before visiting the clinic and didn't eat for exactly two hours after dosing.

I rinsed the cup with two squirts of water, drank that, then tossed the cup in the trash. "Mmm," I said, "Is this cherry?"

"Tropical punch," she said.

My second day of work started in four hours, so I returned to my apartment and crawled back into bed. I lay beside my two cats but failed to drift to sleep. Outside the morning sky was gradually lighting blue. My tired itchy eyes made me wish that I could sleep in late. As I did most mornings, I looked forward to the day when I no longer had to drag myself up to dose before sunrise, a time when I could rely on myself rather than medication for sobriety, could eat a bowl of cereal upon waking and never have to bury the take-out bottles deep in the garbage bin where no one would spot my name printed on the label. Soon, I thought, very soon.

* * *

The first time I tried heroin, I smoked it off of tin foil. My close friend JT scored ten dollar's worth from a guy he worked with at the copy shop. Three friends and I were hanging out at Chris' house, as we did nearly every day, and together we filled our virgin lungs with JT's quarry. If any of us found this a troubling milestone in our adolescent development, we showed no sign of it.

It wasn't something I bragged about or was even remotely proud of, but by the time I turned twenty, my friends and I had tried nearly every chemical in the modern street pharmacopeia. But I hadn't done heroin yet, and I was curious.

The gooey brown tar came smeared across a square of white cellophane. Following his coworker's directions, JT sliced the wad into tiny bits with a knife, placed the bits on the foil and brushed a flame beneath it. In the heat of his Bic, the tar instantly liquefied, sliding sideways across the foil. The way it sizzled and moved atop the aluminum seemed terrifying and unpredictable, almost a wholly new element with no familiar earthly properties. As the liquid vaporized, we inhaled its sour plume through a section of cut soda straw. After a few puffs, our pupils constricted to tiny points. The world turned sepia. We talked a congenial rapid fire, marveling at this new sensation and the low croak in our voices. We smoked until the wad was gone. We sat on the living room couch and talked through a euphoric languor. Then I got queasy.

I excused myself and lay on Chris' mom's bed. Her room was dark. All the curtains were pulled. A swamp cooler filled the air with dense, intra-uterine moisture, and I fought the urge to vomit while experiencing a turbulent ecstasy. Neither able to sleep nor stand, I sprawled on my back for nearly an hour. I wondered why people liked doing a drug that made them so ill. I wondered when I would do it again.

I wasn't drawn to drugs by some romanticized sense of squalor. The mythic allure of the junkie living in a burned out tenement in 1970's Manhattan, the boozy down-and-out musician playing dive bars while trying to make a name for himself—none of the iconic stereotypes of drug users attracted me. But drugs were recreation, and because I lived so close to the Mexican border, they were easy to get.

My friends and I were seventeen, eighteen, nineteen. Drugs seemed harmless because we thought they were fun. Like the time we took acid on vacation in a southern California motel room and stayed up all night cackling at Richard Pryor movies. And the time we ate mushrooms and took photos beside animated Sesame Street characters in a toy store in the mall. And the times we tripped on mushrooms while camping outside of Sedona's famous red rock formations, and the head of an ax flew off while Jason chopped wood.

I also lacked purpose. I was preoccupied by the pressure to choose a profession and a practical major. Because I'd been drawing all of my life, I started college as a drawing major, which I considered as useful a degree as having no degree at all. Poultry science students had more career opportunities. Walking past the university's buildings everyday only drew my dilemma into sharper relief. Other students buzzed around these buildings with a sense of purpose. Here were America's future DNA researchers, oil company employees, and CPAs. What would I become? I had hobbies, but none of them provided such promising career tracks. I liked to hike, to read, to journal, draw, take photographs, identify native animals and plants, and see bands play. If anything, I had too many interests.

My parents tried to help me focus. "Is there a link between them?" my dad would ask. "An umbrella category to haul them all under?" As encouraging as he and my mother were, their involvement only added to my stress because I recognized the subtext: sometimes you just had to pick something and go with it. Dad never liked any of his jobs in construction or retail clothing, but held them because he had to support his family, and he did so without complaint. Information like that only fueled my agitation.

After two years of study, I accepted the limitations of my drawing major and searched for other options. I entertained the idea of becoming a National Park ranger, since that's what my favorite writer Ed Abbey had been. It sounded cool to work outdoors all day, to maintain trails and answer visitor questions, or whatever park rangers did. Unfortunately, research revealed that those were highly coveted positions that often required a wildlife biology degree. I couldn't earn that degree. It required math too complicated for my lopsided brain. I considered becoming a wilderness guide in some mountainous place like Colorado or Montana, until I realized that I couldn't handle the snow. And because I'd grown up in Phoenix where the most water I had contact with was in chlorinated pools, I didn't feel qualified to run rivers. At one point I considered putting my personal experience to use as a drug counselor, but first I needed to quit using them.

Eventually I switched the drawing major to an Ecology/Evolutionary Biology major, figuring that fit my love of hiking and nature. When I discovered how much calculus the profession required, I switched to a Philosophy major, keeping the science as a minor as if to further round out my unmarketability. I pictured myself wiping restaurant tables with a wet rag at age forty, discussing Sartre and the fate of the spotted owl with waitresses with library science degrees.

In addition to sleep, inebriation gave me my sole respite from worry. Weed and beer had initially made funny things funnier, and boring things bearable. Now they were medicine to still my mind: suck down the smoke and replace anxiety with laughter. Heroin, though, proved to be the best thought-blotter of all.

* * *

Contrary to popular belief, methadone doesn't get you high. In reasonable amounts, it simply prevents the onset of opioid withdrawal when addicts quit using other drugs. Although methadone acts on the same basic opioid receptors as morphine and heroin, methadone behaves differently in the human body. First of all, methadone is rarely injected; it is primarily swallowed. Once ingested, it is rapidly absorbed by the gastrointestinal tract. From there it diffuses widely into other body tissues, particularly fatty tissue, where it is stored and then released into the plasma as quickly as thirty minutes following consumption. Half-life is the period of time it takes a decaying substance to decrease in volume by half. Although metabolism rates vary greatly between individuals, morphine has an elimination half-life of four to six hours. Methadone has a half-life of fifteen to sixty hours, with a mean of about twenty-two, and therein lies its magic. Methadone's prolonged metabolism allows clinics to administer the medication once every twenty-four hours, a marked improvement from the five to eight daily heroin injections or intranasal squirts the average addict administers themselves.

Methadone's therapeutic benefits were an accidental discovery. Initially, the compound was synthesized in Nazi Germany as a substitute for morphine. Like many European nations at the time, Germany sourced much of its raw pharmaceutical opium from Turkey. Research for synthetic analgesics had already begun in Germany in the 1880s, but Hitler's desire to achieve an economically independent, industrial state intensified these efforts. Hitler also anticipated potential opium shortages due to Allied blockades during the upcoming war. Consequently, scientists at the pharmaceutical laboratories of the I.G. Farbenkonzern, a subsidiary of the important chemical conglomerate Farbwerke Hoechst in Frankfurt, were diligently searching for synthetic opioids to serve both the military and civilian populations.

In 1939, two Hoechst scientists named Bockmühl and Ehrhart synthesized a number of compounds, one of which was 2-dimethylamino-4,4-diphenylheptanon-(5), which they numbered Va 10820, patented and codenamed Amidon. Hoechst produced very limited quantities of Amidon, and it was never used during WWII to treat patients in either military hospitals or casualty clearing stations. Instead, WWII ended, and Allied forces seized all German research records, patents, and trade names. The US Department of Commerce confiscated the Farbwerke Hoechst's documents, gave them to the US Department of State's Technical Industrial Committee for review, and then brought them to the United States. Since the German patent rights were no longer protected, any pharmaceutical company interested in producing Va 10820 could purchase the rights to the formula. The US government sold the rights for one dollar.

In 1946, researchers at the US Public Health's Narcotic Hospital in Lexington, Kentucky used Va 10820 to alleviate heroin withdrawal symptoms while slowly tapering patients from the new drug over a period of one week to ten days. Because the German opioid was only considered a strong analgesic, it never received further testing beyond this limited clinical use. It was only in 1964 that two New York researchers began utilizing methadone's potential for long-term opioid replacement therapy.

In 1947, the Council on Pharmacy and Chemistry of the American Medical Association gave Va 10820 the generic name "methadone." In that same year, the FDA approved commercial production, and the American pharmaceutical company Eli Lilly became the first company to manufacture it in the US. Lilly registered their product under the trade name Dolophine, a word derived from the Latin dolor, meaning pain, and finis, meaning end. It was common practice to give analgesics the suffixes -dol or -phine, not only in English but in German, French, and other languages. Companies in other countries soon followed suit, marketing the narcotic under innumerable trademarked names ranging from Butalgin to Ketalgin to Westadone.

As the news of methadone's use in the Lexington Narcotic Hospital spread, other researchers and doctors started using it as a form of long-term opioid replacement therapy. People opened up clinics in New York City in the 1970s, and they soon multiplied around the City and beyond.

In order to dispense medicine, most modern clinics have firm rules. CODA required that new or early-stage patients had to attend monthly one-on-one meetings with a counselor, attend the weekly "Stabilization" support group, and leave random urine samples, or UAs. If you left dirty UAs, missed too many groups, or ditched too many one-on-ones, nurses withheld your dose for noncompliance. The fear of withdrawal is a powerful motivator, detox the ultimate ultimatum, but CODA offered many incentives for sobriety too. The longer patients stayed clean, the more freedoms the clinic would afford us. If I abstained, as I had been, for one full year, I'd soon have monthly rather than weekly urinalysis, graduate from the weekly group to the monthly "Maintenance Group," and I'd be picking up two weeks' worth of take-out doses at a special designated time well before the clinic's long line formed. Not a bad deal. I scheduled my first group meeting not long after I arrived in Portland; it met once a week at the clinic on my day off work. First, CODA assigned me a counselor.

Her name was Francine. She was a tall, heavyset woman with sagging sail-fish arms, and a voice like melted chocolate. Her small office's window overlooked the clinic's parking lot. Framed family photos lined her desk. She patted my shoulder the first time I came in. I liked her immediately.

Francine sat straight in her chair, studying me as we spoke. Without spending too much time on small talk she said, "So, why did you use heroin?" It wasn't the worst question she could have asked, but it was one of them.

I stared at the compacted carpet fibers and tried to collect my thoughts. "Why did I use?" I figured my reasons were the same as most recovering addicts'—heroin made me feel good, or at least feel better than I felt on my own. I never suffered some childhood trauma that I wanted to run from, but on it, I told Francine, I was calmer, kinder. I worried about nothing and nothing mattered other than each ravishing glacial moment. Like William Burroughs in his book *Junkie*, I could happily stare at my toe for hours, though I was more likely to fall asleep in various places while reading. And I was lazy.

I wasn't thrilled to admit the way heroin made me feel. It seemed the sort of information that enticed young people to try the drug. But saying otherwise would have been as disingenuous as saying I hadn't enjoyed the high during my first months of abuse. "Humans are pretty simple creatures in one respect," I said. "We avoid discomfort and pursue pleasure. We do what feels best." Having studied ecology and philosophy as an undergraduate, my understanding of human behavior—my entire world view—was rooted in the fundamentals of life science and moral theory. "But it's that little—" I stopped to run my hand across my head. I looked up. "I'm sorry. It's really weird talking like this." I drew a deep breath and apologized for the tears I was struggling to hold back. "But, you know, we're really complicated too, right?"

She nodded.

"I used for a ton of different reasons later," I said. "Tons."

When she asked if my friends or family knew I was in a program, I said that they didn't even know I'd had a heroin problem. "You're the first person I have ever spoken to in such detail," I said.

I told Francine a bit about Kari, described our misguided engagement and how I'd secretly used, and I mentioned how the three friends with whom I'd first tried heroin five years earlier had eventually developed an opiate habit. After years of over-drinking, one bottomed out with heroin and later joined AA. One developed a drinking problem and a brief, closet dependence on prescription pain pills, a habit that I heard about later and that he still refused to discuss. Like me, another became a junkie who eventually got on a methadone program. He was the ideal person with which to discuss my problems, yet I'd never broached the subject. Francine said some patients found divulging their secrets therapeutic, but I feared full disclosure would have the opposite effect: that people would grow suspicious of me, retract whatever trust they'd afforded, and then sever our relationship. Even though I'd only snorted heroin for one year, I feared that wouldn't matter to most people. A junkie was a junkie, and once one always one. Also, I didn't want to admit to my past because my lying and sneaking and secrecy shamed me. I wanted people in Portland to embrace me for my other traits, not judge me solely on my weaknesses. I knew it was an idealistic, unrealistic approach, but I intended to start completely from scratch here: a new life affixed to no past other than the good parts. She nodded. She didn't have to outwardly acknowledge the outlandish futility of such thinking for me to recognize it. "Well, if you ever feel it's time," she said, "that's a topic you might explore in group."

Francine adjusted herself in the chair. "So, why didn't you tell Kari any of this?" Now that was the worst question.

* * *

After abandoning my mixed drug recovery group in Tucson, I managed a stint of unsupervised sobriety. As if to add meaning to the ritual of my resistance, I marked my sober days on a wall calendar, starting from zero after my little relapse with weed at a party in Phoenix. I also started adding notes about where Kari and I went on dates. We ate at restaurants and hung out at coffee shops. Sometimes I dragged her to a bookstore and browsed the nature shelves. Other times she took me to her girlfriends' apartments to swim in their pool. Then, on a whim, I drove to south Tucson and scored heroin. Even though I'd snorted and smoked it a few times back in Phoenix, I had no idea why I thought of it unprompted while watching TV alone on this particular night. I had no idea how to score either, but I'd seen enough movies to figure it out.

You find some sketchy looking guy in baggy Dickies and a tank top, someone with sunken cheeks or forearms darkened with fading tattoos, loitering either on a residential side street or in front of the liquor store housed in a corrugated aluminum warehouse topped with an external air conditioning unit, and ask if he has any chiva. When he says no but he knows where to get some, he'll grab your passenger side car door handle and, since you're desperate enough to let him in, direct you to some house with dried red chili garlands dangling on the porch, or busted cars parked in the yard. If you're lucky he'll take you to a small square cut out in the rotting wood of a backyard fence where you hand your money to an unseen stranger like at a fast food window, but that's if cops haven't shut that spot down, or it's early enough that the sellers haven't yet left the ninety-five degree heat to nod out in some air-conditioned room, and you're rarely that lucky. So at the house the man will hold out his hand and ask, "Whadyouwant, ten? Twenty?" You'll say you'll pay when he comes back and he'll say, "Can't, man." You'll pause for effect, maybe raise one brow or tilt your head, a bluff that makes him worry about his own supply and utter his standard response of "I'll be back. I'm not like that," even though you know he is like that because, as honest a person as you once were, you're like that too. The whites of his eyes are taut and mustard-brown, glassy like those of the goldfishes' at the sushi restaurant you used to eat at before you started spending so much money on drugs. His dark hair and clothes stink of sweat, and as he steps into the house holding your bills, you eyeball the property, searching for views of the sides and backyard so you might see him if he sneaks out a rear door. You'll sit in the car counting the seconds that tick by like minutes, knowing how suspicious you look, thinking it would be less obvious if you circled the block in case a cop passes by—which in this neighborhood they often do—but knowing that would only encourage this guy to rip you off. You'll sit there stewing in guilt and his remnant BO, your engine puttering wearily like you, wondering how long it fucking takes to score one fucking balloon, wondering if he's busy breaking pieces off your stuff, cooking it in a spoon at that very minute or has already bailed out the back door to scurry down the alley and that maybe it's time to accept that you got duped or drove around back to see if you can spot him making his escape that punk motherfucker, though you wouldn't know what to do if you did spot him. Then, after forever, he'll come out of the house and slip inside the seat and ask for some of the ridiculously small piece he hands you. "That's not a ten," you'll tell him, and he'll say something like "That's what they gave me" while scanning the street for what you hope are cops rather than an ideal time to jack you. Because he's scary and seated three inches away, you oblige, trying to scrape as small a piece as possible from the gooey brown wafer the dealer smeared on a white plastic square of cut grocery bag, try to make it appear bigger than it actually is by spreading it with your fingernail since the recipient is sitting right there staring at your hands, reminding you that he got it for you bro, shit, come on. Then you'll grumble and hand it to him, and he'll grumble back with something like, "A little more," and you'll either talk tough with "That's all I can spare," or you'll oblige because you're a pansy ass who just wants to evade police and get home already.

When I got home I snorted a bit and was relieved to finally silence my chatterbox mind. No more worries about school, no more thoughts about careers. All the anxiety locked in my muscles drained from my body. I was pleased to be dazed again, but frightened by how much I enjoyed the feeling.

For hours I sat there in my living room chair, staring into space, thinking about nothing deeper than the color of the brown carpet fibers. That night, vivid, hallucinatory dreams filled my head, and I ditched school the next day to sniff some more. I lay on my bed and looked at the ceiling, my body draped across the warm sheets. Then, in a panic, I flushed the remaining dope down the toilet. As the heroin wore off I sat in my chair and cursed myself. All that hard work, the group sessions, for what? I shouldn't have done this.

A few weeks later I went back for more dope. I told myself it was the last time. Months passed. Kari and I spent more time at her house. We watched movies, went to dinner. The spring semester came to a close. Summer school came and went. And then, while packing for a month-long summer roadtrip, I returned to south Tucson for ten dollar's worth—"a special occasion," I told myself. Before I departed, Kari bought a plane ticket to meet me in Seattle. With my truck loaded with hiking gear, camping equipment, and blank journals, I drove across Arizona to Fresno, California in one day, snorting heroin the entire way, and I spent the night inside my camper in a hotel parking lot somewhere amid the San Joaquin Valley's shimmering farm fields. Bronzed by the sun, my mind serene, I felt so good that I went to sleep thinking it was one of the greatest days of my life, rather than the beginning of the end of it.

* * *

When Kari and I returned home from our summer trip where she suffered numerous stings from a swarm of yellow-jackets, her mother made a beeline for me in the driveway. "You saved my daughter," she said. Kari was allergic to bees. Her mother gripped me in a hug that made me both grateful and uneasy.

I said, "I got your daughter into trouble in the first place."

She squeezed me tighter, then leaned back to look into my eyes. "You still took good care of her. Got her to the hospital and all, right?" I nodded. Kari stood beside us smiling.

With minimal thought and surplus excitement, I accepted Kari's offer the following year to move in to her apartment. It was a tiny stucco cottage in what was once an old Tucson motor court—hardwood floors, honeycomb tile, the coolest place I'd lived at that point, and the first I'd shared with someone. We adopted a feral cat, went out for sushi, ordered vegetarian pizzas, and watched movies at home. Our home. Our relationship felt fantastic. So did heroin.

Trying to ignore the fact that I'd already decided to succumb to temptation, I poured my energy into moderating rather than terminating my intake. I scored heroin regularly in South Tucson. I hid my supplies under the seat of my truck. Kari was too trusting and uniformed to recognize the pinprick pupils, brownish eyes, and gravelly voice for what they were. I felt guilty taking advantage of her naïveté, but that didn't stop me from doing it.

She and I went to school, did homework, and occasionally walked home from campus holding hands. Sometimes I snorted a bit in the morning, sometimes late afternoon. I even managed to binge a few days then quit for a few to avoid physical dependence. That didn't work for long.

The first withdrawal was worse than I imagined. Symptoms started while I sat on a bench under a row of olive trees on campus, and detox derailed my life for three days. I sweated, I shivered, my muscles ached. I spent nights curled on our living room sofa in front of a TV I was too besieged to watch. Kari entered our bedroom and emerged the next morning and I hadn't slept a wink. Must be a flu, I told her. How could one nose run this much? I soaked in a bath while she went to class, then acted like I was reading schoolwork in there when she got home. My abdomen knotted up and my bones somehow hurt. In an attempt to lessen my misery, I went to a natural foods store and bought homeopathic tinctures of California poppy, Valerian, and Kava Kava, and I guzzled half the bottles. Nothing worked. To make sure Kari didn't get suspicious, I spent most of the third day lying across the front seat of my air conditioned truck. I'd parked it by a tree in a desert park far from home to avoid discovery. When the fever finally lifted I felt reborn. Never again, I told myself.

As it turned out, all that meant was never another break in my supply.

Although I regularly scored in Tucson, it took too much effort. One day a woman would be selling in an alley, the next day I'd pick someone up at a bus stop because the alley lady wasn't there. Once a guy had me drive him to a motel, and I ended up yelling from my car window as he ran off through the desert with my money. Thankfully, years earlier, someone had introduced my friends and me to a few Phoenix dealers. They were a small group of Latino men employed by a mysterious chain of higher ups who equipped them with cell phones and a revolving fleet of what resembled retired town cars. We knew their fake first names—Carlos, John—but names didn't matter. Once I got their numbers, I started driving the two hundred mile roundtrip to Phoenix.

You'd call from a payphone. They'd ask your location and tell you how long they'd be. Then you'd wait for up to an hour, growing increasingly anxious depending on how close you were to withdrawal. You'd wonder want to do if they didn't show up. But then a black Lincoln Continental with tinted windows would arrive; you'd step in and cruise around the parking lot or maybe the block. The driver would open his door and grab a tiny plastic container from under the car. It was one of those vitamin bins with little dividers for pills. Its magnetized bottom stuck to the chassis so cops wouldn't find it if they got pulled over. Balloons were color coded: one color for heroin, one for cocaine. The contents were folded within crisp squares of plastic then stuffed inside the balloon which was tied in a knot. I always sat in the back seat where the driver would talk to me while connecting with my eyes in the rearview mirror. Sometimes they'd throw in a free balloon, to be "nice."

I stockpiled every few weeks. Then Kari and I rented movies and ate dinner on the couch. Months passed. I nodded out in class. Fell asleep while reading in bookstores.

* * *

One day Kari asked, "So when are you going to propose to me?"

I hadn't thought I should. We weren't really in that kind of love. Despite our childish romanticism, Kari and I never used the term "soul-mates" in reference to each other. We said "I love you," and that was it.

"A magician never reveals his secrets," I said, then hauled my spineless ass to the mall to find affordable rings.

Once equipped with her gold band and small center-mounted diamond, Kari told her friends all about it, how excited she was. We didn't set a date—we were still thinking about it. My mother volunteered to help shop for anything Kari needed, be it stationary or centerpieces. Mom even bought us a copy of *Emily Post's Wedding Etiquette*.

Our parents met, shared a meal, and visited each other's homes. As anaesthetized as I was, I constantly wondered what I'd gotten myself into, but a sham boyfriend deserved a sham engagement. Kari did not.

We would never set a date.

* * *

When I walked into the kitchen many months after the proposal, Kari pointed to the coffee table. "What is this?" A textbook lay on its side, exposing what I'd foolishly left hidden underneath it: the bent spoon, cut straw and tin of Altoids mints containing four balloons.

My head went light. Everything flashed white.

"It's—" What could I say? I braced myself against the doorframe. "It's heroin."

A stream of demands and regrets and obscenities flowed from Kari's mouth, and I agreed with them all: I was a jerk, I had betrayed her, how could I be so sneaky and lowdown to hide something like this. She'd let me move in and this is how I treated her?

She crossed her arms. "Do you have a problem?"

I said I didn't. I'd just bought some on a whim the last time I visited friends in Phoenix. I was stressed, I explained. I thought it would help. It was a mistake. I wouldn't do it again. "Promise," I told her. "I'll throw it out." She stared at me. "Seriously. You can watch me do it."

"It doesn't matter," she said. "You'll just get more." I told her that wasn't true. But when she turned her head before following me to the bathroom, I slipped two balloons in my pocket and flushed the others down the toilet so quickly she couldn't count the total as they swirled in the bowl.

I wish I'd thought of this as the de facto intervention that I needed, but all it meant was I had to be more cautious.

I made excuses to take drives: gotta run to the library. Gotta run and get some groceries. I'll pick up the movie and Indian food, you just stay here and relax honey. Then I'd mix a batch in my truck and snort it while leaning below the dashboard for cover. Kari grew suspicious.

When I returned home she'd say, "Why were you gone so long? I thought you were coming back at six?" When I stayed too long in the bathroom she said, "Are you okay in there? You fall in or something?" I'd crack the bathroom door to feign transparency, sliding the Altoids tin and spoon under the rug behind the toilet. Each hour of every day presented the same enormous risk. I had trouble maintaining the ruse.

Once I dozed off at dinner at her parent's house. Kari and I, her folks, her younger sister Diane, and brother and his wife were seated around the large dining room table. It was antique and dark-stained, set with matching chairs and shiny silver centerpieces. Before her father brought out his expensive decanted port wine, we talked and passed around food. Someone said something, and apparently my eyes were closed when they looked over for my response. I don't remember this. Of course I don't.

Kari's dad was a doctor. He was an affable if distant man who watched a lot of televised sports in his bedroom and, understandably, wanted to protect his daughter. Later that night he asked Kari if I had a drug problem and, to my surprise, she defended me. "No," she told him, "He doesn't have a problem. He doesn't do any of that stuff." That ended the discussion but not his apprehension. Learning of this conversation a decade later, I wondered how Kari failed to make the connection between my narcolepsy and what she'd found in our kitchen the previous year. She knew me back in high school when my friends and I had wild reputations. She must not have been surprised. Maybe she was more naïve than I thought, so innocent that she couldn't even see the signs. Or maybe, as I assume, she chose to ignore them.

She was privately struggling with her own issues: teaching at a Montessori school while questioning the value of her Sociology degree; worrying about her weight; struggling with her high school eating disorder; trying various diets and worrying about whether or not she was pursuing the right career. If my presence offered any comfort for her anxieties, it must have been small. She kept a little log of her calories in a journal each day, then planted herself in front of the TV at night. Maybe she needed to live in as deep a fantasy as I did, one generated not from drugs but from the narcotic of television, snacking, and occasional drinking with her friends. Maybe, like me, she needed to find one thing in life to cling to, something stable to weather the challenging transition from adolescence to adulthood and, for some reason, she chose our relationship. Like me, she seemed unwilling to admit that our relationship was doomed to fail, and so she blocked out any evidence of its disintegration, choosing instead to invest all her hope in us, and me, no matter how misguided. Whatever her reasons, as I filled up on opiates each day, we each lived our separate fantasies: I thought I could get away with using indefinitely, and she thought she was involved in a promising relationship. She never confronted me, never asked "Are you still using?" or "Are you high?" because, like everything else in our relationship, we never talked openly about the issues that mattered most: when were we getting married? Did she really want to move with me to the Pacific Northwest? Why wasn't I as excited discussing her students as I was discussing books? We maintained the fantasy by speaking only of the easy stuff: classes, homework, her day at work, what we should cook for dinner.

It still shocks me to think about how something as obvious as my intoxication can remain secret. But secret and unacknowledged aren't the same things. People often see what they want to see, and sometimes what is secret isn't what is hidden, it's only what's ignored.

* * *

The Phoenix dealers were usually reliable. For months they kept me well-supplied. When they stopped answering their phones, I assumed they'd been caught or their suppliers had dried up, so I went to a neighborhood south of downtown.

I met a middle-aged woman on the street one morning, and after confirming I was cool ("You a cop?" "No."), she became my new reliable. She'd climb into the passenger seat, run inside various unkempt houses, then slip back in my truck. She pinned her thirsty hair down with a comb, and the pink jogging suit she wore smelled like an overstuffed hamper and instant mashed potatoes. Her thin forearms sometimes bore a large and leaking scab. One morning while scratching it she said, "I got this bad abscess, from skin-popping." I didn't know what that meant, but I watched which parts of the upholstery her dirty hands touched so I knew what to disinfect. The clinic that gave her methadone paid no attention to urine tests, though she kind of wished it did. One morning she stared out the passenger side window and said, "Be glad you don't inject."

That summer, my future father-in-law bought me and his family tickets to see the Arizona Diamondbacks. Some of Kari's cousins had flown in from Texas, and while I'd never cared for baseball, I wanted to meet them. They'd heard nice things about me, and I relished that information, figuring that either my ruse was still holding up, or that I wasn't a complete degenerate. On the day of the game, my connection requested I stop at the liquor store on 7th Avenue. It was summer, scorching hot. I'd borrowed Kari's car for its potent air conditioning and assumed that this, like all the other trips, would be a short one.

As my connection stepped from the car, a cop pulled onto the street behind me. Without thinking, I turned right onto 7th and immediately the red and blue lights flared. My slick palms spun the wheel as I ran through my options. If I tossed the drugs out the window, the officer would see. If I pocketed them, the cop would find them, because in that neighborhood there was going to be a pat down. So I did what street dealers do and shoved the balloons in my mouth, all the while praying they hadn't been in anyone else's.

I parked on the highway onramp. "Hi," the officer said. "License and registration please." She stood just behind my doorframe and explained that she pulled me over because of the area's high drug activity. "You know this isn't a safe place to be, right?" I said I did not. I was just getting a soda at the liquor store. When she asked where the soda was, I said I hadn't gone in yet. She told me to step out of the car.

I stood beside Kari's clean gray Acura, answering the officer's questions, which I didn't initially realize were intended to not only extract information but confirm by my awkward lilt that there was something under my tongue.

After a brief exchange she said, "Spit it out Aaron. Don't swallow it. Make this easy on yourself."

My eyes darted wildly. Her voice remained firm: "Come on. Don't make this difficult. Spit it out."

I wondered what would happen if I didn't. Would the balloons burst in my stomach and cause me to OD? Or would I just get really serene and think this was a dream?

Gripping her black belt as if preparing to pounce and pry open my mouth, the officer said, "Do it. Spit it out." I nodded my head and spit the balloons into my palm. I told her I wouldn't make trouble then admitted why I'd come. She sat me on the curb and placed the evidence in her car.

When she returned she said she was sorry for having to do this, but would I please turn around. And right there, in front of passing traffic near a highway my family and I had driven countless times, she bent my arms behind my back, tightened the cuffs around my wrists and wedged me into her narrow back seat. "What happens to my car?" I said. It would be impounded; I could pick it up later. "Later?" I said. Of course—I was going to jail.

I didn't cry. I didn't beg her not to take me. I resigned to my fate and just stared out the window at the gritty side of my city.

The silence of the drive was smothering. If her radio had been squealing at high volume, I was so lost in thought I don't think I would have heard it. My sweaty back pressed my hands against the vinyl. To make conversation, the officer asked where I was born, where my family was. She was surprised this was my first drug arrest. In a moment of clarity, I told her this was exactly what I needed.

Until that moment I had always considered the war on drugs a misguided approach to protecting the citizenry: how could you battle substance abuse by curbing the supply? This was a demand-side issue. You had to make people want to not use drugs and help those who did use with a psycho-social, systems-thinking approach; until then, in our capitalist economy, someone would always be willing to sell. Also, it was wrong to criminalize people with addictions since being hooked on coke wasn't the same as rape or murder. We all had problems, and we medicated in different ways. I still feel that way. But in that moment, the adrenaline and cold handcuffs helped me see things differently. Jail time and parole could either force me to sober up, or lead me toward some darker pole.

I thanked her, saying this arrest would snap me out of it, even though I didn't know if anything could. "Well," she said, "make that happen."

She pulled onto a disheveled residential side street to talk to another officer in a car. Then, without warning, she stepped out, opened my door and uncuffed me—more comfortable, she said. I doubt this would have happened if I wasn't white. When she released me into the jail loading bay I told her I wanted to hug her. She said thanks but that was against policy. "Good luck" were her final words.

Uniformed staff patted me down, put the contents of my pockets inside a plastic bag and checked the bag into an office. Looking at the thugs in line around me, I asked the closest officer if I could be kept with the women. The guy laughed. "They're meaner than the men."

Staff shoved tens of us into a white cinder block cell without air conditioning. Three walls and one pane of glass overlooking a hall. The dense swampy air stunk of armpit and filled my throat like hot oil. Officers led people back and forth past the glass, toward some fate I could only guess. A silver metal toilet sat in one corner. White metal bunks without mattresses hung from the walls.

I sat on the floor while people talked about their charges. "What're you in for?" Drugs, robbery, assault. Beefy Caucasians with sleeveless shirts picked at their fingertips. Sweaty Hispanic men with bandanas over their foreheads told jokes. One told me not to worry; first time drug possession only meant staying overnight. "You'll be in and out," he said. I tried to look unfazed, tough and worldly, but they must've have sensed my alarm. Others explained how the process worked: cops would move us around to different holding cells; we'd see a judge and make a plea; then the lowball cases like mine would go home while others stayed longer awaiting sentencing. The place smelled like cigarette breath and BO.

A payphone hung nearby. The considerate thing would have been to at least tell Kari not to wait for me, that I was okay and offer an excuse for missing the baseball game. Instead I laid face down on the dirty floor under a bunk and tried to wish away the smothering heat and these loud, rough people. I didn't want to get into a heated discussion with my fiancé in front of these men.

As the opiates drained from my system hour by hour, prisoners swapped stories and talked shit. One guy bragged about robbing a convenience store without a gun. "Just stuck my hand in my coat pocket," he said, "with my finger out so it stuck like a barrel. Dumb motherfuckers." He claimed he would've gotten away with it had his companion not tripped while running down an embankment.

A cockroach scurried past my arm.

As predicted, officers passed us cell to cell—filtering out people for what seemed different offenses—and moved us steadily closer to the court room. Lunch arrived: green bologna on soggy bread. "Fucking Sheriff Joe," people said. I traded someone my sandwich for their orange. No way was I getting food poisoning inside a cell.

A chatty thirty-something missing a side tooth said, "Wanna bunk together?" Bunk? I thought. I was only staying overnight. He described the jail's upper levels, where people awaited trial and their impending transfer to prison. "There's mattresses on the beds," he said, "showers too." I tried not to panic, which was hard without the palliative titty-suck force of narcotics. How bad of shape was I in?

By the time an officer led me and the few remaining others into the nearly vacant court, it was past the middle of the night. I sat on a hard wooden bench sweating and in withdrawal. My joints ached. My calf muscles twitched. I sat as straight as possible, trying to resume a modicum of the dignity my parents had raised me with, and also hoping that decorum would earn me some mercy. Instead, when staff called my name, I stood up. The judge read my charge and asked for my plea. "Guilty," I said and sat back down.

Afterwards I lay in a different cell, on a mattress, where my mind jumped between thoughts, mainly the dope I had stashed at home and what I'd tell Kari. Missing all night? She must have been terrified. When they released me onto the street, the sun hadn't risen. I called her on a payphone and reassured her that everything was alright; I'd explain when she arrived. I sat on the steps under a dark blue sky thinking over my story: I could say that her sister Diane had borrowed the Acura to drive some friends to a northern Arizona cabin. I hadn't even heard about their trip or who went, but I knew how to use their trip to my advantage.

Kari pulled up with Diane in the passenger seat, both in a panic. "We were so worried about you," they said. "We called all the hospitals to see if you were in an accident." I kissed Kari on the cheek and thanked them for rescuing me at that ungodly hour. They'd been up all night. "What happened?"

I said I got pulled over for not using my signal. When the cop questioned whose car it was, she searched it and found a Ziploc containing weed under the passenger seat, probably from Diane's trip. "Seeds and stems," I said. "but that's enough in this state for a felony."

Diane shrieked. "Me?" She turned to face me in back, her brows furrowed and eyes wide. "No one I went with even smokes weed."

I told her it was okay. I wasn't mad at her—we can't control what our friends do—and Kari seemed to buy it. Diane stared at her as if searching for clemency, then turned back around and settled into her seat.

It was, without a doubt, the most despicable thing I had ever done. Worse than sneaking behind Kari's back, worse than the lies and using in the first place. Watching Diane's slumped body deflate, the ease with which I threw her to the dogs, it was enough to make me want to cut my own wrists. With nothing to dampen the sting of my malice and virulent guilt, my whole body ached as if someone had cut them for me.

I caught my huge black hockey puck pupils in the rearview mirror and apologized for all the worry I'd caused. The jail phones didn't work, I said. "Your relatives must've thought I was the biggest jerk on earth." No, they assured me, everyone was just confused, no one knew where I had gone. I nodded, but wanted to scream, No! I am the biggest jerk on earth! I'm a fucking mess please help me before anything else comes apart it's so wrecked.

After moments of chilly silence Diane turned around and said, "Aaron, I promise you. We did not have weed in the car."

"I'm just telling you what I know," I said. "It's not your fault." Like I was the nice guy.

We dropped Diane off and drove home. The cats rushed the door, and when Kari went to the bathroom, I went straight to the kitchen cabinet. To save time, I had recently stashed an eye-dropper full of pre-mixed heroin far back behind the spice bottles—that's how much my intake had skyrocketed. By the time Kari returned, my muscles had loosened, my dry eyes were wet. I plopped down on the couch beside her and wrapped her in a hug.

For weeks I couldn't watch TV shows or films involving prison. I had nightmares about unprovoked arrests that had me howling in my sleep. "Ssssh," Kari comforted me, held my head.

To expunge the felony, the state offered first time drug offenders a twelve-month diversion program called TASC. Short for Treatment Assessment Screening Center, the program required random urinalysis, substance abuse counseling and group sessions. If compliant, the state would erase the charge because it would never officially convict me. I asked the clerk on the phone two or three times about the issue of job applications: "Just to be clear, if I complete the program, I can check no on the felony conviction box, right?" Yes, he said, but if my pee came up dirty and didn't quickly get clean, I'd be kicked off TASC, hit with a $1,200 fine, charged with the felony, and remain on probation. If I violated that probation, a judge would determine whether to sentence me to prison for up to 3.75 years. Mandatory urinalysis was the best thing that could happen to me. Without the threat of imprisonment and fines forcing me into treatment— diverting me from recklessness—I'm not sure how long I would have kept avoiding treatment. I do know this: I am the statistical exception. Arrest worked for me, but for most people, criminalization doesn't lead to sobriety, it leads to a life in prison and continued crime, and unfairly affects people of color and low-income populations.

Before my first visit to TASC, I hid in my parent's spare bedroom and called a clinic I'd seen advertised in the Phoenix New Times. I understood the basics of how methadone programs worked—basic chemistry, the long lines—but I asked the doctor a litany of questions anyway, about costs, frequency of visits, what to expect and if it was secret. When the doctor asked why I had decided to utilize methadone, I mentioned TASC and how I needed to avoid dope sickness. He warned that those weren't the best reasons. "This isn't nicotine gum," he said. "You could be on this for years." I wasn't thinking in terms of years. My calendar measured the hours between hits and the days left until the next score. He said, "You have to want to live clean." I did want that. I also wanted to get out of all this trouble without anyone knowing much about it.

I went to the clinic the next morning before Kari went to work. The tiny building sat on a shady side street in a rough part of town I grew up avoiding. People lined up at one window inside, and I checked in at another. A middle-aged nurse with blonde bobbed hair led me into a back room. She was the doctor's wife. They co-owned the clinic. Their son ran the front desk. She sat me on an examination table, took my pulse and heart rate. "How much do you use daily?" she said. As I told her about how things had gotten out of control, I admitted how desperately I wanted my life back. I started to cry. I hadn't cried in months, not after my arrest, not even when apologizing to Kari.

"Do the urinalysis results matter?" I said, sobbing into my shirt. She said they did. "Good," I said. "I need them to matter."

She explained that they were going to get me on a small dose first, based on how much heroin I used, and slowly increase the milligrams until they found the amount that stabilized me. It was an inaccurate science, and I might feel some discomfort in the interim. Discomfort was the main reason I was there. It was a junkie's least favorite word. "Part of the process is hanging in there," she said, and instructed me not to use to compensate. She left and came back with a tiny cup of clear liquid. I drank it down. It would take about thirty minutes to work.

After paying her son at the front desk, he told me he'd see me tomorrow. "Hang in there," he said as I walked out the door. "And don't use."

I drove down the street in the early morning darkness. I parked by some rundown old houses with brown front lawns and hung my arm out the window. Stars showed overhead, cosmic dust dimming at the advance of the sun. This has to be the end, I thought, death feeding new life. After thirty minutes watching the horizon light black to blue, I still didn't feel a thing. So I mixed up a small hit from what remained of my heroin, refusing to believe that the nurse had given me enough.

* * *

You can do a few things with a secret like mine. You can tell it to everyone at once, and unload the biggest burden you've ever carried in one explosive discharge. Or you can disclose it piecemeal, one apology and admission at a time. First you tell people, Hey, I was a heroin addict, then a few months later say, Oh, and I was on methadone too. As anyone at a bar in a strange town will tell you, sometimes it's easier to admit your secrets to people you'll never see again than it is to admit them to the people you know.

How much and for how long Kari bought my lies and excuses remains unclear. But one night out of the blue, at a restaurant, she broke up with me. I was shocked it had taken her so long to come to her senses, and envious of her willingness to do what I was too afraid to do.

"I still don't know what Kari knows or where the wedding ring went," I later said to Francine. Even though Emily Post said it was customary to return the ring, I had called Kari from Portland to tell her that if she didn't want the engagement ring I understood, but the ring was a gift. I thought letting her decide what to do with it was the "adult" thing to do. Really, I just felt guilty for betraying her.

Finally, to lighten the mood, Francine asked how I liked Oregon so far: did I miss Arizona? Was I glad that I moved?

I sobbed. "The smartest decision I ever made besides getting sober was moving up here." I loved it all: nearby hikes, numerous bookstores, the high rate of literacy, the focus on recycling and biking, and mass transit. Portland was a city of youthful dreamers, a place where artists and progressive thinkers cultivated their left-wing predilections and welcomed whatever weirdo moved into their midst. It was liberal and socially conscious—nothing like Phoenix.

"Well it wasn't always that way." Francine said that when you mapped voter registration in the state, you saw that Portland was essentially a Democratic island in a conservative sea. All of Oregon's liberal hot spots were in the Willamette Valley cities of Portland, Corvallis, and Eugene. "The rest of the state is Republican," she said, "farmers, ranchers, loggers, conservatives." She told me about a sign that settlers placed at a fork in the Oregon Trail during the Gold Rush. The sign said "To Oregon," accompanied by an arrow, and stood near a cairn of gold quartz that marked the route south to California. It was designed to filter out both poor illiterate whites and black travelers, so that only those able to read could follow the sign. The literate and "respectable" folks went to Oregon, the reckless adventurers and illiterate rest ended up in California. She said, "Pretty ugly beginning to what became a really great place." I hoped I would turn out the same.

That morning I went home and showered. I pet my cats, waited two hours for the methadone to digest before I ate breakfast, then I went to work. I repeated this routine every week for six years, and in 2006, I got off methadone. In 2010, I celebrated ten years heroin-free. Soon I'll celebrate twenty. I've privately apologized to my ex-fiancé and her sister for my enormous betrayals, and I've confessed my addiction and arrest to friends because transparency, I know now, strengthens rather than weakens such bonds. As French writer and diarist Anaïs Nin said, "Life shrinks or expands in proportion to one's courage." Yet I still can't admit to having been on methadone. All these years later, I've told no one but Rebekah, my wife. Not Kari, not my family or friends. At first I didn't admit it because I felt ashamed. Now, having come clean about heroin in general, I find myself withholding about methadone because I've waited so long to confess, and the longer I wait, the more deceitful I feel. The same internal debate plagues me from long ago: if I admit it now, won't everyone wonder what else I'm hiding? Worse, won't they question everything I say? Then there's the guilt. I feel as guilty for continuing to conceal it from everyone as I do for sneaking to the clinic behind Kari's back in the first place. Admitting to my other secrets felt liberating and morally correct, but unlike Nin's courage, mine seems to have its limits.

After I moved to Oregon, Kari and I talked occasionally on the phone. Months passed. We quit calling. Months turned to years. It's as if I hoped time would expunge my history. Maybe you don't need to come clean to be clean, but my conscious has always felt burdened because part of me believes that the people you wrong this deeply deserve an apology. But maybe I'm projecting. Maybe I'm imagining that because I need forgiveness, Kari needs an apology. Maybe I'm confusing my need to confess with Kari's need to know the truth. Back when we were twenty-five years old, telling her I was on methadone seemed imperative, but she's a mother of two now, married to a good man and enjoying a career. Even though we're still in contact and on friendly terms, I doubt she spends time thinking about those years. Even if she does occasionally reflect on them, what good would knowing I was on methadone do her now? Or maybe I have it wrong: maybe the need to be honest supersedes the fragile relief of an incomplete portrait of reality. Until I come clean, the answers will remain unclear.

That morning after meeting Francine, the only things that were clear to me were what I had done and what I still needed to do. So I showered and rubbed my tired eyes and walked south from my apartment toward the closest light rail stop. I walked past rows of tall elms and maples to my local station. Yards filled with ferns lined the sidewalk. Low clouds stretched infinitely overhead. I drew deep breaths of the moist air, relishing the smell of the temperate zone, the taste of dirt and chlorophyll. Then I stepped onto the light rail, and the doors closed behind me.

WORKS CITED

Here is a selection of works I utilized during the writing of this book. My thanks to all the authors whose research, ideas, and enthusiasm contributed to my own.

BOOKS

Abbey, Edward. *The Journey Home: Some Words in Defense of the American West*. Plume, 1991.

Anderson, J. Seth. *Downtown Phoenix*. Arcadia Publishing, 2012.

Carpenter, Bill. *Uncloudy Days: The Gospel Music Encyclopedia*. Backbeat Books, 2005.

Daum, Meghan. *My Misspent Youth: Essays*. Picador, 2015.

De Mente, Boyé Lafayette. *Japan Unmasked: The Character & Culture of the Japanese*. Tuttle Publishing, 2006.

Diner, Hasia R. *Lower East Side Memories: A Jewish Place in America*. Princeton University Press, 2002.

Ellis, Edward Robb. *The Epic of New York City: A Narrative History*. Basic Books, 2011.

Erickson, Hal. *Television Cartoon Shows: An Illustrated Encyclopedia, 1949 Through 2003*. McFarland, 2016.

Gopnik, Adam. *Through the Children's Gate: A Home in New York*. Vintage, 2007.

Gornick, Vivian. *Fierce Attachments: A Memoir*. Farrar, Straus and Giroux, 2005.

Hess, Alan. *Googie: Fifties Coffee Shop Architecture*. Chronicle Books, 1986.

Hess, Alan. *Googie Redux: Ultramodern Roadside Architecture*. Chronicle Books, 2004.

Hopkinson, Deborah. *Shutting Out the Sky: Life in the Tenements of New York, 1880-1924*. Orchard Books, 2003.

Huxley, Aldous. *The Doors of Perception*. Harper Perennial Modern Classics, 2009.

Kazin, Alfred. *A Walker in the City*. Harvest Book, 1969.

Kerr, Alex. *Dogs and Demons: Tales From the Dark Side of Japan*. Reprint ed., Hill and Wang, 2002.

Lankevich, George J. *American Metropolis: A History of New York City*. NYU Press, 1998.

Logan, Michael F. *Desert Cities: The Environmental History of Phoenix and Tucson*. University of Pittsburg Press, 2006.

Luckingham, Bradford. *Phoenix: The History of a Southwestern Metropolis*. 1st ed., University of Arizona Press, 1989.

McNamee, Gregory, and Virgil Hancock. *Open Range and Parking Lots: Photographs of the Southwest*. University of New Mexico Press, 1999.

McNeil, W. K. *Encyclopedia of American Gospel Music.* 1st ed., Routledge, 2005.

Mitchell, Joseph. *Up in the Old Hotel.* Revised ed., Vintage, 1993.

Nequette, Anne M., and Jeffery R. Brooks. *A Guide to Tucson Architecture.* University of Arizona Press, 2002.

Reisner, Marc. *Cadillac Desert: The American West and Its Disappearing Water.* 2nd ed., Penguin Books, 1993.

Riis, Jacob. *How the Other Half Lives.* Create Space, 2009.

Sante, Luc. *Low Life: Lures and Snares of Old New York.* 1st ed., Farrar, Straus and Giroux, 2003.

Sheraton, Mimi. *The Bialy Eaters: The Story of a Bread and a Lost World.* 1st ed., Broadway, 2000.

Sonnichsen, C. L. *Tucson: The Life and Times of an American City.* Revised ed., University of Oklahoma Press, 1987.

White, E.B. *Here Is New York.* First Edition Thus ed., The Little Bookroom, 1999.

Willis, Ellen. *Out of the Vinyl Deeps: Ellen Willis on Rock Music.* University of Minnesota Press, 2011.

Ahearn, Ashley. "Scientists Say Stop Worrying about Fukushima Radioactivity in Fish." *Oregon Public Broadcasting*, 15 January 2014.

Associated Press. "Radioactive Bluefin Tuna Crossed Pacific to U.S." *CBS News*, 28 May 2012.

Associated Press. "Seventy-Foot Dock from Japan Washes up in Oregon." *CBS News*, 6 June 2012.

BBC. "Japan Tsunami 'Ghost Ship' Drifting to Canada." *BBC*, 24 March 2012.

Buchanan, Susy. "Tough Row To Ho." *Phoenix New Times*, 8 January 2004.

Buesseler, Ken. *Woods Hole Oceanographic Institution*. www.whoi.edu/.

Caplan-Bricker, Nora. "The Fukushima Fearmongers." *New Republic*, 10 March 2014.

Conca, James. "The Fukushima Disaster Wasn't Disastrous Because of The Radiation." *Forbes*, 16 March 2015.

Davis, Rob. "Fukushima Radiation Fears for Fish Along Oregon Coast Unwarranted, Scientists Say." *The Oregonian*, 19 November 2013.

Ellison, Jake. "Bit of Fukushima Radiation Found on NW River Beach, Sparks New Mystery." *Seattle Post Intelligencer*, 12 March 2014.

Floyd, Mark. "Study Finds Only Trace Levels of Radiation from Fukushima in Albacore." Oregon Station University, 28 April 2014.

Geib, Claudia. "The West Coast Is Still Safe from Fukushima Radiation." *PBS*, 16 October 2015.

Griffin, Kevin. "Citizen Scientists Prepare to Test West Coast for Fukushima Radiation." *The Vancouver Sun*, 14 April 2014.

Hanai, Toru and Elaine Lies. "The Children of Japan's Fukushima Battle an Invisible Enemy." *Reuters*, 11 March 2014.

Hume, Mark. "Disease Killing Pacific Herring Threatens Salmon, Scientist Warns." *The Globe and Mail*, 13 August 2013.

International Atomic Energy Agency. "The Radiological Accident in Goiânia." 1988.

Jeong, Eun-Young. "South Korea Bans Fish Caught off Parts of Japan Due to Radiation Fears." *The Associated Press*, 6 September 2013.

JIJI. "More Fukushima Evacuees Are Deciding to Stay Away for Good." *The Japan Times*, 4 March 2015.

Kyodo. "Researchers Find High Cesium in Some Pacific Plankton." *The Japan Times*, 22 May 2013.

Lynch, Rene. "Japanese 'Ghost Ship' Laid to Rest on the Ocean Floor off Alaska." *The Los Angeles Times*, 6 April 2012.

Kiger, Patrick J. "Fukushima's Radioactive Water Leak: What You Should Know." *National Geographic News*, 9 August 2013.

Martini, Kim. "True Facts about Ocean Radiation and the Fukushima Disaster." *Deep Sea News*, 28 November 2013.

Moskin, Julia. "Let the Meals Begin: Finding Beijing in Flushing." *The New York Times*, 30 July 2008.

Murphy, Kim. "Huge Dock Washes up on Oregon Coast." *The Los Angeles Times*, 6 June 2012.

Nakamura, Beth. "Boat Remains, Thought to be Japanese Tsunami Debris, Deliver Asian Fish to Oregon Coast." *The Oregonian*, 15 April 2015.

Oregon Dept. of Parks and Recreation. "More Japanese Tsunami Debris Lands in Florence, Off Siuslaw River." *News Lincoln Country*, 9 April 2013.

Ozick, Cynthia. "The Synthetic Sublime." *The New Yorker*, 22 February 1999.

Pela, Robert L. "No Vacancy at Log Cabin Motel." *Phoenix New Times*, 18 March 2010.

Simms, James. "New Blog On Post-Fukushima Japan, Asia Energy Issues." *Forbes* blog, 20 January 2015.

Space Age City. www.spaceagecity.com/.

Tiki Central. www.tikiroom.com/tikicentral/bb/.

Vollmann, William. "Invisible and Insidious." *Harper's*, March 2015.

Webb, Dewey. "The Way We Whir." *Phoenix New Times*, 21 October 1992.

Webb, Dewey. "Lei'd to Rest: The Valley's Most Exotic Landmark Slowly Sinks Into the Sunset." *Phoenix New Times*, 15 December 1993.

ACKNOWLEDGMENTS

"Dreams of the Atomic Era" in *Cincinnati Review*; "A Secondary Landscape" as a Future Tense Publishing chapbook; "The Stoned Age" in *The Normal School*; "Land Speculation" in *North American Review*; "The Burden of Home" in the *Paris Review*; "Leaving Tatooine" in River Styx; "Tillage" in *Saranac Review*; "Tragedy of the Commons" in *Alligator Juniper*; "It's Really Something You Should Have Examined" in *Passages North*; "My Manhattan Minute" in *Bayou* under a different title; "Ancient History" in *New Ohio Review*; "Between Disappearances" in *Black Warrior Review* and *Tablet*; "Every Supper the Last" in *Third Coast*; "Hey Cowboy" in *Fourth Genre*; "\'ra-di-kəl\" in *Hotel Amerika*; "A Reckless Autonomy in *The Smart Set*; "(Be)Coming Clean," a shorter version, in *Louisville Review*.

CREDITS

If you type enough, pages accrue, but this book is the result of many people's effort, generosity, love, and trust. First, thank you to the magazine editors who believed in these stories and helped improve them: Nina Mason, Kevin Sampsell, Thessaly La Force, Matt Roberts, Sophie Beck, Steven Church, Marcia Aldrich, David Lazar, Amanda Giracca, Kim Groninga, Elissa Cahn, Barry Grass, Wayne Hoffman, Randolph Bates, Jose L. Torres-Padilla, Jeff Fearnside, Ellyn Lichvar, Jason Wilson and Jesse Smith, John Bullock and Damien Cowger, and Shanie Latham and Richard Newman. Many thanks to Powell's alumni Diane Brodie and Mary Winzig, who let me housesit when I needed a quiet place to write and a reminder of who I was. And an extra large, special thanks to Diane for the manna from heaven that got me through a strange time; you went above and beyond. My thanks to Brigid Hughes, David Leavitt, and George Singleton for the example and encouragement along the way, even when they didn't know they were encouraging me. Thanks to Julia Wick and Mark Armstrong at *Longreads* for their support, and for being so engaged in storytelling and literature, and open to experimentation. You are truly good eggs.

I'm indebted to the good people at Curbside Splendor: Naomi Huffman, Catherine Eves, Victor David Giron, Alban Fischer, and Jacob Knabb, for their confidence and dedication to making this happen, and to my teachers Sven Birkerts, Susan Cheever, Bernard Cooper, and Dinah Lenney. Thank you to the tacos who got me through many lean years. Carne and al pastor, you know who you are. And special thanks to my parents, Loraine and Joe, for a life of patient encouragement, understanding, and room to grow. You never suggested I become a lawyer. You never urged me to be more practical. When I got lost, it was because of you that I found my way.

I want to dedicate this book to many people. This is for my uncles Howard and Sheldon, neither of whom lived as long as they should have. This is for my grandma Silvia, who always encouraged me to read and draw and think, who squeezed my cheek and gave me books and told me, "Go enjoy yourself, tatalah." "Are you still writing?" she used to ask. "Good." This is for my granddad Tom Gilbreath, who bought me countless sketchbooks as a kid, who passed on the creative urge through his woodcarving and carpentry, and showed me through example to never give up, because when a job appears that you want but aren't educated enough to do, you have to learn how to do it. This is for Dean, who was there on the road during one of my best times, and who's still with me now, through the hard ones. And for Alex B, whose magical hair and open heart continue to soften my own.

And last but not least, this is for Rebekah, my other half, my light, my Boss Coffee and somehow my biggest fan, you're a person who sees everything and loves me despite it. Does that make sense? Here's the thing. Only you, Schiefy, you, you, you.

AARON GILBREATH is an essayist, journalist, and burrito enthusiast. His essays and articles have appeared in *Harper's*, *The New York Times*, *Paris Review*, *Saveur*, *Kenyon Review*, *Virginia Quarterly Review*, *Tin House*, *Vice*, *The Morning News*, and *Brick*, and been listed as notable in *Best American Essays* and *Best American Travel Writing*. A contributing editor at *Longreads*, he's working on a book about rural California and a travel book about Japan. He lives in Portland, Oregon.